A volume
in
THE DOCUMENTARY HISTORY
of
WESTERN CIVILIZATION

Victorian Culture and Society

Victorian Culture and Society

edited by

EUGENE C. BLACK

WALKER AND COMPANY

New York

First published in the United States of America
in 1974 by the Walker Publishing Company, Inc.

Published simultaneously in Canada
by Fitzhenry & Whiteside, Limited, Toronto.

ISBN: 0-8027-2041-2
Library of Congress Catalog Card Number: 73-78607
Printed in the United States of America.

Volumes in this series are published in association
with Harper & Row, Publishers, Inc.,
from whom paperback editions are available
in Harper Torchbooks.

Acknowledgments

There is no way to thank the many people who have contributed, one way or another, to the making of this book. I would have to thank generations of students, graduate and undergraduate, who have worked with me at Brandeis, colleagues whose constant intellectual challenge is a spur to discipline and imagination. Several individuals have been particularly helpful: Louis Richman and Ophelia Orr in the preparation of the manuscript, Donna Bouvier and Sue Irwin in the collection of materials, and the many people at Harper & Row involved in the book's production.

Contents

III. CULTURAL DIMENSIONS   279

Doctrine

Dogma

Value

Knowledge

Ave Atque Vale

Introduction

Victorianism rings with a misleading tone of stability and order. The age, impervious to a generation of calm, scholarly examination, remains a rhetorical yardstick, the good (or bad) old days to use as a standard against our own hectic century. But whatever the assumptions, the facts remain simple. It was an era of economic, social, and political revolution. Life changed entirely for many people; it was altered substantially for almost all. Then as now, social problems were more pressing and difficult to resolve than the economic ones. Industrial revolution is produced by a confluence of forces, people, and events. Technological innovation, capital, and entrepreneurship will not produce it for themselves. The industrial revolution is economic, psychological, social and cultural. Political stability in Britain provided a veneer of calm. The persistence of political institutions and ruling classes, both of which accommodated modification but resisted overthrow, and the general acceptance of common values among most of the socially dynamic elements in society combined to make pacific adaptation possible. Britain's experience may have been unique, but it remains instructive.

This volume illustrates some of the economic, social, and cultural institutions and values upon which Victorian civilization rested. Neither it nor any selection could be complete or pay tribute to the rich variety of themes and doctrines. The documents here emphasize certain points but only aspects of them. There is no such thing as a Victorian society or a Victorian culture. The closer one comes to the evidence, the more that specific cases resist generalization. The image of Victorians shatters into millions of living, breathing persons bound by geography and chronology but inhabiting individual worlds and lives. As any trade union secretary can testify, shared occupation and economic status do not guarantee social or cultural uniformity. Less articulate people tend, as always, to disappear as individuals and to reemerge as groups or categories, the classified impersonal subjects of external examination.

I have been relatively conventional both in sources and approach. But if these documents treat the more obvious issues, I hope that they raise questions about some of the more subtle and significant questions. Take sport and recreation. These important themes, which I treat cavalierly, almost invariably appear as curiosities or quaint sidelights in the conventional studies of the time. The historian touches upon line bowling or the considerable achievements of W. G. Grace. These remarks suffice to pass the test of awareness, but they say nothing about the unconscious use of village cricket to reenforce a sense of community and social structure. The development of association football, the mass spectator sport, seems to have a more than fortuitous connection with the evolution of industrial society. Or take another and different instance. The sermon was one of the most characteristic forms of communication of ideas and values in the century, and the one example here cannot approximate the range of those musty orations.

I have drawn most of the documents from the endless and invaluable sessional papers, parliamentary debates, the newspapers and journals of opinion so rich in Victoria's century, contemporary literature, correspondence, biographical and autobiographical remains. But there is a range of material that has much to tell, and cannot be represented for lack of space. Here the reader will find no penny dreadfuls, no *Reynold's Weekly*, no temperance tract, no racing tip-sheet, no music hall showbill, no advertisement for narcotic cure-alls. The world of "the other Victorians" was real, but the reader must turn to Stephen Marcus, the feverish fantasies of *My Secret Life* and avowed fancies of *The Pearl*, or (better) the last volume of Mayhew's survey of London.

I wish to raise questions in this volume, not necessarily resolve them. I hope to point the reader toward some of the issues, questions, and materials that must be considered in any thoughtful investigation of the concept "Victorianism." The word describes a variety of forms, institutions, and cultural expressions; it encompasses a revolution no less profound because it was executed with the preservation of external forms.

Generalizations are easiest when drawn from a great distance. Proximity reveals the infinite variety of man's thought, work, and character. Nevertheless, some uniform characteristics or features offer a starting point for the definition of problems.

The little old England of Walpole's time was not one but many lands. Jane Austen found twenty miles a great journey. For most Englishmen the world of the eighteenth century was the world of their parish, the nearest market town, and reached perhaps to the county seat. With more than half of the population illiterate even when Victoria ascended the throne in 1837, there were few incentives to seek broader horizons in the small world of the parish. The many Englands of the Hanoverian century were finally unified in Victorian England. While regional distinctions remained and persist more than a century later—some natural, others contrived—the United Kingdom came, for the first time, to be united. The railroad, that spearhead of early- and mid-Victorian progress, proved the principal instrument in realizing the hope of centuries. Setting aside the economic impact of the railroad, a matter of vast, perhaps crucial importance in Britain's world position, the locomotive steamed through the social and cultural fabric of the country. The railroad provided and recognized mobility (while preserving social distinctions with first-, second-, and third-class carriages). People and goods could be moved across the land in hours, not days. The modern concentration of population and development of urban-suburban complexes as we know them depended upon the train. Railroads provided personal mobility and ratified social mobility with criteria of class now strictly economic.

Unification made possible local and regional specialization. The efficient organization and exploitation of men and resources often proceeded from the implementation of effective transportation. Sometimes it did not. Britain's extraordinary head start in industrialization, coinciding with the global population explosion, provided her such an unchallenged position that she could tolerate, even cultivate, forms of social and economic inefficiency that were to cost her dearly in later decades. The United States was continually wasteful of natural resources. The British inclined to be more careless of human resources.

Local and regional specialization contributed, with the simultaneous population increase and shift to cities and towns, to the concentration of people and things. Urban communities had never sustained their populations on native births. Nineteenth-century London, like its fifteenth-century ancestor, demanded constant migration to maintain its size, let alone grow. Demographic historians sort through mazes of inadequate and confusing statistics, but we may never know precisely when natural increase would sustain the population of a British city. It does appear that the urban death rate was little if at all lower when Victoria died in 1901 than it had been in 1837. The considerable advances in medical science and public health, even substantial urban renewal and the improvement in popular awareness and attitudes, meant very little. The death rate remained shockingly high in an era of burgeoning population increase.

The newly urbanized were people adrift in economic, social, and cultural terms, although they were also emancipated in great measure from traditional controls. The denizens of a Westmoreland village or a Dorsetshire estate were bound to one another by history, if not by kinship. To some degree they replicated the past; they had both a continuity and a community of existence. But who lived in Manchester? Or London? Thousands upon thousands of souls lived and died in grim anonymity—men, women, and children who toiled in mills or breweries or shops or offices. Thousands of Irish migrated to England each year, for to them the world could not be worse and might be better. Highland and Lowland Scots moved by compulsion or choice toward mills and factories. So did the Sussex farm girl for whom the uncertainties of London domestic service seemed preferable to possible spinsterhood and certain poverty in her village.

This concentrated population was built from a society in dissolution. Relationships and roles, defined in the simpler agrarian setting, broke down in urban complexity. Values evolved empirically, often by imitation. Everything changed in subtle as well as obvious ways. Industrial society provided new forms of work and unprecedented economic and social discipline. Only miners, seamen, and members of the armed forces had confronted anything comparable in the preindustrial era. The regimentation of the factory bell and the implementation of precise working functions and hours were new. Men, women, and children did not necessarily work more hours in a week; they usually worked less, but did so on an inflexible schedule. Industrial society provided new social and cultural relationships while inspiring new forms of social and political as well as economic organization. The friendly society, the trade union, or (particularly in the North and Scotland) the cooperative became characteristic although not necessarily novel groups in the redefinition and reorganization of society. There were many interesting elements of continuity. The "local," the neighborhood public house, or beershop, preserved some of the cultural function of the village center. It also provided one of the few (and perhaps the most important) elements of continuity in leisure.

Forms of leisure, like forms of work, changed with the shift to industrial discipline and urban concentration. Much—probably too much—has been made of the loss of fresh air and open fields in the transition from agricultural to industrial, from rural to urban. The shifts were usually but not necessarily related, and there was no inevitable retrogression from one to the next. Sir John Ramsden's well-made housing projects in Huddersfield were probably a more salubrious environment judged by any criteria than the dung-floored cottages on many an estate about which land stewards' handbooks speak with such approval. But there were important changes, and some of them had implications we have but begun to consider. Village sports tended to be participatory. Games might be brutal. They would almost certainly be poorly played, but they directly involved a substantial portion of the community. Rowdyism, fighting, and drinking were shared recreations on the rural and urban scenes, but they changed as the firm hand of the utilitarian regulator or evangelical reformer reached in. Spectator sports came to assume an increasingly important role in urban leisure. We shall probably never know precisely what impact this change had, but it continues to this day, accentuated and caricatured by the inroads of television. One psychological and cultural point seems clear. Mass spectator sports simultaneously reenforce the omnipresence of the community and individual anonymity.

The selections are divided into three broad categories—economic, social, and cultural—with the last, in turn, subdivided again into doctrine, dogma, value, and knowledge. "Queen Victoria as a Moral Force" serves to introduce all of the selections, while that great positivist, Frederic Harrison, summarizes many of the themes in conclusion. The documents will be most profitably employed in conjunction with *British Politics in the Nineteenth Century* (New York: Harper & Row, 1969, Harper Torchbook 1427), for the two volumes develop related and complementary themes.

Prologue

---

1. The Victorian Frame of Reference

VICTORIA GAVE her name to the age. She outlived the Whigs and Tories who had shaken the constitution in Church and State in the early years of her life. She survived Lord Palmerston, that titan of mid-Victorian politics. She mourned the passing of Gladstone and Disraeli. France had liquidated two centuries of European hegemony when she was born; the German century was approaching its first great crisis when she died. The United States was discovering itself and its continent in 1837. By 1901 it was fast moving to world power. Englishmen and things traveled by canal boat, flying coach, and a new gadget, the railroad, when Victoria ascended the throne. Motor vehicles and airplanes were becoming common when she died. The relative novelty of gas light illuminated her youth; electricity brightened her old age. She spanned a world from Keats to Kipling, which included much that is best in English letters.

Her influence derived initially from her position as queen, although her importance was never exclusively political. Her constitutional duties, her political notions, and her determination to be involved meant sixty-three years of political importance. On occasion she was ill-advised on constitutional questions, and sometimes she responded foolishly to political issues. Her powers were limited, but her influence was great. Victoria the person made Victoria the queen. Other sovereigns had political claims more extensive than hers. Franz Josef of Austria-Hungary reigned as long, but his Vienna has only a musty nostalgia, a faintly decadent air humming with waltzes and operettas from those Victorian years. Victoria was not particularly intelligent or perceptive or interesting. But she was a moral force of incalculable weight. She was pleasant when she chose to be, even amusing. She worked hard, met her obligations, and was in herself a mirror of the Victorian public. She embodied those virtues that nineteenth-century Britain adopted as its own, holding them out, not merely to her own dominions, but to the Western world.

William Edward Hartpole Lecky (1832–1903), one of the most distinguished historians of the century, captured Victoria's virtues without attempting to conceal her faults. A Liberal Unionist, he was himself politically active—and committed to Victorian values. Lecky shared most of the queen's prejudices, saw all too clearly the elements undermining Victorian civilization, and viewed the coming of democracy as inherently dangerous. Political constraint, a quality he found so admirable in the late queen and the age that was gone, was vanishing, leaving open the way for demagogues and war.

Recommended Reading

Victoria is well served in two biographies. That of Elizabeth Long-ford, *Queen Victoria: Born to Succeed* (New York: 1965); does not completely supersede Lytton Strachey, *Queen Victoria* (New York: 1921). The current two-volume study by Mrs. C. Woodham Smith (Vol I, London, 1972) should be definitive. Documents 14, 19, and 32 in *British Politics in the Nineteenth Century* (New York: Harper & Row, 1969; Harper Torchbook 1427) deal with particular aspects of Victoria in politics.

W. E. H. Lecky,
Queen Victoria as a Moral Force

At a time when the unprecedented increase of gigantic and rapidly acquired fortunes has deeply infected both English and American society with the characteristic vices of a Plutocracy, the profound feeling of sorrow and admiration elicited by the death of Queen Victoria is an encouraging sign. It shows that the vulgar ideals, the false moral measurements, the feverish social ambitions, the love of the ostentatious and the factitious, and the disdain for simple habits, pleasures, and characters so apparent in certain conspicuous sections of society, have not yet blunted the moral sense or perverted the moral perceptions of the great masses on either side of the Atlantic. To this type, indeed, we could scarcely find a more complete antithesis than in the life and character of the great Queen who has passed away. Nothing more deeply impressed all who came in contact with her than the essential simplicity and genuineness of her nature.

She was a great ruler, but she was also to the last a true, kindly, simple-minded woman, retaining with undiminished intensity all the warmth of a most affectionate nature, all the soundness of a most excellent judgment. Brought up from childhood in the artificial atmosphere of a Court, called while still a girl to the isolation of a throne; deprived, when her reign had yet forty years to run, of the support and counsel of her husband, she might well have

Source: From "Queen Victoria as a Moral Force," in *Historical and Political Essays* (London: 1908), pp. 275–297.

been pardoned if she often found herself out of touch with large sections of her people, and had viewed life through a false medium or in partial aspects. Yet Lord Salisbury probably in no degree exaggerated when he said that if he wished to ascertain the feelings and opinions of the English people, and especially of the English middle classes, he knew no truer or more enlightening judgment than that of the Queen. She thought with them and she felt with them; she shared their ambitions; she knew by a kind of intuitive instinct the course of their judgments; she sympathised deeply with their trials and their sorrows.

She could hardly be called a brilliant woman. It is difficult indeed to judge the full social capacities of anyone who lives under the constant restraints of a royal position, but I do not think that in any sphere of life the Queen would have been regarded as a woman of striking wit, or originality, or even commanding power. The qualities that made her so successful in her high calling were of another kind: supreme good sense; a tact in dealing with men and circumstances so unfailing that it almost amounted to genius; an indefatigable industry which never flagged from early youth till extreme old age; a sense of duty so steady and so strong that it governed all her actions and pleasures, and saved her not only from the grosser and more common temptations of an exalted position, but also in a most unusual degree from the subtle and often half-concealed deflecting influences that spring from ambition or resentment, from personal predilections and personal dislikes. It was these qualities, combined with her unrivalled experience of affairs, and strengthened by long and constant intercourse with the foremost English statesmen of two generations, that made her what she undoubtedly was—a perfect model of a constitutional Sovereign.

The position of a Sovereign under a parliamentary government like ours is a singular and difficult one. There was a school of politicians who were much more prominent in the last generation than in the present one, who regarded the Sovereign, in political life at least, as little more than a figure-head or a cipher, absolved from all responsibility, but also divested of all power, and fulfilling functions in the Constitution which are little more than mechanical. This view of the unimportance of the Monarchy will now be held by few really intelligent men. Those take but a false and narrow view of human affairs who fail to realise the part which sentiment and enthusiasm play in the government of men; and no one who knows England will question that the throne is the centre of a great strength of personal attachment which is wholly different from any attachment to a party or a parliament.

In India and the Colonies this is still more the case. It is not the British Parliament or the British Cabinet that there forms the centre of unity or excites genuine attachment. The Crown is the main link binding the different States to one another, and the pervading sentiment of a common loyalty unites them in one great and living whole. In foreign politics it cannot be a matter of indifference that a Sovereign is closely related to nearly all the greatest rulers in the world, and in frequent, intimate, unconstrained correspondence with them. This is a kind of influence which no Minister, however powerful, can exercise, and it was possessed by Queen Victoria probably to a greater degree than by any Sovereign on record, for there has scarcely ever been one who included among her relations so many of the Sovereigns of the world. Future historians will no doubt have ample means of judging how frequently and how judiciously it was employed in assuaging differences and promoting European peace. All the great offices in Church and State, all the great distributions of honours were submitted to her; and though in a large number of cases this patronage is purely Ministerial or professional, there are many cases in which the Sovereign had a real voice, and a strong objection on her part was usually attended to. In Church patronage and in the distribution of honours she is known to have taken a great interest, and to have exercised a considerable influence.

The one subject on which the Queen was not always in harmony with her people was that of foreign politics. She and the Prince Consort took a keen interest in them, and during his lifetime she followed very implicitly his guidance. The strong German sympathies she imbued from her own marriage were much intensified by the marriages of her children, and especially by that of her eldest daughter to the heir of the Prussian throne. The influence also of Stockmar, who was the closest adviser of her early married life, was not wholly for good, and the theory which the Prince held that the direction of foreign affairs is in a peculiar degree under the care of the Sovereign, and that the Prince, her husband, should be regarded as "her permanent Minister," created during many years much friction. In a constitutional country, where the responsibility of affairs rests wholly on the Minister, who is doubly responsible to the Cabinet and to the Parliament, such a theory can only be maintained with great qualifications.

On the other hand, the government of the country was carried on in the name of the Queen. Foreign despatches were addressed to her and could only be answered with her sanction. The right of the English Sovereigns to be present at the Cabinet Councils of their Ministers was abdicated when George I. came to the throne, but every important departure in policy was submitted to the Queen and required her assent. The testimony of Ministers of all shades of policy supports the belief that this was no idle form. The Queen, though always open to argument and tolerant of contradiction, had her own decided opinions; she exercised her undoubted right of expressing and defending them, and even apart from her royal position, her great experience and her singular clearness and rectitude of judgment made her opinion well worth listening to. . . .

. . . Her nature, which was very frank, made it impossible for her, even if she desired it, to conceal her opinions, and she devoted much time and pains to making herself acquainted with the details of every question as it arose. She made it a rule to sign no paper that she had not read. She did not hesitate fully to apprise her Ministers of her views when they differed from their own, and she enforced her views by argument and remonstrance. She more than once drew up memoranda of her dissent from the opinions of her Foreign Minister, and insisted on their being brought before the Cabinet for consideration. In the formation of a new Ministry she more than once exercised her power of deciding to whom the succession of the first places should be offered. After an adverse vote of the House of Commons, she considered herself fully authorised to decide whether she would accept the resignation of a Minister or submit the issue to the test of a dissolution, and there were occasions on which she remonstrated with her Ministers on their too ready determination to resign.

At the same time it is certain that the Queen fulfilled with perfection that most difficult duty of an able constitutional Sovereign—the duty of yielding her convictions to those of her responsible Ministers and acting faithfully with Ministers she distrusted. To a Sovereign with clear views and a more than common force of character this must often have been very painful, and to have fulfilled it faithfully and with no loss of dignity is no small merit. It is the universal testimony of all who served her, that no

Sovereign ever supported her successive Ministers with a more perfect loyalty or held the scales between contending parties with a more complete impartiality. No one understood better to what point a constitutional Sovereign may press her opinions and at what point she is bound to give way; and while maintaining her rightful authority she never in any degree transgressed its bounds. . . .

She acted in the same way in internal affairs. Few measures that were carried in her time were more repugnant to her than Gladstone's disestablishment of the Irish Church. It abolished an institution of which she was herself the head and which a special clause in the Coronation Oath required her to uphold, and she foretold, not without good reason, that it would not pacify Ireland but would be an encouragement to further agitation. The question, however, had been submitted at a general election to the decision of the country, and after that decision had been unequivocally given in favour of the policy of Gladstone, she frankly accepted it with the assent of the Prime Minister. When a great danger of a conflict between the two Houses of Parliament had arisen, she devoted herself actively in preventing it. . . .

On three very memorable occasions the intervention of the Queen had probably a great effect on English politics. It is well known that at the time when the issue of peace or war with the United States was trembling in the balance on account of the seizure of the Southern envoys on the "Trent," the Queen, acting in accordance with the Prince Consort, by softening and revising the language of an English despatch to America, did very much to prevent the dispute from leading to a great war; that in the proclamation which was issued to the Indian people after the Sepoy Mutiny, she insisted on the excision of some most unfortunate words that seemed to menace the native creeds, and on the insertion of an emphatic promise that they should in no wise be interfered with, and thus probably prevented a new outburst of most dangerous fanaticism; that at the time of the Schleswig-Holstein dispute she contributed powerfully and actively to give a turn to the negotiations that averted a war with Prussia and Austria, which, as is now almost universally recognised, could only have led to a great catastrophe. . . .

On other occasions her remonstrances were disregarded, and courses were pursued to which she strongly objected. The surrender after Majuba was in her opinion a pusillanimous abandonment of the English flag, and it was with extreme reluctance that she acquiesced in it. Still more vehement were her feelings about the long abandonment of General Gordon in the Soudan. She had been indefatigable in urging on the Ministry of Gladstone the duty of speedy measures for his rescue, and when, owing to the long delay of the Ministry, the most heroic of modern Englishmen perished at Khartoum, her indignation knew no bounds . . . This was one of the few occasions in which she allowed her sentiments in hostility to the policy of her Ministers to appear publicly before the world. In general, she had a profound distrust of the policy and judgment of Mr. Gladstone, and she fully shared the dread with which the great body of English statesmen looked upon the Home Rule policy. It was no new sentiment on her part, for she had lived through the Repeal agitation of O'Connell, and as far back as 1843 Sir Robert Peel had somewhat unconstitutionally declared in Parliament that he was authorised by the Queen to state that she, like her predecessor, was resolved to maintain the Union inviolate by all the means in her power.

There can now be no harm in saying—what when both parties were alive was naturally kept in the background—that the relations of the Queen with Mr. Gladstone were usually of a very painful character. She had personally not much to complain of. The skill and firmness with which Mr. Gladstone resisted the attempts to diminish the parliamentary subsidies for her family were fully and gratefully recognised by the Queen, but the main course of his politics, both foreign and domestic, filled her with alarm, and she never appears to have experienced the attraction which his great personal gifts exercised over most of those with whom he came in immediate contact. The extreme copiousness of his vocabulary, the extreme subtlety of his mind and reasoning, and the imperiousness of temper with which he seldom failed to meet opposition, were all repugnant to her. To those who have experienced the sustained emphasis of language with which Mr. Gladstone was accustomed in conversation to enforce his views, there is much truth as well as humour in the saying which was attributed to the Queen, "I wish Mr. Gladstone would not always speak to me as if I was a public meeting." . . . At all times the Queen had decided political opinions, and the experience of a long reign had given her a large measure of not unjustifiable self-confidence. Few persons had studied as she had during all those years the various political questions that arose, and she had had the advantage of discussing them at length with a long succession of the leading statesmen of England. Under such circumstances her opinions had no small weight, and although in the Liberal Government she gave her full confidence to Lord Clarendon and Lord Granville, she looked with the gravest apprehension on the policy of Mr. Gladstone.

It was a painful and irksome position, but it did not lead the Queen to any unconstitutional course. No public act or word ever disclosed her feelings. It was indeed in most cases very slowly, and in small circles and through private channels, that the convictions of the Queen became known.

. . . In an autograph letter to Mrs. Gladstone she spoke with the deep and genuine warmth that was never wanting in her letters of condolence of her sympathy with the bereavement of that lady. She spoke of his illustrious gifts and of his personal kindness to herself, but it was noticed that no sentence in the letter intimated any approbation of his general policy. "Truth in the inmost parts" was indeed a prominent characteristic of the Queen, and she wrote nothing which was not in accordance with her true convictions.

There were occasions when she took independent steps, and some of these had a considerable influence on politics. Louis Napoleon was one of the few great Sovereigns who were not related to her, and to few persons could the *coup d'état* which brought him to the throne have been more repugnant, but the cordial personal relations she established with him undoubtedly contributed considerably to the good relations which for many years subsisted between England and France. Bismarck detested English Court influence and was greatly prejudiced against her, but he has left a striking testimony to the favourable impression which her tact and good sense made upon him when he first came into contact with her. She possessed to a high degree the power of choosing the right moment and striking the true chord, and she appears to have been an excellent judge not only of the feelings of large bodies of men, but also of the individual characters of those with whom she dealt. She had a style of writing which was eminently characteristic and eminently feminine, and it is easy to trace the letters which were entirely her own. Her letters of congratulation, or sympathy, or encouragement on public occasions scarcely ever failed in their effect and never contained an

injudicious word. The same thing may be said of her many beautiful letters to those who were suffering from some grievous calamity. Whether she was writing to a great public character like the
widow of an American President, or expressing her sorrow for
obscure sufferers, there was the same note of true womanly sympathy, so manifestly spontaneous and so manifestly heartfelt, that it
found its way to the hearts of thousands. The tact for which she
was so justly celebrated, like all true tact, sprang largely from
character, from the quick and lively sympathies of an eminently
affectionate nature. No one could have been less theatrical, or less
likely in any unworthy way to seek for popularity; but she knew
admirably the occasions or the methods by which she could strike
the imagination and appeal most favourably to the feelings of her
people. She showed this in the very beginning of her reign when
she insisted, in defiance of the opinion of the Duke of Wellington,
on riding herself through the ranks of her troops at her first
review. She showed it on countless other occasions of her long
reign—pre-eminently in her two Jubilees and in her last visit to
Ireland. It is well known that this visit was entirely her own idea.
To many it seemed rash or even positively dangerous. They dwelt
upon the bitter disaffection of a great portion of the Irish people,
upon the danger of mob outrage or even assassination, upon the
extreme difficulty of preventing a royal visit to Ireland from taking
a party character and being regarded as a party triumph or defeat.
But the Queen, as Sir William Harcourt once truly said, "never
feared her people," and nothing could be more happy than the
manner in which she availed herself of the new turn given to Irish
feeling by the splendid achievements of Irish soldiers in South
Africa, to come over, as if to thank her Irish people in person, and
at the same time to repair in extreme old age a neglect for which
she had been often, and not altogether unjustly, blamed. There
never indeed was a more brilliant and unqualified success. To those
who witnessed the spontaneous and passionate enthusiasm with
which she was everywhere greeted, it seemed as if all bitter feeling
vanished at her presence; and the Irish visit, which was one of the
last, was also one of the brightest pages of her reign. The credit of
its most skilful arrangements belongs chiefly to the officials in
Dublin, but the Irish people will long remember the patient courage with which the aged Queen went through its fatigues; the
tactful kindness and the gracious dignity with which she won the

hearts of multitudes who had never before seen her or spoken to her; the evident enjoyment with which she responded to the cordiality of her reception. One feature of that visit was especially characteristic. It was the Children's Review in Phœnix Park, where, by the desire of the Queen, some fifty thousand children were brought together to meet her. No act of kindness could have gone more directly home to the hearts of the parents, and it left a memory in many young minds that will never be effaced.

It is rather, however, by the example of a life than by any public acts that a constitutional Sovereign can impress her personality on the affections of her people. Of the reign of Queen Victoria it may be truly said that very few in English history have been so blameless as this, which was the longest of all. Her Court was a model of quiet dignity and decorum, singularly free from all the atmosphere of intrigue and from all suspicion of injudicious or unworthy favouritism. She managed it as she managed her family, with a happy mixture of tact and affection; and though she gave her confidence to many she gave it to such persons and in such a way that it seemed never to be abused. No domestic life could in all its relations have beeen more perfect, and her love of children amounted to a passion. . . . Her vast family, spread through many countries, was her abiding interest and delight, and although she had to pay in full measure the natural penalty of many bereavements, she at least never knew the dreary loneliness that clouded the last days of her great predecessor, Elizabeth.

In the early years of her reign she fully filled her place as the leader of English society. In the plays she patronised, in the art she preferred, in the restrictions of her Drawing Rooms, in the fashions she countenanced, in the intimacies she selected or encouraged, her influence was always healthy and pure, and for some years it powerfully affected the tone of English society. Unfortunately, after the great calamity of her widowhood the nerves of the Queen seem to have been shaken, and though she never intermitted her political duties and spent daily many hours over her correspondence, she allowed her social duties to fall too much and too long into abeyance. She still, it is true, occasionally appeared in public ceremonies. She laid the first stones of several hospitals and infirmaries. She presided over the inauguration of several great industrial enterprises. She sometimes opened Parliament in person, and was sometimes present at military and naval reviews. But she scarcely ever appeared in London, except for a few days. She never appeared in a London theatre. She shrank from great crowds and large social gatherings, and buried herself too much in her Highland home. This is one of the few real reproaches that history is likely to bring against her. Her influence on English society was never wholly lost, and it was always an influence for good, but for many years it was exerted less frequently and less powerfully than it should have been and the tone of large sections of society lost something by her retirement.

It may be doubted, however, whether this long retirement really injured her in the minds of her people. Her rare occasional appearances had a greater weight, and the depth of feeling exhibited by her long widowhood became a new title to respect. The transparent simplicity and unselfishness of her character were now generally appreciated, and her own books contributed greatly to make her people understand her. It is in general far from a wise thing for royal personages to descend into the arena of literature unless they possess some special aptitude for it. They expose themselves to a kind of criticism wholly different from that which follows them in their public lives—a criticism more minute and often more deliberately malevolent than that to which an ordinary writer is subject. The Queen wrote pure and excellent English and she had a good literary taste, but she certainly could never have become a great writer; and the complete frankness and unreserve of her Journals, as well as their curious homeliness of thought and feeling, were not viewed with favour in some sections of the fashionable and of the literary world. There were circles in which the word "bourgeois," and there were others in which the word "commonplace," was often pronounced. Yet in this, as on nearly all occasions when the Queen acted on her own impulse, she acted wisely. Her books had at once an enormous circulation, and there can be no doubt that they contributed very widely to her popularity. Multitudes to whom she had before been little more than a name, now realised that she was one with whom they had very much in common. Her evident longing for sympathy produced an immediate response. Her deep domestic affection, her constant interest in her servants, her high spirits, her love of scenery, her love of animals, her power of taking delight in little things, appeared vividly in her pages and came home to the largest classes of her people.

In some respects the Queen was an eminently democratic Sovereign. While maintaining the dignity of her position, rank and wealth were in her eyes always subordinate to the great realities of life and to true human affections. In no one was the touch of Nature that makes the whole world kin more constantly visible. She was never more in her place than in visiting some poor tenant on the morrow of a great bereavement, or uttering words of comfort by the sick bed of some humble dependant. Men of all ranks who came in contact with her were struck with her thoughtful kindness, and her royal gift of an excellent memory never showed itself more frequently than in the manner in which she remembered and inquired after the fortunes and happiness of obscure persons related to those with whom she spoke.

Her religious opinions were brought very little before the public. Beyond a deep sense of Providential guidance and of the comforting power of religion, little is to be gathered from her published utterances; but she seemed equally at home in the Scotch Presbyterian and the Anglican Episcopal Church, and her marked admiration for such men as Dean Stanley and Norman Macleod, and for the preaching of Principal Caird, gives some clue to the bias of her opinions. Her mind was not speculative but eminently practical, and while she patronised good works of the most various kinds, there is reason to believe that those which most appealed to her personal feelings were those which directly contributed to alleviate the sufferings, or promote the material welfare, of the poor. She devoted the greater part of her Jubilee present to institutions for providing nurses for the sick poor, and this is said to have been one of the charities in which she took the warmest and most constant interest.

She is said not to have had any sympathy with the movement for the extension of political power to women, which became so conspicuous in her reign; but her own success in filling for sixty-three years the highest political position in the nation will always be quoted in its support. Considering, indeed, how comparatively small has been the number of reigning female Sovereigns, it is remarkable how many in modern times have shown themselves preeminently capable. Isabella of Spain, Catherine of Russia, Maria Theresa of Austria, and our own Elizabeth, all rise far above the level of ordinary Sovereigns. Some of these seem figures of a larger and stronger mould than Queen Victoria, but they governed under very different constitutional conditions, and, with one exception, there are serious blots on their memory. . . . In spite of the saying of Burke, the age of chivalry is not wholly dead. The sex of Queen Victoria no doubt gave an additional touch of warmth to the loyalty of her people, and many of the qualities that made her most popular are intensely, if not distinctively, feminine. They would not, however, have given her the place she will always hold in English history, if they had not been united with what men are accustomed to regard as more peculiarly masculine—a clear, well-balanced mind, singularly free from fanaticisms and exaggerations, excellently fitted to estimate rightly the true proportion of things.

In the last years of her reign the political horizon greatly cleared. Lord Beaconsfield, during his later Ministries, obtained not only her fullest political confidence, but also won a warmer degree of personal friendship than she had bestowed on any Minister since the death of Lord Melbourne; and her relations with his successor, Lord Salisbury, appear to have been perfectly harmonious. The decisive rejection by the country of the Home Rule policy removed a great incubus from her mind, and she was fully in harmony with the strong Imperialist sentiments which now began to prevail in English thought, and especially with the warmer feeling towards our distant colonies which was one of its chief characteristics. Her own popularity also rapidly grew. She had keenly felt and bitterly resented the reproaches which had at one period been frequently brought against her for her neglect of social and ceremonial duties during many years of her widowhood. Her censors, she maintained, made no allowance for her loneliness, her advancing years, her feeble health, the overwhelming and incessant pressure of her more serious political duties. But her two Jubilees, bringing her once more into close touch with her people, put an end to these reproaches. The Queen found with pleasure and perhaps with surprise how capable she still was of performing great public functions, and the vast outburst of spontaneous loyalty and affection of which she became the object gave her deep and unconcealed pleasure. To those, however, who were closely in connection with her it was touching to observe the gracious and unaffected modesty with which she received the homage of her subjects. Flattery was one of the things she disliked the most, and all who knew her best were struck with the singularly modest view she always took of herself. But blending with this modesty, and even with a shyness which she never wholly conquered, was the craving of a deeply affectionate and womanly nature for sympathy, and this craving was now abundantly gratified.

Still, with all this there was much that was melancholy in her later days. She had survived nearly all the intimacies of her youth. Death had made—especially in very recent times—many gaps in the circle of those who were nearest to her, and several of her children and of her children's husbands had preceded her to the tomb. Her sight had greatly failed. She was bowed down by physical infirmity, and her last year was saddened by a long, sanguinary, and inglorious war. Yet almost to the very end she continued with unabated courage to fulfil her daily task, and there was no sign that she had lost anything of her quick sympathy and her admirable judgment and tact. Her life was a most harmonious whole in which mind and character were happily attuned,

Like perfect music set to noble words.

PART I

Economic Structure

BRITAIN WAS still agricultural when Victoria came to the throne in 1837. The pace of industrialization, the explosion in productivity, combined with demographic revolution and urban concentration to suggest a misleadingly rapid shift of the nation to city and factory in early Victorian years. The urban-rural balance tilted to the city only in the 1840s. The railroad network provided a national market for labor just as it did for other commodities, but more than two decades passed before the trunk and principal branch lines could be completed. Investment and commercial statistics are impressive for the 1830s and 1840s, but they display no pattern of sustained, systematic growth. There is even evidence for a drop in the rate of growth during the 1830s, which would have been felt most severely in industrial and commercial sectors of the economy.[1]

EVOLUTION OF AGRICULTURE

The broad outline of the traditional picture is correct. Britain did urbanize and industrialize, and agriculture did not share fully in national economic growth. But agriculture, shaken by unrest in 1830,[2] sustained a slow evolution in form. Classic mixed farming—a balance of cropland and pasture, of cereal grain and livestock produced by the first agricultural revolution—gradually gave way to specialized, intensive farming. Agriculture remained labor intensive until the last quarter of the century, from whence, to the First World War, machinery and specialization made increasing inroads. Victorian farming came to resemble Victorian manufacturing rather than the balanced, self-sufficient mixed farm so dear to the heart of Arthur Young and his fellow agricultural reformers of the eighteenth century. Artificial fertilizers reduced dependence upon domestic livestock and made

1. P. Deane and W. A. Cole, *British Economic Growth, 1688–1959* (Cambridge: 1962), p. 172; P. Deane, "Contemporary Estimates of National Income in the First Half of the Nineteenth Century," *Economic History Review*, 2d series, VIII (1956), 353; R. S. Neale, "The Standard of Living, 1780–1844: A Regional and Class Study," *Economic History Review*, 2d series, XIX (1966), 590–606, esp. App. B.

2. E. Hobsbawn and G. Rude, *Captain Swing* (London: 1969).

possible intensive cereal cropping and crop specialization without fear
of exhausting the soil. The farmer came increasingly to resemble the
manufacturer, purchasing raw materials and transforming them into a
marketable product—a process that increases in intensity with the
evolution of modern high farming.[3]

British agriculture was a victim of artificial prosperity engendered by
more than two decades of war with France (1793–1815). Farming was
so profitable that there was no real incentive for recapitalization and
improvement. So softened, British agriculture reeled under a postwar
deflation, bad enough in itself, but leading directly into a sustained
price fall lasting until 1849. Agriculture recovered fitfully and un-
evenly. Leases drawn and improvements capitalized at the opening of
the century were fiscal albatrosses. Yet there was continual demand
that agriculture must pay. Standards of consumption and luxury grew
steadily more expensive for the landowning classes, but rent (reflecting
agricultural income) could only be maintained at current rates with
difficulty. Thus the intense political passions engendered by the agitation for the repeal of the corn laws, the protective tariff on agricultural
produce.

English agriculture, suffering from deflation and the imbalanced
burden of taxation, fluttered briefly upward with the new poor law of
1834[4] only to drop again in the recession of 1837. Agriculture continued depressed in the early Victorian years; and, in the case of
Ireland, an almost entirely agricultural country, the failure of the crops
spelled human as well as economic disaster. English landowners and
farmers saw the manufacturer-sponsored campaign against the corn
laws, culminating in repeal in 1846, as threatening economic, social,
and political ruin.[5] Free-traders contended that freight charges served
the function of a protective tariff without placing a bread tax upon the
workingmen of the nation. They were right, but the international
transportation revolution of the third quarter of the nineteenth century destroyed that slender margin and prepared the way for the
British agricultural disaster of the 1870s and 1880s.

The transportation revolution opened the era of British agricultural
prosperity in the 1850s and 1860s. The railroad created a national
market and thus helped to standardize agricultural prices, rationalize
procedures, and stimulate economic efficiency through regional specialization. By the 1850s, moreover, there was nowhere for British
agriculture to go but up. The price rise, rationalization of the market,
and continuing population growth made agriculture pay in mid cen-

3. F. M. L. Thompson, "The Second Agricultural Revolution," *Economic
History Review*, Second Series, XXI (1968), 62–77. Cf. J. D. Chambers and
G. E. Mingay, *The Agricultural Revolution* (London: 1966).

4. See Document 12, *British Politics in the Nineteenth Century* (New
York: Harper & Row, 1969; Harper Torchbook 1427), hereafter cited as
BP19C.

5. See Document 16, *ibid.*

tury. This prosperity displayed many of the characteristics of prosperity in other sectors of the economy during the 1850s and 1860s. Profits tended to accrue at the top. Landowners and, to a lesser degree, farmers were the principal beneficiaries. Rents rose about 30 percent from 1842 to 1878, while wages, always low but particularly depressed during the 1830s and 1840s, rose far more slowly. The concentration of agricultural holdings, a significant feature of British agriculture at the opening of the century, continued.[6] According to the great survey of 1872–1873, 7,400 persons out of a total population of 31,000,000 owned approximately half of the land in Britain. More than 40 percent of England was in estates of 3,000 acres or more. This concentration widened the gulf between those who raised food and those who received rent. Less than one-eighth of England's soil was owned by those who actually farmed it.

Few looked past the immediate glitter of present prosperity. The gloomy predictions of the 1840s appeared foolish to the British agriculturalist of the 1870s. He enjoyed an expanding market to which he provided four-fifths of the food consumed. Continuing population growth and increasing public prosperity expanded demand and maintained prices. The British workingman was earning more and eating better. Potatoes were no longer his staple. Bread consumption remained steady, but demand for meat soared. The British farmer, who had geared himself to adjust for market shifts, could forsee only a prosperous future, but danger was close at hand. To some degree the farmer enjoyed false abundance. Land values rose more rapidly than new investment in land, and landlords enjoyed a situation in which there were more farmers than available farms. Agricultural labor paid the price. Save in regions near industry, which offered optional forms of employment for the laborer, farm wages were low and working conditions wretched. In the face of adversity Joseph Arch initiated his Agricultural Workers Union. For the last time the farm worker had been the principal victim of economic fluctuations, although the results were far from clear when the rains came. Improvement in wages and working conditions, moreover, derived quite as much from the flight from agriculture as an occupation as from trade union pressure.

1879 was almost legendary. The United Kingdom is wet, but this was too much. It rained through the rain. Crops were ruined; sheep died of rot. It was the worst harvest of the century, but prices did not rise as they should have done. They fell. And they continued to fall. Technology and the world market finally exacted their toll. Spurred by the railroad, the great plains of the United States and Canada, together with the East European breadbasket, dumped thousands of tons of grain into the food markets of the Western world. Refrigeration brought imported meat, so even those areas of highest food demand became increasingly competitive.

6. Document 9, "Land and Power." For some of the social implications of land ownership, see Document 20.

The debate still rages as to the extent of damage done British agriculture by the collapse of 1879. It is, in many ways, a matter of splitting hairs. No depression has a universal, total impact. Some inefficient farmers were driven from the land. Others moved to more profitable crops or commodities. There were hard times on the land, and landlords knew it. Overall averages are deceptive, but rents fell approximately 30 percent between 1879 and 1901. Yet the acreage of cultivated land continued to rise until 1890 and declined very slowly until the First World War. There were significant shifts in land use as farmers switched from arable to pasture. In cropland, green crops remained relatively stable, while wheat and cereal grain production fell sharply. The impact and immediacy of collapse was cushioned to some extent by the fact that foreign competition was weakest in those areas where domestic demand was growing most rapidly. Technology, however, held yet another rude shock for those plunging hard into livestock. The little blue cloud of exhaust smoke as yet gave no hint that the internal combustion engine would displace the horse.

Agricultural capital, prices, and rents all fell, but not the wages paid farm labor. For the first time in the nineteenth century the agricultural worker began to enjoy relative prosperity. Laborers earned more in cash wages, much more in real wages, when Victoria died in 1901 than they had when the blow came in 1879. Much of the credit goes to the work of Joseph Arch's union, but credit must be shared with the economic facts of life. Between 1879 and 1901 the number of agricultural workers dropped by more than one-fourth. In the end the principal beneficiary was the British consumer whose choices improved as prices fell. He ate more and better for less.

INDUSTRY

British industrial growth was, in great measure, a slow but reasonably steady process in which change begot change. Britain was also the center and model for the first industrial revolution, a drama that played its middle and last acts in the Victorian years. Economic development usually pays scant attention to the niceties of political chronology. The industrial revolution, as distinguished from British economic growth, is traditionally associated with the spectacular expansion of the cotton textile industry. Late eighteenth-century technological innovation restored the balance between spinning and weaving while providing for an astounding increase in productivity. Vastly increased output at dramatically falling prices generated its own market demand. Steam engines emancipated mills from their dependence upon water power. Eli Whitney's cotton gin slashed the cost of raw material. When the Scottish chemist Andrew Ure rhapsodized on the improving theme of technological progress in 1835,[7] he sang principally of the cotton trade. The largest capital expansion of the textile industry occurred in the first years of Victoria's reign. The number of

7. Document 2.

cotton spindles more than doubled between 1830 and 1850. The number of power looms almost quintupled. Simultaneously, the number of handlooms engaged in cotton production fell to one-sixth of the 1830 total.

Steam power made it all possible. Factory organization—the concentration and specialization of labor—involved a revolution in the way people lived and worked. Labor costs were halved. Spinners and weavers moved into factories. Cotton entrepreneurs found an ample labor market, generally unregulated before 1847, in which there was no threat of competition. Technological improvement lagged in other forms of cloth, particularly wool and linen. But significant foreign competition lay far in the future. The market, domestic and foreign, seemed ever expandable.

Yet each advantage was a wasting asset. Technological advances came to other textiles. Synthetics eventually threatened natural fibers themselves. Other nations industrialized, and cotton textiles were invariably one of the first to appear. Britain's industrial lead—short-lived as it proved to be—was deceptively great. Her labor costs rose; so did cotton prices. Capital improvements cost more and yielded relatively less. Save for a brief setback during the American Civil War, the cotton industry expanded more than 5 percent per year during the first half of the century—more slowly but still impressively during the second half. Production finally began to fall in the 1890s, and by the end of Victoria's reign, cotton had dropped behind coal and the engineering trades.

Wool, the traditional staple of the British economy, proved a technological problem. Wool fibers demanded more delicate and sophisticated machinery than cotton, so innovation proceeded more slowly. Wool was, relatively speaking, of declining importance in British export trade, falling from between 4 and 5 percent of British national income before Victoria to 3.5 percent in midcentury and a mere 1.5 percent by 1901. A midcentury flurry of recapitalization and mechanization slowed by the 1870s. Wool employed no more people in 1901 than it had in 1851, and technology does not account for this relative decline.

Linen, which eighteenth-century governments had been at such pains to develop, also suffered a relative decline, which, after the middle of the century, became absolute. The linen industry remained prosperous in late Victorian years only in Ireland, its traditional center. And for Ireland it was one of the few bright spots in a bleak economic setting. Linen resisted factories and mechanization. It did business the old ways—a domestic industry organized on the putting-out system—until well into the second half of the nineteenth century. Power looms made few and slow inroads.

The relative importance of Victorian industries suggests the chronological shifts in economic structure. Textiles and clothing played their most important role in the economy during the middle of the cen-

tury—years in which the British concentrated intensively on producing and distributing a narrow range of necessities for the world
market. More than one-fifth of the national work force was engaged in
textiles and clothing in 1851. Relative decline became absolute by the
census of 1871.[8] Even then, almost one-third of the factories and
workshops that fell under government regulation produced textiles or
clothing.

The story of textiles is, in many ways, the saga of British industry.
Textiles, excluding clothing, produced something like 14 percent of
national income during the early 1820s. Fortunes accumulated. Entrepreneurial experiments became habits. But the share of national income
fell steadily from 11 percent during the early Victorian years to 9
percent on the eve of the American Civil War. Continued expansion of
cotton textiles sustained this sector of the economy, although the relative decline continued. Textiles probably did not represent 5 percent
of national income by 1901.

Other and newer industries grew and prospered while textiles continued a relative decline. But old habits and notions were hard to
uproot. Investment capital continued to flow into an increasingly less
profitable sector of the economy. It worked for grandfather; it will
work for us. Investment patterns, no less than educational inadequacy,
restricted British economic flexibility just when international competition, principally although not exclusively from Germany and the
United States, made vital the development of new economies. Frozen
attitude and habit, both of labor and management, help to account for
the faltering of the British economy during and after the 1880s.

British economic primacy rested, to a considerable degree, upon
chronology and geography. She had geared her production to the world
market, developing those goods and services the world needed. Her
position, dominating the North Atlantic sea lanes, the waterway from
northern Europe to the world beyond, made much simpler the development and maintenance of commercial supremacy. Europe came
increasingly to dominate the world, and Britain was the country
economically and physically situated to develop and maintain commercial supremacy. Britain's industrial and commercial lead, in turn,
strengthened her financial position and emphasized her role as the
world's banker. The prospects seemed infinite. British railroadmen
exported British technology to build British railroads with British
capital in Argentina. These railroads required British money and
British rolling stock and rails shipped in British merchantmen. British
coal, British iron, British engineering, not to mention British insurance
or British domestic transport, profited enormously from Argentinian
railroads. And these railroads brought Argentinian foodstuffs more
cheaply to the British market. Both Argentinians and Britons prospered. God might or might not be an Englishman, but Mammon
certainly appeared to be.

8. Document 6.

This economic success was misleading. Britain lacked the natural resources of the United States. Britain resisted the drives for economic efficiency and technical education that propelled Germany so far. British industry developed against feeble external competiton and prospered as the rest of Europe, then the world, struggled to develop themselves. Success came too easily. British industry became increasingly set in old ways just when imagination and flexibility were most needed. There was no lack of capacity, no lack of capital in money or science. Much of the basic experimental work in electricity, chemical dyes, and nonferrous metals was done by Britons, but her competitors developed each of those industries more rapidly and effectively than Britain. Cotton, coal, and steam characterized the first industrial revolution and the rationalization of the British economy. Steel, electricity, and the gasoline engine became the turn-of-the-century bellwethers. Once a pioneer, now she lagged. In part, the reasons were beyond her control. She had neither the material edge of the United States nor the technological capacities of Germany. But part of it was simply a failure to move and adapt. Michael Faraday stated the principle of the dynamo in 1831, but Britain did not introduce electric lighting until 1875 and continued to prefer gas. Of course there were the vested interests of gas companies, but more of the difficulty lay in entrepreneurial disinterest, in the spotty and small-scale development of electric companies. Factory and mineowners in the Tyneside joined forces to develop a central electrical supply and grid system, but only in that one region was there substantial electrical development before the First World War. A Briton developed the modern turbine in 1884, but Sir Charles Parsons failed to generate any sudden British move in either electricity or propulsion. Other countries capitalized upon British developments. Only in the closing years of the century did English cities begin to build electric traction systems. The London tubes and provincial tramways were deferred but important dividends.

The British were equally immune to the internal combustion engine. With unconscious humor, Parliament in 1865 limited mechanically propelled vehicles to four miles per hour in the country, two in town. Such vehicles had to be accompanied by a man with a red flag. The act was finally repealed in 1896, twenty years after Dr. Otto's internal combustion engine, nine after Daimler's automobile. Lorries, buses, and automobiles, the highways on which they must run were, like the airplane, children of the turn of the century. Real development began only on the eve of the First World War. The railroad served the Victorians, the automobile their heirs.

Britain had led the world in production and innovation in iron. British inventions by Henry Bessemer and William Siemens made possible the economic conversion of iron to steel. The Gilchrist-Thomas process, by dealing with other impurities, opened the way for the development of the Ruhr Valley steel industry. The United States and Germany, followed shortly by other countries, were to take more advantage of British technology than the British could or would themselves.

Business success is easy to misdefine. Profits and dividends can become their own justification. Those methods and processes that work are not necessarily the best. Every economy has deficient factors. Unfortunately for the British, by the last third of the nineteenth century, theirs were increasingly evident in the same sectors that had produced world economic leadership. Shipbuilding, for example, found adjustment increasingly difficult and expensive just as foreign competition was becoming acute. Shipbuilders converted from sail to steam, from wooden to iron ships—each a psychological as well as a fiscal strain—only to find themselves confronting the still more expensive shift from iron to steel. And what of the shipper? Each wooden sailing ship, every iron steamship, represented a heavy investment to be amortized slowly. When vast recapitalization was needed, the Suez Canal and growing foreign competition sharply cut profits. The story could be repeated in one industry after another. Investment in obsolete plant and equipment was the price paid for having paced the economic race.

Psychological and economic obsolescence haunted British business during the last three decades of the 1800s. Business success did not, of itself, bring social and cultural status. Only when such success was translated into traditional terms—landed estate, public-school and university education, emancipation from the need to earn a living, involvement in the charmed circle of social and political elites—only then could the business family gain social prestige. Of course many businessmen played active political roles while maintaining business interests and activities. Obviously plutocracy could gain a considerable measure of social prestige through the leverage of money and little else. But business, in general, failed to provide the same measure of social status that it did in the United States or, to a considerable degree, in Germany. True social position, as in France, presumed that one was a *rentier*.

British industry had developed as family and partnership enterprise.[9] Corporate organization, restricted by the vagaries of British commercial law and economic habit, imposed an impossible demand— the consistent and continuous development of entrepreneurial attitudes and skills through sequential generations. The second generation often, perhaps usually, continued in any successful business, with a tendency toward broader interests. The second generation was more apt to be simultaneously involved in municipal improvement and political and cultural activities. Given continued economic success, the third generation might opt for the higher (or lower) things in life. Public-school education becomes more common. He looks to Oxford or Cambridge, thinks and acts like a gentleman, and merges imperceptibly

9. Although the railroad, in particular, makes an important exception. See Document 3.

into the "establishment." Simultaneously, the coming of limited liability with shares and directorships provided a new, amusing form of business respectability. One could profit from business, even participate in it, without being functionally involved. Titled members added dignity to a board of directors and by their presence conferred respectability upon the managers of corporate enterprise.

Established firms incorporated slowly but in greater numbers as the century drew to a close. Limited liability, shares, directors, and professional management brought benefits and problems.[10] Families tended to run out of males capable of or interested in continuing the enterprise. New professional business careerists made possible the survival of some firms. British professional management, however, drew substantially from individuals trained as accountants, rather than technicians (those whose expertise was involved with the productive process) or lawyers (whose concern tends to be with corporate structure, regulation, and expansion). To some extent this made corporate business more conservative, although probably more stable.[11] Limited liability and professional management further widened the gap between employer and worker which had grown since the eighteenth century. From small shops where there was little in background or outlook to distinguish master and man, factories, the intensive division of labor, urban concentration and segregation had all depersonalized work relationships.[12]

Throughout the Victorian years labor made its presence felt as an organized entity.[13] By the middle of the century craft unions were capable of regional bargaining. Legal recognition, political success, the refinement of collective bargaining into a fine art made unionism an estate of the realm by the years of Gladstone and Disraeli. The pressures upon organized labor were principally internal and from the ranks of the disorganized below. The Great Depression (1873–1896) actually produced strikingly higher living standards and working conditions for British working people.[14] Higher expectations produced demands for inclusion from the hitherto neglected unskilled. The gasworkers of London, the matchgirls, and the dockers organized, secured recognition, and improved their conditions. The world of organized labor became increasingly restive, but considerably more representative of British workers.

The increasing prosperity, which, despite all short-term fluctuations, Britain enjoyed through the century, was poorly distributed in British society. Mid-Victorian prosperity, for example, looks most

10. Document 4.
11. This is not to suggest that organizational imagination was lost. See Document 10.
12. This suggests the artificial divisions in such volumes. The point is developed in Part II, Social Organization.
13. Document 7.
14. Document 8.

impressive in terms of profits and savings—making money and using it to make more money. Individualism and frugality animated the mill owner and his hand. But there remained the brutal reality of poverty— what even Victorians allowed to be "the submerged tenth." Possibly as much as 30 percent of the population was under- or erratically employed. Britons lived a materially better life in 1901 than they had in 1837. They ate better, were better housed, had more options in life and living. The state came increasingly to regulate those in a position to exploit and protect those incapable of caring for themselves. But even as collectivism increased, the traditional values still found expression in the organizations for mutual self-help, or the cooperative movement.[15]

For all of the hints of decline, in spite of the many points of tension, it was still a self-confident, growing empire that emerged into the twentieth century. There had always been problems, but Britons could always resolve them. There were always threats, but Britain would prevail. She was unique—the greatest and most truly world power since creation.

15. Document 5.

General Bibliography

T. S. ASHTON, *The Industrial Revolution* (London: 1948).

W. ASHWORTH, *An Economic History of England, 1870–1939* (London: 1961)

J. BRUNETT, *Plenty and Want* (London: 1965).

A. K. CAINCROSS, *Home and Foreign Investment, 1870–1913* (Cambridge: 1953).

J. D. CHAMBERS, *The Workshop of the World* (London: 1961).

―――― and G. E. MINGAY, *The Agricultural Revolution, 1750–1913* (London: 1966).

S. G. CHECKLAND, *The Rise of Industrial Society in England, 1815–1885* (London: 1964).

J. H. CLAPHAM, *An Economic History of Modern Britain*, 3 vols. (Cambridge: 1927–1939).

W. H. B. COURT, *A Concise Economic History of Britain from 1760* (Cambridge: 1954).

P. DEANE, *The First Industrial Revolution, 1750–1850* (Cambridge: 1966).

―――― and W. A. COLE, *British Economic Growth, 1688–1959* (Cambridge: 1962).

H. J. DYOS and D. H. ALDCROFT, *British Transport* (Leicester: 1969).

LORD ERNLE [ROLAND E. PROTHERO], *English Farming, Past and Present*, rev. ed. (London: 1927).

M. W. FLINN, *An Economic and Social History of Britain* (London: 1961).

A. D. GAYER, W. W. ROSTOW, and A. SCHWARTZ, *Growth and Fluctuations of the British Economy, 1790–1850*, 2 vols. (Oxford: 1953).

H. J. HABAKKUK, *American and British Technology* (Cambridge: 1962).

J. L. and B. HAMMOND, *The Rise of Modern Industry*, 5th ed. (London: 1937).

E. J. HOBSBAWM, *Industry and Empire* (London: 1968).

W. G. HOFFMAN, *British Industry, 1700–1950*, trans. W. O. Henderson and W. H. Chaloner (Oxford: 1955).

J. R. T. HUGHES, *Fluctuations in Trade, Industry, and Finance, 1850–1869* (Oxford: 1960).

A. J. IMLAH, *Economic Elements in the Pax Britannica* (Cambridge, Mass.: 1958).

L. H. JENKS, *The Migration of British Capital to 1875* (New York: 1927).

C. P. KINDLBERGER, *Economic Growth in France and Britain, 1851–1950* (Cambridge, Mass.: 1964).

D. S. LANDES, *The Unbound Prometheus* (Cambridge: 1969).
P. MATHIAS, *The First Industrial Nation* (London: 1969).
E. M. OJALA, *Agriculture and Economic Progress* (London: 1952).
C. S. ORWIN, *History of English Farming* (London: 1949).
────── and E. WHETHAM, *History of British Agriculture, 1846–1914* (London: 1964).
W. W. ROSTOW, *The British Economy of the Nineteenth Century* (Oxford: 1949).
S. B. SAUL, *Studies in British Overseas Trade, 1870–1914* (Liverpool: 1960).
W. SCHLÖTE, *British Overseas Trade from 1700 to the 1930s*, trans. W. O. Henderson and W. H. Chaloner (Oxford: 1952).
F. M. L. THOMPSON, *English Landed Society in the Nineteenth Century* (London: 1963).

2. *The Entrepreneur: A Philosophy of Manufactures*

INVENTIVE MEN, factory organization, and machine production propelled the industrial revolution. The last quarter of the eighteenth century and the first half of the nineteenth were an unparalleled era of individual enterprise. Industrial entrepreneurship, while indebted to earlier commercial and manufacturing attitudes and methods, demanded a new psychology and novel skills. Let two examples suffice. The industrial entrepreneur had to find and develop fixed capital on an unprecedented scale. Other mercantile activity and previous methods of manufacturing had high degrees of liquidity. Most money invested was circulating capital—inventories, raw materials, goods in process, finished product, and cash for wages. Factories and machinery demanded increasing investment of fixed capital in plant and equipment. The return was slow, the investment difficult to liquidate save at great loss, and most lending institutions hostile or ill-equipped to meet these fiscal needs. The process continued. As investment in manufacturing shifted from cotton textiles to iron foundries and steel mills, the demand for fixed instead of circulating capital rose dramatically.

The industrial entrepreneur had to recruit, train, and retain a labor force of unprecedented size. No schools taught personnel management. There were no civilian examples. Only the state had comparable experience; thus the more than casual analogy between the armed forces and factory workers. Entrepreneurs had to discipline, train, equip, house, and feed their work force. With these problems in hand, entrepreneurs discovered that they had created new ones. Once factory discipline and regimentation had been imposed, the workingmen were themselves different. It was but a short step to the organization of labor unions in spite of a mixture of coercion and concession. The entrepreneurial outlook tended, for obvious reasons, to be commercial. Labor was a commodity, viewed, treated, and responding as such. The factory work force was a ledger entry, like money, raw cotton, or coal. Entrepreneurs, taking this view, were not vicious, nor, in many cases, were they consciously exploiting people. The most successful manufacturers were those who developed amicable bases for their labor relations. Some, like John Fielden of Todmorden or Robert Owen of New Lanark, were highly successful manufacturers who cut a significant figure in radical politics. Both Fielden and Owen were radical authoritarians—intellectually committed to the cause of mankind, convinced they knew how to define and serve it, and intolerant of subordinate dissent.

It was a world for innovation, although not necessarily for imagination. Entrepreneurial survival meant mastering new skills and adapting oneself to the market. Ownership and management still tended to vest in the same hands during the early and mid-Victorian years. The era of shareholders and professional management began (slowly) with the Limited Liability Act of 1855. This concentration of responsibility and authority made each decision more weighty. Mistakes meant ruin, and that reenforced solid pragmatism. But even during the early Victorian years entrepreneurs were moving further away from the excessive individualism of early industrialism. Necessity proved the mother of organizations and institutions. Banking, company law, commercial codes had to be reconstructed to meet the needs of the world's leading economic power. Manufacturers learned to cooperate to provide common services, to cope with the organization of trade unions, and to encourage or resist the intervention of the state.

Andrew Ure (1778–1857) was a Scottish chemist, physician, and scientific writer who championed the new world of machines amd manufacturers. He minimized or dismissed criticisms of the manufacturing system and wrote this extensive treatise to explain what manufacturing was, how it worked, and what were its economic and social consequences.

Recommended Reading

In addition to the considerable literature to be found in *Explorations in Entrepreneurial History*, *The Business History Review*, *Economic History Review*, and *The Journal of Economic History*, consult S. Pollard, *The Genesis of Modern Management* (London: 1965), R. Bendix, *Work and Authority in Industry* (New York: 1956), and a provocative, controversial volume by D. C. McClelland, *The Achieving Society* (New York: 1961).

ANDREW URE,
A PHILOSOPHY OF MANUFACTURES

This island is pre-eminent among civilized nations for the prodigious development of its factory wealth, and has been therefore

Source: From *The Philosophy of Manufactures* (London: 1835), pp. 6–9, 11–14, 16–21, 22–25, 29–32, 40–43.

long viewed with a jealous admiration by foreign powers. This very pre-eminence, however, has been contemplated in a very different light by many influential members of our own community, and has been even denounced by them as the certain origin of innumerable evils to the people, and of revolutionary convulsions to the state. If the affairs of the kingdom be wisely administered, I believe such allegations and fears will prove to be groundless, and to proceed more from the envy of one ancient and powerful order of the commonwealth, towards another suddenly grown into political importance than from the nature of things.

In the recent discussions concerning our factories, no circumstance is so deserving of remark, as the gross ignorance evinced by our leading legislators and economists, gentlemen well informed in other respects, relative to the nature of those stupendous manufactures which have so long provided the rulers of the kingdom with the resources of war, and a great body of the people with comfortable subsistence; which have, in fact, made this island the arbiter of many nations, and the benefactor of the globe itself. Till this ignorance be dispelled, no sound legislation need be expected on manufacturing subjects. To effect this purpose, is a principal, but not the sole aim of the present volume, for it is intended also to convey specific information to the classes directly concerned in the manufactures, as well as general knowledge to the community at large, and particularly to young persons about to make the choice of a profession.

The blessings which physico-mechanical science has bestowed on society, and the means it has still in store for ameliorating the lot of mankind, has been too little dwelt upon; while, on the other hand, it has been accused of lending itself to the rich capitalists as an instrument for harassing the poor, and of exacting from the operative an accelerated rate of work. It has been said, for example, that the steam-engine now drives the powerlooms with such velocity as to urge on their attendant weavers at the same rapid pace; but the handweaver, not being subjected to this restless agent, can throw his shuttle and move his treddles as his convenience. There is, however, this difference in the two cases, that in the factory, every member of the loom is so adjusted, that the driving force leaves the attendant nearly nothing at all to do, certainly no muscular fatigue to sustain, while it procures for him good, unfailing wages, besides a healthy workshop gratis: whereas the non-factory weaver, having everything to execute by muscular exertion, finds the labour irksome, makes in consequence innumerable short pauses, separately of little account, but great when added together; earns therefore proportionally low wages, while he loses his health by poor diet and the dampness of his hovel. . . .

The constant aim and effect of scientific improvement in manufactures are philanthropic, as they tend to relieve the workmen either from niceties of adjustment which exhaust his mind and fatigue his eyes, or from painful repetition of effort which distort or wear out his frame. At every step of each manufacturing process described in this volume, the humanity of science will be manifest. New illustrations of this truth appear almost every day, of which a remarkable one has just come to my knowledge. In the woollen-cloth trade there is a process between carding and spinning the wool, called *slubbing*, which converts the spongy rolls, turned off from the cards, into a continuous length of fine porous cord. Now, though carding and spinning lie within the domain of automatic science, yet slubbing is a handicraft operation, depending on the skill of the slubber, and participating therefore in all his irregularities. If he be a steady, temperate man, he will conduct his business regularly, without needing to harass his juvenile assistants, who join together the series of card rolls, and thus feed his machine; but if he be addicted to liquor, and passionate, he has it in his power to exercise a fearful despotism over the young pieceners, in violation of the proprietor's benevolent regulations. This class of operatives, who, though inmates of factories are not, properly speaking, factory workers, being independent of the moving power, have been principal source of the obloquy so unsparingly cast on the cotton and other factories, in which no such capricious practices or cruelties exist. The wool slubber, when behind hand with his work, after a visit to the beer-shop, resumes his task with violence, and drives his machine at a speed beyond the power of the pieceners to accompany; and if he finds them deficient in the least point, he does not hesitate to lift up the long wooden rod from his slubbing-frame, called a billy-roller, and beat them unmercifully. I rejoice to find that science now promises to rescue this branch of the business from handicraft caprice, and to place it, like the rest, under the safeguard of automatic mechanism. . . .

The processes that may be employed, to give to portions of inert matter, precise movements resembling those of organized beings, are innumerable, as they consist of an indefinite number and variety of cords, pulleys, toothed-wheels, nails, screws, levers, inclined-planes, as well as agencies of air, water, fire, light, &c., combined in endless modes to produce a desired effect. Ingenuity has been long exercised on such combinations, chiefly for public amusement or mystification, without any object of futility. . . .

Self-acting inventions . . . , however admirable as exercises of mechanical science, do nothing towards the supply of the physical necessities of society. Man stands in daily want of food, fuel, clothing, and shelter; and is bound to devote the powers of body and mind, of nature and art, in the first place to provide for himself and his dependents a sufficiency of these necessaries, without which there can be no comfort, nor leisure for the cultivation of the taste and intellect. To the production of food and domestic accommodation, not many automatic inventions have been applied, or seem to be extensively applicable; though, for modifying them to the purposes of luxury, many curious contrivances have been made. Machines, more or less automatic, are embodied in the coal-mines of Great Britain; but such combinations have been mainly directed, in this as well as other countries, to the materials of clothing. These chiefly consist of flexible fibres of vegetable or animal origin, twisted into smooth, tenacious threads, which are then woven into cloth by being decussated in a loom. Of the animal kingdom, silk, wool, and hair, are the principal textile products. The vegetable tribes furnish cotton, flax, hemp, besides several other fibrous substances of inferior importance.

Wool, flax, hemp, and silk, have been very generally worked up among the nations of Europe, both in ancient and modern times; but cotton attire was, till sixty years ago, confined very much to Hindostan, and some other districts of Asia. No textile filaments however are, by their facility of production as well as their structure, so well adapted as those of cotton to furnish articles of clothing, combining comfort with beauty and convenience in an eminent degree. Hence we can understand how cotton fabrics, in their endless variety of textures and styles, plain, figured, and coloured, have within the short period of one human life, grown into an enormous manufacture, have become an object of the first desire to mankind all over the globe, and of zealous industry to the most civilized states. This business has received its great automatic development in

England, though it was cultivated to a considerable extent on handi-craft principles in France a century ago, and warmly encouraged by the government of that country, both as to the growth of the material and its conversion into cloth. The failure of the French however to establish a factory system prior to the English is a very remarkable fact, and proves clearly that mechanical invention, for which the former nation have long been justly celebrated, is not of itself sufficient to found a successful manufacture. . . .

The term *Factory*, in technology, designates the combined oper-ation of many orders of work-people, adult and young, in tending with assiduous skill a system of productive machines continuously impelled by a central power. This definition includes such organi-zations as cotton-mills, flax-mills, silk-mills, woollen-mills, and cer-tain engineering works; but it excludes those in which the mechanisms do not form a connected series, nor are dependent on one prime mover. Of the latter class, examples occur in iron-works, dye-works, soap-works, brass-foundaries, &c. Some authors, in-deed, have comprehended under the title *factory*, all extensive establishments wherein a number of people co-operate towards a common purpose of art; and would therefore rank breweries, distil-leries, as well as the workshops of carpenters, turners, coopers, &c., under the factory system. But I conceive that this title, in its strictest sense, involves the idea of a vast automaton, composed of various mechanical and intellectual organs, acting in uninterrupted concert for the production of a common object, all of them being subordinated to a self-regulated moving force. If the marshalling of human beings in systematic order for the execution of any techni-cal enterprise were allowed to constitute a factory, this term might embrace every department of civil and military engineering; a latitude of application quite inadmissible. . . .

Prior to this period, manufactures were everywhere feeble and fluctuating in their development; shooting forth luxuriantly for a season, and again withering almost to the roots, like annual plants. Their perennial growth now began in England, and attracted capital in copious streams to irrigate the rich domains of industry. When this new career commenced, about the year 1770, the annual consumption of cotton in British manufactures was under four millions of pounds weight, and that of the whole of Christendom was probably not more than ten millions. Last year the consump-tion in Great Britain and Ireland was about two hundred and seventy millions of pounds, and that of Europe and the United States together four hundred and eighty millions. This prodigious increase is, without doubt, almost entirely due to the factory system founded and upreared by the intrepid native of Preston. If then this system be not merely an inevitable step in the social progression of the world, but the one which gives a commanding station and influence to the people who most resolutely take it, it does not become any man, far less a denizen of this favoured land, to vilify the author of a benefaction, which, wisely administered, may become the best temporal gift of Providence to the poor, a blessing destined to mitigate, and in some measure to repeal, the primeval curse pronounced on the labour of man, "in the sweat of thy face shalt thou eat bread." Arkwright well deserves to live in honoured remembrance among those ancient master-spirits, who persuaded their roaming companions to exchange the precarious toils of the chase, for the settled comforts of agriculture.

In my recent tour, continued during several months, through the manufacturing districts, I have seen tens of thousands of old, young, and middle-aged of both sexes, many of them too feeble to get their daily bread by any of the former modes of industry, earning abundant food, raiment, and domestic accommodation, without perspiring at a single pore, screened meanwhile from the summer's sun and the winter's frost, in apartments more airy and salubrious than those of the metropolis, in which our legislative and fashionable aristocracies assemble. In those spacious halls the benignant power of steam summons around him his myriads of willing menials, and assigns to each the regulated task, substituting for painful muscular effort on their part, the energies of his own gigantic arm, and demanding in return only attention and dexterity to correct such little aberrations as casually occur in his workmanship. The gentle docility of this moving force qualifies it for impelling the tiny bobbins of the lace-machine with a precision and speed inimitable by the most dexterous hands, directed by the sharpest eyes. Hence, under its auspices, and in obedience to Arkwright's polity, magnificent edifices, surpassing far in number, value, usefulness, and ingenuity of construction, the boasted monuments of Asiatic, Egyptian, and Roman despotism, have, within the short period of fifty years, risen up in this kingdom, to show to what extent, capital, industry, and science may augment the resources of a state, while they meliorate the condition of its citizens.

Such is the factory system, replete with prodigies in mechanics and political economy, which promises, in its future growth, to become the great minister of civilization to the terraqueous globe, enabling this country, as its heart, to diffuse along with its commerce, the life-blood of science and religion to myraids of people still lying "in the region and shadow of death."

When Adam Smith wrote his immortal elements of economics, automatic machinery being hardly known, he was properly led to regard the division of labour as the grand principle of manufacturing improvement; and he showed, in the example of pinmaking, how each handicraftsman, being thereby enabled to perfect himself by practice in one point, became a quicker and cheaper workman. In each branch of manufacture he saw that some parts were, on that principle, of easy execution, like the cutting of pin wires into uniform lengths, and some were comparatively difficult, like the formation and fixation of their heads; and therefore he concluded that to each a workman of appropriate value and cost was naturally assigned. This appropriation forms the very essence of the division of labour, and has been constantly made since the origin of society. The ploughman, with powerful hand and skilful eye, has been always hired at high wages to form the furrow, and the ploughboy at low wages, to lead the team. But what was in Dr. Smith's time a topic of useful illustration, cannot now be used without risk of misleading the public mind as to the right principle of manufacturing industry. In fact, the division, or rather adaptation of labour to the different talents of men, is little thought of in factory employment. On the contrary, wherever a process requires peculiar dexterity and steadiness of hand, it is withdrawn as soon as possible from the *cunning* workman, who is prone to irregularities of many kinds, and it is placed in charge of a peculiar mechanism, so self-regulating, that a child may superintend it. Thus,—to take an example from the spinning of cotton—the first operation in delicacy and importance, is that of laying the fibres truly parallel in the spongy slivers, and the next is that of drawing these out into slender spongy cords, called rovings, with the least possible twist; both being perfectly uniform throughout their total length. To execute either of these processes tolerably by a hand-wheel, would require a degree of skill not to be met with in one artisan out of a hundred. But fine yarn could not be made in factory-spinning except by taking these steps, nor was it ever made by machinery till

Arkwright's sagacity contrived them. Moderately good yarn may be spun indeed on the *hand-wheel* without any drawings at all, and with even indifferent rovings, because the thread, under the two-fold action of twisting and extension, has a tendency to equalize itself.

The principle of the factory system then is, to substitute mechanical science for hand skill, and the partition of a process into its essential constituents, for the division or graduation of labour among artisans. On the handicraft plan, labour more or less skilled, was usually the most expensive element of production—*Materiam superabat opus;* but on the automatic plan, skilled labour gets progressively superseded, and will, eventually, be replaced by mere overlookers of machines.

By the infirmity of human nature it happens, that the more skilful the workman, the more self-willed and intractable he is apt to become, and, of course, the less fit a component of a mechanical system, in which, by occasional irregularities, he may do great damage to the whole. The grand object therefore of the modern manufacturer is, through the union of capital and science, to reduce the task of his work-people to the exercise of vigilance and dexterity,—faculties, when concentred to one process, speedily brought to perfection in the young. . . .

It was indeed a subject of regret to observe how frequently the workman's eminence, in any craft, had to be purchased by the sacrifice of his health and comfort. To one unvaried operation, which required unremitting dexterity and diligence, his hand and eye were constantly on the strain, or if they were suffered to swerve from their task for a time, considerable loss ensued, either to the employer, or the operative, according as the work was done by the day or by the piece. But on the equalization plan of self-acting machines, the operative needs to call his faculties only into agreeable exercise; he is seldom harassed with anxiety or fatigue, and may find many leisure moments for either amusement or meditation, without detriment to his master's interests or his own. As his business consists in tending the work of a well regulated mechanism, he can learn it in a short period; and when he transfers his services from one machine to another, he varies his task, and enlarges his views, by thinking on those general combinations which result from his and his companions' labours. Thus, that cramping of the faculties, that narrowing of the mind, that stunting of the frame, which were ascribed, and not unjustly, by moral writers, to the division of labour, cannot, in common circumstances, occur under the equable distribution of industry. How superior in vigour and intelligence are the factory mechanics in Lancashire, where the latter system of labour prevails, to the handicraft artisans of London, who, to a great extent, continue slaves to the former! The one set is familiar with almost every physico-mechanical combination, while the other seldom knows anything beyond the pin-head sphere of his daily task.

It is, in fact, the constant aim and tendency of every improvement in machinery to supersede human labour altogether, or to diminish its cost, by substituting the industry of women and children for that of men; or that of ordinary labourers, for trained artisans. In most of the water-twist, or throstle cotton mills, the spinning is entirely managed by females of sixteen years and upwards. The effect of substituting the self-acting mule for the common mule, is to discharge the greater part of the men spinners, and to retain adolescents and children. The proprietor of a factory near Stockport states, in evidence to the commissioners, that by such substitution, he would save 50*l.* a week in wages, in consequence of dispensing with nearly forty male spinners, at about 25*s.* of wages each. This tendency to employ merely children with watchful eyes and nimble fingers, instead of journeymen of long experience, shows how the scholastic dogma of the division of labour into degrees of skill has been exploded by our enlightened manufacturers.

They are, in truth, much better acquainted with the general economy of the arts, and better qualified to analyse them into their real principles, than the recluse academician can possibly be, who from a few obsolete data, traces out imaginary results, or conjures up difficulties seldom encountered in practice. He may fancy, for example, that in a great establishment, where several hundred people are employed in producing fine goods, much time and expense must be incurred in verifying the quality and quantity of the work done by each individual. But this verification forms an integral step in the train of operations, and therefore constitutes no appreciable part of the cost of the manufactured article. Thus, for example, the reeling of yarn into hanks measures its length; the weighing of a few miscellaneous hanks determines the grist of the whole; and the *taker-in of work* rapidly ascertains its soundness.

For examining the quality of the very fine yarns used in lace-making, he is aided by machines which register rapidly the uniformity of its cohesive strength, and the exact volume which one hundred yards of it occupy. The lace-maker again, on his part, verifies the grist of all the thread he purchases, in the necessary act of filling the circular grooves of his tiny bobbins, preparatory to their entering into his machine.

The university man, pre-occupied with theoretical *formulæ*, of little practical bearing, is too apt to under-value the science of the factory, though, with candour and patience, he would find it replete with useful applications of the most beautiful dynamical and statical problems. In physics, too, he would there see many theorems bearing golden fruit, which had been long barren in college ground. The phenomena of heat, in particular, are investigated in their multifarious relations to matter, solid, liquid, and aëriform. The measure of temperature on every scale is familiar to the manufacturer, as well as the distribution of caloric, and its habitudes with different bodies. The production of vapours; the relation of their elastic force to their temperature; the modes of using them as instruments of power, and sources of heat; their most effective condensation; their hygrometric agency; may all be better studied in a week's residence in Lancashire, than in a session of any university in Europe. And as to exact mechanical science, no school can compete with a modern cotton-mill. . . .

Steam-engines furnish the means not only of their support but of their multiplication. They create a vast demand for fuel; and, while they lend their powerful arms to drain the pits and to raise the coals, they call into employment multitudes of miners, engineers, ship-builders, and sailors, and cause the construction of canals and railways: and, while they enable these rich fields of industry to be cultivated to the utmost, they leave thousands of fine arable fields free for the production of food to man, which must have been otherwise allotted to the food of horses. Steam-engines moreover, by the cheapness and steadiness of their action, fabricate cheap goods, and procure in their exchange a liberal supply of the necessaries and comforts of life, produced in foreign lands.

Improvements in machinery have a three-fold bearing:—

1st. They make it possible to fabricate some articles which, but for them, could not be fabricated at all.

2d. They enable an operative to turn out a greater quantity of work than he could before,—time, labour, and quality of work remaining constant.

3d. They effect a substitution of labour comparatively unskilled, for that which is more skilled.

The introduction of new machines into any manufacture, with the effect of superseding hand labour, is tempered by the system of patents, which maintains them for a certain time at a monopoly price, and thereby obstructs their rapid multiplication. Did we admit the principles on which the use of particular self-acting mechanisms is objected to by workmen, we should not be able, in any case, to define the limits of their application. Had parliament acted on such principles sixty years ago, none of our manufactures could have attained to their present state of profitable employment to either masters or men. The immediate causes of their vast augmentation may be ascribed, under the blessing of Providence, to the general spirit of industry and enterprize among a free and enlightened people, left to the unrestrained exercise of their talents in the employment of a vast capital, pushing to the utmost the principle of the analysis of labour, summoning to their service all the resources of scientific research and mechanical ingenuity; and finally, availing themselves of all the benefits to be derived from visiting foreign countries, not only in order to form new and confirm old commercial connexions, but to obtain an intimate knowledge of the wants, the tastes, the habits, the discoveries and improvements, the productions, and fabrics of other civilized nations. Thus we bring home facts and suggestions; thus we perfect our old establishments, and add new branches to our domestic stock; opening, at the same time, new markets for the sale of our manufacturing and commercial industry, and qualifying ourselves for supplying them in the best and most economical manner. By these means alone, and, above all, by the effect of machinery in improving the quality, and cheapening the fabrication of our various articles of export, notwithstanding an immense load of taxes, and a higher price of grain, our commerce and manufactures have also increased in such a degree, as to surpass the most sanguine calculations of the ablest political economists who have speculated on the prospects of mankind. We should never cease to bear in mind, that we are surrounded by powerful nations, composed of a people equally industrious, and more sober than ourselves, who, released from the turmoil of war, are intent on cultivating the productive arts of peace, and of pushing their commerce and navigation; whose eagerness of competition is stimulated by the view of the rich prizes which we have already won.

The attempts continually made to carry our implements and machines into foreign countries, and to tempt our artisans to settle and superintend them there, evince the high value set by other nations on our mechanical substitutes for hand labour; and as they cannot be directly counteracted, they should be rendered, as far as possible, unavailing, by introducing such successive improvements at home as may always keep us foremost in the career of construction. It would be therefore no less disastrous to the operative, than to the capitalist, were any extraneous obstacles thrown in their way, since any good machine suppressed, or rejected, in this country, would infallibly be received with open arms by some of our neighbours, and most readily by our mechanical rivals in France, Belgium, Germany, and the United States. . . .

The dressing machine does at present 200 pieces of thirty yards each in a week, = 6000 yards, and costs in wages to the dresser 50s. This branch of the trade having in consequence of the high wages been, like the mule spinning, continually disturbed by unions and strikes, has led to the invention of a self-acting machine which will dress at least 6000 yards of warp in two days, under the superintendence of a labourer at 3s. a-day; that is, at a cost in wages of 6s. This mechanism is at the same time greatly simpler and cheaper than the former, and will soon come into general use for coarse calicoes. It affords an instructive warning to workmen to beware of strikes, by proving how surely science, at the call of capital, will defeat every unjustifiable union which the labourers may form.

It is one of the most important truths resulting from the analysis of manufacturing industry, that unions are conspiracies of workmen against the interests of their own order, and never fail to end in the suicide of the body corporate which forms them; an event the more speedy, the more coercive or the better organized the union is. The very name of union makes capital restive, and puts ingenuity on the alert to defeat its objects. When the stream of labour is suffered to glide on quietly within its banks, all goes well; when forcibly dammed up, it becomes unprofitably stagnant for a time, and then brings on a disastrous inundation. Were it not for unions, the vicissitudes of employment, and the substitution of automatic for hand work, would seldom be so abrupt as to distress the operative.

Some may imagine that the present work, which purposes to give a minute analysis and description of the several processes of manufacture, may prove injurious to the trade of this country, by putting foreigners in possession of much useful knowledge, now hardly within their reach. To this I reply, that knowledge is available just in proportion to the capacity and means of the persons who acquire it. Every invention and improvement relative to cotton fabrics is primarily attracted to Manchester as the surest and most productive scene of its development, where it can be most profitable to the inventor, because most profitable to the trade concentred there. Lancashire is the fertile and well-laboured soil in which the seed of factory knowledge will bring forth fruit one hundred fold, whereas abroad it can yield little more than a tenfold return. However well informed the mill proprietors of Great Britain may be, and they unquestionably may bear a comparison in talent as in wealth with the landed aristocracy in any part of the world, still they may profit extremely by the methodical study of the elements of their prosperity. Many of the machines at present employed by them involve the most elegant applications of both physical and mechanical science; such indeed as if duly studied would enable them to understand the operative part of their business as clearly as the commercial, and thus protect them from those hazardous innovations which crafty projectors are perpetually pressing upon their adoption. Prodigious sums are wastefully expended every year by gentlemen manufacturers in this way, which would be saved by a more thorough acquaintance with those principles of science and art which I shall endeavour to expound.

Several individuals who have embarked vast fortunes in factories are to a very great extent the victims at least, if not the dupes, of scheming managers, who are ever ready to display their perverse ingenuity by the substitution of some intricate trap, for a simpler but less showy mechanism. I have known not a few cases, where a complete system of good machines, capable of doing excellent work, has been capriciously turned out of a cotton factory and replaced by another of greater expense, but of less productive powers, and less suited to the style of work, than the old one if skilfully managed. These substitutions are continual in many establishments. They interfere most essentially, and often unnecessarily, with the going of the mill, and are referrible almost always to injudicious choice at first, and capricious alterations afterwards,— circumstances over which the proprietor, from ignorance of the structure of a good machine, cannot always venture to exercise the proper control. There are no doubt many mill-managers perfectly fitted by judgment, knowledge, and integrity to second the sound commercial views of the mill-owner, and to advance the business with a profitable career. These practical men form the soul of our factory system. But with a wrong-headed, plausible manager, the proprietor is sure to be led such a mechanical dance as will bewilder him completely, unless he has acquired a clear insight into the *arcana* of the business by deliberate study of the composition and performance of each machine in his factory. It may be supposed that this species of education can be most easily acquired in the midst of the machinery itself. But this is a mistake which experience speedily proves. . . .

3. Railroads: The Regulation of an Achievement

BRITAIN'S ECONOMIC miracle brought official marvel and confusion. Parliament smiled benignly upon some areas while viewing others with suspicion. No one ever presumed that public services, common carriers, or public utilities should function entirely as free agents, but the degree of control and its effectiveness varied from one sector and time to another. Emigrant shipping was almost overregulated, but the railroad proved so striking an achievement that the British were not certain quite how to handle it.

Britain needed the railroad to mature economically. Only efficient and quick rail service could integrate the economy and, in the true sense of the term, unify the nation. The railroad paced capital formation, technical demand, and technological achievement. The railroad revolution was probably the most important single element clearing away the depression of the 1840s, and the completion of the basic national railroad grid ushered in Britain's prosperous mid-Victorian years. Railroad demand spurred coal, iron, metallurgy, and engineering. Ports were made by the railroad. The railroad summoned new towns like Crewe into existence or changed others like Rugby and Carlisle almost beyond recognition. Railroads employed unskilled and semiskilled labor on a scale previously only matched by the armed forces. The railroad made possible the growth of the modern suburb. It brought unparalleled mobility and unlimited horizons.

Small wonder that such an instrument of progress, while provoking questions, evoked more reverence than regulation.[1] From the Stockton and Darlington (1825) and Manchester and Liverpool (1830), the railroad steamed into British life. Ironically, passenger revenue initially ran far ahead of expectations. Turnpikes suffered, for the railroad only slowly displaced canals as carriers of bulk freight. By the accession of Victoria, the Great Western was begun, the London-Birmingham and London-Bath-Bristol well under way or completed. Both coastal trunk lines to Scotland were finished within ten years, as well as that line thrusting through the heart of the nation from London to York. Parliamentary committees took extraordinary interest in the doings of railroads. They unearthed a wide variety of facts and many serious problems as committees reported in 1838, 1839, and then delivered multiple reports in 1840, 1844, 1845, 1846, and 1852–1853. Reports were not regulations, although every approach to the problem of the railroad was canvassed once or repeatedly in these enquiries. Gladstone's famous six reports of 1844, for instance, recommended sweeping controls and would have permitted the government to revise charges on any line subsequently constructed or even to purchase the line after twenty-one years. The cabinet would not go so far, although it did endorse and Parliament subsequently provided for a regulatory agency, the Railway Board, with limited powers. The government also took pity on the less well-to-do local traveler. It provided that each railroad must run one train per day each way, making each stop but maintaining a reasonable average speed at a cost of not more than 1d. per mile for third-class passengers. Thus began those perpetual targets of satire:

> The idiot who in railway carriages scribbles on window panes,
> We only suffer to ride on the buffer of parliamentary trains.

But the parliamentary train was of vast social consequence; it made the railroad a vehicle for the poor as well as the rich.

The British were so bemused by the railroad achievement that a generation passed before they insisted upon a standard gauge of track. Safety regulations were too often cases of too little and too late. The 1850s and 1860s were overwhelmingly an era of laissez faire in railroad regulation. Even the revelation of outrageous scandals could not force

---

1. The debate about the coming of state regulation of private economic activity takes many forms. Two of the best articles start from opposite assumptions and proceed, not very surprisingly, to opposite conclusions. Oliver MacDonagh studied the emigrant passenger traffic and pursues governmental collectivism. Henry Parris, on the other hand, examined railroads and argues for laissez faire. Oliver MacDonagh, "The Nineteenth-Century Revolution in Government: A Reappraisal," *The Historical Journal*, I (1958), 52–67; Henry Parris, "The Nineteenth-Century Revolution in Government: A Reappraisal Reappraised," *loc. cit.*, III (1961), 17–37. W. L. Burn helps to explain how such contrary things are true in *The Age of Equipoise* (London: 1964).

a bill for the public examination of railroad books through Parliament. The British people and Parliament were aware of the issues and problems involved. In other instances, the emigrant passenger traffic for example, they chose strong regulation. To some degree, although a marginal one, the industry developed its own regulations and rationalization. Business requirements dictated the establishment of the Clearing House, which finally brought order to the bookkeeping about whose cars were on what tracks for how long. It was railroad, not government, initiative that began a program of rationalization through consolidation—not always with a hearty endorsement from Parliament.

The Regulation of Railways Act of 1871 inaugurated a slow change in attitude and policy. The demand for information from railroads meant that a new safety campaign could pay dividends for the public and for the firms. The block system came into being on governmental prodding. Better braking developed. Passengers and freight moved more safely, more reasonably, and at higher profits for the lines. Because of and in spite of government policy, British railroads became efficient, impressive, and generally profitable.

Recommended Reading

Railroad history remains something of a problem. General summaries in order of publication (which may also be in descending order of merit) are W. T. Jackman, *The Development of Transportation in Modern England*, 2 vols. (Cambridge: 1916; reprinted New York: 1962); C. E. R. Sherrington, *A Hundred Years of Inland Transport, 1830–1933* (London: 1934); C. Hamilton Ellis, *British Railway History: An Outline from the Accession of William IV to the Nationalization of the Railways*, 2 vols. (London: 1954–1959); J. Simmons, *The Railways of Britain: An Historical Introduction* (London: 1961); M. R. Robbins, *The Railway Age* (London: 1962); H. Perkin, *The Age of the Railway* (Newton Abbot: 1971).

SELECT COMMITTEE ON RAILWAY COMPANIES AMALGAMATION, REPORT

CONCLUSION AND RECOMMENDATIONS

The following is a summary of the general conclusions to which the Committee have come: —

1. Past amalgamations have not brought with them the evils which were anticipated.

2. Competition between railways exists only to a limited extent, and cannot be maintained by legislation.

Source: From *Parliamentary Papers*, 1872, vol. XIII, pp. xlix–lii.

3. Combination between railway companies is increasing, and is likely to increase, whether by amalgamation or otherwise.

4. It is impossible to lay down any general rules determining the limits or the character of future amalgamations.

5. The most urgent question now pressing for solution is, whether, under the present state of things, the interest of the public is adequately provided for and protected, and if not, whether any and what improvements can be made in railway legislation, consistently with the fair rights of the companies, which would protect the public against certain evils incident to the present system.

6. The self-interest of the companies alone will not effect the object, since their interest is only to a limited extent the interest of the public; and it becomes, therefore, necessary to consider what can be done in the way of statutory obligation.

7. There can be no doubt that the introduction of certain Amalgamation Bills which have been the immediate occasion of the appointment of the Committee affords opportunities for imposing conditions on the companies which may be desirable in the public interest.

8. But it has been impossible to separate the consideration of such conditions from the consideration of measures which it may be expedient to adopt with respect to all railways; and such measures, if adopted by Parliament, might remove some of the objections to the present and future amalgamations.

9. Whilst, therefore, the Committee advise further legislation of a general character, they are of opinion that, in the absence of such legislation, the measures they recommend should be imposed as conditions, so far as applicable, on the companies which are now seeking, or which may hereafter seek, to amalgamate with other companies.

10. The Committee might have recommended that every company seeking amalgamation should submit the whole of its system, whether constructed before 1844 or not, to the conditions for purchase by the Government contained in the Act of that year. But they do not do so, because the terms of that Act do not appear to be suited to the present condition of railway property, or to be likely to be adopted by Parliament, in case of any intention of Parliament at any future time to purchase the railways.

Under these circumstances the Committee now proceed to state the remedial measures which have been suggested, or which have occurred, to them, with the conclusions to which they have come upon each suggestion:—

1. Effectual competition by sea exists, and ought to be guarded, by preventing railway companies from obtaining control over public harbours.

2. Competition by river and canal exists to a partial and limited extent only, and many important links of canal navigation are in the hands of railway companies, whose interest it often is to depreciate them. It is important that an effort should be made to maintain the competition which now exists; and it is still more important, whether competition is maintained or not, that the capacities of inland navigation should be fully utilised and developed. The following recommendations have this object in view:—

1. No inland navigation now in the hands of a public trust should be transferred to, or placed under the control of, a railway company.

2. The utmost facilities should be given for the amalgamation of adjoining canals with one another, or with adjoining inland navigations: and if the trustees of an inland navigation or a canal company apply to Parliament for power to purchase compulsorily a canal from a railway company, such purchase should be favourably regarded by Parliament.

3. No canal should be transferred, to or placed directly or indirectly under the control of, any railway company, nor should any temporary lease of any canal to a railway company be renewed until it has been conclusively ascertained that the canals cannot be amalgamated with or worked by adjacent canals, or by a trust owning adjacent inland navigation.

4. Whenever a railway company applying to Parliament for amalgamation has any canal communication in the district under its ownership or control, the propriety of continuing or modifying such ownership or control should be a subject of investigation by the Joint Committee referred to below.

5. The principles of the Railway and Canal Traffic Act should be strictly carried into effect by requiring every company owning or controlling a canal to maintain it in a state of thorough efficiency; to give every facility for through traffic; and to remove every obstacle, whether in the shape of bar tolls or otherwise, which are imposed for the purpose of impeding

through traffic; and these obligations should be enforced by proceedings before the Commissioners mentioned below.

6. The owners of any canal or inland navigation should have power to make a through toll or rate from or to any place on its own canal, to or from any place on any other canal, or on any railway forming a through route; the toll or rate to be divided between the owners of different parts of the route, as a general rule, according to mileage, but with a provision that if any objection be made to the proposed toll or rate or division as unfair, and no agreement can be come to, the Commissioners mentioned below shall, upon the application of any of the parties interested, decide the matters in dispute.

3. Equal mileage rates are inexpedient.

4. It is impracticable to establish any standard for the revision of rates and fares founded on cost and profit.

5. There would be much difficulty and little, if any, gain to the public in determining a maximum scale of "terminal charges."

6. Immediate reduction of rates and fares, even when practicable, cannot be looked upon as permanently effectual.

7. Periodical revision of rates and fares is impracticable without some standard of revision.

8. Revision of rates and fares founded on a limitation of dividend to a fixed amount is undesirable in the interest of the public.

9. Revision of rates and fares founded on a division of profit above a certain amount between the companies and the public in this country is attended with great, if not insuperable, difficulties.

10. A new and uniform classification of rates is desirable and practicable; and there should be power to alter the classification from time to time, with consent of the Commissioners mentioned below.

11. The companies ought to be compelled, by exhibition of their books at every station, to inform the public what rates they charge for goods to all stations to which they book, distinguishing between mileage and "terminals," and giving all special rates and contracts. If complaint is made that this condition is not properly complied with, the Commissioners mentioned below should have power to enforce it.

12. If a *prima facie* case is made raising a suspicion that any company is charging unequally or unfairly, contrary to the principles of the Railway and Canal Traffic Act, the said Commis-

sioners should have power to call upon the company to state their reasons for such charges.

13. There is serious difficulty in any general legislation on the subject of Workmen's Trains, but where they are proved to be needed, the obligation to run them may properly be imposed as a condition of amalgamation.

14. Whilst on the one hand there may be amalgamations so large as to be objectionable, and whilst on the other, there are cases in which amalgamation is obviously desirable, it is impossible to re-arrange the railway map, or to determine by any general scheme, what amalgamations shall be allowed, and what shall not.

15. In the event of branch railways being wanted and being refused by the existing companies, power should be given to local authorities to make them, or to guarantee the existing companies a moderate return on the necessary capital; and on such guarantee being given, the companies should be bound to make and work the line. If differences should arise between the local authorities and the companies they should be settled by the said Commissioners.

16. The Railway and Canal Traffic Act ought to be explained by enabling every railway company to make through rates and fares from or to any station on its own line, to or from any station on any other line; the rates to be divided as a general rule according to mileage, after allowing for terminals; but with a provision that if any objection be made to the proposed rate or division as unfair, and no agreement can be come to, the Commissioners mentioned below shall, upon the application of any of the companies inter-ested, decide the matters in dispute.

17. Running powers may usefully be given in certain cases, and the propriety of giving them should be carefully considered by the Joint Committee hereafter mentioned. But it is not practicable, or desirable, to give to railway companies generally running powers over the lines of other companies, or to treat these powers as condi-tions to be imposed by general legislation. Differences as to running powers, when given, should be settled by the said Commissioners.

18. The administration of the Railway and Canal Traffic Act ought to be assigned to a special tribunal possessing knowledge of railway management. Such a tribunal will be found in the Railway Commission mentioned below.

19. The fares now paid by the War Office for the conveyance of troops, should be reduced to such an amount as will give to the

companies, having regard to the nature of the service, profit equal to, but not higher than, that derived from ordinary passenger traffic, whether by excursion trains or ordinary trains. These fares, when fixed, should be subject to revision from time to time; and differences, if any, between the War Office and the companies should be settled by the said Commissioners.

20. The Postmaster General ought to have the power of sending mail bags, with or without a guard, by every train to and from every station; such bags to be received and delivered on the platform without booking, or other delay; the payments to be such, as nearly as possible, as the companies charge to the public for similar services. The Postmaster General should also have power, at his own expense, of putting up at any station an apparatus for exchanging bags without stopping. Differences (if any) between the Postmaster General and the companies to be settled by the said Commissioners.

21. To perform the various duties referred to in this Report, a special body should be constituted, entitled the Railway and Canal Commission, which should consist of not less than three members. They should be persons of high standing, of whom one should be an eminent lawyer, and one should be thoroughly acquainted with the details and practice of railway management.

22. Whenever in existing general or special Railway or Canal Acts, provision is made for arbitration between railway or canal companies, the jurisdiction of the arbitrators and umpire should be transferred to the Commissioners.

23. In future Private Bills, reference to the Commissioners should be substituted for similar arbitrations.

24. The present and future Amalgamation Bills, and all Bills involving a transfer of rights in public harbours, or a transfer of the ownership or control of canals or navigations to railway companies, should be referred to a permanent and specially selected Joint Committee. It should be the duty of such Committee to impose the conditions above suggested, so far as applicable, on the companies, and it should also be their duty to consider carefully what special conditions each amalgamation or transfer requires, whether for the protection of the public or of other companies. Care should be taken that no traders or other persons who have any interest in procuring fair terms and conditions from the companies, are excluded by any rule concerning *locus standi* from

appearing before such Committee; and the Committee see no reason why public departments should not have the same right of so appearing before this (and indeed before every) Railway Committee.

25. If the above recommendations are adopted by Parliament, they will not have the effect of preventing the growth of railway monopoly, or of securing that the public shall share, by reduction of rates and fares, in any increased profits which the railway companies may make. But the Committee believe that their effect will be:—

a. To preserve the competition which now exists by sea.

b. To give immediately such support as is practicable to competition by canal; and both immediately and ultimately to develope and utilise the capacities of canals.

c. To let the public know what they are charged, and why they are charged; and to give them better means than at present exist for getting unfair charges remedied.

d. To enforce the harmonious working and development of the present railway and canal systems, so as to produce from them, in the interest of the public, and at the same time of the shareholders, the greatest amount of profitable work which they are capable of doing.

4. Limited Liability: The Shift in Economic Organization

BRITISH ECONOMIC ascendancy was constructed principally by individual, family, and partnership enterprise. Most Englishmen believed that ownership demanded responsibility and accountability. This was ingrained cultural habit. Stunned by the speculative binge and shareholders' disaster of the South Sea Company a century before, England enacted the Bubble Act of 1720 limiting a common partnership to seven members, each of whom was liable "to his last shilling and acre" for the obligations of the concern. Limited liability—the legal restriction of fiscal obligation to the capital investment as represented by shares of ownership—was still available, but joint stock corporations could only be sanctioned by private act of Parliament. This cumbersome, expensive procedure was available only to projectors of vast means, needs, and patience. Canals, then railroads, demanded the mobilization of capital on a scale only available through limited liability ownership. Through them Britons slowly grew accustomed to shares and boards of directors; and through them Britons developed the investment habit.

Industrial growth was the story of expanding small, modest activities onto ever-larger scales—the tale of men ploughing their profits back into the business, driving themselves and their workers, always aware of the penalty for failure. Individual economic opportunity probably never had a greater range for expression than in nineteenth-century Britain, and almost every entrepreneur assumed total responsibility for his business obligations. There was, nevertheless, constant pressure for the modification of company law. Restrictions of the Bubble Act and related legislation were eased in the 1820s, and, with the multiplication of joint stock enterprises in the early Victorian period, there was demand for rationalization—the development of simple, standard, inexpensive procedures for the mobilization of capital through limited liability. The Limited Liability Act of 1837 enabled the Crown, by letters patent, to grant the rights of incorporation (giving a firm corporate legal personality) and limited liability. No one intended to ease responsibility; rather the government hoped to avoid the excessive costs and delays involved in securing private acts of Parliament.

The railroad, which had to be capitalized under the protection of limited liability, introduced new problems. Railway investment absorbed most available capital, and other forms of business enterprise, starving for money, demanded equal opportunity to recruit it. The Companies Act of 1844 made it easier to form enterprises but still withheld the general privilege of limited liability. Here, as in so many things, Victorian economic and moral aspirations generated conflict. The Victorians ranked character high among corporate assets, and limited liability could too easily mean irresponsibility. Logic and economics prevailed. Gladstone's Limited Liability Act of 1855 finally provided general limited liability for those business enterprises willing to apply, issue a prospectus, and publish certain financial information. The Limited Liability Act of 1856, to which this protest was attached as it passed the House of Lords, merely tidied up some minor provisions of the general statute. Lord Overstone and Lord Monteagle were still so distressed by what seemed to them the immorality of the new economic policy that they availed themselves of one of the few actual privileges of a peer, the right formally to enter their protest in the records of the House of Lords. In doing so, they summarized doubts and criticism long raised and still persisting.

In the short run they seemed to be right. The coming of limited liability, as predicted, brought a speculative binge. The unwary investor was fleeced with shocking regularity. Legitimate, established enterprises moved very slowly and only began to turn to limited liability in the next decade. But the movement was under way; the direction clear. Within a generation, the corporate structure of Britain had changed. Shares, managers, and boards of directors replaced the owner-manager. Banks, ironically, were not included in the Act of 1855. When the City of Glasgow Bank failed in 1878, some two hundred spinsters holding an average £240 in shares found themselves liable for £6,610 apiece.[1] Generally, however, corporate enterprise became impersonal, demanding new people and new skills. Careers opened for professional manipulators of men and money. Ownership came less and less to mean participation. Dombey and Son gave way to Imperial Chemical, an alteration in economic organization bringing profound social and cultural changes.

Recommended Reading

In addition to the excellent general studies, particularly Clapham and Checkland, there are important observations on the significance of changes in business structure and entrepreneurship to be found in D. Landes, *The Unbound Prometheus* (Cambridge: 1968), and H. J. Habakkuk, *American and British Technology* (London: 1962). An old but invaluable study, H. W. Macrosty, *The Trust Movement in British Industry* (London: 1907), suggests the limits of the policy of amalgamation and rationalization, although this was not the point he was attempting to establish. The conventional starting point is B. C. Hunt, *The Development of the Business Corporation in England, 1800–1867* (Cambridge, Mass.: 1936), which should be used with two excellent articles by H. A. Shannan, "The Coming of General Limited Liability," in *Essays in Economic History*, E. M. Carus-Wilson, ed. (London: 1954), vol. 1, and "The Limited Companies of 1866–1883," *Economic History Review*, IV (1933). There are many general and individual studies of great merit, but for a classic portrait of late Victorian entrepreneurship, see C. Wilson, *The History of Unilever* (London: 1954), vol. I.

SAMUEL JONES LOYD, LORD OVERSTONE, AND
THOMAS SPRING RICE, LORD MONTEAGLE OF BRANDON,
A PROTEST

JUNE 16, 1856

The Act (19 and 20 Victoria, cap. 47) for the incorporation and regulation of Joint Stock Companies and other associations, received the royal assent on the 14th of July. It was read a second time in the Lords on the 16th of June, by 18 to 5, the principal opposition being from the peers who sign the subjoined protest.

1st, Because the measure is wholly unnecessary, inasmuch as every concern has the means of limiting its liability by trading upon its own capital and not upon the borrowed capital of others. Liability is not necessarily incident to trading, or to the application

1. P. Ripley, *A Short History of Investment* (London: 1934), p. 93.

Source: From J. Thorold Rogers, *Protests of the House of Lords* (London: 1876), pp. 412–416.

of capital to the pursuits of industry, it is the result of taking credit or trading upon borrowed capital; limited liability, therefore, is a measure of protection, not to the capitalist, great or small, but to the speculator, who wishes to trade for his own profit, but with the capital and at the risk of others.

2ndly, Because the principle of limited liability is antagonistic to and will probably prove seriously destructive of the sober and substantial virtues of the mercantile character; by weakening in the mind of the trader the sense of full responsibility for the consequences of all his actions, and limiting the obligation which now rests upon him, to return in full all that he has borrowed from others, the general tone of commercial morality must be deteriorated; by limiting the unfortunate consequences of failure, whilst no corresponding limitation is placed upon the gains which may attend success, the due equipoise between the restraints and the stimulants to enterprise and speculation, upon which depend the solidity and safety of the commercial system, must be disturbed; by enabling parties to put a fixed limit to the amount of possible loss, the chief incentive to caution or vigilance in the conduct of business will be taken away or seriously weakened, whilst by leaving the hope of gain unrestricted and indefinite, a gambling principle will be introduced into commercial transactions, and the risks of trade will assimilate themselves to the chances of the lottery wheel rather than to what they now are, the legitimate results of hopeful industry and cautious enterprise.

3rdly, Because the measure in its present form, unaccompanied by safeguards or any attempt to obviate the clear and acknowledged danger of abuses to which the principle of limited liability must be exposed, is not only in opposition to the Report of the Royal Commission appointed to inquire into the subject, but is contradictory to the practice and experience of every country in the world which has admitted the principle of limited liability into its commercial code. In every other country the privilege of limited liability is surrounded by restrictions which are intended to guard against the danger, first, of excessive and reckless enterprise, naturally generated by the sense of strict limitation of risk; and, second, of fraudulent abstraction, under the form of interest or profits, of that specific and fixed amount of capital which is alone appropriated as the security of the honest creditor. These restrictions indicate the universal conviction of all other countries that against these sources of abuse it is necessary that some proper safeguard be provided; if it be deemed impossible to render such safeguards efficient and satisfactory, the conclusion necessarily arises that a measure ought not to be persisted in which does not admit of effectual protection against injustice to the honest creditor and injury to the public interests.

4thly, Because the effect of the Bill will be to give legal protection and therefore to hold out moral encouragement to dishonest practices in trade.

Profits in trade consist of interest upon capital, remuneration for labour and skill, and premium of insurance on risk. In proportion as the risk in any business is great, profits are usually high; but of these high profits a large share is by every honest trader set aside as the premium reserved against high risks. An unfortunate tradesman coming before the Bankruptcy Court would not be very leniently dealt with, should it appear that, carrying on a very riskful business, he had year by year spent all the great apparent profits, making no reserve out of them to meet the high risks he was incurring. Now, this is the very practice which this Bill directly sanctions, and therefore encourages.

The object of the measure is to enable concerns to limit their liability to a certain fixed sum, which has no reference to the varying magnitude of the risks which they incur, or to the high profits which, through those risks, they are appropriating to themselves, but not reserving for the honest protection of their creditors.

They are, in fact, appropriating and misapplying the premium of insurance, which, under the form of high profits they year by year receive, and in this immoral course they will have the authority and sanction of the Bill.

5thly, Because the tendency of the measure must be to encourage and promote the transference of capital from trading concerns now constituted and conducted with the caution and prudence which the sense of unlimited liability necessarily generates, to Joint Stock Companies, trading with small paid-up capital, and embarking under the protection of limited liability upon risks which no person would otherwise venture to encounter. When loss occurs a heavy portion of it will be made to fall upon the unfortunate creditor, who deserves our sympathy, while the adventurers, who ought to be the victims of their own reckless speculations, will remain comparatively safe under the ægis of limited liability. Meanwhile the sober calculations and legitimate transactions of real trade will give way to a general spirit of speculation, in hazardous enterprises, and jobbing in shares,—a state of things of which the history of 1824 and 1825 affords a practical illustration, and at the same time holds out a warning example.

6thly, Because many very important advantages arise from the high moral character and commercial credit founded upon the full and punctual discharge of all its obligations which this country at present enjoys throughout the world. If the effect of the measure shall be, as is predicted by its supporters, to restrict rather than to increase credit, by filling the community with a mass of concerns notoriously undeserving of public confidence, the consequence must be serious injury to our commercial character abroad, a diminution of the confidence which other countries repose in the engagements of our merchants and traders, an interruption to the ease and freedom with which all our trading intercourse with the world is at present conducted, and in the end absolute pecuniary loss to the country.

7thly, Because the measure is singularly inappropriate to the present state of this country as regards capital and enterprise. There is abundance of capital in this country; we are the lenders of our surplus capital to every nation in the world; any sudden demand, any new opening for speculation, is at once supplied with inexhaustible funds; whilst we are subject to the frequent recurrence of periods of undue and dangerous inflation of credit and speculation. When these periods occur the tendency of the measure must be to extend and intensify these evils, by giving facility for the wide-spread introduction of Joint Stock Companies, reckless in their procedure because protected by limited liability, and filling the community with the instruments of gambling in the form of shares upon which little or nothing has been paid up. The real want to the country is, competent and duly qualified men (in whom confidence is duly blended with caution, and the spirit of mercantile enterprise is regulated by experience and the sense of responsibility), to wield successfully the vast resources of capital and credit which the country is prepared to place at their command.

The evil to the correction of which the Bill is apparently directed, namely, insufficient supply of capital to meet the demands of industry and enterprise, does not in fact exist, whilst the real difficulty is one which legislation cannot effectually remedy.

8thly, Because the period chosen for the introduction of this measure is peculiarly unfavourable to the safety of the experiment. After a long continued heavy drain of the precious metals from this country, the reflux has apparently commenced. A great accumulation of bullion may be reasonably anticipated. Under such circumstances, credit and a blind spirit of speculation are always developed to a dangerous extent. On the present occasion this danger will be rendered more formidable by the effect (the character and extent of which is yet to be ascertained) of the recent extraordinary discoveries of gold. The time is therefore approaching, according to all probability, at which the prudence and firmness of the community will, through the natural course of events, be subjected to a severe trial.

At such a moment it is eminently inexpedient and dangerous to introduce a change in the law seriously affecting the mutual relation of the debtor and creditor interest, and which must, in the first instance at least, exercise a powerful influence on credit and speculation. Important changes of the laws, which affect our monetary or commercial system, however sound may be the principles on which they rest, are almost invariably followed by rapid and excessive development, leading to temporary but serious embarrassment.

The crisis of 1825 was preceded by, and was intimately connected with, the rapid development of the warehousing system which resulted from the Acts passed in 1822.

The crisis of 1837–9 was closely connected with the sudden and excessive expansion of the Joint Stock Banking system which occurred in the years immediately preceding.

The crisis of 1847 followed closely upon the extensive reduction of important duties introduced by Sir R. Peel, and the sudden outburst of the railway system.

Experience therefore compels us to anticipate a similar crisis as the necessary result of the first development of that great change in our monetary and commercial system which is involved in this abrupt and unqualified introduction of the principle of limited liability.

If this crisis occurs simultaneously with the effect of a strong influx of the precious metals on the return of peace, and of the recent extraordinary addition to the total amount of the precious metals through the gold discoveries, the firmness and prudence of the country may be subjected to a trial too powerful to be withstood, and an artificial expansion of credit may ensue, causing monetary embarrassment and great mercantile disasters.

5. Cooperation: An Early Experiment

CHARLES BRAY (1811–1884) was a Coventry ribbon manufacturer with literary and philosophical pretensions and a determination to serve his fellow man. An ardent exponent of phrenology, one of the more common eccentricities of the age, he also was a tireless promoter of experiments in social uplift for the working classes. He admired Robert Owen's vision, although he believed Owen's communitarian objectives too grandiose. Like Owen, he was concerned not merely with the economic welfare of his own employees, but with the total content of their lives. Ribbon weaving, moreover, was still conducted on the putting-out principle, so Bray's concern was with developing institutions that would create a sense of practical community—that would assist men to help themselves. Shortly after the failure of his cooperative, he wrote:

> In 1845 or 6, I forget the exact date, I set up a Working Man's Club. Many of my workmen (ribbon weavers) came from the country, and having often when they brought in their work to wait till the afternoon for something they wanted from the warehouse, were thus forced to go to the public-house. I found[ed] a Reading-room, with papers and periodicals, a smoking-room, with tea, coffee or lunch; rooms upstairs for friendly assemblies or smaller social gatherings, and beds for people coming from a distance. This I afterwards opened to the operative class at large. But it did not prosper. My own weavers evidently preferred the public-house, and were glad of any excuse to go there. Nor was it so well managed as it should have been, and there was a refinement about it that was in advance of the time, so that after losing about £100 by it I was obliged to close it. Such clubs are succeeding everywhere now [the 1880s], and are helping forward the educational progress of the age. But this club and the Co-operative Store gave great offence to the publicans and small shopkeepers, who combined, and at the next election turned me out of the City council. I was never afterwards returned.[1]

Bray's experiment, like so many others, came to grief, but it was one of many lurchings in the direction of the modern cooperative movement. Popular capitalism or, if one can use the expression without political overtones, peoples' capitalism, ran its self-assertive course through the Victorian years. It was to become still more important in the early twentieth century, although its strength was always regional.

1. C. Bray, *Phases of Opinion and Experiences during a Long Life* (London: 1885), pp. 67–68.

The cooperative movement appealed to the area of classical industrialization, the North country and Scotland. Every principal community had its cooperative by midcentury, most unimportant ones by the turn of the century. Although briefly popular, the Midlands and South lost interest in cooperation, and the movement never made any significant impact on Ireland.

The successful experiment launched by a handful of Owenites at Rochdale in 1844 became the model for consumer cooperatives. The patronage refund, a capitalist fillip, seems to have turned the trick in securing support. Cooperation appealed to a broad, but well-defined section of Victorian society. The small-salaried people and substantial wage earners, that group hovering uneasily between the established middle classes and the rank and file of workers, made it their movement. They set the policies. They managed the societies on their own time without pay. They, together with the regularly employed workers, were their own best customers. This merger of petty bourgeois and aristocracy of labor demonstrated the basic community of Victorian values. The poor could not afford the value for money cooperative merchandise represented. They needed the credit that private shops charging higher prices were willing to advance.

The cooperatives were not only economic institutions; they reflected shared values in one part of the public. The policies—good merchandise, fair prices, modest return on investment, long-term prospects rather than short-term rebates—appealed to men who could afford to make choices. The cooperative movement, however collectivistic and communitarian in appearance, bespoke the essential conservatism of a potentially revolutionary element in British society.

Recommended Reading

The cooperative still needs thoughtful, objective study. Of the available volumes, G. D. H. Cole, *A Century of Co-operation* (London: 1945), is the best.

CHARLES BRAY,
AN EARLY EXPERIMENT

Accordingly the next year, 1843, I helped to establish "The Coventry Labourers' and Artizans' Co-operative Society." The first aim of this Society was to furnish working men with gardens, as healthy occupations, and to help them to counteract in part the ill effects of confinement at the loom. The physical and moral benefit was much greater than the pecuniary, although a man could make about 2s. a week out of the 8th of an acre. The great diffi-

Source: From *Phases of Opinion and Experience During a Long Life,* (London: 1855), pp. 64–67.

culty was to procure land, as most of the land round the city was Lammas, that is, subject to the Freemen's right of pasturage during part of the year. Landholders would not let land to working men, nor to a Society, but they agreed to let it to myself, either as individually responsible or in conjunction with Mr. Cash, of Sherborne House. Ultimately we were able to get about 400 gardens, the gardens were much in demand, and the rent was paid in advance, so that I did not run any great risk. Besides the rent each member paid a penny a week towards the expenses of the Society and this soon amounted to a considerable sum. This was put out in loans at a high rate of interest to buy looms, pigs, pay rent in advance, &c. The Society then began to trade on its own account. Boat-loads of coal were brought direct from the pits and distributed among the members at cost price, thus effecting a considerable saving. Then, flour mills were taken, for the rent of which, I, as President, was again obliged to be (individually) responsible. A store was afterwards opened for the sale of flour, bread, groceries, &c. Of course this took several years to accomplish, and so far we had a time of uninterrupted prosperity. At least 1,000 of the leading and most respectable working men of the city belonged to the Society; all had shares on which a large interest was paid, so that the difficulty was to keep men out for whose benefit it was not intended. But one fatal error mixed up with the business by which we ultimately were wrecked. Our Society was on the Credit System. The Societies that gave credit were failing all over the country, and this fact I was constantly pointing out to our Committee. But the transition from Credit to a Ready Money System was not easy, particularly as old and leading members, who were on the Committee, as I *afterwards* discovered, were largely in debt to the Society. I was always met with the reply, "You're a gentleman, and don't require credit—a working man does"—a great mistake, for the chief benefit conferred by Co-operative Societies depends on the Ready Money System—the provident habits involved in not getting into debt. And so it proved in our case. In 1859 ribbons went partly out of fashion, and there was a great strike of the operatives to keep up wages when ribbons were not wanted. This, of course, failed. In 1860 and following years ribbons went more and more out of fashion; ladies wore their bonnets on the neck and not on the head, and then they wore none at all, or only an apology for one, and we had a time of great distress, ribbon-making being then the staple industry of the place.

Of course the Protectionists, the political opponents of the Government, attributed this distress to Free Trade and the French Treaty, but the real fact was simply that ribbons were not wanted. At the close of 1859 the Society showed a loss of about £400, equal to 4s. in the pound of each man's capital. This led to a panic. It was said everywhere by the members themselves, in their ignorance of business, that the Society was insolvent, although it had £1,600 more than was required to satisfy all demands upon it. Every one wanted his money; every one wanted to sell out. But the money of course could not be had, being invested in Mills and Stock, and consequently every one got into debt to the Society to the amount of his shares if he could, and then refused to pay. One man would order a sack of flour, another a flitch of bacon, and as no money was coming in the concern soon collapsed. Efforts were, of course, made to bring these debtors to book, but such was the distress in the town that they were attended with little success. The looms and other securities on which money had been advanced by the loan department of the Society had vanished, as also in many cases had the people owning them; for a population of 41,000 had been reduced to 37,000. Debts put into the Court did not produce 1s. in the pound, and distress warrants were mostly returned endorsed "No effects." On January 1st, 1864, there were still 322 persons indebted to the Society to the amount of £316 15s. 6d. Of these it was reported that some had gone through the Debtor's Court, others had left the town or died, others were at work on the Commons, or on the mills at the workhouse, and others were too poor to pay a farthing. I conclude enough money was got in to pay all the liabilities of the Society, for I was never called upon to advance any part of the sum for which I had become responsible, but I doubt if any of the shareholders who had not scrambled for the stock ever got anything. It is quite impossible that such societies can succeed except upon a ready money system. . . .

6. Occupations of the People, 1851–1901

THE CENSUS OF 1841 was the first attempt to enumerate all Britons by occupation. It was helpful but misleading. Classifications were, as they continued to be, confusing and confused. Time and specialization helped. Is, for example, the housewife who spins for a woolens manufacturer on a part-time basis to be counted as in manufacturing, "generally in Household Duties," or "working the Land" because she also assists her husband in the fields? Occupational specialization was a necessary prerequisite for adequate census material. Increasing urbanization also helped, for the home tends increasingly to be a nonproductive consuming center while income is earned on a job elsewhere. Sufficient ambiguities remain that precise details cannot be established until the enumerators' papers have been closely studied. We can, however, allow for shifts in categories in 1851, 1861, and 1871 and gain considerable understanding about the changing of work—who did what, where, and how in the mid-Victorian period.

Omitting categories that defied classification—"gentlemen, or men of independent means," 10,604 of them in 1851, or 157,402 persons under the age of twenty that year "chiefly supported by members of the community; as pensioners, as dependent relatives, as almspersons, as paupers, as lunatics, as prisoners; while others are vagrants in barns and tents"—the greatest weakness in the 1851 census was its underestimation of employed women and children. The enumerators tended to disregard part-time occupations. This was all the more confusing because families acted as economic units in early Victorian Britain, not merely when self-employed, but also when hired by employers. Census takers also had some difficulty, then as now, in distinguishing between manufacturing and commerce in given commodities.

Some generalizations are helpful and useful. The total number of persons employed in agriculture reached its peak in the middle of the century, although agriculture had already begun a relative decline as a source of employment. The absolute loss was in farm laborers, for the number of farmers remained about the same from the middle of the nineteenth century until well after the First World War. One troublesome point. Industry had come to employ approximately one-third of Britain's labor force by 1841. While the number employed in industry rose steadily, even dramatically, throughout the Victorian years, the proportion remained almost constant until the First World War. The great shift in ratio between agricultural and industrial employment took place before Victoria ascended the throne during the years after Waterloo.

In those years for which we have the best data, some few of which are given here, the striking changes are to be found in transportation (up three-quarters in the last half of the century), mining (up two-thirds in the same period), and in the broad, general category of commerce and trade (which almost doubles). The statistics show several striking features. The number of recognized occupations more than doubles during the second half of the century. These new jobs, moreover, were almost all urban. Yet in the growing complexity of the economy, there was little drive to eliminate unproductive occupations. Domestic service mushroomed, particularly between 1851 and 1871, with the growing prosperity of the middle classes and employed a significant percentage of the total British working force. Household servants alone amount to one-tenth to one-eighth of the employed population. The labor market, in short, remained saturated through the Victorian years.

CENSUS 1851—SUMMARY TABLES

Table XXIV—Occupations of Males and Females—Under 20 Years—20 Years and Upwards

Occupations	ENGLAND AND WALES			
	Under 20 Years of Age		20 Years of Age and upwards	
	Males	Females	Males	Females
Total	4,064,212	4,046,800	4,717,013	5,099,584
Persons of Specified Occupations and Conditions	4,051,774	4,017,117	4,669,401	5,036,789
CLASSES				
The Queen	"	"	"	1
Class I. Persons engaged in the general or local Government of the Country	1,319	75	63,160	2,169
„ II. Persons engaged in the Defence of the Country	7,320	"	78,498	"
„ III. Persons in the Learned Professions (with their immediate Subordinates), either filling Public Offices, or in private Practice	10,265	52	86,093	1,329
„ IV. Persons engaged in Literature, the Fine Arts, and the Sciences	3,861	7,703	34,924	59,866
„ V. Persons engaged in the Domestic Offices, or Duties of Wives, Mothers, Mistresses of Families, Children, Relatives*	2,874,888	3,236,481	17,844	2,759,173
„ VI. Persons engaged in entertaining, clothing, and performing personal Offices for Man	105,439	401,301	456,242	1,164,639
„ VII. Persons who buy or sell, keep, let, or lend, Money, Houses, or Goods of various Kinds	16,846	2,238	114,257	48,008
„ VIII. Persons engaged in the Conveyance of Men, Animals, Goods, and Messages	90,294	4,760	245,449	6,747
„ IX. Persons possessing or working the Land, and engaged in growing Grain, Fruits, Grasses, Animals, and other Products	335,133	100,233	1,224,629	351,452
„ X. Persons engaged about Animals	9,101	99	63,010	496
„ XI. Persons engaged in Art and Mechanic Productions, in which Matters of various Kinds are employed in combination	104,584	4,617	544,250	10,628
„ XII. Persons working and dealing in Animal Matters	84,832	79,992	270,049	149,233
„ XIII. Persons working and dealing in Matters derived from the Vegetable Kingdom	151,490	137,779	532,774	256,540
„ XIV. Persons working and dealing in Minerals	183,527	23,962	590,096	33,075
„ XV. Labourers and others—Branch of Labour undefined	56,192	2,134	282,779	7,448

CENSUS 1851—SUMMARY TABLES

Table XXIV—Occupations of Males and Females—Under 20 Years—20 Years and upwards—continued

Occupations	ENGLAND AND WALES			
	Under 20 Years of Age		20 Years of Age and upwards	
	Males	Females	Males	Females
Classes—continued				
,, XVI. Persons of Rank or Property not returned under any Office or Occupation	560	1,637	30,701	117,178
,, XVII. Persons supported by the community, and of no specified Occupation*	16,123	14,054	34,646	68,807
Other Persons of no stated Occupations or Conditions	12,438	29,683	47,612	62,795
SUB-CLASSES				
The Queen	,,	,,	,,	1
Class I. Persons engaged in the general or local Government of the Country:				
Sub-class 1. Officers of National Government	1,083	63	33,830	1,178
,, 2. Officers of Local Government	173	12	26,039	991
,, 3. Officers of East India Government	63	,,	3,291	,,
Class II. Persons engaged in the Defence of the Country:				
Sub-class 1. Army—at home	5,100	,,	55,440	,,
,, 2. Navy—ashore or in port	2,220	,,	23,058	,,
Class III. Persons in the Learned Professions (with their immediate Subordinates), either filling Public Offices, or in private practice:				
Sub-class 1. Clergymen and Ministers	38	,,	25,978	,,
,, 2. Lawyers	442	,,	15,387	,,
,, 3. Physicians and Surgeons	1,721	,,	17,469	,,
,, 4. Church Officers	159	8	3,987	856
,, 5. Law Clerks, Court Officers, and Stationers	4,610	1	11,739	12
,, 6. Chemists and Surgical Instrument Makers	3,295	43	11,533	461
Class IV. Persons engaged in Literature, the Fine Arts, and the Sciences:				

CENSUS 1851—SUMMARY TABLES

Table XXIV—Occupations of Males and Females—Under 20 Years—20 Years and upwards—continued

Occupations	ENGLAND AND WALES			
	Under 20 Years of Age		20 Years of Age and upwards	
	Males	Females	Males	Females
Sub-classes—continued				
Sub-class 1. Authors	120	3	2,442	106
" 2. Artists	851	59	6,985	468
" 3. Scientific Persons	21	3	397	21
" 4. Teachers	2,869	7,638	25,100	59,271
Class V. Persons engaged in the Domestic Offices, or Duties of Wives, Mothers, Mistresses of Families, Children, Relatives:*				
Sub-class 1. Wives (not otherwise described)	"	14,929	"	2,262,120
" 2. Widows (not otherwise described)	"	77	"	233,285
" 3. Children and relatives at home (not otherwise returned)	1,708,696	2,095,283	13,900	262,864
" 4. Scholars†	1,166,192	1,126,192	3,944	904
Class VI. Persons engaged in entertaining, clothing, and performing personal Offices for Man:				
Sub-class 1. In Boarding and Lodging	287	173	27,229	38,611
" 2. " Attendance (Domestic Servants, &c.)	33,784	282,242	90,811	580,768
" 3. " Providing Dress	71,368	118,886	338,202	545,260
Class VII. Persons who buy or sell, keep, let, or lend, Money, Houses, or Goods of various Kinds:	16,846	2,238	114,257	48,008

* Classes V. and XVII, include those of the Persons described who are not returned in any of the other Classes.

† The return of scholars here given—derived from the statements of the householders respecting their children—will, from various causes, belonging to the various schools, in Great Britain and Islands in the British Seas, 1,353,338 males and 1,139,503 female children; viz., in England 8,666 male and 7,066 female children besides those "under tuition at home," whose education was superintended by a private tutor or governess generally differ, more or less, from the Returns of the Educational Census. From the latter, it appears that there were on the day of the Census, and Wales, 1,139,324 male and 969,268 female children; in Scotland, 205,348 male and 163,169 female children; and in the Islands in the British Seas. The number of the latter class is stated in the subsequent Tables.

48

CENSUS 1851—SUMMARY TABLES

Table XXIV—Occupations of Males and Females—Under 20 Years—20 Years and upwards—continued

Occupations	ENGLAND AND WALES			
	Under 20 Years of Age		20 Years of Age and upwards	
	Males	Females	Males	Females
Sub-classes—continued				
Class VIII. Persons engaged in the Conveyance of Men, Animals, Goods, and Messages:				
Sub-class 1. Carriers on Railways	2,385	4	22,797	51
" 2. " " on Roads	6,556	61	65,416	2,073
" 3. " " on Canals	4,732	437	32,128	2,066
" 4. " " on Seas and Rivers	12,503	8	85,942	329
" 5. Warehousemen and Storekeepers	2,650	1,195	11,274	1,713
" 6. Messengers and Porters	61,469	3,055	27,892	515
Class IX. Persons possessing or working the Land, and engaged in growing Grain, Fruits, Grasses, Animals, and other Products:*				
Sub-class 1. In Fields and Pastures	326,906	100,047	1,152,767	349,395
" 2. " Woods	1,003	"	6,989	16
" 3. " Gardens	7,224	186	64,873	2,041
Class X. Persons engaged about Animals	9,101	99	63,010	496
Class XI. Persons engaged—in Art and Mechanic Productions:				
Sub-class 1. In Books	8,323	1,527	26,793	3,257
" 2. " Plays (Actors)	101	162	1,217	555
" 3. " Music	1,663	158	8,338	674
" 4. " Pictures and Engravings	1,640	82	7,018	245
" 5. " Carving and Figures	653	1,517	2,268	1,628
" 6. " Shows and Games	577	211	2,152	790
" 7. " Plans and Designs	645	8	4,079	23

* A certain number of persons connected with the land, as proprietors or otherwise are returned in several of the other classes, where they are Classes VII and XVI.

CENSUS 1851—SUMMARY TABLES

Table XXIV.—Occupation of Males and Females—Under 20 Years—20 Years and upwards—continued

Occupations	ENGLAND AND WALES			
	Under 20 Years of Age		20 Years of Age and upwards	
	Males	Females	Males	Females
Sub-classes—continued				
„ 8. „ Medals and Dies	109	5	349	8
„ 9. „ Watches and Philosophical Instruments	3,634	134	16,463	328
„ 10. „ Arms	1,776	46	5,784	186
„ 11. „ Machines	8,983	208	39,636	294
„ 12. „ Carriages	2,313	19	13,077	165
„ 13. „ Harness	2,492	187	13,589	531
„ 14. „ Ships	5,097	„	21,716	27
„ 15. „ Houses	57,153	18	335,663	709
„ 16. „ Implements	5,833	2	30,811	107
„ 17. „ Chemicals	3,592	333	15,297	1,101
Class XII. Persons working and dealing—in Animal Matters:				
Sub-class 1. In Animal Food	15,106	831	77,617	33,481
„ 2. „ Grease, Bones, Horn, Ivory, Whalebone, Intestines	1,735	221	9,396	581
„ 3. „ Skins	3,540	83	21,384	408
„ 4. „ Feathers and Quills	67	60	524	318
„ 5. „ Hair and Fur	1,803	1,377	6,746	2,082
„ 6. „ Wool	47,756	47,996	114,350	60,997
„ 7. „ Silk	14,825	29,424	40,032	51,366
Class XIII. Persons working and dealing—in Matters derived from the Vegetable Kingdom:				
Sub-class 1. In Vegetable Food	18,286	1,419	87,856	16,464
„ 2. „ Drinks and Stimulants	15,136	1,116	125,377	47,999
„ 3. „ Gums and Resins	1,203	337	6,027	642
„ 4. „ Timber	965	155	5,725	299
„ 5. „ Bark	331	17	1,454	83

CENSUS 1851—SUMMARY TABLES

Table XXIV—Occupation of Males and Females—Under 20 Years—20 Years and upwards—continued

Occupations	ENGLAND AND WALES			
	Under 20 Years of Age		20 Years of Age and upwards	
	Males	Females	Males	Females
Sub-classes—continued				
6. " Wood	2,935	2	29,251	22
7. " Furniture	9,234	1,128	40,203	5,412
8. " Utensils	2,532	7	14,867	99
9. " Tools	1,800	130	5,579	332
10. " Cane, Rush, and Straw	5,513	13,241	14,017	15,281
11. " Hemp	5,548	1,248	14,296	3,570
12. " Flax, Cotton	84,007	116,265	175,598	161,134
13. " Paper	4,000	2,714	12,524	5,203
Class XIV. Persons working and dealing—in Minerals:				
Sub-class 1. In Coal	60,772	1,638	162,745	2,551
2. " Stone, Clay	16,115	1,051	96,131	1,001
3. " Earthenware	9,872	5,509	20,518	7,472
4. " Glass	3,112	382	8,083	606
5. " Salt	218	12	1,573	57
6. " Water	109	2	1,503	41
7. " Precious Stones	158	47	581	79
8. " Gold and Silver	3,736	666	13,710	826
9. " Copper	6,462	2,378	16,386	1,599
10. " Tin	7,707	1,734	19,317	1,356
11. " Zinc	81	,,	378	8
12. " Lead	5,802	565	18,766	480
13. " Brass and other Mixed Metals	9,215	3,347	26,157	4,943
14. " Iron and Steel	60,168	6,631	204,248	12,056

CENSUS 1851—SUMMARY TABLES

Table XXIV—Occupation of Males and Females—Under 20 Years—20 Years and upwards—continued

ENGLAND AND WALES

Occupations	Under 20 Years of Age		20 Years of Age and upwards	
	Males	Females	Males	Females
Sub-classes continued				
Class XV. Labourers and others—Branch of Labor undefined:				
Sub-class 1. Labourers	50,515	1,395	274,079	5,785
” 2. Other Persons of indefinite Employments . . .	5,677	739	8,700	1,663
Class XVI. Persons of Rank or Property not returned under any Office or Occupation:	560	1,637	30,701	117,178
Class XVII. Persons supported by the community, and of no specified Occupation:†				
Sub-class 1. Living on Income from voluntary Sources and Rates .	11,767	11,337	25,756	63,545
” 2. Prisoners of no specified Occupations	580	456	808	1,076
” 3. Vagrants of no specified Occupations	3,776	2,261	8,082	4,186
Persons of no specified Occupations or Conditions	12,438	29,683	47,612	62,795

† Paupers, prisoners, and other persons in public institutions, as well as persons described as superannuated or retired, are referred to the respective occupations which they have described themselves as following. This observation applies especially to persons included in occupations when the nature of their former employment is stated, the residue only being returned in Class XVII.

CENSUS 1861–SUMMARY TABLES

Table XVIII–England and Wales—Occupations of Males and Females, distinguishing those under 20 Years of Age from those of 20 Years and upwards–In Classes, Orders, and Sub-orders

Classes, Orders, and Sub-orders	All Ages			Under 20 Years of Age		20 Years of Age and Upwards	
	Persons	Males	Females	Males	Females	Males	Females
All Persons	20,066,224	9,776,259	10,289,965	4,545,686	4,536,980	5,230,573	5,762,985
Persons of Specified Occupations and Conditions	19,915,334	9,724,817	10,190,517	4,542,300	4,524,821	5,182,517	5,665,696
Classes							
Class I. Professional	481,957	385,345	96,612	46,138	16,872	339,207	79,740
" II. Domestic	11,426,720	3,473,916	7,952,804	3,290,319	4,032,347	183,597	3,920,457
" III. Commercial	623,710	585,420	38,290	116,616	4,536	468,804	33,754
" IV. Agricultural	2,010,454	1,631,652	378,802	344,692	60,261	1,286,960	318,541
" V. Industrial	4,828,399	3,262,510	1,565,889	682,085	401,479	2,580,425	1,164,410
" VI. Indefinite and Non-productive	544,094	385,974	158,120	62,450	9,326	323,524	148,794
Orders							
Order							
1. Persons engaged in the General or Local Government of the Country	87,350	83,436	3,914	3,783	194	79,653	3,720
2. Persons engaged in the Defence of the Country	131,944	131,944	—	19,205	—	112,739	—
3. Persons engaged in the Learned Professions or engaged in Literature, Art, and Science (with their immediate Subordinates)	262,663	169,965	92,698	23,150	16,678	146,815	76,020
4. Persons engaged in the Domestic Offices or Duties of Wives, Mothers, Mistresses of Families, Children, Relatives (not otherwise returned)	10,058,938	3,263,133	6,795,805	3,250,845	3,648,376	12,288	3,147,429
5. Persons engaged in entertaining, and performing Personal Offices for Man	1,367,782	210,783	1,156,999	39,474	383,971	171,309	773,028

I. Professional Class

II. Domestic Class

CENSUS 1861—SUMMARY TABLES

Table XVIII—England and Wales—Occupations of Males and Females, distinguishing those under 20 Years of Age from those of 20 Years and upwards—In Classes, Orders, and Sub-orders—continued

Classes, Orders, and Sub-orders	All Ages			Under 20 Years of Age		20 Years of Age and Upwards	
	Persons	Males	Females	Males	Females	Males	Females
III. Commercial Class							
6. Persons who buy or sell, keep, or lend Money, Houses, or Goods of various Kinds	183,643	154,234	29,409	23,414	1,864	130,820	27,545
7. Persons engaged in the Conveyance of Men, Animals, Goods, and Messages	440,067	431,186	8,881	93,202	2,672	337,984	6,209
IV. Agricultural Class							
8. Persons possessing or working the Land, and engaged in growing Grain, Fruits, Grasses, Animals, and other Products*	1,924,110	1,545,667	378,443	332,628	60,185	1,213,039	318,258
9. Persons engaged about Animals	86,344	85,985	359	12,064	76	73,921	283
V. Industrial Class							
10. Persons engaged in Art and Mechanic Productions, in which Matters of various kinds are employed in combination	953,289	893,222	60,067	155,542	10,862	737,680	49,205
11. Persons working and dealing in the Textile Fabrics and in Dress	2,231,617	890,423	1,341,194	213,471	350,953	676,952	990,241
12. Persons working and dealing in Food and Drinks	430,220	347,614	82,606	55,306	5,504	292,308	77,102
13. Persons working and dealing in Animal Substances	56,092	49,257	6,835	8,538	2,539	40,719	4,296
14. Persons working and dealing in Vegetable Substances	144,184	125,310	18,874	20,962	6,544	104,348	12,330
15. Persons working and dealing in Minerals	1,012,997	956,684	56,313	228,266	25,077	728,418	31,236

* In addition to those here returned, many persons connected with the land, as proprietors or occupiers, are classed under other heads according to their professions and occupations. This remark applies especially to persons referred to Orders 6 and 17.

CENSUS 1861—SUMMARY TABLES

Table XVIII—England and Wales—Occupations of Males and Females, distinguishing those under 20 Years of Age from those of 20 Years and upwards—In Classes, Orders, and Sub-orders—continued

Classes, Orders, and Sub-orders	All Ages			Under 20 Years of Age		20 Years of Age and Upwards	
	Persons	Males	Females	Males	Females	Males	Females
VI. Indefinite and Non-productive Class							
16. Labourers and others—Branch of Labour undefined	355,802	342,522	13,280	58,508	4,997	284,014	8,283
17. Persons of Rank or Property, not returned under any Office or Occupation	110,299	22,870	87,429	331	788	22,530	86,641
18. Persons supported by the Community and of no specified Occupation	77,993	20,582	57,411	3,611	3,541	16,971	53,870
Sub-orders							
1. Officers of National Government	48,474	46,543	1,931	3,410	167	43,133	1,764
2. Officers of Local Government	37,671	35,688	1,983	369	27	35,319	1,956
3. Officers of East India and Colonial Government	1,205	1,205	—	4	—	1,201	—
Sub-order							
2. 1. Army (in England and Wales)†	91,005	91,005	—	11,928	—	79,077	—
2. Navy (Ashore or in Port)†	40,939	40,939	—	7,277	—	33,662	—
I. Professional Class							
3. 1. Clergymen, Ministers, and Church Officers	38,536	35,483	3,053	455	260	35,028	2,793
2. Lawyers, Law Court Officers, and Law Stationers	34,991	34,970	21	6,203	3	28,767	18
3. Physicians, Surgeons, and Druggists	38,441	35,995	2,446	4,938	23	31,057	2,423
4. Authors and Literary Persons	3,580	3,395	185	144	5	3,251	180
5. Artists	13,397	12,318	1,079	1,596	182	10,722	897
6. Musicians, Teachers of Music	15,191	10,470	4,721	1,381	822	9,089	3,899
7. Actors, Actresses	4,068	2,934	1,134	382	264	2,552	870
8. Teachers	110,364	30,347	80,017	7,577	15,116	22,770	64,901
9. Scientific Persons	4,095	4,053	42	474	3	3,579	39

† For Returns of the entire Army and Navy, distinguishing Officers and Men, abroad and and at home, see Appendix to Report in Vol. III.

CENSUS 1861–SUMMARY TABLES

Table XVIII–England and Wales–Occupations of Males and Females, distinguishing those under 20 Years of Age from those of 20 Years and upwards–In Classes, Orders, and Sub-orders—continued

Classes, Orders, and Sub-orders	All Ages			Under 20 Years of Age		20 Years of Age and Upwards	
	Persons	Males	Females	Males	Females	Males	Females
II. Domestic Class							
4. 1. Wives (not otherwise described)	2,650,096	—	2,650,096	—	20,287	—	2,629,809
2. Widows (not otherwise described)	269,142	—	269,142	—	69	—	269,073
3. Children and Relatives at home (not otherwise described)§	3,989,652	1,710,395	2,279,257	1,701,969	2,032,383	8,426	246,874
4. Scholars (so described)	3,150,048	1,552,738	1,597,310	1,548,876	1,595,637	3,862	1,673
5. 1. In Board and Lodging	159,134	73,336	85,798	709	949	72,627	84,849
2. Attendance (Domestic Servants, &c.)	1,208,648	137,447	1,071,201	38,765	383,022	98,682	688,179
6. 1. Mercantile Men [and Women]	118,180	114,651	3,529	18,979	181	95,672	3,348
2. Other General Dealers	65,463	39,583	25,880	4,435	1,683	35,148	24,197
III. Commercial Class							
7. 1. Carriers on Railways	53,542	53,385	157	7,134	12	46,251	145
2. ,, on Roads	104,054	101,608	2,446	11,544	86	90,064	2,360
3. ,, on Canals and Rivers	35,817	35,553	264	6,128	46	29,425	218
4. ,, on Seas and Rivers	141,848	141,405	443	20,550	21	120,855	422
5. Engaged in Storage	24,416	20,095	4,321	4,128	1,739	15,967	2,582
6. Messengers and Porters	80,390	79,140	1,250	43,718	768	35,422	482
IV. Agricultural Class							
8. 1. In Fields and Pastures (Agriculturists)	1,833,652	1,457,075	376,577	323,330	60,000	1,133,745	316,577
2. ,, Woods (Arboriculturists)	8,926	8,917	9	995	2	7,922	7
3. ,, Gardens (Horticulturists)	81,532	79,675	1,857	8,303	183	71,372	1,674
9. Persons engaged about Animals	86,344	85,985	359	12,064	76	73,921	283

§ It is probable that a considerable number of the children here returned were under tuition, although not described as "Scholars" in the Householders' Schedules.

56

CENSUS 1861–SUMMARY TABLES

Table XVIII–England and Wales–Occupations of Males and Females, distinguishing those under 20 Years of Age from those of 20 Years and upwards–In Classes, Orders, and Sub-orders–continued

Classes, Orders, and Sub-orders	All Ages			Under 20 Years of Age		20 Years of Age and Upwards	
	Persons	Males	Females	Males	Females	Males	Females
10. 1. In Books	54,293	46,983	7,310	12,898	2,499	34,085	4,811
2. " Musical Instruments	6,586	6,365	221	1,073	29	5,292	192
3. " Prints and Pictures	6,310	5,875	435	1,146	141	4,729	294
4. " Carving and Figures	8,749	4,149	4,600	870	2,027	3,279	2,573
5. " Tackle for Sports and Games	4,187	2,427	1,760	425	381	2,002	1,379
6. " Designs, Medals, and Dies	2,810	2,762	48	601	11	2,161	37
7. " Watches and Philosophical Instruments	25,623	24,888	735	4,442	202	20,446	533
8. " Surgical Instruments	1,029	798	231	141	58	667	173
9. " Arms	13,744	13,031	713	3,544	290	9,487	423
10. " Machines and Tools	117,418	110,772	6,646	24,971	2,699	85,801	3,947
11. " Carriages	20,128	19,896	232	3,691	22	16,289	210
12. " Harness	19,414	18,109	1,305	3,512	444	14,597	861
13. " Ships	43,779	43,704	75	8,230	11	35,474	64
14. " Houses and Buildings	505,671	480,092	25,579	69,995	149	410,097	25,430
15. " Furniture	63,916	55,600	8,316	10,271	1,336	45,329	6,980
16. " Implements	39,623	39,526	97	6,813	5	32,713	92
17. " Chemicals	20,009	18,245	1,764	3,003	558	15,242	1,206
11. 1. In Wood and Worsted	238,814	132,942	105,872	35,936	43,413	97,006	62,459
2. " Silk	117,989	45,121	72,868	10,231	23,521	34,890	49,347
3. " Cotton and Flax	563,014	238,643	324,371	82,250	134,930	156,393	189,441
4. " Mixed Materials (1, 2, 3)	83,170	57,481	25,689	14,631	7,954	42,850	17,735
5. " Dress	1,205,747	399,166	806,581	65,476	139,483	333,690	667,098
6. " Hemp and Other Fibrous Materials	22,883	17,070	5,813	4,947	1,652	12,123	4,161

V. Industrial Class

CENSUS 1861—SUMMARY TABLES

Table XVIII—England and Wales—Occupations of Males and Females, distinguishing those under 20 Years of Age from those of 20 Years and upwards—In Classes, Orders, and Sub-orders—continued

Classes, Orders, and Sub-orders	All Ages			Under 20 Years of Age		20 Years of Age and upwards	
	Persons	Males	Females	Males	Females	Males	Females
12. 1. In Animal Food	141,185	102,836	38,349	17,156	1,264	85,680	37,085
2. „ Vegetable Food	136,354	115,485	20,869	19,306	2,054	96,179	18,815
3. „ Drinks and Stimulants	152,681	129,293	23,388	18,844	2,186	110,449	21,202
13. 1. In Grease, Gut, Bones, Horn, Ivory, and Whalebone	12,040	11,186	854	1,831	258	9,355	596
2. „ Skins, Feathers, and Quills	29,756	28,360	1,396	4,437	479	23,923	917
3. „ Hair	14,296	9,711	4,585	2,270	1,802	7,441	2,783
14. 1. In Gums and Resins	14,659	11,777	2,882	2,329	971	9,448	1,911
2. „ Wood	79,066	76,076	2,990	10,949	1,144	65,127	1,846
3. „ Bark	2,352	2,236	116	521	25	1,715	91
4. „ Cane, Rush, and Straw	17,302	16,048	1,254	2,428	304	13,620	950
5. „ Paper	30,805	19,173	11,632	4,735	4,100	14,438	7,532
15. 1. In Mining	330,446	330,352	94	95,696	7	234,656	87
2. „ Coal	48,238	43,554	4,684	5,346	1,898	38,208	2,786
3. „ Stone, Clay	144,773	142,170	2,603	20,884	1,370	121,286	1,233
4. „ Earthenware	47,144	32,981	14,163	9,343	5,905	23,638	8,258
5. „ Glass	15,603	14,211	1,392	4,023	557	10,188	835
6. „ Salt	2,527	2,404	123	295	38	2,109	85
7. „ Water	2,173	2,147	26	134	—	2,013	26
8. „ Gold, Silver, and Precious Stones	21,576	18,600	2,976	4,705	1,370	13,895	1,606
9. „ Copper	9,733	5,752	3,981	1,213	2,452	4,539	1,529
10. „ Tin and Quicksilver	22,878	18,434	4,444	5,139	2,636	13,295	1,808
11. „ Zinc	760	743	17	164	14	579	3
12. „ Lead and Antimony	4,997	4,027	970	1,062	495	2,965	475
13. „ Brass and other mixed Metals	45,577	41,612	3,965	11,124	1,668	30,488	2,297
14. „ Iron and Steel	316,572	299,697	16,875	69,138	6,667	230,559	10,209

V. Industrial Class continued

58

CENSUS 1861–SUMMARY TABLES

Table XVIII–England and Wales–Occupations of Males and Females, distinguishing those under 20 Years of Age from those of 20 Years and upwards–In Classes, Orders, and Sub-orders–continued

Classes, Orders, and Sub-orders	All Ages			Under 20 Years of Age		20 Years of Age and upwards	
	Persons	Males	Females	Males	Females	Males	Females
16. 1. General Labourers	309,883	306,544	3,339	47,605	681	258,939	2,658
2. Other Persons of indefinite Occupations	45,919	35,978	9,941	10,903	4,316	25,075	5,625
17. Persons of Rank or Property, not returned under any Office or Occupation	110,299	22,870	87,429	331	788	22,539	86,641
18. 1. On Income from voluntary Sources and Rates*	72,724	18,320	54,404	2,375	2,467	15,945	51,937
2. Prisoners and others of Criminal Class, of no specified Occupation*	3,366	1,144	2,222	951	840	193	1,382
3. Vagrants and Gipsies	1,903	1,118	785	285	234	833	551
Persons of no stated Rank, Profession, or Occupation	150,890	51,442	99,448	3,386	12,159	48,056	87,289

VI. Indefinite and Non-productive Class

*Paupers, prisoners, and other persons in public institutions, as well as persons described as superannuated or retired, are referred to specific occupations when the nature of their former employment has been stated, the residue only being classed under Order 18.

CENSUS 1871—SUMMARY TABLES

Table XVII—ENGLAND AND WALES—Occupations of Males and Females, distinguishing those under 20 Years of Age from those of 20 Years and upwards—In Classes, Orders, and Sub-orders.*

Classes, Orders, and Sub-orders	All Ages			Under 20 Years of Age		20 Years of Age and upwards	
	Persons	Males	Females	Males	Females	Males	Females
All Persons	22,712,266	11,058,934	11,653,332	5,192,766	5,189,687	5,866,168	6,463,645
Classes							
I. Professional Class	684,102	486,118	197,984	105,615	97,877	380,503	100,107
II. Domestic Class	5,905,171	244,728	5,660,443	44,508	744,793	200,220	4,915,650
III. Commercial Class	815,424	758,187	57,237	155,538	8,500	602,649	48,737
IV. Agricultural Class	1,657,138	1,470,442	186,696	303,908	52,771	1,166,534	133,925
V. Industrial Class	5,137,725	3,615,727	1,521,998	719,430	427,569	2,896,297	1,094,429
VI. Indefinite and Non-Productive Class	8,512,706	4,483,732	4,028,974	3,863,767	3,858,177	619,965	170,797
Orders							
Order							
1. Persons engaged in the General or Local Government of the Country	106,286	99,892	6,394	7,356	842	92,536	5,552
Class I. { 2. Persons engaged in the Defence of the Country	136,491	136,491	—	22,000	—	114,191	—
3. Persons engaged in the Learned Professions or in Literature, Art, and Science (with their immediate Subordinates)	441,325	249,735	191,590	76,259	97,035	173,476	94,555

*The classification of Occupations adopted in 1871 is essentially identical with that of 1861. The only variations of importance occur in Classes II. and VI.

The change has had the effect of bringing now into Class II., Order 4, all Women (Wives, Widows, Daughters, or others) who have no specified occupation, but are usually employed in household duties. In 1861 the Wives of Innkeepers, Publicans, Lodging-house-keepers, Shopkeepers, Shoemakers, Butchers, and Farmers were placed in the same orders (namely, 5, 6, 8, 11, and 12) as their Husbands, whom they often assist in business; but this, it must be borne in mind, is the case with other as well as with such Wives. As it may be assumed the great

Table XVII–ENGLAND AND WALES–Occupations of Males and Females, distinguishing those under 20 Years of Age from those of 20 Years and upwards–In Classes, Orders, and Sub-orders–continued

Classes, Orders, and Sub-orders	All Ages			Under 20 Years of Age		20 Years of Age and upwards	
	Persons	Males	Females	Males	Females	Males	Females
Class II. 4. Wives and Women engaged generally in Household Duties but assisting in certain cases in the Husbands' Business	4,271,657	–	4,271,657	–	257,613	–	4,014,044
5. Persons engaged in entertaining, and performing Personal Offices for Man . . .	1,633,514	244,728	1,388,786	44,508	487,180	200,220	901,606
Class III. 6. Persons who buy or sell, keep or lend Money, Houses, or Goods of various Kinds	287,164	242,338	44,826	40,775	3,911	201,563	40,915
7. Persons engaged in the Conveyance of Men, Animals, Goods, and Messages . . .	528,260	515,849	12,411	114,763	4,589	401,086	7,822
Class IV. 8. Persons possessing or working the Land, and engaged in growing Grain, Fruits, Grasses, Animals, and other Products . . .	1,559,037	1,372,942	186,095	288,760	52,630	1,084,182	133,465
9. Persons engaged about Animals . . .	98,101	97,500	601	15,148	141	82,352	460

majority of Women of no specified occupation are mainly employed in Household and Family Duties, they are all classed together in these Tables.

Class VI. now comprises Persons whose occupations are indefinite or not stated, Persons of Rank or Property not returned under any office or occupation, and Scholars and Children under the age of 15. Thus Scholars and Children under the age of 15 not returned as engaged in any directly productive occupation, now form by themselves Order 18; whereas in 1861 they were grouped under Class II., Order 4. Students and Scholars of ages 15 and upwards are now in Class I., Order 3; in 1861 they were included in Class II.

With the foregoing exceptions no changes of importance have been made in the various Sub-orders, Orders, and Classes of the classification of 1861.

Note.–The number of persons referred to the particular Classes, Orders, and Sub-orders must not be taken to represent the total number following the Occupations included therein; for example, in addition to the persons returned in Class IV., Order 8, many persons connected with the land as Proprietors or Occupiers are classed under other heads according to the Occupations in which they are principally engaged. See notes at foot of Table XVIII.

CENSUS 1871—SUMMARY TABLES

Table XVII—ENGLAND AND WALES—Occupations of Males and Females, distinguishing those under 20 Years of Age from those of 20 Years and upwards—In Classes, Orders, and Sub-orders—continued

Classes, Orders, and Sub-orders	All Ages			Under 20 Years of Age		20 Years of Age and upwards	
	Persons	Males	Females	Males	Females	Males	Females
Class V.							
10. Persons engaged in Art and Mechanic Productions, in which Matters of various kinds are used in combination	1,144,571	1,086,723	57,848	184,308	14,241	902,415	43,607
11. Persons working and dealing in the Textile Fabrics and in Dress	2,150,791	852,268	1,298,523	200,804	365,033	651,464	933,490
12. Persons working and dealing in Food and Drinks	464,051	398,167	65,884	65,366	8,326	332,801	57,558
13. Persons working and dealing in Animal Substances	56,351	47,676	8,675	7,569	3,105	40,107	5,570
14. Persons working and dealing in Vegetable Substances	165,340	137,816	27,524	22,632	10,170	115,184	17,354
15. Persons working and dealing in Minerals	1,156,621	1,093,077	63,544	238,751	26,694	854,326	36,850
16. Labourers and others—Branch of labour undefined	802,303	753,921	48,382	159,095	19,278	594,826	29,104
Class VI.							
17. Persons of Rank or Property not returned under any Office or Occupation	168,895	25,510	143,385	371	1,692	25,139	141,693
18. Scholars and Children not engaged in any directly Productive Occupation	7,541,508	3,704,301	3,837,207	3,704,301	3,837,207	—	—
Sub-orders							
Class I.							
Sub-order							
1. Officers of National Government	53,874	50,560	3,314	6,714	756	43,846	2,558
2. Officers of Local Government	51,438	48,358	3,080	628	86	47,730	2,994
3. Officers of East India and Colonial Government	974	974	—	14	—	960	—

Table XVII–ENGLAND AND WALES–Occupations of Males and Females, distinguishing those under 20 Years of Age from those of 20 Years and upwards–In Classes, Orders, and Sub-orders–continued

Classes, Orders, and Sub-orders	All Ages			Under 20 Years of Age		20 Years of Age and upwards	
	Persons	Males	Females	Males	Females	Males	Females
2. 1. Army†	93,793	93,793	—	14,659	—	79,134	—
2. Navy†	42,698	42,698	—	7,341	—	35,357	—
3. 1. Clergymen, Ministers, and Others connected with Religion	44,562	39,478	5,084	334	169	39,144	4,915
2. Lawyers and Law Stationers	37,327	37,276	51	6,608	9	30,668	42
3. Physicians, Surgeons, and Druggists	44,214	41,221	2,993	5,455	124	35,766	2,869
4. Authors, Literary Persons, and Students	139,143	61,085	78,058	51,926	75,504	9,159	2,554
5. Artists	16,562	14,728	1,834	1,903	318	12,825	1,516
6. Musicians	18,861	11,786	7,075	1,308	1,269	10,478	5,806
7. Actors	7,324	5,117	2,207	812	541	4,305	1,666
8. Teachers	127,140	32,901	94,239	7,472	19,098	25,429	75,141
9. Scientific Persons	6,192	6,143	49	441	3	5,702	46
4. 1. Wives and others mainly engaged in Household Duties	3,883,830	—	3,883,830	—	256,285	—	3,627,545
2. Wives assisting generally in their Husbands' Business	387,827	—	387,827	—	1,328	—	386,499
5. 1. Engaged in Board and Lodging	139,103	86,851	52,252	1,477	1,466	85,374	50,786
2. Attendants (Domestic Servants, &c.)	1,494,411	157,877	1,336,534	43,031	485,714	114,846	850,820
6. 1. Mercantile Persons	189,807	183,054	6,753	33,581	677	149,473	6,076
2. Other General Dealers	97,357	59,284	38,073	7,194	3,234	52,090	34,839

Class I. continued (rows 2 and 3); Class II. (row 4); Class III. (rows 5 and 6)

† For returns of the entire Army and Navy, distinguishing Officers and Men, abroad and at home, see Appendix to Report, Vol. IV.

CENSUS 1871–SUMMARY TABLES

Table XVII–ENGLAND AND WALES–Occupations of Males and Females, distinguishing those under 20 Years of Age from those of 20 Years and upwards–In Classes, Orders, and Sub-orders–continued

	Classes, Orders, and Sub-orders	Persons	All Ages		Under 20 Years of Age		20 Years of Age and upwards	
			Males	Females	Males	Females	Males	Females
Class III. continued	7. 1. Carriers on Railways	84,900	84,625	275	12,059	24	72,566	251
	2. " on Roads	124,786	122,296	2,490	11,613	85	110,683	2,405
	3. " on Canals and Rivers	33,240	32,823	417	5,156	103	27,667	314
	4. " on Seas and Rivers	141,403	140,949	454	18,846	17	122,103	437
	5. Engaged in Storage	45,338	38,150	7,188	8,298	3,179	29,852	4,009
	6. Messengers and Porters	98,593	97,006	1,587	58,791	1,181	38,215	406
Class IV.	8. 1. Agriculturists	1,447,481	1,264,031	183,450	277,197	52,311	986,834	131,139
	2. Arboriculturists	7,861	7,855	6	665	2	7,190	4
	3. Horticulturists	103,695	101,056	2,639	10,898	317	90,158	2,322
	9. 1. Persons engaged about Animals	98,101	97,500	601	15,148	141	82,352	460
Class V.	10. 1. Workers and Dealers in Books	74,441	64,170	10,271	18,801	3,866	45,369	6,405
	2. " Musical Instruments	8,216	7,924	292	1,402	49	6,522	243
	3. " Prints and Pictures	5,801	5,494	307	993	81	4,501	226
	4. " Carving and Figures	10,595	5,462	5,133	1,287	1,859	4,175	3,274
	5. " Tackle for Sports and Games	4,376	2,754	1,622	491	336	2,263	1,286
	6. " Designs, Medals, and Dies	4,715	4,578	137	1,003	47	3,575	90
	7. " Watches and Philosophical Instruments	26,720	25,888	832	4,067	248	21,821	584

Table XVII—ENGLAND AND WALES—Occupations of Males and Females, distinguishing those under 20 Years of Age from those of 20 Years and upwards—In Classes, Orders, and Sub-orders—continued

Classes, Orders, and Sub-orders	All Ages			Under 20 Years of Age		20 Years of Age and upwards	
	Persons	Males	Females	Males	Females	Males	Females
8. „ Surgical Instruments	1,234	1,004	230	181	34	823	196
9. „ Arms	15,619	13,017	2,602	2,672	1,338	10,345	1,264
10. „ Machines and Tools	174,704	167,429	7,275	31,992	2,632	135,437	4,643
11. „ Carriages	55,790	55,360	430	9,316	53	46,044	377
12. „ Harness	23,011	21,181	1,830	3,751	641	17,430	1,189
13. „ Ships	45,164	45,066	98	6,099	24	38,967	74
14. „ Houses and Buildings	593,252	579,326	13,926	87,296	238	492,030	13,688
15. „ Furniture	71,006	61,179	9,827	10,381	1,694	50,798	8,133
16. „ Chemicals	29,927	26,891	3,036	4,576	1,101	22,315	1,935
11. 1. Workers and Dealers in Wool and Worsted	253,490	128,984	124,506	38,663	56,011	90,321	68,495
2. „ Silk	82,053	28,865	53,188	6,593	17,508	22,272	35,680
3. „ Cotton and Flax	562,015	223,217	338,798	78,415	138,627	144,802	200,171
4. „ Mixed Materials	116,913	71,745	45,168	17,927	15,061	53,818	30,107
5. „ Dress	1,115,247	384,794	730,453	55,193	135,782	329,601	594,671
6. „ Hemp and other Fibrous Materials	21,073	14,663	6,410	4,013	2,044	10,650	4,366
12. 1. Workers and Dealers in Animal Food	132,599	117,501	15,098	20,104	1,440	97,397	13,658
2. „ Vegetable Food	145,196	123,141	22,055	20,182	2,838	102,959	19,217
3. „ Drinks and Stimulants	186,256	157,525	28,731	25,080	4,048	132,445	24,683

Class V. continued

CENSUS 1871—SUMMARY TABLES

Table XVII—ENGLAND AND WALES—Occupations of Males and Females, distinguishing those under 20 Years of Age from those of 20 Years and upwards—In Classes, Orders, and Sub-orders—continued

Classes, Orders, and Sub-orders	All Ages			Under 20 Years of Age		20 Years of Age and upwards	
	Persons	Males	Females	Males	Females	Males	Females
Class V. continued							
13. 1. Workers and Dealers in Grease, Gut, Bones, Horn, Ivory, and Whalebone	11,134	10,258	876	1,579	216	8,679	660
2. " Skins, Feathers, and Quills	30,703	27,928	2,775	4,044	1,076	23,884	1,699
3. " Hair	14,514	9,490	5,024	1,946	1,813	7,544	3,211
14. 1. Workers and Dealers in Gums and Resins	25,059	20,875	4,184	4,199	1,396	16,676	2,788
2. " Wood	81,239	74,764	6,475	10,204	2,898	64,560	3,577
3. " Bark	2,193	2,043	150	324	42	1,719	108
4. " Cane, Rush, and Straw	16,860	15,756	1,104	2,109	202	13,647	902
5. " Paper	39,989	24,378	15,611	5,796	5,632	18,582	9,979
15. 1. Miners	376,783	371,105	5,678	98,909	2,920	272,196	2,758
2. Workers and Dealers in Coal	68,860	64,453	4,407	7,911	1,603	56,542	2,804
3. " Stone, Clay	152,673	149,567	3,106	20,965	1,731	128,602	1,375
4. " Earthenware	52,620	34,398	18,222	8,995	7,679	25,403	10,543
5. " Glass	20,284	18,497	1,787	5,094	706	13,403	1,081
6. " Salt	2,861	2,720	141	330	38	2,390	103
7. " Water	3,347	3,326	21	167	2	3,159	19
8. " Gold, Silver, and Precious Stones	27,139	23,353	3,786	5,084	1,587	18,269	2,199
9. " Copper	5,758	5,598	160	1,022	65	4,576	95

CENSUS 1871–SUMMARY TABLES

Table XVII—ENGLAND AND WALES—Occupations of Males and Females, distinguishing those under 20 Years of Age from those of 20 Years and upwards—In Classes, Orders, and Sub-orders—continued

Classes, Orders, and Sub-orders	All Ages			Under 20 Years of Age		20 Years of Age and upwards	
	Persons	Males	Females	Males	Females	Males	Females
Class V. continued							
10. " Tin and Quicksilver	26,119	23,224	2,895	6,236	1,619	16,988	1,276
11. " Zinc	1,728	1,716	12	294	2	1,422	10
12. " Lead and Antimony	3,727	3,173	554	798	213	2,375	341
13. " Brass and other Mixed Metals	54,366	49,982	4,384	12,369	1,876	37,613	2,508
14. " Iron and Steel	360,356	341,965	18,391	70,577	6,653	271,388	11,738
16. 1. General Labourers	516,605	509,456	7,149	83,550	1,412	425,906	5,737
2. Other Persons of indefinite Occupations	285,698	244,465	41,233	75,545	17,866	168,920	23,367
Class VI.							
17. 1. Persons of Rank or Property not returned under any Office or Occupation	168,895	25,510	143,385	371	1,692	25,139	141,693
18. 1. Scholars and Children not engaged in any directly Productive Occupation	7,541,508	3,704,301	3,837,207	3,704,301	3,837,207	—	—

CENSUS 1901—SUMMARY TABLES

Occupations or Groups of Occupations	Proportion per Million Persons			Proportion per Million Males			Proportion per Million Females		
	1881	1891	1901	1881	1891	1901	1881	1891	1901
Showing Increase as between 1881 and 1901.—									
General or Local Government of the Country	5,386	6,543	7,826	10,373	12,204	14,149	738	1,312	2,009
Defence of the Country	5,545	5,735	6,643	11,494	11,940	13,865	—	—	—
Professional Occupations and their Subordinate Services	21,674	23,029	23,940	24,781	25,035	25,681	18,778	21,175	22,339
Commercial Occupations—excluding Merchants, Salesmen, Buyers (commodity undefined)	15,638	18,277	23,022	31,666	36,190	43,154	699	1,725	4,502
Conveyance of Men, Goods, and Messages (excluding Platelayers, Gangers, Packers, and Railway Labourers)	41,088	45,428	50,022	83,985	93,209	102,844	1,105	1,272	1,427
Coal and Shale Mine Workers	19,774	23,448	25,418	40,657	48,513	52,824	310	286	203
Metals, Machines, Implements	35,190	35,367	39,051	69,043	69,659	77,003	3,639	3,677	4,136
Ships and Boats	2,801	3,162	3,421	5,794	6,568	7,131	11	15	9
Vehicles	3,280	3,694	4,679	6,750	7,577	9,484	44	105	257
Precious Metals, Jewels, Watches, Instruments, and Games (including Electricity Supply)	4,005	4,317	6,016	7,261	7,864	11,012	970	1,039	1,420
Building and Works of Construction—including Platelayers, Gangers, Packers, Railway Labourers; Lock, Key, and Gas Fittings Makers	39,620	36,279	44,570	81,925	75,307	92,811	189	213	188
Wood, Furniture, Fittings and Decorations	9,326	9,152	10,172	17,368	17,089	19,202	1,829	1,818	1,865
Brick, Cement, Pottery, and Glass	6,638	6,309	6,931	11,154	10,391	11,732	2,429	2,536	2,513
Chemicals, Oil, Grease, Soap, Resin, &c	3,629	4,139	5,080	6,696	7,268	8,401	770	1,248	2,024

CENSUS 1901—SUMMARY TABLES—continued

Occupations or Groups of Occupations	Proportion per Million Persons			Proportion per Million Males			Proportion per Million Females		
	1881	1891	1901	1881	1891	1901	1881	1891	1901
Paper, Prints, Books, and Stationery	8,194	9,968	11,016	12,499	14,778	15,498	4,181	5,524	6,892
Drapers, Linen Drapers, Mercers	4,266	4,853	5,357	5,753	5,728	5,540	2,880	4,044	5,189
Food, Tobacco, Drink, and Lodging	36,849	41,609	42,403	59,088	62,178	63,810	16,121	22,601	22,709
Gas, Water and Sanitary Service (not including Electricity Supply)	1,310	1,858	2,705	2,696	3,853	5,637	18	14	9
Engine Drivers, Stokers, Firemen (not Railway, Marine, or Agricultural)	3,426	3,721	4,198	7,101	7,747	8,762	—	—	—
	267,639	286,888	322,470	496,084	523,098	588,540	54,711	68,604	77,691
Showing Decrease as between 1881 and 1901:—									
Agriculture—On Farms, Woods and Gardens	70,058	58,273	47,304	138,327	116,513	95,510	6,426	4,453	2,956
Fishing	1,538	1,144	943	3,157	2,350	1,955	29	29	13
Skins, Leather, Hair, and Feathers	4,230	4,181	4,160	7,100	6,906	6,599	1,555	1,662	1,916
Workers and Dealers in Textile Fabrics (excluding Drapers)	52,433	48,587	40,268	46,009	43,273	35,021	58,420	53,498	45,095
Workers and Dealers in Dress	49,353	48,812	44,481	37,185	36,885	34,171	60,695	59,834	53,966
General Labourers	28,994	27,028	16,193	59,791	56,092	33,770	290	170	23
Domestic Indoor Service	66,646	65,508	55,084	6,042	5,525	5,287	123,134	120,938	100,897
Charwomen	4,790	4,752	4,416	—	—	—	9,254	9,144	8,479
Laundry and Washing Service	9,327	8,713	8,096	366	653	731	17,680	16,162	14,871
All other Occupations	23,134	24,335	22,405	39,006	40,129	35,466	8,342	9,741	10,384
	310,503	291,333	243,350	336,983	308,326	248,510	285,825	275,631	238,600
Total Occupied	578,142	578,221	565,820	833,067	831,424	837,050	340,536	344,235	316,291

69

Different forms of summary tables are given here to convey some sense of the range of available materials. The summary of occupations for England and Wales by class or order is given for 1851, 1861, and 1871. The retrospective table for 1901 is given, not in absolute numbers, but in proportions per million persons arranged by increasing and decreasing occupations.

Recommended Reading

There is surprisingly little general literature on occupations, save insofar as those data are part of other considerations. G. R. Porter, *The Progress of the Nation* (London: 1847) and Charles Booth, "Occupations of the People of the United Kingdom," *Journal of the Statistical Society*, XLIX (June 1886), remain standard even at this considerable remove. Two important studies are J. Saville, *Rural Depopulation in England and Wales, 1851–1951* (London: 1957), and A. Redford, *Labour Migration in England 1800–1850*, 2d ed. (Manchester: 1964). Ivy Pinchbeck has a provocative study in *Women Workers and the Industrial Revolution, 1750–1850* (London: 1968).

OCCUPATIONS OF THE PEOPLE, 1851, 1861, 1871, 1901

Source: Census of 1851—*Parliamentary Papers, 1852–1953*, vol. LXXXVIII, part 1, pp. ccxviii–ccxix; Census of 1861—*Parliamentary Papers*, 1863, vol. LIII, part 1, pp. xl–xli; Census of 1871—*Parliamentary Papers*, 1873, vol. LXXI, part 1, pp. xxxv–xxxvi; Census of England and Wales, 1901—*General Report* (London: 1904).

7. Trade Unions and Combination

ONE OF THE MOST important nineteenth-century institutions was the modern trade union. British trade unions antedated industrialism, survived a two-decade ban on combinations (1799–1824), and achieved legal and privileged status in 1871 and 1875. The history of trade unionism was anything but smooth. Unions suffered from internal tensions and external pressure. Owenite euphoria led to overcommitment in the 1830s. Unions recovered but slowly in the early years of Victoria's reign from manufacturers' lockouts and government prosecution for the administration of illegal oaths.

Mid-Victorian trade unionism was painfully respectable. Utopianism was gone. Skilled labor developed the art of collective bargaining. Unions built up large benefit funds—and struck most reluctantly. Robert Applegarth of the Amalgamated Society of Carpenters and Joiners conceived of trade unions as an instrument of emancipation. His union's rules, quoted with obvious relish by Asa Briggs, provided:

We shall be faithless to our fellow working men if we omit to record our honest conviction that this much to be desired condition must be preceded by the equally universal spread of the principles of economy and sobriety, which would be accelerated by our meeting for business in public halls or private rooms, where, by the establishment of libraries and listening to the voice of the lecturer on all subjects connected with our interests, we and our sons shall become respectful and respected, and make rapid progress in the onward march of reform.[1]

The "Junta," that effective board of directors for British trade unionism, accepted middle-class Victorian values, sought franchise reform, and constructed a solid institutional foundation for future trade union growth.

Even mid-Victorian unionism had its seamy side. Sheffield remained a center of secretive union activity and violence. The South Wales coal pits still awaited the coming of Mabon and some measure of labor regularity. And the overwhelming majority of British workingmen and women were not unionized. The growth and development of trade unionism after midcentury is the subject of the first portion of this report; the question of industrial relations the business of the second.

The principal underlying facts in the case were simple. The British had not yet turned the corner from the Great Depression (1873–1896), and, as it happened, the statistics we have suggest that the workingman fared better in terms of real wages during the depression than the subsequent two decades. Foreign competition, particularly from Germany and the United States, had reached serious proportions in many sectors of the economy, particularly neutral export markets. As the economic path became rougher, so did conflict within the world of industrial relations. Robert Applegarth claimed that he never had a harsh word with an employer either as a workingman or as a trade unionist. The voice of sweet reason was heard less and less as employers attempted to maintain competitive positions while unionists tried to consolidate gains. And there were challenges within the world of labor. The "New Unionism" of the late 1880s reached into the ranks of the semiskilled and unskilled—seamen, gas stokers, matchgirls, dockworkers, agricultural laborers—and spoke a different language. They were far less tolerant of middle-class Victorian values, for those had little relevance to their culture and slight connection with their aspirations.

This report touches upon a series of aspects of association and organization at the end of the Victorian period, dimensions related to although not necessarily coterminus with trade unionism. The cooperative movement had come far from its humble beginnings in Rochdale in the 1840s, but growth and the depression combined to create new problems. The movement to combination and association,

1. A. Briggs, *Victorian People* (Chicago: 1955), p. 168.

moreover, was not limited to labor. Industry, responding to both domestic and foreign pressures, moved in the direction of formal or informal association. This, too, was a matter of concern in the Commission's report.

Perhaps the most important implication of the general movement analyzed by the Commission was the waning of that cardinal Victorian value, individualism: Combination and association meant group action and collectivization.

Recommended Reading

The literature on trade unionism is considerable and dense. The old, often reprinted classic by S. and B. Webb, *History of Trade Unionism* (London: 1894), is still useful. The best brief summary is H. Pelling, *History of British Trade Unionism* (London: 1963). H. A. Clegg, A. Fox, and A. F. Thompson, *History of British Trade Unionism since 1889* (Oxford, 1964), vol. I, is meticulous. E. J. Hobsbawm's *Labouring Men* (London: 1964) has a series of exciting and useful essays. B. C. Roberts, *The Trade Union Congress, 1868–1921* (London: 1958) is standard as is P. H. J. H. Gosnell, *Friendly Societies in England, 1851–1875* (Manchester: 1961).

ROYAL COMMISSION ON LABOUR,
ASSOCIATIONS AND ORGANISATIONS OF EMPLOYERS AND EMPLOYED

1. ROYAL COMMISSION OF 1867 ON TRADE UNIONS, AND SUBSEQUENT
LEGISLATION; SCOPE OF INQUIRY BY THE PRESENT COMMISSION,
SO FAR AS RELATES TO THESE ASSOCIATIONS

. . . The object of the Royal Commission of 1867 was partly to investigate certain charges which had been made with respect to some then recent acts of violence and intimidation alleged to have been committed by trade unionists, but chiefly to inquire into the organisation and rules of trade unions and other associations, whether of workmen or employers, and the effect produced by such bodies, both on the relations between workmen and employers and on the trade and industry of the country. . . .

In the result of their inquiry the Commission of 1867 recommended certain modifications of the then existing law with a view (1) to secure that no combination of persons for the purpose of determining between themselves, or of stipulating for, the terms on

Source: From "Fifth and Final Report of the Royal Commission on Labour, Part 1," *Parliamentary Papers*, 1894, vol. XXXV, pp. 25–48.

which they will consent to employ or be employed, should be unlawful by reason only that its operation would be in restraint of trade; (2) to give to all such unions as complied with certain conditions facilities for becoming registered, and thereby acquiring legal capacities, rights, and liabilities arising from a status recognised by law, so far as regards legal protection for their property. At the same time the Report of this Commission laid great stress on the importance of maintaining the purely voluntary character of industrial organisations, and of fully protecting the freedom of the individual in the disposal of his labour or of his capital.

These recommendations of the Royal Commission of 1867 were, in substance, carried out by the legislation of the year 1871, and (after a further inquiry into the labour laws by another Commission), the legislation of the year 1875. By the effect of the present governing statute called the "Conspiracy and Protection of Property Act, 1875," combined action for trade purposes is relieved from all penal consequences so long as it does not amount to any breach of ordinary law, or extend to certain special modes of action, and some special cases, carefully defined in that statute.

The Trade Union Act, passed in 1871, contained these important declarations, viz., that—

(1) The purposes of any trade union shall not, by reason merely that they are in restraint of trade, be deemed to be unlawful so as to render any member of such trade union liable to criminal prosecution for conspiracy or otherwise;
(2) The purposes of any trade union shall not, by reason merely that they are in restraint of trade, be unlawful so as to render void or voidable any agreement or trust.

The Act then provides (section 4) that

Nothing in this Act shall enable any court to entertain any legal proceeding instituted with the object of directly enforcing or recovering damages for the breach of any of the following agreements, namely:—
(1) Any agreement between members of a trade union as such, concerning the conditions on which any members for the time being of such trade union shall or shall not sell their goods, transact business, employ, or be employed;
(2) Any agreement for the payment by any person of any subscription or penalty to a trade union;

(3) Any agreement for the application of the funds of a trade union (*a*) to provide benefits to members; or (*b*) to furnish contributions to any employer or workman, not a member of such trade union, in consideration of such employer or workman acting in conformity with the rules or resolutions of such trade union; or (*c*) to discharge any fine imposed upon any person by sentence of a court of justice; or,

(4) Any agreement made between one trade union and another; or,

(5) Any bond to secure the performance of any of the abovementioned agreements. But nothing in this section shall be deemed to constitute any of the above-mentioned agreements unlawful.

A trade union registered under this Act may hold land, not exceeding an acre, and personal estate, in the name of trustees, who may sue or be sued in respect of that property. Any trade union may be registered on showing that its rules contain certain provisions, and that it has otherwise complied with the regulations respecting registry in force under the Act. A trade union when registered is bound to furnish the Office of the Registrar of Friendly Societies with an annual statement of accounts. A considerable number of trade unions have registered themselves under this Act. The Report of the Royal Commission of 1867 contained a recommendation that no trade union should be registered the rules of which prevented the employment or limited the number of apprentices in any trade; prevented the introduction or limited the use of machinery in any trade; prevented any workman from taking a sub-contract or working by the piece or working with non-unionists; or authorised the application of funds in support of any other unconnected union engaged in a conflict with its own employers. The recommendation was opposed by a minority of the Commission, and did not become part of the law.

By the Trade Union Act of 1871 as amended by the Trade Union Act of 1876 a trade union is defined as follows:—

The term "trade union" means any combination, whether temporary or permanent, for regulating the relations between workmen and masters, or between workmen and workmen, or between masters and masters, or for imposing restrictive conditions on the conduct of any trade or business whether such combination would or would not, if the principal Act had not been passed, have been deemed to have been an unlawful combination by reason of some one or more of its purposes being in restraint of trade.

The term, therefore, embraces employers' associations, a certain number of which have, in fact, registered themselves under the Act of 1871. It is to be observed that one effect of the Trade Union Act of 1871 is expressly to make an agreement between two unions, although registered, non-enforceable as against either of them in a court of law. This would, therefore, prevent any agreement between an association of workmen and an association of employers from having, as between such bodies, any binding force at law. It is, however, provided that the Act shall not affect "any agreement between an employer and those employed by him as to such employment." In this Report the term "trade union" is employed in its usual sense as meaning an association of workmen. . . .

We have considered it to be our main object, so far as relates to these associations, whether of employers or employed, and their larger development in the shape of federations of associations, to inquire to what extent their existence or absence, strength or weakness, in various trades and occupations, have affected for good or evil the relations between employers and employed, and are a cause of, or obstacle to, conflicts between these classes. If, and in so far as in the result of this Inquiry it should appear that the increase of strength and organisation in these industrial bodies tends, on the whole (in spite of occasional conflicts of great magnitude), towards the establishment of a kind of industrial peace higher than that which has previously prevailed, this would be a reason, subject to the consideration of the effects of such increase of strength upon the general interests of the community, for favouring any legislation which should offer to those organisations a better legal basis than they already possess. The point was well put in a statement made by a minority of the Royal Commission which inquired into the subject of trade unions in the year 1867:—"The practical problem before us is this: seeing that the bulk of the artizan population consider it their interest to form themselves into these associations, in what way can they be rendered most conducive to public policy?"

2. THE OBJECTS, CONSTITUTION, AND POLICY OF ORDINARY TRADE UNIONS

. . . The total membership amounts, according to the last Return, to 871,000 persons, with an annual income of nearly 1,200,000*l*. Mr. Fenwick, the secretary of the Parliamentary Committee of the Trade Union Congress, said in evidence that a million and a quarter of trade unionists were represented at that Congress in 1892, that there were certainly a million and a half of trade unionists in the country, and that, in his opinion, their number approached two millions. The total number of trade unionists who actually subscribe to their societies is very doubtful and varying, especially in the case of the newer societies of less skilled or general labourers. The figures obtained from the Census of 1891 are of some service in indicating the proportions borne by trade unionists to the total number of persons in England and Wales engaged in manual labour. The industrial class, in the classification used in the Census, excludes the agricultural and fishing population who, in England and Wales, amounted to 1,336,945 persons over 10 years of age, and the persons employed in transport by land and sea, amounting to 983,370, and those employed in domestic and kindred services to the number of 1,900,328, but it includes all those who work in other productive or distributive industrial occupations. Thus limited, the industrial class, at the Census of 1891, numbered 7,336,344 persons over 10 years of age, of whom 5,495,446 were males. These figures include employers, clerks, and officials as well as workmen. Having regard to the small progress which trade unionism has made among the agricultural population, and the persons engaged in domestic service, it is evident that it chiefly exists among the "industrial class" of the Census, and especially among that portion of the five and a half million males who are adult workmen, and engaged in productive as contrasted with distributive enterprise. The class engaged in transport adds an appreciable but very vague and fluctuating contingent, and the industrial population of Scotland and Ireland has also to be taken into account.

The funds of trade unions are supported by entrance fees and by subscriptions varying from about 1d. a week to 1s. or more, and these, in the case of large societies, bring in a considerable annual income. Most trade unions also reserve the right of raising money from their members by special levy for strikes or other extraordinary purposes. Some of the societies have accumulated large reserve funds, and derive some income from investments or from interest on deposit at banks.

The two main divisions of the objects to which trade unions of the normal type apply their funds are (1) trade purposes, viz., in connection with disputes and trade conflicts; (2) friendly and benevolent purposes. In some cases the funds for "trade" and "friendly and benevolent" purposes are kept distinct, but in most cases all purposes are met out of a single fund. It is alleged that the system of a single fund tends to make societies more peacefully disposed, and more cautious how they embark on trade conflicts, inasmuch as strikes seriously impair the funds available for friendly and benevolent purposes. This has sometimes been urged by the leaders of what has been called "new unionism" as a reason for objecting to a society having any benevolent purposes at all, lest its fighting efficiency should be diminished. On the other hand, it is alleged that, apart from the intrinsic merit of the friendly and benevolent purposes, they are very effective in giving solidity and permanency to a trade union, and that without them men are not inclined to hold to a society when there is no immediate prospect of obtaining better trade conditions through its agency. An objection taken to the single fund system is that for the purpose of securing friendly benefits it is financially unsound, and that in the case of some trade unions the solvency of the friendly and benevolent fund virtually depends upon the power of the union to raise special "levies."

Some trade unions apply their funds to not more than one or two objects, others to many. Generalising from the evidence, it may be said that a trade society of the strongest, best established, and wealthiest kind might probably, after meeting its working expenses, apply its income to all or most of the following purposes, viz.: —

(1) Trade disputes, including grants to any men who have been discharged or refused employment by employers, or who have left their employment for trade reasons.

(2) Subscriptions to any larger federation to which the trade union may belong, and grants in aid of men of other trades in their disputes.

(3) Maintenance of members out of work through depression of trade or other legitimate causes, and payments for travelling in search of work, or emigration.

(4) Payments for defraying cost of funerals of members and their wives, and for maintenance to those incapacitated for work by accident, sickness, or in some cases, by old age.

(5) Payments to replace burnt, lost, or broken tools (in some trades), and distress benefits generally.

(6) Educational expenditure, and grants for special benevolent purposes.

(7) Acquisition and circulation of information with regard to trade matters.

(8) Expenditure on parliamentary representation.

(9) Payment of legal expenses of members in connection with trade litigation, including actions brought under the Employers' Liability Act.

Thus a trade society, organised on the most complete scale, not only increases the power of its members in negotiating with regard to the standard rate of wages and other general questions, but acts as an assurance to them against all kinds of risks. It has been suggested by several witnesses that powerful and wealthy trade unions might extend the sphere of their operations by themselves (in alliance, perhaps, with co-operative distributive societies) carrying on to some extent and in some trades operations of manufacturing production; and some attempts of this kind have been made. There are, however, few signs of any great development of this movement at present.

The constitution of these societies varies a good deal, chiefly with regard to the amount of real power which is vested in the hands of the central executive of each. In some cases, as in that of the Durham coal-miners, so many references have to be made in the case of general questions to the local "lodges" or branches, to be decided by ballot, that the central body are little more than delegates acting under immediate instructions, and having to refer points to their constituents even in the midst of negotiations with employers. In other cases, especially where a trade is scattered in various branches all over the country and through districts differing widely in local circumstances from each other, much power and discretion is frequently left with the district or executive committees of local branches. In most unions of this kind, however, the control of the funds possessed by the central executive gives a deciding power in the last resort. Since it alone can finance a branch in case of a strike, the central executive can require that a strike shall be justified to it before being undertaken by the district or local branch. In the case of some societies the permanent officials have much more power than in that of others. In some cases a very complete control is lodged with the central executive of a society, careful provision being made for the rapid circulation of life from all parts of the society through that executive. The Society of the Boiler-makers and Iron Shipbuilders presents an instance of very successful working of a society strongly centralised in this manner.

Generalising from features presented by this and other strong trade unions among the skilled artisans, we are brought to the conclusion that the following are the leading characteristics of the most permanent and successful societies. A typical society of this kind will include, if not all, at least such a proportion of men in a trade as will give it a controlling power in the trade and enable it to treat with employers as representative of the whole, and to make its agreements and decisions binding on the whole trade. It will have a strong central executive council, thoroughly representative of the members and implicitly trusted by them. This machinery will enable the society to negotiate with employers with the least possible friction, either from time to time, as occasion may require, or by way of a permanent joint board for the purpose of settling hour and wage-rate questions, and other points of dispute, and to give undertakings and enter into agreements upon which employers can rely. It was shown in evidence that at least one powerful trade union goes so far as to make itself responsible for the proper fulfilment of contracts made with employers by its members, and to compensate employers from its funds for loss through bad work, recouping itself by fining the members in default.

The chief objects of policy aimed at by trade unions (apart from benefit purposes) may be said to be:

(1) To obtain such conditions as will enable them to deal in a body with their employers, and ultimately perhaps to acquire, so far as possible, a monopoly of employment in their respective trades. The means to this end are the inclusion in the trade union of as many as possible of the men working in each trade; the prohibition of encroachment on their special department of work by men of other trades; and the control by the union of admission to the trade. To achieve the last mentioned object many unions endeavour to insist upon all workmen in the trade passing through a fixed period of apprenticeship before a certain age, and to limit the

proportion of apprentices to journeymen. It is the general policy of some unions to try to prevent their members from working with non-unionists. The extent to which this is enforced varies much with the relative strength of unions, and it is most successfully applied where men work in sets or gangs as, for instance, in iron shipbuilding. It may be added that most unions would probably be willing, and some unions actually offer, to supply employers with suitable workmen, the union acting as an agency for this purpose.

(2) To maintain a minimum wage-rate, and to advance it, or prevent its being reduced, so far as possible.

(3) To maintain a fixed maximum of hours of work, and to reduce it when practicable.

(4) To distribute the available work among members so that as few as possible shall be out of employment. In connection with this, as well as for other reasons, the general policy of many trade unions is opposed to piece-work and to systematic overtime.

(5) In general, to improve the conditions of labour, protect members or groups of members from hard usage on the part of employers and managers, and to maintain trade customs and privileges.

3. IN WHAT INDUSTRIES TRADE UNIONS HAVE BEEN MOST SUCCESSFUL, AND THE REVERSE

The evidence shows that the power and constitution of a trade union have a most important influence upon the character of the relations between employers and employed in the industry. It is, therefore, important to consider in what kind of industries trade unions are found to have been most successful or unsuccessful. To some extent, no doubt, trade unions depend for their permanence and power upon having a succession of able officials and leaders to manage them, and probably personal ability has much to do with their successful launching and establishment. But some industries are, by their nature, more adapted for organisation than others are.

A broad and fundamental distinction may be drawn in the following respect between skilled and unskilled industries.[1] The fact

1. In the category of skilled trades fall, among others, all those connected with the higher grades of shipbuilding and engineering, those of the various artificers in metal and clay, printing and bookbinding, the superior work in building and the trades connected with the decoration of buildings, carpen-

that a trade is skilled, *i.e.* requires training from an early age, or, at any rate, for some considerable time, constitutes it, *ipso facto*, a kind of natural crafts guild, defended from sudden invasion by men of other trades by its difficulty of acquirement, and sometimes, also, by the fact that expensive "kits" of tools must be provided by the workmen. Youths who enter such a trade have to be taught their work by men already in it, and thus a strong society, once established, is able to control the conditions of entrance and practically to compel new comers to join it. The natural facilities which skilled industries possess for organisation may be more or less neutralised in the case of trades in which the workers,

(1) are widely scattered, and frequently on the move, as *e.g.*, sailors;

(2) carry on the work in their own homes, or independently, or in very small groups;

(3) are for the most part women;

(4) have, through the operation of any special cause, to contend against an overstocked or irregular labour market.

On the other hand, when a skilled industry is carried on in more or less large factories, workshops, or mines, and (at any rate in some central districts) brings a large number of workmen into close contact; when, in other words, a trade combines the elements of skill, co-operation in the same work of a number of people, and local contiguity, it seems under all these circumstances to be easy to convert the natural craft thus existing into a formal and permanent trade union. The monopoly possessed by an industry and its consequent facilities for organisation may be further developed by extraneous causes, as for instance by legislation. Coal mining affords a good illustration of this. It is not among the class of highly skilled industries and yet it is one in which, except in the West of Scotland, trade unionism has had remarkable success. The natural monopoly for which in some trades workmen are mostly indebted to their special skill is obtained by the coal miners not

---

tering and coach-building, the great textile industries, the make-up of the better description of clothing, the preparation of many articles of luxury, the more skilled work in railways, and some agricultural work. Mining, and the manufacture of iron and steel, may also be included in this list, and many smaller industries, involving a certain fineness of work.

only from the fact that their industry is concentrated in certain districts, and that they have practical possession of the villages adjacent to the pits in which they work, but also through the operation of the provision in the Coal Mines Regulation Act of 1887, Rule 39, which reads as follows:—"No person not now employed as a coal or ironstone getter shall be allowed to work alone as a coal or ironstone getter in the face of the workings until he has had two years' experience of such work under the supervision of skilled workmen, or unless he shall have been previously employed for two years in or about the face of the workings of a mine," a provision intended to secure greater safety in mines, but which also renders it impossible for employers to bring in new men, in case of a strike, to take the place of the strikers.

Unskilled or general labour, that is, labour in occupations which require little or no training, stands on a very different footing from skilled labour in respect to the facilities which it affords for strong and enduring organisation. The evidence shows that trade societies among the class of unskilled labourers have been apt to rise suddenly and rapidly, enrol a great number of members, and then as quickly decline. Those who try to organise labour of this class meet with many difficulties. Among these are the comparative poverty, less regular habits, and frequently the roving disposition of this class of workmen. The chief difficulty, however, appears to be that workmen in these departments of labour do not possess the natural monopoly which belongs to men in skilled trades. If they strike, their employers usually find it easy at very short notice to obtain men of the same class to take their places. Inasmuch as the power to fight by way of strike is the primary basis of trade unions, weakness in this respect often deters men from joining or holding to unions of unskilled labour. Various cases were brought to our notice in which an unsuccessful strike by an association of this kind resulted in the loss of a great part of its members. Upon the whole it is not as yet shown by experience that it is easy, if, indeed, it is practicable, to mould into a permanent organisation men working at an occupation which is not of the nature of a craft requiring special training. Such an organisation, not being built upon the foundation of a natural monopoly of skill, is apt to fall away and perish in times of trade depression or other adverse circumstances.

It has already been observed that benefit funds for friendly purposes are of service in giving solidity and permanency to trade unions, and inducing members of these societies to remain in them even when there is no immediate prospect of gaining by means of them better trade conditions. The comparative poverty of workers in unskilled occupations, and the smallness of the subscriptions which they are able to afford, makes it difficult for their organisations to support funds of this kind, even if, as a matter of policy, they were disposed to establish them. The result of this is that an association of this kind is usually limited to merely fighting purposes, and its prosperity and numerical strength is apt to depend upon its success in trade conflicts.

An effect of the absence, in the case of unskilled or general labourers, of the natural monopoly, secured by specific skill to workmen in trades which require much training, is a tendency towards the use in industrial conflicts of more or less violent methods of action to prevent the introduction of non-unionist or "free" labourers to take the place of unionists who have struck or been locked out. Another consequence of the weakness, due to the absence of this natural monopoly, of any particular section of general labour appears to be the attempt to bring various sections not, strictly speaking, engaged in the same occupation, to the assistance of each other in industrial conflicts. The most striking illustrations of this tendency were afforded by the contest between the Shipping Federation (of shipowners) and the Seamen's Union in and about the year 1891, when the attempt was made, by inducing dock-labourers in various parts to refuse to work on ships not exclusively manned with union crews, to compel shipowners to employ such crews only.[2] It may be added that a further consequence of the difficulty of organising general or unskilled labour is an inclination on the part of leaders of this portion of the industrial population to look rather to the action of the State than to that of trade unions as a means of achieving their ends. A marked difference in this respect runs, on the whole, through the evidence given by the representatives of skilled trades and that given by repre-

2. A further and equally striking illustration is afforded by the great Australian strikes amongst wharf labourers, seamen and marine officers, miners, and shearers, in 1890 and 1891, which originated in a refusal on the part of the employers to employ none but union shearers, and was taken up by the other trades with the object of enforcing the exclusive employment of union labour.

sentatives of industries which either from want of the monopoly given by specific skill or (as in the case of the miners in the West of Scotland) from other special causes, are weak in organisation.

Some of the leading characteristics of unskilled and feebly organised labour, which have been here referred to, will be considered more in detail in other parts of this Report. It is in this class of industries that there is chiefly to be found the spirit or policy frequently called "new unionism," in contrast to the older unionism of the skilled trades which occupied the attention of the Royal Commission of 1867. The chief feature of the annual trade union congresses held in recent years, appears to be the rise in numerical representation and importance of this "new unionism." The spirit characteristic of the movement seems to be due to the particular circumstances of unskilled or general labour, and especially to the natural difficulties which attend its organisation, but this spirit has, no doubt to some and probably to a considerable extent, influenced or modified the views held by representatives of the skilled trades, especially with regard to the substitution in certain important matters, notably that of hours of work, of State action for independent attempts by trade unions to obtain concessions from employers.

4. ORGANISATIONS OF EMPLOYERS

Formal organisations of employers usually make their appearance at a later date than those of the workmen, and arise for purposes of joint resistance when individual employers find themselves too weak to cope with the growing strength of trade unions. Some associations of employers are, however, of old standing, were originally formed for watching legislation affecting the trade, or for tempering competition by agreement among themselves, and have subsequently developed into instruments of mutual protection against the action of trade unions. Employers' associations are of various degrees of solidity and compactness in different trades, varying, perhaps, with the degree in which these qualities are found in the associations of workmen in those trades. Employers frequently seem to combine rather unwillingly, and the trade competition between them often makes it difficult for them to hold together. Just as in some trades many workmen remain outside the organisations, so also many employers remain outside the employers' associations, and it often seems to happen that non-associated employers employ non-associated men.

5. AMALGAMATIONS AND FEDERATIONS

In recent years there has been a decided tendency towards (*a*) the amalgamation of trade unions with one another; (*b*) the federation of trade unions in the same trades; (*c*) the federation of trade unions' associations in different trades with a view to obtaining a greater force in industrial warfare. The same tendency has been visible in the case of employers' associations. A distinction must be drawn between cases (*b*) and (*c*). A federation of unions in the same trade is really often an incomplete amalgamation. Of this kind of combination the Miners' Federation is a conspicuous instance.

A combination of unions or associations in different trades is rather a mere alliance. Of this kind, perhaps, may be said to be the federation recently formed among various trades engaged in shipbuilding and engineering. This federation was established in reply to the formation of an employers' "National Federation of Shipbuilders and Engineers," which was formed for the purpose of mutual protection and resistance to what the employers in question considered to be encroachments on the part of trade unions with regard to "free labour," apprenticeship rules, and so forth. It is alleged on both sides that the whole force of either federation would only be exercised by way of general strike or lock-out in extreme cases. In Durham and Northumberland the various classes of workmen employed in the mines are organised in the first place in their sectional associations, which, again, are federated for the purpose of dealing with employers.

Among the unskilled trades large schemes of amalgamation or federation have also of late appeared, and attempts have been made to carry them into practical effect by means of "sympathy strikes," such as those of dock and riverside labourers on behalf of the policy of the Seamen's Union. On the other side, the "Shipping Federation" of ship-owning firms and local associations, organised to resist these movements, is remarkable both for its extent and power and for the fact that, being incorporated as a limited joint stock company, it has a legal personality.

It has not, as yet, been shown by experience that trades of a totally distinct character from each other can be permanently amalgamated or federated together. For this purpose a certain natural affinity of occupation would seem to be necessary. But the annual trade union congresses bring the various associations which take part in them into a certain connection, the chief object of which is to secure common action in matters requiring legislative treatment.

In many industrial centres "Trade Councils" also exist, composed of the representatives of different and independent trades, and these have a great and apparently increasing influence in consolidating for common action, in some circumstances, the forces of local trades. It is usually one of their professed objects to assist in organising labour as yet unorganised.

6. MIXED ASSOCIATIONS

One outcome of the recent conflicts with regard to employment of "free labour" has been the development of certain institutions by which employers and those immediately in their employ have, in some cases, become formed into a kind of mixed association. The institution by the Shipping Federation of its registry system would seem to be an attempt to move in this direction, and the re-organisation of dock labour at Southampton after the strike of 1890 is an instance of the same tendency.

In a certain sense such an institution as the Board of Conciliation and Arbitration for the Manufactured Iron and Steel Trade of the North of England may be regarded as having formed the employers and men who belong to it into a kind of mixed organisation, although each side in this case has its separate association. For this Board, which meets regularly twice a year, and has its standing joint committee, is composed of one employer and one elected workman from each of the works in association, so that it may be said to form a complete industrial parliament.

There are some cases also in the same trade where single large works, for instance, the "Barrow Steel Works" have a kind of mixed assembly or tribunal of their own for settling trade disputes. Any system under which representatives of employers and workmen in a trade meet periodically in conference or joint committee, as in the South Wales coal mining trade, may be considered as tending in the same direction. The same thing may also be said of some systems of organised profit-sharing, especially where, as in the case of the South Metropolitan Gas Company, the system is worked under the supervision of a joint committee.

7. REPRESENTATIONS MADE AS TO THE INJURIOUS OR BENEFICIAL EFFECTS OF TRADE UNIONS

The employers who have given evidence have usually recognised a legitimate province for trade unions in bargaining as to wages and hours and watching over the general interests of their members, and admitted that strong organisations, acting within those limits, tend on the whole to improve industrial relations, and to make their members act in a better informed way and a more reasonable spirit. . . . But the view has also been put forward, even by those who hold these opinions, that the action and rules of trade unions have been in some respects prejudicial to the efficiency of production and to the industrial prosperity of the country.

The allegations upon this point are as follows: —

(1) That trade unions have a growing tendency to interfere with details of business, and so to take away that concentration of command which is necessary for successful management, and hamper employers in carrying on their business according to the methods which they believe to be best.

(2) That trade unions often misjudge the true position of affairs, and by ill-timed and excessive demands, as well as by placing employers under apprehension of these, discourage enterprise and further investment of capital in this country, to the detriment of all concerned, including ultimately, if not immediately, their own members. As a proof that trade unions have done less than is frequently believed in the way of raising wages, it is contended that wages have in many cases risen as much and as fast in unorganised as in organised employments. It is urged that the extension of machinery in manufactures, and the development of railways and steam navigation, are the main causes of the increased demand for labour and consequent advance of wages during the last half century.

(3) That though organisations may tend to diminish the frequency of industrial conflicts, they extend their range; and that such conflicts on a large scale, especially in industries which supply raw material, are far more injurious to associated and dependent trades than are more frequent conflicts on a small scale.

(4) That workmen with a powerful union behind them are apt

to become too confident as to their position, and to think that they cannot be discharged or punished, and so are likely to become indolent, careless or insubordinate, especially in cases where the foremen are unionists with divided allegiance.

(5) That the action of trade unions has a tendency to bring about a uniformity of wages and hours, both as between individual workmen and as between different localities; and that by insisting on a minimum wage which, in effect, determines the standard, and by seeking to abolish overtime and piece work, they are reducing workmen to a dead level of enterprise, discouraging work of more than average merit, and taking away from individual workmen the motive power of ambition and self-interest. A few independent workmen, in evidence, concurred with this view, which was put forward by many employers in trades where the unions are most powerful. It is further alleged that the uniformity of wages and hours which trade unions sometimes enforce as between different localities, tends to injure localities possessing less natural advantages in favour of those possessing greater ones, because the former places can only compete with the latter by means of lower wages (usually compensated for by lower cost of living) or longer hours.

(6) That trade unions injure trades by the rigidity of their rules. It was said, for instance, that if, at the commencement of the iron ship-building industry, the workmen had enforced their present rigid limitations on apprenticeship, the industry, for want of sufficient hands, could never have developed to its present dimensions. It is also pointed out that the rigid organisation of the different trades in some cases gives rise to a too complete division of work, which prevents men from doing work for which they are qualified and which would at times conveniently fall to their lot, thus occasioning bad economy in production. This was the cause of the recent "demarcation" disputes between various trades in the North of England. In the case of some trades connected with ship-building, it was alleged by representatives of "unskilled labourers" employed in them, and admitted by those of the skilled workmen, that the organisation of the latter, as a rule, makes it difficult for those men who start in the lower class to rise to the higher kind of work, even if they have acquired sufficient experience and skill. The rule or practice of refusing to work with non-unionists may also be mentioned under this head.

The representatives of trade unions claim that, even supposing it to be possible to prove some drawbacks, the existence of these societies is essential to preserve the independence of workmen and to protect their interests. In proof of the benefits of trade unionism they point to the position of workmen in various trades before and after these associations were formed, and maintain that the action of trade unions has secured improved wages, hours and conditions of labour not only directly for organised workmen, but indirectly for those not organised. The refusal of unionists to work with non-unionists is often justified on the ground that the latter without cost to themselves have reaped the benefits secured by the sacrifices and exertions of the organised workmen.

These witnesses deny that their organisations tend to enforce a dead level of wages, except with regard to "minimum rates," and represent that in almost every trade there are found many men in receipt of wages above what is known as the "minimum of the trade," in consequence of their being better workmen. They deny, then, that these organisations take away the motive of self-interest and therefore diminish the energy of the individual workman, but they allege that, in the interests of large bodies of workmen, it is necessary to some extent to restrain by rules the natural desire of the individual workman to work overtime, for the sake of higher wages, and other modes by which he might seek to benefit himself at the cost of his fellow workmen as well as of his own health and strength, or that of his offspring. This action is not, they maintain, injurious in the long run to the general interests of industry, inasmuch as association raises the "*morale*" of the employed, disciplines and educates them, and by rendering their work more intelligent, increases its value. It is necessary, they say, that their rules shall place a check upon the natural temptation of the employers to excessive competition with one another at the expense of the employed, by way of cheapness of goods and speed of production attained by overwork and under-pay, but on the whole, and in the long run, these rules, by their steadying effect, are good for the trade of the country. They allege that the action of strong trade unions is beneficial even to employers by preventing them from destroying each other through unlimited competition. It is usually admitted on both sides that strong organisations have been proved by experience to be almost a condition precedent to the success of voluntary methods or institutions of conciliation and arbitration, so far as these institutions extend beyond the limits of a single establishment to a whole trade or district, and will be no less essential for the purpose of any further development of such institutions, whether voluntary or created by the action of the State.

We have not lost sight of the fact that the concern of the community, as a whole, with regard to the strength of organisation of employers and employed, and the agreement between them which it may be possible to obtain, is not limited to the effect of such strength or agreement upon the interests of these classes. Our attention has chiefly been devoted to the interests of employers and employed in particular trades, not because these interests are the only ones which need to be considered, but because such a course appeared to be most in accordance with the special reference made to us, and because it seeemed to us to be more important that our enquiry should be thorough, so far as it went, than that it should cover a very wide area. Even when thus limited our task remained a very heavy one. It should also be observed that specific evidence can more easily be obtained with regard to the interests of particular industrial groups than as to the general interests of the public. In order to take a complete view of the whole question it would be necessary to consider not merely the effect of the action of trade unions and employers' associations upon the workmen and employers engaged in particular industries, but in addition, the effect of a highly developed system of such organisations upon the interests of the community at large and upon the wage-earning classes generally, whether unionists or non-unionists.

We have thought it desirable to call attention in a concise manner to the fact that agreement between a strong combination of employers on the one side, and workmen on the other, may possibly be attained, in some cases, by measures which tend to repress individual energy and freedom of industrial experiment. One result of such agreement may be to place difficulties in the way of new men endeavouring to work their way into a trade by means of methods of production not sanctioned by the existing trade custom. Such changes, though not immediately convenient to the employers and employed already engaged in a trade, have often, in the end, by enhancing the efficiency of production, conferred important benefits upon the public, and have contributed to the ultimate prosperity of the trade itself. The danger is not great in those trades which produce chiefly for foreign markets, nor, again, in those which are subject to intense foreign competition in the home market, but even in these trades, the growth of international combinations may make it possible to subordinate public to private interest. In the numerous trades in which foreign competition does not exist, or is not very keen, the pressure and the support of a strong union of workmen may give cohesion to associations of employers. Hitherto such associations have seldom been able to impose their collective will upon all the employers engaged in a trade. There appears, however, to be some danger that, under the pressure of, and in alliance with, strong combinations of workmen, such associations might obtain virtually the same power with regard to fixing prices and determining the methods of production that similar associations have derived in earlier times from legal monopolies.

It must further be pointed out that unskilled labour, which it is more difficult to organise, may eventually suffer if skilled trades become close corporations, and, in any case, it is clear that a complete combination of employers and employed in any one great trade for the purpose of raising prices to an artificial level would, if successful, not only impose a tax upon the public but upon those engaged in related and dependent industries. It is obvious also that, where unionists are very strong, their refusal to work with non-unionists may altogether deprive the latter of employment; especially if they are for one reason or another unable to earn the minimum wages fixed by the trade union.

We desire to point out the existence of these various disadvantages which a very complete organisation of industry might involve, without expressing any opinion as to the proximity of dangers of this kind. Having called attention to the existence of such dangers we are free to pass to an examination of the influence which associations of employers and employed exert upon the relations of these classes, and of the methods by which questions arising between them are settled.

8. The Great Depression

THE GREAT DEPRESSION (1873–1896) was the first severe, sustained jolt to the evolving world economy of the nineteenth century. From the accession of Queen Victoria in 1837 to the beginning of the depression, world trade had more than quintupled. Britain led the way, providing and handling much of the goods, financing it for much of the world.

Investments abroad grew from £150,000,000 (1837) to almost £1,000,-000,000 (1873). In the closest approach the world would ever see to free trade in men, money, and merchandise, the workshop of the world was the particular beneficiary. In this prosperity Britain never had a favorable goods balance of trade. The working of the world market actually depended on the continued willingness of the British to purchase more than they sold. But Britain consistently enjoyed a net favorable balance of trade. Her invisible exports—shipping, financing, investments, and exported technology—covered the goods deficit and turned a handsome profit.

The Great Depression was a misnomer. While the word "Unemployed" officially entered the English language in the course of it, real wages rose. For those at work, conditions were much better than they were to be during the years of so-called recovery (1896–1912). The last quarter of the nineteenth century saw a sustained price fall. In part this could be ascribed to an enormous rise in world productivity coupled with the growth of liquidity generated by the gold strikes in California and Australia. The transportation revolution meant more rapid and far-reaching distribution and markedly reduced prices. The prolonged deflation—perhaps a more accurate term than depression—was hard on some sectors, good for others. British agriculture suffered as the wheat belts of the United States and Canada poured their produce across the Atlantic, but the British consumer ate better for less. Surplus raw steel gave ironmasters nightmares, but the machine tool industry prospered as prices fell. One contemporary economist aptly described the slump as a depression of interest, profits, and prices.

For the British the depression coincided with the first visible challenge to their economic supremacy. Although Britain's actual position improved, it was relatively threatened. Britain in 1880 produced one-third of the world's steel. Production increased five times by the death of Victoria, but Britain manufactured one-seventh of the world total. She had already slid to third place behind the United States and Germany.

Britain did not recover from the depression by modernization, although new sectors within the economy fared better than many of the old. Rather she directed more and more of her exports to the underdeveloped parts of the world. Increasingly she came to depend upon her invisibles—her financing, her shipping, her business services. Growing deficits in commodity trade balances were more than covered by increasing profits from financial services. British export goods, however, were still heavily textile. The growth of the Asiatic textile industry, particularly in India and Japan, boded ill for the future.

Britain neither modernized nor rationalized in response to the depression. The old plants, old technology, old methods represented a substantial investment still yielding dividends. And, in spite of gloomy analysis and prognosis, Britain was still "first." Later, with the lead clearly lost and deficient sectors in the economy past mere rehabilitation, critics (guided by hindsight) pointed to failures of education, faulty management decisions, and inadequate functional integration. At the time, one commission after another sought an explanation for the coming of this sustained recession, what it meant to Britain, and what might be done about it.

Recommended Reading

In addition to the general works cited in the introduction, there is a substantial specialist literature. Derek H. Aldcroft has edited an interesting collection, *The Development of British Industry and Foreign Competition, 1875–1914* (Toronto, 1968). A valuable, classical introduction to the problem is H. L. Beales, "The 'Great Depression' in Industry and Trade," *Economic History Review*, 1st series, V (1934), 65–75, which should be read with A. E. Musson, "The Great Depression in Britain, 1873–1896: A Reappraisal," *Journal of Economic History*, XIX (1959), 199–228, and C. Wilson, "Economy and Society in Late Victorian Britain," *Economic History Review*, 2d series, vol. XVIII (1965), 183–198. An excellent recent short summary is S. B. Saul, *The Myth of the Great Depression, 1873–1896* (London: 1969).

ROYAL COMMISSION ON THE DEPRESSION, REPORT

We propose in the first place to deal with the nature of the depression.

Upon this question there have been some inevitable differences according to the points of view from which the several witnesses and those from whom we have received information have regarded it.

Those who may be said to represent the producer have mainly dwelt upon the restriction, and even the absence, of profit in their respective businesses. It is from this class, and more especially from the employers of labour, that the complaints chiefly proceed. On the other hand, those classes of the population who derive their incomes from foreign investments or from property not directly connected with productive industries, appear to have little ground of complaint; on the contrary, they have profited by the remarkably low prices of many commodities.

As regards the artizans and labourers, the question is rather more complicated. It resolves itself into two: (*a*) whether the reduction

Source: From "Third and Final Report of the Royal Commission on the Depression in Trade and Industry," *Parliamentary Papers*, 1886, vol. XXIII, pp. xi–xxv.

of profits, which has told upon so many of the employers, has prejudicially affected the employed by causing a scarcity of employment; (b) whether reductions have been made in their wages, and, if so, whether such reductions have been compensated, or more than compensated, by the low prices of commodities, or by the shortening of their hours of work.

There is, however, yet another point of view to be taken. We have to consider the economical condition of the country as a whole, apart from the vicissitudes of particular industries; and to inquire into the national production of wealth, as well as into its distribution among different classes. If the aggregate quantity of commodities produced is on the increase, and is growing at a more rapid rate than the population, we cannot regard the depression in particular industries, or among particular classes of producers as an indication of a corresponding national loss.

We must not, however, close our eyes to the sufferings which, even in a time of general prosperity, certain classes of producers may have to undergo; and we must bear in mind that what seriously affects one class cannot be without influence on the condition of others.

We are satisfied that in recent years, and more particularly in the years during which the depression of trade has prevailed, the production of commodities generally and the accumulation of capital in this country has been proceeding at a rate more rapid than the increase of population; and in support of the view that our material prosperity is increasing, we might refer to such statistics as those of pauperism, education, crime, savings banks, &c. These, however, supply us only with indirect evidence on the subject, and though their united testimony is valuable, they can apply only to the condition of particular classes or sections of the community.

The statistics of our internal trade are very imperfect, and it is, therefore, not easy to measure the growth of our actual production; but some useful evidence is afforded by the returns of our foreign trade, and by the statistics of the consumption of raw material.

The information obtained from both of these sources appears to point to the conclusion that our production has increased at a rate which, if not quite so rapid as at some previous periods in our history, is still in advance of the rate of increase of population.

It is true that the statistics of our foreign trade show an apparent falling off in some respects, but this is almost entirely due to the continuous fall in prices which has been in progress since 1873, and more particularly to the fall in the prices of raw materials.

A fall of prices may involve a reduction in the profits of those immediately engaged in producing or dealing in the commodities affected; but it is not necessarily injurious to the community at large.

When due allowance is made for the fall of prices, and especially for the fall in the price of the raw material of our manufactures, we think it will be found that the actual products of British labour and capital have largely increased.

The real growth of our foreign trade and of our producing power will be readily seen from the following figures. . . .

Declared value of imports and exports in 1873, 1879, and 1883, compared with the computed values, on the assumption that the values of the whole trade are affected by differences in prices as are the values of enumerated articles.

Imports

	Declared values	Values computed at the prices of 1873
	£ mlns. sterling	£ mlns. sterling
1873	371	371
1879	363	438
1883	427	512

Exports

1873	255	255
1879	191½	273
1883	240	349

From these figures it will be seen that the aggregate of our foreign trade in the year 1883, if valued at the prices of 10 years previously, would have amounted to 861,000,000*l.* instead of 667,000,000*l.*

We understand that corresponding calculations for the years 1884 and 1885 have not yet been made; and they would no doubt necessitate some modifications of these figures. The total falling off in the value of our foreign trade in the year 1885 as compared with 1883 was 82,678,597*l.* But if due allowance is made for the further fall of prices which occurred between 1883 and 1885, and which is estimated at from 1 to 12 per cent., the volume of trade will probably be found to have diminished but very slightly in those years.

The assertion is so constantly made that the value of our foreign trade is declining, that it may not be out of place here to call attention to the fact that the average annual value of the aggregate imports and exports during the years 1880–84 (which was the latest period for which the figures were available when we commenced our inquiry) is greater, both absolutely and relatively to population, than in any previous quinquennial period.

Period	Average Annual Value of our Foreign Trade	Amount per Head of Population		
	Million £	£	s.	d.
1865–69	516	16	19	1
1870–74	636	19	19	3
1875–79	632	18	16	6
1880–84	706	20	0	1

And this increase has taken place in spite of the fall in prices above referred to.

We do not, however, think that too much importance should be attached to the returns of values. In order to test the progressive increase of trade generally, or of particular branches of trade, it is obviously essential that the measure applied should be invariable, and it is manifest that an invariable measure cannot be found in the pound sterling. A ton in weight or a yard in length are the same in one year as in another, and always bear the same relation to the commodities to which they may be applied. But this is not the case with the pound sterling, the value or purchasing power of which varies according to the supply of, and the demand for, the metal of which it is composed. For these reasons we think that quantities are, for our present purpose, a much better criterion than values.

As regards quantities, we have a sound basis for calculation in the statistics of the consumption of raw material, whether produced at home or imported from abroad.

. . . The production of coal, and of pig iron, and the consumption of raw cotton, and of imported wool have largely increased in the five years 1880–84 as compared with preceding periods, and that this increase has been greater than the increase of population.

We see no reason to doubt that with some unimportant exceptions this increase will be found in all the industries of the country.

Period	Coal		Pig Iron		Raw Cotton		Raw Wool	
	Average Quantity Raised	Per Head of Popu- lation	Average Quantity Produced	Per Head of Popu- lation	Net Imports (Annual Average)	Per Head of Popu- lation	Net Imports (Annual Average)	Per Head of Popu- lation
	Million tons	Tons	Million tons	Tons	Million cwts.	lbs.	Million lbs.	lbs.
1865–69	103	3.29	4.1	.14	8.1	29.8	144.0	4.0
1870–74	120	3.79	4.9	.16	11.2	39.3	180.5	5.6
1875–79	133	3.97	6.4	.19	11.0	36.6	197.4	5.8
1880–84	156	4.43	8.1	.23	13.2	41.8	217.1	6.1

Slight fluctuations in the quantity produced from year to year will necessarily always occur, and the statistics of any particular industry will not always show a progressive increase steadily maintained. It appears indeed, from the figures above referred to, that some of the minor industries exhibit a progressive decline, but these are industries chiefly engaged in the production of raw material which is being displaced by increased importation from abroad. Others again, and among them will be found the important industries of coal, iron, and woollens, are not now at their highest point, though their present position is far in advance of what it was even in the productive years from 1871 to 1873.

But we see no indications that, taking the industries of the country as a whole, and having regard to the figures of a series of years, there is any diminution in the aggregate of commodities produced by British capital and British labour.

Besides the statistics of production, we may point, in support of this opinion, to the growth of the goods traffic on railways and of the tonnage employed in the shipping trade, while the increased consumption of all the necessaries and common luxuries of life, and especially of food, affords evidence of the same kind from another point of view.

In stating this general conclusion, however, there is one important branch of industry which must be excepted. We refer, of course, to agriculture. There can be little doubt that the quantity of agricultural produce raised in the country during the last few years has materially decreased, and that even the fairly good seasons of the last three years have scarcely compensated for the diminished production of the eight years which preceded them, while the steady fall in prices has, of course, affected the agriculturist even more seriously than the diminished yield of the soil.

| Period | Goods Traffic Conveyed by Railway | | Tonnage Entered and Cleared with Cargoes | | | |
| | | | In the Foreign Trade | | In the Coasting Trade | |
	Annual Average	Per Head of Population	Annual Average	Per Head of Population	Annual Average	Per Head of Population
	Million Tons	Tons	Million Tons	Tons	Million Tons	Tons
1865–69	—*	—	27.98	.92	36.35	1.19
1870–74	—*	—	36.18	1.13	38.21	1.19
1875–79	207	6.18	42.38	1.26	46.48	1.39
1880–84	253	7.16	52.22	1.48	50.08	1.42

* The complete figures for these periods cannot be given.

This fact, as we shall show later on when we proceed to discuss the causes of the depression, has had a very important influence upon the situation.

It is indisputable that among the classes more immediately connected with the production of the large amount of wealth above alluded to the complaints of diminished profits and restricted markets are widespread and persistent, and it is impossible to doubt that, whatever may be the condition of the community as a whole, certain sections of it are suffering, or are at any rate in less prosperous circumstances than they were a few years back.

The complaints which are made are by no means of a uniform character; but, so far as we are able to judge, there is a general agreement on all hands that business though not absolutely less in quantity is carried on with the smallest possible margin of profit, and in very many cases with no profit at all.

While, however, we find this opinion too generally expressed to admit of much doubt as to its being substantially accurate, we may point out that the only statistics on the subject which are available do not altogether support it.

The gross amount of property and profits assessed to the income tax in the United Kingdom in the year 1885 was 631,000,000l., and in the year 1884, 629,000,000l. Both of these amounts are largely in excess of the figures of any previous year, and we notice that since 1880 no year has shown a decrease when compared with the year immediately preceding.

Nor, again, does the increase in these amounts, when compared with the growth of population, point to a very different conclusion. The amount assessed per head in both 1885 and 1884 was 17.6l., a figure which has been exceeded in only one year previously, namely, 1876, when it was 17.7*l.*; while in the year 1872, notwithstanding the highly profitable character of the trade at that time, the amount per head of population was only 15.3*l.*

These figures, however, include the assessment on lands, tenements, and houses, and have therefore a less direct bearing upon the point which we are now considering than the figures of Schedule D., under which the large proportion of commercial profits are assessed.

The gross amount assessed under that schedule in the year 1885 was 293,000,000*l.*, and in the year 1884, 291,000,000*l.*, both of these figures being the highest then recorded.

Comparing these figures also with the growth of population we find that the amount per head was 8.2*l.* in 1884, 8.1*l.* in 1885, and that to meet with figures exceeding these amounts we must go back to the years 1875 and 1876, when the amounts were 8.2*l.* and 8.3*l.* respectively.

Too much stress, however, should not be laid upon these figures, as it is well known that the growth of the income tax assessment is largely attributable to the increased efficiency of collection in late years. There is, moreover, reason to believe that in some cases the tax is paid on profits which have not been earned, owing to the unwillingness of traders to make known the fact that they have sustained losses, and notwithstanding the option given them by law to be assessed by the Special Commissioners of Income Tax at Somerset House. Due weight should also be given to the fact that the assessment is made on an average of years, and a diminution of profit may, therefore, not be immediately apparent in the returns.

At the same time we think that, at a moment when there appears to be a general agreement among all classes of traders that business has for some time been carried on at a loss or with the smallest possible margin of profit, it is worthy of remark that the amount of profits brought under the notice of the tax collector has actually increased with great steadiness throughout the last five years, a period which the universal testimony of those best qualified to form an opinion pronounces to have been the least profitable in the commercial history of the country.

In addition to this absence of profit there are two other features of the depression which, though neither so marked nor so universal, are worthy of notice.

On the one hand the natural tendency to equilibrium which

results from the mutual reaction of supply and demand appears to have been obstructed for a longer period than usual. The continually increasing production which we have noticed above is maintained and stimulated by some other cause than the spontaneous demand for commodities. Such a state of things should, according to all previous experience, lead to a restriction of production until the legitimate demand had again made itself felt. And one of the most remarkable features of the present depression is that production should be maintained on its present scale for such a length of time in the face of unremunerative prices and a market apparently over supplied.

There is also, in consequence of the unremunerative character of the trade of the country, less inducement to the capitalist to embark his capital in productive enterprise. This has resulted in a diminution of the current rate of both profits and interest, which has tended to create among the capitalist class a sense of depression corresponding to that which we have noticed as prevailing among the employers of labour.

The diminution in the return on capital would have had a much more serious effect if it had not been accompanied by a heavy fall in the prices of nearly all articles of ordinary consumption, which has enabled those with fixed incomes payable in gold to maintain a position not less prosperous than that which they enjoyed in the years of inflated trade and high prices.

We may therefore sum up the chief features of the commercial situation as being—

(*a*) a very serious falling off in the exchangeable value of the produce of the soil;

(*b*) an increased production of nearly all other classes of commodities;

(*c*) a tendency in the supply of commodities to outrun the demand;

(*d*) a consequent diminution in the profit obtainable by production; and

(*e*) a similar diminution in the rate of interest on invested capital.

The diminution in the rate of profit obtainable from production, whether agricultural or manufacturing, has given rise to a widespread feeling of depression among all the producing classes.

Those, on the other hand, who are in receipt of fixed salaries or

who draw their incomes from fixed investments have apparently
little to complain of; and we think that, so far as regards the purchasing power of wages, a similar remark will apply to the labouring
classes.

We must, however, point out that the displacement of labour,
which is always proceeding owing to the increased use of machinery or other changes in the methods of production, cannot fail
to create a certain amount of distress of a more or less temporary
character among the working classes, who are naturally less able to
adapt themselves to sudden changes than those whose capital is in a
more moveable form. This distress, which is to some extent at all
times inevitable, was aggravated during the last winter by the
exceptional severity of the weather. On this point we may refer to
the results of an inquiry instituted by the Local Government Board
in the early part of the year, from which it would appear that the
winter of 1885–86 was marked by a general want of employment
such as has not been felt for five or six years.

The demand for labour must of necessity be always fluctuating
and uncertain, and within the last year or two this irregularity has
been more marked than usual; but, notwithstanding the occurrence
of periods of temporary distress, such as that above referred to, we
think that the statistics of pauperism and the increasing consumption of the commodities most in demand by the working classes
prove that their thrift has increased, and that their general prosperity has not materially diminished in recent years.

We trust that the steps recently taken by the Board of Trade for
the collection, arrangement, and publication of statistics, and other
information relating to labour will result in still further advancing
the interests of the working classes.

III

We have hitherto dealt with the nature and extent of the
depression.

It remains to indicate the causes which have assisted to produce
the state of things above described.

We have shown that the production of the more important
classes of commodities has on the whole continued to increase; and
there can be no doubt that the cost of production tends to diminish. It is difficult, therefore, to understand how the net product of
industry, which constitutes the wealth of the country, can have

failed to increase also. There is, moreover, sufficient evidence that capital has on the whole continued to accumulate, throughout the period which is described as depressed, though there has been a sensible depreciation in the value of some kinds of capital.

How then are we to account for the general sense of depression which undoubtedly exists and is becoming perhaps more intense every year?

We have observed above that the complaint proceeds chiefly from the classes who are more immediately and directly concerned in production; and there can be no doubt that of the wealth annually created in the country a smaller proportion falls to the share of the employers of labour than formerly.

The view, therefore, which we are disposed to adopt is that the aggregate wealth of the country is being distributed differently, and that a large part of the prevailing complaints and the general sense of depression may be accounted for by the changes which have taken place in recent years in the apportionment and distribution of profits.

The reward of capital and management has become less; and the employment of labour is, for the time at least, not so full and continuous; so that even where the rate of wages has not been diminished the total amount earned by the labourer has been less, owing to irregular or partial employment.

Putting aside for a moment the condition of the classes who are immediately dependent upon agriculture for their incomes (on which subject we shall have some further remarks to make), and taking those only who are assessed under Schedule D. of the Income Tax Acts, and who may be assumed to represent the classes engaged directly in commercial enterprise, it will be seen that the total amount of profits on which the tax has been paid has increased, and so has the number of persons assessed.

From the Reports of the Commissioners of Inland Revenue it appears that between the years 1874–5 and 1884–5 the number of incomes assessed under Schedule D., amounting to 200*l*. a year and upwards, increased from 184,354 to 239,367, being an increase of nearly 30 per cent.

But it is to be observed that the number increased at a much more rapid rate at the lower end of the scale than at the upper, as the following table, compiled from the Reports, will show:—

Schedule D.—Trades and Professions only

Number of Persons assessed in the years 1874–75, 1879–80, and 1884–85 in the undermentioned Classes:—

Incomes from	1874–75	1879–80	1884–85	Increase 1884–85 over 1874–75	Rate per cent. of Increase
£ £	No.	No.	No.	No.	
200 to 1,000	162,435	197,775	215,790	53,355	32.85
1,000 to 2,000	11,944	12,011	13,403	1,459	12.21
2,000 to 3,000	3,797	3,604	4,038	241	6.34
3,000 to 4,000	1,857	1,664	1,914	57	3.07
4,000 to 5,000	1,003	898	1,074	71	7.07
5,000 to 10,000	2,035	1,671	1,928	−107	−5.25
10,000 and upwards	1,283	1,020	1,220	−63	−4.91
Total	184,354	218,643	239,367	55,013	29.84

From this table it would appear that the number of persons with incomes of less than 2,000*l.* a year has increased at a more rapid rate than the population (which in the period in question increased about 10 per cent.), while the number of persons with incomes above 2,000*l.* has increased at a less rapid rate, and the number with incomes above 5,000*l.* has actually diminished; and further, that the lower the income the more rapid the rate of increase.

We think, therefore, that, whether the aggregate amount of profits is increasing or not, there is distinct evidence that profits are becoming more widely distributed among the classes engaged in trade and industry; and that while the larger capitalists may be receiving a lower return than that to which they have been accustomed, the number of those who are making a profit, though possibly a small one, has largely increased.

This view is further confirmed by the figures given in the above table for the year 1879–80, which was undoubtedly a year of very general depression; it will be seen that there was a decrease in the number of assessments in all classes above the limit of 2,000*l.* a year, while in the classes below that limit there was in all cases a considerable increase.

But whatever may be the facts as to a change in the distribution of profits we think that it can scarcely be doubted that capitalists generally, and especially those directly engaged in production, obtain a smaller return than formerly.

It is, we believe, generally recognised that the accumulation of capital, which is always progressing in a civilized country, and the greater severity of the competition which results from this accumulation, tend to lower the rate of profit.

This tendency is of course checked by any expansion of trade which may be caused by the creation of a new demand; but its general effect is, we think, worthy of notice here, as there has been in recent years a marked absence of such expansion.

The great destruction of capital which is involved in a war, such as that of 1870–71, naturally stimulates production until the waste of capital is repaired. But when this has been done and consumption returns to its normal level, the world's capacity of production will naturally be in excess of its ordinary requirements; and the inevitable result of such a state of things is, either a restriction of production, or a reduction in the rate of profit.

Having regard to the difficulty of curtailing production owing to the loss of capital which would frequently ensue, we are inclined to consider this tendency to a diminution in the rate of profit as one of the more permanent elements in the condition of industry in this country, unless it should be counteracted by a corresponding expansion of trade.

In addition to the natural result of an accumulation of capital which is proceeding at a more rapid rate than the demand which will alone enable it to be profitably employed, one of the commonest explanations of this depression or absence of profit is that known under the name of over-production; by which we understand the production of commodities, or even the existence of a capacity for production, at a time when the demand is not sufficiently brisk to maintain a remunerative price to the producer, and to afford him an adequate return on his capital.

We think that such an over-production has been one of the prominent features of the course of trade during recent years; and that the depression under which we are now suffering may be partially explained by this fact.

Over a series of years it would naturally be expected that the supply of commodities would accommodate itself to the demand in such a manner as to ensure the maintenance in the long run of an adequate price and an adequate profit.

A general over-production is of course impossible, but it may often happen that there is an over-production of one class of commodities which is unable to find a remunerative market owing to the lack of purchasing power on the part of some section of the community which produces other classes of commodities; and we think that the course of trade in the last 10 years affords an example of this phenomenon.

On the one hand the purchasing power of a large section of the community—that, namely, which depends directly upon the productive capacity of the soil—has been seriously crippled. Bad seasons and the competition of the produce of other soils which can be cultivated under more favourable conditions than our own have reduced the quantity or the exchangeable value of the commodities which the agricultural classes have to offer for the products they desire.

Meanwhile, a process of an exactly opposite kind has been going on in other branches of industry.

Most of those commodities, the production of which is independent of the seasons and of the natural qualities of the soil, have been produced in steadily increasing quantities.

Machinery is being continually made more perfect, new processes which cheapen the cost of production are being continually introduced, and the quantity of this class of commodities which is annually placed upon the market is thus steadily increasing.

This tendency, which is under ordinary circumstances perfectly natural and usual, has been intensified in recent years owing to the stimulus given to production by the great demand for all manufactured goods which followed the war of 1870–71.

A demand which was only temporary, and which might have been satisfied in the course of a very short period, was treated as if it were of a permanent character; and manufacturers in this country and elsewhere enlarged their power of production accordingly, as if the demand could be expected to continue. This it might very possibly have done if it had not been checked by the falling off in the productive power of the soil above alluded to.

By the operation of these two forces the natural tendency to an equilibrium between supply and demand has been impeded; and to this extent we think that over-production has had a distinct effect in bringing about the depression now complained of.

The remarkable feature of the present situation, and that which in our opinion distinguishes it from all previous periods of depression, is the length of time during which this over-production has continued.

A temporary excess of supply over demand will naturally occur from time to time in the case of all commodities. The producing power will for the moment frequently outrun the consuming power; but these variations, as we pointed out above, usually correct themselves within a very short period. They carry their own remedy with them, and do no harm to the world at large, though an individual producer may occasionally suffer.

But it is more difficult to account for systematic over-production continued during a long period, and resulting, according to the unanimous testimony of the witnesses who appeared before us, in little or no profit to the producing classes.

We are disposed to think that one of the chief agencies which have tended to perpetuate this state of things is the protectionist policy of so many foreign countries which has become more marked during the last ten years than at any previous period of similar length.

The high prices which protection secures to the producer within the protected area naturally stimulate production and impel him to engage in competition in foreign markets. The surplus production which cannot find a market at home is sent abroad, and in foreign markets undersells the commodities produced under less artificial conditions.

The natural growth of the industries of foreign countries possessing in many cases the population and other resources required for successful manufacturing enterprise has also contributed to produce the same result.

The relation between production and demand has been further disturbed by the operation of the Limited Liability Acts.

The capital invested in small sums by a large number of individual shareholders in public companies, is as a rule contented with a lower rate of interest than the ordinary producer will require upon the capital which he employs at his sole and unlimited risk.

The field which the Limited Liability Acts have opened for the employment of capital has also created a class of "promoters," whose interest lies rather in the creation of an industrial undertaking and the speedy sale of its shares at a premium than in its permanent prosperity. Little consideration is, therefore, given to the important question, whether there exists a legitimate opening for extended production, and for the steady employment of additional labour.

The limitation of the liability tends to encourage a less cautious or more speculative system of trading than can be safely pursued by a trader who is liable to the full extent of his operations. The result is that production is often carried on under limited liability for some length of time at a rate of profit which would have compelled the ordinary producer to have restricted his out-put at a much earlier period.

Even the loss of capital which has resulted from the failure of a large number of these companies has not produced all the effect which might have been expected in curtailing their operations, as the losses are spread over a large number of individuals, and are therefore less severely felt. Moreover, new undertakings are constantly formed upon the ruins of those which have failed, and profiting by the depreciation of the property to which they succeed are able to continue operations on the same scale as before.

We do not offer any opinion as to how far trading carried on under these conditions is beneficial or otherwise to the community; but we desire to note the fact that they have exercised an important influence upon the extent of production and the rate of profit obtainable on the capital employed in it.

A cause of a more temporary character which has tended unduly to increase the quantity of commodities placed upon the market arises from a change in the method of distribution in recent years. More direct and rapid communication between the producer and the consumer has caused the stocks formerly held in intermediate hands to become available for consumption without replacement. The goods so held have, in consequence of this change, been placed upon the market and have increased to an abnormal extent the ordinary supply. We believe that this operation has had more effect in depressing prices and profits than might at first sight be supposed.

In addition to these special causes, others of a more general character have arisen tending to retard the natural approximation of supply to demand which usually takes place during periods of depression.

Among these may be mentioned the more limited possibilities of new sources of demand throughout the world, and the larger amount of capital seeking employment—itself a consequence of the increasing wealth of the nation.

The effect of these causes will, in our opinion, be gradually to minimize those abnormal inflations which used to be described as "good trade," and to render less frequent those severe, though comparatively short, periods of depression known as "panics." In former times over-production was suddenly and palpably arrested by financial disaster, while the recuperative process of a largely extending demand quickly repaired the mischief. In future more stability in the ratio of supply to demand may be expected with a more regular though reduced rate of profit.

Another element of great importance in the situation is the serious fall in prices, to which we have above referred. There can be little doubt that production and commercial enterprise are stimulated to a greater extent by rising than by falling prices.

Whatever may be the inconveniences of a rise in prices it certainly encourages a greater activity in production and an extension of credit. When prices are rising capital is constantly endeavouring to find new means of employment; and a spirit of enterprise animates all the classes engaged in commercial operations.

In times when prices are falling, on the other hand, speculation even of a perfectly legitimate kind is checked, and production tends to diminish. Suppose a manufacturer to borrow a fixed sum at a fixed rate of interest. This he has to repay, whatever the result of his operations may be. Meanwhile prices may fall. Not only does he buy his raw material at the higher price and sell his goods at the lower; but he has also to pay interest and repay principal on the higher value; and in addition to this it is found that wages do not respond to such movements as quickly as the prices of commodities.

The trader too is affected in the same way; he does not know what the value of his stock will be at the year's end or what profit he will be able to secure upon his capital; and when trade is crippled it is natural that production should halt.

The fall of prices, which has been in progress during the greater part of the last ten years, has become much more marked in the last two; and its full effect in checking production and depressing trade has therefore scarcely become apparent.

But the slight diminution in the production of some of our leading industries, which we have noticed above . . . affords some evidence that this influence is beginning to operate; and should prices continue to fall we think that a further curtailment of production can hardly fail to ensue.

We . . . [believed] that this fall in prices, so far as it has been caused by an appreciation of the standard of value, was a matter deserving of the most serious independent inquiry; and we do not therefore think it necessary to investigate at length the causes which have brought it about. But we desire to give it a leading place in the enumeration of the influences which have tended to produce the present depression.

There can also, we think, be little doubt that the demand for commodities has fallen off in quarters where formerly our goods found a certain and remunerative market.

First, as regards our home market. We have, as above pointed out, suffered a serious loss in our purchasing power by reason of the deficient or unremunerative character of the produce of the soil. Sir James Caird estimates the loss in the purchasing power of the classes engaged in or connected with agriculture at 42,800,000*l*., during the year 1885, and the loss in several of the preceding years must, no doubt, have been equal to or even greater than this. This amount has been lost to the markets in which it was formerly spent, and cannot fail to have had an important influence upon the demand for manufactured goods.

An effect of a similar kind, though less in degree, has been produced by the increased competition in our own market of foreign manufactured or partly manufactured goods, the importation of which appears to grow at a slightly more rapid rate than the population, having been 1.97*l*. per head in the period 1870–4 and 2.35*l*. per head in the period 1880–4.

To this may be added the falling off in our "entrepôt" trade owing to the increasing tendency of foreign countries to supply themselves directly instead of through our markets.

Secondly, our trade with foreign countries is becoming less profitable in proportion as their markets are becoming more difficult of access owing to restrictive tariffs. It will be observed from the annexed Table that the value of our exports to the principal protectionist countries was larger, in proportion to our population, in the years 1880–84 than in any of the four quinquennial periods under review, with the exception of the five years 1870–74, during which, as is well known, our export trade was abnormally inflated; while, if due allowance is made for the high range of prices which prevailed in the two earlier of the four periods, it will probably be found that the volume of exports in the years 1880–84 was larger than in any preceding period. But, notwithstanding this increase there can be little doubt that the obstruction to our trade caused by the growing stringency of the commercial policy of those countries tends to make it far less profitable.

Average Annual Value of British and Irish Produce exported to the following countries (in thousands of £)

Years	France	Germany	Spain	Italy	Russia	United States	Total	Per Head of Population
								£
1865–69	10,995	19,964	2,184	5,474	4,147	23,522	66,286	2.18
1870–74	16,156	26,308	3,414	6,388	7,592	33,023	92,881	2.91
1875–79	15,098	20,212	3,442	6,005	6,525	17,991	69,273	2.06
1880–84	16,860	18,082	3,640	6,532	5,984	28,684	79,782	2.26

Further, in neutral markets, such as our own colonies and dependencies, and especially in the East, we are beginning to feel the effects of foreign competition in quarters where our trade formerly enjoyed a practical monopoly.

The increasing severity of this competition both in our home and in neutral markets is especially noticeable in the case of Germany. A reference to the reports from abroad will show that in every quarter of the world the perseverance and enterprise of the Germans are making themselves felt. In the actual production of commodities we have now few, if any, advantages over them; and in a knowledge of the markets of the world, a desire to accommodate themselves to local tastes or idiosyncrasies, a determination to obtain a footing wherever they can, and a tenacity in maintaining it, they appear to be gaining ground upon us.

We cannot avoid stating here the impression which has been made upon us during the course of our inquiry that in these respects there is some falling off among the trading classes of this country from the more energetic practice of former periods.

Less trouble appears to be taken to discover new markets for our produce, and to maintain a hold upon those which we already possess; and we feel confident that, if our commercial position is to be maintained in the face of the severe competition to which it is now exposed, much more attention to these points must be given by our mercantile classes.

There is also evidence that in respect of certain classes of products the reputation of our workmanship does not stand so high as it formerly did. The intensity of the competition for markets, while in many respects it has legitimately diminished the cost of production, has also tended to encourage the manufacture of low-priced goods of inferior quality, which have not only failed to give satisfaction themselves, but have also affected the reputation of other classes of goods to which no such exception could be taken.

The reputation of British workmanship has also suffered in another way by the fraudulent stamping of inferior goods of foreign manufacture with marks indicating British origin.

This appears to be particularly the case with the hardware goods of Birmingham and Sheffield which have secured so wide a reputation in the markets of the world.

We regret, however, to be obliged to add that the practice of fraudulent marking appears from the evidence before us to be not unknown in this country.

Considerable importance is attached by some witnesses who have appeared before us to the effect upon trade of legislative restrictions on the employment of labour and to the action of the working classes themselves by strikes and similar movements in making production in this country more costly than elsewhere.

But we do not think that either of these causes has materially affected the general prosperity of the country.

With regard to the comparative efficiency of labour carried on under the conditions which prevail in this country and foreign countries respectively there would appear to be great difference of opinion. But those who have had personal experience of both appear to incline to the view that the English workman, notwithstanding his shorter hours and higher wages, is to be preferred. . . .

But whatever may be the comparative advantage of the longer hours which are worked abroad, we cannot recommend, and we feel satisfied that public opinion in this country would not accept, any legislative measure tending to an increase in the present number of hours of labour.

There is no feature in the situation which we have been called upon to examine so satisfactory as the immense improvement which has taken place in the condition of the working classes during the last twenty years. At the present moment there is, as we have already pointed out, a good deal of distress owing to the want of regular work, but there can be no question that the workman in this country is, when fully employed, in almost every respect in a better position than his competitors in foreign countries, and we think that no diminution in our productive capacity has resulted from this improvement in his position.

As regards the future, should any symptoms present themselves that foreign competition is becoming more effective in this respect, it must be for the country and the workman himself to decide whether the advantages of the shorter hours compensate for the increased cost of production or diminished output. We believe that they do, and on social as well as economical grounds we should regret to see any curtailment of the leisure and freedom which the workman now enjoys. No advantages which could be expected to accrue to the commerce of the country would in our opinion compensate for such a change.

It is, however, right to point out that, while the share of the aggregate wealth produced in the country which now falls to labour is larger than it was twenty years ago, a corresponding diminution has taken place in the share which falls to capital: in other words that while wages have risen profits have fallen; and that this is obviously a process which cannot be continued beyond a certain point. This point has we think been very nearly, if not quite, attained already. A time may therefore come when capital will lose all inducement to lend itself to the work of production; and if the employer is driven out of the field, the labourer will necessarily suffer with him.

We may add that in our opinion the unfavourable elements in the existing condition of trade and industry cannot with any justice be attributed to the action of trade unions and similar combinations.

The administration of these associations has not infrequently laid them open to criticism; but we feel bound to record our opinion that, in recent years, they have, on the whole, been conducted with propriety and judgment.

We have no evidence to connect the depression of trade directly with the increase, or with the incidence, of taxation. On the contrary, several witnesses distinctly negatived the allegation of trade having been hampered to any appreciable extent by such taxation.

Of the fact of the increase, especially in local taxation, there is no doubt. At the same time it will probably be found that relatively to the population and the wealth of the country the burden of taxation is now far lighter than in previous periods; and that in this respect we are in a more favourable position than that of the foreign countries who compete with us in the markets of the world.

Among the causes which are said to have aggravated the prevailing depression, scarcely any have been so persistently put forward as the difficulties connected with the transport of goods.

The complaints under this head may be divided into three classes: —

(a) That the railway companies regulate their charges so as to favour one district or place or trade at the expense of another, and the importer of foreign goods at the expense of the home producer.

(b) That the cost of transit in this country is excessive as compared with the charges made for similar services in other countries, and that consequently our home trade is being crippled or destroyed to the advantage of our foreign competitors, who are able to place their goods in our markets at a less expense than the home producers, who carry on their operations at a much less distance.

(c) It is contended that if the water communications of the country were properly developed, an effective competition would thus be established which would regulate the monopoly now possessed by the railways.

With regard to the first of these points we would observe that even if the allegation made were proved, it could only account for a partial or local depression of trade, and would throw no light on the general depression of the trade of the country which we are considering. What one trade or locality loses must obviously be gained by the trade or locality which is preferentially treated.

While as regards the complaint that goods imported from abroad are carried at lower rates, over identical lengths of line than English goods, it must be borne in mind that if the companies are compelled to withdraw these advantages in the case of imported goods, it may be found necessary to follow the same treatment with regard to the low rates now in force for goods intended for export, and in fact to abolish altogether the so-called "through rates." This would probably meet with as much opposition from the exporter as the existing practice arouses on the part of the home producer.

As regards the second point, it is no doubt true that railway carriage on the continent is cheaper than in this country. This is due partly to the lower initial cost of railways on the continent, and partly to the longer distances to be traversed, which make the rate per mile much lower. Until, however, it can be proved that the railway companies are making an undue rate of profit on their capital (now on an average about 4 per cent.), we do not think that any steps could be taken to reduce the charges in this country, which, it must be remembered, have the sanction of an Act of Parliament.

But, apart from this question, we are inclined to think that what is really felt is, not the comparative cheapness of land transport on the continent, but the cheapness of the sea transport between the continent and this country; and we notice that the complaints under this head proceed generally from the inhabitants of inland towns who have no means of transport except those afforded by the railways, and not from those who can bring to bear upon the railways the natural competition afforded by the sea. The inland producer, who can only move his goods by railway, is, in fact, at a disadvantage compared with the foreign producer, or the producer on the sea coast, who enjoys the benefit of the cheaper water carriage.

We can see no justification for depriving the latter class of the natural advantages which their position gives them.

On the other hand, it is fair to point out that the position of the inland producer has been distinctly improved by the introduction of railways, which enable him to compete on much better terms than formerly with those who have the natural advantage of the seaboard.

As regards the third point, we find ourselves more able to agree with the complainants; and we think that measures should certainly be adopted, both to permit of the free development of canals wherever they are likely to be useful, and to prevent their being controlled by the railway companies, as appears to be the case in many parts of the country.

Among the causes of minor or less general importance which are stated to have contributed to the prevailing depression we may mention the excessive royalties alleged to be demanded by the owners of the mineral wealth of the country.

We refer to the subject rather because it is believed by some persons to have contributed to the present depressed condition of the coal and iron industries than because we think it possesses any intrinsic importance.

It is, however, stated that the average amount of royalty on the constituent elements of a ton of pig iron in this country varies from 3s. to 6s. 3d., while in France and Germany it is only from 6d. to 1s. But we see no reason to doubt that the price charged by the owners of the minerals, whatever it may be, is, or at any rate was at the time when it was fixed, the fair market price of the commodity, settled in the same fashion and by the same forces as such prices usually are.

Complaints are also made that the conditions usually attached to mineral leases are of an oppressive or onerous character, and tend to hamper production; but the remedy appears to lie entirely in the hands of the parties concerned, and will probably be applied at the proper time if it is really required.

Among the minor causes of the depression a place should also be given to the following:—

The demand for railway material, which at various times during the last ten years has been so great not only in America but in other parts of the world, has latterly fallen off.

The substitution of steel for iron, both in railway construction and in shipbuilding, and the consequent economy of material, is another element of the same kind.

While the excessive production of shipping in 1882–83 has had its natural result in depressing both the shipping and shipbuilding industries.

If then we consider the combination of (a) bad seasons, (b) fall in the price of agricultural produce, (c) diminished demand for iron in the construction of both railways and ships, and (d) want of employment for the shipping already built, we can account by special or local causes for a depression in a sufficiently large number of important trades and industries to influence all.

We have now reviewed the more prominent features of our commercial position, and the forces which have contributed to bring it about.

We have shown that while the general production of wealth in the country has continuously increased, its distribution has been undergoing great changes; that the result of these changes has been to give a larger share than formerly to the consumer and the labourer, and so to promote a more equal distribution; that the condition of the large class who depend upon the produce of the soil is unsatisfactory, and the number of the unemployed is a matter of serious importance; but that the general condition of the country affords encouragement for the future; that trade, though less profitable, shows little tendency to diminish in volume; but that owing to the nature of the times the demand for our commodities does not increase at the same rapid rate as formerly; that our capacity for production is consequently in excess of our requirements, and could be considerably increased at short notice; that this is due partly to the competition of the large amount of capital which is being steadily accumulated in the country, partly to the stimulus given to production by the events of 1870–71, which has been maintained longer than was warranted by the demand for commodities, and partly to a falling off in the purchasing power of at least one important section of the community; that our position as the chief manufacturing nation of the world is not so undisputed as formerly, and that foreign nations are beginning to compete with us successfully in many markets of which we formerly had a monopoly.

We have also shown that some elements in the situation above described are independent of our own control; namely, the depression in agriculture, which is not likely to exhibit any material improvement until the competition of soils superior to our own has worked itself out; the fall in the rate of profit which it is the natural tendency of the accumulation of capital to effect, unless accompanied by a corresponding expansion of trade or some periodical destruction of wealth such as is caused by a great war; and the protectionist policy of foreign countries. While other elements again are to a great extent dependent on causes within our own power to remove; such as the deterioration in the quality of some branches of our manufactures; the want of care or enterprise which permits our foreign rivals, with less natural facilities or aptitude for production, to compete with us in markets which have been, and might again be, our own; and any defects which may be found to exist in our domestic legislation on commercial matters.

IV

We have consequently but few definite recommendations to make.

The great object to be aimed at is, we need hardly say, the

cheapening of the cost of production so far as it can be done consistently with the maintenance of sound quality and good workmanship. In the competition for business, which has become so
intense during the last few years, this will be the only means of
securing success; and we have natural advantages in this respect
such as are possessed by few of our rivals.

We think also that the increasing severity of the competition of
foreign countries is a matter deserving more serious attention than
it has received at the hands of our commercial and industrial
classes. We cannot, perhaps, hope to maintain, to the same extent as
heretofore, the lead which we formerly held among the manufacturing nations of the world. Various causes contributed to give us a
position far in advance of other countries, which we were well able
to hold for many years; but those causes could not have been
expected to operate permanently, and our supremacy is now being
assailed on all sides.

But if we do not possess to their full extent the same natural
advantages as we formerly enjoyed, we have still the same physical
and intellectual qualities which gave us so commanding a lead; and
we see no reason why, with care, intelligence, enterprise, and
thoroughness, we should not be able to continue to advance.

In order to do so, however, it is obvious that we must display
greater activity in the search for new markets, and greater readiness to accommodate our productions to local tastes and peculiarities.

Even in matters of so little apparent importance as weights and
measures it would seem that our disinclination to adapt ourselves to
the requirements of our customers has not been without its effect.

In the matter of education we seem to be particularly deficient as
compared with some of our foreign competitors; and this remark
applies not only to what is usually called technical education, but
to the ordinary commercial education which is required in mercantile houses, and especially the knowledge of foreign languages.

Suggestions have been offered by several witnesses as to the
assistance which might be afforded to our trade by Your Majesty's
Diplomatic and Consular Officers abroad, especially in reporting
information with regard to the requirements of foreign markets,
and in answering inquiries from merchants and others on such
matters.

We gladly recognise the efforts which have been recently made to utilise the services of these officers more effectually; but we doubt if their functions could be usefully extended in the direction referred to above. It is very important, having regard to their position and duties in foreign countries, that they should be neither directly nor indirectly engaged in commercial operations, and we fear that inconvenience would be felt if they assumed in any degree the character of agents for mercantile houses.

Any general information which they may acquire with regard to the trade of the district in which they reside, and which is likely to be generally useful at home, should, of course, be reported and made public at once; and this is already provided for in their annual reports. But we should deprecate any change in their position which would bring them into closer relations with individual firms.

Nor do we think that it would be desirable for them to take a more active part in pressing particular schemes or enterprises set on foot by British traders in foreign countries. The representatives of some of our competitors may have been more active in this respect in some cases than our own consular and diplomatic officers; but such action must, we think, tend to lower the reputation of the country and to diminish the usefulness of the officer concerned.

As regards the reports themselves, we doubt if any useful purpose is served by requiring an annual report from each consulate. The consul should, we think, be instructed to report any information which appears to him of interest as soon as he obtains it, and it should be as promptly published at home when received. A large proportion of the statistics and tables which now appear in the reports might be omitted without disadvantage, and the reports confined to matters of more immediate and practical interest.

In connexion with the development of new markets for our goods, we desire to call special attention to the important subject of commercial geography. . . .

In the course of our inquiry we have frequently experienced the want of accurate statistics with regard to the details of our home trade. We would strongly recommend that steps should be taken to procure fuller information both as to the production of the leading industries of the country, and as to the distribution of our industrial population.

If annual returns on some or all of these points could not conveniently be prepared, they might be issued at intervals of two, or at most three, years.

With regard to the group of questions affecting the charges for railway carriage, we think (*a*) that greater facilities should be afforded to the public for readily ascertaining the rates which the companies profess to charge, together with any modification of those rates which they make in favour of any individuals, or any classes of their customers; (*b*) that a cheap and effective procedure should be provided for obtaining a legal decision on any disputed point, and for enforcing the decision, when given; (*c*) that greater attention should be paid to the development of the water communications of the country, and that no railway company should be allowed either directly or indirectly to control or own a canal; (*d*) that every facility should be afforded by Parliament for the construction of light railways or tramways in those parts of the country which may be found to be insufficiently supplied with the means of communication, or which are susceptible of further development in this respect.

We think that legislation is also required to make more effective the existing provisions of the law with regard to the counterfeit marking or fraudulent description of goods, and that negotiations should be entered into with foreign countries with a view to obtain similar protection for our manufactures abroad.

We refrain from making any specific suggestions for amending the law relating to limited liability; but we are of opinion that in some respects it is capable of improvement.

It is most desirable that the creation of unsound companies should be checked, and that in every case where the facilities afforded by the Limited Liability Acts are taken advantage of, the *bona fides* of the promoters should be, as far as possible, ensured.

Several proposals for the amendment of the Acts have been laid before us; but we think that the details of any new legislation on the subject would require to be further considered and discussed by those who have a more practical acquaintance than we possess with the working of the existing law.

To the suggestions which will be found in the evidence of the witnesses on this subject, we may add that the creation of unsound companies might be to some extent restricted if the fee for registration, which is now very low in proportion to the nominal capital embarked, were increased; and the attention of the Legislature might, in our opinion, be advantageously directed to this point, both in the interests of the revenue and of legitimate trading.

In conclusion, we desire to express our sense of the ready assistance which we have received in the course of our inquiry from the several bodies and individual witnesses whom we have consulted; and we would also commend to the careful attention of all classes of Your Majesty's subjects the valuable and complete collection of information as to the economical condition and prospects of the country which will be found in the appendices to our several reports, and a list of which is annexed to this document. We think that while, on the one hand, the information which we have been able to collect will tend to dispel much of the misapprehension which appears to prevail on the subject of our commercial position, and to encourage a more hopeful view of the situation, it will also show that if our position is to be maintained it must be by the exercise of the same energy, perseverance, self-restraint, and readiness of resource by which it was originally created. . . .

9. Land and Power

THE SOOT OF industrial cities and smog of London obscure the continuing importance of land through Victoria's reign. Agriculture was a significant, if declining, sector of Britain's economy. There was money to be made feeding the growing nation. There were horses to be raised to transport it. Agricultural produce and livestock produced an income well in excess of £200,000,000 in 1870. Estate rents represented the principal source of income for most of the gentry-aristocracy. Land conferred social and political, as well as economic, benefits upon its owners. At the beginning and end of Victoria's reign, the landed interests found themselves on the defensive. Something approximating class (or interest) war rocked the nation in the 1830s and 1840s as upstart manufacturing and commercial interests contested the landed elements over the symbolic issue of free trade and protection. After a generation of agricultural prosperity, the collapse of farm prices in 1879 and their continued depression beneath tons of North American and East European grain dropped income from land by more than 30 percent. This was an economic blow with social and political consequences, for, in the words of Lady Bracknell, "land [had] ceased to be a profit or a pleasure. It [gave] one position and prevented one from keeping it up."

Three distinct elements were involved in British agriculture. Most of the land was owned in large parcels. A trifle more than 4,200 people owned half of Great Britain—more than 18,500,000 acres. This land was occupied and worked by tenant farmers at their own risk, usually on long (nineteen-year) lease in Scotland but normally as tenants-at-will in England, Wales, or Ireland, subject to eviction on six-months' notice. The landlord provided all fixed capital (sometimes sharing drainage costs with the farmer), while the farmer put up the capital for equipment, seed, fertilizer, wages, and moveables. Any permanent improvement, whether made by the landlord or the tenant, became the property of the landlord. Landlords financed most of the agricultural revolution, although tenants amortized the costs with higher rents. Increasing agricultural specialization during the nineteenth century saw farmers contributing a larger share of agricultural working capital. As they came increasingly to underwrite the costs of farming, they came to demand compensation for improvements, better lease arrangements, and greater freedom in establishing farming practices.

Farms were generally too large to be worked by a farmer and his family, so almost every farm had some laborers. Wages were poor; living conditions deplorable. The organization of agriculture was at least partly to blame. Landlords then, like agricultural investors today, were not anxious to improve estate cottages. The farm laborer, after all, was a lower breed of animal, dirty, irresponsible, careless, destructive. Also he was the farmer's problem. The farmer, for his part, declined to put his money into improvements which, as soon as they were completed, ceased to be his. Only after Joseph Arch's agricultural union made successful inroads during the 1870s did agricultural wages and living conditions begin a fairly steady improvement.

These selections are concerned with one aspect of this problem: land ownership. One-third of all the land in Britain was owned by less than 1,000 persons; four-fifths of the nation was owned by no more than 7,000. Summary figures, of course, hide important qualifications. A great landowner might have 10,000 acres with a rent roll of £20,000, but a few very substantial peers pulled national averages up. The Duke of Sutherland, for example, owned 1,358,545 acres (mostly barren land in the Scottish highlands) with a rent roll of £141,667, while the Duke of Buccleuch enjoyed half again as much income from one-third of the acreage. The Dukes of Northumberland and Bedford and the Earl of Derby also drew more income from much less acreage. For those obliged or preferring to live grandly, however, even such incomes were insufficient. The Duke of Devonshire, whose rent roll exceeded £130,000 from almost 200,000 acres was £1,000,000 in debt by the middle of the century. Even before the collapse of farm prices in 1879, agricultural income could not sustain high society. The aristocratic oligarchy was slowly losing control of the nation in political, social, and economic terms. The last eroded first.

The selections given here are, first, the summary tables from the Local Government Return of 1873, often called the New Domesday Book. Then, to give some qualitative weight to the raw data, there are two selections from John Bateman's analysis, *The Great Landowners of Great Britain*, which discusses what the numbers mean in somewhat tart terms.

OWNERS OF THE LAND, ENGLAND AND WALES, SCOTLAND, AND IRELAND

SUMMARY of ENGLAND and WALES
(exclusive of the Metropolis)

	Number	Extent of Lands			Gross Estimated Rental	
		A.	R.	P.	£.	s.
Total Number of Owners of less than 1 acre	703,289	151,171	2	26	29,127,679	2
Total Number of Owners of 1 acre and under 10 acres	121,983	478,679	2	27	6,438,324	15
Ditto 10 acres " 50 "	72,640	1,750,079	3	38	6,509,289	18
Ditto 50 " 100 "	25,839	1,791,605	2	23	4,302,002	12
Ditto 100 " 500 "	32,317	6,827,346	3	11	13,680,759	16
Ditto 500 " 1,000 "	4,799	3,317,678	—	11	6,427,552	4
Ditto 1,000 " 2,000 "	2,719	3,799,307	—	28	7,914,371	10
Ditto 2,000 " 5,000 "	1,815	5,529,190	—	13	9,579,311	13
Ditto 5,000 " 10,000 "	581	3,974,724	3	24	5,522,610	6
Ditto 10,000 " 20,000 "	223	3,098,674	2	30	4,337,023	4
Ditto 20,000 " 50,000 "	66	1,917,076	1	31	2,331,302	12
Ditto 50,000 " 100,000 "	3	194,938	3	36	188,746	12
Ditto 100,000 " and upwards	1	181,616	2	38	161,874	9
Ditto no areas	6,448	-	-	-	2,881,452	13
Ditto no rentals	113	1,423	2	28	—	
Total	972,836	33,013,514	2	4	99,352,301	6

Source: from *British Sessional Papers*, 1876, vol. LXXX. 21, 33, 25.

Summary of Scotland

	Number	Estimated Acreage of Property	Gross Annual Value	
		Acres	£	s.
Total Number of Owners of less than 1 acre	113,005	28,177	5,800,045	18
Total Number of Owners of 1 acre and under 10 acres	9,471	29,327	1,433,106	4
Ditto 10 acres " 50 "	3,469	77,619	843,471	12
Ditto 50 " 100 "	1,213	86,483	380,345	7
Ditto 100 " 500 "	2,367	556,372	1,674,773	7
Ditto 500 " 1,000 "	826	582,741	1,263,523	13
Ditto 1,000 " 2,000 "	591	835,242	1,179,755	16
Ditto 2,000 " 5,000 "	587	1,843,378	1,946,506	18
Ditto 5,000 " 10,000 "	250	1,726,869	1,043,519	3
Ditto 10,000 " 20,000 "	159	2,150,111	965,166	3
Ditto 20,000 " 50,000 "	103	3,071,728	945,914	10
Ditto 50,000 " 100,000 "	44	3,025,616	588,788	1
Ditto 100,000 " and upwards	24	4,931,884	623,147	16
Ditto no areas	11	—	10,739	12
Ditto no rentals	11	1,147	—	
Total	132,131	18,946,694	18,698,804	—

Summary of Ireland

	Number of Owners	Extent A.	R.	P.	Valuation £.	s.
Total Number of Owners of less than 1 acre	36,144	9,065	1	30	1,366,448	—
Total Number of Owners of 1 acre and under 10 acres	6,892	28,968	—	35	498,917	6
Ditto 10 acres " 50 "	7,746	195,525	3	4	480,181	12
Ditto 50 " 100 "	3,479	250,147	—	—	313,374	8
Ditto 100 " 500 "	7,989	1,955,536	1	2	1,772,570	19
Ditto 500 " 1,000 "	2,716	1,915,528	—	6	1,332,435	9
Ditto 1,000 " 2,000 "	1,803	2,514,743	3	36	1,452,982	19
Ditto 2,000 " 5,000 "	1,198	3,675,267	1	22	1,997,210	7
Ditto 5,000 " 10,000 "	452	3,154,628	—	11	1,583,472	18
Ditto 10,000 " 20,000 "	185	2,478,493	—	19	1,113,673	13
Ditto 20,000 " 50,000 "	90	2,558,850	—	30	1,071,616	12
Ditto 50,000 " 100,000 "	14	1,023,677	—	29	397,829	2
Ditto 100,000 " and upwards	3	397,079	3	18	37,644	10
Ditto no valuation	5	46	3	—	—	
Total	68,716	20,157,557	1	2	13,418,357	15
Total in Printed Return (Summary of Ireland)	68,758	20,159,678	—	10	13,419,258	—
Add Errors in Totalling, Printing, &c.	8	2,404	3	9	2,697	19
Deduct in Totalling, Printing, &c.	68,766	20,162,082	3	19	13,421,955	19
	50	4,525	2	17	3,598	4
Total as Classified	68,716	20,157,557	1	2	13,418,357	15

Recommended Reading

Orwin and Lord Ernle (cited in the general bibliography) are particularly useful. E. L. Jones, *The Development of English Agriculture* (London: 1968), F. M. L. Thompson, *English Landed Society in the Nineteenth Century* (London: 1963), and David Spring, *The English Landed Estate in the Nineteenth Century* (Baltimore: 1963).

JOHN BATEMAN,
NOTES ON THE FOREGOING TABLES

SUMMARY TABLE OF ENGLAND AND WALES

No. of Owners	Class	Extent in Acres
400	Peers and Peeresses	5,728,979
1,288	Great Landowners	8,497,699
2,529	Squires	4,319,271
9,585	Greater Yeomen	4,782,627
24,412	Lesser Yeomen	4,144,272
217,049	Small Proprietors	3,931,806
703,289	Cottagers	151,148
14,459	Public Bodies { The Crown, Barracks, Convict Prisons, Lighthouses, &c.	165,427
	Religious, Educational, Philanthropic, &c.	947,655
	Commercial and Miscellaneous	330,466
	Waste	1,524,624
973,011—Total		34,523,974

These figures are compiled from those at the foot of each County in the Return of 1873. They do not harmonise exactly with the summary at the beginning of the Blue Book, but that summary itself varies from the County summaries in many instances—in Durham, for instance, by some 2,800 acres.

These tables (and the dissertation thereon) were compiled for "English Land and English Landlords," by Hon. George Brodrick, published by the Cobden Club in 1880, the dissertation being somewhat toned down so as not to offend men of extreme Liberal views.

"STATISTICS!—why they may be made to prove anything," said an eminent civil engineer to the Compiler a few weeks ago. "The London death-rate, for instance, is the greatest lie I know; for the bulk of the great middle class, as is well known to Doctordom, if it can possibly manage it, goes into the country to die."

A lie of this kind was the original cause of the compilation of the much-abused "Return of Landowners, 1873,"—viz., that in the

Source: From *The Great Landowners of Great Britain and Ireland* (London: 1883), pp. 495–499, 515–528.

census tables of 1871 some 30,000 persons only were entered under the head of "Landowners;" which so-called fact was much gloated over by those who would fain apply Mr. Bright's *"blazing principles"* to our existing land system. This lie vanished with the publication of the Government return of 1873, in the year 1876; the landowners being found to come to something like a million.

Still it was evident that, useful as this compilation might be, it was marred by several serious blots, such as the non-entry of the Metropolitan area, the omission, in some counties at least, of the woods which in 1873 were still unrated, and the occasional double entry of one and the same man, especially where he was blessed with a double-barrelled name, such as Burdett-Coutts or Vernon-Harcourt, to say nothing of grosser cases, where some four surnames are strung together, rope-of-onion fashion, like Butler-Clarke-Southwell-Wanderforde   or   Douglas-Montagu-Scott-Spottiswoode.

A study of the Blue Book convinced me that something like 10 per cent., if not more, of the landowners thus appeared more than once; and, when compiling "The Great Landowners of Great Britain," I wrote to every large owner begging a correction, the answers proved that my surmise was perfectly right. One instance may be given.

Case of CAPT. EDWARDS-HEATHCOTE, copied verbatim from the Return (his real initials being J. H.) : —

Staffs	Name of Owner	Address of Owner	Extent of Lands			Gross Estimated Rental	
			A.	R.	P.	£.	s.
Page 19, line 19	Edwards, H. T. H.	Apedale Hall	962	3	0	1,587	12
Page 27, line 42	Heathcote, Capt. E.	Audley	—	—	—	9,703	16
Page 27, line 44	Heathcote, J. E.	Newcastle, Stafford	44	0	20	154	0
Page 27, line 45	Heathcote, J. H. E.	Apedale Hall	—	—	—	1,097	0

Capt. Heathcote's real acreage is much over the amount with which the Return credits him. The property lies in at least four parishes,—principally in Audley, in which, I believe, Apedale Hall stands; and Newcastle is his post town.

Having considerably weeded out these double, treble, and multiple entries before compiling "The Great Landowners," I have used that work, as well as the Government returns, in compiling the foregoing tables, using only such corrections as had been sent up to Christmas, 1877, but none of later date. Curiously enough, these corrections would not materially alter the totals in each column, because the cases of over-estimation in the Return are very nearly balanced by others which tell in an opposite way.

The 3rd Class (squires), and the 4th and 5th (greater and lesser yeomen) are averaged on the scales of 1,700, 500, and 170 acres, in all cases but Cambs., Northumberland, Rutland, Staffordshire, and Merioneth, where, if the usual averages had been strictly adhered to, the result on Class 6 would have been to make a "small proprietor" in Cambs. owner of but 11¼ acres, whereas he really holds 6¼; while a Northumbrian in the same class would have been lord of nearly 50 acres. Suspecting this to be false, I worked out the actual extent of the lands held by the "squires" on Tyneside, which proved them to hold 355 acres apiece more than their fellow-squires nearer Cockaigne.

As to Staffordshire, a county very familiar to me, the staggering fact came out, after totalising the lands proper to each class, that the 6th Class landowner in Staffordshire was the pariah of his race, and not only a pariah, but one degraded so utterly as to be owner of but 11 acres; while a semi-Cockney of the same class in Surrey, which county most nearly approached him, held 13 acres of the soil. Still, though every statistical dodge has been tried to raise the 6th Class Staffordshire pariah from his low estate, every dodge, though it somewhat softens down his evil case, still fails to rid him of his disgrace. He, as owner of but 12⅕ acres, is still *the* pariah of England.

The fact may perhaps thus be accounted for. At a very rural petty sessions in Northern Stafford, colloquies like the following were often taking place:—

MILD ASSAULT CASE

Chairman of Justices loq.: "Prisoner, we have decided to convict you. You had no business to take the law into your own hands, and to give the man (though we must own you had much provocation) two black eyes, to knock him down, kick him, kneel on his stomach, throw his hat into the fire, knock out the ashes of your pipe into his left eye, and, finally, to use very bad language towards him."

Prisoner: "Noh, sur, A knows A didna oughta a doon it leastways, not quoit so mooch on it; but ye see, sir. A wasna 'ardly sober at the toime."

Chairman of Justices (severely): "Drunkenness is no excuse." (*To Head Constable*): "Shallcross! what's this man's position?"

Shallcross: "Milks three caaws, sir."

Prisoner: "A dunna: you're a loiar."

Chairman of Justices (excitedly): "Really! you mustn't," &c.

Prisoner: "But A ony milks two—t'other's a cawf."

Chairman (after consulting Colleagues): "Very well, then, we fine you fifteen shillings, or twenty-one days."

This police case only illustrates the fact that in the humbler walks of life, in both Cheshire (a small-averaged county) and Staffordshire, the position and respectability of a man is gauged by the number of cows, or rather "caaws," he milks.

To my certain knowledge, there are hundreds, nay thousands, of colliers who hold from four to eight acres, milk two or three cows, and willingly slave in the pits or iron-works to provide the rent in case they are tenants, or the interest on the inevitable mortgage in case (as 33,000 of them are) they are freeholders.

The prevalence of this mania for cow-milking as the badge of respectability in Mercia, as contrasted with the counter mania for the same badge in the form of keeping a "servant gal" or a "one-oss shay" in Middlesex, accounts for the large number and small extent of Mercian sixth-class holdings. Rutlandshire is greedily seized upon by the host of pundits who have dilated on the Government Return as a text to preach a statistical sermon upon, viz., by *The Pall Mall Gazette* (of yore), *The Spectator*, Mr. Frederick Purdy.—Hon. Lyulph Stanley, M.P., Mr. Lambert, and others whose names have escaped me,—or at least by most of them; 'tis a tempting text—only 4¼ pages long, as compared with 185 pages for York—but to me the sermons in figures thereon preached seem, like the London death-rates to my host of last August, to savour of the lie statistical. Rutlandshire folk may be estimable, astute, or both, but somehow they have not managed to keep possession of the acres, of all others (Leicestershire not excepted), most glorious for a fox-hunting gallop.

For instance, among foreigners owning their soil are the following:—

Adderley, Sir Charles (now Lord Norton, a Warwickshire man).
Aveland, Lord (who is classed as a Lincolnshire Peer, his principal property being there).
Belgrave, Mr., of Maydwell, in Northamptonshire.
Brooke, Sir W. de C., Bart, also of Northamptonshire.
Hankey, Mr., of Balcombe, Sussex.
Lonsdale, Lord, from the North Country.
Northwick, Lord, a Worcestershire Peer.
Richards, Mr. Westley, of Birmingham (name dear to lovers of the trigger).
Exeter, Lord (who is classed as a Northamptonshire Peer).
Pochin, Mr., of Edmondthorpe, Leicestershire.
Pierrepoint, Mr., of Chippenham, Wilts.
Rutland, Duke of, a Leicestershire Peer.
Kennedy, Mr., "of London" (a somewhat vague address).
De Stafford, Mr., a Northamptonshire man.
Blake, Mr., of Welwyn, in Herts.
Laxton, Mr., from Huntingdonshire.

These sixteen persons among them own nearly 37,000 acres, or two-fifths of the whole county.

Again, the unwary statistician who can only succeed in finding five persons ranging from 1,000 acres to 5,000 might be misled by supposing that "*Mr. Fludyer*," who figures for 1,100 acres, and "*Mr. Hudyer*," who owns 1,500, are two separate persons; whereas Sir John Fludyer tells me that he is the person aimed at in the Returns of 1873, under both the letters F and H.

Where landowners only reach five in the third class, a mistake of one is serious, and any generalization therefore based on Rutlandshire alone would affect England as judged thereby to the extent of one-fifth at the least.

Merioneth deserves special distinction as exemplifying Class 6 in its highest stage of ownership; yet a walk through two counties would bring a wayfarer from this paradise of small proprietors into Staffordshire, its lowest type of degradation. A glimpse at the column devoted to "waste" will show the reason why—a reason in itself sufficient to prove that the parochial magnates who compiled the crude materials for the Return had many curious eccentricities.

"Waste" figures for only 416 acres in Merionethshire—certainly a most bucolic part of the Queen's dominions, if not exactly (as may be said of Connaught or Webster-Ross) "west of the law." There is no doubt that a dozen spots could be picked on its wild mountain ranges where no policeman could be found within half-a-dozen miles. Contrast this with the neighbouring counties of Brecon, Denbigh, Montgomery, and Radnor, where the waste reaches a total of 215,000 acres, or say 53,000 acres each. Yet Merioneth is a wilder county than any of the four. The obvious moral is that in Merioneth all *joint* lands have been equally divided in the rate-books among the participants, while in the four neighbouring counties they figure not as *joint*, but as *waste* lands. As to waste, though no uniform system of excision from other lands has been adopted in the Return, it may be roughly taken as a fact, that generally (but by no means always) they include, in the southern counties, heaths, charts, unfenced land, and, in some cases, salt marshes; and, in the northern ones, all such land as is entered in the valuable agricultural returns published of late years annually as "mountain pasture" and "barren heath." But on what principle can one reconcile figures like the following:—Kent—waste, five thousand odd acres, Surrey—forty thousand? Kent is more than twice the size of Surrey, and as a fact contains, though perhaps in smaller proportion to its area, quite as much "heath," "common" and "chart" as Surrey. We must guess that in the rate-books of Kent these wastes swell the estates of the local Lords of the Manor.

The northern counties contain vast areas of "waste." Much of this is "waste" only in name, being unfenced, heathery-furzy-ferny-swampy-rocky pasture, much of it at a level of some 1,000 to 2,000 feet over sea-level, and affording fair pasturage to the hardy local sheep and cattle, though useless as nourishment to a 3,000 guinea shorthorn. These "wastes" are locally divided into what are called *cattle-gates*, each *gate* representing sufficient summer feed for one beast. In Kendal, Hexham, or Carlisle such cattle-gates are as saleable as an "eligible building plot" is in Kennington, Hoxton, or Camberwell; in no sense are they wastes; they are rather the rough survivals of some fossilized communal land system.

Let me with true Tory barbarity banish a few of the south-country land-law agitators, to try the experiment of settling themselves as virtuous and contented agriculturists on five-acre plots, carved out of the braes of Skiddaw, treeless, undrained, exposed to all the winds, and handsomely fenced with rough posts and rotten colliery rope. I fear the contentment would vanish, whether or not the virtue should remain. The agitator (specially if eloquent) is a proverbially thirsty soul: picture his horror at finding the nearest beer-house eight miles off, and the friendly grog-shop another five! Meanwhile, let him bear in mind a few simple facts—that in the northern counties he may have to keep his wife and bairns without such aids to digestion as onions, gooseberries, strawberries, carrots, apples, cherries, cabbages, and peas, none of which flourish in Northumbria over the 1,000 feet level, besides combining all trades in his own proper person—such as stonemason, waller, butcher, plasterer, shoemaker, painter, glazier, and possibly accoucheur. The case of the southern wastes is equally unpromising in a money-making or self-supporting point of view. Many a Kentish "chart," if parcelled out into ten-acre freeholds, would scarce support a four-year old baby with a healthy appetite on each of them. Their only advantage over the northern moors is their much larger allowance of bright sunshine—a commodity of which the supply is now regularly registered in the daily weather reports.

Irish ills, Irish grievances, we hear not a little of these nowadays: one grievance under which St. Patrick's protégés suffer is often overlooked, *i.e., the want of bright sunshine.*

Lord Beaconsfield, touching on matters Irish, alluded to this when he spoke of "The incessant rain-drip on shores washed by a melancholy ocean."

Ireland is Nature's buffer and umbrella to break the wild violence of the storms so oft and so unkindly sent us from New York, and the gutter to carry off the superfluous rain. England thereby benefits. Western England gets ofttimes more than it desires of rainfall. Corn-growing is but a secondary interest there. Cattle and cheese make the profits, and pay the rents. Irishmen should follow suit; instead of increasing the numbers of a starving peasantry, and glueing them to the soil, they should leave the ungrateful soil to itself, and to the cattle whom it could, under an intelligent system of breeding and rearing, carry with ease; or if they must continue to cultivate the soil, cultivate it where the sun does occasionally shine often enough to ripen a crop of oats—or something better.

Meanwhile, the Irish coasts swarm with fish which they seldom even try to catch. Any capitalist who introduces a new manufac-

ture or handicraft is sure to suffer in purse, even if he escapes a
bullet in the head.

Why, again, may I ask, is it that an Irishman will only dig a
pratie out of his own easily dug, friable peat soil? He does not care
for the same job on the stiffer lands of New York, Ohio, or Illinois.
No; he severely sticks to town life and its joy, the whisky-shop; he
hardly even enters the country parts of Yankee land. No; the
industrious Irish peasant, as I know him best in Co. Mayo, loves to
work ten minutes, then to rest on his long-handled spade for
another twenty, then perhaps he does a furious spurt of labour for
a quarter of an hour, which deserves to be rewarded, as it generally
is, by well-earned rest against the nearest cabin wall, and a pipe of
tobacco as a soother, and so on *ad lib*. Irish soil for the Irish!—hur-
rah, t'would demean a bold peasant to delve in stiff clays, such as
the East Saxon hirelings of our East Saxon agricultural prophet,
Mechi, delve and moil in, from six till six, or something like seven
hours more work than the most industrious Galway or Mayo man
ever did in a day.

> French peasants thrive; Irish peasants don't.
> French peasants work; Irish peasants won't.

Yet, according to Roman Catholic lights, France ought to be a
blighted and heaven-accursed country, where Gambetta exercises
his wicked will over the priesthood, and mightily oppresses them,
while our British Premier has taken the best of care to denude Erin
of the only educated men who could hold their own against the
rural Irish priest.

The climate of these islands, I fear, is not suitable for what the
French call "the small culture." No man on an average British plot
of $2\frac{1}{2}$ acres can raise and support a healthy family. I would put the
smallest desirable peasant-holding at from $4\frac{1}{2}$ to 6 acres, and these
only in the eastern—*i.e.*, the drier—half of England. In the western
counties, where the bulk of the land is under permanent pasture,
and corn growing is a secondary interest, the minimum should be
raised to what would keep four cows; and this minimum would
vary much in different counties—say from 9 acres in the vale of
Evesham, to 45 or 50 in northwestern Devonshire. Desirable as it
is in every way to encourage the subdivision of the soil on political
grounds, specially from the moderate Tory point of view, it cannot be too strongly urged that if a man buys a small freehold (as

we all hope he may be able to do when Sir Charles Dilke carries his intended (?) measure for the hanging of all conveyancing counsel and solicitors whose deeds of conveyance exceed 40 lines), that man should have some other trade or means of livelihood than the tillage of the soil. We cannot stand an indefinite increase in the number of acres under such crops as lettuce, radishes, cabbage, celery, and onions; the supply would soon exceed the demand, and the cultivator would starve. 217,000 "small proprietors" are already in our midst—men who own some twenty acres apiece—and it will be well for England when the number is quadrupled. Beyond that point it would so far do harm as to (I believe) materially reduce the amount of food grown on the fair face of Old England. In view of the terrible competition of American produce, large capital, open-handed use of all manures, close-fistedness in bargaining, and credit enough to avoid having to sell at bad prices, combined with a largish area to work on, and much knowledge of the business, are the only conditions under which the British farmer can hold his own. Men of this stamp are far too wise to aspire to the ownership of the lands they till.

When divided by the number of small proprietors in Class VI., the four million acres they hold shows the following approximate average size of holdings in each county:—

Staffs., 12⅕	Somerset, 16	Clamorgan, 21¼
Flint, 12⅓	Cambs., 16⅙	Anglesea, 21⅓
Surrey, 13	Carnarvon, 16⅔	Beds., 21⅓
Hereford, 13⅓	Notts., 16⅔	Suffolk, 22¾
Worcester, 13⅗	York (E.R.), 16¾	Durham, 24⅗
Gloucester, 13⅚	Huntington, 17	Westmoreland, 25½
Dorset, 14	Essex, 17½	Pembroke, 26
Middlesex, 14¹⁄₁₀	Warwick, 17⅔	Cornwall, 26⅛
Cheshire, 14⅔	Denbigh, 17¾	York (N.R.), 26¾
Rutland, 14¾	Oxon, 18¼	Devon, 27¼
Salop, 15	Berks, 18⅓	Northumberland, 27⅔
Lancashire, 15½	Leicester, 18¾	Cumberland, 29
York (W.R.), 15½	Norfolk, 19¼	Carmarthen, 29⁹⁄₁₀
Herts, 15⅔	Kent, 19¾	Montgomery, 31¹⁄₁₀
Wilts, 15⅔	Monmouth, 19⅚	Brecon, 31⅖
Lincoln, 15⅚	Bucks, 20	Radnor, 33½
Hampshire, 15⅘	Sussex, 20¹⁄₁₀	Cardigan, 39½
Derby, 15⅚	Northampton, 20⅓	Merioneth, 41⅙

It may be noted how closely the averages of many neighbouring counties run—the four northern counties and their neighbour, the North Riding; the three cider-making counties of Gloucester, Hereford, and Worcester; Lancaster and the West Riding; Kent and Sussex; and, though divided by the "silvery Thames," it is hard to raise a distinction between a small holding in Oxon and its fellow in Berks.

The two classes of yeomen show also a few curious facts; notably, the very large proportion of them who have the prefix "Rev." to their names. Of course it may so happen that in some parts of the country the rate-collectors, following the example of the Vicar of Owston and his Diocesan of Lincoln, refuse this prefix to our non-performing clerics, and thus simplify the labour of cleric-extraction from the ranks of the yeomen; but I take it that as a rule not only "Church Parsons," but their brethren "Ministers of Religion" who so often (and wisely) are associated with them in the modern toast-list, and even "Holy Romans," are entered in the Return of 1873 as "Reverends."

Their total number is 3,185, out of a total landed yeomanry of 33,998; in other words, not far short of ten per cent. Names with the clerical prefix are thickest in Northampton, Leicester, and Rutland, where about one in five of my yeomen is a cleric. This, of course, means that the glebe-land has not been entered, as the Local Government Board directed, as the property of "The vicar of Blank," but in the vicar's name, as "Rev. J. Smith."

After all, "yeomen" is but a makeshift title for holders of between 100 and 1,000 acres. If called out for a yeomanry drill, 'twould be diverting not a little to see, dressed in line, Mr. Goschen (halting between two opinions), Sir R. Cross (smiling on his neighbour), a popular Protestant Dean, arguing a theological point with the Ex-President of the E.C.U., while his rear-rank man, Mr. Coupland, who rules in Leicestershire, might talk fox-hunting with the Poet-Laureate and an eminent Hebrew financier. Still, as no better name suggests itself, we must content ourselves with calling them "yeomen."

It is much to be hoped that, if ever a revision of the Great Return of 1873 is made, a separate volume will be given to all town properties, as it is essentially absurd to mix the rental (say 10,000*l.*) derived from a row of warehouses in Bristol, covering three acres, with 50*l.* more derived from fifty acres of Gloucestershire clay. This is always done in the present Return; thus—

Extent, 53 acres; rental, 10,050*l.*

Let us also hope that, ere then, our rulers, even if they do not proceed to the violent measure with which I have saddled Sir Charles Dilke, will shatter the legal bonds which fetter and prevent the free sale of land, and the expansion thereby of Class 6—a class which, if multiplied fourfold, would add greatly to the stability of our fatherland and its institutions. Could they but effect this (I could hardly say so much in 1882), I for one (Tory though I be), shall not regret that, for what I hope is but a short space, the tree-planter of Hughenden succumbed to the woodcutter of Hawarden.

APPENDICES

I.—A Table showing the Distribution of the Area of the United Kingdom among the Great Landowners themselves, divided into Six Classes.

Class I. No. of persons holding 100,000 acres and upwards				44
" II. Do.	do.	between 50,000 and 100,000 acres		71
" III. Do.	do.	between 20,000 and 50,000 acres		299
" IV. Do.	do.	between 10,000 and 20,000 acres		487
" V. Do.	do.	between 6,000 and 10,000 acres		617
" VI. Do.	do.	between 3,000 and 6,000 acres		982
				2,500

This table excludes holders of large areas the rental of which does not reach 3,000*l.;* a list, however, of the more noteworthy of these exceptions is given further on. This and the following tables do not take in the Metropolian area, the Isle of Man, or the Channel Islands, or the estate of the HON. C. W. WHITE.

Holders of between 2,000 and 3,000 acres, or of between 2,000*l. and* 3,000*l.* rental from estates of over 3,000 acres   1,320

This table, as well as Tables II., III., and IV., was compiled in 1879; the alterations which have since taken place in the distribution of English land would not materially alter it, or them. Some men have increased their wealth, or, in the expressive North country phrase, "kept a scrattin of it together," while divers eminent firms of auctioneers have been kept busy dispensing the dirty acres of those more unfortunate or more lavish. In this the "merrie month of May" chaos reigns in Ireland; in half that distracted kingdom the peasantry are now virtually owners of the soil,—paid for though it may have been, and in many cases was, with Saxon cash, the fruit of Saxon toil and industry.

I may mention that, since the Premier has taken the *détenus* of Kilmainham into his confidence, but two Irish landowners have taken the pains to correct the figures contained in the body of this work. Are they in hiding in caves or bullet-proof huts? (they can hardly think that letters of inquiry dated from the Carlton Club

II.—A Table showing the Landed Incomes of such of her Majesty's Subjects as possess 3,000 acres rented at 3,000*l.* per annum and upwards, divided into Six Classes.

Class I.	Landed incomes of 100,000*l.* and upwards		15
" II.	Landed incomes of between 50,000*l.* and 100,000*l.*		51
" III.	Landed incomes of between 20,000*l.* and 50,000*l.*		259
" IV.	Landed incomes of between 10,000*l.* and 20,000*l.*		541
" V.	Landed incomes of between 6,000*l.* and 10,000*l.*		702
" VI.	Landed incomes of between 3,000*l.* and 6,000*l.*		932
			2,500
	Holders of 2,000*l.* rental and below 3,000*l.* or under 3,000 acres		1,320

III.—A List of some of the Holders of Exceptionally Large Estates, the Rental of which is under 2,000*l.* per annum.

	County	Acres	Value
			£
Forbes, Charles H., of Kingairloch	Argyll	30,000	1,873
Grierson, Andrew, of Quendale	Zetland	22,006	1,131
Hill (late), Lord George A., of Ballyvar	Donegal	24,189	1,308
Macdonald, John Allan, of Glenaladale	Inverness	24,000	1,550
Macpherson of Glendale	Inverness	35,022	1,257
Nicolson, Lady, of Nicolson	Zetland	24,785	1,314
Robertson, Mrs., of Struan	Perth	24,000	1,239
Smith, Thomas V., of Acharanich	Argyll	22,050	1,800

IV.—A List of the Number of Great Landowners who are
Members of the following Clubs:—

Political Clubs

Tory	Carlton	642
	Junior Carlton	112
	Conservative	65
	St. Stephen's	37
		856

Liberal	Brooks's	216
	Reform	103
	Devonshire	29
		348

Service Clubs

United Service	107
Junior United Service	72
Army and Navy	120
Guards	70
Naval and Military	22
	391

Learned Clubs

Athenæum	145
Oxford and Cambridge	79
United University	61
New University	16
	301

Other Clubs

Travellers'	286
White's	169
Boodle's	145
Arthur's	119
St. James's	86
Garrick	55
Turf	54
Marlborough	52
Union	50
National	35
Windham	29
St. George's	28
Raleigh	13
	1,121

are likely to contain dynamite); or do they consider that Irish
proprietorship is so utterly illusory under the present régime that
to correct is a work of supererogation?

Some changes have come over clubland since 1879. The "Scottish," "Royal Irish," "Bachelors'," and "Salisbury" have, for good
or evil, added themselves to the already lengthy list of clubs, while

the "Junior Naval and Military" has resolved itself into a political club as the "Beaconsfield," thus adding to the disproportionate number of Great Landowners who belong to Tory clubs; which disproportion is far more affected by the numerous (and somewhat late) secessions of Whigs who cannot stomach recent Radical legislation. In Liberal circles it is rumoured that the late internecine feud at the "Reform" has numerically strengthened the "Devonshire" not a little.

10. Industrial Reorganization: The Coal Trust Proposal

BRITAIN FLIRTED uneasily with industrial reorganization while her major competitors turned to trusts and cartels. The British made a number of false starts but few successful moves toward rationalization and combination. The Bradford Dyers Association completed a formal trust agreement in textiles. The chemical industry established its Salt Union. Price-fixing agreements were concluded in iron. Most projected combinations were stillborn, however foresighted. Sir George Elliot, an eminent, imaginative mineowner in South Wales, was troubled by the utter disorder of the coal trade during the industrial dispute of 1893. Seeking rationality, he proposed a national coal trust, regionally administered, which would allocate to each producer his proportionate share in new, hopefully much enhanced, profits.

Coal had come to be Britain's key industry. For a few brief decades it was the monopoly fuel. There was a steady rise in domestic need, an overwhelming demand for exports. Britain fueled the industrialization of Europe. Less than one-tenth of British coal was exported, including that consumed for ship fuel in 1860. This amounted to little more than 2 percent of the value of British exports. By the first decade of the twentieth century, exports had increased sevenfold, accounting for more than one-third of total output and one-tenth of all British export trade. Over 3,000 mines employed more than 1,000,000 miners by the end of the century. Between 1875 and 1914 coal output more than doubled, with the most dramatic growth in South Wales and Yorkshire. Coal paid the highest wages in the land, handsome dividends, too. Mineral royalties were the quickest path to great wealth in Victorian Britain.[1]

The coal trade grew with sharply rising costs. Demand rose at 4 percent per year, outstripping the combined productive capacity of Britain, the United States, and Germany. This concealed the real deficiencies in the British coal industry. World demand, Britain's

1. I. Lubin and H. Everett, *The British Coal Dilemma* (New York: 1927), p. 29. There is an excellent summary by A. J. Taylor, "The Coal Industry," in D. H. Aldcroft, *The Development of British Industry and Foreign Competition* (London: 1968), pp. 37–70.

geographic position, the accident of geology that gave her easy access from coal pithead to the sea, all concealed the organization of the industry in uneconomic units, the obsolete technology, and the diminishing resources. While demand stayed high, more labor at higher wage rates meant sharply falling productivity. Output per manshift dropped almost 20 percent between 1880 and 1910. The most accessible coal had already been mined, and there were few undeveloped fields. Mines had to plunge deeper, exploit thinner seams, and do so with few benefits of new technology. Electricity only began to come to the pits at the turn of the century. The industry was undermechanized, although the scale of the individual enterprise was so small that heavy investment in cutting machines would probably not have been justifiable. As the industry grew, so did strong unionization. The decline in output can be at least partially linked to increasing prosperity and higher wage levels. Absenteeism grew as the miners, like others, began to consume leisure.

Most collieries were small, employing 50 to 1000 miners. Mine managers were apprenticed, rather than trained—thus very good on small or local matters, more apt to be deficient on larger, more theoretical issues. Adaptation tended to stay within the confines imposed by new safety regulations rather than the possibilities of new methods. The future was left to care for itself with the presumption that the market must have coal at any price. Sir George's plan excited some discussion but no serious interest. Geography and chronology enabled the weak and inefficient to survive. After the First World War, with growing competition from other fuels and the market in collapse, mineowners, managers, and miners still resisted reorganization. Only when disaster overtook the industry was rationalization possible, and even so, it took thirty years.

Recommended Reading

Two of the best works on the general problem are still J. W. Jenks, *Industrial Combination in Europe: Reports of the United States Industrial Commission* (Washington: 1901), vol. XVIII, and H. W. Macrosty, *The Trust Movement in British Industry* (London: 1907). An excellent study of one modern industrial giant is C. H. Wilson, *The History of Unilever*, 2 vols. (London: 1954). See, also, Ashworth, Clapham, Habakkuk, Kindleberger, and Landes from the general bibliography.

A Projected Coal Trust

Next after water and bread coal is recognized to be the most general necessity of English life. To waste it is to waste the tissues

Source: *The Times*, September 20, 1893.

of our strength; to economize the production and to prolong the duration of the supply is proportionately to prolong the period during which we may hope to hold a first place among nations. It is no exaggeration therefore to say that there can hardly be a proposal of greater importance to consider than one which would materially affect our manner of dealing with this vast possession.

Such a proposal is contained in a scheme for the consolidation and common working of all the coal interests of the United Kingdom, which, after years of consideration and consultation between coal experts and other eminent authorities, it has been decided to lay before the public. The name of Sir George Elliot, who is the proposer and originator of the scheme, is too well known to call for comment. There is perhaps no one in Great Britain who is better qualified by practical experience to take the position of leader in the movement which he has initiated. He claims that the object of the great change which his scheme seeks to compass is in no way the creation of a monopoly or trust for the sole benefit of the proprietors, but a combination which shall be a benefit not only to the coalowners, lessees, workmen, and consumers, but to the nation at large. It is on this level that the scheme challenges consideration, and in so far as it makes good its right to this high ground, it ranks for judgment among the great political commercial conceptions of the day. The very interesting difference which exists between such a proposal and the proposals of the chartered companies, in which the public has also been asked to recognize other than purely financial aims, is that, while the schemes of the chartered companies have dealt mainly with the expansion of the Empire abroad, this scheme follows the other leading current of political life, and associates itself directly with the development of social questions at home. It is the first time that a commercial scheme of any magnitude has attempted to do this.

It differs also from the chartered companies in the fact that it requires no political sanction for its formation. The co-operation which it needs for success is in the first instance solely the co-operation of the coal lessees of the United Kingdom, who are invited to exchange their interest in the properties at present worked by them for shares and debentures in a United Coal Company. This company shall then undertake the working of the entire coal deposit of the country, with all the attendant responsibilities involved by the employment of so vast a body of labour, and the sole command of the home supply of fuel. The scheme works out in ably devised detail the conditions under which it is proposed that such an amalgamation of competing interests should be accomplished.

The present yearly output of the coalfields of Great Britain is 182,000,000 tons, which, at an average selling price of 7s. 3d. a ton, represents a gross value to the coalowners and lessees of £65,975,-000 per annum. From this £54,000,000 must be deducted to cover the average cost price of 6s. per ton at the pit bank. The remaining £11,375,000 represents roughly the profit which may be made under the present system of working by the coal lessees. About 20 per cent. of the quantity of coal now produced is consumed in the working of ironstone and in the manufacture of iron and steel. As a great deal of this is raised and worked by the great ironmasters themselves, who would evidently have nothing to gain in joining a scheme based on any general principle of profit-making, it has been left out of consideration, and the calculation is based on a present annual output of 145,000,000 tons. It is estimated that the sums required to represent the whole capitalized interest of the lessees would be slightly under £110,000,000. This figure does not greatly exceed the share value of the London and North-Western or even of the Midland Railway, and, in view of the fact that the amalgamated value of the railways of Great Britain would come to nearly £900,000,000, it will probably be a matter of surprise to many people to learn that the capitalized value of the amalgamated coalfields would be so relatively small. The capital sum to be dealt with, although considerable, is not therefore of such unmanageable magnitude as the first thought of a consolidation of the coal interests of the United Kingdom would suggest. The basis of co-operation on which it is proposed to carry out the scheme dispenses with the necessity to raise any greater proportion of this sum in cash than may be required to free the collieries from present obligations. For this purpose it is proposed, probably with some foreknowledge of the chances of carrying out such a proposal with success, that a body of bankers shall be formed who shall agree to take debentures, at a price to be agreed upon, from any colliery proprietor, to an amount not exceeding one-third of those allotted to him. It is a further detail of this proposal that any one so applying for the exchange of his debentures into cash should set aside an equal amount of his shares, giving to the bankers an option for 12 months to take the same at par. The total amount of cash required will not, it has been estimated, be likely to exceed the provision thus made for it.

The figures disclose nothing impracticable in this part of the scheme. The question of its working feasibility turns mainly upon the advantages which the coal lessees might hope to gain in return for their co-operation. Many of these advantages are obvious. In the first place, as a united body owning the whole coal wealth of the country, they would—paradoxically as the statement may at first sight seem—have a larger mass of available coal in their possession than any added computation of their individual properties would now give. A lessee under existing conditions is obliged to leave on the boundary of the royalty a solid rib of coal varying in width from 40 to 100 yards, which is a total loss to himself and to the nation. A consolidation of royalties, doing away with the necessity of boundaries for any but engineering purposes, would bring nearly the whole of this coal into the market, and, together with the facilities which a different method of working would give for the hauling of small coal now allowed to go to waste, would, it has been estimated, add fully 10 per cent. to the annual output. This would mean, if all other conditions remain as they are, an increase of 10 per cent. upon the existing collection of profits in the coal trade. But the saving in coal itself is only one of the economies which the substitution of co-operation for the present system of competitive development might be expected to introduce. The expenses of pumping, ventilation, and underground haulage are among the most considerable items of cost in the process of raising coal. All of these might, it is claimed, be much reduced if the area to be treated were regarded only in the light of the physical peculiarities, and dealt with without consideration of arbitrary divisions. Pumping power, instead of being distributed as now, would then be concentrated in the most advantageous points to deal with water at its source, and thus avoid the disastrous deep level floodings which are so frequent a cause of waste and expense. The ventilation of large areas unimpeded by artificial obstructions would be safer and more economical than the present system, under which the coal beds are honeycombed with separate mines and ventilated, as it were, in every cell. The saving in underground haulage alone which would be effected by the abolition of eccentric surface boundaries would be considerable. With the existing system coal may have to be hauled for distances of as much as two miles from the pit bottom, owing simply to the irregular configuration of an estate, while coal from the very same bed is being taken up by a neighbouring colliery on a different estate, within a few hundred yards. The enormous expense which this underground transit entails in keeping the passage ways open and timbered, merely for lack of a more convenient right of way over neighbouring ground, illustrates vividly the waste and friction, now unavoidable, which under a system of united ownership would disappear. Briefly, the effect of amalgamation, it is contended, would be to remove all the artificial factors which now stand for so much in the sum of the coal mining industry, and to leave science and nature face to face. The different coal districts would then be treated each as a whole, according to its geological peculiarities. Under a more fully organized method of working, the whole of the coal, good and bad, could be, systematically extracted, instead of being as now, largely wasted for the sake of bringing up only those kinds which produce the highest market prices. Beyond this, it is anticipated that there would be an additional and important saving in the cost of distribution, as each group of collieries, having no longer an individual interest in seeking distant custom, would naturally supply that part of the country in which its coal can be most easily delivered.

The more the scheme is considered the less doubtful does it appear that the value of the coal property of the country as a whole would be increased by its adoption. The value of the whole being greater, it seems to follow as a mathematical deduction that the value of the parts must be proportionately increased, and the existing coal-owners and lessees must gain by accepting the share which is proposed to them in the general scheme. There remain, however, two very important points for their consideration, and these are fully dealt with in the scheme. One is the management of the proposed new system, and the other is the still more delicate and knotty question of the appraisement of the value of their existing properties, together with the manner in which the profits of the proposed associated should be shared.

With regard to management, it is proposed to create a central representative council, the unit of representation being a given number of tons of coal. Thus the several coal districts of England, Scotland, Wales, would be entitled for every average annual output of 5,000,000 tons, or any other quantity that may be fixed, to elect a representative upon the central council, which will be charged with the general management, supervision, and control of the business of the company. Under this central council it is proposed to create about 30 district committees, which would be immediately concerned with the working of the collieries and local business of their respective clients. These committees would also be elective, and would consist of representatives chosen in a fixed proportion by the shareholders and the miners. Existing managers and factors would continue in the majority of cases to be employed, and when that is impossible it is proposed to give liberal compensation. But the district committee would absorb and take over the duties of numerous existing boards of directors, and thus cause a considerable ultimate saving in the expenses of management.

The appraisement of existing values in coal properties has been looked upon as in some respects one of the most practical of the difficulties to be met. It has, however, to be bourne in mind that such appraisement is at the present time constantly made for purposes of sale or for division rendered necessary by the death of a colliery proprietor. The principle of procedure would not be new, it would only need application on an extended scale; and, in order to secure the greatest possible impartiality in the carrying out of so large an operation, it is proposed to place the appraisement of values in the hands of bodies of experts nominated by the colliery proprietors for approval by a central council. These bodies of experts would then take evidence and make all investigations which might be found necessary in order to arrive at an equitable estimate of the value of each property. Further, it is proposed as a guide for their deliberations that a sum of about 15s. per ton for coal of ordinary quality, calculated on the average annual output of the last few years, should be taken as the level from which differing values should be approximately determined. Many collieries will be found to be worth more than this; others, again, will be worth less; and there are various exceptional conditions which it will be the duty of the boards of experts to take into consideration, but it is believed that a fair estimate of annual output calculated at 15s. a ton will be found to represent the capital value of the entire coal beds of the United Kingdom. Should this calculation prove to be mistaken, it is not a matter of vital importance to the scheme, for, as the collieries themselves will represent the bulk of the unlimited capital and the owners will claim profits only in proportion to the capital value of their shares, it will matter little—so long as the appraisement is relatively just—what figure the sum of the united value may reach.

This brief outline serves to indicate the nature of the advantages which the colliery proprietors might expect to draw from an amalgamation of their interests. Such advantages have already been enjoyed in other countries by the American system of combination, and, if a combination in coal were all that Sir George Elliot's scheme proposes to effect, it would be travelling over common ground. But the scheme does not stop here; it is of wider scope. The labour which is directly employed upon the coal properties of Great Britain amounts to something not far short of a million of men. The interests of a million of human beings, who, with the wives and families dependent upon them, may be estimated to form nearly an eighth part of the population of the kingdom, have a weight and importance which the dislocation of industry that has followed upon successive strikes does not allow any of us to forget. Sir George Elliot has studied the coal industry on every essential side; he has a right to speak with authority upon the needs, the aspirations, and the fair requirements of the great body of English miners, and it is from the point of view of the enlightened pitman that the proposals which affect the workman's share in the new scheme have been conceived. They are put forward with a confident assurance that their adoption will relegate strikes to a closed chapter of the history of the coal trade. The guiding principle appears to have been the same as that which has prompted the application of the system of local self-government throughout our political organization. The men are to be made, as far as possible, responsible for their own affairs. In the first place it is proposed that the question of wages should be determined by the district committees, on which it is to be remembered that the miners are represented by their elected directors, and these committees shall be empowered to deal with the special features of each mine so as to obtain, as far as possible, an approximately uniform scale of wage throughout the country. It is laid down as an axiom that the scale shall be calculated on a liberal basis as compared with other classes of labour. The general employment of the best appliances, which will become possible under one responsible system of management, and the added facilities for pumping the ventilation will, it is estimated, greatly ameliorate the average conditions under which work is carried on, and lessen the existing risks to life. It is claimed that this uniformity in wages and conditions of labour must in itself remove the cause of many partial and local strikes. Among ameliorating measures it is also proposed to establish a general insurance fund for worn-out and disabled workmen and their families. The amount of the insurance fund may be fixed by a subsequent decision of the central board; but it is suggested that 1*d*. per ton upon the entire present output would provide a sum for this purpose of £758,333 a year.

But these proposals are only nibbles at the great principle of admitting the claims of labour to share with capital in the profit-earning power of industrial enterprise. The principle is accepted wholly in a clause of the scheme which includes a certain limited interest upon capital as part of the working expenses, and provides that the workmen shall share equally with the coal lessees in any further profit that is made. Nothing in the scheme is more interesting and novel than the section which deals with the division of profits. From what has been already said it will have become evident that the interests of the labour employed in the mines have been no less practically safeguarded than the interests of the landlords and the coal lessees. But of late we have heard of proposals put forward that the men and masters should enter into combination to raise the price of coal and thus satisfy their own requirements at the public expense. Such an amalgamation of coal interests as that contemplated in the present scheme would offer a field of rare opportunity for unscrupulous action of the kind, and there could be little question of enlisting public sympathy in its accomplishment, unless the strongest guarantees were given against any such possible abuse of the position. Sir George Elliot appears to have appreciated this aspect of the question, and accepts all the obligations of the high ground which he has taken. He offers to secure for the men and masters every advantage which some of them have imagined that they might gain from the simple process of allowing wages to govern price, but he proposes to get out of the increased volume and better working of the available coal supply what the authors of so impossible a combination propose to take out of the public purse. In doing this he claims that a substantial benefit will be conferred upon the nation at large, but it is not merely by the additional value that will be given to an important article of primary production that he seeks to justify the public utility of his project. The interests of the public are more directly safeguarded by a clause which admits the consumer to immediate participation in the benefits of the economy which is contemplated. The scheme accepts in its entirety the principle of the limitation of interest, and one of its essential conditions is the provision that the price of coal shall never be raised above the figure which is required to give an interest of 5 per cent. upon the debentures, and to reach a maximum of 15 per cent. upon the stock, without the sanction of the Board of Trade. It has been estimated that an average selling price at the pit bank of 7s. 3d. a ton at the present annual rate of output would suffice to give the interest required. The purchaser, it is claimed, would thus be protected from the possibility of extortionate prices in the future, and, in order to give full effect to this guarantee, it is proposed to invest the Board of Trade, wither in the articles of association of the company or, if necessary, with Parliamentary sanction, with all functions essential to the exercise of its arbitrating powers. More than this, it is provided that, in the event of the Board of Trade sanctioning an increase of dividend beyond 15 per cent., the purchaser shall receive, in the form of discount, a share equal to that of the labourer and the lessee in the profit made. It is also believed that a considerable benefit will accrue to the poorer part of the population by the power which will be acquired of working coal hitherto wasted and distributing it at a low price to the consumer. It is a matter of common knowledge that the poor, who cannot afford to store coal in the cheap season, at present pay a considerably higher price in proportion to their consumption than the rich. The distribution of water at equal rates to poor and rich proved to be only a matter of organization when water supply was dealt with on a large scale. The details of the manner in which the principle is to be applied to coal have not been fully worked out, but it is believed that, when there is but one salesman for coal throughout the country and the prices of that salesman are regulated by a decision of the Board of Trade, the fluctuations of retail prices must be greatly checked, and the creation of agencies of distribution where coal could be obtained at a fixed published rate would be like the distribution of water, a mere question of subsequent organization.

The scheme thus becomes a three-sided one, in which the lessee, the labourer, and the public are invited to amalgamate their interests. Treating coal as an article of general utility, the production of which is too important to be left to the haphazard incidence of the competitive market, it proposes nothing less than at the same time to reform the method of supply and to regulate the price of consumption. It is to this two-edged nature that the scheme owes the unique quality of the interest which it arouses. The whole appears to have been thought out on a strictly utilitarian basis. No one interest is allowed to override the others, but it is sought to demonstrate that the advantage of each is co-ordinate with the profit of all.

The definite proposal which the scheme embodies may be summed up in set terms as follows: —

The coal lessees of the United Kingdom shall amalgamate their existing interests in a co-operative company, charged with the entire working of the coal deposit of the country, taking payment in the form of one-third debentures and two-thirds stock. All stock shall be interminable. A reserve fund shall be formed for opening further collieries to take the place of those annually exhausted and to provide for extensions and sinkings; an insurance fund for the workmen shall be set aside, and a sinking fund for the redemption of capital shall also provide the means for rendering the consolidated property permanent. All further earnings will be applied, first, in paying interest on the debentures at 5 per cent.; secondly, in paying a minimum dividend of 10 per cent. upon the stock. In view of the exceptional nature of the property concerned, it is believed that the dividend upon the stock need never be less than 10 per cent., but the profits shall not exceed 5 per cent. more without the approval of the Board of Trade, and such 5 per cent., if paid, shall be divided equally between the lessee and the workman. In the event of the Board of Trade sanctioning an advance in price sufficient to yield any interest beyond 15 per cent., the whole further profit will then be divided equally in thirds between the workmen, the coal lessees, and the purchaser. As in such an arrangement the purchaser pays the whole difference and only receives back a third in the form of discount, the interest of the workmen and the coal lessees will manifestly be to bring pressure to bear upon the Board of Trade to sanction an advance in price. The interest of the public will be to bring pressure to resist an advance. Between these two fires the Board of Trade is called upon by the terms of the scheme to protect the several interests of all parties concerned. If upon consideration it should be found that the political composition of the Board of Trade would render it inexpedient in the public interest to invest it with ultimate powers of control, it is proposed to substitute referees, who shall be appointed by high judicial authority, say the Lord Chief Justice. The principle of limiting the interest on capital is, it is admitted, one that has long been recognized in this country in the supply of gas and water, and there need be no difficulty in the application of the same principle to coal.

If the calculations on which this proposal is based are correct, the coal owners, it is believed, would gain a security for their dividend which would be scarcely less than that of Government stocks. The public would gain the advantage of a steady, moderate price, which would be safeguarded from the fluctuations caused by strikes and other accidental circumstances, and would not be altered without the sanction of the Government. The workmen would gain better conditions of labour, better wages, and a share in the profits. The nation would gain in the more economical, and at the same time more thorough and systematic, development of the coal deposits.

All this is a great deal to promise, and to submit proposals for a scheme of this magnitude is manifestly a very different thing from carrying it to a successful issue. The first and most practical question for consideration is whether the coal lessees of Great Britain will be disposed as a body to consider that they serve their own interests by exchanging their present chances of a higher rate of profit for the practical certainty of 10 per cent. which the new scheme claims to offer. A majority of two-thirds of the coal lessees of this country would be required in order to insure the success of the working of the scheme. Many of them have already been consulted, and, as it is believed that one effect of the better security would be to increase the capital value of coal property from the present figure of five or seven years' purchase to something like 20 years' purchase, little doubt is entertained that the requisite number would be found willing to join the enterprise. The amount of existing obligations, such as mortgages, &c. to which coal properties may be subject is also, by the necessarily private nature of many such obligations, difficult to estimate beforehand. It is believed by the supporters of the scheme that the readiness with which debentures could be disposed of would meet all requirements likely to arise on this head, and it is, in general terms, presumable that an interest in the security of a property can hardly be regarded as an injury to the interests of a mortgagee. But in its financial aspect the scheme must be regarded as an immense conversion scheme, and experience with the conversion of many public debts has shown that arguments in general terms are not always received as absolutely satisfactory in individual application. For all these reasons it is clear that many obstacles remain to be disposed of before it can become possible for the proposals embodied in the scheme to be carried into effect. Should these be removed and the full practicality of the measure be established, it will still be for the various parties involved to watch with care over the maintenance of the economic theory of the balance of interests upon which it takes its stand. Without attempting to predict its fate, it may be safely said, that the conception and publication of the scheme will in any case have submitted for consideration one of the most interesting possibilities of industrial development which has been witnessed in this generation.

PART II

Social Organization

BRITAIN'S POPULATION doubled twice in the course of the nineteenth century. This impressive, even overwhelming growth was achieved in spite of vast outward migration overseas and the almost halving of Ireland's population. England and Wales more than doubled between 1837 and 1901. Scotland grew by 80 percent, while Ireland fell from 8,000,000 to 4,500,000. There was no decline in infant mortality, the rate being about the same in 1841 and 1901, nor did the death rate change significantly among those over sixty-five. But the death rate did drop steadily during the last third of the century. Fewer people died during their most productive years.

Large Victorian families continued into the 1870s—an average slightly under six children. Growing concern with the costs of child-rearing and the demands of status led to later marriage and smaller families. By the Edwardian era, average family size was 4⅔, reaching toward the 3⅓ of the 1920s. The British population, statistically, became slightly more mature, better balanced between males and females, and overwhelmingly urban. The population moved geographically as well as quantitatively. Millions emigrated overseas. Millions more were uprooted in their own land. Victoria ruled a nation more urban than rural by 1851. By the 1880s the urban population was more than double that of the countryside. Overseas migration almost devoured the natural population increase briefly in the mid-Victorian years, but the statistics are misleading. The drain of Irish population after the famine accounts for most of it, although emigration from the remainder of the kingdom was also substantial. Those concerned that the nation might no longer be able to man the fleet could have taken consolation in the fact that the pressure of population imposed no difficulty in the recruitment of increasing numbers of domestic servants.

Approximately 30 percent of the Victorian population were males over fifteen, one-third, women over fifteen, and slightly more than one-third, children under fifteen. It was a man's society, more so, if such a thing be possible, than that of the past or that which was to come. One adult woman in five worked, the number fluctuating slightly through the century. Half were engaged in industry, half in domestic service. Some women, of course, gave part-time aid to husbands in shop or field, but 80 percent of adult women were dependent upon others for their livelihood. Textiles employed women early; the sweated trades late.[1] Overwhelmingly, however, women were engaged in domestic and related service industries. To this extent the typewriter was an instrument of emancipation. The 7,000 women who held secretarial positions in 1881 blossomed to 90,000 by 1901. What would eventually be felt to be a demeaning task was initially a stage in emancipation.

In the second half of the century agricultural employment fell most sharply. White collar workers (overwhelmingly male) made the most substantial gains. The number of clerks doubled in the 1860s and again in the 1870s. People were increasingly engaged to provide goods and services for other people rather than to make things. Increasing specialization multiplied the number of people who stood between the producer and the consumer. The middle classes, particularly the lower middle classes, grew much more rapidly than the population as a whole. The world of casual labor shrank slowly. There was always demand for the unskilled in those armies of navvies who built the railroads or the casual workers on Britain's bustling docks.

Rural society remained relatively stable. It was deferential, had already undergone the trauma of enclosure, now moved calmly from balanced farming to specialized agriculture, and was not particularly mechanized. The most dramatic changes were on the Celtic fringe— sweeping away the crofters of the Scottish highlands or starving out the redundant agrarian population of Ireland. Specialization came to country as well as factory, and the rural hierarchy grew more complex. New specialists arose in market towns, and a rural middle class evolved among farmers. Few generalizations are possible about the pool of agrarian labor. They fared well when there was nonagricultural competition for hands, poorly in outreaches where men had to compete for jobs. Even in the same district, opposites prevailed. One village would have tidy cottages, fringe benefits in the form of surplus produce and meat, generous customs on the estate, a legitimate garden patch, and ample opportunities for illegitimate poaching. The next village would have cramped, filthy cottages, niggardly wages, no benefits, and a trigger-happy gamekeeper on the estate. Human attrition, measured out by the law of supply and demand, finally reduced the agricultural labor force to levels at which it could organize and secure its welfare in the face of agrarian depression.

Throughout the Victorian years British society was an enormous triangle in which more than 70 percent of the population were definably working class. The initial problem for the early Victorian laboring population was adaptation—to towns, to factories, to a larger and increasingly complex world. Many skilled artisans found themselves in direct competition with new forms of production. Handloom weavers were a classic but not unique example. The constant objects of official handwringing, they were forced to adapt themselves to their environ-

1. Document 17. See also occupational censuses, Document 6.

ment with little effective assistance.[2] There were few institutions besides those workingmen developed for themselves or those established by philanthropy to temper the workings of economic law. Victorians were happier about protecting the children of the lower orders. Humanitarian impulses to aid children in the mines led, incidentally, to the removal of all women from the pits.[3] The motives were somewhat mixed. Mineowners were already phasing out women, partly in response to pressure from men. They found the reform a convenience.

In social terms the Victorian age was certainly a middle-class era. No part of British society grew more rapidly; none advanced its position or asserted its values more effectively. Middle-class virtues colored the lives of peer and worker alike, and that social and cultural ascendancy had its costs. Hard work, frugality, achievement, family loyalty appealed to the merchant prince or petty shopkeeper, to the aspiring cotton spinner, ironmaster, or ambitious physician. But the patriarchal structure of Victorian middle-class society was overbearing. Women were, in all respects, "inferior," albeit many a Victorian woman ruled from within the family. But the woman's role demanded that she fulfill herself through her husband or the males in her family. Exploitation awaited women of the lower orders; those socially more fortunate could anticipate a life of subordination.[4]

The middle classes, of course, evade definition. They run from Bob Cratchit to Mr. Gladstone, from the petty tradesman to the professional and large merchant or manufacturer. It includes those people who conceived of themselves as middle class or were defined by others as middle class. It was a group with vaguely shared attitudes and criteria of education, life style, function, and income. The middle classes included every religious faith in Britain, those who controlled commerce and industry, almost all those in the liberal arts, and a substantial portion of those who consumed religion, goods and services, literature and the arts. It was family centered, assessing itself by wealth and education, obsessively concerned with respectability and achievement. Its values (see Part III) were neither homogeneous nor consistent, but they gave a tone to the age.

They gloried in the family, inculcating from earliest youth an ethic of hard work built upon the principle of deprivation, discipline, and suppression. Yet control of children in the home or at school was ultimately built upon dependency. Because place of residence and place of work were rarely the same in an increasingly urban world, employed children became increasingly independent. Family discipline and authority were best preserved in middle- and upper-class families where boarding school merely extended the principles of deference,

2. Document 11.
3. Document 12.
4. Document 13.

order, and suppression. Discomfort and deprivation were imposed in the most affectionate home to inculcate the principles of love and morality.[5] The application and preservation of the patriarchal principle depended upon economic control and the accepted inferiority of women. Only in 1870 did married women win the right to hold property in their own name.[6]

Prosperity, educational opportunity, new jobs for women, gradual legal emancipation all helped; but the feminist movement of the nineteenth century was still principally an activity of the well-to-do addressed to the problem of establishing individual rights—winning, as it were, what men had secured for more than a century. The emancipation of women proceeded slowly, not always consistently, to the establishment of legal personality. The fundamental issues of role and equality were barely touched.

Society inhabited an increasingly urban world. Towns and cities multiplied, themselves demanding new services, thus intensifying occupational specialization. Financial, insurance, commercial, and maintenance facilities evolved with the ports of Liverpool and London. A railroad center like Crewe demanded its own specialized facilities and manpower. The urban world itself generated more and increasingly specialized jobs. From rent collectors to bankers, shop assistants to actuaries, the need for more people to serve more people grew. There was more crime, more poverty, more madness. Self-help could never begin to provide elementary sanitary facilities, a water supply, or transportation.

Work and the family bound urban society together. Families themselves became increasingly anonymous, more segregated, more intensely class conscious. At the nether end of the social scale the family could not be sustained. It disintegrated into the "outlaw" world inhabited by the low, the unredeemed. The submerged world of the slum served to remind respectable society that only rigorous moral and social discipline could preserve civilization.[7] Hell might or might not exist in the next world; it certainly did in this. The respectable kept themselves to themselves, gloried in labor, saved, achieved. Steady artisans and petty bourgeois looked at their work and leisure and found it good.[8]

There were, however, important distinctions between the working and middle classes. Working-class life and living were dominated by a sense of total insecurity—no unemployment insurance, no medical or health plans. Only self-help or mutual aid organizations insulated the working man against economic adversity. The savings bank, the friendly society, the cooperative, or in some instances the trade

5. Document 15.
6. Document 14.
7. Document 18.
8. Document 19. On this point, see G. M. Young, "The Happy Family," *Victorian Essays*, ed. W. D. Handcock (London: 1962), pp. 116–123.

union—these were his institutions. The pawnshop remained the sole refuge for those without access to the world of self-help and mutual aid. Beyond that lay the strained resources of philanthropy and the less than tender mercies of the poor law.[9]

The aristocracy of labor and lower middle classes overlapped considerably in income and prospects but differed principally in how money was spent. The lower middle classes, significantly, aspired to imitate middle-class life styles, while the working man was more likely to consume leisure or comfort. The lower middle classes were principally concerned with creating and preserving a gap between themselves and the class below, from which, most often, they themselves had sprung.

Victorian prosperity did mean enhanced standards of life and expectations. Diet improved, not merely for the better off but for society as a whole. Meat consumption, for example, rose far more substantially than the total population. Even making allowance for extraordinary wastage in the upper and middle classes, there was little comparison between the early and late Victorian years. Refrigeration and economic linkages with tropical areas made the exotic routine. The banana joined the apple as a staple consumption fruit. Sweets, tea, and sticky confections became habits. Jam was on the typical working-class table. In early Victorian years consumption had been limited to a few necessities for most Britons. As the century progressed, consumption of a wide range of consumer goods flourished. The cooperative movement in the North, the increasing number of multiple shops in the rest of the country responded to and helped to accelerate the demand for goods among the lower classes. Factory production meant cheap consumer goods; by the last third of the century it was providing an enhanced standard of living for most Britons.[10]

Affluence and aspiration generated ambition. The passive and exploited came, increasingly, to demand recognition and their rights. Poverty became unthinkable for the first time in history. The poor and deprived were no longer passive, the rich and privileged too frightened or guilty to resist. Economic opportunity—the options and possibilities generated by the nineteenth-century economy and the world market—made dreams possibilities, occasionally realities.

The established orders, displaying an extraordinary capacity to adapt to circumstances, showed their mettle. The landed elite retreated very slowly, fighting minor rearguard actions in politics and economics, most gradually of all, in social prestige. To the extent that the fortunes of those who ruled the land were bound up in its economic vitality, the collapse of 1879 and subsequent hard times on the land drained the economic foundations of their power. The aristocratic role became more costly, the resources less ample. Political reform and civil

9. Document 12, *BP19C*.

10. E. J. Hobsbawm, *Industry and Empire* (London: 1968). Chapter viii develops these points in detail.

service had executed a revolution in slow motion. While mineral royalties or urban and suburban land development provided windfall profits for some landed proprietors, most found themselves badly squeezed with the decline of agriculture.[11]

Upper-class lifestyle reflected expanding, not contracting resources. The Victorian wealthy had always displayed a capacity for consumption on the grand scale, but Victorian constraint was obsolete by the end of the century. Prince Edward lived in a different world. The Marlborough House set could never have amused Victoria. High society came to be, more than ever, a mixture of the highly bred and excessively rich. The life style of conspicuous consumption proved so expensive that a reticent aristocracy was forced to come to grips with plutocracy.[12] Luxury, the season, hunting, travel—life in that fraction of 1 percent of the social world became an exhibition of magnificence. In high society, but trickling down the scale, the Victorian certitudes melted.

11. Document 20. See also, documents 16, 20, 25, 30, *BP19C*.
12. Document 21.

General Bibliography[13]

J. L. BANKS, *Prosperity and Parenthood* (London: 1954).

A. BRIGGS, *The Age of Improvement* (London: 1959).

——, *Victorian Cities* (New York: 1965).

——, *Victorian People* (Chicago: 1955).

—— and J. SAVILLE, *Essays in Labour History*, 2 vols. (London: 1967–1971).

W. L. BURN, *The Age of Equipoise* (London: 1964).

S. G. CHECKLAND, *The Rise of Industrial Society in England, 1815–1885* (London: 1964).

G. D. H. COLE, *Short History of the British Working Class Movement*, rev. ed. (London: 1948).

——, *Studies in Class Structure* (London: 1955).

—— and R. POSTGATE, *The Common People*, rev. ed. (London: 1946).

H. J. DYOS, *Victorian Suburb* (Leicester: 1961).

R. C. K. ENSOR, *England, 1870–1914* (Oxford: 1936).

W. L. GUTTSMAN, *The British Political Elite, 1832–1936* (London: 1963).

E. HALÉVY, *Imperialism and the Rise of Labour* (London: 1929).

——, *Victorian Years* (London: 1948).

J. L. and B. HAMMOND, *The Age of the Chartists* (London: 1930).

E. J. HOBSBAWM, *Industry and Empire* (London: 1968).

——, *Labouring Men* (London: 1964).

R. LEWIS and A. MAUDE, *The English Middle Classes* (New York: 1950).

—— and ——, *Professional People* (London: 1952).

H. M. LYND, *England in the Eighteen Eighties* (New York: 1946).

D. C. MARSH, *The Changing Social Structure of England and Wales, 1871–1951* (London: 1958).

H. PELLING, *The Origins of the Labour Party* (London: 1954).

——, *Popular Politics and Society in Late Victorian Britain* (London: 1968).

H. PERKIN, *The Origins of Modern English Society* (London: 1971).

S. POLLARD, *A History of Labour in Sheffield* (Liverpool: 1959).

N. J. SMELSER, *Social Change in the Industrial Revolution* (Chicago: 1959).

D. SOUTHGATE, *The Passing of the Whigs* (London: 1962).

D. THOMSON, *England in the Nineteenth Century* (Harmondsworth: 1950).

---

13. In addition to the relevant works cited in Part I.

F. M. L. Thompson, *English Landed Society in the Nineteenth Century* (London: 1963).

G. M. Trevelyan, *A Social History of England* (London: 1944), vol. IV.

R. K. Webb, *Modern England* (New York: 1968).

A. F. Weber, *The Growth of Cities in the Nineteenth Century* (New York: 1899).

R. Williams, *Culture and Society, 1780–1950* (London: 1959).

G. M. Young, *Early Victorian England*, 2 vols. (Oxford: 1934).

———— and W. D. Handcock, *English Historical Documents, 1833–1874* (London: 1956).

11. Technology and Life: The Conventry Ribbon Weavers

Avowed or tacit assumptions underlie the continuing debate over the social impact of the industrial revolution. Some are simple, a few complex, ranging from articles of faith or conviction to elaborate speculations. Some proceed on the assumption that country life is better than city life or that the primitive is superior to the sophisticated. Others presume the working of some philosophic dialectic. Some authors, like many Victorians, are appalled at the evidence of man's inhumanity to man and indict modernization, urbanization, and the factory system. Others find the flaw in man, not his environment.

The historian's problems are ones of perspective and reference. The early Victorians and their immediate forebears pioneered the technique of elaborate investigation, then used the reports to root out the evils they revealed. For the first time we, as historians, have considerable evidence about the world we seek to describe. We cannot safely presume that this represented regression from the past. Daniel Defoe wrote proudly of child labor—not a child of six but can make his own way in the world—in Somersetshire more than a century before. Scrutiny of apprenticeship in eighteenth-century London or Leicester might show worse, not better conditions.

Just as cotton textiles are considered the bellwether of the industrial revolution, the handloom weaver is seen as its first casualty. The victims of technology labored increasing hours for a decreasing return. No contemporary minimized the problem, as repeated investigations by Parliament and royal commissions will testify. But the early Victorian had no answer beyond permitting the free play of market economy while offering emigration and education as "auxiliary measures." The royal commissioners, like the Reverend Thomas Robert Malthus who offered "moral restraint" as an escape clause for society, held out little hope for acceptance.

The commissioners were proven right by results in the most basic sense. Market economy, the simple working of the law of supply and demand, finally resolved the problem in spite of blue books, charity, and chartism. The early and mid-Victorians had the power but not the conviction to reorder and reorganize their society. Assistant Commissioner Fletcher suggests some of the reasons why in this portion of his report. Although he discusses the crucial issues of wages and productivity in considerable detail, his findings focus on "morality."

Recommended Reading

The debate is almost endless. In addition to the studies cited in the General Bibliography for this section, A. J. Taylor summarizes the arguments in "Progress and Poverty in Britain, 1780–1850: A Reappraisal," *History*, new series, XLV (1960), 16–31; or there is the more recent summary by P. Deane in *The First Industrial Revolution* (Cambridge: 1965), chap. xv. For the weavers, see D. Bythell, *The Handloom Weavers* (London: 1969).

J. FLETCHER, ESQ.
MORAL CONDITION OF THE RIBBON WEAVERS

. . . The following picture of their former grossness may shock the imagination, and impress a belief that all the features portrayed are peculiar to Coventry. But it should be borne in mind that the notions and habits of every uncultivated people are gross, and, when, they are brought together in masses, also vicious; for a lower state of intelligence will suffice for the self-government of men labouring almost in solitude about the fields, and pillowed nightly by fatigue, than is demanded to meet the mutual incitements, and the facilities for vicious indulgence, incident to every manufacturing community.

The changes which have taken place in the manners and habits of the class of employers at Coventry, during the present century, were these the subject of immediate investigation, would present a series of very curious pictures, to which a good index is afforded by the historical succession of buildings in its ancient streets. Forty years ago, the mass of the labouring population of this city, and of the weaving district to the north of it (composed chiefly of weavers, colliers, and farm servants), undisturbed by schools or by sectarianism, remained in a state of barbarism, as gross as was consistent with the perpetuation of the race; the men without intelligence and without religion, working badly at irregular hours, and

Source: From "Reports from Assistant Commissioners on the Hand-Loom Weavers, Midland District," *Parliamentary Papers*, 1840, vol. XXIV, pp. 71–75.

sotting in dirt and disorder nearly the rest of their time, including the whole of Sunday. But intelligence has penetrated even this mass of ignorance and vice; being aided in its diffusion beyond the middle classes by the Sunday-schools, which here came into operation towards the close of the last century, and were seconded, about 1810, by the establishment of rival Lancasterian and National day-schools. The first object of these spontaneous labours to improve the moral condition of the labouring poor, was naturally to implant in their minds the principles of Christianity. The doctrines instilled were not always in accordance with the canons of the Established Church; and hence the rivalry, here, as elsewhere in England, which has made the great purpose of instruction, to develop every faculty, and guide its application by a heart-stirring religion and a healthy morality, be too often overlooked for the inculcation of mere words, to the abasement rather than to the improvement of the character. Circumstances peculiar to our country have thus withheld it from the more enlightened course pursued in Protestant Christendom generally, where religion, is inculcated rather as the guide of secular knowledge than as a substitute for it; and these influences are still in full action, thwarting every attempt to advance our moral cultivation in the same ratio as the development of our physical resources. Still considerable advance has been made, and the population engaged in the ribbon weaving now divides itself morally into two distinct portions;—that engaged in the engine-weaving in the city and suburbs, among which superior habits and intelligence prevail; and the dispersed and ignorant inhabitants of the rural parishes, employed chiefly in the single-hand trade, and retaining most of their original barbarism with an accession of vice.

The present mayor of Coventry thus describes the manners and habits of the journeymen weavers of the city in his youth:—

"The whole trade of journeymen subsisted on the community for two months in the year at least. They were the chief recipients of the numerous charities of the city, and the poor's rates were much resorted to; for when out of work, they had only these resources, and running into debt with the huckster. They were room-keepers: they rented one or two rooms. Some of the two months' relief which they borrowed, they afterwards worked out; but they were always in arrear.

"There were no schools but the charity (endowed) schools, and day-schools, at about 6*d*. per week, to which the undertakers sent their children; but the journeymen, themselves ignorant, knew not the advantages of instruction for their children, and never thought about getting it for them. Generally speaking, they had no personal pride, and were not in a condition to appear in public on Sunday. They would make themselves rather smarter at the club feast-day, once or twice a-year, but generally they were not cleaned on the Sunday, which is a very good test as to the rest of their habits.

"Nearly all were in some club. The club was for mutual maintenance during illness, and for funerals on the death of a member or of his wife. The subscriptions were generally one shilling fortnightly on Monday, and the payments out varied according to the state of the funds. On the club-nights, the rule was to spend 4*d*. in drink. There were no other savings made, except by some very few journeymen. It was most difficult to encounter the shop habits. There was no habit of saving when they had employment against the time when they had not. The man gave what he thought right to the wife on Saturday night, with which she must get through the week as she could. He spent the rest in drink. The houses had little furniture, and that of the coarsest sort. The breakfast was generally of milk. A dinner generally a bit of meat or bacon, and potatoes. Tea was commonly brought to the men at the shop by the wife or one of the children.

"The improvement which has since taken place has been stimulated by the example of those who have prospered by regulating their conduct. The Sunday-schools were the first institutions by which those who were easier in circumstances and better informed, first showed an interest in the intellectual improvement of the lower and more ignorant. This was followed up by the establishment of schools on the plans of Lancaster and Bell. Sunday-schools had existed previous to 1800, and the children could not be unfeeling to the solicitude shown for their improvement. The Lancasterian school was established about 1810; the national school came soon after. These opened the way for active minds, and the improvement of the general mass has ensued. Indeed vice, there can be no doubt, reigned jointly with ignorance, and their sway was co-extensive. There were formerly no means of adult improvement collectively whatever, and ninety-nine out of every hundred never thought of books. The more provident hands were generally those working at home. The home work greatly conduces to moral conduct, for the good influence of the woman is lost in the shop."

This will be recognized as a faithful picture of labourer's life half a century ago, elsewhere than at Coventry. The description here given of the former habits of the men, certainly gives but a mean opinion of the vaunted morality resulting from the old apprentice-ship system, as compared with the half-pay apprenticeship, except that there appears to have been a less early emancipation of the young people from bonds which restrained them from thoughtless marriages, at the same time that they sought the excitement of more active though ruder sports than they now do. The relations of the boy with the family of his master, or that of his parents, are not, by this half-pay system left in so healthy, although perhaps a less rude state. His connexion with that of his master is in fact no more than that of any journeyman, while his receipt of wages makes him feel himself little other than a lodger in the house of his parents. A boy would feel it a degradation to be denied the receipt of his own apprentice wages, which in some instances would now be paid to his parents, but that other apprentices receive theirs directly; and the parents of some of the apprentices are of charac-ter so bad, that it is right they should do so. The local magistrates have a strong feeling against the system of half-pay apprenticeship, which, says one of the factory proprietors, compels him to take a boy before them when refractory, or his overlooker would be punished for castigating him, instead of which the boy is subjected to the contamination of a prison.

But of all the industrial circumstances affecting the moral habits of the men, none can have so much influence as those which result from their working dispersedly at their own homes, or in company at a shop or factory. It is the prevalence of the latter system, counteracting the domestic apprenticeship, to which we ought properly to attribute any excess of disorders that formerly pre-vailed, beyond those incident to a state of barbarous ignorance among every people. The picture above given of the former state of the trade certainly produces features obnoxious to the very com-plaints now loudly urged against the increasing factory system, which is a reverting to the old shop system on a larger scale; "the feeling of good-fellowship leading to drinking, and absence from home, and its decencies. To escape being flouted, the man must take part in the habits of the mass among whom he is thrown, and in this mass the general level is low; while the weaver at home can pursue his own course, and has no restrictions on self-improvement. The factory system is the great propagator of '*socialism.*' The men have no centre for their habits in a home, and in the power of forming an individual character." One of the most respectable factory masters says, "Some of our men bring their wives to pick up for them; and the influence of the wife is good, binding the man to work, and binding him to decency; but the influence of the factory generally is decidedly bad, especially upon the the young unmarried men and women."

An officer of the directors of the poor "thinks that the dissolute portion of the Coventry city weavers, are not more than one-sixth, if so much, and these are chiefly of the journeyman's journeyman class. This dissolute portion never save a farthing in any shape, although they may be earning good wages, as at Mr. Day's factory. There are at present very few of any sort of weavers on the rates; but the moment there is a slackness of trade, these come on, and very few others do. The better class of weavers are decent, well-doing people, with habits generally good. They are not drinkers in the bad sense of the term, though to take a couple of glasses of ale and a pipe, costing altogether 5d., in the smoking-room of a public-house, is a common habit with them. Their modes of saving are in the purchase of looms, and in benefit clubs at public-houses. Their providence is generally limited to this, and they save in no other shape. The homes of the weavers of this class are generally cleanly, and many of them have wives who were born in the country, and are larger in person and cleanlier in habits than the town girls: they are better managers. Many weavers' wives are making good earnings at weaving, winding, and warping; and the women have their benefit clubs as well as the men, held like theirs at the public-houses, where they are exposed to the like temptations, against which their frailty is not proof. Their providence is thus limited, and in good times they are not frugal, as the poultry market bears testimony. But their expenditure on the whole is better directed, and they maintain themselves in a state of far higher decency than is seen in other weaving districts. . . . It is generally the wives of dissolute weavers who themselves are dissolute, the rest are, for the most part, tidy and well-conducted."

This evidence as to the present habits of the city weavers was borne out by my own observation in making the circuit of different parts of the town. In several streets I went into the habitations of every weaver; and the houses of the first hand journeymen presented a neatness and cleanliness which could not well be surpassed. No one who had seen the squalor of Spitalfields or Macclesfield, but must have felt the liveliest gratification at witnessing this superiority of habits. But I was equally struck with the excessive number of vagabonds to be found at evening in the taprooms of the low public-houses; in person, in dress, and in occupations appearing as though they belonged to the metropolitan fraternity of St. Giles's, as I cannot doubt that some did. These are chiefly the men above alluded to, who "enjoy only strolling and sotting, and, if they have families, leave the poor women to struggle through with them as they can." The general habits with regard to diligence will be detailed minutely in describing the hours of work. Industry is the rule, and idleness the exception.

Dram-drinking has increased, but ale is the old-accustomed beverage. The amount of crime in the city is not large. The greater number of commitments are of young delinquents, for petty offenses of various kinds, chiefly larcenies committed by bad apprentices, or apprentices abandoned by their masters. The young people from 14 to 18, both weavers and watchmakers, are many of them very disorderly, and resort to the beer-houses for card-playing, expecially the half-pay apprentices. There are also gangs who make some part of their subsistence by depredations.

It is remarkable that while the benefit clubs are exceedingly numerous, and not fewer than twenty are in contract with the self-supporting dispensary for attendance on their members, there are not more than 100 weavers depositors in the Savings' Bank. This is but a modern institution, and the weavers have certainly to some extent distrusted it. Some were apprehensive that they should never get their money back again; while others were fearful that if the manufacturers, who were on the Committee, should be aware that they were able to make savings, their wages would be reduced. The clerk to the bank "is confident that this feeling has existed, but thinks it is gradually wearing away. Last Monday the deposits were greater than ever has before been known; upwards of 400*l*. being brought in on that day. The proportion of weavers is increasing, but it is yet only about one-forth of the whole number, and of these at least half are unmarried females." Weavers, watchmakers, and dyers, are, however, the principal subscribers to the self-supporting dispensary, hereafter noticed.

There is inevitably a considerable want of economy and management in the expenditure of their earnings, owing to occupation in the trade preventing the women from acquiring a proper domestic education. The women are more than usually fond of dress, and the well-conducted men have notions of appearance which sometimes show themselves very characteristically. Of want of integrity there was no complaint.

The character of the city weavers as to "diligence, providence, frugality, honesty, and temperance," these few data will sufficiently indicate; and it may be well to notice the influences now acting upon this character in adults. There are in the city four churches and eleven other places of worship; four for Independents, two for Baptists, one for Wesleyan, and one for Primitive Methodists, one for Unitarians, one for the Society of Friends, and one for Roman Catholics. But the number is very great of those who go to no place of worship. Tract distributors, going round during the time of worship to give tracts to those who were staying at home, have found a large proportion of the houses in which none of the family were gone to worship. In some instances these were respectable people; but the great body were those who were too indolent and insensible to clean themselves to go. But the Sunday schools are diminishing the latter class, although many who are instructed in them abandon public worship; for, if all who were brought up in them continued their attendance, the existing places of worship would not be large enough as they now amply are.

Among the more active-minded young men the strange theoretical confusion of all the relations of civil life, commonly called "*socialism*," with its community of property and exchange of women, has great sway; but the older men have generally no intellectual excitement whatever. The occupation of the ribbon weaver, especially if he have good silk, leaves his mind at liberty to ruminate; and the loom is here frequently called "the weaver's study." One of the weavers told me that when he has to prepare himself for a speech, he never can do it half so well as in the loom. The intelligence and dexterity of the leaders of the men is, in fact, very remarkable; partly arising from their long practice politically at elections. And I believe the great body of them to be sensitively awake to the seizure of any means of bettering their condition, which could be pointed out to them, except that of self-cultivation, for which the grown up men have for the most part little means of opportunity and less taste. As a key to self-control, to self-respect, and to the respect of others, some of the younger leaders of the men are, however, awakening to its importance to themselves as individuals, and to the class in whose fate they share.

There is a book society connected with the chapels of Cow Lane and Vicar Lane; the library composed chiefly of religious, biographical, and historical works, and books of voyages, travels, and missions; and several booksellers' shops let out, at 2d. per volume, novels and other works which are extensively read by the weavers. But the principal source of useful intelligence is a Mechanics' Institution, to which the entrance fee is 1s., and the subscription 2s.6d. per quarter; terms of which the men with families complain, as being too dear, at the same time that they feel little inclination to make the institution their evening resort. But there are a great many of the young weavers in it, who benefit greatly by the books and lectures, and by the writing, arithmetic, geometry, grammar, and geography classes. Perhaps one-forth of the members are weavers. Somewhat analogous to this institution (for in Coventry nearly all institutions go in pairs, because of its civil and religious parties), there is a Religious and Useful Knowledge Society, having a library of books carefully selected by a Committee almost wholly Episcopalian, and the subscription to which is only 1s. per quarter, without any admission fee.

The Mechanics' Institution was founded in 1828, and at first was of very limited extent and means, but it has now for several years possessed a commodious building in Hertford Street; comprising a library, museum, reading room, four class rooms, a laboratory, and a lecture room, or theatre, 500 or 600 persons, heated by steam, and lighted with gas; the whole erected at an expense of 1700l. "The object of the institution is the instruction of the mechanic and artisan in the principles of those arts more immediately connected with their particular occupations, and the communication of such useful and appropriate knowledge as may assist them in obtaining an honest livelihood, and render them more intelligent and valuable members of society." The library now contains about 2000 volumes, and the tenth annual report, made in October, 1838, thus describes the more recent proceedings:—

> In adverting to the subject of the classes, the Committee have much satisfaction in stating that they have engaged, as a paid teacher, in writing, arithmetic, geometry, and English grammar, a person who has long been accustomed to education, and whose

acquirements, as well as mode of instruction, hold out the promise of great good. The music class is still under efficient superintendence, and will give occasional performances before the members. At the same time they are enabled to state that a plan for the better formation and regulation of the classes has long been in contemplation, and is now, they are happy to say, carried into effect. That more has not been done in this department during the past year is to be attributed not to any insensibility of the Committee to its value, but rather to the deep sense which they entertain of its importance, which has led them to prefer delay to the hurried and imperfect construction of the classes, and therefore to their probable failure.

The Committee beg to call attention to a new feature in the institution—the formation of a museum; and, in referring to the geological and entomological departments, they have to acknowledge, in the former, some valuable contributions from Messrs. Whittem, Troughton, Muddiman, and Davis; in the latter, a large and valuable collection of British insects, from Mr. W. H. Mercer. Miscellaneous contributions have also been received from Messrs. Nankivell, Stephens, Jenkins, and Bicknell.

There is but one branch of the institution remaining which calls for particular attention, that is the reading room. The Committee feel great pleasure in stating that the arrangements adopted for its better regulation have exceeded their most sanguine expectations, and that they are now enabled to offer to the mechanic the comforts of a commodious room, where, after the labours of the day, he may find, in the midst of a well-ordered and respectable society, the blessings either of instruction or relaxation.

It is worthy of notice, as showing the character of some of the rising intelligence, that some sixty or seventy "socialists" have seceded from the institution, and formed themselves into a separate establishment, because the members generally would not submit to the disturbance of the discussions of which they made the institutions the theatre. A prospectus has been issued of an Education Society, to form the groundwork of a Statistical Society. . . .

12. Exploitation: Women and Children in the Mines

THE INDUSTRIAL revolution has a deservedly bad name with historians for "dehumanizing" society, but the most pathological conditions in the early Victorian years were to be found, not in industry, but in other, traditional occupations—farm labor, handloom weaving, and coal mining, to mention but three. Industrialization generated many new problems, but it also created new opportunities. The factory working force was not conscripted. Young men and women went to urban industries because they offered new options and an escape from the bleak routine and limited choices of rural life—for the same reason, in fact, that adventurous spirits had fled to the city since the Dark Ages. Much is made of the fact that traditional agrarian society, while it oppressed and exploited labor, tended to have a floor through which the worker did not sink. But even William Cobbett, that romantic exponent of rural nostalgia, admitted that country life was no longer the good life.

Industrial society was in disarray for the first four decades of the century. It was not more brutal than the past, but it was different. Manufacturers presumed that output was a direct function of hours worked. Save for an interest in preserving their skilled labor and supervisory personnel, most mill owners were hard to convince that workers responded to good treatment. Wildly fluctuating prices, unpredictable markets, and economic uncertainty aggravated the problems among marginal producers who were most vulnerable to the vagaries of the market. The landed classes who dominated the political life of the nation neither would nor could come to grips with the social problem.

Efforts had been made to regularize conditions of industrial competition since the beginning of the century. The first Factory Act of 1802 had been passed explicitly to prevent competitive deterioration in the cotton industry. Subsequent legislation in 1819, 1825, and 1831 sought to prohibit the employment of young children in mills and regulate some of the grosser abuses in factories, but the acts lacked effective sanctions. Not until 1833, with the creation of government factory inspection, did Britain have a regulatory arm for the control of industrial abuse and the necessary flow of information to take action. By the time Victoria became queen, the principle of government regulation had been established. The debate was merely about extent.

There still remained the undeniable and multiplying degradation in older industries and crafts. Pathological abuses, which shook the early Victorian in ways from which he never fully recovered, came to public attention from the coal mines. Mining, an English occupation in the days of the Phoenicians, was not produced by the industrial revolution. The age of iron and steam made coal far more important. Coal mining, for reasons too complex to discuss here, had always been a social as well as an economic problem. Coal was particularly sensitive to fluctuations in demand. London consumed one-quarter of the output in the first third of the century. A mild season meant loss of profits, jobs, wages. The original problem was not technological. Coal deposits do not happen to coincide with real-estate holdings. All of the old abuses of manpower remained, but with the coming of the nineteenth century they became, if anything, more acute. Mine owners generally neither cared about nor felt any responsibility for their workers, and the workers themselves developed and perpetuated, with the butty and subcontract system, the worst of industrial abuses.

The shocking treatment of women and children outstripped human imagination, as this testimony shows. Lord Shaftesbury's commission improved upon the stark words by embellishing the pages with wood-cuts graphically displaying the worst abuses and dangers. No effort was made to amend these degrading conditions. Women and children were removed from work below ground by the Mines and Collieries Act of 1842. The mine owners and operators could not have resisted the demand for an immediate end to this situation, and they wept few tears at seeing the termination of basically uneconomic employment. The best owners, as the testimony indicates, had already begun clearing women and children out of the pits. Their employment was, in an uncomfortable number of instances, defended principally by husbands and fathers for their own convenience.

The abuse and exploitation of human resources did not begin with the industrialization of Britain, nor did it end there. It was industrial, not preindustrial, society that rooted the abuses out, pilloried and amended them. The social conscience is a modern innovation. And again, the worst conditions prevailed, not in new but in old industries and occupations. There was much to be done to improve the lot of man; and Victorians, from the beginning, bent much of their energy to it.

Recommended Reading

For the broad problem of the human impact of industrialization and relative social condition, see the general bibliography for this section. The pessimistic view is currently eloquently sustained by Eric Hobsbawm, whose latest offering on the broad subject is *Industry and Empire* (London: 1968). The soundest new approach seems to me to be that of J. A. Banks, most recently in "Population Change and the Victorian City," *Victorian Studies*, XI (1968), 277–289. Most of the better literature on miners is principally concerned with the later period. Two useful studies on the struggle for factory acts are J. T. Ward, *The Factory Movement, 1830–1855* (London: 1962), and M. W. Thomas, *The Early Factory Legislation* (London: 1948). The most recent study of Shaftesbury is G. F. A. Best, *Shaftesbury* (London: 1964).

SHAFTESBURY COMMISSION, EMPLOYMENT OF GIRLS AND WOMEN IN COAL MINES

1. DISTRICT IN WHICH GIRLS AND WOMEN ARE EMPLOYED UNDERGROUND

In England, exclusive of Wales, it is only in some of the colliery districts of Yorkshire and Lancashire that female Children of

Source: From "First Report of the Children's Employment Commission, Mines," *Parliamentary Papers*, 1842, vol. XV, pp. 24–27, 31–32, 34, 255–261.

tender age and young and adult women are allowed to descend into the coal mines and regularly to perform the same kinds of underground work, and to work for the same number of hours, as boys and men; but in the East of Scotland their employment in the pits is general; and in South Wales it is not uncommon.

West Riding of Yorkshire: Southern Part—In many of the collieries in this district, as far as relates to the underground employment, there is no distinction of sex, but the labour is distributed indifferently among both sexes, excepting that it is comparatively rare for the women to hew or get the coals, although there are numerous instances in which they regularly perform even this work. In great numbers of the coal-pits in this district the men work in a state of perfect nakedness, and are in this state assisted in their labour by females of all ages, from girls of six years old to women of twenty-one, these females being themselves quite naked down to the waist.

"Girls," says the Sub-Commissioner, "regularly perform all the various offices of trapping, hurrying, filling, riddling, tipping, and occasionally getting, just as they are performed by boys. One of the most disgusting sights I have ever seen was that of young females, dressed like boys in trousers, crawling on all fours, with belts round their waists and chains passing between their legs, at day pits at Hunshelf Bank, and in many small pits near Holmfrith and New Mills: it exists also in several other places. I visited the Hunshelf Colliery on the 18th of January: it is a day pit; that is, there is no shaft or descent; the gate or entrance is at the side of a bank, and nearly horizontal. The gate was not more than a yard high, and in some places not above 2 feet. When I arrived at the board or workings of the pit I found at one of the side-boards down a narrow passage a girl of fourteen years of age, in boy's clothes, picking down the coal with the regular pick used by the men. She was half sitting half lying at her work, and said she found it tired her very much, and 'of course she didn't like it.' The place where she was at work was not 2 feet high. Further on were men at work lying on their sides and getting. No less than six girls out of 18 men and children are employed in this pit. Whilst I was in the pit the Rev. Mr. Bruce, of Wadsley, and the Rev. Mr. Nelson, of Rotherham, who accompanied me, and remained outside, saw another girl of ten years of age, also dressed in boy's clothes, who was employed in hurrying, and these gentlemen saw her at work.

She was a nice-looking little child, but of course as black as a tinker, and with a little necklace round her throat. In two other pits in the Huddersfield Union I have seen the same sight. In one near New Mills, the chain, passing high up between the legs of two of these girls, had worn large holes in their trousers; and any sight more disgustingly indecent or revolting can scarcely be imagined than these girls at work—no brothel can beat it. On descending Messrs. Hopwood's pit at Barnsley, I found assembled round the fire a group of men, boys, and girls, some of whom were of the age of puberty, the girls as well as the boys stark naked down to the waist, their hair bound up with a tight cap, and trousers supported by their hips. (At Silkstone and at Flockton they work in their shifts and trousers.) Their sex was recognisable only by their breasts, and some little difficulty occasionally arose in pointing out to me which were girls and which were boys, and which caused a good deal of laughing and joking. In the Flockton and Thornhill pits the system is even more indecent; for though the girls are clothed, at least three-fourths of the men for whom they 'hurry' work *stark naked*, or with a flannel waistcoat only, and in this state they assist one another to fill the corves 18 or 20 times a-day: I have seen this done myself frequently." . . .

Evidence to the same effect is given by all classes of witnesses in this district:—

Thomas Dunn, Esq., of the firm of Hounsfield, Wilson, Dunn, and Jeffcock, chief manager, says: "Girls are worked naked down to their waist, the same as men."—Mr. Thomas Peace, of the firm of Webster and Peace, Hunshelf Bank Coal-Works, says: "There are as many girls as boys employed about here." —Mr. Charles Locke, coal-master and agent at Snafethrope, near Wakefield: "Girls make better hurriers than boys; the boys are often stripped all but a shirt." . . . —Mr. William Bowden, underground steward to Messrs. Hounsfield, Dunn, and Co., at the Soaphouse Colliery, Sheffield: "In Silkstone Pits, believes women and girls work dressed as men, and often naked down to the waist, just the same as men and boys. Decency is disregarded." —Mr. William Hopwood, agent of Barnsley New Colliery: "In most of the pits round Barnsley girls are employed in trapping and in hurrying: they do the same work as the boys." . . . —William Pickard, general steward to Sir John Lister Lister Kaye's Collieries: "I have known a married woman hurrying for a man who worked stark naked, and not any kin to her."

Edward Newman, Esq., solicitor: "I have been an inhabitant of

Barnsley for eighteen years, and been in the constant habit of seeing the colliers and children passing to and from their work. At
Silkstone there are a great many girls who work in the pits, and I
have seen them washing themselves naked much below the waist
as I passed their doors, and whilst they are doing this they will be
talking and chatting with any men who happen to be there with
the utmost unconcern; and men, young and old, would be washing
in the same place at the same time. They dress so well after their
work, and on Sundays, that it is impossible to recognise them. They
wear earrings even whilst they work, and I have seen them with
them nearly two inches long. There is a great deal of slang and loud
talk between the lads and girls as they pass along the streets; and I
conceive that they would behave far more decorously were it not
for the dress and the disguise it affords. I have never heard similar
language pass between men and girls respectably dressed in Barnsley. Their dress, when they come out of the pit, is a kind of skull-
cap which hides all the hair, trousers without stockings, and thick
wooden clogs; their waists are covered." . . .

. . . Rebecca Hough, aged fourteen, examined whilst getting in
the same pit: "I am a regular hurrier; I am used to help the getter.
I often do it three or four times a-week. I help to fill and riddle,
and then I hurry the corves down to the Bullstake. I find the hurrying the hardest work. It is because I don't do much at getting that
it tires me less." —Margaret Westwood, aged fourteen and a half,
examined whilst hurrying and eating in Messrs. Stanfield's and
Briggs's Emryod Pit, Flockton: "I hurry for Charles Littlewood.
I am let to him. He is no kin to me; he works stark naked; he has
no waistcoat on, nor nothing." . . . —Ebenezer Healey, aged thirteen: "There are girls that hurry in the same way, with belt and
chain. Our breeches are often torn between the legs with the chain.
The girls' breeches are torn as often as ours; they are torn many a
time, and when they are going along we can see them all between
the legs naked; I have often; and that girl, Mary Holmes, was so
to-day; she denies it, but it is true for all that." . . .

Lancashire and Cheshire—In the greater portion of the Lancashire coal fields it is the general custom of girls and women to be
employed in the ordinary work of the mines; and an unusually
large proportion appear to be so employed in the mines about
Wigan, Blackrod, Worsley, Hulton, Clifton, Outwood, Bolton,
Lure, St. Helen's, and Prescot.

Henry Eaton, Ringley Bridge, Bolton, surveyor of coal mines:
"I have been sixteen years and upwards connected with coal-mines,
and I have been in almost all the pits in the neighbourhood of Bolton, Bury, Ratcliff, Lure, and Rochdale. There are women in all

the pits in those neighbourhoods. I cannot say in which pits there are the most employed; they are employed in all; they are used as drawers." John Millington, superintendent of the collieries of Mr. Ashton at Hyde: "They [the women, whilst at work] wear a pair of drawers which come down nearly to the knees, and some women a small handkerchief about their necks; but I have seen many a one with her breasts hanging out. The girls are not a bit ashamed amongst their own pit set; it is the same as if they were one family." —Mr. Miller, underlooker at Mr. Woodley's, near Staley-bridge, states that "one reason why women are used so frequently as drawers in the coal-pits is, that a girl of 20 will work for 2s. a-day or less, and a man of that age would want 3s. 6d.: it makes little difference to the coal-master, he pays the same whoever does the work; some would say he got his coal cheaper, but I am not of that opinion; the only difference is that the collier can spend 1s. to 1s. 6d. more at the alehouse, and very often the woman helps him to spend it. Not one woman in a hundred ever becomes a coal-getter, and that is one of the reasons the men prefer them." —Mr. Joseph Hatherton, underlooker at Messrs. Foster's, Ringley-bridge, states that "He has four children in the pits, two girls and two boys. Comes from the neighbourhood of St. Helen's; many women and children are employed in the pits there—many a hundred; the drawers are all women or children there. The girls go down into the pits as soon as the boys, every bit—at eight or nine years old; mine went into them at that time." . . . —Peter Gaskell, collier, at Mr. Lancaster's, near Worsley: "Prefers women to boys as drawers; they are better to manage, and keep the time better; they will fight and shriek and do everything but let anybody pass them; and they never get to be coal-getters, that is another good thing." —Betty Harris, aged thirty-seven, drawer in a coal-pit, Little Bolton: "I have a belt round my waist, and a chain passing between my legs, and I go on my hands and feet. The road is very steep, and we have to hold by a rope, and, when there is no rope, by anything we can catch hold of. There are six women and about six boys and girls in the pit I work in: it is very hard work for a woman. The pit is very wet where I work, and the water comes over our clog-tops always, and I have seen it up to my thighs: it rains in at the roof terribly; my clothes are wet through almost all day long. I never was ill in my life but when I was lying-in. My cousin looks after my children in the day-time. I am very tired when I get home at night; I fall asleep sometimes before I get washed. I am not so strong as I was, and cannot stand my work so well as I used to do. I have drawn till I have had the skin off me; the belt and chain is worse when we are in the family way. My feller [husband] has beaten me many a time for not being ready. I were not used to it at first, and he had little patience: I have known many a man beat his drawer." —Mary Glover, aged thirty-eight, at Messrs. Foster's, Ringley-bridge: "I went into a coal-pit when I was seven years old, and began by being a drawer. I never worked much in the pit when I was in the family way, but since I gave up having children I have begun again a bit. I wear a shift and a pair of trousers when at work. I always will have a good pair of trousers. I have had many a two-pence given me by the boatmen on the canal to show my breeches. I never saw women work naked, but I have seen men work without breeches in the neighbourhood of Bolton. I remember seeing a man who worked stark naked."

William Cooper, aged seven years, thrutcher, at Almond's: "There are about twenty wenches, drawers, in the pit I work in. They are nigh naked; they wear trousers; they have no other clothes except loose shifts." —Robert Hunt, underlooker to Messrs. Foster, Outwood: "It is quite true that women work in the pits when they are in the family way. My last wife worked in a pit from ten years old; and once she worked all day in the pits, and was put to bed at night. That woman you saw in the pit was in the family way [alluding to a person I had seen in the pit]. I cannot say that my wife's health suffered by her working in the pits; she worked in the pits till she was 30. She had four children; two were born alive, but they died afterwards, and two were still-born." William Royle, engineer at Mr. Lancaster's, Patricroft: "His wife was in the family way while she was working in the pits: she has had one child, but it is dead. She had a fall in the pits; she was hooking on to her tub, and she missed her hold and fell backwards, and the doctors said that it was that which had hurt her; she had a very bad time." —Betty Harris, drawer in a coal-pit, Little Bolton: "I worked at drawing when I was in the family way. I know a woman who has gone home and washed herself, taken to her bed, been delivered of a child, and gone to work again under the week." —Betty Wardle: "I have worked in a pit since I was six years old. I have had four children, two of them were born while I worked in the pits. I worked in the pits whilst I was in the family way. I had a child born in the pits, and I brought it up the pit-shaft in my skirt; it was born the day after I were married—that makes me to know." . . .

2. MORAL EFFECTS OF THE EMPLOYMENT OF GIRLS AND WOMEN UNDERGROUND

Before quitting the subject of the employment of girls and women in the pits, we should fail in our duty if we did not notice more particularly, as applying to the districts in which women and girls are employed, the evidence of the serious moral injury to which such employment exposes them. All classes of witnesses bear the strongest testimony to the immoral effects of this practice.

West Riding of Yorkshire: Southern Part—The following may serve as examples of the evidence given on this subject by the several classes of witnesses in this district.—

Matthew Lindley, collier, Day and Twibell's, Barnsley: "I wish the Government would expel all girls and females from mines. I can give proof that they are very immoral, and I am certain that the girls are worse than the men in point of morals, and use far more indecent language. It unbecomes them in every way; there is not one in ten of them that know how to cut a shirt out or make one, and they learn neither to knit nor sew. I have known myself of a case where a married man and a girl who hurried for him had sexual intercourse often in the bank where he worked." —Mr. George Armitage, aged thirty-six years, Hoyland: "I hardly know how to reprobate the practice sufficiently of girls working in pits; nothing can be worse. I have no doubt that debauchery is carried on, for which there is every opportunity; for the girls go constantly, when hurrying, to the men, who work often alone in the bank-faces apart from every one. I think it scarcely possible for girls to remain modest who are in pits, regularly mixing with such company, and hearing such language as they do. I dare venture to say that many of the wives who come from pits know nothing of sewing or any household duty, such as women ought to know—they lose all disposition to learn such things; they are rendered unfit for learning them also by being overworked, and not being trained to the habit of it. I have worked in pits for above ten years, where girls were constantly employed, and I can safely say it is an abominable system. I think that girls ought to be prevented from going into pits, whatever may be the consequence; the effect of preventing them could not be worse than that of letting them be in." —John Cawthra, collier, Messrs. Wilson's Pit: "I think it is not a good system bringing girls into pits; they get bold. It tends to make the girls have bastards very much in some pits; I know, for instance, at Flockton it leads to immoral conduct." —John Simpkin, collier, Drighlington: "I have worked a great deal where girls were employed in pits. I have had children by them myself, and have frequently had connexion with them in the pits. I am sure that this is the case especially in pits about Lancashire." . . .

At a meeting of above 350 working colliers from the surrounding district, held in the Courthouse, Barnsley, before the Sub-Commissioner, among others the following resolution was passed:—"That the employment of girls in pits is highly injurious to their morals, that it is not proper work for females, and that it is a scandalous practice." (Carried with five dissentients only.) . . .

Michael Thomas Sadler, Esq., surgeon, Barnsley: "I strongly

disapprove of females being in pits; the female character is totally destroyed by it; their habits and feelings are altogether different; they can neither discharge the duties of wives nor mothers. I see the greatest differences in the homes of those colliers whose wives do not go into the pits in cleanliness and good management. It is a brutalizing practice for women to be in collieries; the effect on their morals is very bad; it would be advisable to prevent females from going into pits." . . . —Rev. Oliver Levey Collins, Incumbent of Ossett: "There is a good deal of drunkenness and sensuality. Bastardy is sadly too common; they look on it as a misfortune, and not as a crime." . . . —John Thorneley, Esq., one of her Majesty's justices of the peace for the county of York: "I consider it to be a most awfully demoralising practice. The youth of both sexes work often in a half-naked state, and the passions are excited before they arrive at puberty. Sexual intercourse decidedly frequently occurs in consequence. Cases of bastardy frequently also occur; and I am decidedly of opinion that women brought up in this way lay aside all modesty, and scarcely know what it is but by name. I sincerely trust that before I die I shall have the satisfaction of seeing it prevented and entirely done away with." . . .

Lancashire—Similar effects are stated to result from the employment of girls and women in the coal mines of this district. The evidence, says the Sub-Commissioner [J. L. Kennedy], all tends to the following conclusions:—"First. That the employment itself is, from its peculiar severity, unsuited to the physical condition of females, and especially to those of them who are mothers.—Secondly. That, from the nature of the work below ground, it tends more or less to demoralise and brutalise the females employed.—Thirdly. That their employment below ground prevents their attention to the performance of domestic duties, as diminishing their competency for the proper care and training of their children.—And Fourthly. That for these pernicious effects there appear to be no countervailing advantages to the people employed, or to the public.

"There is a growing feeling throughout this district generally against the employment of females in the mines. The trustees of the late Duke of Bridgewater have now excluded married women from the mines belonging to that trust, and girls are not now allowed to enter the pits under twelve years of age. Mr. Peace, the agent for Lord Balcarras, near Wigan, stated to me that his lordship was anxious to discontinue the employment of females in his collieries in the neighbourhood of Haigh, Aspul, and Blackrod; but that the system had been carried on for so many years, and there were so many females employed in them, that it would be impossible to dispense with them on a sudden. Mr. Hilton, near Wigan, stated to me that he should be glad to discontinue the employment of females in his mines, but that it had always been a custom for the men to find their own drawers, and that the masters did not interfere. He mentioned to me that the day before I visited the colliery there had been a disturbance arising from a collier having neglected his wife to 'take up' with a young girl who drew for him in the pits. Violent changes are always to be avoided, but I think it will appear that a stand should be made against this pernicious system." . . .

From the whole of the Evidence which has been collected, and of which we have thus endeavoured to give a digest, we find,—

In regard to Coal Mines—

1. That instances occur in which Children are taken into these mines to work as early as four years of age, sometimes at five, and between five and six, not unfrequently between six and seven, and often from seven to eight, while from eight to nine is the ordinary age at which employment in these mines commences.

2. That a very large proportion of the persons employed in carrying on the work of these mines is under thirteen years of age; and a still larger proportion between thirteen and eighteen.

3. That in several districts female Children begin to work in these mines at the same early ages as the males.

4. That the great body of the Children and Young Persons employed in these mines are of the families of the adult workpeople engaged in the pits, or belong to the poorest population in the neighbourhood, and are hired and paid in some districts by the workpeople, but in others by the proprietors or contractors.

5. That there are in some districts also a small number of parish apprentices, who are bound to serve their masters until twenty-one years of age, in an employment in which there is nothing deserving the name of skill to be acquired, under circumstances of frequent ill-treatment, and under the oppressive condition that they shall receive only food and clothing, while their free companions may be obtaining a man's wages.

6. That in many instances much that skill and capital can effect to render the place of work unoppressive, healthy, and safe, is done, often with complete success, as far as regards the healthfulness and comfort of the mines; but that to render them perfectly safe does not appear to be practicable by any means yet known; while in great numbers of instances their condition in regard both to ventilation and drainage is lamentably defective.

7. That the nature of the employment which is assigned to the youngest Children, generally that of "trapping," requires that they should be in the pit as soon as the work of the day commences, and, according to the present system, that they should not leave the pit before the work of the day is at an end.

8. That although this employment scarcely deserves the name of labour, yet, as the Children engaged in it are commonly excluded from light and are always without companions, it would, were it not for the passing and repassing of the coal carriages, amount to solitary confinement of the worst order.

9. That in those districts in which the seams of coal are so thick that horses go direct to the workings, or in which the side passages from the workings to the horseways are not of any great length, the lights in the main ways render the situation of these Children comparatively less cheerless, dull, and stupifying; but that in some districts they remain in solitude and darkness during the whole time they are in the pit, and, according to their own account, many of them never see the light of day for weeks together during the greater part of the winter season, excepting on those days in the week when work is not going on, and on the Sundays.

10. That at different ages, from six years old and upwards, the hard work of pushing and dragging the carriages of coal from the workings to the main ways, or to the foot of the shaft, begins; a labour which all classes of witnesses concur in stating requires the unremitting exertion of all the physical power which the young workers possess.

11. That, in the districts in which females are taken down into the coal mines, both sexes are employed together in precisely the same kind of labour, and work for the same number of hours; that the girls and boys, and the young men and young women, and even married women and women with child, commonly work almost naked, and the men, in many mines, quite naked; and that all classes

of witnesses bear testimony to the demoralizing influence of the employment of females underground.

12. That, in the East of Scotland, a much larger proportion of Children and Young Persons are employed in these mines than in other districts, many of whom are girls; and that the chief part of their labour consists in carrying the coals on their backs up steep ladders.

13. That when the workpeople are in full employment, the regular hours of work for Children and Young Persons are rarely less than eleven; more often they are twelve; in some districts they are thirteen; and in one district they are generally fourteen and upwards.

14. That in the great majority of these mines night-work is a part of the ordinary system of labour, more or less regularly carried on according to the demand for coals, and one which the whole body of evidence shows to act most injuriously both on the physical and moral condition of the workpeople, and more especially on that of the Children and Young Persons.

15. That the labour performed daily for this number of hours, though it cannot strictly be said to be continuous, because, from the nature of the employment, intervals of a few minutes necessarily occur during which the muscles are not in active exertion, is nevertheless generally uninterrupted by any regular time set apart for rest and refreshment; what food is taken in the pit being eaten as best it may while the labour continues.

16. That in well-regulated mines, in which in general the hours of work are the shortest, and in some few of which from half an hour to an hour is regularly set apart for meals, little or no fatigue is complained of after an ordinary day's work, when the Children are ten years old and upwards; but in other instances great complaint is made of the feeling of fatigue, and the workpeople are never without this feeling, often in an extremely painful degree.

17. That in many cases the Children and Young Persons have little cause of complaint in regard to the treatment they receive from the persons in authority in the mine, or from the colliers; but that in general the younger Children are roughly used by their older companions; while in many mines the conduct of the adult colliers to the Children and Young Persons who assist them is harsh and cruel; the persons in authority in these mines, who must be cognizant of this ill-usage, never interfering to prevent it, and some

of them distinctly stating that they do not conceive that they have any right to do so.

18. That, with some exceptions, little interest is taken by the coal owners in the Children and Young Persons employed in their works after the daily labour is over; at least little is done to afford them the means of enjoying innocent amusement and healthful recreation.

19. That in all the coal-fields accidents of a fearful nature are extremely frequent; and that the returns made to our own queries, as well as the registry tables, prove that of the workpeople who perish by such accidents, the proportion of Children and Young Persons sometimes equals and rarely falls much below that of adults.

20. That one of the most frequent causes of accidents in these mines is the want of superintendence by overlookers or otherwise to see to the security of the machinery for letting down and bringing up the work-people, the restriction of the number of persons that ascend and descend at a time, the state of the mine as to the quantity of noxious gas in it, the efficiency of the ventilation, the exactness with which the air-door keepers perform their duty, the places into which it is safe or unsafe to go with a naked lighted candle, and the security of the proppings to uphold the roof, &c.

21. That another frequent cause of fatal accidents in coal mines is the almost universal practice of intrusting the closing of the air-doors to very young Children.

22. That there are many mines in which the most ordinary precautions to guard against accidents are neglected, and in which no money appears to be expended with a view to secure the safety, much less the comfort, of the workpeople.

23. That there are moreover two practices peculiar to a few districts which deserve the highest reprobation, namely,—first, the practice not unknown in some of the smaller mines in Yorkshire, and common in Lancashire, of employing ropes that are unsafe for letting down and drawing up the workpeople; and second, the practice, occasionally met with in Yorkshire, and common in Derbyshire and Lancashire, of employing boys at the steam-engines for letting down and drawing up the workpeople.

24. That in general the Children and Young Persons who work in these mines have sufficient food, and, when above ground, decent and comfortable clothing, their usually high rate of wages

securing to them these advantages; but in many cases, more especially in some parts of Yorkshire, in Derbyshire, in South Gloucestershire, and very generally in the East of Scotland, the food is
poor in quality, and insufficient in quantity; the Children themselves say that they have not enough to eat; and the Sub-Commis-
sioners describe them as covered with rags, and state that the
common excuse they make for confining themselves to their homes
on the Sundays, instead of taking recreation in the fresh air, or
attending a place of worship, is that they have no clothes to go in;
so that in these cases, notwithstanding the intense labour performed by these Children, they do not procure even sufficient food
and raiment: in general, however, the Children who are in this
unhappy case are the Children of idle and dissolute parents, who
spend the hard-earned wages of their offspring at the public house.

25. That the employment in these mines commonly produces in
the first instance an extraordinary degree of muscular development
accompanied by a corresponding degree of muscular strength; this
preternatural development and strength being acquired at the expense of the other organs, as is shown by the general stunted
growth of the body.

26. That partly by the severity of the labour and the long hours
of work, and partly through the unhealthy state of the place of
work, this employment, as at present carried on in all the districts,
deteriorates the physical constitution; in the thin-seam mines, more
especially, the limbs become crippled and the body distorted; and
in general the muscular powers give way, and the workpeople are
incapable of following their occupation, at an earlier period of life
than is common in other branches of industry.

27. That by the same causes the seeds of painful and mortal
diseases are very often sown in childhood and youth; these, slowly
but steadily developing themselves, assume a formidable character
between the ages of thirty and forty; and each generation of this
class of the population is commonly extinct soon after fifty.

When we consider the extent of this branch of industry, the vast
amount of capital embarked in it, and the intimate connexion in
which it stands with almost all the other great branches of trade
and manufacture, as a main source of our national wealth and
greatness, it is satisfactory to have established, by indubitable
evidence, the two following conclusions:—

1. That the coal mine, when properly ventilated and drained, and when both the main and the side passages are of tolerable height, is not only not unhealthy, but, the temperature being moderate and very uniform, it is, considered as a place of work, more salubrious and even agreeable than that in which many kinds of labour are carried on above ground.

2. That the labour in which Children and Young Persons are chiefly employed in coal mines, namely, in pushing the loaded carriages of coals from the workings to the mainways or to the foot of the shaft, so far from being in itself an unhealthy employment, is a description of exercise which, while it greatly develops the muscles of the arms, shoulders, chest, back, and legs, without confining any part of the body in an unnatural and constrained posture, might, but for the abuse of it, afford an equally healthful excitement to all the other organs; the physical injuries produced by it, as it is at present carried on, independently of those which are caused by imperfect ventilation and drainage, being chiefly attributable to the early age at which it commences, and to the length of time during which it is continued.

There is, however, one case of peculiar difficulty, viz. that in which all the subterranean roadways, and especially the side passages, are below a certain height: by the Evidence collected under this Commission, it is proved that there are coal mines at present in work in which these passages are so small, that even the youngest Children cannot move along them without crawling on their hands and feet, in which unnatural and constrained posture they drag the loaded carriages after them; and yet, as it is impossible, by any outlay compatible with a profitable return, to render such coal mines, happily not numerous nor of great extent, fit for human beings to work in, they never will be placed in such a condition, and consequently they never can be worked without inflicting great and irreparable injury on the health of the Children.

In regard to Ironstone Mines, we find—

That on account of the greater weight of the material to be removed, the labour in these mines, which are worked on a system similar to that of the coal mines, is still more severe than that in the latter, and renders the employment of older and stronger Children a matter of absolute necessity; while the ironstone pits are in general less perfectly ventilated and drained than the coal mines, and are, therefore, still more unhealthy, producing the same physical deterioration and the same diseases, but in a more intense degree.

In regard to Blast Furnaces, for reducing the ores of iron, we find—

That the operations connected with these works involve the absolute necessity of night work; that Children and Young Persons invariably work at night with the adults; that the universal practice is for one set of workpeople to work one week during the day, and the same set to work the following week during the night; and that there is, moreover, in addition to the evil of alternate weeks of night work, a custom bearing with extreme hardship upon Children and Young Persons, namely, that of continuing the work without any interruption whatever during the Sunday, and thus rendering every alternate Sunday the day during which the labour of one set of workpeople is continued for twenty-four hours in succession; a custom which still prevails, notwithstanding that a considerable proportion of the proprietors have dispensed with the attendance of the workpeople during a certain number of hours on the Sunday, without disadvantage to their works.

In regard to Underground Labour in Tin, Copper, Lead, and Zinc Mines, we find—

1. That very few Children are employed in any kind of underground work in these mines before they are twelve years old, and that in many cases even the young men do not commence underground work until they are eighteen years of age and upwards.

2. That there is no instance in the whole kingdom of any girl or woman being employed in underground work in these mines.

3. That it is in the Cornish district alone that Children and Young Persons of any age are constantly employed under ground in considerable numbers.

4. That, in general, the Children and Young Persons employed in these mines have sufficient food, and decent and comfortable clothing.

5. That employment in these mines does not, in general, pro-

duce any apparent injury to the young worker during the period of boyhood and adolescence, but that his employment is essentially, and in every mode in which it has hitherto been carried on, necessarily injurious in after life.

6. That the very general and early deterioration and failure of the health and strength of those who have followed this occupation from boyhood and youth, is increased by certain circumstances which are not necessarily connected with the nature of the employment; among these may be reckoned the practice, almost universal in these mines, of associating the Young Persons in partnership with the adult miners, by which the former are stimulated to exertions greatly beyond their age and powers; and though these Young People, thus excited, work with spirit and without apparent injury for some time, yet in a few years it is proved by experience that they have expended the whole capital of their constitution.

7. That this result is materially hastened by the fatigue of climbing the ladders; these being, with few exceptions, the only means by which the miners can go to and return from their places of work.

8. That these, however, are only the accessory causes of the general and rapid deterioration of the health and strength of the miners; since the primary and ever active agent which principally produces this result is the noxious air of the places in which the work is carried on; the difficulties connected with the purification and renovation of this air, and with the whole subject of ventilation, being incomparably greater in the mines in question than in coal mines.

9. That the ultimate effect of the disadvantageous circumstances under which the miner is obliged to pursue his laborious occupation, is the production of certain diseases (seated chiefly in the organs of respiration), by which he is rendered incapable of following his work, and by which his existence is terminated at an earlier period than is common in other branches of industry, not excepting even that of the collier.

With regard to the surface employments connected with Dressing the Ores of Tin, Copper, Lead, and Zinc, we find—

That these employments, though entered into at very early ages, and in the Cornish district by great numbers of girls as well as boys, are wholly free from the evils connected with underground work; that, with the exception of a very injurious exposure to the enclemency of the weather, which might be obviated by a small expenditure in providing shelter, and with the exception of two or three occupations, such as those of "bucking" and "jigging," for the manual labour of which the substitution of machinery is gradually taking place, there is nothing in this branch of mining industry injurious, oppressive, or incompatible with the maintenance even of robust health, which indeed is described as the general condition of the workpeople; the Children and Young Persons thus employed having commonly sufficient food, and warm and decent clothing, being subjected to no harsh or tyrannical treatment, and enjoying an almost complete immunity from any serious danger.

With regard to the works for Smelting Ores of Tin, Copper, Lead, and Zinc, we find—

That in smelting the ores of lead, near the places at which they are raised, no Children and very few Young Persons are engaged, while those employed in the tin works will require a separate notice in treating of manufactures; but that in the copper works of South Wales, in which the Cornish ores are smelted, and in those of North Wales, which reduce the ores raised in their vicinity, a number of Children and Young Persons are employed, from nine years of age and upwards (in South Wales girls as well as boys), of whom those engaged at the calcining furnaces regularly work with the men twenty-four hours consecutively, on alternate days, without excepting the Sunday; a term of work which is sometimes extended to thirty-six hours, and even to forty-eight hours, when, as in South Wales, the "long watch" includes the Sunday.

We have thus endeavoured to present a faithful account of the "actual state, condition, and treatment" of the Children and Young Persons employed in the "Collieries and Mines" of the United Kingdom, and "of the effects of such employment on their Bodily Health:" the effects of this employment on their "Morals," it appears to us, will best be shown by bringing them into view in our next Report, in connexion with the intellectual, moral, and religious state of the whole of that portion of the working population which is included under the terms of our Commission.

All which we humbly certify to Your Majesty.

THO⁵. TOOKE
T. SOUTHWOOD SMITH
LEONARD HORNER
ROBT. J. SAUNDERS

Westminster, April 21, 1842

13. Women: The Anomolies of Status

ECONOMIC WELL-BEING purchased what Edmund Burke once called "the decent drapery of life," but prosperity and status brought a paradoxical circumscription to many. The Victorian lady was the repository of virtue. She was the homemaker, the mother, the custodian of culture and value. She also had severely limited options in life. Women achieved respectability and status initially by emancipation from the need to work, but it was difficult, almost impossible, to maintain social respectability and meet other than domestic obligations, functions, and responsibilities. She could, within broad limits, do good works, for the obligations of charity were moral responsibilities attached to status in society. But she was, until the later years of the queen's reign, barred from the professions. She might, if talented, follow a career in letters or the arts; but during the early and mid-Victorian years she was, if anything, finding fewer outlets for nascent entrepreneurial or commercial skills.

The Victorians were economically wasteful of manpower. Ample supply dulled the demand for efficiency and invention. And the Victorians were even more wasteful of "womanpower." Most students can recite the names and careers of those few who led active lives outside of the farm, the mill, or domestic service, if poor, and the home, if rich. The oblivion of domesticity was the lot of most ladies. Social ritual developed to meet the needs of frustrated people and talent. Homemaking and the social whirl became increasingly elaborate. Domestic servants were a form of ostentation intended to demonstrate (and incidentally to provide) comfort and ease; but the larger the household staff, the more elaborate and demanding became the task of domestic management. Those who had to work did, but what occupation existed for the indigent lady other than being a governess, a social parasite, or another lady's salaried companion?

Most of those who carved out careers in the liberal arts were, like George Eliot, souls in conscious revolt. Josephine Butler (1828–1906) was a refreshing exception. Her charitable activities brought her into the campaign for the rights and dignity of all women, even prostitutes.

Her most famous campaign was that mounted against the Contagious Diseases Act (1866–1883), which provided for government medical inspection of prostitutes. This legislation, if soundly conceived as a public health measure, was one of the more notorious exceptions to the principle of equality before the law. The Act was, as critics constantly pointed out, self-contradictory. It legalized the activity and penalized its practitioneers. While white slavery and prostitution commanded Mrs. Butler's attention for much of her life, she also contributed, staunch feminist that she was, to the improved higher education of women and social justice on a broad front.

Josephine Butler's aunt, Margaretta Grey (from whose diary this document comes), exerted a considerable influence on this active feminist. It was Margaretta who first raised to Josephine and constantly posed to her and others questions about social options and the waste of women's talent. Josephine Butler duly preserved some of Margaretta Grey's most telling points.

Recommended Reading

There is an extensive but often unsatisfactory literature on the position and status of women, although there are prospects of new, excellent work. D. M. Stenton, *The English Woman in History* (London: 1957), provides an interesting overview. J. Dunbar, *Early Victorian Woman: Some Aspects of Her Life, 1837–57* (London: 1953), and I. Pinchbeck, *Women Workers in the Industrial Revolution* (London: 1930), are helpful for the early period. Josephine Butler had something to say herself in *Women's Work and Women's Culture* (London: 1869), as did John Stuart Mill in *The Subjection of Woman* (London: 1869). J. A. Banks, *Prosperity and Parenthood* (London: 1954), and J. A. and O. Banks, *Feminism and Family Planning* (Liverpool: 1964), are pioneering and important, as is O. R. McGregor, *Divorce in England* (London: 1959). Roger Fulford has the liveliest account of the last phase in *Votes for Women* (London: 1957), although Constance Rover deals more perceptively with many problems in *Women's Suffrage and Party Politics in Britain, 1866–1914* (Toronto: 1967).

MARGARETTA GREY,
DIARY (1853)

It appears to me that, with an increase of wealth unequally distributed, and a pressure of population, there has sprung up among us a spurious refinement, that cramps the energy and circumscribes

Source: Josephine E. Butler, *Memoir of John Grey of Dilston*, rev. ed. (London: 1874), pp. 288–290.

the usefulness of women in the upper classes of society. A lady, to be such, must be a mere lady, and nothing else. She must not work for profit, or engage in any occupation that money can command, lest she invade the rights of the working classes, who live by their labour. Men in want of employment have pressed their way into nearly all the shopping and retail businesses that in my early years were managed, in whole or in part by women. The conventional barrier that pronounces it ungenteel to be behind a counter, or serving the public in any mercantile capacity, is greatly extended. The same in household economy. Servants must be up to their several offices, which is very well; but ladies, dismissed from the dairy, the confectionary, the store-room, the still-room, the poultry-yard, the kitchen-garden, and the orchard, have hardly yet found themselves a sphere equally useful and important in the pursuits of trade and art to which to apply their too abundant leisure. I have always regretted that they have suffered the whole of the medical offices, with the knowledge and application of simples, which used to lie in the province of mothers of families, to pass out of their hands, and that the practice of midwifery, so obviously appropriate to women, should be given up by them. Medical men, in want of occupation, lay claim to this as a province of theirs, and decry all household dabbling in medicine as derogatory to science. Yet I cannot but think that in the earlier times, when living was more simple, and diseases perhaps less complicated, the established home-remedies that were brought into use, taking illness in its incipient stages, were instrumental in warding off diseases which the doctors cannot cure. . . .

We must submit to the changes which the progress of art—I will not say positively of civilisation—forces upon us. What is done with abridged labour and greater effect on a large scale in the factory, need not be done with time and pains by many hands in the family. But what I remonstrate against is the negative forms of employment: the wasting of energy, the crippling of talent under false ideas of station, propriety, and refinement, that seems to shut up a large portion of the women of our generation from proper spheres of occupation and adequate exercise of power. . . . Women have almost universally a broken, desultory education, made up of details, of which the secondary and mechanical often have the precedence of the solid and intellectual. Those studies are left out or vaguely pursued that strengthen the faculties, and give vigour and perseverance to the thinking powers. The education of girls also comes to an end at the time when the serious work of self-improvement properly begins. And the loss might not be great, if what went before were of the kind that brings the faculties into healthful action, and what follows after kept up the stimulus to progress and acquisition of knowledge. But here is the grand downfall; for now regular arrangement of hours and systematic occupation given place to all manner of casualties—visiting, note-writing, dressing, and choosing dresses for morning and evening engagements, being dutifully at hand for any odd job that is required in the way of shopping and making and receiving calls. Life is too often divested of any real and important purpose. The wise and the unwise, the gifted and the imbecile, yield to the impertinence of custom, and limit themselves to what has been the fashion in their circle and station.

It is time to rise out of this, and for women of principle and natural parts to find themselves something to do. There would still be a sufficient quota left to attend to the comfort of parents and the requirements of home, though a reasonable proportion of the talented and earnest chose for themselves some more special calling, and without vows, devoted themselves, as Providence might direct their way, to pursuits in which they were qualified to attain excellence or to rise to superior usefulness. Some children discover at an early age a passion for books, indicative of mental capacity, and directing to study, and the cultivation of lettered acquirements; some, with a taste for reading, show a general curiosity, with love of observation and experimental science. Let these have scope, and we should soon have a superior body of teachers and trainers for our youth, spreading influence through our schools for the commoner and higher classes. Others, perhaps the most numerous class, develop activity, love of employment and despatch, inclining to business occupation, and adapted for carrying out plans that require labour, distribution of employment, and co-operation. How would the morbid listlessness and insipidity that pervade some family circles be broken up by having one or two of their members withdrawn for such destinations! It need not prevent marriage; though it would beneficially divert the thoughts from that as the grand event in life, by which so many of the unemployed lose precious time in vain speculation, frustrated inclination, and disappointed hope. . . . When at any time has society presented, on the one hand, so large an array of respectably educated individuals embarrassed for want of a proper calling, and, on the other, so ponderous a multitude of untrained, neglected poor, who cannot without help rise out of their misery and degradation? What an obstruction to usefulness and all eminence of character is that of being too rich or too genteelly connected to work at anything! How is life sacrificed as to its most important ends, and given to vanity instead of to the service of God! . . . What I plead for is, that those who are led by a necessity of duty, made up of choice, adaptation, and general circumstances, to desire a life of philanthropic usefulness, may have the means opened before them of adopting a profession, acquiring the skill, and following out the practice of the particular line of service for which they are fitted.

14. Women's Rights: Property and Marriage

THE LONG AND torturous road to the recognition of women's rights threaded through hazards of legal disability and social habit. The historian usually recalls a few of the more obvious milestones—the militant suffragettes of the decade before the First World War, Florence Nightingale's campaign to provide a respectable career for nurses, or (a little more subtle) Josephine Butler's efforts to demonstrate that all women really are people and should be treated as such.

The world on the eve of Victoria's accession was still a man's world in spite of a few eccentric if committed challenges. No movement had more profound social implications than the gradual emancipation of the weaker sex. If the suffrage had to wait until 1918, many barriers fell in the Victorian age. In law, medicine, in the universities—however halting the progress and circumscribed the results—down they came. Nor were there more than the conventional restraints of cultural prejudice for the single woman ready to compete in arts and letters. The nub of the problem surrounding the role of women was to be found in the Victorian definition of the family and its legal buttress, the law of property and contract.

The single woman could do what she wished and call her rewards her own. Society might not quite approve, for from our beloved queen to her humblest subject, marriage and family were the proper lot of every woman. The Married Woman's Property Act of 1870, one of the outstanding liberal reforms of Gladstone's first administration ("The Great Ministry," 1868–1874), implied a social revolution. Under its provisions a woman no longer surrendered all of her property rights. It was a crucial step in defining a fundamental freedom within as well as outside the state of matrimony. But the Act also removed one of the legal props upon which the cultural values of the Victorian family were constructed.

Paterson's gloss of the statute and most of his footnotes have been preserved in this selection. The lawyer regarded the statute with considerable misgiving.

Recommended Reading

In addition to the works cited with Document 13, see W. L. O'Neill, *The Woman Movement* (London: 1969).

W. PATERSON,
MARRIED WOMEN'S PROPERTY ACT

This act is a very important one, and will necessarily have a very extensive operation. It reverses the rule of law that by marriage all the personal property of the wife vests in the husband, and as it removes one of the causes so it takes an effective step for abolishing the difference between the two systems which have hitherto existed at common law and equity, as regards husband and wife: and what, therefore, has only been an equitable interest will now, in those cases in which the act applies, become a legal right.

No doubt the old rule of law worked considerable hardship, especially amongst those whose property was not large enough to justify the expense of a settlement, or who by their talents or industry gained an income for themselves. These last alone have been calculated to amount to the large number of 800,000; and many are the cases in which idle and profligate husbands have lived on the earnings and property of their wives, squandering on themselves what should have gone to the support of the wives and children. The Divorce Act, which enabled a wife who had been deserted by her husband to obtain a protection order from a magistrate, gave some relief, as it conferred on her the rights of a *feme sole* over earnings and property she might acquire after such desertion, but its operation, being limited to cases of desertion, was necessarily very small and totally inadequate to meet the existing evil. Hence many plans to relieve the injustice thus felt have been brought forward for some time past, and at last, the present measure, which owes its origin to the Recorder of London, has received the sanction of the Legislature. It does not create that revolution in the social relation of the parties which some of the

Source: From *The Practical Statutes of the Session 1870* (London: 1870), pp. 406–415.

proposed plans were calculated to produce. Still it effects a very considerable change.

The first of these, which enables a married woman to enjoy as her separate property all that she may earn by her own industry and ability, is one which no one can object to, and will probably have a very beneficial effect as a strong encouragement to her labours. The act further provides for four separate species of investments which a woman, either married or about to marry, may make of her money, and which, if made in the mode pointed out by the act will be deemed to be the separate property of such woman. These investments are, first, in savings banks; secondly, in the funds; thirdly, in fully paid up shares or stock of a joint-stock company; and fourthly, in friendly, benefit, building, or such like societies.

There are, in addition to these, three other cases under the act, in which a married woman may have property to her separate use, but these apply only to women who marry after the passing of the act, and they are as follows: first, personal property to which she may become entitled as next of kin; secondly, money not exceeding 200*l.* to which she may become entitled under any deed or will; and thirdly, the rents and profits of freeholds or copyholds which may descend on her as heiress of an intestate.

The act having thus in these eight different instances enabled the married woman to hold money or property as her own, invests her with legal rights, both civil and criminal, in respect of the same. In these instances, her position as a *feme sole* is recognized at law, and she may of course alienate and dispose of all such property in any way she may please without the concurrence of her husband; and as there is no restraint on anticipation, she may assign it all away at once.

The strongest objection to the present measure has been the facility it may afford persons of defrauding their creditors. There is great force in this objection, and although a clause has been introduced for the special purpose of obviating it, there is good reason for fearing that the act may be used to the serious prejudice of creditors. If the husband is not a dissenting party, which, of course, he will not be where creditors are intended to be defrauded, there is nothing to prevent his wife from investing her husband's money in the savings banks, funds, or joint-stock property in her name to her separate use, and so keeping it from the creditors of her husband; and though there is a clause which makes such investment invalid as against such creditors, it will, it is apprehended, succeed in defeating them, unless in the event of the husband's bankruptcy the truth should be discovered under the searching inquiries which may then be instituted. This, therefore, gives a greater facility to defraud creditors than a man formerly had by means of a post-nuptial settlement, which last had been found so mischievous that by the Bankrupt Act of last year such voluntary settlement when made by a trader was declared to be void if he became bankrupt within two years after its date; and even afterwards it was to be void if he became bankrupt at any time within ten years from its date, and the parties claiming under it failed to prove that the bankrupt was able at the time of the settlement to pay all his debts without the aid of the settled property. The protection to creditors given by this 91st section of the Bankrupt Act may now be said to be gone, for an investment by the wife under the present act is a much more simple mode than a deed of settlement, and such investment, instead of, like the settlement, being absolutely void within two years as against the bankrupt's trustee, will be good unless shewn to have been made out of moneys of the husband in fraud of his creditors, and the onus of shewing this will be on the creditors.

In conclusion it may be here observed, that as the natural consequence of the reversal of the rule of common law which gave the wife's personal property to her husband, the latter is freed by the act from the liability the common law put on him for his wife's debts, contracted by her before marriage. Further than this, a married woman having separate property is to be liable to the parish for the maintenance of her husband and children when they have become chargeable to the parish.

THE STATUTE

An Act to amend the Law relating to the Property of Married Women—[*9th August,* 1870]

Whereas it is desirable to amend the law of property and contract with respect to married women:

Be it enacted by the Queen's most excellent Majesty, by and with the advice and consent of the Lords spiritual and temporal, and Commons, in this present Parliament assembled, and by the authority of the same, as follows:

1. *Earnings of married women to be deemed their own property.*—The wages and earnings of any married woman acquired or gained by her after the passing of this act in any employment, occupation, or trade in which she is engaged or which she carries on separately from her husband, and also any money or property so acquired by her through the exercise of any literary, artistic, or scientific skill, and all investments of such wages, earnings, money, or property, shall be deemed and taken to be property held and settled to her separate use, independent of any husband to whom she may be married, and her receipts alone shall be a good discharge for such wages, earnings, money, and property.[1]

2. *Deposits in savings banks by a married woman to be deemed her separate property—Proviso.*—Notwithstanding any provision to the contrary in the act of the tenth year of George the Fourth, chapter twenty-four, enabling the Commissioners for the Reduction of the National Debt to grant life annuities and annuities for terms of years, or in the acts relating to savings banks and post office savings banks, any deposit hereafter made and any annuity granted by the said commissioners under any of the said acts in the name of a married woman, or in the name of a woman who may marry after such deposit or grant, shall be deemed to be ten separate property of such woman, and the same shall be accounted for and paid to her as if she were an unmarried woman;[2] provided that if any such deposit is made by, or such annuity granted to, a married woman by means of moneys of her husband without his consent, the court may, upon an application under section nine of this act, order such deposit or annuity or any part thereof to be paid to the husband.

3. *As to a married woman's property in the funds.*—Any married woman, or any woman about to be married, may apply to the

1. The married woman may bring an action in her own name for the recovery of such wages, earnings, money, and property: (see *post*, sec. 11.) She may, it would seem, invest the amount when received on any security, without restriction as to its being such as is mentioned in the four following sections, and such investment will be deemed to be to her separate use. This, and the other property declared by the act in the subsequent sections to be her separate property may, of course, be disposed of by her as if she were sole, such right of alienation being one of the incidents of her being able to hold property as her own.

2. By sect. 11 the married woman may bring an action in her own name for the recovery of such property. She may alienate the property as a *feme sole.*

governor and company of the Bank of England, or to the governor and company of the Bank of Ireland, by a form to be provided by the governor of each of the said banks and company for that purpose, that any sum forming part of the public stocks and funds, and not being less than twenty pounds, to which the woman so applying is entitled, or which she is about to acquire, may be transferred to or made to stand in the books of the governor and company to whom such application is made in the name or intended name of the woman as a married woman entitled to her separate use, and on such sum being entered in the books of the said governor and company accordingly the same shall be deemed to be the separate property of such woman, and shall be transferred and the dividends paid as if she were an unmarried woman; provided that if any such investment in the funds is made by a married woman by means of moneys of her husband, without his consent, the court may, upon an application under section nine of this act, order such investment and the dividends thereof, or any part thereof, to be transferred and paid to the husband.

4. *As to a married woman's property in a joint stock company.*—Any married woman, or any woman about to be married, may apply in writing to the directors or managers of any incorporated or joint stock company that any fully paid up shares, or any debenture or debenture stock, or any stock of such company, to the holding of which no liability is attached, and to which the woman so applying is entitled, may be registered in the books of the said company in the name or intended name of the woman as a married woman entitled to her separate use, and it shall be the duty of such directors or managers to register such shares or stock accordingly, and the same upon being so registered shall be deemed to be the separate property of such woman, and shall be transferred and the dividends and profits paid as if she were an unmarried woman; provided that if any such investment as last mentioned is made by a married woman by means of moneys of her husband without his consent, the court may, upon an application under section nine of this act, order such investment and the dividends and profits thereon, or any part thereof, to be transferred and paid to the husband.

5. *As to a married woman's property in a society.*—Any married woman, or any woman about to be married, may apply in writing to the committee of management of any industrial and

provident society, or to the trustees of any friendly society, benefit building society, or loan society, duly registered, certified, or enrolled under the acts relating to such societies respectively, that any share, benefit, debenture, right, or claim whatsoever in, to, or upon the funds of such society, to the holding of which share, benefit, or debenture no liability is attached, and to which the woman so applying is entitled, may be entered in the books of the society in the name or intended name of the woman as a married woman entitled to her separate use, and it shall be the duty of such committee or trustees to cause the same to be so entered, and thereupon such share, benefit, debenture, right, or claim shall be deemed to be the separate property of such woman, and shall be transferable and payable with all dividends and profits thereon as if she were an unmarried woman; provided that if any such share, benefit, debenture, right, or claim has been obtained by a married woman by means of moneys of her husband without his consent, the court may, upon an application under section nine of this act, order the same and the dividends and profits thereon, or any part thereof, to be transferred and paid to the husband.

6. *Deposit of moneys in fraud of creditors invalid.*—Nothing herein-before contained in reference to moneys deposited in or annuities granted by savings banks or moneys invested in the funds or in shares or stock of any company shall as against creditors of the husband give validity to any deposit or investment of moneys of the husband made in fraud of such creditors, and any moneys so deposited or invested may be followed as if this act had not passed.[3]

7. *Personal property coming to a married woman to be her own.*—Where any freehold, copyhold, or customaryhold property shall during her marriage become entitled to any personal property as next of kin or one of the next of kin of an intestate, or to any sum of money not exceeding two hundred pounds under any deed

---

3. This section will, as stated in the introduction to the statute, probably give the creditors very slight protection, as the onus will be on them to show that the investment was made out of the husband's moneys; and section 9, which gives a summary remedy for determining the ownership of the property, is limited to the husband and wife, and does not extend to any third party. It would seem that to enable the creditors to follow the moneys the wife may have so invested, they must show not only that the investment was out of moneys of the husband, but that it was made in fraud of such creditors, therefore they must show that the husband at the time of such investment was insolvent.

or will, such property shall, subject and without prejudice to the trusts of any settlement affecting the same, belong to the woman for her separate use, and her receipts alone shall be a good discharge for the same.[4]

8. *Freehold property coming to a married woman to be her own.*—Where any woman married after the passing of this act shall descend upon any woman married after the passing of this act as heiress or co-heiress of an intestate, the rents and profits of such property shall, subject and without prejudice to the trusts or any settlement affecting the same, belong to such woman for her separate use, and her receipts alone shall be a good discharge for the same.[5]

9. *How questions as to ownership of property to be settled.*—In any question between husband and wife as to property declared by this act to be the separate property of the wife, either party may apply by summons or motions in a summary way either to the Court of Chancery in England or Ireland according as such property is in England or Ireland, or in England (irrespective of the value of the property) the judge of the county court of the district in which either party resides, and thereupon the judge may make such order, direct such inquiry, and award such costs, as he shall think fit; provided that any order made by such judge shall be subject to appeal in the same manner as the order of the same judge made in a pending suit or on an equitable plaint would have been and the judge may, if either party so require, hear the application in his private room.

10. *Married woman may effect policy or insurance—As to insurance of a husband for benefit of his wife.*—A married woman may effect a policy of insurance upon her own life or the life of her husband for her separate use, and the same and all benefit thereof, if expressed on the face of it to be so effected, shall enure

4. The personal property acquired as next of kin is not like the property acquired under deed or will limited to money. It would therefore include leaseholds. The married woman, it is apprehended, will be entitled to sue for the property which is hers by this section in her own name (see *post*, sect. 11); although the 11th section says, "property by this act declared to be her separate property," and this 7th section uses instead the expression "separate use." There is no distinction for this purpose between the two forms of expression; and sect. 1, to which the 11th section must apply also like the present one, says "separate use" instead of "separate property."

5. See *ante*, note 4, as to the married woman suing in her own name for these rents.

accordingly, and the contract in such policy shall be as valid as if made with an unmarried woman.

A policy of insurance effected by any married man on his own life, and expressed upon the face of it to be for the benefit of his wife or of his wife and children, or any of them, shall enure and be deemed a trust for the benefit of his wife for her separate use, and of his children, or any of them, according to the interest so expressed, and shall not, so long as any object of the trust remains, be subject to the control of the husband or to his creditors, or form part of his estate. When the sum secured by the policy becomes payable, or at any time previously, a trustee thereof may be appointed by the Court of Chancery in England or in Ireland according as the policy of insurance was effected in England or in Ireland, or in England by the judge of the county court of the district, or in Ireland by the chairman of the Civil Bill Court of the division of the county, in which the insurance office is situated, and the receipt of such trustee shall be a good discharge to the office. If it shall be proved that the policy was effected and premiums paid by the husband with intent to defraud his creditors, they shall be entitled to receive out of the sum secured an amount equal to the premiums so paid.

11. *Married women may maintain an action.*—A married woman may maintain an action in her own name for the recovery of any wages, earnings, money, and property by this act declared to be her separate property,[6] or of any property belonging to her before marriage, and which her husband shall, by writing under his hand, have agreed with her shall belong to her after her marriage as her separate property,[7] and she shall have in her own name the

6. It is a pity the act should constantly change the expression, and in one part call the property "her separate property" and in another part call it "for her separate use." It is submitted that the act intends to make no distinction between the two, and this power of suing extends to all such cases. It must obviously extend to the 1st section, and yet there the property is expressly declared to be "settled to her separate use."

7. The property here referred to is evidently different property from what is specified in sections 2, 3, 4, and 5, and which, whether there is any agreement in writing or not between the wife and husband, the former may invest so as to be her separate property in the mode pointed out by those sections. Before her marriage the wife may have had money invested on mortgage or other security which is not such as is specified in sects. 2, 3, 4, and 5. Such will not be her separate property unless the husband agrees to it in writing, and then it will be only so in equity except that this section unables her to bring an action for it in her own name.

same remedies, both civil and criminal, against all persons whomsoever for the protection and security of such wages, earnings, money, and property, and of any chattels or other property purchased or obtained by means thereof for her own use, as if such wages, earnings, money, chattels, and property belonged to her as an unmarried woman; and in any indictment or other proceeding it shall be sufficient to allege such wages, earnings, money, chattels, and property to be her property.

12. *Husband not to be liable on his wife's contracts before marriage.*—A husband shall not, by reason of any marriage which shall take place after this act has come into operation, be liable for the debts of his wife contracted before marriage, but the wife shall be liable to be sued for, and any property belonging to her for her separate use shall be liable to satisfy such debts as if she had continued unmarried.

13. *Married woman to be liable to the parish for the maintenance of her husband.*—Where in England the husband of any woman having separate property becomes chargeable to any union or parish, the justices having jurisdiction in such union or parish may, in petty sessions assembled, upon application of the guardians of the poor, issue a summons against the wife, and make and enforce such order against her for the maintenance of her husband as by the thirty-third section of "The Poor Law Amendment Act, 1868," they may now make and enforce against a husband for the maintenance of his wife who becomes chargeable to any union or parish. Where in Ireland relief is given under the provisions of the acts relating to the relief of the destitute poor to the husband of any woman having separate property, the cost price of such relief is hereby declared to be a loan from the guardians of the union in which the same shall be given, and shall be recoverable from such woman as if she were a *feme sole* by such and the same actions and proceedings as money lent.

14. *Married woman to be liable to the parish for the maintenance of her children.*—A married woman having separate property shall be subject to all such liability for the maintenance of her children as a widow is now by law subject to for the maintenance of her children: Provided always, that nothing in this act shall relieve her husband from any liability imposed upon him by law to maintain her children.

15. *Commencement of act.*—This act shall come into operation at the time of the passing of this act.

16. *Act not to extend to Scotland.*—This act shall not extend to Scotland.

17. *Short title.*—This act may be cited as the "Married Women's Property Act, 1870."

15. Socialization: Child and Family

FATHER WAS God in that patristic universe called the home—a wrathful, forbidding figure. Love for father, like love of God on the evangelical Christian model, was animated by fear. The Victorian family revolved around the mother, the day-to-day authority who provided comfort, a haven, even an escape. Socialization defined the child's world and role. Upbringing insured acceptance, not appreciation. Children in the middle and upper classes mingled considerably with servants. They thus developed, or thought they developed, a sense of easy familiarity, understanding, and sympathy with the lower orders. From earliest childhood they proceeded to a sense of caste. The family—that congerie of father, mother, aunts, uncles, and servants—taught the creed of obedience, morality, loyalty. Discipline lay at the heart of socialization. Each child must learn order and self-restraint through encouragement and suppression. Enforcement of the culture was simple and direct. Manliness, honor, duty, deference, the orderly life. God sanctioned it. The family taught it. The world approved.

Augustus Hare (1834–1903), raconteur, water colorist, author of travel guides, described his own childhood in considerable detail. The youngest son of a middle-class family, he was adopted by his godmother and aunt, Maria Hare, at the age of one. He grew up in that traditional world of the Anglican clerical household, briefly attended Harrow, and took his degree at University College, Oxford. He remained with his adoptive mother, living abroad until her death in 1870. For the last thirty years of his life, he wrote about and lived in cultivated high society. Augustus was taught no trade, animated by no sense of purpose beyond that of living the life style to which he was bred. He made no striking contribution to English art or letters, but he did explain almost unintentionally an important dimension of socialization. He was not caught up in the quest for manliness, the drive for achievement. But he was taught a code, and he was prepared for life in the world of the privileged classes.

Recommended Reading

The problems suggested here are considered in several selections in Part III. For the general problem, W. E. Houghton, *The Victorian Frame of Mind* (New Haven: 1957). Among other important works, see J. A. Banks, *Prosperity and Parenthood* (London: 1954), G. Avery and A. Bull, *Nineteenth-Century Children: Heroes and Heroines in English Children's Stories* (London: 1965), and E. E. Buxton, *Family Sketchbook* (London: 1954). O. A. Sherrard, *Two Victorian Girls*, ed. A. R. Mills (London: 1966), gives two interesting diaries. R. Smith has a fascinating local study in "Early Victorian Household Structure: A Case Study of Nottinghamshire," *International Review of Social History*, XV (1970), 69–84.

AUGUSTUS HARE,
ON CHILDHOOD AND BOYHOOD

But, to return to our own life, at one we had dinner—almost always roast-mutton and rice-pudding—and then I read aloud—Josephus at a *very* early age, and then Froissart's Chronicles. At three we went out in the carriage to distant cottages, often ending at the Rectory. At five I was allowed to "amuse myself," which generally meant nursing the cat for half-an-hour and "hearing it its lessons." All the day I had been with my mother, and now generally went to my dear nurse Lea for half-an-hour, when I had tea in the cool "servants' hall" (where, however, the servants never sat—preferring the kitchen), after which I returned to find Uncle Julius arrived, who stayed till my bedtime.

As Uncle Julius was never captivating to children, it is a great pity that he was turned into an additional bugbear, by being always sent for to whip me when I was naughty! These executions generally took place with a riding-whip, and looking back dispassionately through the distance of years, I am conscious that, for a delicate child, they were a great deal too severe. I always screamed dreadfully in the anticipation of them, but bore them without a sound or a tear. I remember one very hot summer's day, when I had been very naughty over my lessons, Froissart's Chronicles having been particularly uninteresting, and having produced the very effect which Ahasuerus desired to obtain from the reading of the book of the records of the chronicles, that Uncle Julius was summoned. He arrived, and I was sent upstairs to "prepare." Then, as I knew I was going to be whipped anyway, I thought I might as well do something horrible to be whipped *for*, and, as soon as I reached the head of the stairs, gave three of the most awful, appalling and eldrich shrieks that ever were heard in Hurstmonceaux.

Source: From *The Story of My Life* (London: 1896), vol. I, pp. 104–111, 114–116, 168–169, 178–187.

Then I fled for my life. Through the nursery was a small bedroom, in which Lea slept, and here I knew that a large black travelling "imperial" was kept under the bed. Under the bed I crawled, and wedged myself into the narrow space behind the imperial, between it and the wall. I was only just in time. In an instant all the household —mother, uncle, servants—were in motion, and a search was on foot all over the house. I turn cold still when I remember the agony of fright with which I heard Uncle Julius enter the nursery, and then, with which, through a chink, I could see his large feet moving about the very room in which I was. He *looked under the bed*, but he saw only a large black box. I held my breath, motionless, and he turned away. Others looked under the bed too; but my concealment was effectual.

I lay under the bed for an hour—stifling—agonised. Then all sounds died away, and I knew that the search in the house was over, and that they were searching the garden. At last my curiosity would no longer allow me to be still, and I crept from under the bed and crawled to the window of my mother's bedroom, whence I could overlook the garden without being seen. Every dark shrub, every odd corner was being ransacked. The whole household and the gardeners were engaged in the pursuit. At last I could see by their actions—for I could not hear words—that a dreadful idea had presented itself. In my paroxysms I had rushed down the steep bank, and tumbled or thrown myself into the pond! I saw my mother look very wretched and Uncle Julius try to calm her. At last they sent for people to drag the pond. Then I could bear my dear mother's expression no longer, and, from my high window, I gave a little hoot. Instantly all was changed; Lea rushed upstairs to embrace me; there was great talking and excitement, and while it was going on, Uncle Julius was called away, and every one . . . forgot that I had not been whipped! That, however, was the only time I ever escaped.

In the most literal sense, and in every other, I was "brought up at the point of the rod." My dearest mother was so afraid of over-indulgence that she always went into the opposite extreme: and her constant habits of self-examination made her detect the slightest act of especial kindness into which she had been betrayed, and instantly determine not to repeat it. Nevertheless, I loved her most passionately, and many tearful fits, for which I was severely punished as fits of naughtiness, were really caused by anguish at the thought that I had displeased her or been a trouble to her. From never daring to express my wishes in words, which she would have thought it a duty to meet by an immediate refusal, I early became a coward as to concealing what I really desired. I remember once, in my longing for childish companionship, so intensely desiring that the little Coshams—a family of children who lived in the parish—might come to play with me, that I entreated that they might come to have tea in the summer-house on my Hurstmonceaux birthday (the day of my adoption), and that the mere request was not only refused, but so punished that I never dared to express a wish to play with any child again. At the same time I was *expected* to play with little Marcus, then an indulged disagreeable child whom I could not endure, and because I was not fond of *him*, was thought intensely selfish and self-seeking.

As an example of the severe discipline which was maintained with regard to me, I remember that one day when we went to visit the curate, a lady (Miss Garden) very innocently gave me a lolly-pop, which I ate. This crime was discovered when we came home by the smell of peppermint, and a large dose of rhubarb and soda was at once administered with a forcing-spoon, though I was in robust health at the time, to teach me to avoid such carnal indul-gencies as lollypops for the future. For two years, also, I was obliged to swallow a dose of rhubarb every morning and every evening because—according to old-fashioned ideas—it was sup-posed to "strengthen the stomach!" I am sure it did me a great deal of harm, and had much to do with accounting for my after sickli-ness. Sometimes I believe the medicine itself induced fits of fretful-ness; but if I cried more than usual, it was supposed to be from want of additional medicine, and the next morning senna-tea was added to the rhubarb. I remember the misery of sitting on the backstairs in the morning and having it in a teacup, with milk and sugar.

At a very early age I was made to go to church—once, which very soon grew into twice, on a Sunday. Uncle Julius's endless sermons were my detestation. I remember some one speaking of him to an old man in the parish, and being surprised by the state-ment that he was "not a good winter parson," which was explained to mean that he kept the people so long with his sermons, that they could not get home before dark.

With the utmost real kindness of heart, Uncle Julius had often the sharpest and most insulting manner I have ever known in speaking to those who disagreed with him. I remember an instance of this when Mr. Simpkinson had lately come to Hurstmonceaux as my uncle's curate. His sister, then a very handsome young lady, had come down from London to visit him, and my mother took her to church in the carriage. That Sunday happened to be Michaelmas Day. As we were driving slowly away from church through the crowd of those who had formed the congregation, Uncle Julius holding the reins, something was said about the day. Without a suspicion of giving offence, Miss Simpkinson, who was sitting behind with me, said, in a careless way, "As for me, my chief association with Michaelmas Day is a roast goose." Then Uncle Julius turned round, and, in a voice of *thunder*, audible to every one on the road, exclaimed, "Ignorant and presumptuous young woman!" He had never seen her till that day. As she said to me years after, when she was a wife and mother, "That the Archdeacon should call me ignorant and presumptuous was trying, still I could bear that very well; but that he should dare to call me a *young woman* was not to be endured." However, her only alternative was to bear the affront and be driven two miles home, or to insist upon getting out of the carriage and walking home through the mud, and she chose the former course, and afterwards my uncle, when he knew her good qualities, both admired and liked her. . . .

From MY MOTHER'S JOURNAL

Lime, June 18, 1839.—During a week spent in London, Augustus was part of every day with his brothers and sister. Their first meeting was at Sheen. Augustus was much excited before they came, and when he saw his brothers, threw himself on my neck and kissed me passionately. They were soon intimate, and he was very much delighted at playing with them, and was not made fretful by it. There seemed to be a strong feeling of affection awakened towards them, unlike anything he has shown to other children. I have begun to teach Augustus to draw, but it is wearisome work from his inattention. . . . His delight in flowers and knowledge of their names is greater than ever, and it is equally necessary to control his gratification in this as in other pleasures. The usual punishment for his impatience over dressing is to have no garden flowers.

In all the books of education I do not find what I believe is the useful view taken of the actual labour of learning to read—that of forcing the child's attention to a thing irksome to it and without interest. The task is commonly spoken of as a means to an end, necessary because the information in books cannot otherwise be obtained, and it is to be put off till the child's interest in the information is excited and so made a pleasure to him. Now it seems to me to be an excellent discipline whereby daily some self-denial and command may be acquired in overcoming the repugnance to doing from duty that which has in itself no attraction. In the first struggle to fix the attention and learn that which is without interest, but which *must be done*, a habit is gained of great importance. And in this way nothing is better suited to the purpose than the *lesson* of reading, even though little progress may be made for a long time.

I find in giving any order to a child, it is always better not to *look* to see if he obeys, but to take it for granted it will be done. If one appears to doubt the obedience, there is occasion given for the child to hesitate. "Shall I do it or no?" If you seem not to question the possibility of non-compliance, he feels a trust committed to him to keep and fulfils it. It is best never to repeat a command, never to answer the oft-asked question "why?"

Augustus would, I believe, always do a thing if *reasoned* with about it, but the necessity of obedience without reasoning is specially necessary in such a disposition as his. The will is the thing that needs being brought into subjection.

The withholding a pleasure is a safe punishment for naughtiness, more safe, I think, than giving a reward for goodness. "If you are naughty I must punish you," is often a necessary threat; but it is not good to hold out a bribe for goodness—"If you are good I will give you such a thing."

. . . My own experience of Harnish [School] is one of the many instances I have known of how little the character of the head of an establishment affects the members of it, unless his spirituality is backed up by a thorough knowledge of the world. The greater portion of Mr. Kilvert's scholars—his "little flock of lambs in Christ's fold"—were a set of little monsters. All infantine immoralities were highly popular, and—in such close quarters—it would have been difficult for the most pure and high-minded boy to escape from them. The first evening I was there at nine years old, I was compelled to eat Eve's apple quite up—indeed, the Tree of the Knowledge of Good and Evil was stripped absolutely bare: there was no fruit left to gather.

I wonder if children often go through the intense agony of anguish which I went through when I was separated from my mother. Perhaps not, as few children are brought up so entirely by and with their parents in such close companionship. It was leaving my mother that I minded, not the going to school, to which my misery was put down: though, as I had never had any companions, the idea of being left suddenly amongst a horde of young savages was anything but comforting. But my nervous temperament was tortured with the idea that my mother would die before I saw her again (I had read a story of this kind), that our life was over, that my aunts would persuade her to cease to care for me,—indeed, the anguish was so great and so little understood, that though it is more than fifty years ago, as I write this, I can scarcely bear to think of it. . . .

The winter of 1844–45 was the first of many which were made unutterably wretched by "Aunt Esther." Aunt Lucy had chastised me with rods, Aunt Esther did indeed chastise me with scorpions. Aunt Lucy was a very refined person, and a very charming and delightful companion to those she loved, and, had she loved me, I should have been devoted to her. Aunt Esther was, from her own personal characteristics, a person I never could have loved. Yet my uncle was now entirely ruled by her, and my gentle mother considered her interference in everything as a cross which was "sent to her" to be meekly endured. The society at the Rectory was now entirely changed: all the relations of the Hare family, except the Marcus Hares, were given to understand that their visits were unwelcome, and the house was entirely filled with the relations of Aunt Esther—old Mr. and Mrs. Maurice; their married daughter Lucilla Powell, with her husband and children; their unmarried daughters—Mary, Priscilla, and Harriet[1]—Priscilla, who now never left her bed, and who was violently sick after everything she ate (yet with the most enormous appetite), often for many months together.

With the inmates of the house, the whole "tone" of the Rectory society was changed. It was impossible entirely to silence Uncle Julius, yet at times even he was subdued by his new surroundings, the circle around him being incessantly occupied with the trivialities of domestic or parochial detail, varied by the gossip of such a tenth-rate provincial town as Reading, or reminiscences of the

1. Harriet survived all her sisters for many years, as the wife of Edward Plumptre, Dean of Wells. She died in 1890. A charming account of her has appeared in Boyd's "Twenty-five Years at St. Andrews:" I thought her most unlike it.

boarding-school which had been their occupation and pride for so many years. Frequently also the spare rooms were filled by former pupils—"young ladies" of a kind who would announce their engagement by "The infinite grace of God has put it into the heart of his servant Edmund to propose to me," or "I have been led by the mysterious workings of God's providence to accept the hand of Edgar,"[2]—expressions which Aunt Esther, who wrote good and simple English herself, would describe as touching evidences of a Christian spirit in her younger friends.

But what was far more trying to me was, that in order to prove that her marriage had made no difference in the sisterly and brotherly relations which existed between my mother and Uncle Julius, Aunt Esther insisted that my mother should dine at the Rectory *every* night, and as, in winter, the late return in an open carriage was impossible, this involved our sleeping at the Rectory and returning home every morning in the bitter cold before breakfast. The hours after five o'clock in every day of the much-longed-for, eagerly counted holidays, were now absolute purgatory. Once landed at the Rectory, I was generally left in a dark room till dinner at seven o'clock, for candles were never allowed in winter in the room where I was left alone. After dinner I was never permitted to amuse myself, or to do *anything*, except occasionally to net. If I spoke, Aunt Esther would say with a satirical smile, "As if you ever *could* say anything worth hearing, as if it was ever *possible* that any one could want to hear what you have to say." If I took up a book, I was told instantly to put it down again, it was "disrespect to my Uncle." If I murmured, Aunt Esther, whose temper was absolutely unexcitable, quelled it by her icy rigidity. Thus gradually I got into the habit of absolute silence at the Rectory—a habit which it took me years to break through: and I often still suffer from the want of self-confidence engendered by reproaches and taunts which never ceased: for a day—for a week —for a year they would have been nothing: but for *always*, with no escape but my own death or that of my tormentor! Water dripping for ever on a stone wears through the stone at last.

The cruelty which I received from my new aunt was repeated in various forms by her sisters, one or other of whom was always at the Rectory. Only Priscilla, touched by the recollection of many

2. Actual cases.

long visits during my childhood at Lime, occasionally sent a kindly message or spoke a kindly word to me from her sick-bed, which I repaid by constant offerings of flowers. Most of all, however, did I feel the conduct of Mary Maurice, who, by pretended sympathy and affection, wormed from me all my little secrets—how miserable my uncle's marriage had made my home-life, how I never was alone with my mother now, &c.—and repeated the whole to Aunt Esther.

From this time Aunt Esther resolutely set herself to subdue me thoroughly—to make me feel that any remission of misery at home, any comparative comfort, was as a gift from her. But to make me feel this thoroughly, it was necessary that all pleasure and comfort in my home should first be annihilated. I was a very delicate child, and suffered absolute agonies from chilblains, which were often large open wounds on my feet. Therefore I was put to sleep in "the Barracks"—two dismal unfurnished, uncarpeted north rooms, without fireplaces, looking into a damp courtyard, with a well and a howling dog. My only bed was a rough deal trestle, my only bedding a straw palliasse, with a single coarse blanket. The only other furniture in the room was a deal chair, and a washing-basin on a tripod. No one was allowed to bring me any hot water; and as the water in my room always froze with the intense cold, I had to break the ice with a brass candlestick, or, if that were taken away, with my wounded hands. If, when I came down in the morning, as was often the case, I was almost speechless from sickness and misery, it was always declared to be "temper." I was given "saurkraut" to eat because the very smell of it made me sick.

When Aunt Esther discovered the comfort that I found in getting away to my dear old Lea, she persuaded my mother that Lea's influence over me was a very bad one, and obliged her to keep me away from her.

A favourite torment was reviling all my own relations before me—my sister, &c.—and there was no end to the insulting things Aunt Esther said of them.

People may wonder, and oh! how often have I wondered that my mother did not put an end to it all. But, inexplicable as it may seem, it was her extraordinary religious opinions which prevented her doing so. She literally believed and taught that when a person struck you on the right cheek you were to invite them to strike you on the left also, and therefore if Aunt Esther injured or insulted me in one way, it was right that I should give her the opportunity of injuring or insulting me in another! I do not think that my misery cost her nothing, she felt it acutely; but *because* she felt it thus, she welcomed it, as a fiery trial to be endured. Lea, however, was less patient, and openly expressed her abhorrence of her own trial in having to come up to the Rectory daily to dress my mother for dinner, and walk back to Lime through the dark night, coming again, shine or shower, in the early morning, before my mother was up.

I would not have any one suppose that, on looking back through the elucidation of years, I can see no merits in my Aunt Esther Hare. The austerities which she enforced upon my mother with regard to me she fully carried out as regarded herself. "Elle vivait avec elle-même comme sa victime," as Mme. de Staël would describe it. She was the Inquisition in person. She probed and analysed herself and the motive of her every action quite as bitterly and mercilessly as she probed and analysed others. If any pleasure, any even which resulted from affection for others, had drawn her for an instant from what she believed to be the path—and it was always the thorniest path—of self-sacrifice, she would remorselessly denounce that pleasure, and even tear out that affection from her heart. She fasted and denied herself in everything; indeed, I remember that when she was once very ill, and it was necessary for her to see a doctor, she never could be persuaded to consent to it, till the happy idea occurred of inducing her to do so on a Friday, by way of a penance! To such of the poor as accepted her absolute authority, Aunt Esther was unboundedly kind, generous, and considerate. To the wife of the curate, who leant confidingly upon her, she was an unselfish and heroic nurse, equally judicious and tender, in every crisis of a perplexing and dangerous illness. To her own sisters and other members of her family her heart and home were ever open, with unvarying affection. To her husband, to whom her severe creed taught her to show the same inflexible obedience she exacted from others, she was utterly devoted. His requirement that she should receive his old friend, Mrs. Alexander, as a permanent inmate, almost on an equality with herself in the family home, and surround her with loving attentions, she bowed to without a murmur. But to a little boy who was, to a certain degree, independent of her, and who had from the first somewhat resented her interference, she knew how to be—oh! she was—most cruel.

Open war was declared at length between Aunt Esther and myself. I had a favourite cat called Selma, which I adored, and which followed me about at Lime wherever I went. Aunt Esther saw this, and at once insisted that the cat must be given up to her. I wept over it in agonies of grief: but Aunt Esther insisted. My mother was relentless in saying that I must be taught to give up my own way and pleasure to others; and forced to give it up if I would not do so willingly, and with many tears, I took Selma in a basket to the Rectory. For some days it almost comforted me for going to the Rectory, because then I possibly saw my idolised Selma. But soon there came a day when Selma was missing: Aunt Esther had ordered her to be . . . hung!

From this time I never attempted to conceal that I loathed Aunt Esther. I constantly gave her the presents which my mother made me save up all my money to buy for her—for her birthday, Christmas, New Year, &c.—but I never spoke to her unnecessarily. On these occasions I always received a present from her in return—"The Rudiments of Architecture," price nine-pence, in a red cover. It was always the same, which not only saved expense, but also the trouble of thinking. I have a number of copies of "The Rudiments of Architecture" now, of which I thus became the possessor.

16. Domestic Service

SOCIAL HISTORIANS concerned with the wrongs of labor, a theme to which critics have warmed from Robert Owen and the first Sir Robert Peel at the opening of the industrial era to the present, almost invariably speak of categories like mill workers, agricultural laborers, miners, handloom weavers, or even skilled artisans and craftsmen. All of these are useful and important groups. About them we know a great deal and shall undoubtedly learn more. Yet the largest single category of labor, and one that increased sharply during the Victorian era, is domestic service.

While the handloom weaver fought a losing battle against machinery, the miner struggled against the brutality of the butty system, and millhands developed trade unions to preserve what few advantages they had—the political establishment was willing to investigate, make token gestures, even (on occasion) intervene with a degree of decision. But in the largest and fast growing category of domestic servants, no one took the faintest interest. The servant, somewhat in the manner of the Victorian woman, was a casualty of the sanctity of the Victorian home. To be sure, Victorian culture demanded that servants be properly treated, but gross abuses were frighteningly common. Nothing protected the backstairs maid from the unwanted attentions of the scion of the house. Should she complain, she would be discharged. Should she acquiesce and be caught, she would be discharged. Should she become pregnant, she would be discharged.

Servants might respond in kind and often did. They could embezzle (the coachman, oats for the horses; the cook, food; the housemaid or valet, trinkets and small change), they could perform slovenly work with ill grace, or they might respond in countless ways to domestic abuse. Because servants often did become pregnant or turn to drink or petty theft, the middle and upper classes could always remind themselves of the essential weakness of character in the lower orders.

In no other situation were "workers" more isolated than in domestic service. They lived in and were part of a household, and yet they were excluded from the nexus of family relationships. Because domestic servants were one of the first "commodities" acquired by those successful in the great world, they became increasingly victims in awkward, novel relationships. Ellen W. Darwin touched on a series of aspects of the problem of domestic service. She aroused considerable indignation, quite as much perhaps because she dared to open the taboo doors of the Victorian home as for her advanced views on the general question of labor and social relations.

Recommended Reading

The literature is scanty, but see M. Lochhead, *The Victorian Household* (London: 1964), and E. Hull, ed., *Miss Whetan's Journal of a Governesss*, 2 vols. (Newton Abbot: 1969).

ELLEN W. DARWIN,
DOMESTIC SERVICE[1]

In the sixteenth century, those who took an interest in education were apologetic. If they were not drawn to the profession by necessity, they felt it incumbent on them to explain and defend

1. It will be seen that the following remarks and suggestions apply most strongly to the ordinary middle-class household, where there are about two to five servants in the kitchen. Also, they are most applicable to female servants, the male servants, in obedience to the working of economic law, commanding not only much higher wages, but claiming also a position of comparative freedom and independence.

Source: From *The Nineteenth Century* 39 (August 1890), pp. 286–296.

their interest in a subject then considered so trivial. Nowadays, explanations and apologies would be considered superfluous on the part of those who state their views on education. But they would, perhaps, not be considered superfluous in an introduction to a treatise on Domestic Service. In any case, surprise, and possibly derision, would be excited if it were stated that domestic service is a problem as momentous as that of Capital and Labour, and as complicated as that of Individualism and Socialism. Social theorists and philanthropists are dealing energetically with the state of the working classes, and with the relations of one class to another. But they are silent on this—a most important and significant side of human life, where the individuals of the two great classes, commonly known as Capital and Labour, come into the closest and most direct personal relationship.

With this problem women have dealt single-handed and alone. In all civilised ages they must have given thought, or at least time, to it. The management of the household was, and probably will continue to the end of time to be, their business. In the times of slavery and feudalism, though difficulties may have arisen, their task must have been easier than it is now. The principles by which to settle their difficulties were plain. But slavery and feudalism have passed away. Faint echoes of them are heard occasionally in the speech of some British matron roused on the subject of domestic grievances; and perhaps there still hangs about the idea of domestic relations an odour of stale and ineffectual feudalism. However it may be, domestic relations have lagged behind in the course of progress, and do not seem to have adjusted themselves to the modern spirit of human relations. The consequence is, that the domestic machinery is continually jarring. Most women who are mistresses of households must have felt at times that it was strangely hard to work: many servants must have felt that it can be turned into a yoke of tyranny and injustice. But most women have been taught—and with many it is an instinct—that the household (and of the household the management of servants is the principal part) must take up a great deal of time, and probably give a good deal of worry. There is by no means a plentiful supply of employment for women, and women who are poor, and not particularly well-educated, must earn their livelihood and work as servants. Thus urged by a sense of duty on the one side and necessity on the other, the domestic machinery goes round, but with many more, I think, of those "various entanglements, weights, blows, clashings, motions by which things severally go on," than occur in the workings of other human relations. Over this friction a silence reigns. Its causes have never been fundamentally inquired into: one side is silent through necessity, and the other through a certain callousness and reserve.

Of course there are exceptions—cases where things work in harmony, because on both sides there are people of character who, in spite of great obstacles thrown in their way, have succeeded in understanding each other. These instances I cannot help regarding as exceptions. The obstacles are increasing, and slowly, but surely, domestic service as a profession is going downhill.

I see a vista of irritable mistresses and irritated servants; there is the desperate cry for lady-helps, and the growth of flats, where the difficulties of housekeeping can be avoided. The voice of servants, as a class, is never heard. But there remains one great and significant fact: it is well known that in manufacturing districts, where there is ample employment for women, servants belonging to that part of the country are rarely to be found, showing that the women of those parts prefer the hard work and the long hours of factory-life to the comparative ease and comfort, but, at the same time, dependence, of domestic service. Does this not show emphatically that, as employment for women increases, domestic service will be avoided more and more by women of capacity, of character, and independence—the very women who are wanted in the profession which offers, more than any other, positions of trust and responsibility? As at present constituted, it not only discourages people of the highest type of character from entering it, but its tendency is to have a deteriorating effect on many of those who do so, and this because it denies them many of the essentials of a healthy, independent, and natural life.

The relation between employer and servant is infinitely complicated by the fact that it is by no means a purely business one. Wages are, indeed, settled roughly by the laws of supply and demand, though until there are trade-unions among servants none can tell how exactly. For a certain amount of money and board and lodging they undertake to do a certain amount of badly-defined work. But here the business relation ends, and the human relation, tremendous in its scope and importance, begins. It is with this latter that I am concerned. The profession is, on the whole, well paid, compared to the other branches of female industry; and I think that most servants would allow that wages are of small importance, in comparison with the other factors of their position. For their life, so to speak—for comfort, happiness, freedom, and development—they are dependent on the character of their master and mistress, especially on that of the mistress, who gives the tone to the house, and by her choice and treatment of servants ultimately decides the tone of the kitchen, and its possibilities of being a place in which it is tolerable to live. It is, practically speaking, a servant's life which is governed in this vague and uncertain way.

It cannot be argued for one minute that the dependence of servant and employer is mutual. The master and mistress depend on having good servants for a certain amount of their material well-being, and some mistresses who are sensitive to personal relations are uncomfortable when these personal relations go wrong. But it is mainly for material comfort that the mistress depends on the servant. There, beyond a vague feeling of responsibility, which generally takes the form of filling up what leisure the servant may have with work designed to keep her out of mischief, her necessary connection with her servant ends. She has her independent life—her husband, her children, her interests, her social duties, her friends and acquaintances.

The servant is cut off from both her family and her class. She sees, perhaps, her family for a fortnight in the year, possibly not for so long. The severing of family ties is, indeed, a penalty which domestic service shares in common with many other of the professions of the poor. Yet it none the less remains a stern and cruel fact. In addition to this, a servant's intercourse with the outside world must be fitted into two or three hours on the Sunday; and, perhaps, if she is in an easy situation, she may have an hour or two during the week. But, on the whole, a servant's society is that of the three or four other servants in the kitchen, with whom she is very lucky if she can form a friendship of circumstances. I think I may say, without exaggeration, that this is the only form of society which mistresses encourage. Whatever advantages it may be supposed are opened to her by being continually in contact with the wealthier and leisured classes, it cannot be denied that it is thoroughly unhealthy to separate a human being from her people. I mean, by "her people," not only her family, but the class in which she was born, and whose interests and hopes and struggles she inherits understanding of, and sympathy with. For servants are not a class in themselves, though the tendency of domestic service is to make them so. They are part of the great working class, which has its distinctive social life, different from that of the leisured classes, but not necessarily inferior.

Some there are, who have turned their back on their own class— *i.e.*, on the wealthy and leisured and cultivated—who say that only in the class that works day by day for its livelihood, that faces daily the struggle for life, is solid character, simplicity, honesty, strength, resolution, and real heroism to be found. In literature, the labouring class has many champions, Carlyle not amongst the least. Still, putting aside what genius, enthusiasts, poets, and, above all, revolutionists have said, common sense must recognise that, if the struggle for life is not so severe as to sap all energy and hope, it brings out and intensifies those qualities of resolution, strength, and independence which we look upon as the basis of character. For on the weaknesses and vices of the poorer classes retribution is swift: ruin and misery follow quickly on helplessness, incompetency, laziness, and dishonesty. We have, with some inconsistency, put the fate of our country into the hands of the labouring class; but when we come to deal with them personally, we are slow to recognise in them an equality, much less a superiority, in those solid virtues which are called out by the honest, and therefore successful, struggle with the sternest realities of life, and which are apt to languish in easy circumstances. I do not wish to contrast the working and the leisured classes, or to try and answer that question, as old as our civilisation, and yet every day pathetically fresh, why one human being should work all day, and barely get enough to eat, and another should sit at ease, and yet have more than is good for him in every respect. I only wish to emphasise strongly, that those whose circumstances are so entirely different from ours must, their common human nature being taken into account, possess, not only a distinctive individuality, but naturally, also, a distinctive social life, and that this distinctive social life is healthy, vigorous, independent, and not wanting in high standards and in stirring interests and hopes. Also, that the intercourse in this life is close and intimate, and perhaps more necessary and stimulating, in proportion as it is founded more on mutual wants and mutual sympathies, and less (as with the richer classes) on the idea of enjoyment.

From this life in which they were brought up, to which their fathers, mothers, brothers, and probable husbands belong, servants are cut off, owing, to a certain extent, to the necessities of their position, but far more to custom and habit, which, it seems to me, are grounded on prejudice—on a certain unfounded distrust of the class to which they belong.

No amount of kindness, or even of genial companionship, on the part of master and mistress, can compensate to them for being cut off from this independent social life. And what is offered to them instead? They are connected with the wealthier classes principally as ministering to their material well-being. They have a clear and complete view of their luxury. With their attention to their own comfort, with the ugly, squalid corners of their lives, with their bad tempers, with their efforts to keep up the appearance that convention demands, they are intimate. No people contemplate so frequently and so strikingly the unequal distribution of wealth: they fold up dresses whose price contains double the amount of their year's wages; they pour out at dinner wine whose cost would have kept a poor family for weeks. And of the amusements and occupations, of the higher interests and of the higher life of the leisured classes, of which comfort and ease and luxury is only supposed to be the basis, they have no share, and, probably, very little understanding. Cut off from their own general life, they remain spectators from the outside of that of others; and it cannot be said that its appearance is always elevating, or even intelligible, except from the standard of self-indulgence. What they gain by constant association with the weathier classes are, principally, external qualities—politeness, a certain amount of outward refinement, a high standard of cleanliness for themselves and of comfort for others; sometimes they find a patron, but rarely a friend.

The limits of the tolerableness, or the intolerableness, of such a life, vary as human nature varies. Mistresses are of all sorts—the fussy, the fidgety, the callous, the indifferent, the kind and protecting, the competent, the incompetent, the just, the unjust, and, lastly, the bullying. It cannot be denied that many opportunities in dealing with servants are open to those who are born with this instinct in their nature. Happily, one knows that these opportunities are limited by the endurance of the servant: the young and sanguine soon rebelling and leaving; the older, more experienced, and less sanguine, bearing much, knowing that change in the comparative dark is not always for the better. In Ecclesiasticus it is written: "Be not as a lion in thy house, nor frantic among thy servants." I have always wished that a way could have been found to put this among the Ten Commandments.

But though the Ten Commandments are silent on the subject, there must be some maxims of public opinion, some generalisations from the common experience of mankind, or, rather, of womankind, to which to appeal. There ought to be some guide to an inexperienced mistress as to how she is to treat the servant, and some guide to the servant as to how she is to be treated. There is, indeed, a strong public opinion with regard to servants which, unfortunately, seems to have been generalised from unfortunate facts. "You inquire into the stuffing of your couch when anything galls you there, whereas eider-down and perfect French springs excite no attention." When things go smoothly (to the enormous credit of the servants in most cases), it is, perhaps, natural that the domestic arrangements should excite no attention. But when things go wrong, and the comfort of the house suffers, then occurs vast disturbance, and the incompetency, the untrustworthiness, the obstinacy, the laziness of servants is insisted on. It is, as a rule, only when servants take advantage of their situation and responsibilities that attention is aroused; it is then that vague generalisations are made, and vague principles formed for future guidance. Thus there comes to be a very low idea of the capacity of servants for performing their duties, though there is a very high ideal of the duties themselves. Tradition teaches that mistresses must continually guard against being taken advantage of—no little carelessness, no little omission, must be passed over; the ideal mistress must superintend and watch, and her attitude of mind, if it cannot be said to be exactly suspicious, must be apprehensive. The leisure of servants is called idleness, and jealously watched, and it is feared that, if the mistress does not fill it up, Satan must. This atmosphere if apprehension, even if we do not allow it to be called one of mistrust, is certainly not genial or encouraging to live in. In theory it surrounds the whole class, though in practice it may be frequently tempered by the personal discrimination of a master or mistress. If it is necessary, then it is obvious that the worst of the working class choose the profession. If it is not so, it is irksome, cruel, and harmful.

It is, indeed, true that it is easy for a servant to take advantage of

her position: there are infinite opportunities of doing work badly
—of neglecting it, of scamping it—and for carelessness and deceit;
many opportunities of concealing for a long time, from the strictest
of mistresses, bad work and bad conduct. It is for this very reason
that a servant's post is one of trust and responsibility. The position
of cook—the task of being economical with the resources of
others—is a position of great responsibility. To care for the furniture, the linen, the china, the plate, as if it were your own, demands
a great amount of character. To be steady; to be satisfied with the
smallest enjoyment possible; to be always polite; to control your
temper under all circumstances; to get on well with your fellow-
servants, with whom you are in the closest contact, and whom you
may dislike, or, indeed, detest, demands a high sense of duty,
strength, and resolution. But shall we encourage people of character and self-respect to enter a profession where so much is demanded of them when they know (for no pains are taken to
conceal it) that they have to assert themselves against a spirit
which, *a priori*, does not consider them worthy of much respect or
capable of much independence? Many who do so may have their
characters wrecked in the struggle; others may emerge, still with a
high sense of duty, but embittered and permanently irritated.

And here I must make a digression. In speaking of servants, so
far I have meant the average trained servant and the mature human
being. The quite young girl, whose character is still unformed, and
who has been trained to no domestic work, must, of course, go
through the mill, and learn her work and the duties incumbent on
her profession. And here comes in the office and the talents which
are in themselves "magnificently useful," but exceptional, and
which are wrongly supposed to belong to every mistress of a
house. The training of girls, especially of young servants, requires
capacity and genius, and it is only given to a few to possess these
qualities. Those who do and who happen to be at the head of a
household, may be said to have found their vocation. As a rule, I
should think, unless the mistress possesses this exceptional genius, the
training of young and inexperienced servants is best done by an
older and trained servant (who should, of course, be paid for the
additional responsibility and the trouble of teaching). Experienced
servants will understand, better than an ordinary mistress, how to
teach the work that has to be learned; and they will, perhaps,
administer better the discipline that has to be submitted to. Those

who have never gone through it themselves will either be too lenient or too harsh; whereas the older servant may, from having more fellow-feeling, teach better, and more quickly and intelligibly, the hard lesson, that life to them—the children of the labouring class—will have few outlooks, few pleasures, and small leisure, but is mainly made up of hard work, responsibilities, and duties.

This is by no means a callous age, indifferent to the hardships and sufferings of the poor: philanthropy flourishes exceedingly, and to the rather wicked and to the very poor we are entirely kind. But philanthropy rather spoils manners to the individual: it is apt to make people think that, in their relations with others, they must constantly be on the watch to do good or improve. This is not, by any means, the spirit to introduce into domestic relations. We need, rather, that behaviour which is the basis of all true ties between human beings, and which lies at the bottom of all courtesy. I mean, a certain respect and belief, which every human being has the right to claim of another, whatever his station may be, till he has definitely proved that he is unworthy of it. Especially is this tone necessary in domestic service, where the business relation and the human relation are so inextricably mixed up with each other, and both so close and personal, and where it seems to me important to make the employed feel that her subordination in work to her mistress does not extend to her character and her life. If the wealthier classes feel they owe more to their less fortunate brethren, let them cultivate a certain tolerance and forbearance, and faith in human nature. Faith is thought to be an excellent thing till it comes to be applied to human character. It is then that it is thought to be dangerous. But whatever the danger be—and, as a rule, it is most blindly and gratuitously exaggerated—it seems to me that it is better to be taken advantage of a thousand times than to suspect once unjustly.

There are, also, some definite changes to be made in order to put the profession on a higher and more attractive level. They involve a practical extension of the theory of belief and trust in servants. First, every servant should have, at least, every day, two hours' definite leisure, during which she is her own mistress, and not bound to answer the calls of the bell. This *might* call for a little more expense, but I should think, on the whole, would only involve a little trouble in arrangement. This leisure they must employ exactly as they wish; and an endeavour must be made to break down the prejudice that even the best mistresses and the best servants have, and which is so injurious, as tending to make them a class to themselves—viz., that it is not desirable that servants should form friendships outside their own class. The maxim of a superior servant, encouraged by mistresses, is that "she should keep herself to herself." If this meant only a proper reserve, there would be little objection to it; but it means, unfortunately, that she should eschew friendship and acquaintances. "It is a mere and miserable solitude to want true friends," says Bacon in his essay on Friendship, "without which the world is but a wilderness." And to me it seems that the only way to keep a servant's life healthy and wholesome and stirring, and, indeed, the life of any one cut off from their family, and family interests and family affections, is to give them every chance of making friends and acquaintances. To feel yourself part of a larger life, to be occasionally taken out of yourself by interests other than those that concern your immediate surroundings, to have a call on your sympathies, to hear of the happiness and calamities of your friends and your neighbours, is necessary to any healthy-minded individual, especially to those who do not feed their sympathies and emotions through books. To live in very close contact with three or four people who have, none of them, much change, or chance of impersonal interests, whose faces may be "a gallery of pictures, and their talk but a tinkling cymbal," because there is no love is, to generate discontent, bad temper, and that disposition to quarrel and take offence which is characteristic, not only of servants, but of every one who lives a starved and limited life. But here the distrust which I have mentioned as making part of the atmosphere in which servants live comes out very strikingly. We are, perhaps, the most backward of all nations to recognise how necessary is that freedom of spirit which happiness and a little enjoyment and change give, to preserve the mind healthy and wholesome. Here, perhaps, the philanthropists have done harm. Kind and sympathetic and energetic people are urged on by love of their kind, and the desire to make the world a better place for the less fortunate, to give what help they can. But they are brought into communication, not with the real working class, from which servants should be drawn, but with those who have fallen out of the ranks, either through misfortune, or helplessness, or immorality. Philanthropic work brings people into contact with

the fringe that surrounds every class: but we should no more judge
the working class by the fringe that surrounds it, than the
wealthier and leisured class should be judged by the fringe that
surrounds it. If this fringe seem larger in proportion, it is because in
the poorer class nothing can be concealed. In the wealthier classes a
decent reserve (except from servants) can be thrown over immorality and drunkenness and deviations from honesty; a foolish
mistake is not followed instantly by ruin. It is cases where human
nature has sinned and fallen which are mostly before the eyes of
those engaged in good works, who thus become to have the same
desponding view of the poorer and hard-working class that a
lawyer in the Divorce Court will probably have of marriage in
general.

The temptations of the poorer class seem many and strong; but,
in proportion as their work and success depends on their resistance
to them, so they are strong. Public opinion and the traditions of
respectability are, perhaps, stronger in their class than in ours; and
what is more frequently observable among the best of the working
class, than that they have a sense of reputation carried to the
degree of hardness? Of course, I do not mean that there ought to
be no check or guard against the dangers of intercourse, especially
when beauty and high spirits and impulsiveness seem to aggravate
these dangers. For this reason, if for no other, it is necessary that a
servant be kept as much as possible in connection with her family.
No mistress, if she feels the moral responsibility of having servants
under her roof, would hesitate to throw, if it were possible, some
of the responsibility on the shoulders naturally fitted to bear it—
that of the parents and family. This is only one reason among the
many for encouraging communication with relations. A great
majority of servants of the highest character forfeit a life of independent employment which, perhaps, would be less lucrative, in
order to support parents and relations. The feeling that leads them
to do this, and to give up very often the chance of saving for their
own old age, must make separation for long a hardship.

There is one peculiar relic of feudalism—one might almost say
barbarism—in the custom of engaging servants, which needs reform. It is strange, to say the least of it, that the mistress should be
entitled to have a written and formal character of the servant, and
that the servant, to whom the situation is everything that is most
important in life, should have no formal opportunity given her

of judging of the situation, of hearing of the character of the household. This, which common justice demands, could be easily remedied without any extra machinery by the following plan: every mistress should choose a referee, or two referees, among her servants past or present, who have been with her not less than two years; she should give the names and addresses of these two referees to the servant whom she is inclined to engage, before she writes for her character from her last mistress. I cannot imagine any reasonable objection to this plan. If carried largely into practice, it could become the test of any theory about domestic service. Mistresses could then gather statistics and make generalisations as to the situations which were most highly recommended and most sought after by the best and most competent of servants. It might also put spirit into the custom of character-giving, which is said by some to be so formal. Personally, I have never found it so. It puts a vast amount of irresponsible power into the hands of one fallible human being; and though I think it may rarely be abused, it adds tremendously to the unnecessary and injurious dependence of servants.

In what I have said, my aim has been to show the great importance of putting Domestic services on a higher level, in order to secure and preserve that high average of character and ability which is absolutely necessary for the sort of work and behaviour required of them. The profession can never be made superior to any other independent one that offers itself to women. There is a certain dependence in it which, even under the best of circumstances, can never be done away with. The case of the governess profession is an analogous one. Since the birth of high schools, though the work is infinitely harder, and the pay less, governesses to private families are comparatively hard to find; the independent life of the high schools absorbs them. This fact, and the general progress of civilisation, has brought about a considerable change in the position of the private governess. The post is extremely well paid, and care is taken to make it attractive. Things have improved since the time when the Brontës[2] lived and suffered as private

2. "She (Charlotte Brontë) said that none but those who had been in the position of a governess could ever realise the dark side of 'respectable' human nature: under no great temptation to crime, but daily giving way to selfishness and ill-temper, till its conduct towards those dependent on it sometimes amounts to a tyranny of which one would rather be the victim than the inflicter" (*Life of Charlotte Brontë*, Mrs. Gaskell).

governesses; and though independence and freedom is vitally necessary to genius, yet it is equally necessary to the average mind. Why cannot we make the same change with regard to servants before we are driven to it by the rapidly increasing growth of independent employment for women, or before we reach that stage through which America is passing at present, where, we are told by American ladies, servants have it *all* their own way. What mistress would not rejoice in a high average among servants of good temper, ability, and character, to whom she need only teach the "little ways" of her household, and not the fundamental duties and responsibilities of work and life: so many women's lives are usurped by duties they are incompetent to perform, by attempting to teach work of which they know nothing, and inculculating virtues which they cannot practise.

There is also another consideration which forces itself strongly on some. In Stevenson's *Inland Voyage*, the "Cigarette" and the "Arethusa" feel that their superior, though tough, beefsteak is not improved, but rather spoilt, by the plate of bread-berry which the working man eats sitting side by side with them at the inn-table. "You may have a head knowledge that people live more poorly than yourself, but it is not agreeable—I was going to say it was against the etiquette of the universe—to sit at the same table and pick your own superior diet from among their crusts." In the same way, one has a head knowledge that thousands of lives, by no fault of their own, are limited, and dulled, and spiritually starved compared to ours. This we bear with equanimity: indeed, if we did not, it would be like hearing the grass grow, and we should perish under the burden of our sensibilities. But this fact stares one in the face, and meets one at every turn, in one's relations with the servants with whom one lives side by side. Custom may dull any sensibility: and it very properly dulls a good many, else life would not be possible; but it seems to me that with some it had better not interfere.

17. The Sweated Trades

OUR CONCEPTION of the industrial revolution and the conversion to factory industrialism often blinds us to the many areas in which handwork continued. Even in factories hand processes continued to predominate over automated until well into the twentieth century. The sophisticated machine tool industry, essential to automation, began effective development only about the middle of the century. The exploitation of machine production, moreover, tended to be confined to a relatively limited area, principally capital goods.

While handloom weavers disappeared save in luxury trade by the last third of the century, handwork continued throughout the Victorian age to be the basis of the clothing industry. The putting-out system and the sweatshop were characteristic of clothing manufacture. But sweated trades were limited neither to clothing nor, geographically, to London, as the selection from this investigation might imply. The situation was, if anything, worse in the provincial cities and in Edinburgh. Leather goods, nail and chain making, and other industries included in this inquiry were just as depressing. The sweater in chain and nail manufacture, for instance, was called—with unconscious humor—a "fogger." He acted as agent for the master in putting out work, drove "a coach and horses through the [Truck] Act," routinely cheated and exploited the workers, and had little difficulty in resisting the incursion of trade unionism.

The second part of this selection is the committee's summary and recommendations. They merit careful reading, for they suggest both the limits that still existed on government intervention in private matters and those areas considered to be legitimate concerns. Even here, in the Victorian twilight, the committee believed that moral suasion would derive from its investigation. The public conscience would force masters to behave and workers to be provident.

Recommended Reading

In addition to the general works cited for Parts I and II, see B. Webb, *My Apprenticeship* (London: 1926).

SELECT COMMITTEE OF THE HOUSE OF LORDS,
REPORT ON THE SWEATING SYSTEM

TAILORING

(1) London

Every cause which tends to produce and perpetuate sweating is at work in the most concentrated form in the clothing trades. In reference to those trades, therefore, we have found it necessary to take a large body of evidence, much of which is of the greatest interest and importance.

It is stated that some years ago a tailor, who was properly trained

Source: From *Parliamentary Papers*, 1890, vol. XVII, pp. iv–viii, xxv–xxxii, xlii–xlv.

in his calling, could make either a complete suit of clothes, or any part of it: he knew his business throughout. Sweating has been known for 50 years. The parcelling out of work must have had its origin in the fact that the journeyman tailor took his work home to be done by himself, and possibly by other members of his family. There were obviously advantages to the journeyman tailor and employer in this arrangement. There was little subdivision, the tailor made the garments from end to end; the only subdivision then being that the least important part of the work was put into the hands of the workmen's own apprentices. In the opinion of many witnesses the gradual lapse of the system of thorough apprenticeship increases the sweating, and is extremely prejudicial to the interest of trade and to the public. Now, excepting in the very best bespoke trade, a man generally confines himself to one particular kind of garment, or to a certain portion only of a garment, the making of which is easily learnt. Now, instead of the thoroughly practical tailor being employed, the trade is divided into different sections. There are foremen or cutters, basters, machinists, fellers, buttonholers, pressers, and general workers, one witness indeed stating that there were 25 subdivisions. "Sub-division is so minutely carried out that a man who can press a coat cannot necessarily press a waistcoat, and a waistcoat presser is equally unqualified to press trousers. If the labour was not so much subdivided there would not be half the evils connected with sweating." This is borne out by Mr. Burnett, Labour Correspondent of the Board of Trade. "Except for the best kinds of clothing, the old-fashioned tailor has been crushed out; and although for the highly skilled man the rates of remuneration may be as high, or higher than before," (and this high remuneration is shown to exist) "the great bulk of the cheap clothing is in the hands of a class who are not tailors at all in the old sense of the term;" the trade is governed by no rules at all, at least as regards the lower grades; the hours are anything a sweater likes to make them; each sweater has his own method of engaging and paying his workers. The question as to what is a day, or half a day, is differently interpreted by different masters. It is the usual thing for seven and a-half, eight, and nine hours to be regarded as half a day.

In some cases the man known as a sweater is merely an agent, knowing nothing of the business. Sometimes he acts the part of a foreman, and directs the work of every branch, understanding the whole business thoroughly. Sometimes he works as hard as any of his employés.

Sometimes work is sent down into the country to be done in cottages. A witness thought it did not go through more than one hand before reaching the worker, "for the price paid for the labour is so limited that there is not a chance of filtration."

The conditions under which life is carried on as described by some witnesses are deplorable in the extreme. These witnesses have seen people working with the garments on their backs to keep the worker warm; Mr. Monro knowing of a case of a child with measles being covered by one of these garments. "Three or four gas jets may be flaring in the room, a coke fire burning in the wretched fire-place, sinks untrapped, closets without water, and altogether the sanitary condition abominable." A witness told us that in a double room, perhaps 9 by 15 feet, a man, his wife, and six children slept, and in the same room ten men were usually employed, so that at night eighteen persons would be in that one room. These witnesses alluded to the want of sanitary precautions and of decent and sufficient accommodation, and declared that the effect of this, combined with the inadequate wage earned, had the effect of driving girls to prostitution. As to sanitary arrangements; in a sweater's den, with which witness is acquainted, there is one water-closet for all workers, male and female, about twenty-two persons. The medical officer stated to witness that one water-closet was insufficient for more than twenty persons. If the owner of the shop is required to make an additional water-closet he refuses, and he says he will reduce his hands. This may be done in the slack season, but in the busy season he will take more hands on, and the state of things is as bad as ever. Referring to workshops in Prince's-street, there is a shop in which the water-closet is in the shop itself; the females sit within three feet of the door of it, and the water-closet fits into a corner, not behind an ordinary fire-place, but behind a big furnace, used for heating irons, so that it is the hottest corner in the room. There is great want of decency, and it is easy to imagine what follows on such contamination. The workshop of witness is in a yard, or what was a yard. Three machines are at work; there is one fire-place and eight or nine gas jets, also a sky-light, which, when broken, exposes the workers to the rain. On complaints being made, the sweater says, "If you can't work, go home." Witness works in a room nine feet square, and in some cases only 130 cubic feet of air are obtainable per person. In nine out of ten cases the windows are broken and filled up with canvas; ventilation is impossible, and light insufficient. The Rev. R. C. Billing, now Bishop of Bedford, said that the poor people, who formerly occupied two or three rooms, are now, for the most part, driven to occupy one room. There they live by day and night, and there is to be found all the trade refuse in the room, creating an immense danger not only to themselves but to their neighbours. "You can tell where work is being done on the Sabbath by the blinds being drawn; there is no holiday at all."

Work is precarious, and wages, such as they are, are irregularly paid. "Sometimes," one of the workmen told us, "we have nothing to do for weeks and weeks, but have to go idle, and the wages are not paid regularly. One sweater pays on Friday, one pays on Saturday, one pays on Sunday, and one pays nothing; you have to summon him for it." Statements with regard to wages paid in this trade differ very widely, as it is inevitable they should do, considering the subdivisions already referred to, the irregular nature of the work, and the different degrees of skill required. A paper handed in, of Mr. Burnett's, attempts, on the basis of careful but limited inquiries, to give the average rate of wages in various branches. From this it would appear that the highest rate paid for men's work is 10s. a day, and that it runs down to 2s. 6d.; women occasionally get 6s. a day, but the average is very low. For a slop coat from 2s. to 3s. 9d. was formerly paid; the rate is now 1s. 6d. to 2s. 3d. A good coat, for which a man got 10s. 2d. a few years ago, now brings to the maker only 6s. 6d. Mr. Burnett added the following example: "a few doors further down was an establishment where cloaks are now made for 4s. 6d., and six or seven years ago were paid 8s.: Witney coats, which were then made for 10s. 3d., are now made for 5s. 6d.;" and this was the case of a man whom Mr. Burnett described as a first-rate tailor. He paid good wages, and even in prosperous times it was difficult for him to clear 3l. a week for himself. A woman makes a vest out-right for 5d., and she is able to make four a day. Mr. Arnold White produced a coat which was made for 7½d., and by working 15 hours a woman could make four such in the day, earning 2s. 6d.; but out of this she had to pay 3d. for getting the button-holes worked, and 4d. for trimmings. It is not clearly established, in the opinion of the Committee, whether or how far this lowering of prices is due to the more extended use of machinery.

As regards the abstracts from the Factory and Workshops Act for the protection of workers, witness produces one and describes what is done with it. It is written in English, and generally everyone in the room is a foreigner and unlikely to be able to read a word of English. This document is stowed away in a drawer where it gets grimy with age. On a visit from the Inspector it is produced and put up. On the occasion of the next whitewashing it is stowed away again.

As the workshops are described by witnesses to be miserable dens; so is the food stated to be of the poorest description. "I am almost ashamed to say what my food is." Ordinary diet, a cup of tea and a bit of fish. Mrs. Killick, 22 years a trouser finisher, was glad to get a bit of cleaning and washing to support her family. The money earned was hardly sufficient to buy food. Her food is chiefly a cup of tea and a bit of fish. "Meat I do not expect; I might get meat once in six months."

Regarding hours of work, the evidence tends to show much evasion of the Factory Acts and overtime working of females. Many difficulties are experienced by inspectors in endeavouring to find the workshops, the worst being the most difficult to find. Monro said he had a factory for two years before it was visited by the inspector. Mr. Holley considers Clause 69 in the Factory Act is more protection to the sweater than the worker. As regards instances of overwork, Mrs. Killick works from 6 a.m. to 8 p.m.; Mrs. Hayes, from 6 or 7 a.m. to 10 p.m., or midnight; whether this takes place subject to the jurisdiction of the Factory Inspector is not very clearly stated. It is true that the Factory Act requires the employers of children, young persons, and women, to keep in books, provided for the purpose, a register of overtime as a check on the infringement of the law with regard to overtime, but according to some witnesses evasion of the law in this particular is easy and constantly practised. As regards men's hours, sometimes they work 18, 20, or even 22 hours at a stretch; a witness once worked 40 hours, from 6 a.m. on Thursday till 10 p.m. on Friday; a witness went to work the day before appearing before the Committee, at 6.30 a.m. and worked till 2.30 a.m. of the following day; one hour for dinner, no tea time; worked harder here than in Warsaw, and made less. A witness stated that he got 5s. per diem when at work; his hours were from 8 a.m. to 11 p.m., and employment was very irregular. The Rev. R. C. Billing has seen hands at work at 2 a.m., and has found them again at work at 7 a.m. the same morning.

The foregoing statements disclose the case of the workers as given by them in evidence. The evidence is of an extremely contradictory nature, and very strong statements against employers were sworn to by some witnesses, and circumstantially denied by the employers. Mr. Moses, who is a contractor and master tailor, and who attended as representative of the master tailors and journeymen, challenges all the figures and statements set forth in Mr. Burnett's Report, contradicts several of Lyons' statements, and, from knowledge of his character, throws great doubt upon his credibility as a witness. He stated, "Our hands are paid 25 per cent, better now than they were six or seven years ago." He admitted that some of the low class houses did give out work at starvation prices. In answer to a statement of Plattman, one of the witnesses, that workmen are afraid to combine for fear of being discharged, he stated that he, in conjunction with masters and journeymen, "had endeavoured to promote and encourage combination for the mutual advantage of masters and journeymen tailors." He rebutted a statement of the Rev. R. C. Billing as to the feeling between Jews and Gentiles, and said, emphatically, that it was good. He does not admit the enormous amount of misery in the lowest class of employés, and thinks the case has been over-stated. As regards the employment of inspectors with technical knowledge, he would be afraid of it, "for, if a man were employed from the ranks of the workers, he would use arbitrary powers; that is the only objection I would have." The evidence of Mr. Moses was supported by that of work-women in his employ, but Mr. Burnett showed that the scale of wages spoken to by Mr. Moses was not invariably adhered to in his workshop.

Miss Potter, who has interested herself in the condition of the labouring classes in London, has worked personally in sweaters' shops, with a view to gain practical experience in the subject. She does not agree with Mr. Burnett's definition of sweating. She contends that the worst cases of sweating occur where there is no subcontract. Regarding the coat trade, the best part of it is in the hands of the Jews, who principally employ their own co-religionists of both sexes. They are more skilful workers than the Gentiles.

Last winter there were only 62 Jewish tailoresses on the Jewish register out of work, though there were many tailors. The best class of bespoke work pays very good wages. Machinists, 7s. to 9s. 6d.; pressers, 5s. to 8s. 6d.; and women rarely under 2s. 6d. to 5s. s. The worst sweating takes place in the lowest stratum, where there are no contracts. (There are contracts in the upper stratum.) She adds, "There is nothing to complain of in the wages in the coat trade, but hours are irregular and shops insanitary." Her remarks, however, apply only to the branch of the trade which she knew best, that is to say, "the bespoke trade with the West End shops and City." For such work as this the sweaters, whether Jews or Gentiles, pay very good wages, though the hours are long. Miss Potter said that lower wages are, as a rule, paid to out-workers than to those working in workshops, because "the outdoor work is very irresponsible, and very bad, so that the employers have to take it out in one way or another. There is an enormous amount of goods spoiled and not brought in to time, and that sort of thing, so that the honest have to pay for the dishonest." She confirmed a statement of Mr. Moses, to the effect that Jewish contractors would not take the lowest class of work. "There is the very lowest layer of the coat trade," she said, "that work is done by men and women at their own homes. It really does not pay the contractor to take it out. That is the sort of coat that is done for 7d. or 8d.; it hardly pays the Jewish contractor to take that coat out, so that that is done to a great extent by Gentile women." This remark, it must be remembered, applies only to better grades of the coat trade, and not to the small slop shops, or to the sweater who carries on his business in his own house. The prices which Mr. Burnett found would appear to contradict Miss Potter's evidence, but the figures are reconcilable, as they apply to different classes of goods. Mr. Burnett saw a man making some boys' Chesterfield coats, they were remarkably well made, and beautifully hand-stitched. His price for them was 3s. 6d. He was busy with some others which were heavily trimmed with fur, for these he received 4s. 6d. He was making some big official overcoats for the officers of the Water Company, which were also remarkably well made and stitched with silk, and he received only 3s. 6d. for these kinds of coats also. At another place 10 persons were employed making slop coats at 9d. each. In Fashion-street a man was making double-breasted coats, boys' coats, with eight button-holes, at 1s. 4d. He said that every time he takes more coats out further reductions are attempted. A firm, which has the reputation among sweaters of being the best-paying house in the trade, was paying 4s. 6d. each for coats which were sold at 2l. 2s. In Green-street an employer produced an order ticket for 60 black diagonal coats, at 1s. 2d. each; these coats were braided with five pockets, three of which had flaps. Another sweater, Mr. Burnett also stated, was busy with pilot overcoats, with velvet collars, silk stitched, at 2s. 9d. each, for which he had to find his own trimmings. In Spitalfields a Polish Jew, with a staff of five males and four females, often worked in the slack season on coats for which he received only 9d. each. In Miss Potter's opinion pauper immigration has no effect on tailoring, for, in busy times, machinists and pressers make their own terms. She states that Jews and Gentiles can work peaceably together. Miss Potter speaks strongly on the inefficiency of sanitary inspection; is further of opinion that at the East End the Gentile is generally going downwards, while the position of the Jew is improving. The Gentile makes money to drink, the Jews to save. Except as to sanitation, the coat-maker can take care of themselves. In her opinion the standard of life of the Polish Jews is so low that they can do with very much less than the English. They live on very little, and are as little particular about quality as about quantity. They are capable of thriving where an Englishman could not live, and she further gives it as an opinion that Jews and Gentiles do not compete; Gentiles do not follow the coat trade, and Jews only make coats. "They work, as it were, in water-tight compartments." In regard to the registration of workshops, she fears it would drive the trade into lower channels unless the registration included home work. She considers the landlords should be made responsible for sanitation. In her opinion, if a sweater makes a large profit it is a sign that he pays his hands well.

With regard to factories and their inspection, the evidence mostly tends in one direction. That the inspection is insufficient, and that more efficient inspection would check much evil. That the inspectors, while anxious to do their duty, have very great difficulty in finding the workshops. That in the case of workshops where they have not the right of entry, but can only enter with consent, the forms to be gone through for compulsory powers take some time to obtain, and therefore allow the sweater to do away with what is objectionable, that is, to hide or dismiss the women working overtime. So that, in reality, the system as at present pursued is more in favour of the sweater than the worker. Suggestions have been made by witnesses that every workshop should be registered, whereby notice will be given to authorities of the existence of such shops, and suggestions were made as to the fees for registration. It is also recommended that the Factory Inspector should have some sanitary powers, and be able to act at once without having to see the sanitary officer, who is a local official. Mr. Holley had made inquiries in large provincial towns in England as to the carrying out of Section 15 of the Act of 1878 for giving notice of workshops, and found it had never been carried into effect; his principal complaint not being of the wording of the Act, but the want of its enforcement, and this want of enforcement is also a complaint with the best employers, because they know that, in the absence of such inspection, illegal overtime can be carried on, thus producing unfair competition. This witness considered that the onus of registration should be on the employer. A manager, on giving work out to a new middleman, should be bound to give notice to the inspector. He is not in favour of free entry everywhere, but suggests greater facilities for finding workshops, and would favour the appointment of a practical sub-inspector, who should be acquainted with the locality.

In respect of the causes conducing to this state of things, Mr. Hollington says, "We have room for the educated labour but we have not room for the unskilled labour. My contention is . . . that the cause of sweating is the surplus or surfeit of uneducated or unskilled labour. That is the whole origin of the thing, and is caused by the immigration of Jews, and by the Jewish Board of Guardians, and the large proportion of women who work at the trade. That is what the surplus is composed of."

This statement as to Jewish immigration was contradicted by Mr. Stephany and Mr. Alexander, both officials of the Jewish Board of Guardians. Mr. Shipton states that he knows no trade, where union is strong, which is affected by foreign labour or goods. He thinks that public exposure has already had a healthy effect. He looks to combination for the amelioration of the existing state of things. Mr. White, in the course of his evidence, points out that combination is almost impossible owing to the different languages spoken by immigrants, and also to the fear among workers of joining societies. Various witnesses speak to the promotion of sweating by foreigners, owing to their being able to work at starvation wages, which naturally defeats attempts at fixing "log" prices. This statement as to immigration is combated by Miss Potter, Stephany, and Alexander. Mr. Stephany does not think the number of foreigners is increasing. Very few sweaters apply to the Jewish Board of Guardians for relief. He quoted figures to show that the emigration of Jews exceeded the immigration; in 1887, 536 went out, 249 came in. Wages are not bad, but the number of days on which work is procurable are few in the week. He considers that some of the worst cases named in Mr. Burnett's Report are isolated cases.

Mr. Alexander remarks that subdivision of labour tends to cheapen and quicken production; he, therefore, is of opinion that it is a boon to the poor consumer. Mr. Alexander acknowledges that the sanitary condition of workshops is bad, but does not admit that the Jewish workshops are worse than others. Messrs. Stephany and Alexander agree that sweating does not lead to immorality, and Mr. Alexander states that the opening up of the trade to girls has enabled many to get work and aid in maintaining the family. He further says that the Jewish Board do all they can to prevent the Jewish poor entering crowded trades, and issue warnings in Poland and Russia against their co-religionists coming here. The Jewish Board of Guardians sent Home 627 cases in 1886, 146 in 1887. He has endeavoured to ascertain the existence of a supposed organisation for procuring labour from abroad, but has been unable to discover one, and he contends that one great reason why the Jews live so much cheaper than the Gentiles is their sobriety.

In giving a summary of sweating as carried on in the clothing trade in the Provinces, it is unnecessary to deal with the subject at any great length. In all essential points the system pursued in provincial cities and towns is identical with that in the metropolis. The prices paid for work are often lower. . . .

CHAIN AND NAIL-MAKING

These industries do not give employment to a great number of persons, but in scarcely any that have come under our notice is so much poverty to be found, combined with such severe work and so many hardships. We have taken a great deal of evidence in regard to the circumstances of the people, and we now proceed to give a summary of the more important of the facts that have been brought before us. Some general information was furnished by Mr. R. Juggins, secretary of the Midland Counties Trades Federation, which consists of a combination of trade societies, such as the chain-makers, nail-makers, rivet-makers, and other workers in iron. Chain-making is carried on chiefly at Cradley Heath, and in villages comprised within an area of three or four miles. It is a small industry, not more than from two to three thousand persons being engaged in it. The larger descriptions of chains, known as cable chains, are made in factories; block chains, cart-horse back-bands, dog chains, and other smaller kinds, are made in the district, in small shops attached to the homes of the workers. In most cases there is a workshop at the back of the house, fitted up with an anvil, a stone block, and other appliances. The occupier of the shop may let it out, wholly or in part, to four or five other persons. A shop of the kind described, with a dwelling-house attached to it, lets for from 3s. to 3s. 6d. a week.

The business is carried on in this way: the worker receives a certain weight of iron, and he has to return a corresponding weight of chain, less an allowance, which is, or ought to be, four pounds in the bundle weighing half a hundredweight, for waste in working. It is stated that workmen can occasionally save some iron out of the allowance for waste, which they work up on their own account, and sell to "foggers" at low rates, to the general detriment of the trade. One of the most common charges, however, brought by the workers is, that the necessary weight for waste is not allowed them, and consequently they are unable to return the requisite weight of chain.

The sweater in these trades is known as the "fogger." He goes to the master, takes out the work, and distributes it among the men and women. When it is done he takes it back to the master. Sometimes the fogger works himself, but more frequently he acts merely as a go-between. It is also stated in evidence that the workpeople are compelled in many cases to buy the provisions and other things they require at the fogger's shop, or at a shop kept by his relations or friends; in fact, that he manages to get the workers into his power, and obliges them to deal at his shop, under penalty of refusing to give them work. When the fogger has a shop, the prices he charges for his wares are said to be of an exorbitant character. For American bacon, which an ordinary tradesman sells for 5½d. a pound, they charge 8d.; for sugar they make their customers pay a halfpenny per pound above the usual price; for tea they charge more by 50 per cent. than other shops. It is also stated that the fogger does not always wait for orders, but sends in articles to the men, which they are obliged to take, for fear of losing their work. Mr. Bassano, a magistrate, and chairman of the local board, gave it as his opinion that these practices used to be "very prevalent indeed," but he thought they were now declining. . . .

Mr. Parry stated plainly that many of the foggers carried on truck as a regular system. They simply drive a coach and horses through the Act; they tell the men, or at least it is understood, 'If you do not buy my groceries, we will not buy your nails.' " Nearly all the foggers in his district keep public-houses or shops. It is easy for them to evade the Act by placing their shops in the hands of a relation, or by carrying it on in a way which shall secure for them the profit, while relieving them of all risk. Mr. Hoare, the above-mentioned factory inspector, however, believes that since the strike of 1887, and since the sittings of this Committee began, the abuses complained of have largely decreased.

Various other charges have been made against the "fogger." To understand them it is necessary to explain the system of working, which is this: Chains are paid for by the cwt. Less work is required for a cwt. of the larger than of the smaller chains, and consequently the smaller the size of the rods used in making the chain the larger is the payment per cwt. The sizes of iron run downwards from No. 1, which is the largest. The harder and better the iron the more difficult it is to work. The fogger is often accused of giving out iron of the wrong size or quality. This complaint was put before us, among others, by a woman in the trade. The large masters, she said, would not be bothered to give her the small quantity of work she was able to do. She therefore had to take it from a fogger. He gave a certain sized iron, which he called No. 5, but which was really No. 6, and the woman only received 13s. per cwt. for making it, instead of 17s., which is the regulation price.

Another charge made against the fogger is that he exacts an excessive price for repairing tools, or makes a charge without doing the repairs at all, in which latter case the workers have to pay twice over for the necessary repairs, also that he charges for carriage though it is often done for him by the masters.

It is also stated that occasionally material in an unsuitable condition, that is, bent or crooked iron rods, is served out, and that the

workers have to straighten it at their own expense, no allowance
being made to them for so doing.

It is a subject of complaint also that an excessive allowance is
charged for the weight of the bags in which the nails are weighed.
Nails and bags are weighed together, and 2 lbs. per bag is deducted
in calculating the weight of nails to be paid for. In reality, it is
stated, the bags weigh only 1 lb., and the workman is consequently
defrauded of the value, to him, of 1 lb. of nails per bag of ½ cwt.
of nails. In nail-making it is stated that an inordinately large sum is
charged by the fogger for carriage. Twopence a bundle of ½ cwt.
is charged for carrying the iron and nails to and from the shop, the
distance frequently being very small. A witness declared she could
get the carriage done cheaper, but was compelled to pay the sums
mentioned or she would have got no more work.

A more favourable view of the fogger is given by some of the
masters. Mr. Green, member of a firm of chain and nail manufacturers, stated that he had never heard the word fogger till he came
before the Committee; that the persons in question were merely
large shopmen. He did not seem to think that cheating went on,
but he assented to the view that masters and men alike would be
better off without the foggers. Mr. Reay, another manufacturer,
considered that the foggers were not of much use to the manufacturers. They were brought into existence, he said, by the workpeople themselves. This he explained in the following manner: "As
the master does not go into an outlying district, perhaps, above
once a fortnight, the workperson wants money, and goes to one of
these foggers and says, 'I have some nails, will you buy them of
me?' and he sells them, and gets the money there and then. The
master might not go into that district for a week or fortnight or so;
that is the way they have been created."

The fogger, it is said, in however large a way of business he may
be, differs from a master in that he never sends chain direct to
market, but supplies the master in the locality. Some of the alleged
malpractices of foggers are also imputed to the masters. It is further
alleged against them that they make use of foggers to beat down
prices and to do, through them, things which they would be
ashamed to do themselves. The masters and foggers are also accused of giving out iron of such an inferior quality that it cannot
be worked up, and the workers have to change it at their own
expense. . . .

A grave complaint against the masters is that it is customary for them to give out a considerable quantity of iron, sufficient to keep the hands employed for five or six weeks after a notice for an advance of wages has been given, and to insist upon the iron being worked up at the old rates, after the advance demanded on the notice has been agreed to. On this point a witness read a portion of a letter from her husband: "I am still at play; I have had orders to work the iron up at the old price, but it breaks my heart to do it." On the other hand, it is stated that if prices fall after an order is given out the hands have to accept the reduced wage; thus suffering the disadvantage of falling prices without fully reaping the benefit of rising prices.

Another cause of suffering described by Mr. Bassano is "the curse of long reckonings." Sometimes, it appears, a settlement is not made for months. "I can remember," said Mr. Bassano, "some few cases where there had not been a reckoning for years. In those cases, the workman is entirely at the mercy of the master. The master keeps books, the workman keeps none."

Untested chains of various kinds are sold and exported as tested chains under a bogus certificate. Mr. Hingley, M.P. for North Worcestershire, gave evidence on this point. These bogus certificates are fabricated by "the so-called manufacturer, the warehouse-master, or the small manufacturer." The buyers alone can take action in the matter, but, it would appear, they never do. Possibly the true explanation of this forbearance was given by a witness who said he thought this practice of giving bogus certificates was confined to the export trade.

The witnesses show that a hard week's work on common chain, averaging twelve hours a day for five days out of the week, provides no more than a bare subsistence for the men or women engaged in it. The Rev. H. Rylett, a minister at Dudley, acquainted with the district, stated that the women get from 4s. 6d. to 6s. to 6d. a week. A man can make about three cwt. of chain in a week, for which he receives 5 s. per cwt., so that he would earn about 15s. One of the workwomen said that she could usually earn 5s. a week, or something like that, out of which she had to pay 1s. for firing. Another stated that, working from seven in the morning till seven at night, she could make about a cwt. of chain in a week, for which she was paid from 4s. to 6s. 6d., the price varying. "We do not live very well," she said; "our most living is bacon; we get a bit of butter sometimes." Caroline Cox, aged just 15, stated that she did not get as much as she would like to eat, even of bread and potatoes; and Mr. Ker, certifying surgeon under the Factory Acts for the Halesowen district, told us that children do not get enough to eat, even of the poorest food, and the factory inspector said that two years ago the people were near starving. Jane Smith, aged 14 years and 9 months, who points and helps to cut nails, began to work when she was about 13, works from 7 to 7, and is not strong enough for the work. Mr. Hoare said that children used to begin work at 8, and now begin at 12 or 13. Mr. W. Price, who himself began work at 9, said that children now begin at 11 or 12, and that the Education Act forbidding children under 13 to work for more than half-time is evaded. A girl of eighteen stated that she worked twelve hours a day, and that her net earnings would be about 7s. 1d. Sometimes she had bacon for her dinner; never fresh meat. She gave the weight of the heavier of the hammers she used at from 7 to 8 lbs., but Mr. Hoare who weighed them found they weighed 1 lb. and 2½ lb. respectively. It may be here mentioned that the price of a dog chain which is made by these women for three farthings is, in London, from 1s. to 1s. 3d. The value of the materials would be about 2d. A still more extraordinary case is that mentioned by Mr. Juggins, who stated that cart chains, costing, as far as value of labour and material were concerned, 1½d. and 7d. respectively, had been sold in Southport for from 4s. 6d. to 5s., in Liverpool for 5s. and in London for 7s. A male chainmaker stated that he earned 14s. or 15s. a week, working from seven till seven, except on Mondays, when he finished at six, and on Saturdays at three. A nailmaker said that out of his week's work only about 8s. 6d. remained for himself, after deducting firing and other charges; "and I have worked for that amount of money," he added, "till I did not know where to put myself." In another case a husband and wife work together, and there are three children, two at school and none at work. The man does the "heading," the woman the "pointing," of the nails. Their united work brings in from 18s. to 1l. a week; out of that about 2s. 3d. for "breeze," about 5s. for carriage, 2s. 6d. for rent of house and shop, schooling of the children, 6d., 6d. to 9d. for deductions on account of under weight, and the man has to devote from half a day to a day to repairing his tools. Eighteen shilling or 1l. does not represent their average weekly earnings over a year, as some weeks they do not get any work at all. Their general hours of work were from seven in the morning till nine at night, with half-an hour for breakfast, an hour for dinner, and half-an-hour for tea for the man. The witness herself had no regular time for meals, "on account of there being no one in the house to do the work besides myself." The hands employed in factories are better paid, the cases which we have cited being taken from the persons who work in their own homes. Mr. George Green, a member of a firm of nail and chain makers carrying on business near Dudley, stated that the average wages per week, taken from the books of his firm, running over four weeks, were, "for women 8s. 2d., young women 9s. 4d., youths 12s. 7d., less 12½ per cent., which would be about the cost of their breeze and the rent of their workshop." Referring to men's wages, Mr. Green said he paid by the "list," and that they were getting "on an average 26s. 11d. net"; but in 1888 he thought they would only have been earning "about 22s." These were the wages paid for special quality of work and for superior labour. In the case of the men, thirteen in number, employed on the premises, these amounts represented individual earnings, but as outworkers employ help, the 26s. 11d., in the majority of cases, must be considered as representing the wages of more than one person. With regard to the half-inch chain, the men would only get 24s. 6d. per week. Out of that sum, Mr. Green said, "you will have to deduct 25 per cent."

We have stated that twelve hours appear to make an ordinary full day's work, but the Rev. H. Rylett said, "it is quite a common thing for these people to work ten to twelve hours a day, and even thirteen or fourteen hours a day. I have heard of cases of that. I have frequently gone through this district, and it is as common as possible to find these people working . . . up to 8 and 9 o'clock at night. In fact, you may go through the district when it is pitch dark, and there are no lamps in some parts, and you will hear these little forges going and people working in them, and you wonder when they are going to stop." One man, a chainmaker of Cradley Heath, said that he began work at about 7.30 in the morning and kept at it till about 9 at night. It is right, however, to say that the number of hours of work is the subject of much dispute. While Mr. Homer doubts the possibility of a man being capable of working from 60 to 70 hours a week, Mr. Priest, while he admits that 70 hours is exceptional, "could mention scores of instances of working

60 to 65 hours." One of the inspectors, Mr. Hoare, stated that in the factories there is no difficulty in enforcing the Act, but with regard to the small shops it is impossible to control the hours of work. When the inspector is about, "runners" are sent round to warn the people. "These people who profess to want to be so much more inspected do all they can to thwart your finding out how things are, by sending boys and girls round, or by giving signals from one shop to another." Mr. Hoare added that since the inquiry began the inspectors have been looked upon in a more friendly spirit.

Mr. Homer said that the Union had failed to shorten hours, as the men would break away from the rule restricting the hours of work. He added that the race had deteriorated in the last ten years. A woman told us that she carried a quarter of a mile, on her neck, chain weighing, it would seem, on an average, half a cwt. Another woman carried a cwt. of chain 20 or 30 yards, and Mr. Hoare said that women carried a 60 lb. bundle of nails a mile.

Before, and for some time after, the appointment of your Committee, startling statements appeared in various public journals with regard to the employment of women in these trades, and the immorality which was alleged to be one of the consequences. We found nothing whatever to justify these imputations on the character of the people. As a rule, they are well conducted, and although it may be objected that some of the work is unfit for women to do, there is no warrant for the assertion that it is indecent. . . .

Several remedies were proposed by the witnesses, some of which we may enumerate. It is suggested that co-operative warehouses and shops should be set up, by the aid of subscriptions. A similar suggestion was that "the Government should advance sufficient capital to build factories and establish agencies throughout the country;" in short, that these industries should be placed under the special care of the Government, and practically subsidised at the expense of the nation. The nail trade in many of its branches as now carried on in these districts is gradually dying out, most descriptions of hand work being superseded by the greater use of machinery. Hand-made nails, are it is stated, better for certain purposes than those made by machinery, and it has been suggested that the Government should buy these nails for soldiers' boots. Evidence has been given to us that the wrought hob, though in the

first instance more expensive than the cast hob, is in the long run
considerably more economical.

We cannot close this summary without mentioning that in these
trades, we had to contend with a certain indisposition on the part
of the workpeople to come forward and give evidence. There was
no proof of intimidation in any shape that would have enabled us
to reach it, but there seemed to be a general feeling that if a witness
came to tell the Committee all he knew, it would be the worse for
him in his own neighbourhood. The people appeared unwilling to
talk about their hardships or their wrongs.

The homes in which these poor people live are generally of the
most squalid and deplorable kind. The Rev. H. Rylett told us, "I
was in a house only the other day; the fireplace was a wreck, and
there had not been a bit of whitewash or anything of that kind
done in that house for seven years; and a woman who stood near
said, 'I have lived seventeen years in my house, and the landlord has
done nothing to it.' " The drains are at the best defective; sometimes there are no drains whatever. One of the women stated:
"there is no drain from my house; we throw the water down, and
it runs anywhere; it goes down afore the people's doors, and has to
get out how it can." Many a time, she added, there had been illness
in the family; "we have had the measles and fever a good bit sometimes." Mr. Ker, certifying surgeon for the district, testified that
heaps of manure are often to be found opposite the workshops and
dwellings. In some cases, there is only one privy provided for three
houses, and that is in a detestable condition. Typhoid is "much
more common than it ought to be." Mr. A. Smith, Sanitary Commissioner of the "Lancet," said that the people at Cradley threw all
their slops into the main street, whence some of it flows into surface wells, the water of which is used for drinking purposes. There
is water supplied by a company, but the people prefer the well
water, but this preference may be accounted for by the fact that
they can get well water for nothing, whereas they have to pay for
the other. "I found cases," said Mr. Smith, speaking of the condition of the houses, "where there were holes in the roof, where
buckets had to be kept in the bedrooms to catch the water pouring
through the roof. I found other houses so extremely damp that
there was actually fungus growth on the wall, not on a level with
the floor, but breast high." The district "is all left to hazard." In
some respects, we believe there has been an improvement in sanita-

tion since the Committee began its inquiries. The mortality among children under five is great; more than half the total deaths. This is ascribed in part to early marriages and unhealthy parentage. It is "a common thing" for girls and boys to marry at fifteen or sixteen, and to bring on themselves the charge of a family when in a state not far removed from starvation.

Mr. Bassano mentioned a place called "Tibbet's Garden." "It is" he said, "about the worst place in all Rowley Regis. It is a sort of cottage property whereon very poor people have got isolated cottages; not a court, or a row, or a street, or anything of that sort; but an open space with houses dotted about it, just as if they had come down in a shower, and undoubtedly it is the most insanitary part of all our parish. The people are so extremely poor that it has been just a matter of putting them into the workhouse to carry out any works, and then to recover the expenses from them, because they have not the money to do it themselves." The Local Board are, however, he told us, doing all they can do considering the poverty of the parish to improve the sanitary condition of it.

CONCLUSIONS AND RECOMMENDATIONS

We have endeavoured to extract from the principal witnesses a clear idea of what they understood by the term "sweating."

> The replies received were neither clear nor consistent. It was urged by some that sweating is an abuse of the sub-contract system, and consequently that there can be no sweating where there is no sub-contracting. Others, on the contrary, maintained that sub-contracting is by no means a necessary element of sweating, which consists, according to them, in taking advantage of the necessities of the poorer and more helpless class of workers, either by forcing them to work too hard or too long, or under insanitary conditions, or for "starvation wages," or by exacting what some witnesses call "an undue profit" out of their labour.

Mr. Arnold White observes, that the broadest definition he can give to the term sweating is the "grinding the faces of the poor."

We do not propose to enter upon any discussion of the various definitions placed before us.

It is enough to say that we considered our inquiry should embrace—

I. The means employed to take advantage of the necessities of the poorer and more helpless class of workers.

II. The conditions under which such workers live.

III. The causes that have conduced to the state of things disclosed.

IV. The remedies proposed.

Such having been the scope of our inquiry, and ample evidence having been brought before us on every matter comprised within its scope, we are of opinion that, although we cannot assign an exact meaning to "sweating," the evils known by that name are shown in the foregoing pages of the Report to be—

1. A rate of wages inadequate to the necessities of the workers or disproportionate to the work done.
2. Excessive hours of labour.
3. The insanitary state of the houses in which the work is carried on.
   These evils can hardly be exaggerated.

The earnings of the lowest classes of workers are barely sufficient to sustain existence.

The hours of labour are such as to make the lives of the workers periods of almost ceaseless toil, hard and often unhealthy.

The sanitary conditions under which the work is conducted are not only injurious to the health of the persons employed, but are dangerous to the public, especially in the case of the trades concerned in making clothes, as infectious diseases are spread by the sale of garments made in rooms inhabited by persons suffering from small-pox and other diseases.

We make the above statements on evidence of the truth of which we are fully satisfied, and we feel bound to express our admiration of the courage with which the sufferers endure their lot, of the absence of any desire to excite pity by exaggeration, and of the almost unbounded charity they display towards each other in endeavouring by gifts of food and other kindnesses to alleviate any distress for the time being greater than their own.

As a rule, however, it must be remembered that the observations made with respect to sweating apply, in the main, to unskilled or only partially skilled workers, as the thoroughly skilled workers can almost always obtain adequate wages.

When we come to consider the causes of and the remedies for the evils attending the conditions of labour which go under the name of sweating, we are immediately involved in a labyrinth of difficulties. First, we are told that the introduction of sub-contractors or middlemen is the cause of the misery. Undoubtedly, it appears to us that employers are regardless of the moral obligations which attach to capital when they take contracts to supply articles and know nothing of the condition of the workers by whom such articles are made, leaving to a sub-contractor the duty of selecting the workers and giving him by way of compensation a portion of the profit. But it seems to us that the middleman is the consequence, not the cause of the evil; the instrument, not the hand which gives motion to the instrument, which does the mischief. Moreover, the middleman is found to be absent in many cases in which the evils complained of abound.

Further, we think that undue stress has been laid on the injurious effect on wages caused by foreign immigration, inasmuch as we find that the evils complained of obtain in trades, which do not appear to be affected by foreign immigration.

We are of opinion, however, that certain trades are, to some extent, affected by the presence of poor foreigners, for the most part Russian and Polish Jews. These Jews are not charged with immorality or with vice of any description, though represented by some witnesses as being uncleanly in their persons and habits. On the contrary, they are represented on all hands as thrifty and industrious, and they seldom or never come on the rates, as the Jews support by voluntary contributions all their indigent members. What is shown is that the Jewish immigrants can live on what would be starvation wages to Englishmen, that they work for a number of hours almost incredible in length, and that until of late they have not easily lent themselves to trade combinations.

Machinery, by increasing the sub-division of labour, and consequently affording great opportunities for the introduction of unskilled labour is also charged with being a cause of sweating. The answer to this charge seems to be, that in some of the largest clothing and other factories in which labour is admitted to be carried on under favourable conditions to the workers, machinery, and sub-division of labour to the greatest possible extent, are found in every department of the factory.

With more truth it may be said that the inefficiency of many of the lower class of workers, early marriages, and the tendency of the residuum of the population in large towns to form a helpless community, together with a low standard of life and the excessive supply of unskilled labour, are the chief factors in producing sweating. Moreover, a large supply of cheap female labour is available in consequence of the fact that married women working at unskilled labour in their homes, in the intervals of attendance on their domestic duties and not wholly supporting themselves, can afford to work at what would be starvation wages to unmarried women. Such being the conditions of the labour market, abundant materials exist to supply an unscrupulous employer with workers helplessly dependent upon him.

The most important question is, whether any remedy can be found for this unhappy state of a portion of the labouring class. With respect to the low wages and excessive hours of labour, we think that good may be effected by the extension of co-operative societies, and by well-considered combination amongst the workers. We are aware that home-workers form a great obstacle in the way of combination, inasmuch as they cannot readily be brought to combine for the purpose of raising wages. To remove this obstacle we have been urged to recommend the prohibition by legislation of working at home, but we think such a measure would be arbitrary and oppressive, not sanctioned by any precedent in existing law, and impossible to be effectually enforced.

We now proceed to make recommendations in respect of the evils, which appear to us, under existing circumstances, to require immediate Parliamentary interference.

It will be seen from our report above that the sanitary condition of work-places is regulated by the Factory and Workshop Act, 1878, and the Public Health Act, 1875.

Under the factory law work-places for the purposes of sanitation are divided into three classes:—

(1) Factories,
(2) Workshops, and
(3) Domestic workshops.

We are of opinion that all work-places included under the above descriptions should be required to be kept in a cleanly state, to be lime-washed or washed throughout at stated intervals, to be kept free from noxious effluvia, and not to be overcrowded; in other words, to be treated for sanitary purposes as factories are treated under the factory law.

In considering the question of out-workers, our attention has been drawn to a section of a statute that has been for six years in force in the Colony of Victoria, which we print in the Appendix. It provides that a list of the names and addresses of all home-workers should be kept by every occupier of a factory or work-room, and be open to inspection by an authorised inspector. We recommend this provision to the consideration of the House.

We are also of opinion that an adequate number of inspectors should be appointed to enforce a due observance of the law. It has been suggested that the inspector should be assisted by workmen having practical knowledge of the trades inspected, and paid only the wages of artizans, but we doubt whether the disadvantages arising from the division of responsibility would not outweigh any advantage to be derived from their technical knowledge.

We think that inspectors should have power to enter all work-places within their jurisdiction at reasonable times without a warrant.

We consider that the establishment of County Councils provides in every county a body capable of being trusted with the control and superintendence of sanitary inspection.

To carry into effect the foregoing recommendations amendments will be required of the Factory and Workshop Act, 1878, the Public Health Act, 1875, and the Local Government Act, 1888.

We are of opinion that greater facilities should be given to factory inspectors for inspecting the workplaces within their jurisdiction by registration of owners, or by requiring notice to be given to the inspectors of the establishment of new work-places, and the discontinuance of old. Some means should also be devised for enabling sanitary inspectors to discover readily the names and addresses of the owners of insanitary workplaces and houses.

We think it a disadvantage that different departments of the Government should be concerned with matters relating to the labour question. The Factory Inspectors are appointed by and under the control of the Home Office. The Board of Trade supplies the public, through its Labour Correspondent, with information as to the conditions of labour and the state of the industrial classes, and requires for that purpose the aid and co-operation of the Factory Inspectors. The Local Government Board have a medical department, which, for the purpose of promoting hygiene, ought to be in constant communication with the Factory Inspectors. We suggest that it would be advisable to bring the officers employed in the above-mentioned functions into closer relation with each other.

We find that the provisions of the Truck Acts are much contravened in the Cradley Heath District, and probably in other places also, and we should wish the administration of those Acts to be more strictly enforced through the medium of the local authorities or otherwise.

Our attention has been directed to the manner in which "the viewers" or inspectors of Government work perform their duty. We are of opinion that considerable laxity has prevailed amongst them, and that bad work has not unfrequently escaped detection. We are aware of the difficulties which necessarily stand in the way of procuring competent and impartial viewers, but we think that greater care should be taken in selecting the best men and a stricter supervision exercised over their conduct.

Evidence has been brought before us proving that the use of the "oliver," or heavy sledge-hammer, used for cutting cold iron, is unfit work for women or girls, with the exception of the "light oliver," adapted for making hobnails; and we recommend that women and girls should be prohibited by law from working the "oliver" when the hammer exceeds a certain specified weight.

We also recommend that women and girls should be prohibited by law from making chains the links of which are made of iron exceeding a certain specified thickness.

We have received considerable evidence attributing to the disuse of the apprenticeship system the incompleteness of the education of the workman. The remedies suggested are, on the one hand, a renewal of the apprenticeship system; and, on the other, the promotion of a larger system of technical education. We think that the encouragement of technical education for all classes of artizans is more likely to prove an efficient remedy than a recurrence to the old system of apprenticeship.

We are glad to find that efforts are being made to put an end to the grave scandal of sweating in the making up of Government contracts for clothing and accoutrements. Proposals to this end have been made as follows:—First, to insist on the observance of the conditions now commonly annexed to such contracts, which hitherto it has been no one's duty to enforce, namely, that the work should be done in factories; and, secondly, a proposal has been made by Mr. Nepean, the Director of Contracts, to bind contractors not to pay less than a specified minimum rate of wages approved by the Department. Mr. Nepean believes that the increased cost will be compensated for by the excellence of the work. Municipal and other public bodies will, we hope, observe with care these efforts to contend with the evils of sweating, and take, as we are aware that some of them have already taken, every precaution in their power to ensure fair and reasonable terms to the worker. We think that practical experience alone can determine how this result may best be effected.

We cannot conclude without expressing our earnest hope that the exposure of the evils which have been brought to our notice will induce capitalists to pay closer attention to the conditions under which the labour which supplies them with goods is conducted. When legislation has reached the limit up to which it is effective, the real amelioration of conditions must be due to increased sense of responsibility in the employer and improved habits in the employed. We have reason to think that the present inquiry itself has not been without moral effect. And we believe that public attention and public judgment can effectually check operations in which little regard is shown to the welfare of workpeople and to the quality of production, and can also strongly second the zealous and judicious efforts now being made to encourage thrift, promote temperance, improve dwellings, and raise the tone of living.

18. The Other Side of Society: Shadwell

THE VICTORIAN urban problem was a microcosm of Victorian life. Some problems of the city are timeless, deriving almost by definition from the concentration of people and things. Poverty was not new; nor was conspicuous consumption. Social distinctions were no greater than they had been. One related difficulty was new and was observed by countless critics from Dickens and Engels to Mayhew and Booth. City dwellers ceased to live intersecting lives. Where rich and poor, masters and men had once tumbled over one another in everyday life, now regions within cities increasingly tended to become vast, homogeneous social agglomerations. The transportation revolution made possible the flight to the suburbs, and those most capable of effecting change displayed little interest in it. There was no need so long as the problem was somewhere else. People could and did live their lives without ever really confronting the "other" world.

Factory concentration sped the process of social segregation in the industrial city. The men had to live near their work. New slums were built for them or made in formerly middle-class housing. Previously blighted areas disintegrated under the impact of the poorest people in the city. Immigration and the pressure of population led to segregation and concentration of the urban dwellers. Habit and custom initially brought Irish migrants together. Economic exploitation and social discrimination compounded their isolation and continued their brutalization.

Slum survival demanded more discipline than most people had—and more luck. Prostitution and theft were always the easier way; drink the escape from frightening reality. The slum was its own progenitor, and it did not matter whether it was sprawling Ancoats in Manchester or Shadwell in London. The slum housed the underworld—the masses, those who lived lives apart, those beyond the pale of respectability, those who lacked the will to improve. The Victorians surveyed the poor, described them, analyzed them. But they could not bring themselves to launch a frontal attack upon poverty. There was always the workhouse for the relief of destitution and private charity to meet the special case of need. Victorians did not like slums, poverty, or exploitation, but their social and cultural habits prevented them from confronting their social problem. Their religion taught them that a man must seek salvation to achieve it, and they carried this code into day-to-day life. The debate about the deserving and undeserving poor continues to our day.

Shadwell was an old slum, a district lying just north of the London docks in the heart of the East End. It was, as Hippolyte Taine observed, by no means unique. He could as easily have described the rabbit warrens of Victoria, lying almost within sight of the Houses of Parliament and Buckingham Palace.

Recommended Reading

In addition to Taine, Mayhew, Dickens, or other contemporaries: A. Briggs, *Victorian Cities* (London: 1963); W. Booth, *In Darkest England and the Way Out* (London: 1890); W. Ashworth, *The Genesis of Modern British Town Planning* (London: 1954); H. J. Dyos, *Victorian Suburb: A Study of the Growth of Camberwell* (Leicester: 1961), and his article "The Slums of Victorian London," *Victorian Studies*, XI (1967), 5–40; T. C. Barker and J. R. Harris, *A Merseyside Town in the Industrial Revolution: St. Helens, 1750–1900* (Liverpool: 1954); J. J. Tobias, *Crime and Industrial Society in the Nineteenth Century* (New York: 1968).

HIPPOLYTE TAINE,
SHADWELL

Shadwell, one of the poor neighbourhoods, is close at hand; by the vastness of its distress, and by its extent, it is in keeping with the hugeness and the wealth of London. I have seen the bad quarters of

Source: From *Notes on England*, trans. W. F. Rae (New York: 1872), pp. 33–36.

Marseilles, of Antwerp, of Paris, they do not come near to it. Low houses, poor streets of brick under red-tiled roofs cross each other in every direction, and lead down with a dismal look to the river. Beggars, thieves, harlots, the latter especially, crowd Shadwell Street. One hears a grating music in the spirit cellars; sometimes it is a negro who handles the violin; through the open windows one perceives unmade beds, women dancing. Thrice in ten minutes I saw crowds collected at the doors; fights were going on, chiefly fights between women; one of them, her face bleeding, tears in her eyes, drunk, shouted with a sharp and harsh voice, and wished to fling herself upon a man. The bystanders laughed; the noise caused the adjacent lanes to be emptied of their occupants; ragged, poor children, harlots—it was like a human sewer suddenly discharging its contents. Some of them have a relic of neatness, a new garment, but the greater number are in filthy and unseemly tatters. Figure to yourself what a lady's bonnet may become after passing during three or four years from head to head, having been crushed against walls, having had blows from fists; for they receive them. I noticed blackened eyes, bandaged noses, bloody cheek-bones. The women gesticulate with extraordinary vehemence; but most horrible of all is their shrill, acute, cracked voice, resembling that of an ailing screech-owl.

From the time of leaving the Tunnel, street boys abound—barefooted, dirty, and turning wheels in order to get alms. On the stairs leading to the Thames they swarm, more pale-faced, more deformed, more repulsive than the scum of Paris; without question, the climate is worse, and the gin more deadly. Near them, leaning against the greasy walls, or inert on the steps, are men in astounding rags; it is impossible to imagine before seeing them how many layers of dirt an overcoat or a pair of trousers could hold; they dream or doze open-mouthed, their faces are begrimed, dull, and sometimes streaked with red lines. It is in these localities that families have been discovered with no other bed than a heap of soot; they had slept there during several months. For a creature so wasted and jaded there is but one refuge—drunkenness. "Not drink!" said a desperate character at an inquest. "It were better then to die at once."

A trader said to me, "Look after your pockets, sir," and a policeman warned me not to enter certain lanes.

I walked through some of the broader ones; all the houses,

except one or two, are evidently inhabited by harlots. Other small streets, dusty courts, reeking with a smell of rotten rags, are draped with tattered clothes and linen hung up to dry. Children swarm. In a moment, in a narrow court, I saw fourteen or fifteen around me—dirty, barefooted, the little sister carrying a sucking child in her arms, the year-old nursling whose whitish head had no hair. Nothing is more lugubrious than these white bodies, that pale flaxen hair, these flabby cheeks encrusted with old dirt. They press together, they point out the gentleman with curious and eager gestures. The motionless mothers, with an exhausted air, look out at the door. One observes the narrow lodging, sometimes the single room, wherein they are all huddled in the foul air. The houses are most frequently one-storied, low, narrow—a den in which to sleep and die. What a place of residence in winter, when, during the weeks of continuous rain and fog, the windows are shut! And in order that this brood may not die of hunger, it is necessary that the father should not drink, should never be idle, should never be sick.

Here and there is a dust-heap. Women are labouring to pick out what is valuable from it. One, old and withered, had a short pipe in her mouth. They stand up amidst the muck to look at me; brutalised, disquieting faces of female Yahoos; perhaps this pipe and a glass of gin is the last idea which floats in their idiotic brain. Should we find there anything else than the instincts and appetites of a savage and of a beast of burden? A miserable black cat, lean, lame, startled, watches them timidly out of the corner of its eye, and furtively searches in a heap of rubbish. It was possibly right in feeling uneasy. The old woman, muttering, followed it with a look as wild as its own. She seemed to think that two pounds weight of meat were there.

I recall the alleys which run into Oxford Street, stifling lanes, encrusted with human exhalations; troops of pale children, nestling on the muddy stairs, the seats on London Bridge, where families, huddled together with drooping heads, shiver through the night; particularly the Haymarket and the Strand in the evening. Every hundred steps one jostles twenty harlots; some of them ask for a glass of gin; others say, "Sir, it is to pay my lodging." This is not debauchery which flaunts itself, but destitution—and such destitution! The deplorable procession in the shade of the monumental streets is sickening; it seems to me a march of the dead. That is a plague-spot—the real plague-spot of English society.

19. Recreation: The Best Day of the Week

THE CLATTER of clogs on cobblestone streets and the clang of the factory bell were characteristic, symbolic sounds of Victorian discipline. Working time defined in hours rather than tasks, days, weeks, or seasons was, to a considerable degree, a by-product of industrial urbanization. Factories worked by the clock, the shop and counting house fixed hours, and the home adjusted to them acquiring its own time discipline. The Victorian ethic of work made scant provision for relaxation. Work was presumed to produce pleasure. The busy man is happy and content. There is no joy like that of completing a good job well. The Victorian revolution—industrial, demographic, urban—was as much a change of leisure as labor.

This is not to say that the Victorians were a joyless crew, but there was something different about Victorian recreation. For proper Victorians of every class the family was the center in leisure as in life.

> Domesticity is the taproot which enables the nation to branch wide and high. The motive and end of their trade and empire is to guard the independence and privacy of their homes. Nothing so much marks their manners as the concentration of their household ties.[1]

The family was the cardinal sign of respectability, and recreation was, to an unprecedented degree, familial. Family meals, the ritual of tea, family strolls in the park, visiting relatives on Sunday, family holidays—all reenforced the significance of this core of Victorian life.

Economic and social success conferred, as one of its benefits, token or real emancipation. The possibility of finding employment, even as a domestic servant, provided daughters a degree of independence. While the industrious mechanic could only escape the domestic toils of the family by pleading a higher purpose (an adult education course or a meeting of his friendly society did very nicely), the more prosperous professional could flee to the fraternal comforts of his club. Social rituals developed in London and provincial cities for those still outside of the charmed circle designed to occupy the time of individual members of more successful, more prosperous, or more privileged families. These circles overlapped with those that revolved around the country house weekend, offering bucolic pleasures spiced with the adventure of field sports. All too often these proved to be a licensed slaughter of game reserved to an elite by vigorously enforced game laws. "Le weekend" entered the French vocabulary just as it spread to the furthest reaches of the Empire.

1. Ralph Waldo Emerson, *English Traits* (Boston: 1903), p. 109.

But there was another side to the coin of leisure. Economic and social privilege conferred, even demanded, that the Victorian travel, acquire cultivation, indulge in costly hobbies, and perform a plenitude of good or useless works. The last suggests the potency of the work ethic as ritual even in the remote reaches of high society. Such advantages and responsibilities were there for those who needed to do nothing, and the degree to which one could share in them implied social standing.

There was comparable discrimination at the opposite end of the social scale. A proper man could have a pint in a pub, but he must not patronize a gin palace. The music hall should, perhaps, have been a source of family delight, but any woman attending might anticipate trouble or insult. Constables or no, a lady never went out unescorted, and one explanation for family activities probably derives from this elementary problem of security. The respectable family had much to be said for it. It meant gradual emancipation from the brutal sports of the market town, although the rough and tumble of the past did not vanish in the soot and slime of the industrial city or sprawling metropolis. The life of the underworld became, if anything, more savage. Saturday night in Deptford, if we are to credit a visiting Frenchman, was apt to mean drunken women, stripped to the waist in a gaslit gin palace, slashing each other with broken bottles to the delight of an intoxicated crowd. The violent pleasures of the slum have altered little since Hogarth, and that principally upon superficial points.

Thomas Wright (1790–1875) had a gift for simple, revealing description. This Manchester workingman achieved renown for salvaging ex-convicts and parolees. He was offered a job as inspector of prisons, but rejected it in favor of an annuity that would permit him to continue his good works. He was always conscious of belonging to the working classes and proud of it. He talks about the people among whom he lived and worked, and if he displays reformist zeal in many things, his description rings true.

Recommended Reading

There is much more literature on work than leisure which suggests, among other things, that we still essentially accept Victorian priorities. Middle-class England may be seen through its satirical mirror in A. Adburgham, *A Punch History of Manners and Modes, 1841–1940* (London: 1961), and is penetratingly dissected by G. M. Young in "The Happy Family," *Victorian Essays*, ed. W. D. Handcock (London: 1962), pp. 116–123. J. A. Banks cast his perceptive sociologist's eye on the problem in *Prosperity and Parenthood* (London: 1954), and there are several essays of somewhat uneven merit in B.B.C., *Ideas and Beliefs of the Victorians* (London: 1949). For one of the great problems, see B. Harrison, *Drink and the Victorians* (London: 1970).

THOMAS WRIGHT,
WORKING MEN'S SATURDAYS

When "from six to six" was the order of the day for six days a week, working men regarded the seventh with the sentiment expressed by the lover of "Sally in our Alley," when he sings—

> Of all the days that's in the week
> I dearly love but one day,
> And that's the day that always comes
> 'Twixt Saturday and Monday.

But among those who enjoy the benefits of the Saturday half-holiday, this tone of feeling has been considerably modified; and, indeed, it is now a stock saying with many working men, that *Saturday* is the best day of the week, as it is a short working day, and Sunday has to come; and this latter is a much more important consideration to the working man than to the uninitiated it would appear to be.

The working man has necessarily to deter the transacting of many little pieces of business to the end of the week; and when he had to work till six o'clock on Saturdays, by the time he had washed himself and changed his clothes, taken his tea, and got through the deferred pieces of business, he was generally thoroughly tired, and it was near bed-time, and Sunday was upon him before he knew where he was. And though, in point of fact, this did not lessen the material comforts of the day of rest, yet every one knows that the previous contemplation and mind-picturing of pleasures to come is in itself a pleasure of no mean order, in some cases (and the working man's long "lie in" on a Sunday morning is one of these) anticipation not only lends enchantment to the view, but really gives an added charm to the realization of the looked-for joy. On "week days" the working man wakes or is roused from his toil-worn sleep, or from delightful dreams of a new and blissful state of society, in which it is permitted to all working men to lose a quarter every day in the week, about five or half-past five o'clock in the morning, in order that he may be at his work by six. And when awake he *must* get up, however much he may feel disposed

Source: From *Some Habits and Customs of the Working Class* (London: 1867), pp. 184–203.

to have another turn round, for workshop bells are among the things that wait for no man, and the habitual losing of quarters is a practice that leads to that unpleasant thing—to working men—"the sack," and so, to slightly alter a line from the "Three Fishers," "Men must work, while women may sleep." Early rising *may* make a man healthy, wealthy, and wise; but there can be no doubt that it is a great bore when it is compulsory, and when the heavy-sleeping working man, or the one who acts upon the plan of gaining length of days by stealing a few hours from the night, reluctantly "tumbles out," he thinks to himself, "I shall be in there again pretty soon tonight." But when night comes, and he has had a good wash and a good tea, he feels like a giant refreshed; and having settled himself comfortably by the fireside, or gone out for his evening stroll, he feels almost as unwilling to go to bed early as he does to leave it, and thus morning after morning he has to fight his battles o'er again. Sometimes he does not wake until a little after his usual hour; he will then hastily consider whether he can get to his work in time, decide to try it, spring out of bed, huddle on his clothes, and, without waiting to light his pipe, rush off, and just come in sight of the workshop gate in time to see it shut, and to join with two or three equally unfortunate mates in heaping curses loud and deep upon the gatekeeper. But on Sunday morning there is none of this. On that morning, when from force of habit the working man wakens at his usual time—I know several enthusiastic individuals who have themselves "called" on that morning the same as any other, in order that they may make sure of thoroughly enjoying the situation—and for a confused moment or two thinks about getting up, he suddenly remembers him that it is Sunday, and joyously drawing the clothes tighter around him, he consumes time generally, and morning quarters in particular, and resolves to have a long "lie in," and in many instances to have breakfast in bed. And on all these things the working man who benefits by the half-holiday movement can, when taking it easy on a Saturday afternoon, pleasingly ponder.

For only working men can thoroughly appreciate or understand all that is embodied in that chiefest pleasure of the working man's Sunday, "a quarter in bed." To any late-rising, *blasé* gentlemen who may be in search of a new pleasure, I would strongly recommend the adoption of some plan—(if nothing better occurred to them, they might commit some offence against the law, that would

lead to a term of imprisonment "without the option of a fine")—
that would for a time make rising at a fixed and early hour compulsory, and when the morning arrives upon which they can once
more indulge in a "lie in," they may exclaim, *Eureka!* for they will
have found a new and great pleasure.

The working half of Saturday is up at one o'clock, and that
wished-for hour seems to come round quicker on that day than
any other. In a well ordered workshop every man is allowed a
certain time each Saturday for "tidying up," sweeping of the floor
and benches, cleaning and laying out in order of the tools. This is
completed a minute or two before one o'clock; and when the
workmen, with newly-washed hands and their shop jackets or
slops rolled up under their arms, stand in groups waiting for the
ringing of the bell, it is a sight well worth seeing, and one in which
the working man is, all things considered, perhaps seen at his best.
He is in good humour with himself and fellow-workman; is in his
working clothes, in which he feels and moves at ease, and not
unfrequently looks a nobler fellow than when "cleaned;" and is
surrounded by the machinery with which he is quite at home.
When the bell rings the men leave the works in a leisurely way that
contrasts rather strongly with the eagerness with which they leave
at other times; but once outside the workshop gates, the younger
apprentices and other boys immediately devote themselves to the
business of pleasure. They will be seen gathering together in a
manner that plainly indicates that there is "something in the wind."
The something in the wind may be a fight that is to come off
between Tommy Jones, *alias* "Bubbly," and Billy Smith, otherwise
"The Jockey," owing to the latter sportingly-inclined young
gentleman having openly boasted that he could take Mary Ann
Stubbins for a walk any time he liked; Miss S. being a young lady
of fourteen, the daughter of a retail greengrocer and generally
regarded as the lady-love of Bubbly, it being notorious that she
gives him much larger ha'p'orths of apples than any other boy,
and—when her father is not looking—supplies him with roasting
potatoes free of charge. Or the something in the wind may be a
hunt after a monstrous rat that is believed to haunt a neighbouring
pond; or perhaps the something is the carrying out of a hostile
demonstration against the butcher who rents the field adjoining the
workshop, and who has been so unreasonable as to object to their
catching his pony and riding it by three at a time.

The first proceeding of the workmen upon reaching home is to get their dinner, which they eat upon Saturday and Sunday only in a leisurely manner; and after dinner the smokers charge, light, and smoke their pipes, still in a leisurely and contemplative manner unknown to them at other times. By the time they have finished their pipes it is probably two o'clock, and they then proceed to clean themselves up—that phrase being equivalent among "the great unwashed" to the society one of performing your toilet. The first part of the cleaning-up process consists in "a good wash," and it is completed by an entire change of dress. A favourite plan of cleaning-up on Saturday afternoons is—among those who live within easy reach of public baths—to take their clean suits to the bath, and put them on after they have bathed, bringing away their working suits tied up in a bundle. Some of the higher-paid mechanics present a very different appearance when cleaned up from that which they presented an hour or two before, when we saw them sauntering out of the shop gates. Working-class swelldom breaks out for the short time in which it is permitted to do so in all the butterfly brilliance of "fashionably" made clothes, with splendid accessories in collars, scarves, and cheap jewellery. But neither the will nor the means to "come the swell" are given to all men, and a favourite Saturday evening costume with the mass of working men consists of the clean moleskin or cord trousers that are to be worn at work during the ensuing week, black coat and waistcoat, a cap of a somewhat sporting character, and a muffler more or less gaudy. Of course, the manner in which working men spend their Saturday afternoon is dependent upon their temperaments, tastes, and domestic circumstances. The man who goes home from his work on a Saturday only to find his house in disorder, with every article of furniture out of its place, the floor unwashed or sloppy from uncompleted washing, his wife slovenly, his children untidy, his dinner not yet ready or spoilt in the cooking, is much more likely to go "on the spree" than the man who finds his house in order, the furniture glistening from the recent polishing, the burnished steel fire-irons looking doubly resplendent from the bright glow of the cheerful fire, his well-cooked dinner ready laid on a snowy cloth, and his wife and children tidy and cheerful. If the man whose household work is neglected or mismanaged is, as sometimes happens, of a meek character, and has been unfortunate enough to get for a wife a woman who is a termagant as well as a sloven, or one of those lazy, lackadaisical, *London-Journal*-reading ladies with whom working men are more and more curst, he will have to devote his Saturday afternoon to assisting in the woman's work of his own house. But when the husband is not of the requisite meekness of spirit, he hastens from the disorderly scene, and roams about in a frame of mind that predisposes him to seek the questionable comforts of the public-house, or to enter upon some other form of dissipation. On the other hand, the man who has a clever and industrious wife, whose home is so managed that it is always cosy and cheerful when he is in it, finds there a charm, which, if he is endowed with an ordinary share of manliness and self-respect, will render him insensible to the allurements of meretricious amusements. In no rank of society have home influences so great a power for good or evil, as among the working classes. Drunkenness is in many cases, doubtless, the result of innate depravity, and a confirmed drunkard is rarely to be reclaimed by home comforts, which to his degraded mind offer no charm; but at the same time there can be no doubt in the mind of any person who is acquainted with the manners and habits of the working classes, that thousands of working men are driven by lazy, slovenly, mismanaging wives, to courses which ultimately result in their becoming drunkards and disreputable members of society.

There has been a great deal written and said about what is called modern servantgalism; and while there could, no doubt, be a good deal said respecting illtempered, ignorant, selfish, and "genteel" mistresses, there is equally little room for doubt that the complaints against modern female servants are "founded on facts." To those whose lot it is to employ servant girls, the combination of vanity, affectation, ignorance, and impudence, which go to make up servantgalism, may afford amusement as well as cause annoyance. But it is no joke when we consider that these servant girls, and their compeers the shop and dressmaker girls, are the class who become the wives of working men and the mothers of their children. Servantgalish ideas and sentiments are, in a general way, the result of the universal fastness of the age, of the all-pervading desire for the possession of wealth, and the love of display, which developes Robsons and Redpaths, causes Jones, ex-greengrocer, to publicly intimate that it is his intention to be known for the future by the name of Fitzherbert, and brings so many "fashionably attired" young men before the magistrates. But while the general character of the age we live in may in a great measure be held responsible for the vanity, love of dress and high notions which characterize the female domestic mind, and in a still more remarkable degree the minds of the "young ladies" of millinery and other establishments, there is a *special* element which contributes directly to the generation and fostering of the worst spirit of servantgalism. That special element is the devotion of those females to the perusal of the tales published in the cheap serials, of which they (the class of females in question) are the chief supporters. The miscellaneous parts of these serials, the "household receipts," "sayings witty and humorous," and the "ladies' page," may, though dull, be harmless and even instructive; nor is there anything immoral in the tales, which are the chief and most injurious features of these publications. On the contrary, it is the tremendous triumph and excessive reward—of which a rich, titled and handsome husband is invariably a part—awarded in them, to virtue, as embodied in the person of a "poor but virtuous maiden," which is the most objectionable part of these tales; and which, taken in conjunction with the distorted views of life which they contain, and the exaggerated splendour and luxury of their accessories, make them the most pernicious of all works, not of a directly immoral character, that can be placed in the hands of poor, half-educated, and not particularly strong-minded girls. That poor but virtuous maidens occasionally find rich and titled husbands is doubtless true, but still constantly harping on this string, and mingling the sensational adventures of the stock virtuous maiden, and the poor clerk or travelling artist, who ultimately turns out to be a rich nobleman, with splendid carriages, gorgeous dresses, dazzling jewellery, and luxurious boudoirs, is scarcely the way to make the general run of poor but virtuous maidens contented with their position in life. For neither their type of mind, nor the nature of their education is of a kind that fits them for making fine distinctions, and they are wont to argue in this wise, "Are not we, too, poor and virtuous? and should not we therefore also get rich husbands, be dressed in gorgeous garments, and wear costly jewellery, and lounge in magnificently furnished boudoirs?" The discontented and hankering spirit which these stories create in the silly girls who read them, render them particularly liable to become a prey to any "fashionably attired" scamp, who can use the high-flown language of the stories themselves. To uninterested observers the ideas of those whose minds are inflamed by these absurd tales may appear simply ludicrous; but to those upon whom they have a direct bearing they have a sad as well as a grotesque aspect. Household duties are neglected in order to find time to read the tales, or discuss with some sympathetic soul the probable means whereby some "lowly heroine" will ultimately defeat the schemes of the intriguing and demoniac Duchess of Bloomington, and marry that mysterious young gentleman with the raven locks and marble brow, at present employed in the shawl department of the West-end emporium at which the duchess deals, and whom she and the reader know to be the true heir to the richest earldom in England. And when the tale-tainted wife begins to contrast the manners and language of her commonplace husband with those of Lord Cecil Harborough, or the Honourable Algernon Mount Harcourt, the result may be imagined. In short, these publications pander to a very dangerous kind of vanity. I am fully aware that the labouring classes have benefited largely by cheap literature, but at the same time I am bound to say, speaking from an extensive experience among those classes, that the particular class of cheap literature of which I have been speaking exercises a most injurious influence upon them, and is frequently the insidious cause of bitter shame and misery, as well as a potent cause of the squalor and mismanagement so often found in the homes of even the higher-paid portion of the working classes.

Taking it for granted that the representative working men have tolerably comfortable homes, their methods of spending their Saturday afternoons will then depend upon their respective tastes and habits. The steady family man who is "thoroughly domesti-cated" will probably settle himself by the fireside, and having lit his pipe, devote himself to the perusal of his weekly newspaper. He will go through the police intelligence with a patience and perse-verance worthy of a better cause, then through the murders of the week, proceed from them to the reviews of books, and "varieties original and select," take a passing glance at the sporting intelli-gence, and finally learns from the leading articles that he is a cruelly "ground-down" and virtually enslaved individual, who has no friend or well-wisher in this unfairly constituted world save only the "we" of the articles. This is generally about the range of a first reading. The foreign intelligence, news from the provinces, answers to correspondents, and "enormous gooseberry" para-graphs, being left for a future occasion. By the time such first reading has been got through tea-time is near—for an early tea, a tea to which all the members of the family sit down together, and at which the relishes of the season abound to an extent known only to a Saturday and a pay-day, is a stock part of a working man's Saturday. The family man, whom the wives of other working men describe to their husbands as "something like a husband," but who is probably regarded by his own wife as a bore, and by his shop-mates as a mollicot—will go marketing with or for his wife, and will consider his afternoon well spent if he succeeds in "beating-down" a butterman to the extent of three-halfpence. The unmar-ried man who "finds himself," and who is of a scraping disposition, or cannot trust his landlady, will also spend his afternoon in marketing. Many of the unmarried, and some of the younger of the married men of the working classes, are now members of vol-unteer corps, workshop bands, or boat clubs, and devote many of their Saturday afternoons to drill, band practice, or rowing. When not engaged in any of the above pursuits, the men of this class go for an afternoon stroll—sometimes to some suburban semi-country inn, at others "round town." In the latter case, they are much given to gazing in at shop windows—particularly of newsagents, where illustrated papers and periodicals are displayed, and outfitters, in which the young mechanic who is "keeping company" with a "young lady," and upon whom it is therefore incumbent to "cut a dash," can see those great bargains in gorgeous and fashionable scarfs marked up at the sacrificial price of 1s. 11¾d. Those men who are bent upon improving their general education, or mastering those branches of learning—generally mathematics and mechanical drawing—which will be most useful to them, spend their Saturday afternoons in reading. Other men again, who are naturally of a mechanical or artistic turn of mind, and industriously inclined, employ their Saturday afternoon in constructing articles of the class of which so much has been seen during the last two years at industrial exhibitions; or in making, altering, or improving some article of furniture. But whatever may be the nature of their Satur-day afternoon proceedings, working men contrive to bring them to a conclusion in time for an early (about five o'clock) tea, so as to leave themselves a long evening.

Burns' "Cotter's Saturday Night," though one of the best of his many fine poems, and an enchanting picture of natural and *possible* "rural felicity," and probably a truthful description of the *best* pastoral life of the period, would be in no respect applicable as a description of the Saturday nights of the present generation of working men and their families. How cotters of the agricultural labourer class spend their Saturday nights I am not in a position to say, but it is quite certain that if compared with the model cotter of the poem, the artisan class of the present day would show a decided falling off in moral picturesqueness. The "intelligent artisan" (I merely state the fact) does not spend his Saturday night by his ain fireside, or devote it to family worship, and however "halesome parritch"—"thick dick" he would call it—may be, he would emphatically object to it as a Saturday night's supper. The lover of the modern Jenny, when going courting on Saturday night, will *not* rap gently at the door, but will give an authoritative ran tan upon the knocker; and on being admitted will not be "sae bashfu' and sae grave." On the contrary, he will have a free-and-easy, almost patronizing manner, will greet Jenny in an off-handed style, and tell her to look sharp and get her things on; and while she is dressing, he will enter into familiar conversation with her father, incidentally telling him to what place of amusement he is going to take Jenny, and perhaps informing him that he has put a crown on the Cheshire Nobbler for that pugilistic celebrity's forthcoming encounter with the Whitechapel Crusher. When Jenny is ready he will take his departure with her, merely observing that he will see her home all right, and feeling proudly conscious that he has fully impressed his parents-in-law that are to be with the fact that he is a young man who "knows his way about." In other words, he is not a Scotch cotter, but an English mechanic.

After tea those men who have been out during the afternoon generally stay in for an hour's rest before setting forth on their evening ramble in search of amusement, while those who have been at home, go out in order to get through any business they may have on hand before the amusement begins. Saturday being the only time at which working men can safely indulge in any amusement that involves staying out late at night, and being moreover a time when they are flush of money, and when they can get to the entrance of any place of entertainment in time to take part in the first rush, and so secure a good seat, they avail themselves of this combination of fortuitous circumstances, and hence the crowded state of theatre galleries on that night, and the notice on music-hall orders that they are not available on Saturdays. The theatre is the most popular resort of pleasure-seeking workmen, and the gallery their favourite part of the house. Two or three mates generally go together, taking with them a joint-stock bottle of drink and a suitable supply of eatables. Or sometimes two or three married couples, who have "no encumbrance," or who have got some neighbour to look after their children, make up a party, the women carrying a plentiful supply of provisions. To the *habitués* of the stalls and boxes the eating and drinking that goes on in the gallery may appear to be mere gluttony, though the fact really is that it is a simple necessity. There is scarcely a theatre gallery in England from the back seats of which it is possible to see and hear with any degree of comfort, or in a manner that will enable you to comprehend the action of the piece without standing during the whole of the performance, and standing up in a gallery crowd is a thing to be contemplated with horror. In order to get a place in the gallery of a well attended theatre on a Saturday night from which you can witness the performance while seated, it is necessary to be at the entrance at least half an hour before the doors open, and when they do open you have to take part in a rush and struggle the fierceness of which can only be credited by those who have taken part in such encounters. And when you have at length fought your way up the narrow, inconvenient, vault-like staircase, and into a seat, and have recovered sufficiently to reconnoitre your position, you find yourself one of a perspiring crowd, closely packed in an ill-lighted, ill-ventilated, black hole of Calcutta like pen, to which the fumes of gas in the lower parts of the house ascend. It is not unlikely, too, that you find yourself seated next to some individual who has been rendered ferociously quarrelsome by having been half strangled in the struggle at the doors, and who, upon your being unavoidably pressed against him, tells you in a significant manner, not to "scrouge" *him* whoever else you scrouge. To endure this martyrdom some substantial nourishment is absolutely necessary, and the refreshments of the gods provided by the theatrical purveyors of them, being of a sickly and poisonous, rather than an ambrosial character, consisting for the most part of ale and porter, originally bad, and shaken in being carried about until it has become muddy to the sight and abominable to the taste; rotten fruit, and biscuits stale to the degree of semi-putrefaction; those gods who take a supply of refreshments with them when they go to a theatre, display, not gluttony, but a wise regard for their health and comfort. After the theatres, the music-halls are the most popular places of Saturday night resort with working men, as at them they can combine the drinking of the Saturday night glass, and the smoking of the Saturday night pipe, with the seeing and hearing of a variety of entertainments, ranging from magnificent ballets and marvellous scenic illusions to inferior tumbling, and from well-given operatic selections to the most idiotic of the so-called comic songs of the Jolly Dogs class. Music-halls being practically large public-houses, it is not, as a matter of course, permitted to take refreshments into them. The refreshments supplied in these halls, however, are generally moderately good, but at the same time more than moderately dear, while the waiters, who, in accordance with the usage of these establishments, have to be pecuniarily "remembered" each time that they refill your glass or bring you the most trifling article, haunt you in an oppressive and vampirish manner if you venture to linger over your drink; and, all things considered, it is not too much to say that, notwithstanding the comparatively low prices of admission to them, music-halls are about the dearest places of amusement that a working man can frequent. Next to the theatres and music-halls, the shilling, sixpenny, and threepenny "hops" of the dancing academics and saloons which abound in manufacturing districts, are the amusements most affected by the younger and more spruce of unmarried working men. And it is at these cheap dancing *academies* (which, not being connected, as the *saloons* generally are, with public-houses, are looked upon as exclusive and genteel establishments) that unfortunate working men generally make the acquaintance of those young ladies of the millinery and dressmaking persuasion, who entertain secret hopes of one day marrying a gentleman; but who, unhappily for society in general and the working classes in particular, become the slovenly mismanaging wives of working men. Other men spend their Saturday nights at public-house "free-and-easies," from which they will come home happy if the comic or sentimental song—the learning of which has been their sole mental labour during the past week—has been favourably received by their free-and-easy brethren.

Of course there are some of my class who prefer above all things to spend a quiet Saturday evening in a reading-room, or at a working man's club, though the members of these clubs are by no means so numerous, nor is the success of the institutions themselves so great as might be supposed from so much having been written and said about them. But, however differently working men may spend the bulk of their Saturday night, it is an almost invariable practice with those of them who are not teetotallers, to "drop in" some time during the night at some house of call, in order to have a pipe and glass in company with the friends or shopmates who frequent the house. For though drunkenness is happily giving way to "manly moderation" among the working classes, they have not yet reached the bigoted stage of anti-alcoholic belief that would decree that because they are virtuous, there should be no more pipes and ale.

And while the men of the artisan class (the class that has chiefly benefited by the Saturday half-holiday movement) now look upon Saturday as in many respects the best day of the week, their wives and families also regard it as a red-letter day. For on that day Mrs. Jones, the blacksmith's wife, gets the new bonnet or dress without which, she assures her husband, she is not fit to be seen out of doors; or the new article of parlour furniture, lacking which—since she has seen a similar piece of furniture at her neighbour Mrs. Brown's house—she is, she tells Jones, quite ashamed when any decent body calls to see them. On that day, little Billy Jones gets the new jacket, and his sister Polly the new frock, which will draw upon them the envy or admiration of their companions at Sunday school on the following day, and each of them will on Saturday receive the penny which is their weekly allowance of pocket-money, but which, owing to the promptings of their "sweet tooth," and the advice of not altogether disinterested, though for the time being extraordinarily affectionate playmates, they will spend a few hours after they have got it, and experience in consequence much remorse whenever during the ensuing week they see a great bargain in the way of toffee. On Saturday night too Billy and Polly are indulged in the dissipation of sitting up late, in order that they may have a share of the hot supper, which, like a tea with relishes, is also a characteristic of a working man's Saturday.

That the Saturday half-holiday movement is one of the most practically beneficial that has ever been inaugurated with a view to the social improvement of "the masses," no one who is acquainted with its workings will for a moment doubt. It has made Saturday a day to be looked forward to by the working man with feelings of pleasurable anticipation, to be regarded as the day on which he can enjoy many things, which but for it he would not have the opportunity of enjoying; and do many things tending to his own improvement, or the comfort of his family, to the doing of which he had formerly to devote that portion of his Saturday night which he can now spend in some recreation. It enables them to view their relative position in a rosier light than that in which they were wont to regard it, and to see that though they may often have to work whilst others play, they can also sometimes play when many others have to work: and disposes them to think that, notwithstanding that there are many hardships incidental to their station in life, they are not *quite* so "ground down," robbed and oppressed, as sundry spouters and writers who live on and by them would have them to believe.

But there is one aspect of the Saturday half-holiday movement in which those sections of the working classes who have benefited by it have been weighed and found wanting. They have not as a body given the practical aid which, without any inconvenience to themselves or their families, they might have done, and which as working men they ought to have done, to the extension of the movement among the less fortunate sections of their own class. In the manufacturing trades the Saturday half-holiday is an almost general thing, and many of the largest employers of labour in those trades—both companies and private firms—now pay their workmen on Friday night, with an express view to facilitating early shopping and marketing on Saturdays. And yet it is notorious that the late shopping of the artisan class is the sole means of keeping thousands of shops open till eleven and twelve o'clock on Saturday nights, and consequently of keeping tens of thousands of shopmen and assistants at work till those late hours; thus making Saturday the worst day of the week for them, and compelling them and their families in many instances to do their shopping *on Sundays*. Workmen of the artisan class are disposed to entertain a rather contemptuous opinion of "counter-skippers," but they should bear in mind that even counter-skippers are men and brethren, who feel all the irksomeness of confinement, and are doubtless endowed with bumps that cause them to long for, and would enable them to enjoy, a half-holiday.

It would be simply absurd to suppose that the sections of the working classes who already enjoy the Saturday half-holiday could by any act of theirs *at once* extend the movement to other sections, but still it is in their power to do much towards it. If the men in those trades in which the holiday is established would follow an understood law, to have all Saturday marketing and shopping incidental to the requirements of themselves and families finished, as a general rule, by four o'clock, the result would be that thousands of young men would be released from the bondage of the counter some hours earlier on Saturday night than they are at present. It is in the power of the working classes to do much in this way, and the thoughtlessness and indifference of many working men on such points as these must often give additional pain to those of their own class who suffer by it. And I am sure it must have brought something of shame as well as sorrow to the minds of many thoughtful working men when, in the early part of 1866, the clothiers' assistants in the large clothing establishments at the East-end of London brought their grievance (that of having to work seven days a week, and ninety-four hours for a week's work) before the public, and appealed to "the workmen of London to give them one day's rest out of seven, by not shopping at clothing establishments that continue to keep open on Sundays." Occasions frequently arise in which large sections of the working classes, and sometimes even the general body of them, stand in need of the good opinion or friendly assistance of other sections of society, and it behooves them to show themselves deserving of assistance when their hour of need comes, by showing such brotherly kindness and consideration for each other as may be in their power, even if they *should* have to make a little alteration in their habits to do so. And of the matters in which it is in the power of some sections of the working classes to render material assistance to others, the extension of the Saturday half-holiday movement is one of the most prominent, and one in which aid may be given with little or no self-sacrifice upon the part of the givers.

20. The Obligations of Landed Property: Squire Steadyman

THE ARISTOCRACY and landed gentry derived power and prestige from patrimony in land, but the landed classes also assumed a series of obligations, explicit and implicit, that derived from their role and function. Some—Irish absentee landlords are generically indicted for the fault—gave not a rap for the well-being of their tenants or the welfare of their vicinage. But in England and, indeed, in most of the United

Kingdom, a responsible gentry drew praise other places than Anthony Trollope's *Small House at Allington* for meeting its obligations and serving its constituency.

The function of the gentleman magistrate was circumscribed by reformers who demanded professional standards and skills, and articulated rules through a middle-class bureaucracy. Competitive examinations were neither the forte nor the interest of the fox-hunting squirearchy. Yet many old attributes remained. The formal functions of the justice of the peace might be greatly limited and his direct political powers restricted, but there remained obligations of status, in the first instance, family responsibilities. The maintenance of maiden aunts, mother, unmarried sisters, n'er-do-well brothers, and assorted retired retainers past, present, and future fell on the estate. These were all members of the "extended" family, and however modest it might be, the obligations were real and considerable. The estate, moreover, was a business requiring an agent, the services of a solicitor, a constant if modest input of capital (on which very limited return might be anticipated), and a willingness to absorb dead losses on rent in those inevitable times of tenant misfortune.

Beyond this lie inescapable obligations to the Church, to the hunt, to a political party (he may be disinterested but cannot remain neutral), and to charity. Now and now only has he paid the bills of a country gentleman. John Steadyman, Esq., of Wearywork Hall, Cidershire, is now permitted to live and support his extended family on something like £1,000. It is no easy task.

Recommended Reading

Two interesting studies among many are F. M. L. Thompson, *English Landed Society in the Nineteenth Century* (London: 1963), and David Spring, "The Role of the Aristocracy in the Late Nineteenth Century," *Victorian Studies*, IV (1960), 55–64. G. Kitson Clark has two excellent chapters on the transition within the gentry-aristocracy during the Victorian age in *The Making of Victorian England* (Oxford: 1962).

John Bateman,
A Typical Squire

. . . I will give . . . what I consider a fair specimen of what a "landed income" of 5,000*l.* a-year means when analysed. My typical 5,000*l.* a-year squire shall be called—

Source: From *The Great Landowners of Great Britain and Ireland* (London: 1883), pp. xxiv–xxv.

STEADYMAN, John, of Wearywork Hall, Cidershire.

	g. acres.	an. val.
b. 1825, s. 1860, m. 1851.	3,500	5,000
Deduct for value in the rate-books put upon mansion, grounds, fishponds, &c.	£ 220	
Deduct also the value put upon cottages lived in rent free by old workmen and pensioners of the late Mr. Steadyman	30	
		250
Leaving a clear rent roll of		£4,750

Now deduct as under:—

	£
His late father's two maiden sisters, Jane and Esther Steadyman, who each have a rent charge of 180*l.* per annum. (*N.B.*—Both these old ladies seem immortal)	360
His mother, Lady Louisa Steadyman, a rent charge of	700
His sisters, Louisa, Marian, and Éva (all plain), each 150*l.*	450
His brother, Wildbore Steadyman, who was paid off and emigrated, but almost annually comes down on the good-natured head of the family for say	50
Mortgage on Sloppyside Farm and Hungry Hill (started when his father contested the county), interest	650
Do. on Wearywork End (started when his one pretty sister married Sir Shortt Shortt, Bart., and was paid off), interest	150
His estate agent, Mr. Harrable, salary	150
Keep of a horse for do., 35*l.;* house for do. 45*l.*	80
Average of lawyer's bill (settlements, conveyances, &c.)	60
Average cost of farm repairs, &c.	350
Draining tiles furnished gratis to the tenants	40
Repairs to the family mansion	70
Voluntary church rate, school at Wearywork, do. at Wearywork End, pensions, and purely local charities (*N.B.*—If Mr. S. is a Roman Catholic, which I do not think he is, a private chaplain, chapel, school, &c., would increase this to at least 225*l.*)	175
Subscription to county (Liberal or Tory) registration fund	10
Do. to the Cidershire Foxhounds (25*l.*) and Boggymore Harriers (5*l.*).	30
Do. to the Diocesan—? (everything now-a-days is Diocesan, we shall soon be taking pills from Diocesan dispensaries)	25
Other county subscriptions—hospitals, flower shows, races, &c.	35
Returned 15 per cent. of rents in "hard times," averaging perhaps one year in five (would that we could say so now, 1882)	150
Loss on occasional bankrupt tenants (Mr. Harrable dislikes distraint), average	30
Arrears of rent, say annually 300*l.*, loss of interest thereon at 5 per cent.	15
Income-tax at 4*d.* in the pound on rents paid and unpaid	83
Insurance on all buildings	55
	£3,718

Leaving our worthy squire the magnificent annual sum of 1,032*l.* to live upon. The subscriptions, I think I may say, are hardly over painted—being, as folks say, "the least that can be expected from a person in Mr. S.'s position."

21. Social Mobility: Aristocracy and Plutocracy

VICTORIAN SOCIETY necessarily proved increasingly mobile and flexible as the century progressed. New forms of respectable activity, a growth of professions, and the unparalleled advance in wealth demanded recognition. Escott, a perceptive observer of late Victorian English life, contended that three rival elements, "the aristocratic, the democratic, and the plutocratic" were becoming "closely blended."

> The aristocratic principle is still paramount, forms the foundation of our social structure, and has been strengthened and extended in its operation by the plutocratic, while the democratic instinct of the race has all the opportunities of assertion and gratification which it can find in a career conditionally open to talents.[1]

The point was well taken. Both the traditional aristocracy and aspirants for social status wanted mobility, but not too much of it—the aristocracy to preserve its character and values, the climbers to make the prize worthwhile. The flexibility of the English aristocracy is easy to overstate. It had always recruited new talent, but it remained exclusive and demanding. Its persistence, not its flexibility, made it great. Wealth traditionally merged with aristocracy through marriage, but now-landed gentlemen were shareholders; peers sat on boards of directors. The worlds of city and country merged. But it took time. The first industrial peer was, appropriately, a Strutt, but he was not raised to that estate until the middle of the century, and he was the third generation of those lords of the loom.

Even when the process of social assimilation was well under way, money strove to purify itself through landed estates and gentry function.

Recommended Reading

F. M. L. Thompson, *English Landed Society in the Nineteenth Century* (London: 1963). D. Spring, *The English Landed Estate in the Nineteenth Century* (Baltimore: 1963), and his article "The Role of the Aristocracy in the Late Nineteenth Century," *Victorian Studies*, IV (1960), 55–64.

THOMAS HAY SWEET ESCOTT,
THE STRUCTURE OF ENGLISH SOCIETY

The era of the enlargement of English society dates from the Reform Bill of 1832, and if it has brought with it some contradic-

1. Thomas Hay Sweet Escott, *England: Her People, Polity, and Pursuits* (New York: 1880), pp. 317–325.

Source: From *England: Her People, Polity, and Pursuits* (New York: 1880), pp. 317–324.

tions, anomalies, and inconveniences, it has also been instrumental in the accomplishment of great and undoubted good. It has substituted, in a very large degree, the prestige of achievement for the prestige of position. The mere men of fashion, the fops, dandies, and exquisites, the glory of whose life was indolence, and who looked upon any thing in the way of occupation as a disgrace, have gone out of date never to return. . . . Before the eventful year 1832, there existed a society in England very like the old exclusive society of Vienna. The chief and indeed almost only road to it lay through politics, and politics were for the most part a rigidly aristocratic profession. Occasionally men of the people made their way out of the crowd, and became personages in and out of the House of Commons; but most of the places under Government were in the hands of the great families, as also were the close boroughs, and the tendency was to fill each from among the young men of birth and fashion. The Reform Bill admitted an entirely new element into political life, and threw open the whole of the political area. A host of applicants for Parliamentary position at once came forward, and as a consequence the social citadel was carried by persons who had nothing to do with the purely aristocratic section which had hitherto been paramount. The patrician occupants of the captured stronghold, if they were somewhat taken aback by the blow which had been dealt them, accepted the situation and decided upon their future tactics with equal wisdom and promptitude. If the new-comers were to be successfully competed with, they saw that they must compete with them on the new ground, and must assert their power as the scions of no *fainéant* aristocracy. The impulse given to the whole mass of the patriciate was immense, and the sum of the new-born or newly-displayed energies as surprising as it was satisfactory. The man of pleasure ceased to be the type to which it was expected, as a matter of course, that all those born in the purple should conform.

The activity thus communicated directed itself into an infinite number of channels, and it has continued operative ever since. Our aristocrats of to-day are at least fired by a robust ambition. Many of them take up statesmanship as the business of their lives, and work at its routine duties as if it were necessary to the support of existence. Those whose tastes do not incline them in the direction of the senate, write books, paint pictures, or carve statues. Perhaps, even probably, they are of a theatrical turn, and subsidize a theater, or even manage a company. They go into business, or they dedi-

cate their existence to agricultural enterprise. At least they do
something. Society, in fact, has bidden adieu to its ideal of gilded
and inglorious ease, and in strict conformity with the spirit of its
new departure, selects its *protégés* and favorites upon a new principle. The question asked about any new aspirant to its freedom is
not only, who is he? or how much has he a year? but, in addition,
what has he done? and what can he do? The heroes and lions of
society are not handsome young men, who can do nothing more
than dress well, or dance well. They are seldom even those whose
fame is limited to the hunting-field or the battue. They are men
who have striven to solve the secret of the ice-bound pole, who
have tramped right across the arid sands of a strange continent,
who have scaled heights previously deemed inaccessible, who have
written clever books, painted great pictures, done great deeds, in
one shape or other. It is surely a considerable social advance to
have substituted for the exquisites of a bygone period, as ideals of
life for the rising generation, men who have followed in the track
of Xenophon, or who have been the pioneers of civilization on a
continent.

Thus it may be fairly inferred that whatever its levities and
frivolities, the foundation on which English society rests is essentially serious, the result of the traditional and pre-eminently English habit of taking grave and earnest views of life. Religion is not
now spoken of; what is meant is, that pure enjoyment is not the
idea of the typical Englishman in whatever class. He takes his
pleasures heartily indeed, and with gusto, if he finds them in his
path. Occasionally he may make the mistake of forsaking the true
path of his career and following the phantom of pleasure till it
lands him in disaster. These are our failures. The ordinary Englishman has ambitions, social and professional, and he subordinates all
other things to them. He is bent upon improving his position, or
immortalizing his name. His dominant motive is the desire to rise,
or the resolution to do to the utmost his duty in the sphere of life
in which his lot has been cast. The plan of existence, thus regarded
as the great and only opportunity for the accomplishment of a
definite work, acquires an energizing solemnity. The Englishman
may stumble sometimes, but after the fall he picks himself up and
pushes on to the goal.

A hundred illustrations might be given of the development of
this inborn national tendency in the march of an English genera-

tion from the cradle to the grave. At school the boy who does nothing has neither popularity nor respect. He is without any recognized status in the little world which is the microcosm of the great world to which he will be presently introduced. He may shine at his studies; he may excel in the cricket-ground or on the river. The one essential condition is, he must do some thing if he wishes to have any rank or consideration among his equals and contemporaries. This destiny pursues him throughout. At college the mere loafer is a nonentity; the reading man or the athlete is a personage. In the army no young officer ever yet made a reputation which one of his compeers envied by elegant dawdling. He has devoted himself to professional studies, and secured a place in the ranks of coming men. Or he has been of a less studious turn, and knows more of the stud-book and the racing calendar than of Jomini or Hamley. But he has established his reputation in the hunting-field or on the steeple-chase course, and he has extended or maintained the reputation of his regiment. It is the same whatever the pastime that he has made the business of his life; his character will be assessed by the degree of earnestness and success with which he has taken it up.

The degrees of esteem allotted to the different English professions are exactly what might be expected in a society organized upon such a basis and conscious of such aims. Roughly it may be said professions in England are valued according to their stability, their remunerativeness, their influence and their recognition by the State. These conditions may partially explain the difference which English society draws between the callings of the merchant and the stock-broker. Stock-brokers make immense fortunes; but there attaches to them a suspicion of precariousness infinitely in excess of that which, in some degree or other, necessarily attaches to all fortunes accumulated in commerce or trade. The merchant represents an interest which is almost deserving of a place among the estates of the realm, and with the development of which the prosperity and prestige of England are bound up. His house of business is practically a public institution, and the speculative element—the fluctuation of prices and the uncertainty of markets —enters as little as possible into it. Merchants have from time immemorial been the friends and supporters of monarchs—have taken their place in the popular chamber of the legislature, have been elevated to distinguished stations among the titular aristocracy of the land. We have had not only our merchant-princes, but our merchant-peers and merchant-statesmen. The calling has been recognized in our social hierarchy for centuries, and if not exactly a liberal, is an eminently respectable and dignified profession. Nor is the merchant, as a rule, so much absorbed in the affairs of his own business as to be unable to devote as much time as is necessary to the pursuits of society and the affairs of the country. His operations run in a comparatively equal and tranquil channel, and to hint that he lives in an atmosphere of feverish excitement is equivalent to insinuating a doubt of his solvency. It is different with the stock-broker, whose social position is so sudden that it cannot yet be looked upon as assured—whose wealth, though great, has the garish hue of luck, and the glories associated with which may dissolve themselves at any moment into thin air, like Aladdin's palace, and who himself is popularly supposed to be more or less on the tenter-hooks of expectation and anxiety from morning to night. The merchant drives to his place of business in a family brougham or barouche; the stock-broker drives to the station, where he takes the morning express to the City, in a smart dog-cart, with a high-stepping horse between the shafts, and a very knowing-looking groom at his side.

Such, at least, is the conception formed by the public of the two men of business, and it indicates not incorrectly the corresponding view of English society. The British merchant, as has been said, is very probably a member of Parliament; the instances in which stock-brokers are members of Parliament at the present day might be counted as something less than the fingers of one hand. The life of the ideal stock-broker is one of display; that of the ideal merchant, one of dignified grandeur or opulent comfort. Possessed of a certain amount of education, often acquired at a public school, sometimes both at Eton and Oxford, the stock-broker of the period has decided social aspirations. He makes his money easily, and he spends it lightly in procuring all the luxuries of existence. He marries a handsome wife, sets up a showy establishment, lays in a stock of choice wines, hires a French cook; he has carriages and horses, a box at the opera, stalls at theaters and concerts innumerable. He belongs to one or two good though not always first-rate clubs. He has acquaintances in the highest circles, and congratulates himself on being in society. But the blissful experience is not one in which his wife shares. She has to be content with all the talk, stories, and scandal of society which she hears retailed at her husband's table by the young guardsmen and other patrician guests who readily accept the invitations to a house where cook and cellar are both excellent, where the hostess and such other ladies as may be present are pretty or attractive. As a consequence of this, there is a copious stream of male visitors at the residence of the fortunate speculator in scrip and shares, while the lord and master of the household is occupied in the City. Perhaps an uncharitable world begins to talk; at any rate, the glitter and show of the *ménage* acquire a certain flavor of Bohemianism, between which and the animating spirit of English society the only sympathy that exists is of a purely superficial kind.

Let us continue to apply the test which has been indicated to other departments of English professional life. We live in an age whose boast it is that it can appreciate merit or capacity of any kind. Artists and actors, poets and painters, are the much-courted guests of the wealthiest and the noblest in the land—to be met with at their dinner-tables, in their reception-rooms, and in their counting-houses. To all appearance, the fusion between the aristocracy of birth, wealth, and intellect is complete, and the representatives of each appear to meet on a footing of the most perfect and absolute equality. Still the notion prevails that the admission, let us say, of the painter into society is an act of condescension on society's part; none the less real because the condescension is ostentatiously concealed. Nor does the fact that artists occasionally not only amass large fortunes, but contract illustrious matrimonial alliances, militate against the view. It is only possible where an entire class is concerned to speak generally, and to this, as to every other rule, there are exceptions. Why should the rule—always assuming that it is a rule—exist, and what are the explanations of it? As regards painters, there is this to be borne in mind: their calling is a noble one; but in view of the genius of English society, it labors under certain disadvantages. A vague and unreasoning prejudice still exists against the profession of the artist. The keen-scented, eminently decorous British public perceives a certain aroma of social and moral laxity in the atmosphere of the studio, a kind of blended perfume of periodical impecuniosity and much tobacco-smoke. This laxity, moreover, is to a great extent a tradition of art, which artists themselves do not a little to perpetuate. They are, or they affect to be, for the most part a simple-minded, demonstrative, impulsive, eccentric, vagabond race, even as Thackeray has drawn them in his novels. As a matter of fact, many, perhaps most of them, are the reverse of this—shrewd, hard-headed men of business, with as clear a conception as the most acute trader of the value of twenty shillings. But social verdicts are based for the most part on general impressions; and the popular view of the painter—speaking now, as always, of the guild, not of the individual member of it—is that the calling which he elects to follow lacks definitiveness of status, and that it is not calculated to promote those serious, methodical habits which form an integral part of the foundation of English society.

If this sentiment were to be exhaustively analyzed, it would be found that there entered into it considerations which apply to other professions. Attorneys or solicitors, general practioners, and even illustrious physicians in the daily intercourse of society labor under nearly the same disadvantages as artists. It is therefore natural and logical to ask what is the social differentia of this group of professional men? It is to be found, unless we greatly mistake, in the fact that they are each of them in the habit of receiving money payments direct from those with whom they consort nominally on a footing of social equality. All professional men make their livelihood out of the public in some shape or other. The only thing is that some of them receive the money of the public through an agent, or middleman, and that others do not. A barrister has no immediate pecuniary dealings with his client. An author has no immediate pecuniary dealings with those who read his books or articles. A beneficed clergyman is independent of his congregation for his income. Artists, attorneys, surgeons, dentists, physicians, are paid by fee, or they send in their account and receive—or at least look for—a check in settlement. But this is exactly what a tailor, a wine merchant, a butcher, a grocer, or any other retail dealer does. Thus we arrive at the conclusion that whatever the social disadvantage at which artists, attorneys, and doctors may find themselves, it arises from precisely the same cause as that which exists in the case of persons who derive their income from nothing that can be called a liberal or a learned trade.

To pass on to two of the conditions which, at the outset of this argument, were loosely enumerated as tests of professional dignity. The sphere of the influence exercised by artists, as by actors and musicians, is necessarily restricted within comparatively narrow limits. Neither great paintings, nor good acting, nor musical masterpieces exercise a very appreciable power on our every-day life, and the conduct and current of affairs. A fine picture makes a stir in the artistic world; but it does not mold the thoughts, or regulate the aspirations, or inspire the mind of the world outside. Excellence in the performance of a leading character in a clever play is the theme of much conversation in society; but it is impossible to say that influence attaches to the merit thus displayed. The sentiments to which the artist gives expression on the stage may produce a deep result, and have before now given an impulse to movements which have almost culminated in revolutions. In the same way, the language with which the singer accompanies the melody may convey the most profound, the most tragic effects. But in each of these cases it is the author, the dramatist, or the poet who speaks; and the actor or the vocalist is, so far as the sentiment which he contributes his share, but only his share, to eliciting, little more than the organ which the soul of literature inspires, and through which it speaks. In a scarcely less degree it may be predicated of the professions of the attorney and the doctor, that they are without those opportunities of moving the mind of the thinking public in any given direction. A physician, who is a great authority in his consulting-room, acquires a considerable position; and from the pedestal of that position he may speak with the certainty of being listened to on many non-professional subjects. But he has not gained this authority as doctor. An attorney, again, may be an election agent, and thus affect the destiny of parties in the State. But this branch of the profession is only a rare and accidental development of his calling. The more closely the matter is looked at, the more apparent does it become that none of the professional classes—as professional classes—can be said to have the same power of appealing to the intellect and the moral convictions which supply rules for the guidance of every-day life, and of coloring the views of the people on religious or political matters, as the writer, the clergyman, the barrister who takes a prominent place in his profession. The barrister who practices in court, much more the judge who sits on the bench, materially and perceptibly assists in the manufacture, modeling, and remodeling of the public law, which is a distinct department of public ethics. The author assists his readers, sensibly or insensibly, in their verdicts on public men and public questions—in their formation of those ideas of right and wrong, whose conscious or unconscious influence is the good or evil genius of their mortal existence. Of the clergyman—the preacher—there is no need to speak.

We have said that the esteem in which society holds these different orders of professional laborers is closely proportioned to the extent and character of their influence on the public mind. We may go farther, and say that the State in the recognition of their services judges them by the same standard. Those who rise to the highest titular rank by their own efforts, when they are not chosen on the ground of convenient political ability or party service, or immense wealth expended in a cause of which the Government of the day approves, or of brilliant exploits on the sea and on the field—exploits which decide the fate of nations—are selected from some one or other of the classes that we have just been considering. Artists are occasionally advanced to the honor of knighthood or baronetcy; so are doctors; and such fortune sometimes may come to attorneys. But, unlike the barrister, no attorney can be said to carry the wig of the chancellor, or the robe of the peer, in his bag. Has the coronet which the distinguished author may bequeath to his children ever been placed upon the painter's head? Can Æsculapius himself, in his most sanguine moments, anticipate any dignity analogous to the bishop's miter, which every clergyman may consider he potentially packs up in the portmanteau that he takes with him when he leaves home to do duty for a friend, and possibly to preach before a royal or illustrious personage? No doubt, it may be said with truth that in these days representative members of all professions consort together, and are treated in society on a footing of perfect equality; but we have attempted here to go a little beneath the surface, and to hazard a possible explanation of what are perhaps foolish prejudices and superstitions.

PART III

Cultural Dimensions

THERE IS NO Victorian economy, national investment policy, entrepreneurial or labor behavior. Hundreds of thousands of enterprises, as great as Cunard or as small as Liza Doolittle, flourished or failed on the basis of private decisions. Some businessmen were expansive, others conservative. Some opted for risk investment, others would never abandon the consuls. Some undertakings flourished, others did not. Our generalizations are based upon trends, or the direction of decisions and events on balance. By the same token there is no Victorian society. There were many. The Victorians were at some difficulty to define themselves, although they tried. Beyond the collective expressions—middle class, the people, the respectable, and the low—were innumerable guides to accepted nuances of status. John Smith might be: Lord John Smith, Sir John Smith, Colonel John Smith, Reverend or Doctor John Smith, or John Smith Esq. Behind them stood Mr. John Smith, John Smith, carpenter, John Smith, laborer, and John Smith. Further down the scale we would find Mrs. John Smith.[1] Even these many societies, classes and orders do violence to the individuals they contain.

Very clearly there was no Victorian culture. There were conflicting ideas, contradictory taboos, habits, notions, and an extraordinary range of dogmas. Every line of thought had its countercurrent. Many proved of more consequence than the original. Debate was vigorous, wide-ranging, heard by a considerable audience. The Victorian age was a golden era of English letters. If deficient in music and theater, it refined the novel, produced much that is best in poetry and *belles lettres*, made extraordinary contributions to science, to history, even to philosophy.

We cannot consider the range of Victorian culture. It is too wide and would demand, even at a trivial level, more space than this volume

1. R. S. Neale, "Class and Class Consciousness in Early Nineteenth-Century England," *Victorian Studies*, XII (1968), 21–22. Neale continues, using T. A. Webster's *Encyclopedia of Domestic Economy* (London: 1844) to illustrate the further division of the five privileged groups into nine, ordered by income and number of servants. At the top were incomes in excess £5,000 and more than twenty domestics; the lowest, incomes of £150–200 with a maid of all work. Webster also divided servants into twenty-two rankings.

affords. Cultural dimensions is intended to isolate a few of the assumptions and values in general usage. The section still only hints at the range of concerns and obsessions, suggesting some of the explicit and unspoken assumptions of Victorian civilization. With a fine eye for the cliché, I have chosen four broad categories: doctrine, dogma, value, and knowledge. Doctrine is an effort to suggest a few of the dimensions of political and social philosophy, the effort to translate ideology into practice or to provide a rationale for behavior. Dogma concerns belief in its formal and extended sense. Value is used to indicate a few of the standards to which Victorians ostensibly aspired and the media through which they believed doctrine and dogma could be generated into effective action. Knowledge is addressed more narrowly to the ways in which some Victorians felt that doctrine, dogma, and value could and should be developed, maintained, and transmitted. All of the selections, whatever their other merits or faults may be, are devoted to culture in its narrow, functional sense—as it immediately equated thought and life.

Victorian civilization was infinitely complex, and its culture was in a constant process of adjustment and readjustment. The change was continuous and resisted definition across or in time. The concept of duty, for example, is as old as man in society. Serious Victorians were obsessed by the term. "Duty" underwent perpetual modification to fit the changing needs, circumstances, and values of evolving Britain. This section is not concerned with high culture—with the move from romantic to realistic to naturalistic. Nor do these selections treat, as perhaps they should, the artistic orthodoxy of John Ruskin, the challenge of the pre-Raphaelite Brotherhood, the Aesthetic Movement, or the Decadence. Darwin is scarcely a fair representation of the magnificent achievements of Victorian science. Neither do these selections deal with popular culture in the pejorative sense—sport, gambling, the public house, music halls, temperance literature—or those institutions of culture—schools, museums, libraries.

The Victorian age saw the emergence of a culture-consuming public. Prosperity and social mobility made it possible; the persistence of old institutions and values made it worthwhile. The immensely accelerated emergence of the organized professions, which had begun in the eighteenth century, brought a significant, new element into British society. It was neither hostile to nor part of the old world, but it demanded a place and importance out of all proportion to its numbers of economic power in the new. The law, medicine, education, engineering, or business-related professions like accounting and actuarial services joined the older professions—the clergy, the armed forces, the barristers. Training and skill came to be vital in the quest for status. Among the purveyors to these new and old cultural markets were the authors and artists, the printers, the publishers, all of the dealers in cultural services. Technology made wood pulp paper available, one of the greatest advances in the dissemination of knowledge since the invention of printing. A considerable product could now be delivered on a wide scale at a reasonable price. There were more books and more schools, and these generated a demand for still more books and schools. Britain progressed, in Victorian years, from a Regency elite in which one child in seventeen attended school in 1818 to a mass society with compulsory secondary education in 1902. By the last third of the nineteenth century, when literate but not discriminating lower middle classes were growing more rapidly then any part of British society, the way was clear and the precedents set for the tabloid press and mass culture media to take their dominant place on the British scene.

General Bibliography[2]

A. ADBURGHAM, *A Punch History of Manners and Modes, 1841–1940* (London: 1961).

R. D. ALTICK, *The English Common Leader* (Cambridge: 1957).

P. APPLEMAN, W. A. MADDEN, and M. WOLFE, *1859: Entering an Age of Crisis* (Bloomington: 1959).

N. BENTLEY, *The Victorian Scene* (London: 1968).

J. BOWLE, *Politics and Opinion in the Nineteenth Century* (New York: 1954).

C. C. BRINTON, *English Political Thought in the Nineteenth Century*, 2d ed. (New York: 1949).

BRITISH BROADCASTING CORPORATION, *Ideas and Beliefs of the Victorians* (London: 1959).

J. H. BUCKLEY, *The Victorian Temper* (London: 1951).

S. C. CARPENTER, *Church and People, 1789–1889*, rev. ed. (London: 1959).

O. CHADWICK, *The Victorian Church* (London: 1966).

———, *The Victorian Miniature* (London: 1960).

H. DAVIES, *Worship and Theology in England* (London: 1961–1962), vols. III–IV.

R. DUTTON, *The Victorian House* (London: 1954).

R. EDWARDS and L. G. G. RAMSAY, *The Early Victorian Period, 1830–1860* (London: 1958).

L. EISELEY, *Darwin's Century* (Garden City: 1958).

G. FABER, *Jowett* (Cambridge, Mass.: 1957).

C. C. GILLISPIE, *Genesis and Geology* (Cambridge, Mass.: 1951).

J. GLOAG, *Victorian Comfort* (London: 1961).

V. H. H. GREEN, *Oxford Common Room* (London: 1957).

E. HALEVY, *The Growth of Philosophic Radicalism* (London: 1928).

J. F. C. HARRISON, *Learning and Living, 1790–1960* (London: 1961).

G. HIMMELFARB, *Darwin and the Darwinian Revolution* (New York: 1959).

———, *Victorian Minds* (New York: 1968).

G. HOBHOUSE, *1851 and the Crystal Palace* (London: 1950).

J. HOLLOWAY, *The Victorian Sage* (London: 1953).

W. E. HOUGHTON, *The Victorian Frame of Mind* (New Haven: 1957).

W. IRVINE, *Apes, Angels and Victorians* (New York: 1955).

---

2. See also works cited in the general bibliographies for Parts I and II and the thorough annual bibliographies in *Victorian Studies*.

H. JACKSON, *Dreamers and Dreams* (New York: 1948).

O. LANCASTER, *Here, of all Places* (Boston: 1958).

O. R. McGREGOR, *Divorce in England* (London: 1957).

S. MARCUS, *The Other Victorians* (New York: 1966).

P. T. MARSH, *The Victorian Church in Decline* (Pittsburg: 1969).

D. NEWSOME, *Godliness and Good Learning* (London: 1961).

V. OGILVIE, *The English Public School* (London: 1957).

M. J. QUINLAN, *Victorian Prelude* (New York: 1941).

D. C. SOMERVELL, *English Thought in the Nineteenth Century* (London: 1929).

W. R. SORLEY, *A History of British Philosophy to 1900* (London: 1965).

M. STURT, *The Education of the People* (London: 1967).

G. R. TAYLOR, *The Angel Makers* (London: 1958).

A. P. THORNTON, *The Habit of Authority* (Toronto: 1966).

J. WARBURG (ed.), *The Industrial Muse* (Oxford: 1958).

R. K. WEBB, *The British Working-Class Reader* (London: 1955).

B. WILLEY, *More Nineteenth-Century Studies* (London: 1956).

————, *Nineteenth-Century Studies* (London: 1949).

R. WILLIAMS, *Culture and Society* (London: 1958).

————, *The Long Revolution* (New York: 1961).

G. M. YOUNG, *Early Victorian England*, 2 vols. (London: 1934).

————, *Victorian England, Portrait of an Age* (London: 1936).

————, *Victorian Essays*, ed. W. D. Handcock (London: 1962).

Doctrine

22. A Definition of Liberalism: John Stuart Mill

THE VICTORIAN years were the golden age of liberalism. This was no novel doctrine. Britons had, while evading logical conclusions, accepted liberty as the natural state of man. Liberty—the idea of freedom—had its prescriptive appeal as well as the attraction of self-interest. Liberty meant freedom from the constraints of the Anglican Church for dissenters. Liberty meant freedom from obsolete and inhibiting regulations for the entrepreneur. Liberty meant careers open to talents for aspiring professionals. Liberalism had its philosopher and spokesman. Jeremy Bentham (1748–1832) had framed the elements of a political philosophy well suited to the early Victorian age. Utilitarianism, the simple notion that selfishness—individuals pursuing pleasure and avoiding pain—would produce political progress and social peace, was convivial doctrine for the most dynamic elements in society. Prescription—the sanction of history—meant little, for the past seemed an encumbrance to be swept aside. "Does it work?" was a better test. The notions of Benthamite utilitarianism and classical economy were convivial to different people in search of different things. Nor were these doctrines ever accepted without limitation. Laissez faire never applied to children. They were not free contracting agents.

The thrust of liberal ideology bothered many of its champions. One was John Stuart Mill (1806–1873). Mill was an influential thinker but scarcely a profound intellect. He was constantly involved, always reformulating his ideas. His treatise *On the Subjugation of Women* (1869) is still one of the finest treatments of the question. He was concerned with the insufficiency of Benthamism. He shared, with his friend Thomas Carlyle, a moral revulsion at the contemporary pursuit of the narrowest self-interest, and he felt certain that human happiness would not come merely from a Benthamite remodeling of institutions and values. This led him to question the most important premises of liberalism and to attempt their philosophic and analytical reformulation. *The Principles of Political Economy* (1847) stated that laissez faire should never permit exploitation, that the state had obligations to provide for its citizens, and that the state had both the right and duty to interfere in a range of private matters. It could intervene in the relations of parents and children. The state must provide free, compulsory education. The state should intervene, even in free contracts, against foolishness just as it must in instances of fraud or coercion. *On Liberty* (1859) raised profound questions about the nature of democracy pointing to the potential tyranny of the majority. The American experience reported by de Tocqueville put him on his guard.

Finally, he turned to the basic liberal philosophy, Utilitarianism. He contended that Bentham was still right with some modifications. Rationalism was right. He accepted the pleasure-pain principle but emphasized the distinction between "higher" and "lower" pleasures. Thus, even with modification and emphasis upon the qualitative as opposed to the quantitative nature of this hedonistic philosophy, Mill restated the liberal commitment. Happiness is the only objective of human life.

Recommended Reading

The literature is, needless to say, overwhelming. Maurice Cowling, *Mill and Liberalism* (Cambridge: 1963), is the best place to start. M. S. Packe's excellent biography, *John Stuart Mill* (New York: 1954), should be used together with J. M. Robson, *The Improvement of Mankind: The Social and Political Thought of John Stuart Mill* (London: 1968).

JOHN STUART MILL,
UTILITARIANISM

WHAT UTILITARIANISM IS

A passing remark is all that needs be given to the ignorant blunder of supposing that those who stand up for utility as the test of right and wrong, use the term in that restricted and merely colloquial sense in which utility is opposed to pleasure. . . . Those who know anything about the matter are aware that every writer, from Epicurus to Bentham, who maintained the theory of utility, meant by it, not something to be contradistinguished from pleasure, but pleasure itself, together with exemption from pain; and instead of opposing the useful to the agreeable or the ornamental, have always declared that the useful means these, among other things. Yet the common herd, including the herd of writers, not only in newspapers and periodicals, but in books of weight and pretension, are perpetually falling into this shallow mistake. Having caught up the word utilitarian, while knowing nothing whatever about it but its sound, they habitually express by it the rejection, or the neglect, of pleasure in some of its forms; of beauty, of ornament, or of amusement. Nor is the term thus ignorantly misapplied solely in disparagement, but occasionally in compliment; as though it implied superiority to frivolity and the mere pleasures of the moment. And this perverted use is the only one in which the word is popularly known, and the one from which the new generation are acquiring their sole notion of its meaning. Those who introduced the word, but who had for many years discontinued it as a distinctive appellation, may well feel themselves called upon to resume it, if by doing so they can hope to contribute anything towards rescuing it from this utter degradation.

The creed which accepts as the foundation of morals, Utility, or the Greatest Happiness Principle, holds that actions are right in proportion as they tend to promote happiness, wrong as they tend to produce the reverse of happiness. By happiness is intended pleasure, and the absence of pain; by unhappiness, pain, and the privation of pleasure. To give a clear view of the moral standard set up by the theory, much more requires to be said; in particular, what things it includes in the ideas of pain and pleasure; and to what extent this is left an open question. But these supplementary explanations do not affect the theory of life on which this theory of morality is grounded—namely, that pleasure, and freedom from pain, are the only things desirable as ends; and that all desirable things (which are as numerous in the utilitarian as in any other

Source: From *Utilitarianism* (London: 1863), chap. ii. Several deletions of detail have been made.

scheme) are desirable either for the pleasure inherent in themselves, or as means to the promotion of pleasure and the prevention of pain.

Now, such a theory of life excites in many minds, and among them in some of the most estimable in feeling and purpose, inveterate dislike. To suppose that life has (as they express it) no higher end than pleasure—no better and nobler object of desire and pursuit—they designate as utterly mean and grovelling; as a doctrine worthy only of swine. . . .

When thus attacked, the Epicureans have always answered, that it is not they, but their accusers, who represent human nature in a degrading light; since the accusation supposes human beings to be capable of no pleasures except those of which swine are capable. . . . The comparison of the Epicurean life to that of beasts is felt as degrading, precisely because a beast's pleasures do not satisfy a human being's conceptions of happiness. Human beings have faculties more elevated than the animal appetites, and when once made conscious of them, do not regard anything as happiness which does not include their gratification. I do not, indeed, consider the Epicureans to have been by any means faultless in drawing out their scheme of consequences from the utilitarian principle. To do this in any sufficient manner, many Stoic, as well as Christian elements require to be included. But there is no known Epicurean theory of life which does not assign to the pleasures of the intellect, of the feelings and imagination, and of the moral sentiments, a much higher value as pleasures than to those of mere sensation. It must be admitted, however, that utilitarian writers in general have placed the superiority of mental over bodily pleasures chiefly in the greater permanency, safety, uncostliness, etc., of the former—that is, in their circumstantial advantages rather than in their intrinsic nature. And on all these points utilitarians have fully proved their case; but they might have taken the other, and, as it may be called, higher ground, with entire consistency. It is quite compatible with the principle of utility to recognise the fact, that some *kinds* of pleasure are more desirable and more valuable than others. It would be absurd that while, in estimating all other things, quality is considered as well as quantity, the estimation of pleasures should be supposed to depend on quantity alone.

If I am asked, what I mean by difference of quality in pleasures, or what makes one pleasure more valuable than another, merely as a pleasure, except its being greater in amount, there is but one possible answer. Of two pleasures, if there be one to which all or almost all who have experience of both give a decided preference, irrespective of any feeling of moral obligation to prefer it, that is the more desirable pleasure. If one of the two is, by those who are competently acquainted with both, placed so far above the other that they prefer it, even though knowing it to be attended with a greater amount of discontent, and would not resign it for any quantity of the other pleasure which their nature is capable of, we are justified in ascribing to the preferred enjoyment a superiority in quality, so far outweighing quantity as to render it, in comparison, of small account.

Now it is an unquestionable fact that those who are equally acquainted with, and equally capable of appreciating and enjoying, both, do give a most marked preference to the manner of existence which employs their higher faculties. Few human creatures would consent to be changed into any of the lower animals, for a promise of the fullest allowance of a beast's pleasures; no intelligent human being would consent to be a fool, no instructed person would be an ignoramus, no person of feeling and conscience would be selfish and base, even though they should be persuaded that the fool, the dunce, or the rascal is better satisfied with his lot than they are with theirs. They would not resign what they possess more than he for the most complete satisfaction of all the desires which they have in common with him. If they ever fancy they would, it is only in cases of unhappiness so extreme, that to escape from it they would exchange their lot for almost any other, however undesirable in their own eyes. A being of higher faculties requires more to make him happy, is capable probably of more acute suffering, and certainly accessible to it at more points, than one of an inferior type; but in spite of these liabilities, he can never really wish to sink into what he feels to be a lower grade of existence. We may give what explanation we please of this unwillingness; we may attribute it to pride, a name which is given indiscriminately to some of the most and to some of the least estimable feelings of which mankind are capable: we may refer it to the love of liberty and personal independence, an appeal to which was with the Stoics one of the most effective means for the inculcation of it; to the love of power, or to the love of excitement, both of which do really enter into and contribute to it: but its most appropriate appellation is a sense of dignity, which all human beings possess in one form or other, and in some, though by no means in exact, proportion to their higher faculties, and which is so essential a part of the happiness of those in whom it is strong, that nothing which conflicts with it could be, otherwise than momentarily, an object of desire to them. Whoever supposes that this preference takes place at a sacrifice of happiness—that the superior being, in anything like equal circumstances, is not happier than the inferior—confounds the two very different ideas, of happiness, and content. It is indisputable that the being whose capacities of enjoyment are low, has the greatest chance of having them fully satisfied; and a highly endowed being will always feel that any happiness which he can look for, as the world is constituted, is imperfect. But he can learn to bear its imperfections, if they are at all bearable; and they will not make him envy the being who is indeed unconscious of the imperfections, but only because he feels not at all the good which those imperfections qualify. It is better to be a human being dissatisfied than a pig satisfied; better to be Socrates dissatisfied than a fool satisfied. And if the fool, or the pig, are of a different opinion, it is because they only know their own side of the question. The other party to the comparison knows both sides.

It may be objected, that many who are capable of the higher pleasures, occasionally, under the influence of temptation, postpone them to the lower. But this is quite compatible with a full appreciation of the intrinsic superiority of the higher. Men often, from infirmity of character, make their election for the nearer good, though they know it to be the less valuable; and this no less when the choice is between two bodily pleasures, than when it is between bodily and mental. They pursue sensual indulgences to the injury of health, though perfectly aware that health is the greater good. It may be further objected, that many who begin with youthful enthusiasm for everything noble, as they advance in years sink into indolence and selfishness. But I do not believe that those who undergo this very common change, voluntarily choose the lower description of pleasures in preference to the higher. I believe that before they devote themselves exclusively to the one, they have already become incapable of the other. Capacity for the nobler feelings is in most natures a very tender plant, easily killed, not only by hostile influences, but by mere want of sustenance; and in the majority of young persons its speedily dies away if the occupations to which their position in life has devoted them, and the society into which it has thrown them, are not favourable to keeping that higher capacity in exercise. Men lose their high aspirations as they lose their intellectual tastes, because they have not time or opportunity for indulging them; and they addict themselves to inferior pleasures, not because they deliberately prefer them, but because they are either the only ones to which they have access, or the only ones which they are any longer capable of enjoying. It may be questioned whether any one who has remained equally susceptible to both classes of pleasures, ever knowingly and calmly preferred the lower; though many, in all ages, have broken down in an ineffectual attempt to combine both. . . .

I have dwelt on this point, as being a necessary part of a perfectly just conception of Utility or Happiness, considered as the directive rule of human conduct. But it is by no means an indispensable condition to the acceptance of the utilitarian standard; for that standard is not the agent's own greatest happiness, but the greatest amount of happiness altogether; and if it may possibly be doubted whether a noble character is always the happier for its nobleness, there can be no doubt that it makes other people happier and that the world in general is immensely a gainer by it. Utilitarianism, therefore, could only attain its end by the general cultivation of nobleness of character, even if each individual were only nobleness, there can be no doubt that it makes other people happier, ness is concerned, were a sheer deduction from the benefit. But the bare enunciation of such an absurdity as this last, renders refutation superfluous.

According to the Greatest Happiness Principle, as above explained, the ultimate end, with reference to and for the sake of which all other things are desirable (whether we are considering our own good or that of other people), is an existence exempt as far as possible from pain, and as rich as possible in enjoyments, both in point of quantity and quality; the test of quality, and the rule for measuring it against quantity, being the preference felt by those who in their opportunities of experience, to which must be added their habits of self-consciousness and self-observation, are best furnished with the means of comparison. This, being, according to the utilitarian opinion, the end of human action, is necessarily also the standard of morality; which may accordingly be defined, the rules and precepts for human conduct, by the observance of which an existence such as has been described might be, to the greatest extent possible, secured to all mankind; and not to them only, but, so far as the nature of things admits, to the whole sentient creation.

Against this doctrine, however, arises another class of objectors, who say that happiness, in any form, cannot be the rational purpose of human life and action; because, in the first place, it is unattainable: and they contemptuously ask, what right hast thou to be happy? a question which Mr. Carlyle clenches by the addition, What right, a short time ago, hadst thou even *to be?* Next, they say, that men can do *without* happiness; that all noble human beings have felt this, and could not have become noble but by learning the lesson of Entsagen, or renunciation; which lesson, thoroughly learnt and submitted to, they affirm to be the beginning and necessary condition of all virtue.

The first of these objections would go to the root of the matter were it well founded; for if no happiness is to be had at all by human beings, the attainment of it cannot be the end of morality, or of any rational conduct. Though, even in that case, something might still be said for the utilitarian theory; since utility includes not solely the pursuit of happiness, but the prevention or mitigation of unhappiness; and if the former aim be chimerical, there will be all the greater scope and more imperative need for the latter, so long at least as mankind think fit to live, and do not take refuge in the simultaneous act of suicide recommended under certain conditions by Novalis. When, however, it is thus positively asserted to be impossible that human life should be happy, the assertion, if not something like a verbal quibble, is at least an exaggeration. If by happiness be meant a continuity of highly pleasurable excitement, it is evident enough that this is impossible. A state of exalted pleasure lasts only moments, or in some cases, and with some intermissions, hours or days, and is the occasional brilliant flash of enjoyment, not its permanent and steady flame. Of this the philosophers who have taught that happiness is the end of life were as fully aware as those who taunt them. The happiness which they meant was not a life of rapture; but moments of such, in an existence made up of few and transitory pains, many and various pleasures, with a decided predominance of the active over the passive, and having as the foundation of the whole, not to expect more from life than it is capable of bestowing. A life thus composed, to those who have been fortunate enough to obtain it, has always appeared worthy of the name of happiness. And such an existence is even now the lot of many, during some considerable portion of their lives. The present wretched education, and wretched social arrangements, are the only real hindrance to its being attainable by almost all.

The objectors perhaps may doubt whether human beings, if taught to consider happiness as the end of life, would be satisfied with such a moderate share of it. But great numbers of mankind have been satisfied with much less. The main constituents of a satisfied life appear to be two, either of which by itself is often found sufficient for the purpose: tranquillity, and excitement. With much tranquillity, many find that they can be content with very little pleasure: with much excitement, many can reconcile themselves to a considerable quantity of pain. There is assuredly no inherent impossibility in enabling even the mass of mankind to unite both; since the two are so far from being incompatible that they are in natural alliance, the prolongation of either being a preparation for, and exciting a wish for, the other. It is only those in whom indolence amounts to a vice, that do not desire excitement after an interval of repose: it is only those in whom the need of excitement is a disease, that feel the tranquillity which follows excitement dull and insipid, instead of pleasurable in direct proportion to the excitement which preceded it. When people who are tolerably fortunate in their outward lot do not find in life sufficient enjoyment to make it valuable to them, the cause generally is, caring for nobody but themselves. To those who have neither public nor private affections, the excitements of life are much curtailed, and in any case dwindle in value as the time approaches when all selfish interests must be terminated by death: while those who leave after them objects of personal affection, and especially those who have also cultivated a fellow-feeling with the collective interest of mankind, retain as lively an interest in life on the eve of death as in the vigour of youth and health. Next to selfishness, the principal cause which makes life unsatisfactory is want of mental cultivation. A cultivated mind—I do not mean that of a philosopher, but any mind to which the fountains of knowledge have been opened, and which has been taught, in any tolerable degree, to exercise its faculties—finds sources of inexhaustible interest in all that surrounds it; in the objects of nature, the achievements of art, the imaginations of poetry, the incidents of history, the ways of mankind, past and present, and their prospects in the future. It is possible, indeed, to become indifferent to all this, and that too without having exhausted a thousandth part of it; but only when one has had from the beginning no moral or human interest in these things, and has sought in them only the gratification of curiosity.

Now there is absolutely no reason in the nature of things why an amount of mental culture sufficient to give an intelligent interest in these objects of contemplation, should not be the inheritance of every one born in a civilised country. As little is there an inherent necessity that any human being should be a selfish egotist, devoid of every feeling or care but those which centre in his own miserable individuality. Something far superior to this is sufficiently common even now, to give ample earnest of what the human species may be made. Genuine private affections, and a sincere interest in the public good, are possible, though in unequal degrees, to every rightly brought up human being. In a world in which there is so much to interest, so much to enjoy, and so much also to correct and improve, every one who has this moderate amount of moral and intellectual requisites is capable of an existence which may be called enviable; and unless such a person, through bad laws, or subjection to the will of others, is denied the liberty to use the sources of happiness within his reach, he will not fail to find this enviable existence, if he escape the positive evils of life, the great sources of physical and mental suffering—such as indigence, disease, and the unkindness, worthlessness, or premature loss of objects of affection. The main stress of the problem lies, therefore, in the contest with these calamities, from which it is a rare good fortune entirely to escape; which, as things now are, cannot be obviated, and often cannot be in any material degree mitigated. Yet no one whose opinion deserves a moment's consideration can doubt that most of the great positive evils of the world are in themselves removable, and will, if human affairs continue to improve, be in the end reduced within narrow limits. Poverty, in any sense implying suffering, may be completely extinguished by the wisdom of society, combined with the good sense and providence of individuals. Even that most intractable of enemies, disease, may be indefinitely reduced in dimensions by good physical and moral education, and proper control of noxious influences; while the progress of science holds out a promise for the future of still more direct conquests over this detestable foe. And every advance in that direction relieves us from some, not only of the chances which cut short our own lives, but, what concerns us still more, which deprive us of those in whom our happiness is wrapt up. As for vicissitudes of fortune, and other disappointments connected with worldly circumstances, these are principally the effect either of gross imprudence, of ill-regulated desires, or of bad or imperfect social institutions. All the grand sources, in short, of human suffering are in a great degree, many of them almost entirely, conquerable by human care and effort; and though their removal is grievously slow—though a long succession of generations will perish in the breach before the conquest is completed, and this world becomes all that, if will and knowledge were not wanting, it might easily be made—yet every mind sufficiently intelligent and generous to bear a part, however small and unconspicuous, in the endeavour, will draw a noble enjoyment from the contest itself, which he would not for any bribe in the form of selfish indulgence consent to be without.

And this leads to the true estimation of what is said by the objectors concerning the possibility, and the obligation, of learning to do without happiness. Unquestionably it is possible to do without happiness; it is done involuntarily by nineteen-twentieths of mankind, even in those parts of our present world which are least deep in barbarism; and it often has to be done voluntarily by the hero or the martyr, for the sake of something which he prizes more than his individual happiness. But this something, what is it, unless the happiness of others, or some of the requisites of happiness? It is noble to be capable of resigning entirely one's own portion of happiness, or chances of it: but, after all, this self-sacrifice must be for some end; it is not its own end; and if we are told that its end is not happiness, but virtue, which is better than happiness, I ask, would the sacrifice be made if the hero or martyr did not believe that it would earn for others immunity from similar sacrifices? Would it be made if he thought that his renunciation of happiness for himself would produce no fruit for any of his fellow creatures, but to make their lot like his, and place them also in the condition of persons who have renounced happiness? All honour to those who can abnegate for themselves the personal enjoyment of life, when by such renunciation they contribute worthily to increase the amount of happiness in the world; but he who does it, or professes to do it, for any other purpose, is no more deserving of admiration than the ascetic mounted on his pillar. He may be an inspiring proof of what men *can* do, but assuredly not an example of what they *should*. . . .

Meanwhile, let utilitarians never cease to claim the morality of self devotion as a possession which belongs by as good a right to them, as either to the Stoic or to the Transcendentalist. The utilitarian morality does recognise in human beings the power of sacrificing their own greatest good for the good of others. It only refuses to admit that the sacrifice is itself a good. A sacrifice which does not increase, or tend to increase, the sum total of happiness, it considers as wasted. The only self-renunciation which it applauds, is devotion to the happiness, or to some of the means of happiness, of others; either of mankind collectively, or of individuals within the limits imposed by the collective interests of mankind.

I must again repeat . . . that the happiness which forms the utilitarian standard of what is right in conduct, is not the agent's own happiness, but that of all concerned. As between his own happiness and that of others, utilitarianism requires him to be as strictly impartial as a disinterested and benevolent spectator. In the golden rule of Jesus of Nazareth, we read the complete spirit of the ethics of utility. To do as you would be done by, and to love your neighbour as yourself, constitute the ideal perfection of utilitarian morality. As the means of making the nearest approach to this ideal, utility would enjoin, first, that laws and social arrangements should place the happiness, or (as speaking practically it may be called) the interest, of every individual, as nearly as possible in harmony with the interest of the whole; and secondly, that education and opinion, which have so vast a power over human character, should so use that power as to establish in the mind of every individual an indissoluble association between his own happiness and the good of the whole; especially between his own happiness and the practice of such modes of conduct, negative and positive, as regard for the universal happiness prescribes; so that not only he may be unable to conceive the possibility of happiness to himself, consistently with conduct opposed to the general good, but also that a direct impulse to promote the general good may be in every individual one of the habitual motives of action, and the sentiments connected therewith may fill a large and prominent place in every human being's sentient existence. If the impugners of the utilitarian morality represented it to their own minds in this its true character, I know not what recommendation possessed by any other morality they could possibly affirm to be wanting to it; what more beautiful or more exalted developments of human nature any other ethical system can be supposed to foster, or what springs of action, not accessible to the utilitarian, such systems rely on for giving effect to their mandates.

The objectors to utilitarianism cannot always be charged with representing it in a discreditable light. On the contrary, those among them who entertain anything like a just idea of its disinterested character, sometimes find fault with its standard as being too high for humanity. They say it is exacting too much to require that people shall always act from the inducement of promoting the general interests of society. But this is to mistake the very meaning of a standard of morals, and confound the rule of action with the motive of it. It is the business of ethics to tell us what are our duties, or by what test we may know them; but no system of ethics requires that the sole motive of all we do shall be a feeling of duty; on the contrary, ninety-nine hundredths of all our actions are done from other motives, and rightly so done, if the rule of duty does not condemn them. It is the more unjust to utilitarianism that this particular misapprehension should be made a ground of objection to it, inasmuch as utilitarian moralists have gone beyond almost all others in affirming that the motive has nothing to do with the morality of the action, though much with the worth of the agent. He who saves a fellow creature from drowning does what is morally right, whether his motive be duty, or the hope of being paid for his trouble; he who betrays the friend that trusts him, is guilty of a crime, even if his object be to serve another friend to whom he is under greater obligations. But to speak only of actions done from the motive of duty, and indirect obedience to principle: it is a misapprehension of the utilitarian mode of thought, to conceive it as implying that people should fix their minds upon so wide a generality as the world, or society at large. The great majority of good actions are intended not for the benefit of the world, but for that of individuals, of which the good of the world is made up; and the thoughts of the most virtuous man need not on these occasions travel beyond the particular persons concerned, except so far as is necessary to assure himself that in benefiting them he is not violating the rights, that is, the legitimate and authorised expectations, of any one else. The multiplication of happiness is, according to the utilitarian ethics, the object of virtue: the occasions on which any person (except one in a thousand) has it in his power to do this on an extended scale, in other words to be a public benefactor, are but exceptional; and on these occasions alone is he called on to consider public utility; in every other case, private utility, the interest or happiness of some few persons, is all he has to attend to. Those alone the influence of whose actions extends to society in general, need concern themselves habitually about so large an object. In the case of abstinences indeed—of things which people forbear to do from moral considerations, though the consequences in the particular case might be beneficial—it would be unworthy of an intelligent agent not to be consciously aware that the action is of a class which, if practised generally, would be generally injurious, and that this is the ground of the obligation to abstain from it. The amount of regard for the public interest implied in this recognition, is no greater than is demanded by every system of morals, for they all enjoin to abstain from whatever is manifestly pernicious to society.

The same considerations dispose of another reproach against the doctrine of utility, founded on a still grosser misconception of the purpose of a standard of morality, and of the very meaning of the words right and wrong. It is often affirmed that utilitarianism renders men cold and unsympathising; that it chills their moral feelings towards individuals; that it makes them regard only the dry and hard consideration of the consequences of actions, not taking into their moral estimate the qualities from which those actions emanate. If the assertion means that they do not allow their judgment respecting the rightness or wrongness of an action to be influenced by their opinion of the qualities of the person who does it, this is a complaint not against utilitarianism, but against having any standard of morality at all; for certainly no known ethical standard decides an action to be good or bad because it is done by a good or a bad man, still less because done by an amiable, a brave, or a benevolent man, or the contrary. These considerations are relevant, not to the estimation of actions, but of persons; and there is nothing in the utilitarian theory inconsistent with the fact that there are other things which interest us in persons besides the rightness and wrongness of their actions. The Stoics, indeed, with the paradoxical misuse of language which was part of their system, and by which they strove to raise themselves above all concern about anything but virtue, were fond of saying that he who has that has everything; that he, and only he, is rich, is beautiful, is a king. But no claim of this description is made for the virtuous man by the utilitarian doctrine. Utilitarians are quite aware that there are other desirable possessions and qualities besides virtue, and are perfectly willing to allow to all of them their full worth. They are also aware that a right action does not necessarily indicate a virtuous character, and that actions which are blamable, often proceed from qualities entitled to praise. When this is apparent in any particular case, it modifies their estimation, not certainly of the act, but of the agent. I grant that they are, notwithstanding, of opinion, that in the long run the best proof of a good character is good actions; and resolutely refuse to consider any mental disposition as good, of which the predominant tendency is to produce bad conduct. This makes them unpopular with many people; but it is an unpopularity which they must share with every one who regards the distinction between right and wrong in a serious light; and the reproach is not one which a conscientious utilitarian need be anxious to repel.

If no more be meant by the objection than that many utilitarians look on the morality of actions, as measured by the utilitarian standard, with too exclusive a regard, and do not lay sufficient stress upon the other beauties of character which go towards making a human being lovable or admirable, this may be admitted. Utilitarians who have cultivated their moral feelings, but not their sympathies nor their artistic perceptions, do fall into this mistake; and so do all other moralists under the same conditions. What can be said in excuse for other moralists is equally available for them, namely, that, if there is to be any error, it is better that it should be on that side. As a matter of fact, we may affirm that among utilitarians as among adherents of other systems, there is every imaginable degree of rigidity and of laxity in the application of their standard: some are even puritanically rigorous, while others are as indulgent as can possibly be desired by sinner or by sentimentalist. But on the whole, a doctrine which brings prominently forward the interest that mankind have in the repression and prevention of conduct which violates the moral law, is likely to be inferior to no other in turning the sanctions of opinion against such violations. It is true, the question, What does violate the moral law? is one on which those who recognise different standards of morality are likely now and then to differ. But difference of opinion on moral questions was not first introduced into the world by utilitarianism, while that doctrine does supply, if not always an easy, at all events a tangible and intelligible mode of deciding such differences. . . .

[Mill proceeds to deal with several fallacies in great detail, then concludes:] If utility is the ultimate source of moral obligations, utility may be invoked to decide between them when their demands are incompatible. Though the application of the standard may be difficult, it is better than none at all: while in other systems, the moral laws all claiming independent authority, there is no common umpire entitled to interfere between them; their claims to precedence one over another rest on little better than sophistry, and unless determined, as they generally are, by the unacknowledged influence of considerations of utility, afford a free scope for the action of personal desires and partialities. We must remember that only in these cases of conflict between secondary principles is it requisite that first principles should be appealed to. There is no case of moral obligation in which some secondary principle is not involved; and if only one, there can seldom be any real doubt which one it is, in the mind of any person by whom the principle itself is recognised.

23. A Critique of Modernity: John Henry Newman

JOHN HENRY NEWMAN (1801–1890) may have been the most profound thinker among Victorian men of letters. He certainly ranks among the greatest of English religious figures, although he was as suspect and isolated in the Roman Catholic Church as he had been in the Anglican Church. Newman gave the Oxford Movement distinction (see Document 26) and an intellectual quality it otherwise would have lacked. Newman also did more than any man to soften the harsh anti-Catholic prejudices which had become English conventions.

Newman struck out at the narrowness, the smaller than life-size view that seemed to him to characterize the liberal conception. Man was grander than the materialists would have him. A calculus of happiness would deprive him of his fantasy, his dreams, his soul. Newman was, in this sense, part of the Romantic revolution—demanding sentiment, feelings, mystery, the unseen. His hostility to liberalism was not political. He had no desire to resurrect some outdated past. His critique derived from his concern for the Church, a spiritual concern in the deepest sense of the term. The Church was the bastion against the corruption of modernism. Erastianism forced the Church into the petty world of transient phenomena; liberalism sought to strip away the dogmatism and authority, which the Church must have.

Newman never ignored or rejected the mundane world and contemporary society, but he addressed himself to the human condition throughout time, not in the transitory world of the nineteenth century. History was apocalyptic, not progressive. Newman never joined the strident voices of reaction. He provided a conceptual rationale for but never participated in some of the banalities of feudal revivalism. He shared with Mill the notion that truth depended upon the existence of error, contending that error alone can force us to think clearly and precisely. Only thus can we understand our faith.

This selection sets forth a series of propositions, not altogether fairly, around which the Low Church-High Church controversy revolved. Behind the attack on Erastian liberalism, however, lies a fundamental challenge to the utilitarian conception.

Recommended Reading

Newman is his own best spokesman in the *Apologia Pro Vita Sua,* but A. D. Culler, *The Imperial Intellect* (New Haven: 1955), M. Trevor, *Newman,* 2 vols. (London: 1962), D. J. De Laura, *Hebrew and Hellene in Victorian England* (Austin: 1969), and T. Kenny, *The Political Thought of John Henry Newman* (London: 1957), are recent additions to a voluminous literature.

JOHN HENRY NEWMAN,
ON LIBERALISM

I conclude this notice of Liberalism in Oxford, and the party which was antagonistic to it, with some propositions in detail, which, as a member of the latter, and together with the High Church, I earnestly denounced and abjured.

1. No religious tenet is important, unless reason shows it to be so.

Therefore, e.g. the Doctrine of the Athanasian Creed is not to be insisted on, unless it tends to convert the soul; and the doctrine of the Atonement is to be insisted on, if it does convert the soul.

2. No one can believe what he does not understand.

Therefore, e.g. there are no mysteries in true religion.

3. No theological doctrine is any thing more than an opinion which happens to be held by bodies of men.

Source: From *Apologia Pro Vita Sua* (London: 1864), pp. 294–296.

Therefore, e.g. no creed, as such, is necessary for salvation.

4. It is dishonest in a man to make an act of faith in what he has not had brought home to him by actual proof.

Therefore, e.g. the mass of men ought not absolutely to believe in the divine authority of the Bible.

5. It is immoral in a man to believe more than he can spontaneously receive as being congenial to his moral and mental nature.

Therefore, e.g. a given individual is not bound to believe in eternal punishment.

6. No revealed doctrines or precepts may reasonably stand in the way of scientific conclusions.

Therefore, e.g. Political Economy may reverse our Lord's declarations about poverty and riches, or a system of Ethics may teach that the highest condition of body is ordinarily essential to the highest state of mind.

7. Christianity is necessarily modified by the growth of civilization, and the exigencies of times.

Therefore, e.g. the Catholic priesthood, though necessary in the Middle Ages, may be superseded now.

8. There is a system of religion more simply true than Christianity as it has ever been received.

Therefore, e.g. we may advance that Christianity is the "corn of wheat" which has been dead for 1800 years, but at length will bear fruit; and that Mahometanism is the manly religion, and existing Christianity the womanish.

9. There is a right of Private Judgment: that is, there is no existing authority on earth competent to interfere with the liberty of individuals in reasoning and judging for themselves about the Bible and its contents, as they severally please.

Therefore, e.g. religious establishments requiring subscription are Anti-christian.

10. There are rights of conscience such, that every one may lawfully advance a claim to profess and teach what is false and wrong in matters, religious, social, and moral, provided that to his private conscience it seems absolutely true and right.

Therefore, e.g. individuals have a right to preach and practise fornication and polygamy.

11. There is no such thing as a national or state conscience.

Therefore, e.g. no judgments can fall upon a sinful or infidel nation.

12. The civil power has no positive duty, in a normal state of things, to maintain religious truth.

Therefore, e.g. blasphemy and sabbath-breaking are not rightly punishable by law.

13. Utility and expedience are the measure of political duty.

Therefore, e.g. no punishment may be enacted, on the ground that God commands it: e.g. on the text, "Whoso sheddeth man's blood, by man shall his blood be shed."

14. The Civil Power may dispose of Church property without sacrilege.

Therefore, e.g. Henry VIII. committed no sin in his spoliations.

15. The Civil Power has the right of ecclesiastical jurisdiction and administration.

Therefore, e.g. Parliament may impose articles of faith on the Church or suppress Dioceses.

16. It is lawful to rise in arms against legitimate princes.

Therefore, e.g. the Puritans in the 17th century, and the French in the 18th, were justifiable in their Rebellion and Revolution respectively.

17. The people are the legitimate source of power.

Therefore, e.g. Universal Suffrage is among the natural rights of man.

18. Virtue is the child of knowledge, and vice of ignorance.

Therefore, e.g. education, periodical literature, railroad travelling, ventilation, drainage, and the arts of life, when fully carried out, serve to make a population moral and happy.

All of these propositions, and many others too, were familiar to me thirty years ago, as in the number of the tenets of Liberalism, and, while I gave into none of them except No. 12, and perhaps No. 11, and partly No. 1, before I began to publish, so afterwards I wrote against most of them in some part or other of my Anglican works.

24. Moral Collectivism: The Revolt of John Ruskin

IF NEWMAN APPEALED to a prescriptive past and Mill to a utilitarian present, John Ruskin (1819–1900) found neither conception to his taste. He shared a moral revulsion against contemporary society with both Newman and Mill, but he attempted to suggest a different answer. It partook of socialism, of utopianism, of communitarianism. But fundamentally his position was ethical and apolitical.

History has mistreated Ruskin. It is a canard, even allowing for the grain of truth, to call him a man who wrote twenty-six volumes about which he knew little. Ruskin established himself as an art critic, resurrected Turner, one of England's finest painters, and contributed to the British obsession with the Italian renaissance. His audience elevated him to the status of an oracle; he did not seek it. In his later, declining years his worse side became more obvious. His views became, increasingly, parodies of themselves.

Ruskin was concerned that art should be moral and uplifting—a view that has been out of favor for the better part of a century. He also rejected the notion that industrial society must be ugly. William Morris, with his fraternal, aesthetic socialism, was to preserve and extend Ruskin's vision. Ruskin's comments on industrial society were often wrong in particulars but conceptually sound. He believed that industry should serve man, not the other way around. Industry could and should provide man the material needs for a good life at a just price. Industry should help to make man better, not merely provide him things. Ruskin's notions about minimum wages, prices reasonably related to worth, limits on profits, and the value of labor shocked contemporaries but look restrained today.

Ruskin did subtitle this work a study in political economy, but that had little to do with his principal interest. He often indulged in misleading advertising. How many unsophisticated farmers bought *On the Construction of Sheepfolds* only to discover that it was a tract on municipal architecture? Ruskin was a moralist, not an economist. The economic system as he comprehended it was culturally and morally destructive. Beauty and truth could never be served in a society where one man sought the greatest reward for himself while allotting as little as possible to his colleagues or customers. It was the economic system, argued Ruskin, which poisoned the proper relationship of man to man and men to their community.

Recommended Reading

There is a considerable literature on Ruskin. J. D. Rosenberg, *The Darkening Glass* (New York: 1961), is one of the best of several biographies. Sir Kenneth Clark has some useful observations in *Ruskin Today* (London: 1964), and J. T. Fair considers the problem presented here in *Ruskin and the Economists* (Nashville: 1957). For socialism, esthetic and otherwise, see *BP19C*.

John Ruskin,
On Mastership

The simplest state of it, then, is this:[1] a wise and provident person works much, consumes little, and lays by a store; an improvident person works little, consumes all his produce, and lays by no store. Accident interrupts the daily work, or renders it less productive; the idle person must then starve, or be supported by the provident one, who, having him thus at his mercy, may either refuse to maintain him altogether, or, which will evidently be more to his own interest, say to him, "I will maintain you, indeed, but you shall now work hard, instead of indolently, and instead of being allowed to lay by what you save, as you might have done, had you remained independent, *I* will take all the surplus. You would not lay it up for yourself; it is wholly your own fault that has thrown you into my power, and I will force you to work, or starve; yet you shall have no profit of your work, only your daily bread for it; [and competition shall determine how much of that[2]]." This mode of treatment has now become so universal that it is supposed to be the only natural—nay, the only possible one; and the market wages are calmly defined by economists as "the sum which will maintain the labourer."

The power of the provident person to do this is only checked by the correlative power of some neighbour of similarly frugal habits, who says to the labourer—"I will give you a little more than this other provident person: come and work for me."

The power of the provident over the improvident depends thus, primarily, on their relative numbers; secondarily, on the modes of agreement of the adverse parties with each other. The accidental

1. In the present general examination I concede so much to ordinary economists as to ignore all *innocent* poverty. I adapt my reasoning, for once, to the modern English practical mind, by assuming poverty to be always criminal; the conceivable exceptions we will examine afterwards.

2. [I have no terms of English, and can find none in Greek nor Latin, nor in any other strong language known to me, contemptuous enough to attach to the bestial idiotism of the modern theory that wages are to be measured by competition.]

Source: From *Minerva Pulveris: Six Essays on the Elements of Political Economy* (New York: 1872), pp. 131–155.

level of wages is a variable function of the number of provident and idle persons in the world, of the enmity between them as classes, and of the agreement between those of the same class. *It depends, from beginning to end, on moral conditions.*

Supposing the rich to be entirely selfish, *it is always for their interest that the poor should be as numerous as they can employ, and restrain.* For, granting that the entire population is no larger than the ground can easily maintain—that the classes are stringently divided—and that there is sense or strength of hand enough with the rich to secure obedience; then, if nine-tenths of a nation are poor, the remaining tenth have the service of nine persons each;[3] but, if eight-tenths are poor, only of four each; if seven-tenths are poor, of two and a third each; if six-tenths are poor, of one and a half each; and if five-tenths are poor, of only one each. But, practically, if the rich strive always to obtain more power over the poor, instead of to raise them—and if, on the other hand, the poor become continually more vicious and numerous, through neglect and oppression,—though the *range* of the power of the rich increases, its *tenure* becomes less secure; until, at last, the measure of iniquity being full, revolution, civil war, or the subjection of the state to a healthier or stronger one, closes the moral corruption, and industrial disease.

It is rarely, however, that things come to this extremity. Kind persons among the rich, and wise among the poor, modify the connexion of the classes: the efforts made to raise and relieve on the one side, and the success of honest toil on the other, bind and blend the orders of society into the confused tissue of half-felt obligation, sullenly-rendered obedience, and variously-directed, or mis-directed, toil, which form the warp of daily life. But this great law rules all the wild design: that success (while society is guided by laws of competition) *signifies always so much victory over your neighbour* as to obtain the direction of his work, and to take the profits of it. *This is the real source of all great riches.* No man can become largely rich by his personal toil.[4] The work of his own

3. I say nothing yet of the quality of the servants, which, nevertheless, is the gist of the business. Will you have Paul Veronese to paint your ceiling, or the plumber from over the way? Both will work for the same money; Paul, if anything, a little the cheaper of the two, if you keep him in good humour; only you have to discern him first, which will need eyes.

4. By his art he may; but only when its produce, or the sight or hearing of it, becomes a subject of dispute, so as to enable the artist to tax the labour of multitudes highly, in exchange for his own.

hands, wisely directed, will indeed always maintain himself and his family, and make fitting provision for his age. *But it is only by the discovery of some method of taxing the labour of others that he can become opulent.* Every increase of his capital enables him to extend this taxation more widely; that is, to invest larger funds in the maintenance of labourers,—to direct, accordingly, vaster and yet vaster masses of labour, and to appropriate its profits.

There is much confusion of idea on the subject of this appropriation. It is, of course, the interest of the employer to disguise it from the persons employed; and, for his own comfort and complacency, he often desires no less to disguise it from himself. And it is matter of much doubt with me, how far the foul and foolish arguments used habitually on this subject are indeed the honest expression of foul and foolish convictions;—or rather (as I am sometimes forced to conclude from the irritation with which they are advanced) are resolutely dishonest, wilful, and malicious sophisms, arranged so as to mask, to the last moment, the real laws of economy, and future duties of men. . . .

. . . "Riches" mean eternally and essentially this; and God send at last a time when those words of our best-reputed economist shall be true, and we *shall* indeed "all know what it is to be rich;" that it is to be slave-master over farthest earth, and over all ways and thoughts of men. Every operative you employ is your true servant: distant or near, subject to your immediate orders, or ministering to your widely-communicated caprice,—for the pay he stipulates, or the price he tempts,—all are alike under this great dominion of the gold. The milliner who makes the dress is as much a servant (more so, in that she uses more intelligence in the service) as the maid who puts it on; the carpenter who smooths the door, as the footman who opens it; the tradesmen who supply the table, as the labourers and sailors who supply the tradesmen. Why speak of these lower services? Painters and singers (whether of note or rhyme,) jesters and story-tellers, moralists, historians, priests,—so far as these, in any degree, paint, or sing, or tell their tale, or charm their charm, or "perform" their rite, *for pay,*—in so far, they are all slaves; abject utterly, if the service be for pay only; abject less and less in proportion to the degrees of love and of wisdom which enter into their duty, or *can* enter into it, according as their function is to do the bidding and the work of a manly people;—or to amuse, tempt, and deceive, a childish one.

There is always, in such amusement and temptation, to a certain extent, a government of the rich by the poor, as of the poor by the rich; but the latter is the prevailing and necessary one, and it consists, when it is honourable, in the collection of the profits of labour from those who would have misused them, and the administration of those profits for the service either of the same persons in future, or of others; and when it is dishonourable, as is more frequently the case in modern times, it consists in the collection of the profits of labour from those who would have rightly used them, and their appropriation to the service of the collector himself.

The examination of these various modes of collection and use of riches will form the third branch of our future inquiries; but the key to the whole subject lies in the clear understanding of the difference between selfish and unselfish expenditure. It is not easy, by any course of reasoning, to enforce this on the generally unwilling hearer; yet the definition of unselfish expenditure is brief and simple. It is expenditure which, if you are a capitalist, does not pay *you*, but pays somebody else; and if you are a consumer, does not please *you*, but pleases somebody else. . . .

"Impossible, absurd, Utopian!" exclaim nine-tenths of the few readers whom these words may find.

No, good reader, *this* is not Utopian: but I will tell you what would have seemed, if we had not seen it, Utopian on the side of evil instead of good; that ever men should have come to value their money so much more than their lives, that if you call upon them to become soldiers, and take chance of a bullet through their heart, and of wife and children being left desolate, for their pride's sake, they will do it gaily, without thinking twice; but if you ask them, for their country's sake, to spend a hundred pounds without security of getting back a hundred-and-five,[5] they will laugh in your face. . . .

5. I have not hitherto touched on the subject of interest of money; it is too complex, and must be reserved for its proper place in the body of the work. The definition of interest (apart from compensation for risk) is, "the exponent of the comfort of accomplished labour, separated from its power;" the power being what is lent: and the French economists who have maintained the entire illegality of interest are wrong; yet by no means so curiously or wildly wrong as the English and French ones opposed to them . . . it never seeming to occur to the mind of the compiler, any more than to the writers whom he quotes, that it is quite possible, and even (according to Jewish proverb) prudent, for men to hoard as ants and mice do, for use, not

There are, therefore,—let me finally enforce, and leave with the reader, this broad conclusion,—three things to be considered in employing any poor person. It is not enough to give him employment. You must employ him first to produce useful things; secondly, of the several (suppose equally useful) things he can equally well produce, you must set him to make that which will cause him to lead the healthiest life; lastly, of the things produced, it remains a question of wisdom and conscience how much you are to take yourself, and how much to leave to others. A large quantity, remember, unless you destroy it, *must* always be so left at one time or another; the only questions you have to decide are, not *what* you will give, but *when*, and *how*, and *to whom*, you will give. The natural law of human life is, of course, that in youth a man shall labour and lay by store for his old age, and when age comes, shall use what he has laid by, gradually slackening his toil, and allowing himself more frank use of his store; taking care always to leave himself as much as will surely suffice for him beyond any possible length of life. What he has gained, or by tranquil and unanxious toil continues to gain, more than is enough for his own need, he ought so to administer, while he yet lives, as to see the good of it again beginning, in other hands; for thus he has himself the greatest sum of pleasure from it, and faithfully uses his sagacity in its control. Whereas most men, it appears, dislike the sight of their fortunes going out into service again, and say to themselves,—"I can indeed nowise prevent this money from falling at last into the hands of others, nor hinder the good of it from becoming theirs, not mine; but at least let a merciful death save me from being a witness of their satisfaction; and may God so far be gracious to me as to let no good come of any of this money of mine before my eyes."

Supposing this feeling unconquerable, the safest way of rationally indulging it would be for the capitalist at once to spend all his fortune on himself, which might actually, in many cases, be quite the rightest as well as the pleasantest thing to do, if he had just

---

usury; and lay by something for winter nights, in the expectation of rather sharing than lending the scrapings. My Savoyard squirrels would pass a pleasant time of it under the snow-laden pine-branches, if they always declined to economize because no one would pay them interest on nuts.

[I leave this note as it stood: but, as I have above stated, should now side wholly with the French economists spoken of, in asserting the absolute illegality of interest.]

tastes and worthy passions. But, whether for himself only, or through the hands, and for the sake, of others also, the law of wise life is, that the maker of the money should also be the spender of it, and spend it, approximately, all, before he dies; so that his true ambition as an economist should be, to die, not as rich, but as poor, as possible, calculating the ebb tide of possession in true and calm proportion to the ebb tide of life. Which law, checking the wing of accumulative desire in the mid-volley, and leading to peace of possession and fulness of fruition in old age, is also wholesome, in that by the freedom of gift, together with present help and counsel, it at once endears and dignifies age in the sight of youth, which then no longer strips the bodies of the dead, but receives the grace of the living. Its chief use would (or will be, for men are indeed capable of attaining to this much use of their reason), that some temperance and measure will be put to the acquisitiveness of commerce.[6] For as things stand, a man holds it his duty to be temperate in his food, and of his body, but for no duty to be temperate in his riches, and of his mind. He sees that he ought not to waste his youth and his flesh for luxury; but he will waste his age, and his soul, for money, and think he does no wrong, nor know the *delirium tremens* of the intellect for disease. But the law of life is, that a man should fix the sum he desires to make annually, as the food he desires to eat daily; and stay when he has reached the limit, refusing increase of business, and leaving it to others, so obtaining due freedom of time for better thoughts. How the gluttony of business is punished, a bill of health for the principals of the richest city houses, issued annually, would show in a sufficiently impressive manner.

I know, of course, that these statements will be received by the modern merchant as an active border rider of the sixteenth century would have heard of its being proper for men of the Marches to get their living by the spade, instead of the spur. But my business is only to state veracities and necessities; I neither look for the acceptance of the one, nor hope for the nearness of the other. Near

6. The fury of modern trade arises chiefly out of the possibility of making sudden fortunes by largeness of transaction, and accident of discovery or contrivance. I have no doubt that the final interest of every nation is to check the action of these commercial lotteries; and that all great accidental gains or losses should be national,—not individual. But speculation absolute, unconnected with commercial effort, is an unmitigated evil in a state, and the root of countless evils beside.

or distant, the day *will* assuredly come when the merchants of a state shall be its true ministers of exchange, its porters, in the double sense of carriers and gate-keepers, bringing all lands into frank and faithful communication, and knowing for their master of guild, Hermes the herald, instead of Mercury the gain-guarder.

And now, finally, for immediate rule to all who will accept it.

The distress of any population means that they need food, house-room, clothes, and fuel. You can never, therefore, be wrong in employing any labourer to produce food, house-room, clothes, or fuel; but you are *always* wrong if you employ him to produce nothing, (for then some other labourer must be worked double time to feed him); and you are generally wrong, at present, if you employ him (unless he can do nothing else) to produce works of art or luxuries; because modern art is mostly on a false basis, and modern luxury is criminally great.

The way to produce more food is mainly to bring in fresh ground, and increase facilities of carriage;—to break rock, exchange earth, drain the moist, and water the dry, to mend roads, and build harbours of refuge. Taxation thus spent will annihilate taxation, but spent in war, it annihilates revenue.

The way to produce house-room is to apply your force first to the humblest dwellings. When your bricklayers are out of employ, do not build splendid new streets, but better the old ones; send your paviours and slaters to the poorest villages, and see that your poor are healthily lodged, before you try your hand on stately architecture. You will find its stateliness rise better under the trowel afterwards; and we do not yet build so well that we need hasten to display our skill to future ages. . . .

The way to get more clothes is—not, necessarily, to get more cotton. There were words written twenty years ago which would have saved many of us some shivering, had they been minded in time. Shall we read them again?

[And Ruskin quotes Thomas Carlyle on the Futility of a civilization that depends upon "selling manufactured cotton at a farthing an ell cheaper than any other people. A most narrow stand for a great nation to base itself on!"]

The way to produce more fuel is first to make your coal mines safer, by sinking more shafts; then set all your convicts to work in them, and if, as is to be hoped, you succeed in diminishing the supply of that sort of labourer, consider what means there may be, first, of growing forest where its growth will improve climate;

secondly, of splintering the forests which now make continents of fruitful land pathless and poisonous, into faggots for fire;—so gaining at once dominion icewards and sunwards. Your steam power has been given (you will find eventually) for work such as that: and not for excursion trains, to give the labourer a moment's breath, at the peril of his breath for ever, from amidst the cities which it has crushed into masses of corruption. When you know how to build cities, and how to rule them, you will be able to breathe in their streets, and the "excursion" will be the afternoon's walk or game in the fields round them.

"But nothing of this work will pay?"

No; no more than it pays to dust your rooms, or wash your doorsteps. It will pay; not at first in currency, but in that which is the end and the source of currency,—in life; (and in currency richly afterwards). It will pay in that which is more than life,—in light, whose true price has not yet been reckoned in any currency, and yet into the image of which, all wealth, one way or other, must be cast. For your riches must either be as the lightning, which,

> Begot but in a cloud,
> Though shining bright, and speaking loud,
> Whilst it begins, concludes its violent race;
> And, where it gilds, it wounds the place;—

or else, as the lightning of the sacred sign, which shines from one part of the heaven to the other. There is no other choice; you must either take dust for deity, spectre for possession, fettered dream for life, and for epitaph, this reversed verse of the great Hebrew hymn of economy (Psalm cxii.):—"He hath gathered together, he hath stripped the poor, his iniquity remaineth for ever:"—or else, having the sun of justice to shine on you, and the sincere substance of good in your possession, and the pure law and liberty of life within you, leave men to write this better legend over your grave:—

"He hath dispersed abroad. He hath given to the poor. His righteousness remaineth for ever."

Dogma

25. Protestantism: A Dogma for Introspection

VICTORIAN CIVILIZATION was Christian and overwhelmingly Protestant. Almost three-fifths of England was Anglican, two-fifths Protestant sects; barely two in a hundred were Roman Catholic in the early Victorian years. Presbyterianism dominated Scotland; Roman Catholicism, Ireland save for Protestant Ulster. The Victorians believed in God. They certainly believed, if they bothered to raise the question at all, that God was an Englishman. Never in history has a national culture succeeded more completely in convincing itself that the highest morality and self-interest were identical.

The late G. M. Young spoke of utilitarian philosophy and evangelical discipline as the driving forces of early Victorian England. Utilitarianism reached considerably beyond the ill-defined circle of philosophic radicals; Protestant evangelicalism, beyond sect and creed. Both provided purpose and momentum in a society undergoing revolution in slow motion. Protestant evangelicalism provided a necessary psychic intensity and mental discipline, which made it attractive to people indifferent or hostile to its theology. Evangelicalism, both in the Church of England and Nonconformist creeds, was necessary for an increasingly urban, anonymous society. A patriarchal rural society can function with less explicit constraints and guides. The traditional hierarchy, traditional culture, traditional structure provide a broad framework. Work-time discipline adapts to the demands of days, months, or seasons rather than the precise ordering of shop clock and factory bell.

Evangelicalism developed in the eighteenth century as part of the general religious revival that ran as a countercurrent to the emotional aridity of Enlightenment philosophy and deistic theology. It was a religion of experience, demanding conversion and salvation, sustained through life by good works. The great work of Evangelicalism in the late eighteenth and early nineteenth centuries had been to stimulate movements for social and moral reform. The campaign against slavery and the slave trade, the concern for the insane, prisoners, chimney sweeps, and the deprived are all to the credit of the movement. We may appreciate the degree to which Evangelicals rooted out the grosser abuses and some of the violence of Hanoverian England, but even Victorians began to balk at the intellectual and cultural constraints imposed. Sabbatarianism, censorship, the attempts to regulate lives by legislation and social coercion are less admirable. The control of behavior we associate with the Victorians preceded the Victorian age.[1] The Victorians devoted considerable energy to emancipating themselves from the constraints Evangelicalism had placed on life and living. But even after the formal framework was gone, the Victorians retained or attempted to retain the rigor, the intense concentration, the disciplined pursuit of moral objectives.[2] In its secular form Evangel-

---

1. See, in particular, M. J. Quinlan, *Victorian Prelude* (New York: 1941).
2. See Documents 29, 30, 31, and 37. Here, as elsewhere, I have drawn heavily upon G. M. Young, *Victorian England: Portrait of an Age* (London: 1936).

icalism was respectability. The functional code persisted long after belief had degenerated into ritual.

But the ritual and its media were important. Family prayers persisted. Church attendance continued high. The sermon, the acknowledged vehicle for conveying the Truth, would be a model for the secular didactic essay. Gladstone wrote four thousand sermons. Sir Robert Peel's father trained his son for a parliamentary career by having him repeat the Sunday sermon after the service. The emphasis on purpose, serious self-examination, and the sense of superiority were conveyed thousands of times every week to millions of Victorians. Such words went far to condition a Victorian frame of mind.

Recommended Reading

All of the literature cited in the general bibliography bears to some extent on this problem. Horton Davies, *Worship and Theology in England* (London: 1961–1962), vols. III and IV, and O. Chadwick, *The Victorian Church* (London: 1966), deal with the formal aspects of Evangelicalism. A perceptive treatment of its impact may be found in G. Best, "Popular Protestantism," in R. Robson, *Ideas and Institutions of Victorian Britain* (London: 1967), pp. 115–142, G. M. Young, or W. E. Houghton.

REV. ROBERT MURRAY M'CHEYNE, SERMONS FOR SABBATH EVENINGS

"And the Lord said, Simon, Simon, behold, Satan hath desired to have you, that he may sift you as wheat: but I have prayed for thee, that thy faith fail not; and when thou art converted, strengthen thy brethren."—LUKE xxii, 31, 32.

These words were spoken in an hour of calm, and solemn, and holy enjoyment. The disciples had, for the first time, eaten of that bread, and drunk of that cup, which all true disciples are to partake of till He come. Every bosom, but that of the traitor, was filled with peace. Like a family of affectionate children, every one clung closer to him than another. Eye hath not seen, ear hath not heard, heart hath not conceived, the tender joy that flowed into the hearts of Peter, Nathaniel, and John at such a moment. And yet this was the very time the Saviour chose to repeat this solemn word of warning, "Simon, Simon, behold, Satan hath desired to have you, that he may sift you as wheat: but I have prayed for thee, that thy

Source: From "The Believer's Danger, Encouragement, and Duty," *Sermons for Sabbath Evenings,* 3d ed. (London: 1858), pp. 335–352.

faith fail not: and when thou art converted, strengthen thy brethren."

Dear friends, you have been at the same table—some of you have had the same calm and solemn, and holy enjoyment. The Saviour is the same yesterday, and to-day, and for ever. Satan, too, is the same; or, rather, he is more skilful and powerful now than he was in the apostles' days. He has been gaining skill these eighteen hundred years, and his anger is hotter now, for he knows that his time is short. This, then, is the very message of the Saviour to you—"Simon, Simon, behold, Satan hath desired to sift you as wheat."

Learn from these words a lesson of danger, of encouragement, and of duty. Learn,

I. *The Christian's danger:* Satan hath desired to have you all, that he may sift you as wheat. Observe,

1. *The saints are the peculiar objects of Satan's hatred.* "Satan hath desired to have you." In the plural, "to have all of you who are my true disciples." Jesus is "the searcher of hearts," not only of the heart of man, but of devils also. He knew well what was in Satan's heart. It was not the Jewish priests and scribes he desired. It was not the soldiers that crucified him. It was not even poor guilty Judas. These were his own already—but you, my disciples, you whom I have chosen, and washed in my blood—he desires *you*. So it is still with every one of you who is a child of God. I am commissioned to say, "Satan hath desired *you*." Just as the spider spreads its web, not to catch the flies that are already caught, but to ensnare those that are hovering about at liberty; just as the slave-ship that hovers on the coast of Africa is hovering there, not for the sake of the miserable captives that are already crowded in the hold, but in order to entrap some of those who are walking at liberty on the shore; so Satan spreads his nets chiefly for those that are Christ's freemen—who walk in the liberty wherewith Christ maketh his people free. It is not for the drunkard, the swearer, the unclean, that Satan is so full of snares. These are already in his possession. They are his palace, his children, his goods. But is there any of you awakened, brought nigh, filled with his free Spirit—oh, then it is you that Satan hath desired. His heart is even now panting and contriving how to get you ensnared.

Do you ask why?

(1) Because you were once his prey: "Ye were sometime dark-

ness, but now are ye light in the Lord." If a lamb has been in the mouth of a lion, and has been delivered out of it, the lion will be more enraged at the lamb than if it had never had it in its mouth; so you who have been in the lion's mouth, but have been saved out of it, you are much more the objects of his hatred than others. "Such were some of you; but ye are washed, but ye are justified, but ye are sanctified." Doubtless, when Satan passed round the Lord's table, he observed some of you there that once drank the cup of devils; and he would gnash his teeth for very soreness of heart. Ah! how he desires to have you back again! "God be thanked that you were the servants of sin, but ye have obeyed from the heart that form of doctrine which was delivered unto you."

(2) Because you are in the image of God. Satan is the great enemy of God. He hates God, because he is holy, and just, and true. What was said of Elymas the sorcerer is eminently true of the devil: "O full of all subtilty and mischief, thou child of the devil, thou enemy of all righteousness." But you that are born again are growing up into the image of God. I doubt not that Satan, as he looked upon us at the Lord's table, saw many of you, who have been created anew after the image of God in righteousness and true holiness. This would call out all his enmity, for he is the enemy of all righteousness. Some of you, perhaps, feel that you have made a step in holiness—that you have received more of the Spirit than you ever had before—that you have been more completely changed into God's holy image. Oh! remember, then, Satan is more enraged than ever against you. He is more determined than ever to cast you down. "Simon, Simon, Satan hath desired you."

(3) Because your fall would be more to him than the falls of many Christless sinners. When Christless persons fall into sin, Satan does not gain nearly so much as when a Christian falls. His great design is to pull out the stones of the living temple, that the temple of God may fall to ruins. Often, in great battles, the cruel command has been given to the soldiers, to aim chiefly at the officers—in order that the men, being left without their officers, might fall into confusion. This is just what the devil does; Christians are like the officers in Christ's army—they are the standard-bearers—and the devil hurls all his fiery darts at them.

Christians are the lights of the world. Satan's great design is to blow out the lights, that the whole world may be left in darkness.

Some of you may have felt this already. You have felt that you are more marked out by Satan than the rest of your family. Perhaps some in your family are the dead in trespasses and sins, and yet they have not been assaulted by Satan as you have been. Satan hath desired to have you. You are just like King Ahab in the battle with the Syrians. The King of Syria said, "Fight ye not with small or great, but only with the King of Israel." So Satan has commanded all his angels, "Fight ye not against small or great, but only against the Christians." Remember, you are marked men. "Put on, then, the whole armour of God, that ye may be able to stand in the evil day; and having done all, to stand."

Observe again.

2. *Satan's prayer:* "He hath desired to have you, that he may sift you as wheat." The object of passing wheat through the sieve is to separate the chaff from the wheat; it is said of Christ in the great day of his coming—"Whose fan is in his hand, and he will thoroughly purge his floor." This is the very thing which Satan wishes to be permitted to do. He thinks that Christians are hypocrites— and all he desires from God is, that he may be allowed to try them. We will give two examples:—

(1) *That of Job.* God said to Satan (1.8): "Hast thou considered my servant Job, that there is none like him in the earth, a perfect and an upright man, one that feareth God and escheweth evil?" Satan said, "Doth Job fear God for nought!" And then God said, "Behold, all that he hath is in thy power." Here Satan got leave to sift Job like wheat. On the very day when Job rose up early and offered burnt-offerings for himself and for his children— when his heart was overflowing with holy joy—on that day, Satan was allowed to sift him like wheat. His oxen, his sheep, his camels, his ten children, all were taken from him in one day. Satan wanted to persuade him that he was no child of God—that God was his enemy—that God had no love for him. So with some of you. Some of you are God's dear children, perhaps have received great joy at his table—perhaps it is to prepare you for Job's sifting. Remember, if it come, it is no strange thing. Satan hath desired you, to sift you like wheat.

(2) *That of the Apostles.* They had enjoyed a season of sweet communion with Christ—their joy had been full—they had heard words that filled their hearts to overflowing; yet it was that very night that Satan obtained leave to sift them as wheat: "All ye shall be offended because of me this night, and ye shall be scattered

every one to his own, and shall leave me alone. And they all forsook him and fled."

Dear friends, some of you may have found that the same thing is true still. Like the apostles, you were filled with peace, your joy was full; one little week has passed, and have you not been sifted like wheat? have you not been offended in Christ—forsaken him and fled?

"Beware, lest by any means, as the serpent beguiled Eve through his subtilty, so your minds should be corrupted from the simplicity that is in Christ?"

"Oh foolish Galatians, who hath bewitched you, that ye should not obey the truth, before whose eyes Christ hath been evidently set forth crucified?"

Learn,

II. *The safety of all God's children.*

1. *Satan needs to ask leave before he can do any thing to God's children.*—When Satan entered into Judas, he asked no leave. He said, "I will go to my house, whence I came out;" so he went, and took with him seven other devils, more wicked than himself; and the latter end of that man is worse than the beginning. When the strong one armed keepeth his palace, his goods are in peace. Dear friends, if you are Christless, Satan can go in and out of your heart at his pleasure. But, Christians, *you* are not his—you are bought with a price—you are Christ's—the hairs of your head are all numbered. Although Satan be very strong and mighty—perhaps the strongest and mightiest of all the creatures—still you may look him in the face and say, "Thou canst do nothing at all against me, except it be given thee from above." Oh, dear Christians, "keep yourselves in the love of God," and "you shall never perish, neither shall any pluck you out of the Father's hand." "And the very God of peace shall bruise Satan under your feet shortly.

2. *Jesus prays for them:* "I have prayed for thee." Oh, how lovely in the eyes of a believer is Christ—a living intercessor! There is not, in the whole Bible, a more refreshing scene than this. Peter was quite ignorant of his danger—he saw no coming storm— he feared no coming evil; on the contrary, he was quite bold— "Lord, I am ready to go with thee; though all men forsake thee, yet will not I." But the Saviour saw all the danger; he marked the first movement of Satan's wing, and said, "I have prayed for thee."

In time of war it is common to set watchmen upon the high

towers, and upon the tops of the mountains, to look out for an enemy; and when he sees the first appearance of the white sail over the bosom of the deep, it is his part to blow the trumpet and warn the people. But Christ is better than all watchmen—his eye never shuts. "He that keepeth Israel neither slumbers nor sleeps." His watch-tower is the throne of heaven, where he sits at the right hand of the Father. He sees all the dangers of your path—he sees every enemy, every temptation, every snare; and his word is, "I have prayed for thee, that thy faith fail not." "He is able to save to the uttermost all that come unto God by him, seeing he ever liveth to make intercession for them."

Oh! but some will say, I fear he does not pray for me, for my heart is so wicked—I am so much tempted—I am so much tried by diverse lusts and passions. But observe, "I have prayed for thee," he says to Peter. Peter was the very one that was most tempted; he was the very one who was going to deny Christ with oaths and curses; yet it was for him peculiarly that Jesus prayed.

Oh yes, if you are only joined to the Lord Jesus; though you may have a dreadful thorn in the flesh—though you may have some strong master-passions—some besetting sin that often drives you to despair—still, "Fear not thou worm Jacob; and ye few men of Israel, be not afraid, I will help thee." Jesus prays peculiarly for thee, more than for all besides. When a tender mother bends her knees at the footstool of God's throne—when she goes over all her children—beginning with the little one in the cradle, till she comes to her grown up lads—when she carries them on her heart to God, and pleads like Jacob, "I will not let thee go until thou bless me,"— which of all her children occupies most of her prayer? Is it not the one that is in greatest danger—is it not the son who has gone to sea, who is borne by rough winds over many waters, and whose soul, perhaps, has not yet found the haven of peace? Does she not linger over his name? It is no vain repetition, when she says, again and again, "Oh that Ishmael might live before thee!"

Oh! dear friends, the heart of Christ is more tender than a mother's; the child that he prays for is the one most in danger; so that if you are tempest-tossed, afflicted and not comforted, still stay upon your God, for Jesus says, "I have prayed for thee, that thy faith fail not."

Learn,

III. *The duty of restored backsliders.*—Some will ask, Do we need to be converted a second time? To this I answer,—That when a believer has fallen into sin, he needs to be brought back to Christ in the very same way that he was brought at the first.

1. It needs the same power to bring him back.—Some of you dear Christians, may have ventured to sin a little, thinking that you could easily come back again. When Peter denied his Lord, doubtless he thought that he could easily restore his soul: but no,—he went out and wept bitterly, for he found that he had fallen by his iniquity—that he had fallen into darkness and into utter helplessness. Remember, it is written, "*I* will heal their backslidings." It is a work of God. And again, "*He* restoreth my soul." Remember, He only can do it. "Oh! Israel, thou hast destroyed thyself; but in *me* is thine help."

2. *The return requires just the same work as conversion.*— There is nothing more remarkable than the blindness which sin brings along with it. Some of you, perhaps, have fallen into sin, and are saying this day, "Now I am sure I believed last Sabbath-day, and, therefore, though I have sinned, I may still take peace to-day." Ah, no! this is false; you cannot live upon the experiences of last Sabbath any more than you can live upon the food you took a week ago: you must be brought, guilty, helpless, and undone, to a present closing with the Saviour; you must be turned again. And now consider,

IV. *Your duty.* "Strengthen thy brethren." It is sweet to observe how anxiously Peter strengthened his brethren. He was the first of the apostles who said, "The Lord is risen indeed." And in his epistle, how affectionately does he say, "Be sober, be vigilant, because your adversary, the devil, as a roaring lion, walketh about, seeking whom he may devour; whom resist, stedfast in the faith."

Go you and do likewise, all converted souls. When a sailor has been saved from shipwreck, is it not natural to think that his first care will be to save his fellows? so let it be with you.

Can you not tell your friends and neighbours the evil of sin?— that it is an evil thing, and bitter to forsake God, and not to have his fear in you; that thought it be for the moment sweet to the taste, yet it is bitter afterwards, and its wages, death?

Can you not tell of the deceitfulness of the heart—that it is deceitful above all things, and desperately wicked?

Can you not tell the grace of the Lord Jesus—that he thought upon you in your low estate, for his mercy endureth for ever; that he saved you out of the hands of your enemies, for his mercy endureth for ever?

Can you not imitate the poor blasphemer, who, having found mercy through the blood of Jesus, left this message to the companions of his wickedness, "Tell them, that since I have found mercy, none that seek it need despair."

Oh! let this be your prayer, "Restore unto me the joy of thy salvation; and uphold me with thy free Spirit. Then will I teach transgressors thy ways; and sinners shall be converted unto thee." Support the weak—comfort the feeble-minded—"When thou art converted strengthen thy brethren."

26. The Love of God: Anglo-Catholicism

ANGLICANISM HAS been a source of controversy and confusion since the days of Henry VIII. It is but is not Protestant. The particular manifestation of the Catholic side of the Victorian church worked against facts and logic. The Anglo-Catholic movement, which evolved from the Oxford Movement, flew in the face of two centuries of prejudice and habit. "No Popery!" was totally ingrained in respectable English life. The Ecclesiastical Titles dispute of 1851 arose from the reconstruction of Roman Catholic dioceses in the United Kingdom. Lord John Russell parlayed anti-Catholicism into an electoral victory and the prime ministership with the applause of the substantial middle classes.

The history of the Oxford Movement is usually written around John Henry Newman, certainly its most gifted intellect. When Newman defected to Rome, accounts lapse into vague observations or silence. But the Anglo-Catholic movement had a continuing influence on the Anglican Church and English life. It never lost a class aspect. It was not a popular movement. It always had about it the effete, withdrawn quality of the common room or intellectual cocktail party.

Anglo-Catholicism was antievangelical, anti-Erastian, antilatitudinarian. It grew out of a protest against the interference of a secular parliament with the Church. The issue was badly needed reform in the Anglican establishment in Ireland. Francis Keble's sermon "On National Apostasy" (July 14, 1833) triggered the Tractarian movement. This, in turn, opened a heated debate on the nature of the Church and the role of churchmen. The leader of the Anglo-Catholic party came to be Dr. Edward Pusey (1800–1882); "Puseyite," the term used to identify the Catholic wing in the Church of England. Puseyites contended that Protestantism had destroyed papal authority (correct in itself) but had permitted the state to dominate the Church (a grave error). By contending that individual judgment and scriptural authority are accessible to all, Protestantism meant the rise of schism, even unbelief. Only those who fully understand the Bible can teach it. The individual cannot understand the depth of scriptural truth. One must master tradition—the writings of the Church fathers—as well as the scriptures to understand, and that labyrinth is beyond the ken of any save a clergy. Thus the Puseyites summoned clergymen to "be a priest," to "magnify their office," to become true figures of authority armed with awesome powers. Resurrect ritual symbols. Rebuild the devotional life. Remove Protestantism without Romanizing the Church.

Pusey lacked the intellect of Newman, the popular appeal of Keble. He was not a skillful ecclesiastical politician. He had background and wealth, fitted well his Oxford don environment, and brought character and dedication to the movement. His writing and thought were thorough but turgid. Pusey was hostile to novelty of any kind. He believed that old ways were best, and he never sought to comprehend any others. He translated a considerable body of devotional literature and was a great champion of the Christian mystics. To obey was to be at one with the will of God. Pusey shared with the Evangelicals the belief that each person could choose between good and evil. Faith and conviction were insufficient. One's salvation must be judged by good works as well as immense moral earnestness.

Nineteenth-century theologians had a much easier time with hell and damnation than with God and love. Pusey, in this selection, addresses himself to that. This reassertation of the principles of authority and prescription had modest influence. The leading Tractarians were part of a university culture, a leisured and cultivated society. The impact of Puseyism was more appearance than reality. Ecclesiastical vestments returned. Crucifixes appeared on altars. More heat than light was generated by prolonged debates on the virtues of candles and confession. The ritual became more Catholic, but the impact was felt principally among the privileged classes. For the Victorian world the outward changes were more clear. They seemed yet another part of that Gothic revival—of a piece with Wembly Pugin, Sir Gilbert Scott, and the Cambridge Camden Society. Nevertheless, the change in tone and appearance was there—another countercurrent in Victorian culture.

Recommended Reading

In addition to the general works previously cited, see Owen Chadwick's excellent series of readings, *The Mind of the Oxford Movement* (London: 1960). One of the more provocative studies of the Tractarians is G. Faber, *Oxford Apostles* (Harmondsworth: 1954), which should be supplemented with M. R. O'Connell, *The Oxford Movement* (New York: 1969). O. Chadwick, *Victorian Miniature* (London: 1960), is a sensitive reading of one parish. K. S. Inglis, *Churches and the Working Classes in Victorian England* (London: 1963), P. T. Marsh, *The Victorian Church in Decline* (Pittsburg: 1969), and D.

Bowen, *The Idea of the Victorian Church* (Montreal: 1968), are also useful.

EDWARD BOUVERIE PUSEY, ### ON SANCTIFICATION

Faint not, any who would love Jesus, if ye find yourselves yet far short of what He Himself Who is Love saith of the love of Him. Perfect love is Heaven. When ye are perfected in love, your work on earth is done. There is no short road to Heaven or to love. Do what in thee lies by the grace of God, and He will lead thee from strength to strength, and grace to grace, and love to love.

Be diligent by His Grace to do no wilful sin; for sin, wilfully done, kills the soul, and casts out of it the love of God.

Seek to love nothing out of God. God re-makes a broken heart and fills it with love. He cannot fill a divided heart.

Think often, as thou canst, of God. For how canst thou know or love God, if thou fillest thy mind with thoughts of all things under the sun and thy thoughts wander to the ends of the earth, and thou gatherest them not unto God? Nothing (except wilful sin) so keepeth men torpid and lukewarm and holdeth them back from any higher fervour of love, as the being scattered among things of sense, and being taken up with them away from God.

Bring all things, as thou mayest, nigh to God; let not them hurry thee away from Him.

Be not held back by any thought of unworthiness or by failures, from the child-like love of God. When we were dead in trespasses and sins, Christ died for us; when we were afar off, Christ recalled us; when lost, Christ sought us; how much more may we reverently love Him, and hope that we are loved by Him, when He has found us, and we, amid whatever frailties, would love Him by Whom we have been loved!

Be diligent, after thy power, to do deeds of love. Think nothing too little, nothing too low, to do lovingly for the sake of God. Bear with infirmities, ungentle tempers, contradictions; visit, if thou mayest, the sick; relieve the poor; forego thyself and thine own ways for love; and He Whom in them thou lovest, to Whom in them thou ministerest, will own thy love, and will pour His own love into thee. "The love of God," says a holy man, "produceth

Source: From *Sermons During the Season from Advent to Whitsuntide*, vol. II, *Parochial Sermons* (Oxford: 1853), pp. 59–62.

the love of our neighbour and kindleth it"; the love of our neighbour winneth the love of God.

Where, above all, shouldest thou seek for His love, but in the Feast of His Love? Without It, ye cannot have any true love. In It, Jesus willeth to come to thee, to dwell in thee, to abide in thee. Canst thou be warm, if thou keep away from the sun or the fire? Canst thou have any fire of love, if thou keep away from JESUS? or canst thou think to find Him, if thou seek Him not where He is to be found? He has said: "Except ye eat the Flesh of the Son of Man and drink His Blood, ye have no life in you." How should ye have life, if ye have not Him Who is Life? How should ye have Him, if ye refuse to come to Him? Come to Him, longing for His Love; come to Him that He may come to you; pray Him to enter into your soul and pour His Love into you, and He will come, and, if you forsake Him not, will dwell in you everlastingly.

"Charity never faileth." How then is all lost, which tendeth not to love! O abyss of love, torrent of pleasure, life of them that believe, paradise of delights, comfort of our pilgrimage, reward of the blessed, root of all good, strength in all strife, rest in all weariness! Why will ye "labour for that which is not bread," and toil for that which satisfieth not; why seek for pleasures which perish in the grasp, and when tasted, become bitterness; why heap up things ye must part with, or why love vanities, when ye have before you love which cannot weary, cannot sate, cannot change, cannot fail; for Love is the Essence, the Bliss, the Being, the Glory of God; and this may be yours for evermore. God in Whom are all things, Who is All-Goodness, willeth that ye love Him eternally, and be eternally filled with His Love, and enter into His Joy, the Joy of the Everlasting Father in His Co-Equal Son through the Spirit, of both Proceeding, the Bond of Both, and that ye should rest in the Bosom of His Love, and His Love rest upon you and fill you for ever. Will ye not then cast out now, for these few years, what hinders in you the Love of God, that ye may have for ever His Love which passeth all understanding, and be one with God, being filled with the Love of God Who is Love?

27. The Morality of Mammon

EVANGELICAL DISCIPLINE and Catholic holiness provided dogmatic values, a rhetoric of morality. Some Victorians, however, observed that there was a gap between the phrases and life. One of these was Arthur

Hugh Clough (1819–1861). Art is not necessarily better for being social. Many of the most distinguished artists have lived and worked almost totally detached from their world and times. Victorian artists prided themselves on being engaged in the real world. Clough, at this level, represented an ideal. The son of a successful Liverpool cotton merchant, he was one of the young men who fell under the sway of Dr. Thomas Arnold at Rugby College. Clough, not Thomas Hughes's oxlike Tom Brown, was the man Arnold sought to produce—one in whom the best of the old and new would be blended. But the message was lost in the medium. Manliness came to be the muscular Christianity of Charles Kingsley and the games obsession of the late-Victorian public school. Clough was ill-suited to this. As Lytton Strachey unkindly put it, Clough "had weak knees and lived with the highest ends in view."

ARTHUR HUGH CLOUGH,
THE LATEST DECALOGUE (1862)

Thou shalt have one God only; who
Would be at the expense of two?
No graven images may be
Worshipped, except the currency:
Swear not at all; for, for thy curse
Thine enemy is none the worse:
At church on Sunday to attend
Will serve to keep the world thy friend:
Honour thy parents; that is, all
From whom advancement may befall;
Thou shalt not kill; but need'st not strive
Officiously to keep alive:
Do not adultery commit;
Advantage rarely comes of it:
Thou shalt not steal; an empty feat,
When it's so lucrative to cheat:
Bear not false witness; let the lie
Have time on its own wings to fly:
Thou shalt not covet, but tradition
Approves all forms of competition.

28. Hebraism and Hellenism

MATTHEW ARNOLD (1822–1888) is often underestimated. This poet, critic, school inspector, Oxford professor, and international dogmatist

Source: From "The Latest Decalogue" (1862).

was an abler, more perceptive social critic than many of his contemporaries and most of his later imitators. Arnold attempted to understand and define industrial civilization. He appreciated the continuity of past and present, realized that culture consists of what men were and what they are. In this he differed from liberal relativists. Truths were absolute and unchanged through time. Arnold was in the conservative tradition, but like his distinguished predecessors Coleridge, Cobbett, and Carlyle, he had his radical side. Arnold was, unlike John Henry Newman, a thinker in the mainstream of the nineteenth-century development.

Mid-Victorian Britain, Arnold contended, faced a cultural crisis. Society consisted of Barbarians (aristocracy), Philistines (middle class), and Populace (working classes). Industrial Victorian Britain was principally a Philistine achievement with staggering but costly material gains. The price, Arnold, like most conservative and radical critics, argued, was too high. Industrialization had degraded and pauperized the Populace, brutalized and shrunk their lives. The Philistine world was ugly, narrow, and mean. What else could be expected from the puritanical ethic of middle-class, individualistic, industrial society?

Humane values were increasingly cultural casualties. Arnold called such values "sweetness and light," an appellation borrowed from Jonathan Swift. Liberal utilitarianism and laissez-faire political economy were poisoning society and its culture. There is a quality of rural nostalgia about Arnold, particularly in his poetry, but this longing after the simpler, fuller, and better life of a rural past contrasted to an urban present was not a protest without an alternative. Arnold was not trying to repeal the industrial revolution. He sought to amend it. Sentiment and feeling had given way to self-interest and utility. Mass culture compounded and accelerated this decay in thought and action. Arnold accepted one crucial liberal assumption. Comprehension would slowly correct social and cultural flaws. Philistines were not beyond salvation, and it was his task to educate them. Matthew Arnold was, in effect, pursuing his father's Broad Church campaign. Anglicanism, the "Establishment" of *Culture and Anarchy*, had been the basis of much that was best in English culture. A modernized (and essentially secularized) Church must be the moral and cultural basis of social salvation. To explain the sources of "sweetness and light" and to demonstrate the limitations of the contemporary pursuit of happiness, Arnold establishes his cultural dichotomy between the two principal influences of his world—Hebraism and Hellenism.

Recommended Reading

Arnold is usually his own best spokesman. The student can, however, profitably start with F. Neiman, *Matthew Arnold* (New York: 1968), and L. Trilling, *Matthew Arnold* (New York: 1949).

MATTHEW ARNOLD,
HEBRAISM AND HELLENISM

This fundamental ground is our preference of doing to thinking. Now this preference is a main element in our nature, and as we study it we find ourselves opening up a number of large questions on every side.

Let me go back for a moment to Bishop Wilson, who says: "First, never go against the best light you have; secondly, take care that your light be not darkness." We show, as a nation, laudable energy and persistence in walking according to the best light we have, but are not quite careful enough, perhaps, to see that our light be not darkness. This is only another version of the old story that energy is our strong point and favourable characteristic, rather than intelligence. But we may give to this idea a more general form still, in which it will have a yet larger range of application. We may regard this energy driving at practice, this paramount sense of the obligation of duty, self-control, and work, this earnestness in going manfully with the best light we have, as one force. And we may regard the intelligence driving at those ideas which are, after all, the basis of right practice, the ardent sense for all the new and changing combinations of them which man's development brings with it, the indomitable impulse to know and adjust them perfectly, as another force. And these two forces we may regard as in some sense rivals,—rivals not by the necessity of their own nature, but as exhibited in man and his history,—and rivals dividing the empire of the world between them. And to give these forces names from the two races of men who have supplied the most signal and splendid manifestations of them, we may call them respectively the forces of Hebraism and Hellenism. Hebraism and Hellenism, between these two points of influence moves our world. At one time it feels more powerfully the attraction of one of them, at another time of the other; and it ought to be, though it never is, evenly and happily balanced between them.

The final aim of both Hellenism and Hebraism, as of all great spiritual disciplines, is no doubt the same: man's perfection or salvation. The very language which they both of them use in schooling us to reach this aim is often identical. Even when their

Source: From *Culture and Anarchy* (London: 1869), chap. IV.

language indicates by variation,—sometimes a broad variation, often a but slight and subtle variation,—the different courses of thought which are uppermost in each discipline, even then the unity of the final end and aim is still apparent. To employ the actual words of that discipline with which we ourselves are all of us most familiar, and the words of which, therefore, come most home to us, that final end and aim is "that we might be partakers of the divine nature." These are the words of a Hebrew apostle, but of Hellenism and Hebraism alike this is, I say, the aim. When the two are confronted, as they very often are confronted, it is nearly always with what I may call a rhetorical purpose; the speaker's whole design is to exalt and enthrone one of the two, and he uses the other only as a foil and to enable him the better to give effect to his purpose. Obviously, with us, it is usually Hellenism which is thus reduced to minister to the triumph of Hebraism. . . . The aim and end of both Hebraism and Hellenism is, as I have said, one and the same, and this aim and end is august and admirable.

Still, they pursue this aim by very different courses. The uppermost idea with Hellenism is to see things as they really are; the uppermost idea with Hebraism is conduct and obedience. Nothing can do away with this ineffaceable difference. The Greek quarrel with the body and its desires is, that they hinder right thinking; the Hebrew quarrel with them is, that they hinder right acting. "He that keepeth the law, happy is he," "Blessed is the man that feareth the Eternal, that delighteth greatly in his commandments,"—that is the Hebrew notion of felicity; and, pursued with passion and tenacity, this notion would not let the Hebrew rest till, as is well known, he had at last got out of the law a network of prescriptions to enwrap his whole life, to govern every moment of it, every impulse, every action. The Greek notion of felicity, on the other hand, is perfectly conveyed in these words of a great French moralist: *"C'est le bonheur des hommes,"*—when? when they abhor that which is evil?—no; when they exercise themselves in the law of the Lord day and night?—no; when they die daily?—no; when they walk about the New Jerusalem with palms in their hands?—no; but when they think aright, when their thought hits: *"quand ils pensent juste."* At the bottom of both the Greek and the Hebrew notion is the desire, native in man, for reason and the will of God, the feeling after the universal order,—in a word, the love of God. But, while Hebraism seizes upon certain plain, capital intimations of the universal order, and rivets itself, one may say, with unequalled grandeur of earnestness and intensity on the study and observance of them, the bent of Hellenism is to follow, with flexible activity, the whole play of the universal order, to be apprehensive of missing any part of it, of sacrificing one part to another, to slip away from resting in this or that intimation of it, however capital. An unclouded clearness of mind, an unimpeded play of thought, is what this bent drives at. The governing idea of Hellenism is *spontaneity of consciousness;* that of Hebraism, *strictness of conscience.*

Christianity changed nothing in this essential bent of Hebraism to set doing above knowing. Self-conquest, self-devotion, the following not our own individual will, but the will of God, *obedience,* is the fundamental idea of this form, also, of the discipline to which we have attached the general name of Hebraism. Only, as the old law and the network of prescriptions with which it enveloped human life were evidently a motive-power not driving and searching enough to produce the result aimed at,—patient continuance in well-doing, self-conquest,—Christianity substituted for them boundless devotion to that inspiring and affecting pattern of self-conquest offered by Jesus Christ; and by the new motive-power, of which the essence was this, though the love and admiration of Christian churches have for centuries been employed in varying, amplifying, and adoring the plain description of it, Christianity, as St. Paul truly says, "establishes the law," and in the strength of the ampler power which she has thus supplied to fulfil it, has accomplished the miracles, which we all see, of her history.

So long as we do not forget that both Hellenism and Hebraism are profound and admirable manifestations of man's life, tendencies, and powers, and that both of them aim at a like final result, we can hardly insist too strongly on the divergence of line and of operation with which they proceed. . . .

Both Hellenism and Hebraism arise out of the wants of human nature, and address themselves to satisfying those wants. But their methods are so different, they lay stress on such different points, and call into being by their respective disciplines such different activities, that the face which human nature presents when it passes from the hands of one of them to those of the other, is no longer the same. To get rid of one's ignorance, to see things as they are, and by seeing them as they are to see them in their beauty, is the simple and attractive ideal which Hellenism holds out before human nature; and from the simplicity and charm of this ideal, Hellenism, and human life in the hands of Hellenism, is invested with a kind of aërial ease, clearness, and radiancy; they are full of what we call sweetness and light. Difficulties are kept out of view, and the beauty and rationalness of the ideal have all our thoughts. "The best man is he who most tries to perfect himself, and the happiest man is he who most feels that he *is* perfecting himself,"— this account of the matter by Socrates, the true Socrates of the *Memorabilia*, has something so simple, spontaneous, and unsophisticated about it, that it seems to fill us with clearness and hope when we hear it. But there is a saying which I have heard attributed to Mr. Carlyle about Socrates,—a very happy saying, whether it is really Mr. Carlyle's or not,—which excellently marks the essential point in which Hebraism differs from Hellenism. "Socrates," this saying goes, "is terribly *at ease in Zion*." Hebraism,—and here is the source of its wonderful strength,—has always been severely preoccupied with an awful sense of the impossibility of being at ease in Zion; of the difficulties which oppose themselves to man's pursuit or attainment of that perfection of which Socrates talks so hopefully, and, as from this point of view one might almost say, so glibly. It is all very well to talk of getting rid of one's ignorance, of seeing things in their reality, seeing them in their beauty; but how is this to be done when there is something which thwarts and spoils all our efforts?

This something is *sin;* and the space which sin fills in Hebraism, as compared with Hellenism, is indeed prodigious. This obstacle to perfection fills the whole scene, and perfection appears remote and rising away from earth, in the background. Under the name of sin, the difficulties of knowing oneself and conquering oneself which impede man's passage to perfection, become, for Hebraism, a positive, active entity hostile to man, a mysterious power which I heard Dr. Pusey the other day, in one of his impressive sermons, compare to a hideous hunchback seated on our shoulders, and which it is the main business of our lives to hate and oppose. The discipline of the Old Testament may be summed up as a discipline teaching us to abhor and flee from sin; the discipline of the New Testament, as a discipline teaching us to die to it. As Hellenism speaks of thinking clearly, seeing things in their essence and beauty, as a grand and precious feat for man to achieve, so Hebraism speaks of becoming conscious of sin, of wakening to a sense of sin, as a feat of this kind. It is obvious to what wide divergence these differing tendencies, actively followed, must lead. As one passes and repasses from Hellenism to Hebraism, from Plato to St. Paul, one feels inclined to rub one's eyes and ask oneself whether man is indeed a gentle and simple being, showing the traces of a noble and divine nature; or an unhappy chained captive, labouring with groanings that cannot be uttered to free himself from the body of this death.

Apparently it was the Hellenic conception of human nature which was unsound, for the world could not live by it. Absolutely to call it unsound, however, is to fall into the common error of its Hebraising enemies; but it was unsound at that particular moment of man's development, it was premature. The indispensable basis of conduct and self-control, the platform upon which alone the perfection aimed at by Greece can come into bloom, was not to be reached by our race so easily; centuries of probation and discipline were needed to bring us to it. Therefore the bright promise of Hellenism faded, and Hebraism ruled the world. Then was seen that astonishing spectacle, so well marked by the often-quoted words of the prophet Zechariah, when men of all languages and nations took hold of the skirt of him that was a Jew, saying:—*"We will go with you, for we have heard that God is with you."* And the Hebraism which thus received and ruled a world all gone out of the way and altogether become unprofitable, was, and could not but be, the later, the more spiritual, the more attractive development of Hebraism. It was Christianity; that is to say, Hebraism aiming at self-conquest and rescue from the thrall of vile affections, not by obedience to the letter of a law, but by conformity to the image of a self-sacrificing example. To a world stricken with moral enervation Christianity offered its spectacle of an inspired self-sacrifice; to men who refused themselves nothing, it showed one who refused himself everything;—*"my Saviour banished joy!"* says George Herbert. When the *alma Venus*, the life-giving and joy-giving power of nature, so fondly cherished by the Pagan world, could not save her followers from self-dissatisfaction and ennui, the severe words of the apostle came bracingly and refreshingly: "Let no man deceive you with vain words, for because of these things cometh the wrath of God upon the children of disobedience." Through age after age and generation after generation, our race, or all that part of our race which was most living and progressive, was *baptized into a death;* and endeavoured, by suffering in the flesh, to cease from sin. Of this endeavour, the animating labours and afflictions of early Christianity, the touching asceticism of mediæval Christianity, are the great historical manifestations. Literary monuments of it, each in its own way incomparable, remain in the Epistles of St. Paul, in St. Augustine's Confessions, and in the two original and simplest books of the Imitation.[1]

Of two disciplines laying their main stress, the one, on clear intelligence, the other, on firm obedience; the one, on comprehensively knowing the grounds of one's duty, the other, on diligently practising it; the one, on taking all possible care (to use Bishop Wilson's words again) that the light we have be not darkness, the other, that according to the best light we have we diligently walk,—the priority naturally belongs to that discipline which braces all man's moral powers, and founds for him an indispensable basis of character. And, therefore, it is justly said of the Jewish people, who were charged with setting powerfully forth that side of the divine order to which the words *conscience* and *self-conquest* point, that they were "entrusted with the oracles of God;" as it is justly said of Christianity, which followed Judaism and which set forth this side with a much deeper effectiveness and a much wider influence, that the wisdom of the old Pagan world was foolishness compared to it. No words of devotion and admiration can be too strong to render thanks to these beneficent forces which have so borne forward humanity in its appointed work of coming to the knowledge and possession of itself; above all, in those great moments when their action was the wholesomest and the most necessary.

But the evolution of these forces, separately and in themselves, is not the whole evolution of humanity,—their single history is not the whole history of man; whereas their admirers are always apt to make it stand for the whole history. Hebraism and Hellenism are, neither of them, the *law* of human development, as their admirers are prone to make them; they are, each of them, *contributions* to human development,—august contributions, invaluable contributions; and each showing itself to us more august, more invaluable, more preponderant over the other, according to the moment in

1. The two first books.

which we take them, and the relation in which we stand to them. The nations of our modern world, children of that immense and salutary movement which broke up the Pagan world, inevitably stand to Hellenism in a relation which dwarfs it, and to Hebraism in a relation which magnifies it. They are inevitably prone to take Hebraism as the law of human development, and not as simply a contribution to it, however precious. And yet the lesson must perforce be learned, that the human spirit is wider than the most priceless of the forces which bear it onward, and that to the whole development of man Hebraism itself is, like Hellenism, but a contribution.

Perhaps we may help ourselves to see this clearer by an illustration drawn from the treatment of a single great idea which has profoundly engaged the human spirit, and has given it eminent opportunities for showing its nobleness and energy. It surely must be perceived that the idea of immortality, as this idea rises in its generality before the human spirit, is something grander, truer, and more satisfying, than it is in the particular forms by which St. Paul, in the famous fifteenth chapter of the Epistle to the Corinthians, and Plato, in the *Phædo*, endeavour to develop and establish it. Surely we cannot but feel, that the argumentation with which the Hebrew apostle goes about to expound this great idea is, after all, confused and inconclusive; and that the reasoning, drawn from analogies of likeness and equality, which is employed upon it by the Greek philosopher, is over-subtle and sterile. Above and beyond the inadequate solutions which Hebraism and Hellenism here attempt, extends the immense and august problem itself, and the human spirit which gave birth to it. And this single illustration may suggest to us how the same thing happens in other cases also.

But meanwhile, by alternations of Hebraism and Hellenism, of a man's intellectual and moral impulses, of the effort to see things as they really are, and the effort to win peace by self-conquest, the human spirit proceeds; and each of these two forces has its appointed hours of culmination and seasons of rule. As the great movement of Christianity was a triumph of Hebraism and man's moral impulses, so the great movement which goes by the name of the Renascence[2] was an uprising and reinstatement of man's intel-

2. I have ventured to give to the foreign word *Renaissance*,—destined to become of more common us amongst us as the movement which it denotes comes, as it will come, increasingly to interest us,—an English form.

lectual impulses and of Hellenism. We in England, the devoted children of Protestantism, chiefly know the Renascence by its subordinate and secondary side of the Reformation. The Reformation has been often called a Hebraising revival, a return to the ardour and sincereness of primitive Christianity. No one, however, can study the development of Protestantism and of Protestant churches without feeling that into the Reformation too,—Hebraising child of the Renascence and offspring of its fervour, rather than its intelligence, as it undoubtedly was,—the subtle Hellenic leaven of the Renascence found its way, and that the exact respective parts, in the Reformation, of Hebraism and of Hellenism, are not easy to separate. But what we may with truth say is, that all which Protestantism was to itself clearly conscious of, all which it succeeded in clearly setting forth in words, had the characters of Hebraism rather than of Hellenism. The Reformation was strong, in that it was an earnest return to the Bible and to doing from the heart the will of God as there written. It was weak, in that it never consciously grasped or applied the central idea of the Renascence, —the Hellenic idea of pursuing, in all lines of activity, the law and science, to use Plato's words, of things as they really are. Whatever direct superiority, therefore, Protestantism had over Catholicism was a moral superiority, a superiority arising out of its greater sincerity and earnestness,—at the moment of its apparition at any rate,—in dealing with the heart and conscience. Its pretensions to an intellectual superiority are in general quite illusory. For Hellenism, for the thinking side in man as distinguished from the acting side, the attitude of mind of Protestantism towards the Bible in no respect differs from the attitude of mind of Catholicism towards the Church. . . .

In the sixteenth century, therefore, Hellenism re-entered the world, and again stood in presence of Hebraism,—a Hebraism renewed and purged. Now, it has not been enough observed, how, in the seventeenth century, a fate befell Hellenism in some respects analogous to that which befell it at the commencement of our era. The Renascence, that great re-awakening of Hellenism, that irresistible return of humanity to nature and to seeing things as they are, which in art, in literature, and in physics, produced such splendid fruits, had, like the anterior Hellenism of the Pagan world, a side of moral weakness and of relaxation or insensibility of the moral fibre, which in Italy showed itself with the most startling plainness, but which in France, England, and other countries was very apparent too. Again this loss of spiritual balance, this exclusive preponderance given to man's perceiving and knowing side, this unnatural defect of his feeling and acting side, provoked a reaction. Let us trace that reaction where it most nearly concerns us.

Science has now made visible to everybody the great and pregnant elements of difference which lie in race, and in how signal a manner they make the genius and history of an Indo-European people vary from those of a Semitic people. Hellenism is of Indo-European growth, Hebraism is of Semitic growth; and we English, a nation of Indo-European stock, seem to belong naturally to the movement of Hellenism. But nothing more strongly marks the essential unity of man, than the affinities we can perceive, in this point or that, between members of one family of peoples and members of another. And no affinity of this kind is more strongly marked than that likeness in the strength and prominence of the moral fibre, which, notwithstanding immense elements of difference, knits in some special sort the genius and history of us English, and our American descendants across the Atlantic, to the genius and history of the Hebrew people. Puritanism, which has been so great a power in the English nation, and in the strongest part of the English nation, was originally the reaction in the seventeenth century of the conscience and moral sense of our race, against the moral indifference and lax rule of conduct which in the sixteenth century came in with the Renascence. It was a reaction of Hebraism against Hellenism; and it powerfully manifested itself, as was natural, in a people with much of what we call a Hebraising turn, with a signal affinity for the bent which was the master-bent of Hebrew life. Eminently Indo-European by its *humour*, by the power it shows, through this gift, of imaginatively acknowledging the multiform aspects of the problem of life, and of thus getting itself unfixed from its own over-certainty, of smiling at its own over-tenacity, our race has yet (and a great part of its strength lies here), in matters of practical life and moral conduct, a strong share of the assuredness, the tenacity, the intensity of the Hebrews. This turn manifested itself in Puritanism, and has had a great part in shaping our history for the last two hundred years. Undoubtedly it checked and changed amongst us that movement of the Renascence which we see producing in the reign of Elizabeth such wonderful fruits. Undoubtedly it stopped the prominent rule and direct development of that order of ideas which we call by the name of Hellenism, and gave the first rank to a different order of ideas. Apparently, too, as we said of the former defeat of Hellenism, if Hellenism was defeated, this shows that Hellenism was imperfect, and that its ascendancy at that moment would not have been for the world's good.

Yet there is a very important difference between the defeat inflicted on Hellenism by Christianity eighteen hundred years ago, and the check given to the Renascence by Puritanism. The greatness of the difference is well measured by the difference in force, beauty, significance, and usefulness, betwen primitive Christianity and Protestantism. Eighteen hundred years ago it was altogether the hour of Hebraism. Primitive Christianity was legitimately and truly the ascendant force in the world at that time, and the way of mankind's progress lay through its full development. Another hour in man's development began in the fifteenth century, and the main road of his progress then lay for a time through Hellenism. Puritanism was no longer the central current of the world's progress, it was a side stream crossing the central current and checking it. The cross and the check may have been necessary and salutary, but that does not do away with the essential difference between the main stream of man's advance and a cross or a side stream. For more than two hundred years the main stream of man's advance has moved towards knowing himself and the world, seeing things as they are, spontaneity of consciousness; the main impulse of a great part, and that the strongest part, of our nation has been towards strictness of conscience. They have made the secondary the principal at the wrong moment, and the principal they have at the wrong moment treated as secondary. This contravention of the natural order has produced, as such contravention always must produce, a certain confusion and false movement, of which we are now beginning to feel, in almost every direction, the inconvenience. In all directions our habitual causes of action seem to be losing efficaciousness, credit, and control, both with others and even with ourselves. Everywhere we see the beginnings of confusion, and we want a clue to some sound order and authority. This we can only get by going back upon the actual instincts and forces which rule our life, seeing them as they really are, connecting them with other instincts and forces, and enlarging our whole view and rule of life.

29. Agnosticism: Problems of Morality and Honesty

MANY VICTORIANS had an appalling time with religious belief. Long before Darwin, science and history (particularly science as history) were eroding those much touted Anglican certitudes. Those unaffected by the Tubingen school of historical scholarship or untroubled by astronomical and geological theories often had difficulty with Judaeo-Christian religion as moral philosophy. Eternal punishment sat poorly in the minds of humanitarians, and the morality of many Old Testament prophets did not square well with Victorian ethics. This generated intellectual and emotional problems, for the Victorians had turned truth-telling into a supreme virtue. Some eminent Victorians like Gladstone never wavered in their belief, nor did Gladstone ever evade religious controversy. He believed and proceeded from personal certainty to demand evangelical dedication and mission in political life. The road was not so smooth for many others. Thus, on the one hand, the attraction of authoritarian religious creeds with their dogmatic certitude and discipline; on the other, the tortuous path through Broad Church latitudinarianism, foggy agnosticism, even to avowed secularism.

The Newman brothers almost caricature the problem. John Henry and Francis grew up in an Evangelical home. Both reacted against it, but while John Henry gravitated into High Church Anglicanism and thence to Rome, Francis slid through Broad Church into skepticism. Perhaps each brother watched the other with fascinated horror and moved fearfully but deliberately in the opposite direction.[1]

Less famous but no less significant was the controversy between the Stephen brothers. Both were raised in a demanding Evangelical environment. Their father, Sir James Stephen, who earned the soubriquet "Mr. Oversecretary" while senior civil servant at the Colonial Office, devoted his life to translating Evangelical ethics into secular behavior. Sir Fitzjames Stephen made a lasting mark in the law and as an Anglo-Indian administrator. He remained a devout Anglican, moving almost fashionably to a High Church position. He could be found, to his brother's disgust, defending ritualistic priests in the courts and disputing the shape and thickness of communion wafers. Leslie, that sparkling man of letters and distinguished scholar, moved firmly to agnosticism, for reasons that this selection proclaims. But agnosticism came at a higher price than many wished to pay. Dispense with formal religion, and we lose the sanction of hell and reward of heaven in the afterlife. How then are we to maintain morality? Every distinguished agnostic and doubter sought to salvage ethics, to provide alternative social sanctions. Why will men be good even if there is no demonstrable afterlife?

1. An essay in this direction that does not quite work is William Robbin, *The Newman Brothers* (London: 1966).

Fitzjames was also concerned with this problem and wrote a classic conservative tract to counter the assertions of John Stuart Mill. Social moral indignation, proclaims Fitzjames in *Liberty, Equality, Fraternity*, can serve the function of divine wrath among those whose belief has weakened. Secular law, rigorously enforced, will preserve morality. Psychologists and idealist philosophers extended this view to the point that the guilty, in a basic sense, will their own punishment. Leslie, for his part, argued that religious truth was socially irrelevant. Social belief was a product of conditioning, tradition, and habit. Evolution, moreover, provided an escape from Fitzjames' unanswered question. One need formulate no new principle for ethical behavior. The evolutionary process functioned throughout nature and in society. Study human behavior scientifically and we shall understand the working of evolution in moral problems. Social science replaced religion, observes one of the most distinguished intellectual historians of the period, and evolution replaced God.

> This desire to find metaphysical sanctions gives Victorian agnosticism the appearance of a new non-conformist sect. The power of religion over the very minds which denied it is nowhere more subtly instanced than in [Leslie] Stephen's evolutionary ethics.[2]

"An Apology for Plainspeaking" was an early denunciation of dogmatic systems of thought. Leslie had written a series of articles on the subject for *Fraser's* and collected them into this volume in 1873. He offered hard, unpleasant "truth" as a substitute for comforting illusion. Here and in so many more of his writings this amateur scholar of wide range, flowing style, and much discipline sought to bring order from chaos, for he believed that man could create order. He was proud of the Enlightenment tradition, wrote fondly of it and in it. His conceptions were vast, whether in his *History of English Thought in the Eighteenth Century* (1902) or in the monumental *Dictionary of National Biography;* his concerns, many. Leslie Stephen was an eminent Victorian both for what he did and what he was.

Recommended Reading

There are two excellent, although very different biographies of Leslie Stephen. That by F. W. Maitland (1906) is a delightful memorial by a devoted friend. Lord Annan considers Stephen as a problem in the history of ideas in his more recent (1952) study. One of the best places to start on the problem of religious doubt is Basil Willey, *More Nineteenth-Century Studies* (London: 1956). For a useful study of controversy within the Anglican Church, see A. O. J. Cockshut, *Anglican Attitudes: A Study of Victorian Religious Controversies* (London: 1959), as well as his more recent *The Unbelievers* (London: 1964).

2. N. G. Annan, *Leslie Stephen* (Cambridge, Mass.: 1952), p. 221.

Leslie Stephen,
An Apology for Plainspeaking

All who would govern their intellectual course by no other aim than the discovery of truth, and who would use their faculty of speech for no other purpose than open communications of their real opinions to others, are met by protests from various quarters. Such protests, so far as they imply cowardice or dishonesty, must of course be disregarded, but it would be most erroneous to confound all protests in the same summary condemnation. Reverent and kindly minds shrink from giving an unnecessary shock to the faith which comforts many sorely tried souls; and even the most genuine lovers of truth may doubt whether the time has come at which the decayed scaffolding can be swept away without injuring the foundations of the edifice. Some reserve, they think, is necessary, though reserve, as they must admit, passes but too easily into insincerity.

And thus, it is often said by one class of thinkers, Why attack a system of beliefs which is crumbling away quite fast enough without your help? Why, says another class, try to shake beliefs which, whether true or false, are infinitely consoling to the weaker brethren? I will endeavour to conclude these essays, in which I have possibly made myself liable to some such remonstrances, by explaining why I should think it wrong to be bound by them; I will, however, begin by admitting frankly that I recognise their force so far as this; namely, that I have no desire to attack wantonly any sincere beliefs in minds unprepared for the reception of more complete truths. This volume, perhaps, would be unjustifiable if it were likely to become a text-book for school-girls in remote country parsonages. But it is not very probable that it will penetrate to such quarters; nor do I flatter myself that I have brought forward a single argument which is not already familiar to educated men. Whatever force there may be in its pages is only the force of an appeal to people who already agree in my conclusions to state their agreement in plain terms; and, having said this much, I will answer the questions suggested as distinctly as I am able.

To the first question, Why trouble the last moments of a dying

Source: From *Essays on Freethinking and Plainspeaking* (London: 1907), chap. ix. Extensive cuts of detail have been made.

creed? my reply would be in brief that I do not desire to quench the lingering vitality of the dying so much as to lay the phantoms of the dead. I believe that one of the greatest dangers of the present day is the general atmosphere of insincerity in such matters, which is fast producing a scepticism not as to any or all theologies, but as to the very existence of intellectual good faith. Destroy credit, and you ruin commerce; destroy all faith in religious honesty and you ruin something of infinitely more importance than commerce; ideas should surely be preserved as carefully as cotton from the poisonous influence of a varnish intended to fit them for public consumption. "The time is come," says Mr. Mill in his autobiography, "in which it is the duty of all qualified persons to speak their minds about popular religious beliefs." The reason which he assigns is that they would thus destroy the "vulgar prejudice" that unbelief is connected with bad qualities of head and heart. It is, I venture to remark, still more important to destroy the belief of sceptics themselves that in these matters a system of pious frauds is creditable or safe. Effeminating and corrupting as all equivocation comes to be in the long run, there are other evils behind. Who can see without impatience the fearful waste of good purpose and noble aspiration caused by our reticence at a time when it is of primary importance to turn to account all the forces which make for the elevation of mankind? How much intellect and zeal runs to waste in the spasmodic effort of good men to cling to the last fragments of decaying systems, to galvanise dead formulæ into some dim semblance of life! Society will not improve as it might when those who should be leaders of progress are staggering backward and forward with their eyes passionately reverted to the past. Nay, we shall never be duly sensitive to the miseries and cruelties which make the world a place of torture for so many, so long as men are encouraged in the name of religion to look for a remedy, not in fighting against surrounding evils, but in cultivating aimless contemplations of an imaginary ideal. Much of our popular religion seems to be expressly directed to deaden our sympathies with our fellow-men by encouraging an indolent optimism; our thoughts of the other world are used in many forms as an opiate to drug our minds with indifference to the evils of this; and the last word of half our preachers is, dream rather than work.

To the other question, Why deprive men of their religious consolations? I must make a rather longer reply. . . .

[Leslie Stephen then turns in great detail to what he considers to be the weaknesses of traditional Christian theology and the merits of science.]

To the question, then, from which I started, it seems that an unequivocal reply can be given. Why help to destroy the old faith from which people derive, or believe themselves to derive, so much spiritual solace? The answer is, that the loss is overbalanced by the gain. We lose nothing that ought to be really comforting in the ancient creeds; we are relieved from much that is burdensome to the imagination and to the intellect. Those creeds were indeed in great part the work of the best and ablest of our forefathers; they therefore provide some expression for the highest emotions of which our nature is capable; but, to say nothing of the lower elements which have intruded, of the concessions made to bad passions, and to the wants of a ruder form of society, they are at best the approximations to the truth of men who entertained a radically erroneous conception of the universe. Astronomers who went on the Ptolemaic theory, managed to provide a very fair description of the actual phenomena of the heavens; but the solid result of their labours was not lost when the Copernican system took its place; and incalculable advantages followed from casting aside the old cumbrous machinery of cycles and epicycles in favour of the simpler conceptions of the new doctrine. A similar change follows when man is placed at the centre of the religious and moral system. We still retain the faiths at which theologians arrived by a complex machinery of arbitrary contrivances destined to compensate one set of dogmas by another. The justice of God the Father is tempered by the mercy of God the Son, as the planet wheeled too far forward by the cycle is brought back to its place by the epicycle. When we strike out the elaborate arrangements, the truths which they aim at expressing are capable of far simpler statements; infinite error and distortion disappear, and the road is open for conceptions impossible under the old circuitous and erroneous methods.

We have arrived at the point from which we can detect the source of ancient errors, and extract the gold from the dross. One thing, indeed, remains for the present impossible. The old creed, elaborated by many generations, and consecrated to our imaginations by a vast wealth of associations, is adapted in a thousand ways to the wants of its believers. The new creed—whatever may be its ultimate form—has not been thus formulated and hallowed to our minds. We, whose fetters are just broken, cannot tell what the world will look like to men brought up in the full blaze of day, and accustomed from infancy to the free use of their limbs. For centuries, all ennobling passions have been industriously associated with the hope of personal immortality, and base passions with its rejection. We cannot fully realise the state of men brought up to look for a reward of heroic sacrifice in the consciousness of good work achieved in this world instead of in the hope of posthumous repayment. Nor again, have we, if we shall ever have, any system capable of replacing the old forms of worship by which the imagination was stimulated and disciplined. That such reflections should make many men pause before they reveal the open secret is intelligible enough. But what is the true moral to be derived from them? Surely that we should take courage and speak the truth. We should take courage, for even now the new faith offers to us a more cheering and elevating prospect than the old. When it shall have become familiar to men's minds, have worked itself into the substance of our convictions, and provided new channels for the utterance of our emotions, we may anticipate incomparably higher results. We are only laying the foundations of the temple, and know not what will be the glories of the completed edifice. Yet already the prospect is beginning to clear. The sophistries which entangle us are transparent. That faith is not the noblest which enables us to believe the greatest number of articles on the least evidence; nor is that doctrine really the most productive of happiness which encourages us to cherish the greatest number of groundless hopes. The system which is really most calculated to make men happy is that which forces them to live in a bracing atmosphere; which fits them to look facts in the face and to suppress vain repinings by strenuous action instead of luxurious dreaming.

And hence, too, the time is come for speaking plainly. If you would wait to speak the truth until you can replace the old decaying formula by a completely elaborated system, you must wait for ever; for the system can never be elaborated until its leading principles have been boldly enunciated. Reconstruct, it is said, before you destroy. But you must destroy in order to reconstruct. The old husk of dead faith is pushed off by the growth of living beliefs below. But how can they grow unless they find distinct utterance? and how can they be distinctly uttered without condemning the doctrines which they are to replace? The truth cannot be asserted without denouncing the falsehood. Pleasant as the process might be of announcing the truth and leaving the falsehood to decay of itself, it cannot be carried into practice. Men's minds must be called back from the present of phantoms and encouraged to follow the only path which tends to enduring results. We cannot afford to make the tacit concession that our opinions, though true, are depressing and debasing. No; they are encouraging and elevating. If the medicine is bitter to the taste, it is good for the digestion. Here and there, a bold avowal of the truth will disperse a pleasing dream, as here and there it will relieve us of an oppressing nightmare. But it is not by striking balances between these pains and pleasures that the total effect of the creed is to be measured; but by the permanent influence on the mind of seeing things in their true light and dispersing the old halo of erroneous imagination. To inculcate reticence at the present moment is simply to advise us to give one more chance to the development of some new form of superstition. If the faith of the future is to be a faith which can satisfy the most cultivated as well as the feeblest intellects, it must be founded on an unflinching respect for realities. If its partisans are to win a definitive victory, they must cease to show quarter to lies. The problem is stated plainly enough to leave no room for hesitation. We can distinguish the truth from falsehood, and see where confusion has been reproduced, and truth pressed into the service of falsehood. Nothing more is wanted but to go forward boldly and reject, once for all, the weary compromises and elaborate adaptations which have become a mere vexation to all honest men. The goal is clearly in sight, though it may be distant; and we decline any longer to travel in disguise by circuitous paths, or to apologise for being in the right. Let us think freely and speak plainly, and we shall have the highest satisfaction that man can enjoy—the consciousness that we have done what little lies in ourselves to do for the maintenance of the truths on which the moral improvement and the happiness of our race depend.

Value

30. The Culture of Work: Morley and Carlyle

JOHN MORLEY (1838–1923), ruminating about the formative influences of his youth, contended that the mid-Victorians had suffered unfairly at the hands of their children. H. G. Wells and Lytton Strachey maligned the world of their fathers. The argument has considerable merit. Great men and great works dominated mid-Victorian England. Tennyson's "In Memoriam" and Herbert Spencer's *Social Statics* date from 1850. Buckle's *History of Civilization* raised dramatic, pointed questions in 1848. Darwin's year, 1859, appeared to some contemporaries and many historians to mark the first flood that would wash away most of the foundations of Victorian culture.

> It was easy to reproach us with sunless creeds and declarations of mental insolvency. Supernatural magic was by no means payment of the rational debt in full, and the fortitude of a resolute, open-hearted stoicism is no bankrupt or useless thing.[1]

Thomas Carlyle (1795–1881) would have numbered among the important influences upon young Morley. Carlyle touched every literate young man directly. His notions, his values, his tone reached through every media to each element in the land. He was an early Victorian, a formative influence in the life of nineteenth-century England. In spite of his longevity, he had nothing important to say after *Shooting Niagara* in 1867. Save for his famous biography of *Frederick the Great* (1858–1865), Carlyle's work was done by 1850. Even those who disagreed with Carlyle's ideas felt that he had somehow contributed to the shaping of their lives. Thomas Henry Huxley, the great scientist and controversialist, believed incorrectly that he had learned the importance of work from Carlyle. The dyspeptic Scot had more to say than, "Work is noble; work alone is noble" or "Work for the night is coming in which you no longer work." He asked telling questions about the direction and content of liberal society. From *Sartor Resartus* in 1831, Carlyle declaimed (he never conversed), flexed his verbal muscles, and preached—with more than venial contradiction—that the philosopher points the way and the hero does the job.

Morley responded for liberal society, attempting to balance the good Carlyle had done with the mischief of his thought. This essay, published in 1870, is an apposition of ideas, less profound than Bentham and Coleridge but clearly in the mainstream of Victorian thought. I have reduced the original essay by more than a third. Morley, like good Victorian liberals, did not contend that economy should extend to verbiage.

Recommended Reading

Carlyle's most important work begins with his life of Schiller (1825). His apocalyptic 1830s produced *Sartor Resartus* (1831), *The French Revolution* (1837), and *Chartism* (1839). He developed his "leadership" formula during the 1840s in *Hero-Worship* (1840), *Past*

1. J. Morley, *Recollections*, Vol. I (New York: 1917), p. 19.

and Present (1843), and *Cromwell* (1845). While he continued to turn exciting new phrases, he had few novel ideas by the time he wrote *Latter-Day Pamphlets* (1850). Morley stock collapsed before he died. Carlyle has been of little interest save to cultural historians since the second world war. Both deserve better and receive it in D. A. Hamer, *John Morley: Liberal Intellectual in Politics* (Oxford: 1968), and E. Neff, *Carlyle* (London: 1932).

JOHN MORLEY,
CARLYLE

The new library edition of Mr. Carlyle's works may be taken for the final presentation of all that the author has to say to his contemporaries, and to possess the settled form in which he wishes his words to go to those of posterity who may prove to have ears for them. The canon is definitely made up. The golden Gospel of Silence is effectively compressed in thirty fine volumes. After all has been said about self-indulgent mannerisms, moral perversities, phraseological outrages, and the rest, these volumes will remain the noble monument of the industry, originality, conscientiousness, and genius of a noble character, and of an intellectual career that has exercised on many sides the profoundest sort of influence upon English feeling. . . .

. . . When criticism has done its just work on the disagreeable affectations of many of Mr. Carlyle's disciples, and on the nature of Mr. Carlyle's opinions and their worth as specific contributions, very few people will be found to deny that his influence in stimulating moral energy, in kindling enthusiasm for virtues worthy of enthusiasm, and in stirring a sense of the reality on the one hand, and the unreality on the other, of all that man can do or suffer, has not been surpassed by any teacher now living.

One of Mr. Carlyle's chief and just glories is, that for more than forty years he has clearly seen, and kept constantly and conspicuously in his own sight and that of his readers, the profoundly important crisis in the midst of which we are living. The moral and social dissolution in progress about us, and the enormous peril of sailing blindfold and haphazard, without rudder or compass or chart, have always been fully visible to him, and it is no fault of his if they have not become equally plain to his contemporaries. The policy of drifting has had no countenance from him. That a society

Source: From "Carlyle" (1870).

should be likely to last with hollow and scanty faith, with no government, with a number of institutions hardly one of them real, with a horrible mass of poverty-stricken and hopeless subjects; that, if it should last, it could be regarded as other than an abomination of desolation, he has boldly and often declared to be things incredible. We are not promoting the objects which the social union subsists to fulfil, nor applying with energetic spirit to the task of preparing a sounder state for our successors. The relations between master and servant, between capitalist and labourer, between landlord and tenant, between governing race and subject race, between the feelings and intelligence of the legislature and the feelings and intelligence of the nation, between the spiritual power, literary and ecclesiastical, and those who are under it—the anarchy that prevails in all these, and the extreme danger of it, have been with Mr. Carlyle a never-ending theme. What seems to many of us the extreme inefficiency or worse of his solutions, still allows us to feel grateful for the vigour and perspicacity with which he has pressed on the world the urgency of the problem.

The degree of durability which his influence is likely to possess with the next and following generations is another and rather sterile question, which we are not now concerned to discuss. The unrestrained eccentricities which Mr. Carlyle's strong individuality has precipitated in his written style may, in spite of the poetic fineness of his imagination, which no historian or humorist has excelled, still be expected to deprive his work of that permanence which is only secured by classic form. The incorporation of so many phrases, allusions, nicknames, that belong only to the hour, inevitably makes the vitality of the composition conditional on the vitality of these transient and accidental elements which are so deeply imbedded in it. Another consideration is that no philosophic writer, however ardently his words may have been treasured and followed by the people of his own time, can well be cherished by succeeding generations, unless his name is associated through some definable and positive contribution with the central march of European thought and feeling. In other words, there is a difference between living in the history of literature or belief, and living in literature itself and in the minds of believers. Mr. Carlyle has been a most powerful solvent, but it is the tendency of solvents to become merely historic. The historian of the intellectual and moral movements of Great Britain during the present century, will fail egregiously in his task if he omits to give a large and conspicuous space to the author of *Sartor Resartus*. But it is one thing to study historically the ideas which have influenced our predecessors, and another thing to seek in them an influence fruitful for ourselves. It is to be hoped that one may doubt the permanent soundness of Mr. Carlyle's peculiar speculations, without either doubting or failing to share that warm affection and reverence which his personality has worthily inspired in many thousands of his readers. . . .

It is none the less for what has just been said a weightier and a rarer privilege for a man to give a stirring impulse to the moral activity of a generation, than to write in classic style; and to have impressed the spirit of his own personality deeply upon the minds of multitudes of men, than to have composed most of those works which the world is said not willingly to let die. Nor, again, is to say that this higher renown belongs to Mr. Carlyle, to underrate the less resounding, but most substantial, services of a definite kind which he has rendered both to literature and history. This work may be in time superseded with the advance of knowledge, but the value of the first service will remain unimpaired. It was he, as has been said, "who first taught England to appreciate Goethe;" and not only to appreciate Goethe, but to recognise and seek yet further knowledge of the genius and industry of Goethe's countrymen. His splendid drama of the French Revolution has done, and may be expected long to continue to do, more to bring before our slow-moving and unimaginative public the portentous meaning of that tremendous cataclysm, than all the other writings on the subject in the English language put together. His presentation of Puritanism and the Commonwealth and Oliver Cromwell first made the most elevating period of the national history in any way really intelligible. The Life of Frederick the Second, whatever judgment we may pass upon its morality, or even upon its place as a work of historic art, is a model of laborious and exhaustive narration of facts not before accessible to the reader of history. For all this, and for much other work eminently useful and meritorious even from the mechanical point of view, Mr. Carlyle deserves the warmest recognition. His genius gave him a right to mock at the ineffectiveness of Dryasdust, but his genius was also too true to prevent him from adding the always needful supplement of a painstaking industry that rivals Dryasdust's own most strenuous toil. Take out of the mind of the English reader of ordinary cultivation and the average journalist, usually a degree or two lower than this, their conceptions of the French Revolution and the English Rebellion, and their knowledge of German literature and history, as well as most of their acquaintance with the prominent men of the eighteenth century, and we shall see how much work Mr. Carlyle has done simply as schoolmaster.

This, however, is emphatically a secondary aspect of his character, and of the function which he has fulfilled in relation to the more active tendencies of modern opinion and feeling. We must go on to other ground, if we would find the field in which he has laboured most ardently and with most acceptance. History and literature have been with him, what they will always be with wise and understanding minds of creative and even of the higher critical faculty—only embodiments, illustrations, experiments, for ideas about religion, conduct, society, history, government, and all the other great heads and departments of a complete social doctrine. . . .

It would be a comparatively simple process to affix the regulation labels of philosophy; to say that Mr. Carlyle is a Pantheist in religion . . . a Transcendentalist or Intuitionist in ethics, an Absolutist in politics, and so forth, with the addition of a crowd of privative or negative epithets at discretion. But classifications of this sort are the worst enemies of true knowledge. Such names are by the vast majority even of persons who think themselves educated, imperfectly apprehended, ignorantly interpreted, and crudely and recklessly applied. . . .

These labels are rather more worthless than usual in the present case, because Mr. Carlyle is ostentatiously illogical and defiantly inconsistent; and, therefore, the term which might correctly describe one side of his teaching or belief would be tolerably sure to give a wholly false impression of some of its other sides. The qualifications necessary to make any one of the regular epithets fairly applicable would have to be so many, that the glosses would virtually overlay the text. We shall be more likely to reach an instructive appreciation by discarding such substitutes for examination, and considering, not what pantheistic, absolutist, transcendental, or any other doctrine means, or what it is worth, but what it is that Mr. Carlyle means about men, their character, their relations to one another, and what that is worth.

With most men and women the master element in their opinions is obviously neither their own reason nor their own imagination, independently exercised, but only mere use and wont, chequered by fortuitous sensations, and modified in the better cases by the influence of a favourite teacher; while in the worse the teacher is the favourite who happens to chime in most harmoniously with prepossessions, or most effectually to nurse and exaggerate them. Among the superior minds the balance between reason and imagination is scarcely ever held exactly true, nor is either firmly kept within the precise bounds that are proper to it. It is a question of temperament which of the two mental attitudes becomes fixed and habitual, as it is a question of temperament how violently either of them straitens and distorts the normal faculties of vision. The man who prides himself on a hard head, which would usually be better described as a thin head, may and constantly does fall into a confirmed manner of judging character and circumstance, so narrow, one-sided, and elaborately superficial, as to make common sense shudder at the crimes that are committed in the divine name of reason. Excess on the other side leads people into emotional transports, in which the pre-eminent respect that is due to truth, the difficulty of discovering the truth, the narrowness of the way that leads thereto, the merits of intellectual precision and definiteness, and even the merits of moral precision and definiteness, are all effectually veiled by purple or fiery clouds of anger, sympathy, and sentimentalism, which imagination has hung over the intelligence.

The familiar distinction between the poetic and the scientific temper is another way of stating the same difference. The one fuses or crystallises external objects and circumstances in the medium of human feeling and passion; the other is concerned with the relations of objects and circumstances among themselves, including in them all the facts of human consciousness, and with the discovery and classification of these relations. There is, too, a corresponding distinction between the aspects which conduct, character, social movement, and the objects of nature are able to present, according as we scrutinise them with a view to exactitude of knowledge, or are stirred by some appeal which they make to our various faculties and forms of sensibility, our tenderness, sympathy, awe, terror, love of beauty, and all the other emotions in this momentous catalogue. . . .

The contentiousness of rival schools of philosophy has obscured the application of the same distinction to the various orders of fact more nearly and immediately relating to man and the social union. One school has maintained the virtually unmeaning doctrine that the will is free, and therefore its followers never gave any quarter to the idea that man was as proper an object of scientific scrutiny morally and historically, as they could not deny him to be anatomically and physiologically. Their enemies have been more concerned to dislodge them from this position, than to fortify, organise, and cultivate their own. The consequences have not been without their danger. Poetic persons have rushed in where scientific persons ought not to have feared to tread. That human character and the order of events have their poetic aspect, and that their poetic treatment demands the rarest and most valuable qualities of mind, is a truth which none but narrow and superficial men of the world are rash enough to deny. But that there is a scientific aspect of these things, an order among them that can only be understood and criticised and effectually modified scientifically, by using all the caution and precision and infinite patience of the truly scientific spirit, is a truth that is constantly ignored even by men and women of the loftiest and most humane nature. In such cases misdirected and uncontrolled sensibility ends in mournful waste of their own energy, in the certain disappointment of their own aims, and where such sensibility is backed by genius, eloquence, and a peculiar set of public conditions, in prolonged and fatal disturbance of society. . . .

[Morley then suggests that Carlyle, like Rousseau, exemplified this "triumphant and dangerous sophistry of the emotions." He continues, "With each of them thought is an aspiration and justice a sentiment, and society a retrogression. Each bids us look within our own bosoms for truth and right, postpones reason to feeling, and refers to introspection and a factitious something styled Nature, questions only to be truly solved by external observation and history." Morley argues that Robespierre was the practitioner of this art. "We begin with introspection and the eternities, and end in blood and iron."]

Mr. Carlyle . . . has denounced logic mills, warned us all away from literature, and habitually subordinated discipline of the intelligence to the passionate assertion of the will. There are passages in which he speaks respectfully of Intellect, but he is always careful to show that he is using the term in a special sense of his own, and confounding it with "the exact summary of human *Worth*," as in one place he defines it. Thus, instead of co-ordinating moral worthiness with intellectual energy, virtue with intelligence, right action of the will with scientific processes of the understanding, he has either placed one immeasurably below the other, or else has mischievously insisted on treating them as identical. The dictates of a kind heart are of superior force to the maxims of political economy; swift and peremptory resolution is a safer guide than a balancing judgment. If the will works easily and surely, we may assume the rectitude of the moving impulse. All this is no caricature of a system which sets sentiment, sometimes hard sentiment and sometimes soft sentiment, above reason and method.

In other words, the writer who in these days has done more than anybody else to fire men's hearts with a feeling for right and an eager desire for social activity, has with deliberate contempt thrust away from him the only instruments by which we can make sure what right is, and that our social action is wise and effective. A born poet, only wanting perhaps a clearer feeling for form and a more delicate spiritual self-possession, to have added another name to the illustrious catalogue of English singers, he has been driven by the impetuosity of his sympathies to attack the scientific side of social questions in an imaginative and highly emotional manner. Depth of benevolent feeling is unhappily no proof of fitness for handling complex problems, and a fine sense of the picturesque is no more a qualification for dealing effectively with the difficulties of an old society, than the composition of Wordsworth's famous sonnet on Westminster Bridge was any reason for supposing that the author would have made a competent Commissioner of Works.

Why should society, with its long and deep-hidden processes of growth, its innumerable intricacies and far-off historic complexities, be as an open book to any reader of its pages who brings acuteness and passion, but no patience nor calm accuracy of meditation? Objects of thought and observation far simpler, more free from all blinding and distorting elements, more accessible to direct and ocular inspection, are by rational consent reserved for the calmest and most austere moods and methods of human intelligence. Nor is denunciation of the conditions of a problem the quickest step towards solving it. Vituperation of the fact that supply and demand practically regulate certain kinds of bargain, is no contribution to systematic efforts to discover some more moral regulator. Take all the invective that Mr. Carlyle has poured out against political economy, the Dismal Science, and Gospel according to M'Croudy. Granting the absolute and entire inadequateness of political economy to sum up the laws and conditions of a healthy social state—and no one more than the present writer deplores the mischief which the application of the maxims of political economy by ignorant and selfish spirits has effected in confirming the worst tendencies of the commercial character—yet is it not a first condition of our being able to substitute better machinery for the ordinary rules of self-interest, that we know scientifically how those rules do and must operate? . . .

Has Mr. Carlyle's passion, or have the sedulous and scientific labours of that Bentham, whose name with him is a symbol of evil, done most in what he calls the Scoundrel-province of Reform within the last half-century? Sterling's criticism on Teufelsdröckh told a hard but wholesome truth to Teufelsdröckh's creator. "Wanting peace himself," said Sterling, "his fierce dissatisfaction fixes on all that is weak, corrupt, and imperfect around him; and instead of a calm and steady co-operation with all those who are endeavouring to apply the highest ideas as remedies for the worst evils, he holds himself in savage isolation.". . .

It is, however, a type of Mr. Carlyle's faith in the instinct of nature, as superseding the necessity for patient logical method; a faith, in other words, in crude and uninterpreted sense. Insight, indeed, goes far, but it no more entitles its possessor to dispense with reasoned discipline and system in treating scientific subjects, than it relieves him from the necessity of conforming to the physical conditions of health. Why should society be the one field of thought in which a man of genius is at liberty to assume all his major premises, and swear all his conclusions?

The deep unrest of unsatisfied souls meets its earliest solace in the effective and sympathetic expression of the same unrest from the lips of another. To look it in the face is the first approach to a sedative. To find our discontent with the actual, our yearning for an undefined ideal, our aspiration after impossible heights of being, shared and amplified in the emotional speech of a man of genius, is the beginning of consolation. Some of the most generous spirits a hundred years ago found this in the eloquence of Rousseau, and some of the most generous spirits of this time and place have found it in the writer of the *Sartor*. . . . A man born into a community where political forms, from the monarchy down to the popular chamber, are mainly hollow shams disguising the coarse supremacy of wealth, where religion is mainly official and political, and is ever too ready to dissever itself alike from the spirit of justice, the spirit of charity, and the spirit of truth, and where literature does not as a rule permit itself to discuss serious subjects frankly and worthily— a community, in short, where the great aim of all classes and orders with power is by dint of rigorous silence, fast shutting of the eyes, and stern stopping of the ears, somehow to keep the social pyramid on its apex, with the fatal result of preserving for England its glorious fame as a paradise for the well-to-do, a purgatory for the able, and a hell for the poor—why, a man born into all this with a heart something softer than a flint, and with intellectual vision something more acute than that of a Troglodyte, may well be allowed to turn aside and cry for moons for a season.

Impotent unrest, however, is followed in Mr. Carlyle by what is socially an impotent solution, just as it was with Rousseau. To bid a man do his duty in one page, and then in the next to warn him sternly away from utilitarianism, from political economy, from all "theories of the moral sense," and from any other definite means of ascertaining what duty may chance to be, is but a bald and naked counsel. Spiritual nullity and material confusion in a society are not to be repaired by a transformation of egotism, querulous, brooding, marvelling, into egotism, active, practical, objective, not uncomplacent. The moral movements to which the instinctive impulses of humanity fallen on evil times uniformly give birth, early Christianity, for instance, or the socialism of Rousseau, may destroy a society, but they cannot save it unless in conjunction with organising policy. A thorough appreciation of fiscal and economic truths was at least as indispensable for the life of the Roman Empire as the acceptance of a Messiah; and it was only in the hands of a great statesman like Gregory VII. that Christianity became at last an instrument powerful enough to save civilisation. What the moral renovation of Rousseau did for France we all know. Now Rousseau's was far more profoundly social than the doctrine of Mr. Carlyle, which, while in name a renunciation of self, has all its foundations in the purest individualism. Rousseau, notwithstanding the method of *Emile*, treats man as a part of a collective whole, contracting manifold relations and owing manifold duties; and he always appeals to the love and sympathy which an imaginary God of nature has implanted in the heart. His aim is unity. Mr. Carlyle, following the same method of obedience to his own personal emotions, unfortified by patient reasoning, lands at the other extremity, and lays all his stress on the separatist instincts. The individual stands alone confronted by the eternities; between these and his own soul exists the one central relation. This has all the fundamental egotism of the doctrine of personal salvation, emancipated from fable, and varnished with an emotional phrase. The doctrine has been very widely interpreted, and without any forcing, as a religious expression for the conditions of commercial success.

If we look among our own countrymen, we find that the apostle of self-renunciation is nowhere so beloved as by the best of those whom steady self-reliance and thrifty self-securing and a firm eye to the main chance have got successfully on in the world. A Carlylean anthology, or volume of the master's sentences, might easily be composed, that should contain the highest form of private liturgy accepted by the best of the industrial classes, masters or men. They forgive or overlook the writer's denunciations of Beaver Industrialisms, which they attribute to his caprice or spleen. This is the worst of an emotional teacher, that people take only so much as they please from him, while with a reasoner they must either refute by reason, or else they must accept by reason, and not at simple choice. When trade is brisk, and England is successfully competing in the foreign markets, the books that enjoin silence and self-annihilation have a wonderful popularity in the manufacturing districts. This circumstance is honourable both to them and to him, as far as it goes, but it furnishes some reason for suspecting that our most vigorous moral reformer, so far from propelling us in new grooves, has in truth only given new firmness and coherency to tendencies that were strongly marked enough in the national character before. He has increased the fervour of the country, but without materially changing its objects; there is all the less disguise among us as a result of his teaching, but no radical modification of the sentiments which people are sincere in. The most stirring general appeal to the emotions, to be effective for more than negative purposes, must lead up to definite maxims and specific precepts. As a negative renovation Mr. Carlyle's doctrine was perfect. It effectually put an end to the mood of Byronism. May we say that with the neutralisation of Byron, his most decisive and special work came to an end? May we not say further, that the true renovation of England, if such a process be ever feasible, will lie in a quite other method than this of emotion? It will lie not in more moral earnestness only, but in a more open intelligence; not merely in a more dogged resolution to work and be silent, but in a ready willingness to use the understanding. The poison of our sins, says Mr. Carlyle in his latest utterance, "is not intellectual dimness chiefly, but torpid unveracity of heart." Yes, but all unveracity, torpid or fervid, breeds intellectual dimness, and it is the last which prevents us from seeing a way out of the present ignoble situation. We need light more than heat; intellectual alertness, faith in the reasoning faculty, accessibility to new ideas. To refuse to use the intellect patiently and with system, to decline to seek scientific truth, to prefer effusive indulgence of emotion to the laborious and disciplined and candid exploration of new ideas, is not this, too, a torpid unveracity? And has not Mr. Carlyle, by the impatience of his method, done somewhat to deepen it?

It is very well to invite us to moral reform, to bring ourselves to be of heroic mind, as the surest way to "the blessed Aristocracy of the Wisest." But how shall we know the wisest when we see them, and how shall a nation know, if not by keen respect and watchfulness for intellectual truth and the teachers of it? Much as we may admire Mr. Carlyle's many gifts, and highly as we may revere his character, it is yet very doubtful whether anybody has as yet learnt from him the precious lesson of scrupulosity and conscientiousness in actively and constantly using the intelligence. This would have been the solid foundation of the true heroworship. . . .

[Morley turns to Carlyle's formative years and discusses the derivation of Carlyle's thought from philosophical positions laid down by Coleridge and Byron's emotional *élan*.]

Eager for a firm foothold, yet wholly revolted by the too narrow and unelevated positivity of the eighteenth century; eager also for some recognition of the wide realm of the unknowable, yet wholly unsatisfied by the transcendentalism of the English and Scotch philosophic reactions; he found in Goethe that truly free and adequate positivity which accepts all things as parts of a natural or historic order, and while insisting on the recognition of the actual conditions of this order as indispensable, and condemning attempted evasions of such recognition as futile and childish, yet opens an ample bosom for all forms of beauty in art, and for all nobleness in moral aspiration. That Mr. Carlyle has reached this high ground we do not say. Temperament has kept him down from it. But it is after this that he has striven. The tumid nothingness of pure transcendentalism he has always abhorred. Some of Mr. Carlyle's favourite phrases have disguised from his readers the intensely practical turn of his whole mind. His constant presentation of the Eternities, the Immensities, and the like, has veiled his almost narrow adherence to plain record without moral comment, and his often cynical respect for the dangerous, yet, when rightly qualified and guided, the solid formula that What is, is. The Eternities and Immensities are only a kind of awful background. The highest souls are held to be deeply conscious of these vast unspeakable presences, yet even with them they are only inspiring accessories; the true interest lies in the practical attitude of such men towards the actual and palpable circumstances that surround them. This spirituality, whose place in Mr. Carlyle's teaching has been so extremely misstated, sinks wholly out of sight in connection with such heroes as the coarse and materialist Bonaparte, of whom, however, the hero-worshipper in earlier pieces speaks with some laudable misgiving, and the not less coarse and materialist Frederick, about whom no misgiving is permitted to the loyal disciple. The admiration for military methods, on condition that they are successful, for Mr. Carlyle, like Providence, is always on the side of big and victorious battalions, is the last outcome of a devotion to vigorous action and practical effect, which no verbal garniture of a transcendental kind can hinder us from perceiving to be more purely materialist and unfeignedly brutal than anything which sprung from the reviled thought of the eighteenth century. . . .

This is the kernel of all that is most retrograde in Mr. Carlyle's teaching. He identifies the physical with the moral order, confounds faithful conformity to the material conditions of success, with loyal adherence to virtuous rule and principle, and then appeals to material triumph as the sanction of nature and the ratification of high heaven. Admiring with profoundest admiration the spectacle of an inflexible will, when armed with a long-headed insight into means and quantities and forces as its instrument, and yet deeply revering the abstract ideal of justice; dazzled by the methods and the products of iron resolution, yet imbued with traditional affection for virtue; he has seen no better way of conciliating both inclinations than by insisting that they point in the same direction, and that virtue and success, justice and victory, merit and triumph, are in the long run all one and the same thing. The most fatal of confusions. Compliance with material law and condition ensures material victory, and compliance with moral condition ensures moral triumph; but then moral triumph is as often as not physical martyrdom. Superior military virtues must unquestionably win the verdict of Fate, Nature, Fact, and Veracity, on the battle-field, but what then? Has Fate no other verdicts to record than these? and at the moment while she writes Nature down debtor to the conqueror, may she not also have written her down his implacable creditor for the moral cost of his conquest? . . .

[After discussing some historical examples, Morley continues.]

Apart from its irreconcilableness with many of his most emphatic judgments, Mr. Carlyle's doctrine about Nature's registration of the penalities of injustice is intrinsically an anachronism. It is worse than the Catholic reaction, because while De Maistre only wanted Europe to return to the system of the twelfth century, Mr. Carlyle's theory of history takes us back to times prehistoric, when might and right were the same thing. It is decidedly natural that man in a state of nature should take and keep as much as his skill and physical strength enable him to do. But society and its benefits are all so much ground won from nature and her state. The more natural a method of acquisition, the less likely is it to be social. The essence of morality is the subjugation of nature in obedience to social needs. To use Kant's admirable description, concert *pathologically* extorted by the mere necessities of situation, is exalted into a *moral* union. It is exactly in this progressive substitution of one for the other that advancement consists, that Progress of the Species at which, in certain of its forms, Mr. Carlyle has so many gibes.

That, surely, is the true test of veracity and heroism in conduct. Does your hero's achievement go in the pathological or the moral direction? Does it tend to spread faith in that cunning, violence, force, which were once primitive and natural conditions of life, and which will still by natural law work to their own proper triumphs in so far as these conditions survive, and within such limits, and in such sense, as they permit; or, on the contrary, does it tend to heighten respect for civic law, for pledged word, for the habit of self-surrender to the public good, and for all those other ideas and sentiments and usages which have been painfully gained from the sterile sands of egotism and selfishness, and to which we are indebted for all the untold boons conferred by the social union on man? . . .

. . . He has been too willing to accept its fundamental maxim, that the end justifies the means. He has taken the end for the ratification or proscription of the means, and stamped it as the verdict of Fate and Fact on the transaction and its doer. A safer position is this, that the means prepare the end, and the end is what the means have made it. Here is the limit of the true law of the relations between man and fate. Justice and injustice in the law, let us abstain from inquiring after.

There are two sets of relations which have still to be regulated in some degree by the primitive and pathological principle of repression and main force. The first of these concern that unfortunate body of criminal and vicious persons, whose unsocial propensities are constantly straining and endangering the bonds of the social union. They exist in the midst of the most highly civilised communities, with all the predatory or violent habits of barbarous tribes. They are the active and unconquered remnant of the natural state, and it is as unscientific as the experience of some unwise philanthropy has shown it to be ineffective, to deal with them exactly as if they occupied the same moral and social level as the best of their generation. We are amply justified in employing towards them, wherever their offences endanger order, the same methods of coercion which originally made society possible. No tenable theory about free will or necessity, no theory of praise and blame that will bear positive tests, lays us under any obligation to spare either the comfort or the life of a man who indulges in certain anti-social kinds of conduct. Mr. Carlyle has done much to wear this just and austere view into the minds of his generation, and in so far he has performed an excellent service.

The second set of relations in which the pathological element still so largely predominates are those between nations. Separate and independent communities are still in a state of nature. The tie between them is only the imperfect, loose, and non-moral tie of self-interest and material power. Many publicists and sentimental politicians are ever striving to conceal this displeasing fact from themselves and others, and evading the lesson of the outbreaks that now and again convulse the civilised world. . . .

Yet have we not to confess that there is another side to this kind of truth, in both these fields? We may finally pronounce on a given way of thinking, only after we have discerned its goal. Not knowing this, we cannot accurately know its true tendency and direction. Now, every recognition of the pathological necessity should imply a progress and effort towards its conversion into moral relationship. The difference between a reactionary and a truly progressive thinker or group of ideas is not that the one assumes virtuousness and morality as having been the conscious condition of international dealings, while the other asserts that such dealings were the lawful consequence of self-interest and the contest of material forces; nor is it that the one insists on viewing international transactions from the same moral point which would be the right one, if independent communities actually formed one stable and settled family, while the other declines to view their morality at all. The vital difference is, that while the reactionary writer rigorously confines his faith within the region of facts accomplished, the other anticipates a time when the endeavour of the best minds in the civilised world, co-operating with every favouring external circumstance that arises, shall have in the international circle raised moral considerations to an ever higher and higher pre-eminence, and in internal conditions shall have left in the chances and training of the individual, ever less and less excuse or grounds for a predisposition to anti-social and barbaric moods. This hopefulness, in some shape or other, is an indispensable mark of the most valuable thought. To stop at the soldier and the gibbet, and such order as they can furnish, is to close the eyes to the entire problem of the future, and we may be sure that what omits the future is no adequate nor stable solution of the present.

Mr. Carlyle's influence, however, was at its height before this idolatry of the soldier became a paramount article in this creed; and it is devoutly to be hoped that not many of those whom he first taught to seize before all things fact and reality, will follow him into this torrid air, where only forces and never principles are facts, and where nothing is reality but the violent triumph of arbitrarily imposed will. There was once a better side to it all, when the injunction to seek and cling to fact was a valuable warning not to waste energy and hope in seeking lights which it is not given to man ever to find, with a solemn assurance added that in frank and untrembling recognition of circumstance the spirit of man may find a priceless, ever-fruitful contentment. The prolonged and thousand-times repeated glorification of Unconsciousness, Silence, Renunciation, all comes to this: We are to leave the region of things unknowable, and hold fast to the duty that lies nearest. Here is the Everlasting Yea. In action only can we have certainty. . . .

[Morley discusses Carlyle's relative reticence on the great current questions of faith and doubt, pointing out that insofar as he says anything, he holds to the "God is dead" school.]

Natural Supernaturalism, the title of one of the cardinal chapters in Mr. Carlyle's cardinal book, is perhaps as good a name as another for this two-faced yet integral philosophy, which teaches us to behold with cheerful serenity the great gulf which is fixed round our faculty and existence on every side, while it fills us with that supreme sense of countless unseen possibilities, and of the hidden, undefined movements of shadow and light over the spirit, without which the soul of man falls into hard and desolate sterility. In youth, perhaps, it is the latter aspect of Mr. Carlyle's teaching which first touches people, because youth is the time of indefinite aspiration; and it is easier, besides, to surrender ourselves passively to these vague emotional impressions, than to apply actively and contentedly to the duty that lies nearest, and to the securing of "that infinitesimallest product" on which the teacher is ever insisting. It is the Supernaturalism which stirs men first, until larger fulness of years and wider experience of life draw them to a wise and not inglorious acquiescence in Naturalism. This last is the mood which Mr. Carlyle never wearies of extolling and enjoining under the name of Belief; and the absence of it, the inability to enter into it, is that Unbelief which he so bitterly vituperates, or, in another phrase, that Discontent, which he charges with holding the soul in such desperate and paralysing bondage.

Indeed, what is it that Mr. Carlyle urges upon us but the search for that Mental Freedom, which under one name or another has been the goal and ideal of all highest minds that have reflected on the true constitution of human happiness? His often enjoined Silence is the first condition of this supreme kind of liberty, for what is silence but the absence of a self-tormenting assertiveness, the freedom from excessive susceptibility under the speech of others, one's removal from the choking sandy wilderness of wasted words? Belief is the mood which emancipates us from the paralysing dubieties of distraught souls, and leaves us full possession of ourselves by furnishing an unshaken and inexpugnable base for action and thought, and subordinating passion to conviction. Labour, again, perhaps the cardinal article in the creed, is at once the price of moral independence, and the first condition of that fulness and accuracy of knowledge, without which we are not free, but the bounden slaves of prejudice, unreality, darkness, and error. Even Renunciation of self is in truth only the casting out of those disturbing and masterful qualities which oppress and hinder the free, natural play of the worthier parts of character. In renunciation we thus restore to self its own diviner mind.

Yet we are never bidden either to strive or hope for a freedom that is unbounded. Circumstance has fixed limits that no effort can transcend. . . . [Carlyle makes] a lofty acquiescence in the positive course of circumstance a prime condition at once of wise endeavour and of genuine happiness. The splendid fire and unmeasured vehemence of Mr. Carlyle's manner partially veil the depth of this acquiescence, which is really not so far removed from fatalism. . . . It is fate. Man is the creature of his destiny. As for our supposed claims on the heavenly powers: What right, he asks, hadst thou even to be? Fatalism of this stamp is the natural and unavoidable issue of a born positivity of spirit, uninformed by scientific meditation. It exists in its coarsest and most childish kind in adventurous freebooters of the type of Napoleon, and in a noble and not egotistic kind in Oliver Cromwell's pious interpretation of the order of events by the good will and providence of God.

Two conspicuous qualities of Carlylean doctrine flow from this fatalism, or poetised utilitarianism, or illumined positivity. One of them is a tolerably constant contempt for excessive nicety in moral distinctions, and an aversion to the monotonous attitude of praise and blame. In a country overrun and corroded to the heart, as Great Britain is, with cant and a foul mechanical hypocrisy, this temper ought to have had its uses in giving a much-needed robustness to public judgment. One might suppose, from the tone of opinion among us, not only that the difference between right and wrong marks the most important aspect of conduct, which would be true; but that it marks the only aspect of it that exists, or that is worth considering, which is most profoundly false. Nowhere has Puritanism done us more harm than in thus leading us to take all breadth, and colour, and diversity, and fine discrimination, out of our judgments of men, reducing them to thin, narrow, and superficial pronouncements upon the letter of their morality, or the precise conformity of their opinions to accepted standards of truth, religious or other. Among other evils which it has inflicted, this inability to conceive of conduct except as either right or wrong, and, correspondingly in the intellectual order, of teaching except as either true or false, is at the bottom of that fatal spirit of *parti-pris* which has led to the rooting of so much injustice, disorder, immobility, and darkness in English intelligence. No excess of morality, we may be sure, has followed this excessive adoption of the exclusively moral standard. *"Quand il n'y a plus de principes dans le cœur,"* says De Senancourt, *"on est bien scrupuleux sur les apparences publiques et sur les devoirs d'opinion."* We have simply got for our pains a most unlovely leanness of judgment, and ever since the days when this temper set in until now, when a wholesome rebellion is afoot, it has steadily and powerfully tended to straiten character, to make action mechanical, and to impoverish art. As if there were nothing admirable in a man save unbroken obedience to the letter of the moral law, and that letter read in our own casual and local interpretation; and as if we had no faculties of sympathy, no sense for the beauty of character, no feeling for broad force and full-pulsing vitality.

To study manners and conduct and men's moral nature in such a way, is as direct an error as it would be to overlook in the study of his body everything except its vertebral column and the bony framework. The body is more than mere anatomy. A character is much else besides being virtuous or vicious. In many of the characters in which some of the finest and most singular qualities of humanity would seem to have reached their furthest height, their morality was the side least worth discussing. The same may be said of the specific rightness or wrongness of opinion in the intellectual order. Let us condemn error or immorality, when the scope of our criticism calls for this particular function, but why rush to praise or blame, to eulogy or reprobation, when we should do better simply to explore and enjoy? Moral imperfection is ever a grievous curtailment of life, but many exquisite flowers of character, many gracious and potent things, may still thrive in the most disordered scene.

The vast waste which this limitation of prospect entails is the most grievous rejection of moral treasure, if it be true that nothing enriches the nature like wide sympathy and many-coloured appreciativeness. . . .

[Morley contrasts Macaulay's use of criticism—"only a tribunal before which men were brought to be decisively tried by one or two inflexible tests, and then sent to join the sheep on the one hand, or the goats on the other"—to Carlyle's. Carlyle never dwelt on the trivial, saw the person as a whole, painted them "in all their fulness and colour." Modern criticism, Morley continues, owes much of its "humaner prospect" to Carlyle. "The same principle which revealed the valour and godliness of Puritanism, has proved its most efficacious solvent, for it places character on the pedestal where Puritanism places dogma."]

The second of the qualities which seem to flow from Mr. Carlyle's fatalism, and one much less useful among such a people as the English, is a deficiency of sympathy with masses of men. It would be easy enough to find places where he talks of the dumb millions in terms of fine and sincere humanity, and his feeling for the common pathos of the human lot, as he encounters it in individual lives, is as earnest and as simple, as it is invariably lovely and touching in its expression. But detached passages cannot counterbalance the effect of a whole compact body of teaching. The multitude stands between Destiny on the one side, and the Hero on the other; a sport to the first, and as potter's clay to the second. . . . Here is the end of the Eternal Verities, when one lets them bulk so big in his eyes as to shut out that perishable speck, the human race.

. . . The difference between virtue and vice, between wisdom and folly, is only phenomenal, yet there is difference enough. *"What shadows we are, and what shadows we pursue!"* Burke cried in the presence of an affecting incident. Yet the consciousness of this made him none the less careful, minute, patient, systematic, in examining a policy, or criticising a tax. Mr. Carlyle, on the contrary, falls back on the same reflection for comfort in the face of political confusions and difficulties and details, which he has not the moral patience to encounter scientifically. Unable to dream of swift renovation and wisdom among men, he ponders on the unreality of life, and hardens his heart against generations that will not know the things that pertain unto their peace. . . .

There is no passage which Mr. Carlyle so often quotes as the sublime—

> We are such stuff
> As dreams are made on; and our little life
> Is rounded with a sleep.

If the ever present impression of this awful, most moving, yet most soothing thought, be a law of spiritual breadth and height, there is still a peril in it. Such an impression may inform the soul with a devout mingled sense of grandeur and nothingness, or it may blacken into cynicism and antinomian living for self and the day. . . . As a reaction against religious theories which make humanity over-abound in self-consequence, and fill individuals with the strutting importance of creatures with private souls to save or lose, even such cynicism as Byron's was wholesome and nearly forgivable. Nevertheless, the most important question that we can ask of any great teacher, as of the walk and conversation of any commonest person, remains this—how far has he strengthened and raised the conscious and harmonious dignity of humanity; how stirred in men and women, many or few, deeper and more active sense of the worth and obligation and innumerable possibilities, not of their own little lives, one or another, but of life collectively; how heightened the self-respect of the race? . . .

This renewal of moral energy by spiritual contact with the mass of men, and by meditation on the destinies of mankind, is the very reverse of Mr. Carlyle's method. With him, it is good to leave the mass, and fall down before the individual, and be saved by him. . . . The whole human race toils and moils, straining and energising, doing and suffering things multitudinous and unspeakable under the sun, in order that like the aloe-tree it may once in a hundred years produce a flower. It is this hero that age offers to age, and the wisest worship him. Time and nature once and again distil from out of the lees and froth of common humanity some wondrous character, of a potent and reviving property hardly short of miraculous. This the man who knows his own good cherishes in his inmost soul as a sacred thing, an elixir of moral life. . . .

Mr. Carlyle has indeed written that generation stands indissolubly woven with generation. . . . Man is for Mr. Carlyle, as for the Calvinistic theologian, a fallen and depraved being, without much hope, except for a few of the elect. The best thing that can happen to the poor creature is that he should be thoroughly well drilled. In other words, society does not really progress in its bulk; and the methods which were conditions of the original formation and growth of the social union, remain indispensable until the sound of the last trump. . . .

Every modification of society is one of the slow growths of

time, and to hurry impatiently after them by swift ways of military discipline and peremptory law-making, is only to clasp the near and superficial good. It is easy to make a solitude and call it peace, to plant an iron heel and call it order. . . . Where organic growths are concerned, patience is the sovereign law; and where the organism is a society of men, the vital principle is a sense in one shape or another of the dignity of humanity. The recognition of this tests the distinction between the truly heroic ruler of the stamp of Cromwell, and the arbitrary enthusiast for external order like Frederick. Yet in more than one place Mr. Carlyle accepts the fundamental principle of democracy. "It is curious to consider now," he says once, "with what fierce, deep-breathed doggedness the poor English Nation, drawn by their instincts, held fast upon it [the Spanish War of Walpole's time, in Jenkins' Ear Question], and would take no denial of it, as if they had surmised and seen. For the instincts of simple, guileless persons (liable to be counted stupid by the unwary) are sometimes of prophetic nature, and spring from the deep places of this universe!" If the writer of this had only thought it out to the end, and applied the conclusions thereof to history and politics, what a difference it would have made.

No criticism upon either Mr. Carlyle or any other modern historian, possessed of speculative quality, would be in any sense complete which should leave out of sight his view of the manner and significance of the break-up of the old European structure. The historian is pretty sure to be guided in his estimate of the forces which have contributed to dissolution in the past, by the kind of anticipation which he entertains of the probable course of reconstruction. Like Comte, in his ideas of temporal reconstruction, Mr. Carlyle goes back to something like the forms of feudalism for the model of the industrial organisation of the future; but in the spiritual order he is as far removed as possible from any semblance of that revival of the old ecclesiastical forms without the old theological ideas, which is the corner-stone of Comte's edifice. To the question whether mankind gained or lost by the French Revolution, Mr. Carlyle nowhere gives a clear answer; indeed, on this subject more even than any other, he clings closely to his favourite method of simple presentation, streaked with dramatic irony. No writer shows himself more alive to the enormous moment to all Europe of that transaction; but we hear no word from him on the question whether we have more reason to bless or curse an event that interrupted, either subsequently to retard or to accelerate, the transformation of the West from a state of war, of many degrees of social subordination, of religious privilege, of aristocratic administration, into a state of peaceful industry, of equal international rights, of social equality, of free and equal tolerance of creeds. That this process was going on prior to 1789 is undeniable. Are we really nearer to the permanent establishment of the new order, for what was done between 1789 and 1793? or were men thrown off the right track of improvement by a movement which turned exclusively on abstract rights, which dealt with men's ideas and habits as if they were instantaneously pliable before the aspirations of any government, and which by its violent and inconsiderate methods drove all these who should only have been friends of order into being the enemies of progress as well? There are many able and honest and republican men who in their hearts suspect that the latter of the two alternatives is the more correct description of what has happened. Mr. Carlyle is as one who does not hear the question. He draws its general moral lesson from the French Revolution, and with clangorous note warns all whom it concerns, from king to churl, that imposture must come to an end. But for the precise amount and kind of dissolution which the West owes to it, for the political meaning of it, as distinguished from its moral or its dramatic significance, we seek in vain, finding no word on the subject, nor even evidence of consciousness that such word is needed.

. . . But then, in Mr. Carlyle's belief, there was equally a constructive and highly moral side to all this collapse of traditional Europe as early as the 1740s]. The old fell to pieces because it was internally rotten. The gospel of the new was that the government of men and kingdoms is a business beyond all others demanding an open-eyed accessibility to all facts and realities; that here more than anywhere else you need to give the tools to him who can handle them; that government does by no means go on of itself, but more than anything else in this world demands skill, patience, energy, long and tenacious grip, and the constant presence of that most indispensable, yet most rare, of all practical convictions, that the effect is the inevitable consequent of the cause. Here was a revolution, we cannot doubt. . . .

As to the other great factor in the dissolution of the old state, the decay of ancient spiritual forms, Mr. Carlyle gives no uncertain sound. Of the Reformation, as of the French Revolution, philosophers have doubted how far it really contributed to the stable progress of European civilisation. Would it have been better, if it had been possible, for the old belief gradually as by process of nature to fall to pieces, new doctrine as gradually and as normally emerging from the ground of disorganised and decayed convictions, without any of that frightful violence which stirred men's deepest passions, and gave them a sinister interest in holding one or other of the rival creeds in its most extreme, exclusive, and intolerant form? This question Mr. Carlyle does not see, or, if he does see it, he rides roughshod over it. Every reader remembers the notable passage in which he declares that the question of Protestant or not Protestant meant everywhere, "Is there anything of nobleness in you, O Nation, or is there nothing?" and that afterwards it fared with nations as they did, or did not, accept this sixteenth century form of Truth when it came. . . .

The famous diatribe against Jesuitism in the *Latter-Day Pamphlets*, one of the most unfeignedly coarse and virulent bits of invective in the language . . . is grossly unjust, because it takes for granted that Loyola and all Jesuits were deliberately conscious of imposture and falsehood, knowingly embraced the cause of Beelzebub, and resolutely propagated it. It is one thing to judge a system in its corruption, and a quite other thing to measure the worth and true design of its first founders; one thing to estimate the intention and sincerity of a movement, when it first stirred the hearts of men, and another thing to pass sentence upon it in the days of its degradation. The vileness into which Jesuitism eventually sank is a poor reason why we should malign and curse those who, centuries before, found in the rules and discipline and aims of that system an acceptable expression for their own disinterested social aspirations. It is childish to say that the subsequent vileness is a proof of the existence of an inherent corrupt principle from the beginning; because hitherto certainly, and probably it will be so for ever, even the most salutary movements and most effective social conceptions have been provisional. In other words, the ultimate certainty of dissolution does not nullify the beauty and strength of physical life, and the putrescence of Jesuit methods and ideas is no more a reproach to those who first found succour in them, than the cant and formalism of any other degenerate form of active faith, say monachism or Calvinism, prove Calvin or Benedict or Bernard to have been hypocritical and hollow. To be able, however, to take this reasonable view, one must be unable to believe that men can be drawn for generation after generation by such a mere hollow lie and villainy and "light of hell" as Jesuitism has always been, according to Mr. Carlyle's rendering. Human nature is not led for so long by lies; and if it seems to be otherwise, let us be sure that ideas which do lead and attract successive generations of men to self-sacrifice and care for social interests, must contain something which is not wholly a lie.

Perhaps it is pertinent to remember that Mr. Carlyle, in fact, is a prophet with a faith, and he holds the opposition kind of religionist in a peculiarly theological execration. In spite of his passion for order, he cannot understand the political point of view. The attempts of good men in epochs of disorder to remake the past, to bring back an old spiritual system and method, because that did once at any rate give shelter to mankind, and peradventure may give it to them again until better times come, are phenomena into which he cannot look with calm or patience. The great reactionist is a type that is wholly dark to him. That a reactionist can be great, can be a lover of virtue and truth, can in any sort contribute to the welfare of men, these are possibilities to which he will lend no ear. In a word, he is a prophet and not a philosopher, and it is fruitless to go to him for help in the solution of philosophic problems. This is not to say that he may not render us much help in those far more momentous problems which affect the guidance of our own lives.

31. Self-Help

SELF-HELP IS a promontory by which we recognize the Victorian landscape. At worst it is a set of platitudes; at best it reflects the ethical assumptions of the new society. The rhetoric is confident and earnest; the message simplicity itself.

"Heaven helps those who help themselves" is a well-tried maxim, embodying in a small compass the results of vast human experience. The spirit of self-help is the root of all genuine growth in the individual; and exhibited in the lives of man, it constitutes the true source of national vigour and strength. Help from without is often enfeebling in its effects, but help from within invariably invigorates. Whatever is done *for* men or classes, to a certain extent takes away the stimulus and necessity of doing for themselves; and where men are subject to over-guidance and over-government, the inevitable tendency is to render them comparatively helpless.

Samuel Smiles (1812–1904) did not restrict himself to simple success stories, teaching by precept and example. He spoke of the pride and contentment to be found in the humdrum aspects of life. Success was more important than the cumulation of pounds, shillings, and pence.

> The greatest results in life are usually obtained by simple means, and the exercise of ordinary qualities. The common life of every day, with its cares, necessities, and duties, affords ample opportunity for acquiring experience of the best kind; and its most beaten paths provide the true worker with abundant scope for effort and room for self-improvement. The road of human welfare lies along the old highway of steadfast well-doing; and they who are the most persistent and work in the truest spirit, will usually be the most successful.

Success must be measured in nonmaterial terms. Smiles was preaching secularized evangelicalism. For the religious he restated the doctrine, what shall it profit a man if he gain the whole world but lose his soul. But he couched it in completely secular terms. The ennoblement of man is won by work and duty.

> Certain it is that no bread eaten by man is so sweet as that earned by his own labour, whether bodily or mental. By labour the earth has been subdued, and man redeemed from barbarism; nor has a single step in civilisation been made without. Labour is not only a necessity and a duty, but a blessing: only the idler feels it to be a curse. The duty of work is written on the thews and muscles of the limbs, the mechanism of the hand, the nerves and lobes of the brain—the sum of whose healthy action is satisfaction and enjoyment. In the school of labour is taught the best practical wisdom; nor is a life of manual employment, as we shall hereafter find, incompatible with high mental culture.

Recommended Reading

In addition to the excellent chapter on Smiles in A. Briggs, *Victorian People* (Chicago: 1955), see J. F. C. Harrison, "The Victorian Gospel of Success," *Victorian Studies*, I (1957), 155–164, and K. Fielden, "Samuel Smiles and Self-Help," *Victorian Studies*, XII (1968), 155–176.

SAMUEL SMILES,
MONEY—ITS USE AND ABUSE

How a man uses money—makes it, saves it, and spends it—is perhaps one of the best tests of practical wisdom. Although money ought by no means to be regarded as a chief end of man's life,

Source: From *Self-Help* (London, 1859), chap. x.

neither is it a trifling matter, to be held in philosophic contempt, representing as it does to so large an extent, the means of physical comfort and social well-being. Indeed, some of the finest qualities of human nature are intimately related to the right use of money; such as generosity, honesty, justice, and self-sacrifice; as well as the practical virtues of economy and providence. On the other hand, there are their counterparts of avarice, fraud, injustice, and selfishness, as displayed by the inordinate lovers of gain; and the vices of thriftlessness, extravagance, and improvidence, on the part of those who misuse and abuse the means entrusted to them. "So that," as is wisely observed by Henry Taylor in his thoughtful "Notes from Life," "a right measure and manner in getting, saving, spending, giving, taking, lending, borrowing, and bequeathing, would almost argue a perfect man."

Comfort in worldly circumstances is a condition which every man is justified in striving to attain by all worthy means. It secures that physical satisfaction, which is necessary for the culture of the better part of his nature; and enables him to provide for those of his own household, without which, says the Apostle, a man is "worse than an infidel." Nor ought the duty to be any the less indifferent to us, that the respect which our fellowmen entertain for us in no slight degree depends upon the manner in which we exercise the opportunities which present themselves for our honourable advancement in life. The very effort required to be made to succeed in life with this object, is of itself an education; stimulating a man's sense of self-respect, bringing out his practical qualities, and disciplining him in the exercise of patience, perseverance, and such like virtues. The provident and careful man must necessarily be a thoughtful man, for he lives not merely for the present, but with provident forecast makes arrangements for the future. He must also be a temperate man, and exercise the virtue of self-denial, than which nothing is so much calculated to give strength to the character. John Sterling says truly, that "the worst education which teaches self-denial, is better than the best which teaches everything else, and not that." The Romans rightly employed the same word (virtus) to designate courage, which is in a physical sense what the other is in a moral; the highest virtue of all being victory over ourselves.

Hence the lesson of self-denial—the sacrificing of a present gratification for a future good—is one of the last that is learnt.

Those classes which work the hardest might naturally be expected to value the most the money which they earn. Yet the readiness with which so many are accustomed to eat up and drink up their earnings as they go, renders them to a great extent helpless and dependent upon the frugal. There are large numbers of persons among us who, though enjoying sufficient means of comfort and independence, are often found to be barely a day's march ahead of actual want when a time of pressure occurs; and hence a great cause of social helplessness and suffering. On one occasion a deputation waited on Lord John Russell, respecting the taxation levied on the working classes of the country, when the noble lord took the opportunity of remarking, "You may rely upon it that the Government of this country durst not tax the working classes to anything like the extent to which they tax themselves in their expenditure upon intoxicating drinks alone!" Of all great public questions, there is perhaps none more important than this,—no great work of reform calling more loudly for labourers. But it must be admitted that "self-denial and self-help" would make a poor rallying cry for the hustings; and it is to be feared that the patriotism of this day has but little regard for such common things as individual economy and providence, although it is by the practice of such virtues only that the genuine independence of the industrial classes is to be secured. "Prudence, frugality, and good management," said Samuel Drew, the philosophical shoemaker, "are excellent artists for mending bad times: they occupy but little room in any dwelling, but would furnish a more effectual remedy for the evils of life than any Reform Bill that ever passed the Houses of Parliament." Socrates said, "Let him that would move the world move first himself." Or as the old rhyme runs—

> If every one would see
>   To his own reformation,
> How very easily
>   You might reform a nation.

It is, however, generally felt to be a far easier thing to reform the Church and the State than to reform the least of our own bad habits; and in such matters it is usually found more agreeable to our tastes, as it certainly is the common practice, to begin with our neighbours rather than with ourselves.

Any class of men that lives from hand to mouth will ever be an inferior class. They will necessarily remain impotent and helpless, hanging on to the skirts of society, the sport of times and seasons. Having no respect for themselves, they will fail in securing the respect of others. In commercial crises, such men must inevitably go to the wall. Wanting that husbanded power which a store of savings, no matter how small, invariably gives them, they will be at every man's mercy, and, if possessed of right feelings, they cannot but regard with fear and trembling the future possible fate of their wives and children. "The world," once said Mr. Cobden to the working men of Huddersfield, "has always been divided into two classes,—those who have saved, and those who have spent—the thrifty and the extravagant. The building of all the houses, the mills, the bridges, and the ships, and the accomplishment of all other great works which have rendered man civilized and happy, has been done by the savers, the thrifty; and those who have wasted their resources have always been their slaves. It has been the law of nature and of Providence that this should be so; and I were an impostor if I promised any class that they would advance themselves if they were improvident, thoughtless, and idle."

Equally sound was the advice given by Mr. Bright to an assembly of working men at Rochdale, in 1847, when, after expressing his belief that, "so far as honesty was concerned, it was to be found in pretty equal amount among all classes," he used the following words:—"There is only one way that is safe for any man, or any number of men, by which they can maintain their present position if it be a good one, or raise themselves above it if it be a bad one,—that is, by the practice of the virtues of industry, frugality, temperance, and honesty. There is no royal road by which men can raise themselves from a position which they feel to be uncomfortable and unsatisfactory, as regards their mental or physical condition, except by the practice of those virtues by which they find numbers amongst them are continually advancing and bettering themselves."

There is no reason why the condition of the average workman should not be a useful, honourable, respectable, and happy one. The whole body of the working classes might (with few exceptions) be as frugal, virtuous, well-informed, and well-conditioned as many individuals of the same class have already made themselves. What some men are, all without difficulty might be. Employ the same means, and the same results will follow. That there should be a class of men who live by their daily labour in every state is the ordinance of God, and doubtless is a wise and righteous one; but that this class should be otherwise than frugal, contented, intelligent, and happy, is not the design of Providence, but springs solely from the weakness, self-indulgence, and perverseness of man himself. The healthy spirit of self-help created amongst working people would more than any other measure serve to raise them as a class, and this, not by pulling down others, but by levelling them up to a higher and still advancing standard of religion, intelligence, and virtue. "All moral philosophy," says Montaigne, "is as applicable to a common and private life as to the most splendid. Every man carries the entire form of the human condition within him."

When a man casts his glance forward, he will find that the three chief temporal contingencies for which he has to provide are want of employment, sickness, and death. The two first he may escape, but the last is inevitable. It is, however, the duty of the prudent man so to live, and so to arrange, that the pressure of suffering, in event of either contingency occurring, shall be mitigated to as great an extent as possible, not only to himself, but also to those who are dependent upon him for their comfort and subsistence. Viewed in this light the honest earning and the frugal use of money are of the greatest importance. Rightly earned, it is the representative of patient industry and untiring effort, of temptation resisted, and hope rewarded; and rightly used, it affords indications of prudence, fore-thought and self-denial—the true basis of manly character. Though money represents a crowd of objects without any real worth or utility, it also represents many things of great value; not only food, clothing, and household satisfaction, but personal self-respect and independence. Thus a store of savings is to the working man as a barricade against want; it secures him a footing, and enables him to wait, it may be in cheerfulness and hope, until better days come round. The very endeavour to gain a firmer position in the world has a certain dignity in it, and tends to make a man stronger and better. At all events it gives him greater freedom of action, and enables him to husband his strength for future effort.

But the man who is always hovering on the verge of want is in a state not far removed from that of slavery. He is in no sense his own master, but is in constant peril of falling under the bondage of others, and accepting the terms which they dictate to him. He cannot help being in a measure, servile, for he dares not look the world boldly in the face; and in adverse times he must look either to alms or the poor's rates. If work fails him altogether, he has not the means of moving to another field of employment; he is fixed to his parish like a limpet to its rock, and can neither migrate nor emigrate.

To secure independence, the practice of simple economy is all that is necessary. Economy requires neither superior courage nor eminent virtue; it is satisfied with ordinary energy, and the capacity of average minds. Economy, at bottom, is but the spirit of order applied in the administration of domestic affairs: it means management, regularity, prudence, and the avoidance of waste. The spirit of economy was expressed by our Divine Master in the words "Gather up the fragments that remain, so that nothing may be lost." His omnipotence did not disdain the small things of life; and even while revealing His infinite power to the multitude, he taught the pregnant lesson of carefulness of which all stand so much in need.

Economy also means the power of resisting present gratification for the purpose of securing a future good, and in this light it represents the ascendancy of reason over the animal instincts. It is altogether different from penuriousness: for it is economy that can always best afford to be generous. It does not make money an idol but regards it as a useful agent. As Dean Swift observes, "we must carry money in the head, not in the heart." Economy may be styled the daughter of Prudence, the sister of Temperance, and the mother of Liberty. It is evidently conservative—conservative of character, of domestic happiness, and social well-being. It is, in short, the exhibition of self-help in one of its best forms. . . .

Every man ought so to contrive as to live within his means. This practice is of the very essence of honesty. For if a man do not manage honestly to live within his own means, he must necessarily be living dishonestly upon the means of somebody else. Those who are careless about personal expenditure, and consider merely their own gratification, without regard for the comfort of others, generally find out the real uses of money when it is too late. Though by nature generous, these thriftless persons are often driven in the end to do very shabby things. They waste their money as they do their time; draw bills upon the future; anticipate their earnings; and are thus under the necessity of dragging after them a load of debts and obligations which seriously affect their action as free and independent men.

It was a maxim of Lord Bacon, that when it was necessary to economize, it was better to look after petty savings than to descend to petty gettings. The loose cash which many persons throw away uselessly, and worse, would often form a basis of fortune and independence for life. These wasters are their own worst enemies, though generally found amongst the ranks of those who rail at the injustice of "the world." But if a man will not be his own friend, how can he expect that others will? Orderly men of moderate means have always something left in their pockets to help others; whereas your prodigal and careless fellows who spend all never find an opportunity for helping anybody. It is poor economy, however, to be a scrub. Narrow-mindedness in living and in dealing is generally short-sighted, and leads to failure. The penny soul, it is said, never came to twopence. Generosity and liberality, like honesty, prove the best policy after all. Though Jenkinson, in the *Vicar of Wakefield*, cheated his kind-hearted neighbor Flamborough in one way or another every year, "Flamborough," said he, "has been regularly growing in riches, while I have come to poverty and a gaol." And practical life abounds in cases of brilliant results from a course of generous and honest policy.

The proverb says that "an empty bag cannot stand upright;" neither can a man who is in debt. It is also difficult for a man who is in debt to be truthful; hence it is said that lying rides on debt's back. The debtor has to frame excuses to his creditor for postponing payment of the money he owes him; and probably also to contrive falsehoods. It is easy enough for a man who will exercise a healthy resolution, to avoid incurring the first obligation; but the facility with which that has been incurred often becomes a temptation to a second; and very soon the unfortunate borrower becomes so entangled that no late exertion of industry can set him free. The first step in debt is like the first step in falsehood; almost involving the necessity of proceeding in the same course, debt following debt, as lie follows lie. Haydon, the painter, dated his decline from the day on which he first borrowed money. He realized the truth of the proverb, "Who goes a-borrowing, goes a-sorrowing." The significant entry in his diary is: "Here began debt and obligation, out of which I have never been and never shall be extricated as long as I live." His Autobiography shows but too painfully how embarrassment in money matters produces poignant distress of mind, utter incapacity for work, and constantly recurring humiliations. . . . Fichte, the poor student, refused to accept even presents from his still poorer parents. . . .

It is the bounden duty of every man to look his affairs in the face, and to keep an account of his incomings and outgoings in money matters. The exercise of a little simple arithmetic in this way will be found of great value. Prudence requires that we shall pitch our scale of living a degree below our means, rather than up to them; but this can only be done by carrying out faithfully a plan of living by which both ends may be made to meet. John Locke strongly advised this course: "Nothing," said he "is likelier to keep a man within compass than having constantly before his eyes the state of his affairs in a regular course of account." The Duke of Wellington kept an accurate detailed account of all the monies received and expended by him. . . . Talking of debt his remark was, "It makes a slave of a man. I have often known what it was to be in want of money, but I never got into debt." Washington was as particular as Wellington was, in matters of business detail; and it is a remarkable fact, that he did not disdain to scrutinize the smallest outgoings of his household—determined as he was to live honestly within his means—even while holding the high office of President of the American Union. . . .

Mr. Hume hit the mark when he once stated in the House of Commons—though his words were followed by "laughter"—that the tone of living in England is altogther too high. Middle-class people are too apt to live up to their incomes, if not beyond them: affecting a degree of "style" which is most unhealthy in its effects upon society at large. There is an ambition to bring up boys as gentlemen, or rather "genteel" men; though the result frequently is, only to make them gents. They acquire a taste for dress, style, luxuries, and amusements, which can never form any solid foundation for manly or gentlemanly character; and the result is, that we have a vast number of gingerbread young gentry thrown upon the world, who remind one of the abandoned hulls sometimes picked up at sea, with only a monkey on board.

There is a dreadful ambition abroad for being "genteel." We keep up appearances, too often at the expense of honesty; and, though we may not be rich, yet we must seem to be so. We must be "respectable," though only in the meanest sense—in mere vulgar outward show. We have not the courage to go patiently onward in the condition of life in which it has pleased God to call us; but must needs live in some fashionable state to which we ridiculously please to call ourselves, and all to gratify the vanity of that unsubstantial genteel world of which we form a part. There is a constant struggle and pressure for front seats in the social amphitheatre; in the midst of which all noble self-denying resolve is trodden down, and many fine natures are inevitably crushed to death. What waste, what misery, what bankruptcy, come from all this ambition to dazzle others with the glare of apparent worldly success, we need not describe. The mischievous results show themselves in a thousand ways—in the rank frauds committed by men who dare to be dishonest, but do not dare to seem poor; and in the desperate dashes at fortune, in which the pity is not so much for those who fail, as for the hundreds of innocent families who are so often involved in their ruin.

The late Sir Charles Napier, in taking leave of his command in India, did a bold and honest thing in publishing his strong protest, embodied in his last General Order to the officers of the Indian army, against the "fast" life led by so many young officers in that service, involving them in ignominious obligations. Sir Charles strongly urged, in that famous document—what had almost been lost sight of—that "honesty is inseparable from the character of a thoroughbred gentleman;" and that "to drink unpaid-for champagne and unpaid-for beer, and to ride unpaid-for horses, is to be a cheat, and not a gentleman." Men who lived beyond their means and were summoned, often by their own servants, before Courts of Requests for debts contracted in extravagant living, might be officers by virtue of their commissons, but they were not gentlemen. The habit of being constantly in debt, the Commander-in-chief held, made men grow callous to the proper feelings of a gentleman. It was not enough that an officer should be able to fight: that any bulldog could do. But did he hold his word inviolate?—did he pay his debts? These were among the points of honour which, he insisted, illuminated the true gentleman's and soldier's career. As Bayard was of old, so would Sir Charles Napier have all British officers to be. He knew them to be "without fear," but he would also have them "without reproach." . . .

The young man, as he passes through life, advances through a long line of tempters ranged on either side of him; and the inevitable effect of yielding, is degradation in a greater or a less degree. Contact with them tends insensibly to draw away from him some portion of the divine electric element with which his nature is charged; and his only mode of resisting them is to utter and to act out his "no" manfully and resolutely. He must decide at once, not waiting to deliberate and balance reasons; for the youth, like "the woman who deliberates, is lost." Many deliberate, without deciding; but "not to resolve, *is* to resolve." A perfect knowledge of man is in the prayer, "Lead us not into temptation." But temptation will come to try the young man's strength; and once yielded to, the power to resist grows weaker and weaker. Yield once, and a portion of virtue has gone. Resist manfully, and the first decision will give strength for life; repeated, it will become a habit. It is in the outworks of the habits formed in early life that the real strength of the defence must lie; for it has been wisely ordained, that the machinery of moral existence should be carried on principally through the medium of the habits, so as to save the wear and tear of the great principles within. It is good habits, which insinuate themselves into the thousand inconsiderable acts of life, that really constitute by far the greater part of man's moral conduct.

Hugh Miller has told how, by an act of youthful decision, he saved himself from one of the strong temptations so peculiar to a life of toil. When employed as a mason, it was usual for his fellow-workmen to have an occasional treat of drink, and one day two glasses of whisky fell to his share, which he swallowed. When he reached home he found, on opening his favourite book—*Bacon's Essays*—that the letters danced before his eyes, and that he could no longer master the sense. "The condition," he says, "into which I had brought myself was, I felt, one of degradation. I had sunk, by my own act, for the time, to a lower level of intelligence than that on which it was my privilege to be placed; and though the state could have been no very favourable one for forming a resolution, I in that hour determined that I should never again sacrifice my capacity of intellectual enjoyment to a drinking usage; and, with God's help, I was enabled to hold by the determination." It is such decisions as this that often form the turningpoints in a man's life, and furnish the foundation of his future character. And this rock, on which Hugh Miller might have been wrecked, if he had not at the right moment put forth his moral strength to strike away from it, is one that youth and manhood alike need to be constantly on their guard against. It is about one of the worst and most deadly, as well as extravagant, temptations, which lie in the way of youth. Sir Walter Scott used to say that "of all vices drinking is the most incompatible with greatness." Not only so, but it is incompatible with economy, decency, health, and honest living. When a youth cannot restrain, he must abstain. Dr. Johnson's case is the case of many. He said, referring to his own habits, "Sir, I can abstain; but I can't be moderate."

But to wrestle vigorously and successfully with any vicious habit, we must not merely be satisfied with contending on the low ground of wordly prudence, though that is of use, but take stand upon a higher moral elevation. Mechanical aids, such as pledges, may be of service to some, but the great thing is to set up a high standard of thinking and acting, and endeavour to strengthen and purify the principles as well as to reform the habits. For this purpose a youth must study himself, watch his steps, and compare his thoughts and acts with his rule. The more knowledge of himself he gains, the more humble will he be, and perhaps the less confident in his own strength. But the discipline will be always found most valuable which is acquired by resisting small present gratifications to secure a prospective greater and higher one. It is the noblest work in self-education,—for

> Real glory
> Springs from the silent conquest of ourselves,
> And without that the conqueror is nought
> But the first slave.

Many popular books have been written for the purpose of communicating to the public the grand secret of making money. But there is no secret whatever about it, as the proverbs of every nation abundantly testify. "Take care of the pennies and the pounds will take care of themselves." "Diligence is the mother of good luck." "No pains no gains." "No sweat so sweet." "Work and thou shalt have." "The world is his who has patience and industry." "Better go to bed supperless than rise in debt." Such are specimens of the proverbial philosophy, embodying the hoarded experience of many generations, as to the best means of thriving in the world. They were current in people's mouths long before books were invented; and like other popular proverbs they were the first codes of popular morals. Moreover they have stood the test of time, and the experience of every day still bears witness to their accuracy, force, and soundness. The proverbs of Solomon are full of wisdom as to the force of industry, and the use and abuse of money:—"He that is slothful in work is brother to him that is a great waster." "Go to the ant thou sluggard; consider her ways and be wise." Poverty, says the preacher, shall come upon the idler, "as one that travelleth, and want as an armed man;" but of the industrious and upright, "the hand of the diligent maketh rich." "The drunkard and the glutton shall come to poverty; and drowsiness shall clothe a man with rags." "Seest thou a man diligent in his business? he shall stand before kings." But above all, "It is better to get wisdom than gold; for wisdom is better than rubies, and all the things that may be desired are not to be compared to it."

Simple industry and thrift will go far towards making any person of ordinary working faculty comparatively independent in his means. Even a working man may be so, provided he will carefully husband his resources, and watch the little outlets of useless expenditure. A penny is a very small matter, yet the comfort of thousands of families depends upon the proper spending and saving of pennies. If a man allows the little pennies, the results of his hard work, to slip out of his fingers—some to the beershop, some this way and some that—he will find that his life is little raised above one of mere animal drudgery. On the other hand, if he take care of the pennies—putting some weekly into a benefit society or an insurance fund, others into a savings' bank, and confiding the rest to his wife to be carefully laid out, with a view to the comfortable maintenance and education of his family—he will soon find that this attention to small matters will abundantly repay him, in increasing means, growing comfort at home, and a mind comparatively free from fears as to the future. And if a working man have high ambition and possess richness in spirit,—a kind of wealth which far transcends all mere worldly possessions—he may not only help himself, but be a profitable helper of others in his path through life. That this is no impossible thing even for a common labourer in a workshop, may be illustrated by the remarkable career of Thomas Wright of Manchester, who not only attempted but succeeded in the reclamation of many criminals while working for weekly wages in a foundry.

Accident first directed Thomas Wright's attention to the difficulty encountered by liberated convicts in returning to habits of honest industry. His mind was shortly possessed by the subject; and to remedy the evil became the purpose of his life. Though he worked from six in the morning till six at night, still there were leisure minutes that he could call his own—more especially his Sundays—and these he employed in the service of convicted criminals; a class then far more neglected than they are now. But a few minutes a day, well employed, can effect a great deal; and it will scarcely be credited, that in ten years this working man, by steadfastly holding to his purpose, succeeded in rescuing not fewer than three hundred felons from continuance in a life of villany! He came to be regarded as the moral physician of the Manchester Old Bailey; and where the Chaplain and all others failed, Thomas Wright often succeeded. Children he thus restored reformed to their parents; sons and daughters otherwise lost, to their homes; and many a returned convict did he contrive to settle down to honest and industrious pursuits. The task was by no means easy. It required money, time, energy, prudence, and above all, character, and the confidence which character invariably inspires. The most remarkable circumstance was that Wright relieved many of these poor outcasts out of the comparatively small wages earned by him at foundry work. He did all this on an income which did not average, during his working career, 100*l*. per annum; and yet, while he was able to bestow substantial aid on criminals, to whom he owed no more than the service of kindness which every human being owes to another, he also maintained his family in comfort, and was, by frugality and carefulness, enabled to lay by a store of savings against his approaching old age. Every week he apportioned his income with deliberate care; so much for the indispensable necessaries of food and clothing, so much for the landlord, so much for the schoolmaster, so much for the poor and needy; and the lines of distribution were resolutely observed. By such means did this humble workman pursue his great work, with the results we have so briefly described. Indeed, his career affords one of the most remarkable and striving illustrations of the force of purpose in a man, of the might of small means carefully and sedulously applied, and, above all, of the power which an energetic and upright character invariably exercises upon the lives and conduct of others.

There is no discredit, but honour, in every right walk of industry, whether it be in tilling the ground, making tools, weaving fabrics, or selling the products behind a counter. A youth may handle a yard-stick, or measure a piece of ribbon; and there will be no discredit in doing so, unless he allows his mind to have no higher range than the stick and ribbon; to be as short as the one, and as narrow as the other. "Let not those blush who *have*," said Fuller, but those who *have not* a lawful calling." And Bishop Hall said, "Sweet is the destiny of all trades, whether of the brow or of the mind." Men who have raised themselves from a humble calling, need not be ashamed, but rather ought to be proud of the difficulties they have surmounted. An American President, when asked what was his coat-of-arms, remembering that he had been a hewer of wood in his youth, replied, "A pair of shirt sleeves." A French doctor once taunted Flechier, Bishop of Nimes, who had been a tallow-chandler in his youth, with the meanness of his origin, to which Flechier replied, "If you had been born in the same condition that I was, you would still have been but a maker of candles."

Nothing is more common than energy in money-making, quite independent of any higher object than its accumulation. A man who devotes himself to this pursuit, body and soul, can scarcely fail to become rich. Very little brains will do: spend less than you earn; add guinea to guinea; scrape and save; and the pile of gold will gradually rise. Osterwald the Parisian banker, began life a poor man. He was accustomed every evening to drink a pint of beer for supper at a tavern which he visited, during which he collected and pocketed all the corks that he could lay his hands on. In eight years he had collected as many corks as sold for eight louis d'ors. With that sum he laid the foundations of his fortune—gained mostly by stock-jobbing; leaving at his death some three millions of francs. John Foster has cited a striking illustration of what this kind of determination will do in money-making. A young man who ran through his patrimony, spending it in profligacy, was at length reduced to utter want and despair. He rushed out of his house intending to put an end to his life, and stopped on arriving at an eminence overlooking what were once his estates. He sat down, ruminated for a time, and rose with the determination that he would recover them. He returned to the streets, saw a load of coals which had been shot out of a cart on to the pavement before a house, offered to carry them in, and was employed. He thus earned a few pence, requested some meat and drink as a gratuity, which was given him, and the pennies were laid by. Pursuing this menial labour, he earned and saved more pennies; accumulated sufficient to enable him to purchase some cattle, the value of which he understood, and these he sold to advantage. He proceeded by degrees to undertake larger transactions, until at length he became rich. The result was, that he more than recovered his possessions, and died an inveterate miser. When he was buried, mere earth went to earth. With a nobler spirit, the same determination might have enabled such a man to be a benefactor to others as well as to himself. But the life and its end in this case were alike sordid.

To provide for others and for our own comfort and independence in old age, is honourable, and greatly to be commended; but to hoard for mere wealth's sake is the characteristic of the narrow-souled and the miserly. It is against the growth of this habit of inordinate saving that the wise man needs most carefully to guard himself: else, what in youth was simple economy, may in old age grow into avarice, and what was a duty in the one case, may become a vice in the other. It is the *love* of money—not money itself—which is "the root of evil,"—a love which narrows and contracts the soul, and closes it against generous life and action. Hence, Sir Walter Scott makes one of his characters declare that "the penny siller slew more souls than the naked sword slew bodies." It is one of the defects of business too exclusively followed, that it insensibly tends to a mechanism of character. The business man gets into a rut, and often does not look beyond it. If he lives for himself only, he becomes apt to regard other human beings only in so far as they minister to his ends. Take a leaf from such men's ledger and you have their life.

Worldly success, measured by the accumulation of money, is no doubt a very dazzling thing; and all men are naturally more or less the admirers of worldly success. But though men of persevering, sharp, dexterous, and unscrupulous habits, ever on the watch to push opportunities, may and do "get on" in the world, yet it is quite possible that they may not possess the slightest elevation of character, nor a particle of real goodness. He who recognizes no higher logic than that of the shilling, may become a very rich man, and yet remain all the while an exceedingly poor creature. For riches are no proof whatever of moral worth; and their glitter often serves only to draw attention to the worthlessness of their possessor, as the light of the glowworm reveals the grub.

The manner in which many allow themselves to be sacrificed to their love of wealth reminds one of the cupidity of the monkey—that caricature of our species. In Algiers, the Kabyle peasant attaches a gourd, well fixed, to a tree, and places within it some rice. The gourd has an opening merely sufficient to admit the monkey's paw. The creature comes to the tree by night, inserts his paw, and grasps his booty. He tries to draw it back, but it is clenched, and he has not the wisdom to unclench it. So there he stands till morning, when he is caught, looking as foolish as may be, though with the prize in his grasp. The moral of this little story is capable of a very extensive application in life.

The power of money is on the whole over-estimated. The greatest things which have been done for the world have not been accomplished by rich men, or by subscription lists, but by men generally of small pecuniary means. Christianity has propagated over half the world by men of the poorest class; and the greatest thinkers, discoverers, inventors, and artists, have been men of moderate wealth, many of them little raised above the condition of manual labourers in point of worldly circumstances. And it will always be so. Riches are oftener an impediment than a stimulus to action; and in many cases they are quite as much a misfortune as a blessing. The youth who inherits wealth is apt to have life made too easy for him, and he soon grows sated with it, because he has nothing left to desire. Having no special object to struggle for, he finds time hangs heavy on his hands; he remains morally and spiritually asleep; and his position in society is often no higher than that of a polypus over which the tide floats.

> His only labour is to kill the time,
> And labour dire it is, and weary woe.

Yet the rich man, inspired by a right spirit, will spurn idleness as unmanly; and if he bethink himself of the responsibilities which attach to the possession of wealth and property he will feel even a higher call to work than men of humbler lot. This, however, must be admitted to be by no means the practice of life. The golden mean of Agur's perfect prayer is, perhaps, the best lot of all, did we but know it: "Give me neither poverty nor riches; feed me with food convenient for me." The late Joseph Brotherton, M.P., left a fine motto to be recorded upon his monument in the Peel Park at Manchester,—the declaration in his case being strictly true: "My riches consisted not in the greatness of my possessions, but in the smallness of my wants." He rose from the humblest station, that of a factory boy, to an eminent position of usefulness, by the simple exercise of homely honesty, industry, punctuality, and self-denial. Down to the close of his life, when not attending Parliament, he did duty as minister in a small chapel in Manchester to which he was attached; and in all things he made it appear, to those who knew him in private life, that the glory he sought was *not* "to be seen of men," or to excite their praise, but to earn the consciousness of discharging the every-day duties of life, down to the smallest and humblest of them, in an honest, upright, truthful, and loving spirit.

"Respectability," in its best sense, is good. The respectable man is one worthy of regard, literally worth turning to look at. But the respectability that consists in merely keeping up appearances is not worth looking at in any sense. Far better and more respectable is the good poor man than the bad rich one—better the humble silent man than the agreeable well-appointed rogue who keeps his gig. A well balanced and well-stored mind, a life full of useful purpose, whatever the position occupied in it may be, is of far greater importance than average worldly respectability. The highest object of life we take to be, to form a manly character, and to work out the best development possible, of body and spirit—of mind, conscience, heart, and soul. This is the end: all else ought to be regarded but as the means. Accordingly, that is not the most successful life in which a man gets the most pleasure, the most money, the most power or place, honour or fame; but that in which a man gets the most manhood, and performs the greatest amount of useful work and of human duty. Money is power after its sort, it is true; but intelligence, public spirit, and moral virtue, are powers too, and far nobler ones. . . .

The making of a fortune may no doubt enable some people to "enter society," as it is called; but to be esteemed there, they must possess qualities of mind, manners, or heart, else they are merely rich people, nothing more. There are men "in society" now, as rich as Croesus, who have no consideration extended towards them, and elicit no respect. For why? They are but as moneybags: their only power is in their till. The men of mark in society—the guides and rulers of opinion—the really successful and useful men—are not necessarily rich men; but men of sterling character, of disciplined experience, and of moral excellence. Even the poor man, like

Thomas Wright, though he possess but little of this world's goods, may, in the enjoyment of a cultivated nature, of opportunities used and not abused, of a life spent to the best of his means and ability, look down, without the slightest feeling of envy, upon the person of mere worldly success, the man of moneybags and acres.

32. Sexual Roles: Victorian Progress?

ONE OF SEVERAL ways in which the Victorians dealt with sex was to pretend it did not exist. Where did all those children come from? This was the age of the stork, the cabbage, the doctor's bag. Armies of children were kept in calculated ignorance of the elementary facts of life on the specious notion that knowledge meant abuse—a view, to be sure, sanctioned in *Genesis*. Victorian culture was built upon and reenforced well-defined sexual attitudes. Eighty years of change, as these two medical texts suggest, had eroded but not altered the basic conception of the role of men and women. The Victorians were scarcely a bloodless crew; there was fornication aplenty, homosexuality, masturbation—the full gamut of behavior of years before and after. But the rules of the game were different.

Victorian society, to function, depended on control and self-discipline. The traditional, slightly more relaxed sanctions and controls of the rural community could not work in urban society. Social persecution was invented to maintain cultural discipline, and it functioned with a vengeance in Victorian Britain. Upward social mobility, status consciousness, and drive were the necessary conditions for its success. Only the very high and very low in the social order could secure relative immunity from the demands for conformity. Even there, preference produced much the same behavioral discipline.

The Victorians wallowed in sentiment but avoided licentiousness. They believed (rightly) that sexual drives and fantasies were potentially dangerous and socially disruptive. Therefore they demanded compromises between art and life. Take Victorian sculpture—acres of asexual nudes. Few Victorians indulged in such excesses of virtue as piano "limbs." But from Dr. Thomas Bowdler's sterilizing efforts in Regency England, which put his name in our vocabulary, to the trauma of Ibsen plays, the Victorians attempted to conceal the more explicitly biological aspects of human relations and to deny that they were appropriately subjects of art.

Intention and result stumbled over each other. Sexual education was furtive, whispered, shrouded in mumbo jumbo—a mixture of extremely precise, confusingly general, and just plain wrong. What about the female orgasm? Under these circumstances, confusion may have been the happiest result. The sniggering, after-dark, peer-group orientation of boys, the hesitant half-education of girls had to engender fear and guilt. Although the double standard constrained respectable women, it also inhibited men. Pleasure was for men, procreation for women. But even pleasure was circumscribed and laden with guilt. Prostitution was sordid, even brutal. Masturbation lay burdened with overwhelming taboos. Small wonder that English pornography displayed an obsession with flagellation. Sexual maladjustment remains a problem in far more open societies.

The respectable were oriented toward the home—family recreation, family holidays, a circumscribed social life with relatives and friends very like themselves. The Victorian age was probably an unusual age of marital fidelity. Positive inducement came from the code, but the lethal power of social criticism was a negative bar. No man could misbehave without threatening his own prospects and those of his family. In a culture oriented to achievement, Victorian repression was self-imposed and maintained. Gentlemen, by preference, sought one another's company in the club.

Moral and medical authorities proclaimed the subordination and inferiority of women. Their aspiration must always be toward marriage and the home. The apotheosis of the Victorian mother removed her from worldly circulation. She lived and died in her home. Her only real contact outside this world of her own or others like it was in her church. There she was allowed very limited range for her personality and her creative impulse. Most women were atrociously educated until the last third of the century. Their cultivation tended to be ritualistic rather than intellectual. Women were permitted to dabble in painting or to play the piano. That instrument, thus, came to be an important middle-class status symbol. Music lessons, as a conventional part of middle-class upbringing, date from the Victorian age.

The two selections presented here are from medical texts for lay persons. The ethical emphasis is obvious. They bridge eighty years (1837–1917), and the most striking feature is how little fundamental assumptions changed during that time. In spite of legal emancipation, access to professions, education, the vote, both doctors accept and affirm female inferiority. If it is more subtle by 1917, it is none the less real.

Recommended Reading

Serious consideration of sex in history is relatively recent and of uneven value. Gordon Rattway Taylor develops a fascinating general argument in *The Angel Makers* (London: 1958). Spurred by recent permissiveness and the resurrection of Victorian pornography, Steven Marcus developed a provocative argument in *The Other Victorians* (New York: 1966). Morse Peckham takes a different view of that cultural and historical problem in *Art and Pornography* (New York: 1969). Walter Houghton discusses important aspects of the problem in *The Victorian Frame of Mind* (New Haven: 1957). Other valuable starting points include P. T. Cominos, "Late Victorian Sexual Respectability and the Social System," *International Review of Social History*,

VIII (1963), 18–48, 216–250, J. A. Banks, *Prosperity and Parenthood* (London: 1954), J. A. and O. Banks, *Feminism and Family Planning* (New York: 1964), R. Wood, *Children, 1773–1890* (London: 1969), P. Thompson, *The Victorian Heroine* (London: 1956), and R. Pearsall, *The Worm in the Bud: The World of Victorian Sexuality* (London: 1969).

MICHAEL RYAN,
PHYSIOLOGY OF THE SEXUAL ORGANS

. . . In common with all parts of the body, the brain becomes developed, the intellectual functions are augmented, man is susceptible of the highest conceptions of the mind, the principles of life superabound in his constitution, and he vigorously performs all the noble pursuits assigned him by nature.

Woman, on the contrary, delicate and tender, always preserves some of the infantine constitution. The texture of her organs do not lose all their original softness or assume the strength of those of her companion; her eyes become brilliant and expressive, and all the graces and charms of youth illumine her person. Her bosom throbs with tender inquietudes, her character loses its infantile vivacity, her manner and taste becomes analagous to those of a full grown female, her passions become stronger and more constant, her moral and physical sensibility are greater, and she feels a sentiment hitherto unknown to her—the impulse of love—the desire of marriage.

Amidst this universal disorder of the economy, the excitement of the reproductive organs predominates, and causes the extraordinary and incomprehensible phenomena already described. Nature instinctively points out her rights. Every effort is now made by parents to suppress voluptuous ideas, but the secret thought of amorous pleasure cannot be extinguished. Nevertheless, an enjoyment purely physical or animal is not the object of research; the heart opens to the most tender sentiments, and guides the first movements of the sexes. Until this time they were actuated either by self-love, parental affection, or esteem for the youth of their own sexes; but now paternal tenderness and mere affection are

Source: From *The Philosophy of Marriage in Its Social, Moral, and Physical Relations* (London: 1837), pp. 130–133, 154–157.

Source: From *An Introduction to the Physiology and Psychology of Sex* (London: 1917), pp. 94–99.

insufficient for their happiness. Their well-being exists in another individual, and they think that they cannot enjoy real existence but in the intimate union of their body, soul, and heart, with one of an opposite sex to their own. They meet, their tastes, ages, and sentiments are similar; and now commences the scene of their innocent amours. What delightful reflections are offered to the study of a moral and philosophic mind by the innocent amours of two young persons, who know no other motives for their actions than the pure inspirations of nature and the heart! The strictest chastity presides at their first interviews; a word, a glance, a whisper, the pressure of a trembling hand, are now the enjoyments of happiness. They do not approach each other but with a respectful fear; they dissemble towards each other the nature of the sentiments which agitate them; they look "unutterable things."

In proportion as their visits are more frequent, and their physical love is increased, which it is by the excitement caused by their meetings, their interviews are more numerous, their conversations become longer, more delicate, more intimate; a reciprocal and exclusive confidence is established between them, the trembling hand reposes longer in that of its admirer, they embrace, their hearts palpitate, a secret fire consumes them, and they finally vow to taste legitimate pleasure, after swearing eternal fidelity to each other before the altar.

This, however, is the age at which the youth of both sexes should act in strict accordance with the precepts of religion and morals, as errors committed now are too often irretrievable. The tender sex, which are the objects of the most ardent fire of zealous adoration, and who burn themselves with the same flame, must never yield to the slightest freedom which is contrary to modesty and honour. They must not countenance for a moment obtrusive familiarity, much less the slightest immodest advances, or their ruin and degradation are inevitable. The usual result of impertinent familiarity, of illicit or anticipated love, is disgust, desertion, and indelible disgrace. A virtuous and firm resolution is the only safeguard, and a fixed determination not to remain alone, or beyond the hearing of others, with him who has captivated the heart. The passion of love is as inherent in mankind as the function of digestion or respiration, and must be gratified as well as other wants. It is, however, less essential to individual existence than other functions; but when it is established at puberty, as it is in almost all persons, it must be gratified; and human intervention or laws cannot restrain or extinguish it, except in a very few, if in any, instances.

The secretion of the sexual fluids is intended by nature for the conservation of the species. About the fourteenth or fifteenth year, in temperate climates, the sexual organs of boys become developed, and a fluid is secreted by the testicles, termed seminal or spermatic, which is destined for the perpetuation of the species. This fluid accumulates in receptacles provided for it (*vesiculæ seminales*), and not only excites the sexual organs, but every part of the body. The functions of the mind are improved, the digestion becomes more vigorous, the circulation of blood is more rapid in every organ, which is abundantly nourished, and performs its function with much more energy than before this period of life. Hence, we observe the body developes with rapidity, and the individual in a short time loses the characteristics of boyhood, and acquires those of adolescence, or manhood.

Though the sexual organs rapidly develope from the fourteenth to the twentieth year, yet they do not acquire their complete growth or functions before the twenty-fifth, sometimes not until the thirtieth year; and this is the age most proper for marriage.

The body of man is not fully developed before the twenty-fifth year of age; the spermatic fluid is less abundant and fitted for reproduction; and persons under this age generally beget delicate sickly infants, which seldom arrive at maturity. Sexual indulgence, or unnatural excitement of the virile organ, before the age of twenty-one, according to our laws, but before the age of twenty-five, according to the laws of nature, not only retards the development of the genital organs, but of the whole body, impairs the strength, injures the constitution, and shortens life. . . .

According to Venette, complete efforts do not exceed six or seven acts; and men who exceed this number, "quibus rigidus adhuc in inguine nervus," ejaculate no more, or sometimes have emissions of blood. Tissot relates examples of the last disease in his Traite Sur l'Onanisme. When we remember the limited capacity of the seminal receptacles, we must at once perceive the utter impossibility of numerous coitions, even allowing the secretion of semen to be increased by them. But as the genital power will vary according to age, habit, temperament, occupation, climate, and season, it must differ in different individuals, and cannot be properly estimated, or a positive rule laid down respecting it.

It is not to be supposed that when pleasure is most vivid conception takes place more readily, as the contrary is often the fact, "non
eo quò salacior mulier, eò fecundior;" for when the uterus is in a
state of extreme and too frequent excitement, it often loses its
retentive power. We see this exemplified in the lower orders of
mammiferous animals, over which it is often necessary to pour cold
water after copulation, to excite the contraction of the uterus. The
same reason explains the infertility of prostitutes and courtesans,
who rarely conceive, unless after intercourse with persons whom
they prefer. In fact, a uterus incessantly open and stimulated, has a
tendency to evacuate itself, and repeated venereal enjoyments induce excessive menstruation, mucous discharges, and abortions. In
such cases conception rarely occurs, unless the mind be intently
fixed upon one person, and there is one undivided love. It has been
observed that prostitutes who were infertile for years, have become
mothers after transportation to Botany Bay, when they became
restrained by marriage. In the same manner, when men abuse the
end of marriage, they have no children, because they secrete semen
which is not sufficiently elaborated, and which is too feeble; and
hence polygamy is much less favourable to population than
monogamy. Chastity, on the contrary, augments the vigour of the
organs and amorous ardour, and is the surest means of fecundity.
Hence, those newly married persons who have observed a strict
chastity before their union, procreate immediately, and their offspring is vigorous; while dissipated or aged persons seldom have
children, and if they have, the offspring seldom arrives at the adult
age. For this reason, animals which copulate at certain times only,
engender by one act. But a rigid chastity enfeebles the passion of
love, and may be the cause of infertility.

Abstinence from venereal enjoyment, for a few days or weeks,
favours fecundity, and invigorates both mind and body. The
ancient classic and philosophic authors held that all great intellectual generation required corporeal continence. Minerva, the goddess of genius, and all the muses, were virgins. Horace lauded the
favourite of Apollo for having abstained from women and wine,
"Abstinuit venere et vino, sudavit et alsit," and Virgil wrote still
more forcibly. Bacon observed that no one of great genius, of
antiquity, had been addicted to women; and he stated that among
the moderns, the illustrious Newton had never enjoyed sexual
intercourse. This fact confirms the remark made by Aretæus, and
since verified by all physiologists, that continence, or the reabsorp-

tion of the semen into the animal economy, impressed the whole organism with an extreme tension and vigour, excited the brain, and exalted the faculty of thought. From these effects, courage, magnanimity, all the virtues, and corporeal vigour resulted.

The abuse of enjoyment, on the contrary, enervates the body, destroys the memory, extinguishes the imagination, degrades the soul, and renders it stupid. Thus, idiots who abuse this function are excessively lascivious; and eunuchs are remarkably deficient in genius—they want the organs which are destined to secrete the semen, and this plunges the mind as well as the body into a languor and debility almost infantine. It has also been observed that mental exaltation and madness do not manifest themselves before the age of puberty, nor in old age, but in the adult age especially, by the retention of the sperm or ovarian fluid; and hence, castration and pregnancy have radically cured maniacs. Nothing is more certain than this, that animals and plants shorten their existence by multiplied sexual enjoyments. It was to secure vigour of mind and body that the founders of certain religions prescribed chastity and celibacy to their ministers. This rule is in some degree accordant with physiology; for it is well known that our moral and physical powers are diminished by coition, because we impart a portion of our physical and intellectual endowments to our offspring, and diminish them in ourselves.

A most important train of consequences to society and government follow from this inquiry, which is, that the state of morals has a prodigious influence on the population of empires. It is proved beyond doubt that the population increases much more in the country, and in villages, than in large cities. The citizens pass their youth in dissipation, and marry late for the sake of interest. But in the country, illegitimate unions cannot occur without exposure, as every one knows the conduct of his neighbour; a man marries early in life, he is a stranger to luxury and effeminacy and his offspring is generally healthful, vigorous, and numerous.

S. HERBERT,
PHYSIOLOGY AND PSYCHOLOGY OF SEX

We have thus far given a short survey of the sex phenomena as they appear among animals, and found that they gradually lead up to the manifestations of sex as seen in man. This point has to be kept well in view whilst dealing with the psychical aspect of the human sex impulse. For it is here especially that prejudice or predilection tends to warp our judgments. The primary biological factors of sex in man are so overlaid with a complex fabric of social tradition and custom that it is difficult to arrive at its real significance. Only an unbiased study of all available scientific data will help us towards a proper understanding of the respective spheres of man and woman. To attain this end, we must first of all consider the physical differences of the two sexes in man, so far as they express a fundamental distinction between the male and female organisation.

The most striking feature distinguishing man from woman is, of course, his greater size and strength. The motor energy of man is at least a third greater than that of woman. His greater power and activity is shown not only in the more strongly built limbs, but also in the relatively greater chest development. In woman, on the contrary, the abdominal and pelvic regions are comparatively larger, the vegetative and reproductive functions playing a more important rôle. This tendency of woman is indicated by the greater amount of fatty tissue developed by her, which gives the female figure its beautiful roundness and swelling curves, in contra-distinction to the muscular development of man with his rugged outlines. Though woman is of smaller stature than man, she attains her full height at an earlier age; indeed, there is a period before puberty when girls are actually taller and heavier than boys of the same age. Puberty is reached earlier by woman. But this is not all. In many respects the female remains nearer the infantile type, while man, during his development, approaches more the simian (ape-like) and senile type. This greater youthfulness of woman shows itself in many ways. Thus, the child possesses a relatively larger head and abdomen, but a relatively smaller chest, limbs and face than adult man. In all these points woman is nearer to the child, as also in the more infantile formation of the skull. But this relatively early arrest in growth cannot be interpreted as an inferiority in woman. On the contrary, it has been shown that, just as the young ape is in comparison more human than the adult ape, so the human child is really in advance of the human adult type, which retrogresses somewhat with age to the simian and senile form. In this respect woman leads in the evolution of the race, and man follows.

The most distinctive secondary sex characters of woman lie in the pelvis and the breast, features which are closely bound up with her reproductive function. While the male pelvis is long and narrow, the female pelvis is widened out, the brim being broad and its lower parts more open and separated. This, of course, is an adaptation to the function of child-bearing, a wide maternal pelvis being essential for the birth of the human child, with its large head. Indeed, it has been established as a fact, that the higher the race of man the larger the female pelvis; that is, the differentiation of the sexes as expressed by the female form increases with civilisation. The development of the breast in woman is, of course, an adaptation towards the same end; for suckling is the natural function of a mother.

There exists also a distinct difference in the general metabolism of man and woman. We have already found it a general rule that the male is more active, or katabolic, the female more passive, or anabolic. Now, this has its cause in the different composition of the blood in the two sexes. The blood of man has a higher specific gravity and contains more red blood-corpuscles; the blood of woman is more watery and contains less iron, the iron, as Bunge suggested, being stored in the maternal organism even before the first pregnancy, ready for use for the fœtus. This accounts for the tendency to anæmia and chlorosis shown by growing girls. Altogether, the rate of metabolism is lower in woman, her vital capacity less. On the other hand, she bears illness and injuries better, and has a longer life.

In accordance with these physical differences between man and woman, we find corresponding physiological and psychological characteristics. Man's physiological reaction—i.e., his response to sense-impressions—is more rapid and precise than woman's. Thus, man's activity shows a higher working power, it is quicker and at the same time more effective. Man is capable of powerful spurts. Woman, on the contrary, works at a lower level, but her output of energy is more continuous; she tires less quickly than man.

Coming now to mental characteristics, we find as an outstanding womanly trait the great impressionability of the female mind—its "affectability," as Havelock Ellis has called it. Thus, though women have not, on the whole, a finer discrimination of sense-impressions, they respond much more quickly to new stimuli, and make fresh adjustments more readily. Altogether, women are more excitable and emotional than men. Thus, they are more amenable to hypnotic suggestion, and more liable to convulsions and hysteria. The lesser forms of nervous excitations are also more frequent among women, such as blushing, weeping, laughing, etc. Their nervous organisation is less stable; they respond readily to new stimuli, but become exhausted quickly, thus showing a lack of staying power like children and primitive man. This greater affectability of woman has, of course, also its good side. Thus, women adjust themselves much more easily to new circumstances than man. They have a quick, intuitive apprehension of facts, are more nimble in mind and more resourceful. At the same time, women show less variability than man; they do not reach extremes so often, either of genius or of idiocy. They thus show a greater racial stability, tending more to the norm. This, together with their more passive nature, which inclines them to endurance and self-sacrifice, makes them "in form, function, and instinct, restful to men tortured by their vagrant energies." In short, woman, being nearer to the child, is nearer to Nature, and forms the best *pendant* to the ever-active, striving, restless male. The differentiation of the sexes in their mental respects is thus in full conformity with their respective shares in the reproductive functions. This fundamental distinctive trait of the sexes finds further corroboration in the erotic differences of man and woman.

We have already seen in a previous chapter that it is, as a rule, the male who is active and roaming and seeks the female during mating. The female, on the contrary, plays a more passive rôle, and waits to be wooed. But here a more complex factor is introduced. For the female does not yield immediately, but plays a sort of game of refusal and acceptance. This coyness, characteristic of the human female, is the psychic equivalent of the more primitive instinct, as observed among animals. For the female animal admits the male only during the heat period, and refuses him at any other time. This playfulness, which has its rôle during courtship, tends to heighten the erotic emotion, and thus enhances the process of tumescence in both partners alike. The same emotion is the germ of modesty as developed in the human species. Modesty has, in fact, become one of the most distinctive secondary sex characters of woman. Coquetry, too, a typical feminine trait, is but the social form of the same instinctive female behaviour, and is thus of deep biological and psychological significance. The woman has to be aroused in order to be amenable to passion and love, and it is the task of the male to arouse her. In fact, it may be said, the amatory contest serves the purpose of sexual selection in man.

The aggressive attitude of the male shows itself also in his love for domination, while, once more, the passivity of the female expresses itself in submissiveness and abandonment. This relative passivity of woman has given rise to the idea that the sex instinct of woman is weaker than that of man. But, as Havelock Ellis has pointed out, the passivity of woman as regards the sexual impulse is only apparent. This misconception is due to several facts. First, the sexual impulse in woman tends to develop at a later age than in man; secondly, it remains generally diffuse and in abeyance until it is aroused by love; and, thirdly, woman is capable of submitting to the sexual act in complete passivity. But this last state is by no means the normal one. We have already pointed out that woman takes a relatively active part in the sexual act. In order that she may derive the pleasure of complete orgasm, a proper state of tumescence must be produced in her, which is only possible by appropriate excitation. As a matter of fact, man reaches the climax very much sooner, the orgasm in woman being attained more slowly. Her sex feeling is altogether more diffuse, more extensive, while in man it is intensive, focussed, as it were, in a single point. For this reason, the sex impulse in woman is in need of stimulation. And we must add, as love in woman takes on a more psychical than physical aspect, it is not every man that is capable of rousing the right emotions in a given woman. In fact, while man's sexual impulse may be said to be centred chiefly in the sex act, with woman it is the consequence which is of vital importance. There exists, as Walter Heape has expressed it, a fundamental antagonism between the sexes in this respect. While the male, with his craving for passion and change, has subjugated the female to his own ends, woman, being first and foremost a mother, has built up the family system, and in her turn bent man to her interests. We see here once more the elementary difference in the reproductive organisation of man and woman. To man "love is an episode"; to woman it is her whole life.

33. The Waning of Optimism: Queries about Progress

FROM TIME TO TIME the English have a poet laureate who deserves the job. One such was Alfred, Lord Tennyson (1809–1892). His extensive writings have many of the finest and best remembered moments in the

English language. Tennyson championed most Victorian virtues, but he also had his doubts. Among his early enthusiastic poems was "Locksley Hall," which carried the joy to be alive and hope for the future that animated so many early Victorians. "Locksley Hall Sixty Years After" has lost that easy optimism. He touches upon just a few of the problems—democracy, Ireland, evolution, naturalism, the failures of liberal society—in the section given here, and he does so with forceful lyricism. Gladstone was upset, and wrote a long, critical review of Tennyson's poem. Well he might, for the poet was questioning the assumptions and content of contemporary life.

ALFRED, LORD TENNYSON,
LOCKSLEY HALL SIXTY YEARS AFTER (1886)

. . . .
Truth for truth, and good for good! The Good, the True, the
    Pure, the Just—
Take the charm "for ever" from them, and they crumble into
    dust.

Gone the cry of "Forward, Forward," lost within a glowing
    gloom;
Lost, or only heard in silence from the silence of a tomb.

Half the marvels of my morning, triumphs over time and space,
Staled by frequence, shrunk by usage into commonest common-
    place!

"Forward" rang the voices then, and of the many mine was one.
Let us hush this cry of "forward" till ten thousand years have
    gone.

Far among the vanish'd races, old Assyrian kings would flay
Captives whom they caught in battle—iron-hearted victors they.

Ages after, while in Asia, he that led the wild Moguls,
Timur built his ghastly tower of eighty thousand human skulls,

Then, and here in Edward's time, an age of noblest English names,
Christian conquerors took and flung the conquer'd Christian into
    flames.

Source: From "Locksley Hall Sixty Years After" (1886).

Love your enemy, bless your haters, said the Greatest of the great;
Christian love among the Churches look'd the twin of heathen
    hate.

From the golden alms of Blessing man had coin'd himself a curse:
Rome of Caesar, Rome of Peter, which was crueller? which was
    worse?

France had shown a light to all men, preach'd a Gospel, all men's
    good;
Celtic Demos rose a Demon, shriek'd and slaked the light with
    blood.

Hope was ever on her mountain, watching till the day begun—
Crown'd with sunlight—over darkness—from the still unrisen sun.

Have we grown at last beyond the passions of the primal clan?
"Kill your enemy, for you hate him," still, "your enemy" was a
    man.

Have we sunk below them? peasants maim the helpless horse, and
    drive
Innocent cattle under thatch, and burn the kindlier brutes alive.

Brutes, the brutes are not your wrongers—burnt at midnight,
    found at morn,
Twisted hard in mortal agony with their offspring, born-unborn,

Clinging to the silent mother! Are we devils? are we men?
Sweet St. Francis of Assisi, would that he were here again,

He that in his Catholic wholeness used to call the very flower
Sisters, brothers—and the beasts—whose pains are hardly less than
    ours!

Chaos, Cosmos! Cosmos, Chaos! who can tell how all will end?
Read the wide world's annals, you, and take your wisdom for your
    friend.

Hope the best, but hold the Present fatal daughter of the Past,
Shape your heart to front the hour, but dream not that the hour
    will last.

Ay, if dynamite and revolver leave you courage to be wise:
When was age so cramm'd with menace? madness? written, spoken
    lies?

Envy wears the mask of Love, and, laughing sober fact to scorn,
Cries to Weakest as to Strongest, "Ye are equals, equal-born."

Equal-born? O yes, if yonder hill be level with the flat.
Charm us, Orator, till the Lion look no larger than the Cat,

Till the Cat thro' that mirage of overheated language loom
Larger than the Lion,—Demos end in working its own doom.

Russia burst our Indian barrier, shall we fight her? shall we yield?
Pause! before you sound the trumpet, hear the voices from the
    field.

Those three hundred millions under one Imperial sceptre now,
Shall we hold them? shall we loose them? take the suffrage of the
    plow.

Nay, but these would feel and follow Truth if only you and you,
Rivals of realm-ruining party, when you speak were wholly true.

Plowmen, Shepherd, have I found, and more than once, and still
    could find,
Sons of God, and kings of men in utter nobleness of mind,

Truthful, trustful, looking upward to the practised hustings-liar;
So the Higher wields the Lower, while the Lower is the Higher.

Here and there a cotter's babe is royal-born by right divine;
Here and there my lord is lower than his oxen or his swine.

Chaos, Cosmos! Cosmos, Chaos! once again the sickening game;
Freedom, free to slay herself, and dying while they shout her
    name.

Step by step we gain'd a freedom known to Europe, known to
    all;
Step by step we rose to greatness, —thro' the tonguesters we may
    fall.

You that woo the Voices—tell them "old experience is a fool,"
Teach your flatter'd kings that only those who cannot read can
    rule.

Pluck the mighty from their seat, but set no meek ones in their
    place;
Pillory Wisdom in your markets, pelt your offal at her face.

Tumble Nature heel o'er head, and, yelling with the yelling street,
Set the feet above the brain and swear the brain is in the feet.

Bring the old dark ages back without the faith, without the hope,
Break the State, the Church, the Throne, and roll their ruins down
    the slope.

Authors—essayist, atheist, novelist, realist, rhymster, play your
    part,
Paint the mortal shame of nature with the living hues of Art.

Rip your brothers' vices open, strip your own foul passions bare;
Down with reticence, down with Reverence—forward—naked—
    let them stare.

Feed the budding rose of boyhood with the drainage of your
    sewer;
Send the drain into the fountain, lest the stream should issue pure.

Set the maiden fancies wallowing in the troughs of Zolaism,—
Forward, forward, ay and backward, downward too into the
    abysm.

Do your best to charm the worst, to lower the rising race of men;
Have we risen from out the beast, then back into the beast again?

Only "dust to dust" for me that sicken at your lawless din,
Dust in wholesome old-world dust before the newer world begin.

Heated am I? you—you wonder—well, it scarce becomes mine
    age—
Patience! let the dying actor mouth his last upon the stage.

Cries of unprogressive dotage ere the dotard fall asleep?
Noises of a current narrowing, not the music of a deep?

Ay, for doubtless I am old, and think gray thoughts, for I am
     gray:
After all the stormy changes shall we find a changeless May?

After madness, after massacre, Jacobinism and Jacquerie,
Some diviner force to guide us thro' the days I shall not see?

When the schemes and all the systems, Kingdoms and Republics
     fall,
Something kindlier, higher, holier—all for each and each for all?

All the full-brain, half-brain races, led by Justice, Love, and Truth;
All the millions one at length with all the visions of my youth?

All diseases quench'd by Science, no man halt, or deaf or blind;
Stronger ever born of weaker, lustier body, larger mind?

Earth at last a warless world, a single race, a single tongue—
I have seen her far away—for is not Earth as yet so young?—

Every tiger madness muzzled, every serpent passion kill'd,
Every grim ravine a garden, every blazing desert till'd,

Robed in universal harvest up to either pole she smiles,
Universal ocean softly washing all her warless Isles.

Warless? when her tens are thousands, and her thousands millions,
     then—
All her harvest all too narrow—who can fancy warless men?

Warless? war will die out late then. Will it ever? late or soon?
Can it, till this outworn earth be dead as yon dead world the
     moon?
. . . .
Forward, backward, backward, forward, in the immeasurable sea,
Sway'd by vaster ebbs and flows than can be known to you or
     me.

All the suns—are these but symbols of innumerable man,
Man or Mind that sees a shadow of the planner or the plan?

Is there evil but on earth? or pain in every peopled sphere?
Well be grateful for the sounding watchword "Evolution" here,

Evolution ever climbing after some ideal good,
And Reversion ever dragging Evolution in the mud.

What are men that He should heed us? cried the king of sacred
        song;
Insects of an hour, that hourly work their brother insect wrong,

While the silent Heavens roll, and Suns along their fiery way,
All their planets whirling round them, flash a million miles a day.

Many an Æon moulded earth before her highest, man, was born,
Many an Æon too may pass when earth is manless and forlorn,

Earth so huge, and yet so bounded—pools of salt, and plots of
        land—
Shallow skin of green and azure—chains of mountains, grains of
        sand!

Only That which made us, meant us to be mightier by and by,
Set the sphere of all the boundless Heavens within the human eye,

Sent the shadow of Himself, the boundless, thro' the human soul;
Boundless inward, in the atom, boundless outward, in the Whole.
. . . .
Here is Locksley Hall, my grandson, here the lion-guarded gate.
Not to-night in Locksley Hall—to-morrow—you, you come so
        late.

Wreck'd—your train—or all but wreck'd? a shatter'd wheel? a
        vicious boy!
Good, this forward, you that preach it, is it well to wish you
        joy?

Is it well that while we range with Science, glorying in the Time,
City children soak and blacken soul and sense in city slime?

There among the glooming alleys Progress halts on palsied feet,
Crime and hunger cast our maidens by the thousand on the street.

There the Master scrimps his haggard sempstress of her daily
    bread,
There a single sordid attic holds the living and the dead.

There the smouldering fire of fever creeps across the rotten floor,
And the crowded couch of incest in the warrens of the poor.

Nay, your pardon, cry your "forward," yours are hope and youth,
    but I—
Eighty winters leave the dog too lame to follow with the cry,

Lame and old, and past his time, and passing now into the night;
Yet I would the rising race were half as eager for the light.

Light the fading gleam of Even? light the glimmer of the dawn?
Aged eyes may take the glowing glimmer for the gleam with-
    drawn.

Far away beyond her myriad coming changes earth will be
Something other than the wildest modern guess of you and me.

Earth may reach her earthly-worst, or if she gain her earthly-best,
Would she find her human offspring this ideal man at rest?

Forward then, but still remember how the course of Time will
    swerve,
Crook and turn upon itself in many a backward streaming curve.

Knowledge

34. Science: Evolution

THE SUBSTITUTION of evolution for progress was a revolution in nineteenth-century thought. Charles Darwin (1809–1882) contributed *The
Origin of Species* (1859) and *The Descent of Man* (1871), two of the
most important milestones along the way. But Darwin's contributions,
important as they were, were neither the beginning nor the end of the
movement. The rejection of Newtonian cosmogony began before the

end of the eighteenth century. The world and universe were discovered to be dynamisms, not mechanisms, and that was a revolution in metaphysics.

The eighteenth century suffered from a deficient time sense, but this was no problem so long as history was relatively unimportant to philosophy. The Newtonian mechanistic cosmogony—with or without God the divine watchmaker—could be wound up in 4004 B.C. or 4,000,000,000 B.C. It did not really matter. History did matter in the dynamistic cosmogony of the nineteenth century, and science, considered as history, played a crucial role in redefining philosophy. The important point was not science as science, but science as history. The nebular hypothesis in astronomy; the concept of gradual, natural, uniformitarian change in geology; the first and second laws of thermodynamics in physics—all of these things altered cosmogony, not as science, but as history. They were the story of the universe and the world before man was and after he should cease to be.

Biology contributed evolution. Darwin actually did no more than apply Malthus to the world of plants and animals. We are not here concerned with the much-discussed limitations of his hypothesis (he presented it as nothing more than that). Darwin failed to allow for or understand genetics. Mutation for survival in species is not gradual; it is abrupt. Otherwise the species does not survive at all. The English white moth had to become gray-black practically within a generation to avoid extermination by birds on soot-stained tree trunks. Our concern should be less with what Darwin said as science than what he said as "value." For many, what Darwin implied in *The Origin of Species* and stated in *The Descent of Man* was neither science nor history; it was heresy.

There was no reversing the tide. Darwinian evolution did not destroy Victorian Christianity. Literal interpretation of scripture had already been jolted beyond recovery by other sciences and historical scholarship. Ethical and humane men took moral exception to what they found in their bibles. The overdramatized man-monkey controversy ran its unedifying course fairly quickly in the Huxley-Wilberforce debate of 1860. Those seriously upset by Darwin's findings were already suffering grave doubts. Darwin did no more than accelerate a process already begun, but he did achieve historical immortality. His name will live as long as the concept of evolution.

Darwinism also came to denominate important strands of social, economic, and political thought. Evolution filled the gap left by flagging religious sanction. It provided an unjustified extension of the evolutionary hypothesis to sustain exploitation and racism and to exacerbate the excesses of nationalism in the late nineteenth century. Politics absorbed the rhetoric of science. Supplications could be constructive (arguing for social legislation to make the nation "the fittest") or destructive (defending the perpetual subordination of black Africa as justified by science). All of these were perversions of an elaborate hypothesis worked out in painful detail over a lifetime. The hypochondriac naturalist, who seemed to have made it all possible, approved of few of them.

Recommended Reading

There is, needless to say, an ample literature on the subject. Jacques Barzun links Darwin to central movements in mid-nineteenth century culture in *Darwin, Marx, and Wagner* (Boston: 1941). Gertrude Himmelfarb has written a splendid analysis in *Darwin and the Darwinian Revolution* (New York: 1959). William Irvine constructed a clever, witty dual biography of Darwin and Huxley in *Apes, Angels, and Victorians* (New York: 1955). *Victorian Studies* published a Darwin Anniversary Issue of considerable interest in September 1959 (vol. III, no. 1).

CHARLES DARWIN,
DESCENT OF MAN

Through the means just specified, aided perhaps by others as yet undiscovered, man has been raised to his present state. But since he attained to the rank of manhood, he has diverged into distinct races, or as they may be more fitly called, sub-species. Some of these, such as the Negro and European, are so distinct that, if specimens had been brought to a naturalist without any further information, they would undoubtedly have been considered by him as good and true species. Nevertheless all the the races agree in so many unimportant details of structure and in so many mental peculiarities, that these can be accounted for only by inheritance from a common progenitor; and a progenitor thus characterised would probably deserve to rank as man.

It must not be supposed that the divergence of each race from the other races, and of all from a common stock, can be traced back to any one pair of progenitors. On the contrary, at every stage in the process of modification, all the individuals which were in any way better fitted for their conditions of life, though in different degrees, would have survived in greater numbers than the less well-fitted. The process would have been like that followed by man, when he does not intentionally select particular individuals, but breeds from all the superior individuals, and neglects the inferior. He thus slowly but surely modifies his stock, and uncon-

Source: From *The Descent of Man* (London: 1871), pp. 622–634.

sciously forms a new strain. So with respect to modifications acquired independently of selection, and due to variations arising from the nature of the organism and the action of the surrounding conditions, or from changed habits of life, no single pair will have been modified much more than the other pairs inhabiting the same country, for all will have been continually blended through free intercrossing.

By considering the embryological structure of man,—the homologies which he presents with the lower animals,—the rudiments which he retains,—and the reversions to which he is liable, we can partly recall in imagination the former condition of our early progenitors; and can approximately place them in their proper place in the zoological series. We thus learn that man is descended from a hairy, tailed quadruped, probably arboreal in its habits, and an inhabitant of the Old World. This creature, if its whole structure had been examined by a naturalist, would have been classed amongst the Quadrumana, as surely as the still more ancient progenitor of the Old and New World monkeys. The Quadrumana and all the higher mammals are probably derived from an ancient marsupial animal, and this through a long line of diversified forms, from some amphibian-like creature, and this again from some fish-like animal. In the dim obscurity of the past we can see that the early progenitor of all the Vertebrata must have been an aquatic animal, provided with branchiæ, with the two sexes united in the same individual, and with the most important organs of the body (such as the brain and heart) imperfectly or not at all developed. This animal seems to have been more like the larvæ of the existing marine Ascidians than any other known form.

The high standard of our intellectual powers and moral disposition is the greatest difficulty which presents itself, after we have been driven to this conclusion on the origin of man. But every one who admits the principle of evolution, must see that the mental powers of the higher animals, which are the same in kind with those of man, though so different in degree, are capable of advancement. Thus the interval between the mental powers of one of the higher apes and of a fish, or between those of an ant and scale-insect, is immense; yet their development does not offer any special difficulty; for with our domesticated animals, the mental faculties are certainly variable, and the variations are inherited. No one doubts that they are of the utmost importance to animals in a state of nature. Therefore the conditions are favourable for their development through natural selection. The same conclusion may be extended to man; the intellect must have been all-important to him, even at a very remote period, as enabling him to invent and use language, to make weapons, tools, traps, &c., whereby with the aid of his social habits, he long ago became the most dominant of all living creatures.

A great stride in the development of the intellect will have followed, as soon as the half-art and half-instinct of language came into use; for the continued use of language will have reacted on the brain and produced an inherited effect; and this again will have reacted on the improvement of language. As Mr. Chauncey Wright has well remarked, the largeness of the brain in man relatively to his body, compared with the lower animals, may be attributed in chief part to the early use of some simple form of language,—that wonderful engine which affixes signs to all sorts of objects and qualities, and excites trains of thought which would never arise from the mere impression of the senses, or if they did arise could not be followed out. The higher intellectual powers of man, such as those of ratiocination, abstraction, self-consciousness, &c., probably follow from the continued improvement and exercise of the other mental faculties.

The development of the moral qualities is a more interesting problem. The foundation lies in the social instincts, including under this term the family ties. These instincts are highly complex, and in the case of the lower animals give special tendencies towards certain definite actions; but the more important elements are love, and the distinct emotion of sympathy. Animals endowed with the social instincts take pleasure in one another's company, warn one another of danger, defend and aid one another in many ways. These instincts do not extend to all the individuals of the species, but only to those of the same community. As they are highly beneficial to the species, they have in all probability been acquired through natural selection.

A moral being is one who is capable of reflecting on his past actions and their motives—of approving of some and disapproving of others; and the fact that man is the one being who certainly deserves this designation, is the greatest of all distinctions between him and the lower animals. But in the fourth chapter I have endeavoured to shew that the moral sense follows, firstly, from the enduring and ever-present nature of the social instincts; secondly, from man's appreciation of the approbation and disapprobation of his fellows; and thirdly, from the high activity of his mental faculties, with past impressions extremely vivid; and in these latter respects he differs from the lower animals. Owing to this condition of mind, man cannot avoid looking both backwards and forwards, and comparing past impressions. Hence after some temporary desire or passion has mastered his social instincts, he reflects and compares the now weakened impression of such past impulses with the ever-present social instincts; and he then feels that sense of dissatisfaction which all unsatisfied instincts leave behind them, he therefore resolves to act differently for the future,—and this is conscience. Any instinct, permanently stronger or more enduring than another, gives rise to a feeling which we express by saying that it ought to be obeyed. A pointer dog, if able to reflect on his past conduct, would say to himself, I ought (as indeed we say of him) to have pointed at that hare and not have yielded to the passing temptation of hunting it.

Social animals are impelled partly by a wish to aid the members of their community in a general manner, but more commonly to perform certain definite actions. Man is impelled by the same general wish to aid his fellows; but has few or no special instincts. He differs also from the lower animals in the power of expressing his desires by words, which thus become a guide to the aid required and bestowed. The motive to give aid is likewise much modified in man: it no longer consists solely of a blind instinctive impulse, but is much influenced by the praise or blame of his fellows. The appreciation and the bestowal of praise and blame both rest on sympathy; and this emotion, as we have seen, is one of the most important elements of the social instincts. Sympathy, though gained as an instinct, is also much strengthened by exercise or habit. As all men desire their own happiness, praise or blame is bestowed on actions and motives according as they lead to this end; and as happiness is an essential part of the general good, the greatest-happiness principle indirectly serves as a nearly safe standard of right and wrong. As the reasoning powers advance and experience is gained, the remoter effects of certain lines of conduct on the character of the individual, and on the general good, are perceived; and then the self-regarding virtues come within the scope of public opinion, and receive praise, and their opposites blame. But with the less civilized nations reason often errs, and many bad customs and base superstitions come within the same scope, and are then esteemed as high virtues, and their breach as heavy crimes.

The moral faculties are generally and justly esteemed as of higher value than the intellectual powers. But we should bear in mind that the activity of the mind in vividly recalling past impressions is one of the fundamental, though secondary, bases of conscience. This affords the strongest argument for educating and stimulating in all possible ways the intellectual faculties of every human being. No doubt a man with a torpid mind, if his social affections and sympathies are well developed, will be led to good actions, and may have a fairly sensitive conscience. But whatever renders the imagination more vivid, and strengthens the habit of recalling and comparing past impressions, will make the conscience more sensitive, and may even somewhat compensate for weak social affections and sympathies.

The moral nature of man has reached its present standard partly through the advancement of his reasoning powers, and consequently of a just public opinion, but especially from his sympathies having been rendered more tender and widely diffused through the effects of habit, example, instruction, and reflection. It is not improbable that after long practice virtuous tendencies may be inherited. With the more civilized races, the conviction of the existence of an all-seeing Deity has had a potent influence on the advance of morality. Ultimately man does not accept the praise or blame of his fellows as his sole guide, though few escape this influence, but his habitual convictions, controlled by reason, afford him the safest rule. His conscience then becomes the supreme judge and monitor. Nevertheless the first foundation or origin of the moral sense lies in the social instincts, including sympathy: and these instincts no doubt were primarily gained, as in the case of the lower animals, through natural selection.

The belief in God has often been advanced as not only the greatest, but the most complete of all the distinctions between man and the lower animals. It is, however, impossible, as we have seen, to maintain that this belief is innate or instinctive in man. On the other hand, a belief in all-pervading spiritual agencies seems to be universal; and apparently follows from a considerable advance in man's reason, and from a still greater advance in his faculties of imagination, curiosity, and wonder. I am aware that the assumed instinctive belief in God has been used by many persons as an argument for His existence. But this is a rash argument, as we should thus be compelled to believe in the existence of many cruel and malignant spirits, only a little more powerful than man: for the belief in them is far more general than in a beneficent Deity. The idea of a universal and beneficent Creator does not seem to arise in the mind of man until he has been elevated by long-continued culture.

He who believes in the advancement of man from some low organized form will naturally ask, How does this bear on the belief in the immortality of the soul? The barbarous races of man, as Sir J. Lubbock has shown, possess no clear belief of this kind; but arguments derived from the primeval beliefs of savages are, as we have just seen, of little or no avail. Few persons feel any anxiety from the impossibility of determining at what precise period in the development of the individual, from the first trace of a minute germinal vesicle, man becomes an immortal being; and there is no greater cause for anxiety because the period cannot possibly be determined in the gradually ascending organic scale.

I am aware that the conclusions arrived at in this work will be denounced by some as highly irreligious; but he who denounces them is bound to show why it is more irreligious to explain the origin of man as a distinct species by descent from some lower form, through the laws of variation and natural selection, than to explain the birth of the individual through the laws of ordinary reproduction. The birth both of the species and of the individual are equally parts of that grand sequence of events which our minds refuse to accept as the result of blind chance. The understanding revolts at such a conclusion, whether or not we are able to believe that every slight variation of structure—the union of each pair in marriage—the dissemination of each seed—and other such events, have all been ordained for some special purpose.

Sexual selection has been treated at great length in this work: for, as I have attempted to show, it has played an important part in the history of the organic world. I am aware that much remains doubtful, but I have endeavored to give a fair view of the whole case. In the lower divisions of the animal kingdom, sexual selection seems to have done nothing: such animals are often affixed for life to the same spot, or have the sexes combined in the same individual, or, what is still more important, their perceptive and intellectual faculties are not sufficiently advanced to allow of the feelings of love and jealousy, or of the exertion of choice. When, however, we come to the Arthropoda and Vertebrata, even to the lowest classes in these two great Sub-Kingdoms, sexual selection has effected much.

In the several great classes of the animal kingdom—in mammals, birds, reptiles, fishes, insects, and even crustaceans—the differences between the sexes follow nearly the same rules. The males are almost always the wooers; and they alone are armed with special weapons for fighting with their rivals. They are generally stronger and larger than the females, and are endowed with the requisite qualities of courage and pugnacity. They are provided, either exclusively or in a much higher degree than the females, with organs for vocal or instrumental music, and with odoriferous glands. They are ornamented with infinitely diversified appendages, and with the most brilliant or conspicuous colors, often arranged in elegant patterns, while the females are unadorned. When the sexes differ in more important structures, it is the male which is provided with special sense organs for discovering the female, with locomotive organs for reaching her, and often with prehensile organs for holding her. These various structures for charming or securing the female are often developed in the male during only part of the year, namely, the breeding season. They have in many cases been more or less transferred to the females; and in the latter case they often appear in her as mere rudiments. They are lost or never gained by the males after emasculation. Generally they are not developed in the male during early youth, but appear a short time before the age for reproduction. Hence in most cases the young of both sexes resemble each other; and the female somewhat resembles her young offspring throughout life. In almost every great class a few anomalous cases occur, where there has been an almost complete transposition of the characters proper to the two sexes; the females assuming characters which properly belong to the males. This surprising uniformity in the laws regulating the differences between the sexes in so many and such widely separated classes is intelligible if we admit the action of one common cause, namely, sexual selection.

Sexual selection depends on the success of certain individuals over others of the same sex, in relation to the propagation of the species; while natural selection depends on the success of both sexes, at all ages, in relation to the general conditions of life. The sexual struggle is of two kinds: in the one it is between the individuals of the same sex, generally the males, in order to drive away or kill their rivals, the females remaining passive; while in the other, the struggle is likewise between individuals of the same sex, in order to excite or charm those of the opposite sex, generally the females, which no longer remain passive, but select the more agreeable partners. This latter kind of selection is closely analogous to that which man unintentionally, yet effectually, brings to bear on his domesticated productions, when he preserves during a long period the most pleasing or useful individuals, without any wish to modify the breed.

The laws of inheritance determine whether characters gained through sexual selection by either sex shall be transmitted to the same sex, or to both, as well as the age at which they shall be developed. It appears that variations arising late in life are commonly transmitted to one and the same sex. Variability is the necessary basis for the action of selection, and is wholly independent of it. It follows from this, that variations of the same general nature have often been taken advantage of and accumulated through sexual selection in relation to the propagation of the species, as well as through natural selection in relation to the general purposes of life. Hence secondary sexual characters, when equally transmitted to both sexes, can be distinguished from ordinary specific characters only by the light of analogy. The modifications acquired through sexual selection are often so strongly pronounced that the two sexes have frequently been ranked as distinct species, or even as distinct genera. Such strongly-marked differences must be in some manner highly important; and we know that they have been acquired in some instances at the cost not only of inconvenience, but of exposure to actual danger.

The belief in the power of sexual selection rests chiefly on the following considerations. Certain characters are confined to one sex; and this alone renders it probable that in most cases they are connected with the act of reproduction. In innumerable instances these characters are fully developed only at maturity, and often during only a part of the year, which is always the breeding-season. The males (passing over a few exceptional cases) are the more active in courtship; they are the better armed, and are rendered the more attractive in various ways. It is to be especially observed that the males display their attractions with elaborate care in the presence of the females; and that they rarely or never display them excepting during the season of love. It is incredible that all this should be purposeless. Lastly we have distinct evidence with some quadrupeds and birds, that the individuals of one sex are capable of feeling a strong antipathy or preference for certain individuals of the other sex.

Bearing in mind these facts, and the marked results of man's unconscious selection, when applied to domesticated animals and cultivated plants, it seems to me almost certain that if the individuals of one sex were during a long series of generations to prefer pairing with certain individuals of the other sex, characterised in some peculiar manner, the offspring would slowly but surely become modified in this same manner. I have not attempted to conceal that, excepting when the males are more numerous than the females, or when polygamy prevails, it is doubtful how the more attractive males succeed in leaving a larger number of off-spring to inherit their superiority in ornaments or other charms than the less attractive males; but I have shewn that this would probably follow from the females,—especially the more vigorous ones, which would be the first to breed,—preferring not only the more attractive but at the same time the more vigorous and victorious males. . . .

Everyone who admits the principle of evolution, and yet feels great difficulty in admitting that female mammals, birds, reptiles, and fish, could have acquired the high taste implied by the beauty of the males, and which generally coincides with our own standard, should reflect that the nerve-cells of the brain in the highest as well as in the lowest members of the Vertebrate series, are derived from those of the common progenitor of this great Kingdom. For we can thus see how it has come to pass that certain mental faculties, in various and widely distinct groups of animals, have been developed in nearly the same manner and to nearly the same degree.

The reader who has taken the trouble to go through the several chapters devoted to sexual selection, will be able to judge how far the conclusions at which I have arrived are supported by sufficient evidence. If he accepts these conclusions he may, I think, safely extend them to mankind. . . .

He who admits the principle of sexual selection will be led to the remarkable conclusion that the nervous system not only regulates most of the existing functions of the body, but has indirectly influenced the progressive development of various bodily structures and of certain mental qualities. Courage, pugnacity, perseverance, strength and size of body, weapons of all kinds, musical organs, both vocal and instrumental, bright colours and ornamental appendages, have all been indirectly gained by the one sex or the other, through the exertion of choice, the influence of love and jealousy, and the appreciation of the beautiful in sound, colour or form; and these powers of the mind manifestly depend on the development of the brain.

Man scans with scrupulous care the character and pedigree of his horses, cattle, and dogs before he matches them; but when he comes to his own marriage he rarely, or never, takes any such care. He is impelled by nearly the same motives as the lower animals, when they are left to their own free choice, though he is in so far superior to them that he highly values mental charms and virtues. On the other hand he is strongly attracted by mere wealth or rank. Yet he might by selection do something not only for the bodily constitution and frame of his offspring, but for their intellectual and moral qualities. Both sexes ought to refrain from marriage if they are in any marked degree inferior in body or mind; but such hopes are Utopian and will never be even partially realised until the laws of inheritance are thoroughly known. Everyone does good service, who aids towards this end. When the principles of breeding and inheritance are better understood, we shall not hear ignorant members of our legislature rejecting with scorn a plan for ascertaining whether or not consanguineous marriages are injurious to man.

The advancement of the welfare of mankind is a most intricate problem: all ought to refrain from marriage who cannot avoid abject poverty for their children; for poverty is not only a great evil, but tends to its own increase by leading to recklessness in marriage. On the other hand, as Mr. Galton has remarked, if the prudent avoid marriage, whilst the reckless marry, the inferior members tend to supplant the better members of society. Man, like every other animal, has no doubt advanced to his present high condition through a struggle for existence consequent on his rapid multiplication; and if he is to advance still higher, it is to be feared that he must remain subject to a severe struggle. Otherwise he would sink into indolence, and the more gifted men would not be more successful in the battle of life than the less gifted. Hence our natural rate of increase, though leading to many and obvious evils, must not be greatly diminished by any means. There should be open competition for all men; and the most able should not be prevented by laws or customs from succeeding best and rearing the largest number of offspring. Important as the struggle for existence has been and even still is, yet as far as the highest part of man's nature is concerned there are other agencies more important. For the moral qualities are advanced, either directly or indirectly, much more through the effects of habit, the reasoning powers, instruction, religion, &c., than through natural selection; though to this latter agency may be safely attributed the social instincts, which afforded the basis for the development of the moral sense.

The main conclusion arrived at in this work, namely that man is descended from some lowly organised form, will, I regret to think, be highly distasteful to many. But there can hardly be a doubt that we are descended from barbarians. The astonishment which I felt on first seeing a party of Fuegians on a wild and broken shore will never be forgotten by me, for the reflection at once rushed into my mind—such were our ancestors. These men were absolutely naked and bedaubed with paint, their long hair was tangled, their mouths frothed with excitement, and their expression was wild, startled, and distrustful. They possessed hardly any arts, and like wild animals lived on what they could catch; they had no government, and were merciless to every one not of their own small tribe. He who has seen a savage in his native land will not feel much shame, if forced to acknowledge that the blood of some more humble creature flows in his veins. For my own part I would as soon be descended from that heroic little monkey, who braved his dreaded enemy in order to save the life of his keeper, or from that old baboon, who descending from the mountains, carried away in triumph his young comrade from a crowd of astonished dogs—as from a savage who delights to torture his enemies, offers up bloody sacrifices, practises infanticide without remorse, treats his wives like slaves, knows no decency, and is haunted by the grossest superstitions.

Man may be excused for feeling some pride at having risen, though not through his own exertions, to the very summit of the organic scale; and the fact of his having thus risen, instead of having been aboriginally placed there, may give him hope for a still higher destiny in the distant future. But we are not here concerned with hopes or fears, only with the truth as far as our reason permits us to discover it; and I have given the evidence to the best of my ability. We must, however, acknowledge, as it seems to me, that man with all his noble qualities, with sympathy which feels for the most debased, with benevolence which extends not only to other men but to the humblest living creature, with his god-like intellect which has penetrated into the movements and constitution of the solar system—with all these exalted powers—Man still bears in his bodily frame the indelible stamp of his lowly origin.

35. History: The Use of the Past

HISTORY—CLIO—was the intellectual goddess of the Victorian age. The Victorians, being children of the romantic movement as well as the rationalist enlightenment, had a keen sense of being at a place in time, proceeding from a past, going to a future. Romantic fantasy and scientific conceptions of development fused to enrich the study of history. The distinguished nineteenth-century historians, moreover, wrote history for the reading public, not merely for the edification of other scholars. History was literature; history was philosophy—not merely scholarship. Every thinking Victorian felt that he or she had to understand history. If they did not, they would be unable to understand where and how they had escaped a barbaric past or how to chart their way into the future.

William Edward Hartpole Lecky (1832–1903), a wealthy Anglo-Irishman, was far too skeptical for a career in the Church, disinterested in the armed forces, and drawn to history while disdainful of university posts. A gentleman scholar, he was one of those who brought history and philosophy to the marketplace. He was a man of his age, fascinated by the study of society, ideas, and values. Science had reenforced the belief in relativism. Men and societies were perpetually changing. History was the study of motion. All sorts of forces and influences were at work. Lecky turned a keenly critical and highly literate eye to them. Like Hegel or Comte or Buckle, he perceived of history as a great organic whole. Lecky brought his wisdom and wit with all of his prejudices and presumptions to the study of the past. He still lacked the magnificence of Macaulay. He was not the scholar or historical titan that Stubbs was, or Acton, or Maitland. But Lecky understood, as many historians have not, that historical documents are not prepared with the historian in mind—those that are being highly suspect. He realized that myth was often more important than fact.

Many of Lecky's presumptions were demonstrably untrue. Peaceful industrial societies were not destined to triumph over military states. Nor had mankind seen the end of persecution and ideological tyranny. Lecky's efforts to preserve impartiality laid him open to contemporary and subsequent criticism of banality of thought and conclusion. But Lecky was of a piece with John Stuart Mill—in this sense a classic liberal—finding a measure of truth and importance in opposites. Historical sense and historical understanding were, for Lecky and for many Victorians, necessary to preserve the best of the past while pressing bravely into the future.

Recommended Reading

Histories of history are often the most tedious reading. A narrative with some outdated analysis is G. P. Gooch, *History and Historians in the Nineteenth Century*, rev. ed. (London: 1952). See also, C. F. Mullett, "W. E. H. Lecky," *Some Modern Historians of Britain*, ed. H. Ausubel, J. B. Brebner, and E. M. Hunt (New York: 1951), 128–149.

W. E. H. Lecky,
THE POLITICAL VALUE OF HISTORY

When, shortly after I had accepted the honourable task which I am endeavouring to fulfil to-night, I received from your Secretary a report of the annual proceedings of the Birmingham and Midland Institute,—when I observed the immense range and variety of subjects included within your programme, illustrating so strikingly the intense intellectual activity of this great town,—my first feeling was one of some bewilderment and dismay. What, I asked myself, could I say that would be of much real value, addressing an unknown audience, and relating to fields of knowledge so vast, so multifarious, and in many of their parts so far beyond the range of my own studies? On reflection, however, it appeared to me that in this, as in most other cases, the proverb was a wise one which bids the cobbler stick to his last, and that a writer who, during many years of his life, has been engaged in the study of English history could hardly do better than devote the time at his disposal to-night to a few reflections on the political value of

Source: From "The Political Use of History," *Historical and Political Essays* (London: 1908), pp. 21–42.

history, and on the branches and methods of historical study that are most fitted to form a sound political judgment.

Is history a study of real use in practical, and especially in political, life? The question, as you know, has been by no means always answered in the same way. In its earlier stages history was regarded chiefly as a form of poetry recording the more dramatic actions of kings, warriors, and statesmen. Homer and the early ballads are indeed the first historians of their countries, and long after Homer one of the most illustrious of the critics of antiquity described history as merely "poetry free from the incumbrance of verse." The portraits that adorned it gave some insight into human character; it breathed noble sentiments, rewarded and stimulated noble actions, and kindled by its strong appeals to the imagination high patriotic feeling; but its end was rather to paint than to guide, to consecrate a noble past than to furnish a key for the future; and the artist in selecting his facts looked mainly for those which could throw the richest colour upon his canvas. Most experience was in his eyes (to adopt an image of Coleridge) like the stern light of a ship, which illuminates only the path we have already traversed; and a large proportion of the subjects which are most significant as illustrating the true welfare and development of nations were deliberately rejected as below the dignity of history. The old conception of history can hardly be better illustrated than in the words of Savage Landor. "Show me," he makes one of his heroes say, "how great projects were executed, great advantages gained, and great calamities averted. Show me the generals and the statesmen who stood foremost, that I may bend to them in reverence. . . . Let the books of the Treasury lie closed as religiously as the Sibyl's. Leave weights and measures in the market-place; Commerce in the harbour; the Arts in the light they love; Philosophy in the shade. Place History on her rightful throne, and at the sides of her Eloquence and War."

It was chiefly in the eighteenth century that a very different conception of history grew up. Historians then came to believe that their task was not so much to paint a picture as to solve a problem; to explain or illustrate the successive phases of national growth, prosperity, and adversity. The history of morals, of industry, of intellect, and of art; the changes that take place in manners or beliefs; the dominant ideas that prevailed in successive periods; the rise, fall, and modification of political constitutions; in a word, all the conditions of national well-being became the subjects of their works. They sought rather to write a history of peoples than a history of kings. They looked specially in history for the chain of causes and effects. They undertook to study in the past the physiology of nations, and hoped by applying the experimental method on a large scale to deduce some lessons of real value about the conditions on which the well-being of society mainly depends.

How far have they succeeded in their attempt, and furnished us with a real compass for political guidance? Let me in the first place frankly express my own belief that to many readers of history the study is not only useless, but even positively misleading. An unintelligent, a superficial, a pedantic or an inaccurate use of history is the source of very many errors in practical judgment. Human affairs are so infinitely complex that it is vain to expect that they will ever exactly reproduce themselves, or that any study of the past can enable us to predict the future with the minuteness and the completeness that can be attained in the exact sciences. Nor will any wise man judge the merits of existing institutions solely on historic grounds. Do not persuade yourself that any institution, however great may be its antiquity, however transcendent may have been its uses in a remote past, can permanently justify its existence, unless it can be shown to exercise a really beneficial influence over our own society and our own age. It is equally true that no institution which is exercising such a beneficial influence should be condemned, because it can be shown from history that under other conditions and in other times its influence was rather for evil than for good.

These propositions may seem like truisms; yet how often do we hear a kind of reasoning that is inconsistent with them! How often, for example, in the discussions on the Continent on the advantages and disadvantages of monastic institutions has the chief stress of the argument been laid upon the great benefits which those institutions produced in ages that were utterly different from our own,—in the dark period of the barbarian invasions, when they were the only refuges of a pacific civilisation, the only libraries, the only schools, the only centres of art, the only refuge for gentle and intellectual natures; the chief barrier against violence and rapine; the chief promoters of agriculture and industry! How often in discussions on the merits and demerits of an Established Church in England have we heard arguments drawn from the hostility which the

Church of England showed towards English liberty in the time of the Stuarts; although it is abundantly evident that the dangers of a royal despotism, which were then so serious, have utterly disappeared, and that the political action of the Church of England at that period was mainly governed by a doctrine of the Divine right of kings, and of the duty of passive obedience, which is now as dead as the old belief that the king's touch could cure scrofula! How often have the champions of modern democracy appealed in support of their views to the glories of the democracies of ancient Greece, without ever reminding their hearers that these small municipal republics rested on the basis of slavery, and that the bulk of those who would exercise the chief controlling influence over affairs in a pure democracy of the modern type were absolutely excluded from political power! How often in discussions about the advantages and disadvantages of Home Rule in Ireland do we find arguments drawn from the merits or demerits of the Irish Parliament of the eighteenth century, with a complete forgetfulness of the fact that this Parliament consisted exclusively of a Protestant gentry; that it represented in the highest degree the property of the country, and the classes who are most closely attached to English rule; that it was constituted in such a manner that the English Government could exercise a complete control over its deliberations, and that for good or for ill it was utterly unlike any body that could now be constituted in Ireland!

Or again, to turn to another field: it is quite certain that every age has special dangers to guard against, and that as time moves on these dangers not only change, but are sometimes even reversed. There have been periods in English history when the great dangers to be encountered sprang from the excessive and encroaching power of a monarchy or of an aristocracy. The battle to be then fought was for the free exercise of religious worship and expression of religious opinion, for a free parliament, for a free press, for a free platform, for an independent jury-box. All the best patriotism, all the most heroic self-sacrifice of the nation, was thrown into defence of these causes; and the wisest statesmen of the time made it the main object of their legislation to protect and consolidate them.

These things are now as valuable as they ever were, but no reasonable man will maintain that they are in the smallest danger. The battles of the sixteenth and seventeenth centuries have been definitely won. A kind of language which at one period of English history implied the noblest heroism is now the idlest and cheapest of clap-trap. The sycophant and the self-seeker bow before quite other idols than of old. The dangers of the time come from other quarters; other tendencies prevail, other tasks remain to be accomplished; and a public man who in framing his course followed blindly in the steps of the heroes or reformers of the past would be like a mariner who set his sails to the winds of yesterday.

It is difficult, I think, to doubt that the judgments of all of us are more or less affected by causes of this kind. It is, I imagine, true of the great majority of educated men that their first political impression or bias is formed much less by the events of their own time than by childish recollections of the more dramatic conflicts of the past. We are Cavaliers or Roundheads before we are Conservatives or Liberals; and although we gradually learn to realise how profoundly the condition of affairs and the balance of forces have altered, yet no wise man can doubt the power which the first bias of the imagination exercises in very many cases through a whole life. Language which grew out of bygone conflicts continues to be used long after those conflicts and their causes have ended; but that which was once a very genuine voice comes at last to be little more than an insincere echo.

The best corrective for this kind of evil is a really intelligent study of history. One of the first tasks that every sincere student should set before himself is to endeavour to understand what is the dominant idea or characteristic of the period with which he is occupied; what forces chiefly ruled it, what forces were then rising into a dangerous ascendancy, and what forces were on the decline; what illusions, what exaggerations, what false hopes and unworthy influences chiefly prevailed. It is only when studied in this spirit that the true significance of history is disclosed, and the same method which furnishes a key to the past forms also an admirable discipline for the judgment of the present. He who has learnt to understand the true character and tendencies of many succeeding ages is not likely to go very far wrong in estimating his own.

Another branch of history which I would especially commend to the attention of all political students is the history of Institutions. In the constantly fluctuating conditions of human life no institution ever remained for a long period unaltered. Sometimes with changed beliefs and changed conditions institutions lose all their original utility. They become simply useless, obstructive, and corrupt; and though by mere passive resistance they may continue to exist long after they have ceased to serve any good purpose, they will at last be undermined by their own abuses. Other institutions, on the other hand, show the true characteristic of vitality—the power of adapting themselves to changed conditions and new utilities. Few things in history are more interesting and more instructive than a careful study of these transformations. Sometimes the original objects almost wholly disappear, and utilities which were either never contemplated by the founders or were only regarded as of purely secondary importance take the first place on the scene. The old plan and symmetry almost disappear as the institution is modified now in this direction and now in that to meet some pressing want. The first architects, if they could rise from the dead, would scarcely recognise their creation—would perhaps look on it with horror. The indirect advantages of an institution are sometimes greater than its direct ones; and institutions are often more valuable on account of the evils they avert than on account of the positive advantages they produce. Not unfrequently in their later and transformed condition they exercise wider and greater influence than when they were originally established; for the strength derived from the long traditions of the past and from the habits that are formed around anything that is deeply rooted in the national life gives them a vastly increased importance.

There is probably no better test of the political genius of a nation than the power which it possesses of adapting old institutions to new wants; and it is, I think, in this skill and in this disposition that the political preeminence of the English people has been most conspicuously shown. It is difficult to overrate its importance. It is the institutions of a country that chiefly maintain the sense of its organic unity, its essential connection with its past. By their continuous existence they bind together as by a living chain the past with the present, the living with the dead.

Few greater calamities can befall a nation than to cut herself off, as France did in her great Revolution, from all vital connection with her own past. This is one of the chief lessons you will learn from Burke—the greatest and truest of all our political teachers. Bacon expressed in an admirable sentence the best spirit of English politics when he urged that "men in their innovations should follow the example of Time itself, which indeed innovated greatly, but quietly, and by degrees scarcely to be perceived."

There is a third department of history which appears to me especially valuable to political students. It is the history of those vast Revolutions for good or for ill which seem to have transformed the characters or permanently changed the fortunes of nations, either by a sudden and violent shock or by the slow process of gradual renovation. You will find on this subject, in our country, two great and opposite exaggerations. There is a school of writers, of which Buckle is an admirable representative, who are so struck by the long chain of causes, extending over many centuries, that preceded and prepared Revolutions, that they teach a kind of historic fatalism, reducing almost to nothing the action of Individualities; and there is another school, which is specially represented by Carlyle, who reduce all history into biographies, into the action of a few great men upon their kind.

The one class of writers will tell you with great truth that the Roman Republic was not destroyed by Cæsar, but by the long train of influences that made the career of Cæsar a possibility. They will show how influences working through many generations had sapped the foundations of the Republic—how the beliefs and habits on which it once rested had passed away—how its institutions no longer corresponded with the prevailing wants and ideas—how a form of government which had proved excellently adapted for a restricted dominion failed when the Roman eagles flew triumphantly over the whole civilised world, and how in this manner the strongest tendencies of the time were preparing the downfall of the Republic, and the establishment of a great empire upon its ruins. They will show how the intellectual influences of the Rennaissance, the invention of printing, and a crowd of other causes, many of them at first sight very remote from theological controversies, had in the sixteenth century so shaken the power of the Roman Catholic Church, that the way was prepared for the Reformation, and it became possible for Luther and Calvin to succeed, where Wyckliffe and Huss had failed. They will show how profoundly our theological beliefs are affected by our general conception of the system of the universe, and how inevitably, as Science changes the latter, the former will undergo a corresponding process of modification. Creeds that are no longer in harmony with the general spirit of the time may long continue, but a new spirit will be breathed into the old forms. Those portions which are most discordant with our fresh knowledge will be neglected or attenuated. Although they may not be openly discarded, they will cease to be realised or vitally operative.

In the sphere of politics a similar law prevails, and the fate of nations largely depends upon forces quite different from those on which the mere political historian concentrates his attention. The growth of military or industrial habits; the elevation or depression of different classes; the changes that take place in the distribution of wealth; inventions or discoveries that alter the course or character of industry or commerce, or reverse the relative advantages of different nations in the competitions of life; the increase and, still more, the diffusion of knowledge; the many influences that affect convictions, habits and ideals, that raise, or lower, or modify the moral tone and type—all these things concur in shaping the destinies of nations. Legislation is only really successful when it is in harmony with the general spirit of the age. Laws and statesmen for the most part indicate and ratify, but do not create. They are like the hands of the watch, which move obedient to the hidden machinery behind.

In all this kind of speculation there is, I believe, great truth, and it opens out fields of inquiry that are of the utmost interest and importance. I have, however, long thought that it has been pushed by some modern writers to extravagant exaggeration. As you well know, there is another aspect of history, which, long before Carlyle, was enforced by some of the ablest and most independent intellects of Christendom. Pascal tells us that if Cleopatra's nose had been shorter, the whole face of the world might have been changed, and Voltaire is never tired of dwelling on the small springs on which the greatest events of history turn. Frederick the Great, who was probably the keenest practical intellect of his age, constantly insisted on the same view. In the vast field of politics, he maintained, casual events which no human sagacity can predict play by far the largest part. We are in most cases groping our way blindly in the dark. Occasionally, when favourable circumstances occur, there is a gleam of light of which the skilful avail themselves. All the rest is uncertainty. The world is mainly governed by a multitude of secondary, obscure, or impenetrable causes. It is a game of chance in which the most skilful may lose like the most ignorant. "The older one becomes the more clearly one sees that

King Hazard fashions three-fourths of the events in this miserable world."

My own view of this question is that though there are certain streams of tendency, though there is a certain steady and orderly evolution that it is impossible in the long run to resist, yet individual action and even mere accident have borne a very great part in modifying the direction of history. It is with History as with the general laws of Nature. We can none of us escape the all-pervading force of gravitation, or the influence of the climate under which we live, or the succession of the seasons, or the laws of growth and of decay; yet man is not a mere passive weed drifting helplessly upon the sea of life, and human wisdom and human folly can do and have done much to modify the conditions of his being.

It is quite true that religions depend largely for their continued vitality upon the knowledge and intellectual atmosphere of their time; but there are periods when the human mind is in such a state of pliancy that a small pressure can give it a bent which will last for generations. If Mohammed had been killed in one of the first skirmishes of his career, I know no reason for believing that a great monotheistic religion would have arisen in Arabia, capable of moulding for more than twelve hundred years not only the beliefs, laws, and governments, but also the inmost moral and mental character of a vast section of the human race. Gibbon was probably right in his conjecture that if Charles Martel had been defeated at the famous battle near Tours, the creed of Islam would have overspread a great part of what is now Christian Europe, and in that case it might have ruled over it for centuries. No one can follow the history of the conversion of the barbarians to Christianity without perceiving how often a religion has been imposed in the first instance by the mere will of the ruler, which gradually took such root that it became far too strong for any political power to destroy. Persecution cannot annihilate a creed which is firmly established, or maintain a creed which has been thoroughly undermined, but there are intermediate stages in which its influence on national beliefs has been enormously great. Even at the Reformation, though more general causes were of capital importance, political events had a very large part in defining the frontier line between the rival creeds, and the divisions so created have for the most part endured.

In secular politics numerous instances of the same kind will

occur to every thoughtful reader of history. If, as might easily
have happened, Hannibal after the battle of Cannae had taken and
burned Rome, and transferred the supremacy of the world to a
maritime commercial State upon the Mediterranean; if, instead of
the Regency, Louis XV. and Louis XVI., France had passed during
the eighteenth century under sovereigns of the stamp of the elder
branch of the House of Orange or of Henry IV., or of the Great
Elector, or of Frederick the Great; if, at the French Revolution,
the supreme military genius had been connected with the character
of Washington rather than with the character of Napoleon—who
can doubt that the course of European history would have been
vastly changed? The causes that made constitutional liberty succeed in England, while it failed in other countries where its
prospects seemed once at least as promising, as many and complex;
but no careful student of English history will doubt the prominence among them of the accidental fact that James II., by embrac-
ing Catholicism, had thrown the Church feeling at a very critical
moment into opposition to the monarchical feeling, and that in the
last days of Anne, when the question of the succession was trembling most doubtfully in the balance, his son refused to conform to
the Anglican creed.

Laws are no doubt in a great degree inoperative when they do
not spring from and represent the opinion of the nation, but they
have in their turn a great power of consolidating, deepening, and
directing opinion. When some important progress has been attained, and with the support of public opinion has been embodied
in a law, that law will do much to prevent the natural reflux of the
wave. It becomes a kind of moral landmark, a powerful educating
influence, and by giving what had been achieved the sanction of
legality, it contributes largely to its permanence. Roman law undoubtedly played a great part in European history long after all
the conditions in which it was first enacted had passed away, and
the legislator who can determine in any country the system of
national education, or the succession of property, will do much to
influence the opinions and social types of many succeeding generations.

The point, however, on which I would here especially insist is
that there has scarcely been a great revolution in the world which
might not at some stage of its progress have been either averted, or
materially modified, or at least greatly postponed, by wise states-

manship and timely compromise. Take, for example, the American Revolution, which destroyed the political unity of the English race. You will often hear this event treated as if it were simply due to the wanton tyranny of an English Government, which desired to reduce its colonies to servitude by taxing them without their consent. But if you will look closely into the history of that time—and there is no history which is more instructive—you will find that this is a gross misrepresentation. What happened was essentially this. England, under the guidance of the elder Pitt, had been waging a great and most successful war, which left her with an enormously extended Empire, but also with an addition of more than seventy millions to her National Debt. That debt was now nearly one hundred and forty millions, and England was reeling under the taxation it required. The war had been waged largely in America, and its most brilliant result was the conquest of Canada, by which the old American colonies had benefited more than any other part of the Empire, for the expulsion of the French from North America put an end to the one great danger which hung over them. It was, however, extremely probable that if France ever regained her strength, one of her first objects would be to recover her dominion in America.

Under these circumstances the English Government concluded that it was impossible that England alone, overburdened as she was by taxation, could undertake the military defence of her greatly extended Empire. Their object, therefore, was to create subsidiary armies for its defence. Ireland already raised by the vote of the Irish Parliament, and out of exclusively Irish resources, an army consisting of from twelve to fifteen thousand men, most of whom were available for the general purposes of the Empire. In India, under a despotic system, a separate army was maintained for the protection of India. It was the strong belief of the English Government that a third army should be maintained in America for the defence of the American colonies and of the neighbouring islands, and that it was just and reasonable that America should bear some part of the expense of her own defence. She was charged with no part of the interest of the National Debt; she paid nothing towards the cost of the navy which protected her coast; she was the most lightly taxed and the most prosperous portion of the Empire; she was the part which had benefited most by the late war, and she was the part which was most likely to be menaced if the war was renewed. Under these circumstances Grenville determined that a small army of ten thousand men should be kept in America, under the distinct promise that it was never to serve beyond that country and the West Indian Isles, and he asked America to contribute 100,000*l*. a year, or about a third of its expense.

But here the difficulty arose. The Irish army was maintained by the vote of the Irish Parliament; but there was no single parliament representing the American colonies, and it soon became evident that it was impossible to induce thirteen State legislatures to agree upon any scheme for supporting an army in America. Under these circumstances Grenville in an ill-omened moment resolved to revive a dormant power which existed in the Constitution, and levy this new war-tax by Imperial taxation. He at the same time guaranteed the colonists that the proceeds of this tax should be expended solely in America; he intimated to them in the clearest way that if they would meet his wishes by themselves providing the necessary sum, he would be abundantly satisfied, and he delayed the enforcement of the measure for a year in order to give them ample time for doing so.

Such and so small was the original cause of difference between England and her colonies. Who can fail to see that it was a difference abundantly susceptible of compromise, and that a wise and moderate statesmanship might easily have averted the catastrophe? There are few sadder and few more instructive pages in history than those which show how mistake after mistake was committed, till the rift which was once so small widened and deepened; till the two sections of the English race were thrown into an irreconcilable antagonism, and the fair vision of an United Empire in the East and in the West came for ever to an end.

Or glance for a moment at the French Revolution. It is a favourite task of historians to trace through the preceding generations the long train of causes that made the transformation of French institutions absolutely inevitable; but it is not so often remembered that when the States-General met in 1789 by far the larger part of the benefits of the Revolution could have been attained without difficulty, without convulsion, and by general consent. The nobles and clergy had pledged themselves to surrender their feudal privileges and their privileges in taxation; a reforming king was on the throne, and a reforming minister was at his side. If the spirit of moderation had then prevailed, the inevitable transformation might probably have been made without the effusion of a drop of blood.

Jefferson was at this time the Minister of the United States in Paris. As an old republican he knew well the conditions of free governments, and among the politicians of his own country he represented the democratic section. I know few words in history more pathetic than those in which he described the situation. "I was much acquainted," he writes, "with the leading patriots of the Assembly. Being from a country which had successfully passed through a similar reformation, they were disposed to my acquaintance, and had some confidence in me. I urged most strenuously an immediate compromise to secure what the Government were now ready to yield. . . . It was well understood that the King would grant at this time (1) freedom of the person by Habeas Corpus; (2) freedom of conscience; (3) freedom of the press; (4) trial by jury; (5) a representative legislature; (6) annual meetings; (7) the origination of laws; (8) the exclusive right of taxation and appropriation; and (9) the responsibility of Ministers; and with the exercise of these powers they could obtain in future whatever might be further necessary to improve and preserve their constitution. They thought otherwise," continued Jefferson; "and events have proved their lamentable error; for after thirty years of war, foreign and domestic, the loss of millions of lives, the prostration of private happiness, and the foreign subjugation of their own country for a time, they have obtained no more, nor even that securely."

Let me, in concluding these observations, sum up in a few words some other advantages which you may derive from history. It is, I think, one of the best schools for that kind of reasoning which is most useful in practical life. It teaches men to weigh conflicting probabilities, to estimate degrees of evidence, to form a sound judgment of the value of authorities. Reasoning is taught by actual practice much more than by any *a priori* methods. Many good judges—and I own I am inclined to agree with them—doubt much whether a study of formal logic ever yet made a good reasoner. Mathematics are no doubt invaluable in this respect, but they only deal with demonstrations; and it has often been observed how many excellent mathematicians are somewhat peculiarly destitute of the power of measuring degrees of probability. But history is largely concerned with the kind of probabilities on which the conduct of life mainly depends. There is one hint about historical reasoning which I think may not be unworthy of your notice. When studying some great historical controversy, place yourselves by an effort of the imagination alternately on each side of the battle; try to realise as fully as you can the point of view of the best men on either side, and then draw up upon paper the arguments of each in the strongest form you can give them. You will find that few practices do more to elucidate the past, or form a better mental discipline.

History, again, greatly expands our horizon and enlarges our experience by bringing us in direct contact with men of many times and countries. It gives young men something of the experience of old men, and untravelled men something of the experience of travelled ones. A great source of error in our judgment of men is that we do not make sufficient allowance for the difference of types. The essentials of right and wrong no doubt continue the same, but if you look carefully into history you will find that the special stress which is attached to particular virtues is constantly changing. Sometimes it is the civic virtues, sometimes the religious virtues, sometimes the industrial virtues, sometimes the love of truth, sometimes the more amiable dispositions, that are most valued, and occupy the foremost place in the moral type. The men of each age must be judged by the ideal of their own age and country, and not by the ideal of ours. Men look at life in very different aspects, and they differ greatly in their ways of reasoning, in the qualities they admire, in the aims which they chiefly prize. In few things do they differ more than in their capacity for self-government; in the kinds of liberty they especially value; in their love or dislike of government guidance or control.

The power of realising and understanding types of character very different from our own is not, I think, an English quality, and a great many of our mistakes in governing other nations come from this deficiency. Some thirty or forty years ago especially it was the custom of English statesmen to write and speak as if the salvation of every nation depended mainly upon its adoption of a miniature copy of the British Constitution. Now, if there is a lesson which history teaches clearly, it is that the same institutions are not fitted for all nations, and that what in one nation may prove perfectly successful, will in another be supremely disastrous. The habits and traditions of a nation; the peculiar bent of its character and intellect; the degree in which self-control, respect for law, the spirit of compromise, and disinterested public spirit are diffused through the people; the relations of classes, and the divisions of property, are all considerations of capital importance. It is a great error, both in history and in practical politics, to attach too much value to a political machine. The essential consideration is by what men and in what spirit that machine is likely to be worked. Few Constitutions contain more theoretical anomalies, and even absurdities, than that under which England has attained to such an unexampled height of political prosperity; while a servile imitation of some of the most skilfully-devised Constitutions in Europe has not saved some of the South American States from long courses of anarchy, bankruptcy, and revolution.

These are some of the political lessons that may be drawn from history. Permit me, in conclusion, to say that its most precious lessons are moral ones. It expands the range of our vision, and teaches us in judging the true interests of nations to look beyond the immediate future. Few good judges will deny that this habit is now much wanted. The immensely increased prominence in political life of ephemeral influences, and especially of the influence of a daily press; the immense multiplication of elections, which intensifies party conflicts, all tend to concentrate our thoughts more and more upon an immediate issue. They narrow the range of our vision, and make us somewhat insensible to distant consequences and remote contingencies. It is not easy, in the heat and passion of modern political life, to look beyond a parliament or an election, beyond the interest of a pary or the triumph of an hour. Yet nothing is more certain than that the ultimate, distant, and perhaps indirect consequences of political measures are often far more important than their immediate fruits, and that in the prosperity of nations a large amount of continuity in politics and the gradual formation of political habits are of transcendent importance. History is never more valuable than when it enables us, standing as on a height, to look beyond the smoke and turmoil of our petty quarrels, and to detect in the slow developments of the past the great permanent forces that are steadily bearing nations onwards to improvement or decay.

The strongest of these forces are the moral ones. Mistakes in statesmanship, military triumphs or disasters, no doubt affect materially the prosperity of nations, but their permanent political well-being is essentially the outcome of their moral state. Its foundation is laid in pure domestic life, in commercial integrity, in a high standard of moral worth and of public spirit; in simple habits, in courage uprightness, and self-sacrifice, in a certain soundness and moderation of judgment, which brings quite as much from character as from intellect. If you would form a wise judgment of the future of a nation, observe carefully whether these qualities are increasing or decaying. Observe especially what qualities count for most in public life. Is character becoming of greater or less importance? Are the men who obtain the highest posts in the nation men of whom in private life and irrespective of party competent judges speak with genuine respect? Are they men of sincere convictions, sound judgment, consistent lives, indisputable integrity, or are they men who have won their positions by the arts of a demagogue or an intriguer; men of nimble tongues and not earnest beliefs—skilful, above all things, in spreading their sails to each passing breeze of popularity? Such considerations as these are apt to be forgotten in the fierce excitement of a party contest; but if history has any meaning, it is such considerations that affect most vitally the permanent well-being of communities, and it is by observing this moral current that you can best cast the horoscope of a nation.

36. Liberal Education

WHILE SCIENCE, history, art, and technology poured forth in profusion, the Victorians splashed uneasily down the stream of the dissemination of knowledge. Voluntarism delivered one child in every seventeen to some sort of school in 1818. By 1861, 2,500,000 of the 2,750,000 school-age children of England and Wales attended some sort of school some of the time. The great majority left before the age of eleven, and the quality was to give school inspector Matthew Arnold ample empirical data for *Culture and Anarchy*. The Education Code of 1862 worked some improvement, utilizing the principle of payment by results. There were schoolboards throughout the nation by 1870. Compulsory attendance came in 1876 and 1880. School leaving age was raised to eleven in 1893, twelve in 1899, then in 1900 daringly advanced to the fourteen at which it would remain for most of the twentieth century. The £20,000 stipend to education in the 1833 budget grew with little serious planning or control before the 1860s into compulsory secondary education in 1904.

Victorians had always appreciated the moral value of education. Britons accepted, indeed demanded, that modest provisions on this point be written into the appropriate social legislation from the Factory Act of 1833 and the New Poor Law of 1834. The Education Act of 1904 still spoke with Victorian purpose if with twentieth-century intent by specifying:

. . . it shall be the duty of the local education authority for every area, so far as their powers extend, to contribute towards the spiritual, moral, mental, and physical development of the community by securing that efficient education . . . shall be available to meet the needs of the population of their area.

Education, like so many Victorian phenomena, had both utilitarian and evangelical impulses. Utilitarians saw education as a matter of accumulating information and understanding. This would be sufficient for progress and social peace—or at least so thought Mr. Gradgrind with his "Facts, facts, facts" pilloried by Dickens in *Hard Times*. Evangelicals saw it as a matter of Godliness and seriousness of purpose. They had pioneered the anti-Jacobin brainwashing enterprises of those formidable women Mrs. Sarah Kirkby Trimmer and Hannah More, as well as the more formal and acceptable Sunday School movement of Robert Raikes. The utilitarian argument was constructed upon social justice and political necessity. Evangelical arguments were directed to a moral imperative.

Little changed until effective social demand was felt, and the pressure for social mobility proved irresistable. The middle classes, particularly the professionals, could not effectively bequeath their success as the gentry-aristocracy bequeathed their estates. Even a toehold in the lower middle classes demanded education. The concern always was, as it continues to be, both with the substance of education and the status education brings. Victorian culture, however, was strongly nonacademic, generalized rather than specialized, for at least the first two-thirds of the century. The classics and philosophy, not science or economics, prepared the adolescent for leadership and success.

Public schools and grammar schools were, as they have continued to be, avenues for middle-class adoption, for the fusion of money and blood lines. They preserved elite values while incorporating the successful upwardly mobile. The Taunton Commission (1864) and the Endowed Schools Act (1869), together with the establishment of the Headmasters Conference (1869), marked the first general consolidation and advance since Dr. Thomas Arnold's work at Rugby. Arnold's Godliness gave way to secular manliness—first the bumptious muscular Christianity of Charles Kingsley, then the gamesman underpinnings of imperialism Cecil Rhodes was to find so much to his taste.

Their universities also moved—Oxford and Cambridge glacially, as befitted their ancient dignity. They preserved status, although the University of London was the only institution giving anything resembling real university instruction into the 1850s. As the Anglican closed shop collapsed with the abolition of university religious tests (1854–1871), talent, energy, and imagination could be applied to university reform. From 1850 to 1880 Oxford and Cambridge moved decisively into the nineteenth century. Cambridge did particularly well. Science had never been wholly unknown there. After 1870 it blossomed in such extraordinary enterprises as the Cavendish Laboratories. Women, who became equal beneficiaries of the Education Acts also gained footholds in the ancient universities, although not yet full equality. From Girton (1869) and Newnham (1871) at Cambridge to Somerville and Lady Margaret Hall (1879) at Oxford, they launched on their impressive course.

Thomas Henry Huxley (1825–1895) was one of the heroes of Britain's struggle for educational sanity. His great work as a naturalist and educator has tended to be lost in his colorful career as "Darwin's Bulldog." The demolition of Bishop Wilberforce should never overshadow Huxley's great work in such areas as the systematic development and reorganization of the University of London. During the extraordinarily fertile discussions of education during the 1860s in the movement that would culminate with the Education Act of 1870, Huxley addressed a convocation at the South London Working Men's College. He spoke deftly, to the point, yet ranged over many issues. He reviewed the actual content of an Englishman's education, its shortcomings, the stumbling blocks in the path of reform, and concluded with a sketch (highly relevant today) of what a liberal education should be.

Recommended Reading

H. C. Bibby, *T. H. Huxley* (London: 1959), Mary Sturt, *The Education of the People* (London: 1967), W. H. G. Armytage, *Four Hundred Years of English Education* (Cambridge: 1970), P. W. Musgrove, *Society and Education in England since 1800* (London: 1968), and D. Wardle, *English Popular Education, 1780–1970* (Cambridge: 1970), are useful beginning points. David Newsome treats one important problem in *Godliness and Good Learning* (London: 1961). G. Faber, *Jowett* (London: 1957); V. H. H. Green, *Oxford Common Room* (London: 1957), and J. Sparrow, *Mark Pattison and the Idea of a University* (London: 1967), are useful on university reform. There is also a provocative, thoughtful article by J. P. C. Roach, "Victorian Universities and the National Intelligentsia," in *Victorian Studies*, CXI (1959), 131–150.

THOMAS HENRY HUXLEY,
A LIBERAL EDUCATION; AND WHERE TO FIND IT

The business which the South London Working Men's College has undertaken is a great work; indeed, I might say, that Educa-

Source: From "A Liberal Education and Where to Find It," *The Collected Essays of Thomas Henry Huxley*, vol. III, *Science and Education* (New York: 1897), pp. 76–100.

tion, with which that college proposes to grapple, is the greatest work of all those which lie ready to a man's hand just at present.

And, at length, this fact is becoming generally recognised. You cannot go anywhere without hearing a buzz of more or less confused and contradictory talk on the subject—nor can you fail to notice that, in one point at any rate, there is a very decided advance upon like discussions in former days. Nobody outside the agricultural interest now dares to say that education is a bad thing. If any representative of the once large and powerful party, which, in former days, proclaimed this opinion, still exists in a semi-fossil state, he keeps his thoughts to himself. In fact, there is a chorus of voices, almost distressing in their harmony, raised in favour of the doctrine that education is the great panacea for human troubles, and that, if the country is not shortly to go to the dogs, everybody must be educated.

The politicians tells us, "You must educate the masses because they are going to be masters." The clergy join in the cry for education, for they affirm that the people are drifting away from church and chapel into the broadest infidelity. The manufacturers and the capitalists swell the chorus lustily. They declare that ignorance makes bad workmen; that England will soon be unable to turn out cotton goods, or steam engines, cheaper than other people; and then, Ichabod! Ichabod! the glory will be departed from us. And a few voices are lifted up in favour of the doctrine that the masses should be educated because they are men and women with unlimited capacities of being, doing, and suffering, and that it is as true now, as ever it was, that the people perish for lack of knowledge.

These members of the minority, with whom I confess I have a good deal of sympathy, are doubtful whether any of the other reasons urged in favour of the education of the people are of much value—whether, indeed, some of them are based upon either wise or noble grounds of action. They question if it be wise to tell people that you will do for them, out of fear of their power, what you have left undone, so long as your only motive was compassion for their weakness and their sorrows. And, if ignorance of everything which it is needful a ruler should know is likely to do so much harm in the governing classes of the future, why is it, they ask reasonably enough, that such ignorance in the governing classes of the past has not been viewed with equal horror?

Compare the average artisan and the average squire, and it may be doubted if you will find a pin to choose between the two in point of ignorance, class feeling, or prejudice. It is true that the ignorance is of a different sort—that the class feeling is in favour of a different class—and that the prejudice has a distinct savour of wrong-headedness in each case—but it is questionable if the one is either a bit better, or a bit worse, than the other. The old protectionist theory is the doctrine of trades unions as applied by the squires, and the modern trades unionism is the doctrine of the squires applied by the artisans. Why should we be worse off under one *régime* than under the other?

Again, this sceptical minority asks the clergy to think whether it is really want of education which keeps the masses away from their ministrations—whether the most completely educated men are not as open to reproach on this score as the workmen; and whether, perchance, this may not indicate that it is not education which lies at the bottom of the matter?

Once more, these people, whom there is no pleasing, venture to doubt whether the glory, which rests upon being able to undersell all the rest of the world, is a very safe kind of glory—whether we may not purchase it too dear; especially if we allow education, which ought to be directed to the making of men, to be diverted into a process of manufacturing human tools, wonderfully adroit in the exercise of some technical industry, but good for nothing else.

And, finally, these people inquire whether it is the masses alone who need a reformed and improved education. They ask whether the richest of our public schools might not well be made to supply knowledge, as well as gentlemanly habits, a strong class feeling, and eminent proficiency in cricket. They seem to think that the noble foundations of our old universities are hardly fulfilling their functions in their present posture of half-clerical seminaries, half racecourses, where men are trained to win a cup, with as little reference to the needs of after-life in the case of the man as in that of the racer. And, while as zealous for education as the rest, they affirm that, if the education of the richer classes were such as to fit them to be the leaders and the governors of the poorer; and, if the education of the poorer classes were such as to enable them to appreciate really wise guidance and good governance, the politicians need not fear mob-law, nor the clergy lament their want of flocks, nor the capitalists prognosticate the annihilation of the prosperity of the country.

Such is the diversity of opinion upon the why and the wherefore of education. And my hearers will be prepared to expect that the practical recommendations which are put forward are not less discordant. There is a loud cry for compulsory education. We English, in spite of constant experience to the contrary, preserve a touching faith in the efficacy of acts of Parliament; and I believe we should have compulsory education in the course of next session, if there were the least probability that half a dozen leading statesmen of different parties would agree what that education should be.

Some hold that education without theology is worse than none. Others maintain, quite as strongly, that education with theology is in the same predicament. But this is certain that those who hold the first opinion can by no means agree what theology should be taught; and that those who maintain the second are in a small minority.

At any rate "make people learn to read, write, and cipher," say a great many; and the advice is undoubtedly sensible as far as it goes. But, as has happened to me in former days, those who, in despair of getting anything better, advocate this measure, are met with the objection that it is very like making a child practise the use of a knife, fork, and spoon, without giving it a particle of meat. I really don't know what reply is to be made to such an objection.

But it would be unprofitable to spend more time in disentangling, or rather in showing up the knots in, the ravelled skeins of our neighbours. Much more to the purpose is it to ask if we possess any clue of our own which may guide us among these entanglements. And by way of beginning, let us ask ourselves—What is education? Above all things, what is our ideal of a thoroughly liberal education?—of that education which, if we could begin life again, we could give ourselves—of that education which, if we could mould the fates to our own will, we would give our children? Well, I know not what may be your conceptions upon this matter, but I will tell you mine, and I hope I shall find that our views are not very discrepant.

Suppose it were perfectly certain that the life and fortune of every one of us would, one day or other, depend upon his winning or losing a game at chess. Don't you think that we should all consider it to be a primary duty to learn at least the names and the moves of the pieces; to have a notion of a gambit, and a keen eye for all the means of giving and getting out of check? Do you not think that we should look with a disapprobation amounting to scorn, upon the father who allowed his son, or the state which allowed its members, to grow up without knowing a pawn from a knight?

Yet it is a very plain and elementary truth, that the life, the fortune, and the happiness of every one of us, and, more or less, of those who are connected with us, do depend upon our knowing something of the rules of a game infinitely more difficult and complicated than chess. It is a game which has been played for untold ages, every man and woman of us being one of the two players in a game of his or her own. The chess-board is the world, the pieces are the phenomena of the universe, the rules of the game are what we call the laws of Nature. The player on the other side is hidden from us. We know that his play is always fair, just and patient. But also we know, to our cost, that he never overlooks a mistake, or makes the smallest allowance for ignorance. To the man who plays well, the highest stakes are paid, with that sort of overflowing generosity with which the strong shows delight in strength. And one who plays ill is checkmated—without haste, but without remorse.

My metaphor will remind some of you of the famous picture in which Retzsch has depicted Satan playing at chess with man for his soul. Substitute for the mocking fiend in that picture a calm, strong angel who is playing for love, as we say, and would rather lose than win—and I should accept it as an image of human life.

Well, what I mean by Education is learning the rules of this mighty game. In other words, education is the instruction of the intellect in the laws of Nature, under which name I include not merely things and their forces, but men and their ways; and the fashioning of the affections and of the will into an earnest and loving desire to move in harmony with those laws. For me, education means neither more nor less than this. Anything which professes to call itself education must be tried by this standard, and if it fails to stand the test, I will not call it education, whatever may be the force of authority, or of numbers, upon the other side.

It is important to remember that, in strictness, there is no such thing as an uneducated man. Take an extreme case. Suppose that an adult man, in the full vigour of his faculties, could be suddenly placed in the world, as Adam is said to have been, and then left to do as he best might. How long would he be left uneducated? Not five minutes. Nature would begin to teach him, through the eye, the ear, the touch, the properties of objects. Pain and pleasure would be at his elbow telling him to do this and avoid that; and by slow degrees the man would receive an education which, if narrow, would be thorough, real, and adequate to his circumstances, though there would be no extras and very few accomplishments.

And if to this solitary man entered a second Adam, or, better still, an Eve, a new and greater world, that of social and moral phenomena, would be revealed. Joys and woes, compared with which all others might seem but faint shadows, would spring from the new relations. Happiness and sorrow would take the place of the coarser monitors, pleasure and pain; but conduct would still be shaped by the observation of the natural consequences of actions; or, in other words, by the laws of the nature of man.

To every one of us the world was once as fresh and new as to Adam. And then, long before we were susceptible of any other mode of instruction, Nature took us in hand, and every minute of waking life brought its educational influence, shaping our actions into rough accordance with Nature's laws, so that we might not be ended untimely by too gross disobedience. Nor should I speak of this process of education as past for any one, be he as old as he may. For every man the world is as fresh as it was at the first day, and as full of untold novelties for him who has the eyes to see them. And Nature is still continuing her patient education of us in that great university, the universe, of which we are all members— Nature having no Test-Acts.

Those who take honours in Nature's university, who learn the laws which govern men and things and obey them, are the really great and successful men in this world. The great mass of mankind are the "Poll," who pick up just enough to get through without much discredit. Those who won't learn at all are plucked; and then you can't come up again. Nature's pluck means extermination.

Thus the question of compulsory education is settled so far as Nature is concerned. Her bill on that question was framed and passed long ago. But, like all compulsory legislation, that of Nature is harsh and wasteful in its operation. Ignorance is visited as sharply as wilful disobedience—incapacity meets with the same punishment as crime. Nature's discipline is not even a word and a blow, and the blow first; but the blow without the word. It is left to you to find out why your ears are boxed.

The object of what we commonly call education—that education in which man intervenes and which I shall distinguish as artificial education—is to make good these defects in Nature's methods; to prepare the child to receive Nature's education, neither incapably nor ignorantly, nor with wilful disobedience; and to understand the preliminary symptoms of her pleasure, without waiting for the box on her ear. In short, all artificial education ought to be an anticipation of natural education. And a liberal education is an artificial education which has not only prepared a man to escape the great evils of disobedience to natural laws, but has trained him to appreciate and to seize upon the rewards, which Nature scatters with as free a hand as her penalties.

That man, I think, has had a liberal education who has been so trained in youth that his body is the ready servant of his will, and does with ease and pleasure all the work that, as a mechanism, it is capable of; whose intellect is a clear, cold, logic engine, with all its parts of equal strength, and in smooth working order; ready, like a steam engine, to be turned to any kind of work, and spin the gossamers as well as forge the anchors of the mind; whose mind is stored with a knowledge of the great and fundamental truths of Nature and of the laws of her operations; one who, no stunted ascetic, is full of life and fire, but whose passions are trained to come to heel by a vigorous will, the servant of a tender conscience; who has learned to love all beauty, whether of Nature or of art, to hate all vileness, and to respect others as himself.

Such an one and no other, I conceive, has had a liberal education; for he is, as completely as a man can be, in harmony with Nature. He will make the best of her, and she of him. They will get on together rarely: she as his ever beneficent mother; he as her mouthpiece, her conscious self, her minister and interpreter.

Where is such an education as this to be had? Where is there any approximation to it? Has any one tried to found such an education? Looking over the length and breadth of these islands, I am afraid that all these questions must receive a negative answer. Consider our primary schools and what is taught in them. A child learns:—

1. To read, write, and cipher, more or less well; but in a very

large proportion of cases not so well as to take pleasure in reading, or to be able to write the commonest letter properly.

2. A quantity of dogmatic theology, of which the child, nine times out of ten, understands next to nothing.

3. Mixed up with this, so as to seem to stand or fall with it, a few of the broadest and simplest principles of morality. This, to my mind, is much as if a man of science should make the story of the fall of the apple in Newton's garden an integral part of the doctrine of gravitation and teach it as of equal authority with the law of the inverse squares.

4. A good deal of Jewish history and Syrian geography, and perhaps a little something about English history and the geography of the child's own country. But I doubt if there is a primary school in England in which hangs a map of the hundred in which the village lies, so that the children may be practically taught by it what a map means.

5. A certain amount of regularity, attentive obedience, respect for others: obtained by fear, if the master be incompetent or foolish; by love and reverence, if he be wise.

So far as this school course embraces a training in the theory and practice of obedience to the moral laws of Nature, I gladly admit, not only that it contains a valuable educational element, but that, so far, it deals with the most valuable and important parts of all education. Yet, contrast what is done in this direction with what might be done; with the time given, to matters of comparatively no importance; with the absence of any attention to things of the highest moment; and one is tempted to think of Falstaff's bill and "the halfpenny worth of bread to all the quantity of sack."

Let us consider what a child thus "educated" knows, and what it does not know. Begin with the most important topic of all—morality, as the guide of conduct. The child knows well enough that some acts meet with approbation and some with disapprobation. But it has never heard that there lies in the nature of things a reason for every moral law, as cogent and as well defined as that which underlies every physical law; that stealing and lying are just as certain to be followed by evil consequences, as putting your hand in the fire, or jumping out of a garret window. Again, though the scholar may have been made acquainted, in dogmatic fashion, with the broad laws of morality, he has had no training in the application of those laws to the difficult problems which result from the complex conditions of modern civilisation. Would it not be very hard to expect any one to solve a problem in conic sections who had merely been taught the axioms and definitions of mathematical science?

A workman has to bear hard labour, and perhaps privation, while he sees others rolling in wealth, and feeding their dogs with what would keep his children from starvation. Would it not be well to have helped the man to calm the natural promptings of discontent by showing him, in his youth, the necessary connection of the moral law which prohibits stealing with the stability of society—by proving to him, once for all, that it is better for his own people, better for himself, better for future generations, that he should starve than steal? If you have no foundation of knowledge, or habit of thought, to work upon, what chance have you of persuading a hungry man that a capitalist is not a thief "with a circumbendibus?" And if he honestly believes that, of what avail is it to quote the commandment against stealing, when he proposes to make the capitalist disgorge?

Again, the child learns absolutely nothing of the history or the political organisation of his own country. His general impression is, that everything of much importance happened a very long while ago; and that the Queen and the gentlefolks govern the country much after the fashion of King David and the elders and nobles of Israel—his sole models. Will you give a man with this much information a vote? In easy times he sells it for a pot of beer. Why should he not? It is of about as much use to him as a chignon, and he knows as much what to do with it, for any other purpose. In bad times, on the contrary, he applies his simple theory of government, and believes that his rulers are the cause of his sufferings—a belief which sometimes bears remarkable practical fruits.

Least of all, does the child gather from this primary "education" of ours a conception of the laws of the physical world, or of the relations of cause and effect therein. And this is the more to be lamented, as the poor are especially exposed to physical evils, and are more interested in removing them than any other class of the community. If any one is concerned in knowing the ordinary laws of mechanics one would think it is the hand-labourer, whose daily toil lies among levers and pulleys; or among the other implements of artisan work. And if any one is interested in the laws of health, it is the poor workman, whose strength is wasted by ill-prepared food, whose health is sapped by bad ventilation and bad drainage, and half whose children are massacred by disorders which might be prevented. Not only does our present primary education carefully abstain from hinting to the workman that some of his greatest evils are traceable to mere physical agencies, which could be removed by energy, patience, and frugality; but it does worse—it renders him, so far as it can, deaf to those who could help him, and tries to substitute an Oriental submission to what is falsely declared to be the will of God, for his natural tendency to strive after a better condition.

What wonder, then, if very recently an appeal has been made to statistics for the profoundly foolish purpose of showing that education is of no good—that it diminishes neither misery nor crime among the masses of mankind? I reply, why should the thing which has been called education do either the one or the other? If I am a knave or a fool, teaching me to read and write won't make me less of either one or the other—unless somebody shows me how to put my reading and writing to wise and good purposes.

Suppose any one were to argue that medicine is of no use, because it could be proved statistically, that the percentage of deaths was just the same among people who had been taught how to open a medicine chest, and among those who did not so much as know the key by sight. The argument is absurd; but it is not more preposterous than that against which I am contending. The only medicine for suffering, crime, and all the other woes of mankind, is wisdom. Teach a man to read and write, and you have put into his hands the great keys of the wisdom box. But it is quite another matter whether he ever opens the box or not. And he is as likely to poison as to cure himself, if, without guidance, he swallows the first drug that comes to hand. In these times a man may as well be purblind, as unable to read—lame, as unable to write. But I protest that, if I thought the alternative were a necessary one, I would rather that the children of the poor should grow up ignorant of the knowledge to which these arts are means.

It may be said that all these animadversions may apply to primary schools, but that the higher schools at any rate, must be allowed to give a liberal education. In fact they professedly sacrifice everything else to this object.

Let us inquire into this matter. What do the higher schools, those to which the great middle class of the country sends its children, teach, over and above the instruction given in the primary schools? There is a little more reading and writing of English. But, for all that, every one knows that it is a rare thing to find a boy of the middle or upper classes who can read aloud decently, or who can put his thoughts on paper in clear and grammatical (to say nothing of good or elegant) language. The "ciphering" of the lower schools expands into elementary mathematics in the higher; into arithmetic, with a little algebra, a little Euclid. But I doubt if one boy in five hundred has ever heard the explanation of a rule of arithmetic, or knows his Euclid otherwise than by rote.

Of theology, the middle class schoolboy gets rather less than poorer children, less absolutely and less relatively, because there are so many other claims upon his attention. I venture to say that, in the great majority of cases, his ideas on this subject when he leaves school are of the most shadowy and vague description, and associated with painful impressions of the weary hours spent in learning collects and catechism by heart.

Modern geography, modern history, modern literature; the English language as a language; the whole circle of the sciences, physical, moral and social, are even more completely ignored in the higher than in the lower schools. Up till within a few years back, a boy might have passed through any one of the great public schools with the greatest distinction and credit, and might never so much as have heard of one of the subjects I have just mentioned. He might never have heard that the earth goes round the sun; that England underwent a great revolution in 1688, and France another in 1789; that there once lived certain notable men called Chaucer, Shakespeare, Milton, Voltaire, Goethe, Schiller. The first might be a German and the last an Englishman for anything he could tell you to the contrary. And as for Science, the only idea the word would suggest to his mind would be dexterity in boxing.

I have said that this was the state of things a few years back, for the sake of the few righteous who are to be found among the educational cities of the plain. But I would not have you too sanguine about the result, if you sound the minds of the existing generation of public schoolboys on such topics as those I have mentioned.

Now let us pause to consider this wonderful state of affairs; for the time will come when Englishmen will quote it as the stock example of the stolid stupidity of their ancestors in the nineteenth century. The most thoroughly commercial people, the greatest voluntary wanderers and colonists the world has ever seen, are precisely the middle classes of this country. If there be a people which has been busy making history on the great scale for the last three hundred years—and the most profoundly interesting history—history which, if it happened to be that of Greece or Rome, we should study with avidity—it is the English. If there be a people which, during the same period, has developed a remarkable literature, it is our own. If there be a nation whose prosperity depends absolutely and wholly upon their mastery over the forces of Nature, upon their intelligent apprehension of, and obedience to the laws of the creation and distribution of wealth, and of the stable equilibrium of the forces of society, it is precisely this nation. And yet this is what these wonderful people tell their sons:—"At the cost of from one to two thousand pounds of our hard-earned money, we devote twelve of the most precious years of your lives to school. There you shall toil, or be supposed to toil; but there you shall not learn one single thing of all those you will most want to know directly you leave school and enter upon the practical business of life. You will in all probability go into business, but you shall not know where, or how, any article of commerce is produced, or the difference between an export or an import, or the meaning of the word "capital." You will very likely settle in a colony, but you shall not know whether Tasmania is part of New South Wales, or *vice versa*.

"Very probably you may become a manufacturer, but you shall not be provided with the means of understanding the working of one of your own steam-engines, or the nature of the raw products you employ; and, when you are asked to buy a patent, you shall not have the slightest means of judging whether the inventor is an impostor who is contravening the elementary principles of science, or a man who will make you as rich as Croesus.

"You will very likely get into the House of Commons. You will have to take your share in making laws which may prove a blessing or a curse to millions of men. But you shall not hear one word respecting the political organisation of your country; the meaning of the controversy between free-traders and protectionists shall never have been mentioned to you; you shall not so much as know that there are such things as economical laws.

"The mental power which will be of most importance in your daily life will be the power of seeing things as they are without regard to authority; and of drawing accurate general conclusions from particular facts. But at school and college you shall know of no source of truth but authority; nor exercise your reasoning faculty upon anything but deduction from that which is laid down by authority.

"You will have to weary your soul with work, and many a time eat your bread in sorrow and in bitterness, and you shall not have learned to take refuge in the great source of pleasure without alloy, the serene resting-place for worn human nature,—the world of art."

Said I not rightly that we are a wonderful people? I am quite prepared to allow, that education entirely devoted to these omitted subjects might not be a completely liberal education. But is an education which ignores them all a liberal education? Nay, is it too much to say that the education which should embrace these subjects and no others would be a real education, though an incomplete one; while an education which omits them is really not an education at all, but a more or less useful course of intellectual gymnastics?

For what does the middle-class school put in the place of all these things which are left out? It substitutes what is usually comprised under the compendious title of the "classics"—that is to say, the languages, the literature, and the history of the ancient Greeks and Romans, and the geography of so much of the world as was known to these two great nations of antiquity. Now, do not expect me to depreciate the earnest and enlightened pursuit of classical learning. I have not the least desire to speak ill of such occupations, nor any sympathy with those who run them down. On the contrary, if my opportunities had lain in that direction, there is no investigation into which I could have thrown myself with greater delight than that of antiquity.

What science can present greater attractions than philology? How can a lover of literary excellence fail to rejoice in the ancient masterpieces? And with what consistency could I, whose business lies so much in the attempt to decipher the past, and to build up intelligible forms out of the scattered fragments of long-extinct beings, fail to take a sympathetic, though an unlearned, interest in the labours of a Niebuhr, a Gibbon, or a Grote? Classical history is a great section of the palaeontology of man; and I have the same double respect for it as for other kinds of palaeontology—that is to say, a respect for the facts which it establishes as for all facts, and a still greater respect for it as a preparation for the discovery of a law of progress.

But if the classics were taught as they might be taught—if boys and girls were instructed in Greek and Latin, not merely as languages, but as illustrations of philological science; if a vivid picture of life on the shores of the Mediterranean two thousand years ago were imprinted on the minds of scholars; if ancient history were taught, not as a weary series of feuds and fights, but traced to its causes in such men placed under such conditions; if, lastly, the study of the classical books were followed in such a manner as to impress boys with their beauties, and with the grand simplicity of their statement of the everlasting problems of human life, instead of with their verbal and grammatical peculiarities; I still think it as little proper that they should form the basis of a liberal education for our contemporaries, as I should think it fitting to make that sort of palaeontology with which I am familiar the back-bone of modern education.

It is wonderful how close a parallel to classical training could be made out of that palaeontology to which I refer. In the first place I could get up an osteological primer so arid, so pedantic in its terminology, so altogether distasteful to the youthful mind, as to beat the recent famous production of the head-masters out of the field in all these excellences. Next, I could exercise my boys upon easy fossils, and bring out all their powers of memory and all their ingenuity in the application of my osteo-grammatical rules to the interpretation, or construing, of those fragments. To those who had reached the higher classes, I might supply odd bones to be built up into animals, giving great honour and reward to him who succeeded in fabricating monsters most entirely in accordance with the rules. That would answer to verse-making and essay-writing in the dead languages.

To be sure, if a great comparative anatomist were to look at these fabrications he might shake his head, or laugh. But what then? Would such a catastrophe destroy the parallel? What, think you, would Cicero, or Horace, say to the production of the best sixth form going? And would not Terence stop his ears and run out if he could be present at an English performance of his own plays? Would *Hamlet*, in the mouths of a set of French actors, who should insist on pronouncing English after the fashion of their own tongue, be more hideously ridiculous?

But it will be said that I am forgetting the beauty, and the human interest, which appertain to classical studies. To this I reply that it is only a very strong man who can appreciate the charms of a landscape as he is toiling up a steep hill, along a bad road. What with short-windedness, stones, ruts, and a pervading sense of the wisdom of rest and be thankful, most of us have little enough sense of the beautiful under these circumstances. The ordinary school-boy is precisely in this case. He finds Parnassus uncommonly steep, and there is no chance of his having much time of inclination to look about him till he gets to the top. And nine times out of ten he does not get to the top.

But if this be a fair picture of the results of classical teaching at its best—and I gather from those who have authority to speak on such matters that it is so—what is to be said of classical teaching at its worst, or in other words, of the classics of our ordinary middle-class schools? I will tell you. It means getting up endless forms and rules by heart. It means turning Latin and Greek into English, for the mere sake of being able to do it, and without the smallest regard to the worth, or worthlessness, of the author read. It means the learning of innumerable, not always decent, fables in such a shape that the meaning they once had is tried up into utter trash; and the only impression left upon a boy's mind is, that the people who believed such things must have been the greatest idiots the world ever saw. And it means, finally, that after a dozen years spent at this kind of work, the sufferer shall be incompetent to interpret a passage in an author he has not already got up; that he shall loathe the sight of a Greek or Latin book; and that he shall never open, or think of, a classical writer again, until, wonderful to relate, he insists upon submitting his sons to the same process.

These be your gods, O Israel! For the sake of this net result (and respectability) the British father denies his children all the knowl-edge they might turn to account in life, not merely for the achieve-ment of vulgar success, but for guidance in the great crises of human existence. This is the stone he offers to those whom he is bound by the strongest and tenderest ties to feed with bread.

If primary and secondary education are in this unsatisfactory state, what is to be said to the universities? This is an awful subject, and one I almost fear to touch with my unhallowed hands; but I can tell you what those say who have authority to speak.

The Rector of Lincoln College, in his lately published valuable

"Suggestions for Academical Organisation with especial reference to Oxford," tells us:—

> The colleges were, in their origin, endowments, not for the elements of a general liberal education, but for the prolonged study of special and professional faculties by men of riper age. The universities embraced both these objects. The colleges, while they incidentally aided in elementary education, were specially devoted to the highest learning. . . .
>
> This was the theory of the middle-age university and the design of collegiate foundations in their origin. Time and circumstances have brought about a total change. The colleges no longer promote the researches of science, or direct professional study. Here and there college walls may shelter an occasional student, but not in larger proportions than may be found in private life. Elementary teaching of youths under twenty is now the only function performed by the university, and almost the only object of college endowments. Colleges were homes for the life-study of the highest and most abstruse parts of knowledge. They have become boarding schools in which the elements of the learned languages are taught to youths.

If Mr. Pattison's high position, and his obvious love and respect for his university, be insufficient to convince the outside world that language so severe is yet no more than just, the authority of the Commissioners who reported on the University of Oxford in 1850 is open to no challenge. Yet they write:—

> It is generally acknowledged that both Oxford and the country at large suffer greatly from the absence of a body of learned men devoting their lives to the cultivation of science, and to the direction of academical education.

The fact that so few books of profound research emanate from the University of Oxford, materially impairs its character as a seat of learning, and consequently its hold on the respect of the nation.

Cambridge can claim no exemption from the reproaches addressed to Oxford. And thus there seems no escape from the admission that what we fondly call our great seats of learning are simply "boarding schools" for bigger boys; that learned men are not more numerous in them than out of them; that the advancement of knowledge is not the object of fellows of colleges; that, in the philosophic calm and meditative stillness of their greenswarded courts, philosophy does not thrive, and meditation bears few fruits.

It is my great fortune to reckon amongst my friends resident members of both universities, who are men of learning and research, zealous cultivators of science, keeping before their minds a noble ideal of a university, and doing their best to make that ideal a reality; and, to me, they would necessarily typify the universities, did not the authoritative statements I have quoted compel me to believe that they are exceptional, and not representative men. Indeed, upon calm consideration, several circumstances lead me to think that the Rector of Lincoln College and the Commissioners cannot be far wrong.

I believe there can be no doubt that the foreigner who should wish to become acquainted with the scientific, or the literary, activity of modern England would simply lose his time and his pains if he visited our universities with that object.

And, as for works of profound research on any subject, and, above all, in that classical lore for which the universities profess to sacrifice almost everything else, why, a third-rate, poverty-stricken German university turns out more produce of that kind in one year, than our vast and wealthy foundations elaborate in ten.

Ask the man who is investigating any question, profoundly and thoroughly—be its historical, philosophical, philological, physical, literary, or theological; who is trying to make himself master of any abstract subject (except, perhaps, political economy and geology, both of which are intensely Anglican sciences), whether he is not compelled to read half a dozen times as many German as English books? And whether, of these English books, more than one in ten is the work of a fellow of a college, or a professor of an English university?

Is this from any lack of power in the English as compared with the German mind? The countrymen of Grote and of Mill, of Faraday, of Robert Brown, of Lyell, and of Darwin, to go no further back than the contemporaries of men of middle age, can afford to smile at such a suggestion. England can show now, as she has been able to show in every generation since civilisation spread over the West, individual men who hold their own against the world, and keep alive the old tradition of her intellectual eminence.

But, in the majority of cases, these men are what they are in virtue of their native intellectual force, and of a strength of character which will not recognise impediments. They are not trained in the courts of the Temple of Science, but storm the walls of that edifice in all sorts of irregular ways, and with much loss of time and power, in order to obtain their legitimate positions.

Our universities not only do not encourage such men; do not offer them positions, in which it should be their highest duty to do, thoroughly, that which they are most capable of doing; but, as far as possible, university training shuts out of the minds of those among them, who are subjected to it, the prospect that there is anything in the world for which they are specially fitted. Imagine the success of the attempt to still the intellectual hunger of any of the men I have mentioned, by putting before him, as the object of existence, the successful mimicry of the measure of a Greek song, or the roll of Ciceronian prose! Imagine how much success would be likely to attend the attempt to persuade such men that the education which leads to perfection in such elegances is alone to be called culture; while the facts of history, the process of thought, the conditions of moral and social existence, and the laws of physical nature are left to be dealt with as they may by outside barbarians!

It is not thus that the German universities, from being beneath notice a century ago, have become what they are now—the most intensely cultivated and the most productive intellectual corporations the world has ever seen.

The student who repairs to them sees in the list of classes and of professors a fair picture of the world of knowledge. Whatever he needs to know there is some one ready to teach him, some one competent to discipline him in the way of learning; whatever his special bent, let him but be able and diligent, and in due time he shall find distinction and a career. Among his professors he sees men whose names are known and revered throughout the civilised world; and their living example infects him with a noble ambition, and a love for the spirit of work.

The Germans dominate the intellectual world by virtue of the same simple secret as that which made Napoleon the master of old Europe. They have declared *la carrière ouverte aux talents*, and every Bursch marches with a professor's gown in his knapsack. Let him become a great scholar, or a man of science, and ministers will compete for his services. In Germany, they do not leave the chance of his holding the office he would render illustrious to the tender mercies of a hot canvass, and the final wisdom of a mob of country parsons.

In short, in Germany, the universities are exactly what the Rector of Lincoln and the Commissioners tell us the English universities are not; that is to say, corporations "of learned men devoting their lives to the cultivation of science, and the direction of academical education." They are not "boarding schools for youths," no clerical seminaries; but institutions for the higher culture of men, in which the theological faculty is of no more importance, or prominence, than the rest; and which are truly "universities," since they strive to represent and embody the totality of human knowledge, and to find room for all forms of intellectual activity.

May zealous and clear-headed reformers like Mr. Pattison succeed in their noble endeavours to shape our universities towards some such ideal as this, without losing what is valuable and distinctive in their social tone! But until they have succeeded, a liberal education will be no more obtainable in our Oxford and Cambridge Universities than in our public schools.

If I am justified in my conception of the ideal of a liberal education; and if what I have said about the existing educational institutions of the country is also true, it is clear that the two have no sort of relation to one another; that the best of our schools and the most complete of our university trainings give but a narrow, one-sided, and essentially illiberal education—while the worst give what is really next to no education at all. The South London Working-Men's College could not copy any of these institutions if it would; I am bold enough to express the conviction that it ought not if it could.

For what is wanted is the reality and not the mere name of a liberal education; and this College must steadily set before itself the ambition to be able to give that education sooner or later. At present we are but beginning, sharpening our educational tools, as it were, and, except a modicum of physical science, we are not able to offer much more than is to be found in an ordinary school.

Moral and social science—one of the greatest and most fruitful of our future classes, I hope—at present lacks only one thing in our programme, and that is a teacher. A considerable want, no doubt; but it must be recollected that it is much better to want a teacher than to want the desire to learn.

Further, we need what, for want of a better name, I must call Physical Geography. What I mean is that which the Germans call "Erdkunde." It is a description of the earth, of its place and relation to other bodies; of its general structure, and of its great features—winds, tides, mountains, plains: of the chief forms of the vegetable and animal worlds, of the varieties of man. It is the peg upon which the greatest quantity of useful and entertaining scientific information can be suspended.

Literature is not upon the College programme; but I hope some day to see it there. For literature is the greatest of all sources of refined pleasure, and one of the great uses of a liberal education is to enable us to enjoy that pleasure. There is scope enough for the purposes of liberal education in the study of the rich treasures of our own language alone. All that is needed is direction, and the cultivation of a refined taste by attention to sound criticism. But there is no reason why French and German should not be mastered sufficiently to read what is worth reading in those languages with pleasure and with profit.

And finally, by and by, we must have History; treated not as a succession of battles and dynasties; not as a series of biographies; not as evidence that Providence has always been on the side of either Whigs or Tories; but as the development of man in times past, and in other conditions than our own.

But, as it is one of the principles of our College to be self-supporting, the public must lead, and we must follow, in these matters. If my hearers take to heart what I have said about liberal education, they will desire these things, and I doubt not we shall be able to supply them. But we must wait till the demand is made.

37. Purpose in Education

LIKE THE BENTHAMITE utilitarians who had designed so much of the blueprint for their age, the Victorians displayed considerable inventiveness and an extraordinary capacity to adapt the old to the new. It proved easier, however, to translate and expand institutions than the unspoken assumptions which lay behind them. In many instances, reformers and their opponents were startlingly insensitive to these hypotheses. The rapid growth of the middle classes was not, for example, accompanied by the successful transmission of the social discipline and individual constraint that had made the mobility possible. Education was used to aid the young to make their way in the world, but that failed to go to the heart of the matter. Education was didactic. Students were taught and learned things, whether they were the multiplication tables or the principles of morality. Institutions, teachers, and curriculum served to impede as much as to aid actual learning.

Herbert Spencer (1820–1903), one of history's more engaging eccentrics, is best known for his application of Darwinism to society. He propounded theories that were inappropriate, invented gadgets that did not work. His utopia was to be constructed by competing individuals in an unfettered industrial society. Understandably, he achieved more enthusiastic reception in the United States than the United Kingdom. None of this is entirely fair. Spencer deserves more credit than he has received for his work in the development of sociology. Many of the questions Spencer asked about British society in the mid- and late nineteenth century seem much more appropriate a century later. Didactic as he was, Spencer never insisted that he possessed absolute truth. "Modes of consciousness standing in place of positive answers, must ever remain."[1] He began with the simple assumption "that the moral constitution which fitted man for the predatory state, differs from the one needed to fit him for this social state to which multiplication of the race has led."[2]

Education was the prerequisite for living in a society of free men. But this education must rely upon conviction, not coercion, or the individual would never learn what he must. The only way in which one learns to take charge of life is to take charge of oneself. Any system, any curriculum will fail—it will be knowledge without purpose—that does not begin from the presumption that the child must make himself into the adult. Only so can the foundation be built for a society without violence and exploitation, for a world that can fully realize the idea of progress.

Recommended Reading

Spencer stock has been selling at new lows. J. Rumney, *Herbert Spencer's Sociology* (New York: 1966) may mark the start of a revival.

HERBERT SPENCER,
THE RIGHTS OF CHILDREN

COERCIVE EDUCATION

If coercive education is right, it must be productive of good, and if wrong, evil. By an analysis of its results, therefore, we shall

1. H. Spencer, *The Principles of Sociology and Ethics* (London: 1896), vol. II, pp. 200–201.
2. H. Spencer, *The Rights of Children* (New York: 1879), p. 179.

Source: From *The Rights of Children and the True Principles of Family Governance* (New York: 1879), pp. 172–178.

obtain so much evidence for or against the doctrine that the liberties of children are coextensive with those of adults.

Considering what universal attention the culture of the young has lately received—the books written about it, the lectures delivered on it, the experiments made to elucidate it—there is reason for concluding that as the use of brute force for educational purposes has greatly declined, something radically wrong must be involved in it. But without dwelling on this, let us judge of coercive education not by the effects it is *believed* to produce, but by those it *must* produce.

Education has for its object the formation of character. To curb restive propensities, to awaken dormant sentiments, to strengthen the perceptions and cultivate the tastes, to encourage this feeling and repress that, so as finally to develop the child into a man of well proportioned and harmonious nature—this is alike the aim of parent and teacher. Those, therefore, who advocate the use of authority, and, if need be, force, in the management of children must do so because they think these the best means of compassing the desired object. Paternity has to devise some kind of rule for the nursery. Impelled partly by the creed, partly by custom, partly by inclination, paternity decides in favor of a pure despotism proclaims its word the supreme law, anathematizes disobedience, and exhibits the rod as the final arbiter in all disputes. And of course this system is defended as the one best calculated to curb restive propensities, awaken dormant sentiments, etc., etc., as aforesaid. Suppose now we inquire how the plan works. An unamiable little urchin is pursuing his own gratification regardless of the comfort of others; is perhaps annoyingly vociferous in his play; or is amusing himself by teasing a companion; or is trying to monopolize the toys intended for others in common with himself. Well, some kind of interposition is manifestly called for. Paternity, with knit brows, and in a severe tone, commands desistance, visits anything like reluctant submission with a sharp "Do as I bid you;" if need be, hints at a whipping or the black hole—in short carries coercion, or the threat of coercion, far enough to produce obedience. After sundry exhibitions of perverse feeling the child gives in; showing, however, by its sullenness the animosity it entertains. Meanwhile paternity pokes the fire and complacently resumes the newspaper, under the impression that all is as it should be: most unfortunate mistake!

If the thing wanted had been the mere repression of noise, or the mechanical transfer of a plaything, perhaps no better course could have been pursued. Had it been of no consequence under what impulse the child acted, so long as it fulfilled a given mandate, nothing would remain to be said. But something else was needed. Character was the thing to be changed rather than conduct. It was not the deeds, but the feeling from which the deeds sprung that required dealing with. Here were palpable manifestations of selfishness, and indifference to the wishes of others, a marked desire to tyrannize, an endeavor to engross benefits intended for all; in short, here were exhibitions on a small scale of that unsympathetic nature to which our social evils are mainly attributable. What, then, was the thing wanted? Evidently an alteration in the child's disposition. What was the problem to be solved? Clearly to generate a state of mind which had it previously existed would have prevented the offending actions. What was the final end to be achieved? Unquestionably the formation of a character which would spontaneously produce greater generosity of conduct. Or, speaking definitely, it was necessary to strengthen that sympathy to the weakness of which this ill behavior was traceable.

But sympathy can be strengthened only by exercise. No faculty whatever will grow, save by the performance of its special function; a muscle by contraction, the intellect by perceiving and thinking, a moral sentiment by feeling. Sympathy, therefore, can be increased only by exciting sympathetic emotions. A selfish child is to be rendered less selfish only by arousing in it a fellow-feeling with the desires of others. If this is not done nothing is done.

Observe then how the case stands. A grasping, hard-natured boy is to be humanized, is to have whatever germ of better spirit that may be in him developed; and to this end it is proposed to use frowns, threats, and the stick! To stimulate that faculty which originates our regard for the happiness of others, we are told to inflict pain, or the fear of pain! The problem is—to generate in a child's mind a sympathetic feeling; and the answer is beat it, or send it supperless to bed!

Thus we have but to reduce the subjection theory to a definite form to render its absurdity self-evident. Contrasting the means to be employed with the work to be done, we are at once struck with their utter unfitness. Instead of creating a new internal state which shall exhibit itself in better deeds, coercion can manifestly do nothing but forcibly mold externals into a coarse semblance of such a state. In the family, as in society, it can simply restrain: it cannot educate. Just as the recollection of a jail and the dread of a policeman, whilst they serve to check the thief's depredations, effect no change in his morals, so, although a father's threats may produce in a child a certain outside conformity with rectitude, they cannot generate any real attachment to it. As some one has well said, the utmost that severity can do is to make hypocrites; it can never make converts.

Let those who have no faith in any instrumentalities for the rule of human beings, save the stern will and the strong hand, visit an asylum for the insane. Let all self-styled practical men, who, in the pride of their semi-savage theories, shower sarcasms upon the movements for peace, for the abolition of capital punishments and the like, go and witness to their confusion how a number of lunatics can be managed without the use of force. Let those sneerers at "sentimentalisms" reflect on the horrors of madhouses as they used to be; where was weeping and wailing and gnashing of teeth, where chains clanked dismally, and where the silence of the night was rent by shrieks that made the belated passer-by hurry on shudderingly; let them constrast with these horrors the calmness, the contentment, the tractability, the improved health of mind and body, and the not unfrequent recoveries that have followed the abandonment of the strait-jacket regime; and then let them blush for their creed.

And shall the poor maniac, with diseased feelings and a warped intellect, persecuted as he constantly is by the suggestions of a morbid imagination, shall a being with a mind so hopelessly chaotic that even the most earnest pleader for human rights would make his case an exception, shall he be amenable to a non-coercive treatment, and shall a child not be amenable to it? Will any one maintain that madmen can be managed by suasion, but not children? that moral force methods are best for those deprived of reason, but physical force methods for those possessing it? Hardly. The boldest defender of domestic despotism will not assert so much. If by judicious conduct the confidence even of the insane may be obtained—if even to the beclouded intelligence of a lunatic kind attentions and a sympathetic manner will carry the conviction that he is surrounded by friends and not by demons—and if, under that conviction, even he, though a slave to every disordered impulse, becomes comparatively docile, how much more under the same influence will a child become so. Do but gain a boy's trust; convince him by your behavior that you have his happiness at heart; let him discover that you are the wiser of the two; let him experience the benefits of following your advice, and the evils that arise from disregarding it, and fear not that you will readily enough guide him. Not by authority is your sway to be obtained; neither by reasoning; but by inducement. Show in all your conduct that you are thoroughly your child's friend, and there is nothing you may not lead him to. The faintest sign of your approval or dissent will be his law. You have won from him the key of all his feelings; and, instead of the vindictive passions that severe treatment would have aroused, you may by a word call forth tears, or blushes, or the thrill of sympathy; may excite any emotion you please—may, in short, effect something worth calling education.

THE BEST EDUCATION OF A CHILD

If we wish a boy to become a good mechanic we insure his expertness by an early apprenticeship. The young musician that is to be, passes several hours a day at his instrument. Initiatory courses of outline drawing and shading are gone through by the intended artist. For the future accountant a thorough drilling in arithmetic is prescribed. The reflective powers are sought to be developed by the study of mathematics. Thus all training is founded on the principle that culture must precede proficiency. In such proverbs as "Habit is second nature," and "Practice makes perfect," men have expressed those net products of universal observation on which every education is ostensibly based. The maxims of a village school-mistress and the speculations of a Pestalozzi are alike pervaded by the theory that the child should be accustomed to those exertions of body and mind which will in future life be required of it. Education means this or nothing.

What now is the most important attribute of man as a moral being? What faculty above all others should we be solicitous to cultivate? May we not answer, the faculty of self-control? This it is which forms a chief distinction between the human being and the brute. It is in virtue of this that man is defined as a creature "looking before and after." It is in their larger endowment of this that the civilized races are superior to the savage. In supremacy of this consists one of the perfections of the ideal man. Not to be impulsive, not to be spurred hither and thither by each desire that in turn comes uppermost; but to be self-restrained, self-balanced, governed by the joint decision of the feelings in council assembled, before whom every action shall have been debated and calmly determined. This it is which education—moral education at least—strives to produce.

But the power of self-government, like all other powers, can be developed only by exercise. Whoso is to rule over his passions in maturity, must be practiced in ruling over his passions during youth. Observe, then, the absurdity of the coercive system. Instead of habituating a boy to be a law to himself as he is required in after life to be, it administers the law for him. Instead of preparing him against the day when he shall leave the paternal roof, by inducing him to fix the boundaries of his actions and voluntarily confine himself within them, it marks out these boundaries for him, and says, "cross them at your peril." Here we have a being who, in a few years, is to be his own master, and, by way of fitting him for such a condition, he is allowed to be his own master as little as possible. Whilst in every other particular it is thought desirable that what the man will have to do, the child should be well drilled in doing, in this most important of all particulars, the controlling of himself, it is thought that the less practice he has the better. No wonder that those who have been brought up under the severest discipline should so frequently turn out the wildest of the wild. Such a result is just what might have been looked for. Not only does the physical force system fail to fit the youth for his future position, but it absolutely tends to *un*fit him. Were slavery to be his lot no better method of training could be devised than one which accustomed him to that attitude of complete subordination he would subsequently have to assume. But just to the degree in which such treatment would fit him for servitude, must it unfit him for being a free man among free men.

Ave Atque Vale

38. Retrospect: Frederic Harrison

THE MEMORIAL WAS a Victorian obsession. Biographies, autobiographies, and memoirs, like tombstones, were a way of asserting immortality against the facts of mundane existence. Eminent and lesser

Victorians defended their dogmas, propounded their views, reexamined their lives and world to find them full or wanting. Theirs was, if nothing else, an articulate society.

One of those with much to say was Frederic Harrison (1831–1923), one of England's most dedicated positivists. For over half a century he had commented vigorously on British social and political life. His was the retrospect of a man determined to preserve a faith in science and history in place of his lost formal religion. Like so many leading Victorians, Harrison reacted against a strongly evangelical upbringing. Losing one faith he found another in the doctrines of Auguste Comte propounded with theological fervor at Wadham College, Oxford. Positivism offered a cohesive intellectual system. Man was related to his society and every society to the vast movements of history. Improvement was inevitable. The tools of social science would guarantee continued progress. Positivism alone, contended Harrison, can save us from "the dreadful anarchy" in which we exist.

Harrison was principally a man of words, not action. His essays, as any casual glance through the *Fortnightly Review* will reveal, show his range and rigor. Aimless growth was destructive; purposeless individualism anarchic. There was always about Harrison a revivalist's enthusiasm and a commitment to a higher morality. If he suffered from the reformist's tendency to confuse ends and means, he nevertheless recognized and spoke to many of the most important issues of his age. He saw that the world was smaller and larger than ever. Communication and transportation made it smaller. So did more people and more things. What was the price of progress? Some of his views, notably those on women, were perverse. Others were partially or wholly wrong. But all were seen by a man with that most important Victorian virtue—a conviction of the importance of humanity.

Recommended Reading

The positivists exerted an influence well beyond their numbers. A useful general study is R. Simon, *European Positivism in the Nineteenth Century* (Ithaca: 1963). Harrison is particularly well handled in R. Harrison, *Before the Socialists* (London: 1965).

FREDERIC HARRISON,
A RETROSPECT OF SEVENTY YEARS

As I come to the end of my story, I shall try to gather up my general impressions of the vast changes in habits and in ideas which in a long life it has been my lot to witness. The eighty years which passed between the death of the fourth George and the accession

Source: From *Autobiographic Memoirs* (London: 1911), vol. II, chap. xxxvii.

of George V. (1830–1910) were pre-eminently an age of transition. In all the mechanical arts of civilisation the changes have been greater and more rapid than in any like period of modern history—greater and more rapid even than the effects which followed the invention of gunpowder, of printing, or the various uses of steam. And yet my personal experience satisfies me that the novelties, enormous and bewildering in appearance, have made no profound difference in the life of man. Life, habits, society have not been transformed by a multiplicity of mechanical appliances. The pace has been accelerated, the course remains the same.

It is far otherwise with the world of ideas. There at first sight the advance has not been at all striking. We have to-day in literature no Hume, no Gibbon, no Burke, no Goldsmith, no Byron, no Scott; in politics and war no Chatham, no Wellington; in art no Reynolds, no Gainsborough, no Flaxman, no Garrick, and no Siddons. In spite of the flood of literature and high pressure of universal schooling, some pessimists bewail the decay of intellect and art. And one needs to be a stout optimist to feel that everything in the world of ideas is quite sound and fruitful. And yet, at the root of the matter, the change in mental attitude is decisive. We live in a new world of thought in all things, spiritual, scientific, philosophical, and artistic. The change is less conspicuous, but is wider and deeper than that which followed the Humanists of the Renascence or the age of Galileo, Harvey, and Bacon. It is an age of open questions—in theology, in morals, in politics, in economics. All the old foundations and buttresses of our institutions, our beliefs, and our future hopes have begun to sink. We are in the mid-current of a vast transition.

Of the great change that has come over our own Empire by its enormous expansion, of that which has come over our political action and our resources for war and defence by wholly new international relations—I need say no more. The whole of this book is concerned with my views on these dominant problems. The fact that Great Britain is now only the nerve-centre of a huge aggregate of lands, held together for the time by very various ties—that the whole East and West are in totally new relations—this affects every corner of our lives. But I have discussed both problems at length in other parts of this work. And I pass to things less deep, less controversial, and such as are matters of personal observation and visible contrast.

THE MATERIAL ASPECT

I turn to the new appliances with which life has been armed within my own lifetime. The young will not believe life could be tolerable when travellers had nothing but horses on land and sails at sea; when a letter took an hour to write with a quill pen, and three or four days to be delivered in Edinburgh or Dublin; when the only telegraph was a wooden post, and the only cab was a hackney coach. The explanation of the mystery is, that people had not the least occasion to move about so far, so often, or so fast as they do now. If the appliances were more scanty, life was much easier, much simpler, less of a bustle, and more natural. To adapt a famous *mot* about amusements, we may say that to-day life would be more endurable if it were not for its conveniences. They hardly keep pace with our increasing obligations and difficulties. The vast increase in our means of locomotion does not compensate us for the enormous distances we have to traverse, and the treble pace at which we have to pass from place to place. It is a small gain to multiply our appliances, if the obstacles to be overcome and the volume to be treated are multiplied even faster.

They will tell me that age has dulled my power of enjoyment, or sharpened my sense of inconvenience—I will not believe that it has; but my impression is clear that life on the whole used to be more pleasant, more varied, and more sociable than it is to-day. There was certainly more fun, more originality, more *bonhomie* going about the world. Thackeray and Dickens, Lamb and Tom Moore, Charles Lever and Captain Marryat, tell us of a livelier, jollier age than that recorded in *Middlemarch* and *Fors Clavigera*—to say nothing of our psychologic poetry and divorce court realism. People who gave dinner-parties, balls, or dramatic entertainments invited their friends to their own houses and tried to make every one feel that they were really at home. And when they married their daughters, they seated their relations and a few chosen friends at their own tables, and the occasion was a quiet feast of intimates. There was no mob on the stairs struggling to get a glimpse of a sort of show bazaar. To-day nothing is counted as Society if it be not in a crush. And hospitality means doing the correct thing in regulation style at a gaudy hotel.

In all social and material things a great wave of uniformity has set in—the rule of conformity to conventional standards—which colours life with a sameness and a tameness, makes every one look alike, and obey the fashions of the day. In the journalist's phrase of our age, life and society have been "standardised." This has been done by a process of levelling up and levelling down. The dress, manners, habits, and education of the masses have been assimilated to those of the middle classes—happily by reason of greatly improved wages and conditions of labour. And the dress, manners, habits, and tastes of the wealthier classes have happily taken on a good deal of democratic simplicity, and along with it not a little of democratic vulgarity. Our grandfathers were rowdy enough at times—but our grandmothers held fast to the traditions of gentlewomen. And at the accession of Victoria these traditions had not been cast aside by the example of the New Woman from overseas. Democratic uniformity and the rule of go-as-you-please have "come to stay"—with much of real gain and not a little of incidental evil. Our age in external things has become one of somewhat level commonplace.

The most visible change between the tone current at the accession of Victoria and that at the accession of George V. is the marvellous development of the Press, and with it the millennium of advertisement. Politics, literature, art, manners are now within "the sphere of influence" of the daily Press, which by its volume and myriad voices makes and mars governments, reputations, opinions, and customs. The relations of nations, peace and war, taxation, the Constitution, and social reforms are decided by the struggle between rival speculators who own the Press. It is the most portentous form of demagogy that the world has seen. Some of its works are useful—some are mischievous. But, whether good or bad, they are all in effect matters of trade profit. The Press is not worked to promote opinions, measures, or politics, but simply to swell dividends. And dividends are swollen sometimes by encouraging the public in a beneficial line, sometimes by goading it to its injury or shame. But, as in the main the instincts of the great public are sound, and its good sense usually prevails, the mischiefs done are not so great as the good which ultimately succeeds. All the people cannot be fooled all the time, as Lincoln said. And as the Press is a sort of monstrous megaphone which magnifies and multiplies, the popular voice, the better voice in the long run usually makes itself hear amid the din.

To the eye the most exasperating development of this age is the advertising machine. Life has become a vast, incessant, ubiquitous biograph, whirling round ever before our eyes in order to puff somebody's wares. It is like an insidious, universal plague, stalking into every corner of our existence and every hour of our lives. When we are reading the momentous speech of a Minister, his oration is broken off to make room for a tawdry sketch of a bathycolpic female showing off a new corset. We are interrupted in the middle of the study of an international imbroglio by the contortions of a clerk writhing with backache or a housemaid displaying the sores on her face. When we buy a new book on philosophy, its pages are strewn with gross praises of sensational novels, and everything we touch or see is alive with the verminous wrigglings of the puffing tradesman. Painters, poets, actors, politicians, society beauties, and pot-hunting athletes, nay, noble and royal transparencies, are expected to pay for public notoriety, unless they prefer to remain obscure. Photography, wood pulp, and hungry journalists combine to make the world one great advertising bazaar.

Everything has got closed up. The planet has shrunk, and a considerable number of persons are perpetually going round it, and a vast new industry is employed in carrying them about it and from point to point. Every part of the country in the same way has been closed up, so that in the South of England it is not easy to find an open natural space. Even the moors and mountains are fenced round, so that the visitor must keep to the high roads. He is content to do so, if he can only be whirled along them in motors. When I was a boy the moors and mountains, glens and lakes, were open and virgin, as Nature made them, as if they were in Canada or Colorado. It is true that a vast increase of travelling enables millions to see something of foreign lands, and even of their own, which a century ago was restricted to a small number of the wealthy and leisured class. But against this must be set the enormous growth of cities, which makes city life a thing wholly different from, and far less natural and pleasant than what city life was in my own boyhood. *Mole ruit sua*[1] is the motto which may be fixed on most of the colossal developments of modern life. London ceases to be a city, and becomes a province covered with houses. The Thames, the Tyne, the Clyde, and the Mersey are no longer rivers, but turbid and fuliginous dockyards. The beauty of the Midlands, and of Lancashire and parts of Yorkshire, is engulfed in a pall of soot. And from Richmond to the Nore our silver Thames has become an

---

1. "Force without counsel falls by its own weight"—Horace.

interminable factory rather than a river. One cannot enjoy the charm of a fine sea-coast, because millions are struggling to do the same thing at the same time. It is an excellent thing that they should do so. But the enormous numbers who have to be fed with the two fishes and five loaves to be found in our small island leaves most of them unfed. The miracle does not come off now.

It is certain that not only is the volume of everything grown so as to make fresh difficulties to life, but the racing pace at which everything is carried out greatly increases the strain on the nerves. Ours is essentially the electric age. The one thing sought everywhere is rapidity of movement. To race round the globe in a month or two, to race along lovely countries as fast as an express train, to motor 100 miles in a day, and to fly a mile in a minute—to achieve "records"—these are counted now as the ends of perfect enjoyment. It is a laughable paradox to pretend that this raising the means of locomotion to the nth power increases our means of knowledge and the range of what we can see. To be whirled along a beautiful landscape is not to see it, any more than passing along the Galleries of the Louvre on a bicycle would be studying art. An American globe-trotter going round the world bragged that he had given "seven hours to the Eternal City." We are happy now that in our new motors in seventy minutes we exhaust the beauties of the valley of the Thames or the Wye, of Ullswater or the Lake of Como.

No one can read the delicious account that Ruskin gives of home and foreign travel in the 'forties in his *Praeterita*, without feeling how far more delightful—how far more instructive and satisfying—was a tour in those primitive ages. The memory of my own boyhood and youth enables me to bear witness how exactly true is Ruskin's picture of those days. To travel by *vetturino* in Italy or by post in Tyrol for a week was better than "a personally conducted tour" of three months to all the countries of Europe. The Bay of Naples and the Golden Horn; or the canals of Venice, to-day are veiled in smoke and ring with steam-hooters. The multiplying the means of locomotion and the volume of traffic deforms what is to be seen when we get there, and makes things we want too costly to be bought. Food, dress, housing, literature, art, and amusements are all worked by syndicates of speculators. The poor public is in a perpetual "corner," at the mercy of those who gamble in everything it needs. To be "up to date," to "get on a good thing," in the slang of our day, is the aim of life. Existence has become one long scramble to get to-day things more new, more quick, more gaudy than the newest, quickest, gaudiest thing of yesterday.

Now, though I delight in Ruskin's idylls of old times, and can recall not a few of such joys myself, I am no pessimist, no cynic, nor a convert to his fantastic, impossible, and even inhuman defiance of science, progress, and industrial development. Of course I agree with all reasonable persons that the vast development of industry, the marvellous inventions, discoveries, and resources of the nineteenth century, which the twentieth century seems about to surpass, are of incalculable boon to humanity, and have to be multiplied, used, and popularised in every way. The wonders of anaesthetics, of sanitary science, the glorious reduction of the statistics of disease and of the death-rate, the hardly less beneficial reduction in the birth-rate, and also of the suffering from malady or accident, the extension of the highest opportunities of modern civilisation to the humblest and the poorest, so that neither low birth, nor poverty, nor obscurity are bars to a competent man becoming statesman, artist, poet, or millionaire—all these new gifts of time and all the other glories of progress vaunted by a thousand pens, are so real that it would be blasphemy towards humanity to decry them.

But I say that these vast achievements of modern progress must be taken as subject to two classes of reduction and counter detriment. In the first place, the increase of our appliances and resources by its very volume, variety, and intensity, brings in new embarrassments and complications which at times threaten to undo all the boon they confer. In many a fairy tale the prayer for water, food, or wealth results in a flood or other catastrophe. And so, in the Greek legends of Midas overcome by a surfeit of gold, or Semele consumed by the splendours of Zeus, many a boon eagerly pursued brings its own neutralising evil. Some such disaster threatens the material triumphs of the nineteenth century. These evils are not inevitable consequences of the triumphs; but, for the time, they go far to qualify and deform the best of our successes.

In the second place, the weakening of all the ancient moral and spiritual forces able to discipline and organise great changes in material and social existence, has left the ground open to the craving for enjoyment and the power of wealth. In its thirst after new excitements and diversions, our age rushes after novel pleasures with a reckless indifference to all that is being destroyed and mutilated in the race for the end. Powers unimagined of old— the power to transform the face of our earth, power to race across continents, across oceans and polar ice, or through the bowels of the everlasting Alps, the power to bring the fruits and produce of the antipodes to every market, the power to communicate thought, the power to pass almost at will through the air—this has suddenly come upon a century which had no preparation for it or expecta- tion of it, and was wholly unable to extemporise any adequate means of reducing it to order or of mitigating its inevitable evils. But both classes of evils are remediable and within our control. Were it not so, humanity might count on going from bad to worse, and ending not in progress but in regression. The same energy, the genius, the audacity which has made our marvellous achievements are quite adequate to remedy the evils they bring with them, when these moral and intellectual gifts of man are duly summoned and welcomed. The age of novelties is quite able to invent the blessed novelty of bringing social order and material organisation out of unlicensed freedom. The task of the twentieth century is to disci- pline the chaotic activity of the nineteenth century. And it can only do this by becoming aware of the death-sentence to be passed on Western civilisation if it neglects to organise a new social and spiritual discipline. I am neither thoughtless *optimist* nor despon- dent *pessimist* of the future of our country. I am always, in every- thing, *meliorist*. The better hopes outweigh the menaces of evil. But it will need all our energies and our moral force to bring the good to fruit out of the elements of mischief that surround it.

THE SPIRITUAL ASPECT

In things intellectual, moral, religious, the change is profound and universal. The enormous increase in general *schooling*—I will not call it *education*, the wonderful advance of science, the per- petual debate over moral problems, the renewed activity of all forms of Church—whether Catholic, evangelical, unitarian, or ethical,—all these things blind us to the truth that our age is one of scepticism, dissolution, dissent, and flux. By scepticism I do not mean aggressive negation, but the general sense that what our grandfathers held to be irrefragable truth can no longer be treated as even probable. And this is not merely as to Scripture, Creeds, theological dogmas, but as to the canons of social life, the relations of the sexes, institutions, our philosophy, our political axioms, our manners, our literary and artistic ideals. We want everything new, and unless things are (or pretend to be) new, they arouse indifference or disgust.

There is a universal earth-current that runs from continent to continent, stirring each nation to shed its old life and renew its youth. But the earth-current has no message of what the new thing is to be. It shakes down the ancient walls and leaves the field open and bare. One of our foremost men, with one of the subtlest of minds, has aptly formulated our mental attitude as that of philosophic doubt, of which the obverse face presents to us the foundations of our beliefs. Another of our leading preachers of lay sermons has invented the term and inaugurated the creed of Agnosticism—the creed that we do not know any supreme truth, and indeed would rather not know. Our principal philosopher teaches that the source of the universe and the object of religious reverence is the Absolute Unknowable. And our principal poet—himself as much of a theologian as ever was Milton—enshrines in his fine religious musings the really typical paradox that true faith is to be found in honest doubt. Philosophers, scientists, poets, theologians, all celebrate the apotheosis of doubt.

This tendency to universal doubt falls in with another remarkable tendency of our age, of which it may be either cause or result. I mean the tendency to repudiate—or at least to adjourn—all forms of *Synthesis, i.e.* the co-ordination and organic unification of our ideas. Theologians, of the better sort, warn us against seeking to put our religious belief into creeds—or any cast-iron summary of faith. Beware of coherent dogmas, they cry. It is enough to have religious sympathies about cardinal points, to feel the beauty of the Gospel story, to trust that after all there is something "behind the veil"—of what we know, or even can imagine to be on this earth. The cry of science is to stick carefully to some special group of facts, and never to combine religious or moral ideals with our physical knowledge. Literature, art, learning, and education, like science and theology, must all be kept, they assure us, in detached groups. They cannot be pursued together. And they can only be pursued with success by strict adherence to the boundaries which separate one specialism from another.

This mania for special research in place of philosophic principle, or tabulated facts in lieu of demonstrable theorems and creative generalisations, attenuates the intelligence and installs pedantic information about details, where what man wants are working principles for social life. The grand conceptions of Darwin and of Spencer are too often used by their followers and successors as a text on which to dilate on microscopic or local trivialities which mean nothing. And even Spencer's Synthesis, the only one yet attempted by any English thinker, proves, on being closely pressed, to rest on a substructure of hypotheses, and to ignore two-thirds of the entire scale of the sciences viewed as an interdependent whole. The enormous accumulation of recorded facts in the last century goes on as blindly in this, quite indifferent to the truth that infinite myriads of facts are as worthless as infinite grains of sand on the seashore, until we have found out how to apply them to the amelioration of human life.

It was obvious that the literature of the first half of the nineteenth century greatly surpassed that of the second half. And it is sadly evident that literature in the twentieth century is far inferior even to that of the second half century. Contrast 1910 with 1810, when there were in full career Scott and Byron, Coleridge and Wordsworth, Shelley and Keats, Landor, Campbell, Lamb, Southey, Jeffrey, Tom Moore and Sam Rogers, Maria Edgeworth and Jane Austen, and the lions of the *Edinburgh Review* and of the *Quarterly Review*. What have we to-day to put beside these names in so many different forms of literary art? And yet to-day we have ten thousand men and women who write a correct prose style far better than any but the few chief masters of the age of Southey and Lamb. And as to verse, we may say boldly that there never has been a time in the whole history of English poetry when the second and third class of poems produced have been so good, so right in feeling, so graceful in form, when really beautiful verse is poured out day by day with inexhaustible torrents. And withal, there is not in these tens of thousands one single poem of the truly first order—not a sonnet to be put beside the *Ode to a Skylark* or to the *Grecian Urn*,[2] not an essay that Lamb or Coleridge would be proud to sign; nor is there one of the ten thousand women

2. In 1862 Francis Palgrave made that invaluable collection of poetry, *The Golden Treasury*, which stopped at 1850 and included no living poet. In 1897 was published the *Second Series*, which included the Tennysons, the Brownings, Landor, Keble, Newman, Kingsley, Patmore, and the two Rossettis. We can all see the sad inferiority of his *Second Series* to the *First Series*, even if we limit this to poems written between 1800 and 1850.

novelists who will live in 2010 beside the authors of *Emma* and *Castle Rackrent*.

And this is so, in spite of the vast increase of general education and of all forms of literary product, of all agencies of intellectual cultivation. When the population of our island was one-fifth of its present number, there were hardly half a million of men and women who could read a book with pleasure. There are now at least ten millions—it may be twice as many—who can read with ease and have been through some school. The printed matter available must be one hundred times as great as it then was. And in spite of all this, literature is on the down grade. I hazard the paradox in good faith that the decline is not merely in spite of all this instruction, but is a result of the universal schooling. The incessant education drill, the deluge of printed matter, asphyxiate the brain, dull beauty of thought, and chill genius into lethargic sleep.

To read is not necessarily to learn anything worth knowing, to pore over print may be even enervating or corrupting the mind instead of improving it; and, if ninety per cent of printed stuff is worthless, reading may be worse than waste of time. Incessant schooling on a regulation system may produce uniformity of style and even a certain aptitude to conform to the conventional type. But it is the death of originality; it starves imagination, fancy, and free thought. Schooling by itself, only trains scholars to think on the official pattern, to repeat the facts or the doctrines that are drummed into the open mind, to swallow the food crammed into their jaws, as young starlings are fed when they open their beaks for grubs. It is a subtle and wide field, on which I have no space to enter now—but I seriously maintain that a direct result of our mechanical schooling—misnamed education—and that whether primary, middle, or highest; Board schools, high schools, academies, or universities—is the gradual deterioration of literature into dry specialism and monotonous commonplace.

This is really not a theory but a matter of actual observation. The population of the United States is double ours. The schooling is four or five times as great and as good. The whole of that immense population has the opportunity of getting the best schooling of our age—or rather what our age counts as best. There is in the Republic a wonderful eagerness for cultivation in all its forms, and a plethora of erudition, and yet there is no literature of the higher kind, far less than there was when population and schools were not a tenth of the present. The American Press pours out day

and night a Niagara of print, and in it all there is not one page, one
sonnet, one idea of the highest order, hardly one of the second or
the third. The educational system of Switzerland has the repute of
being the most perfect extant. The natural beauty of that noble
land exceeds that of Greece, and its climate compels a large part of
its sons to long periods of sedentary work at home. And yet there
is no great literature in Switzerland, there never was any, there
never will be any. France, Italy, Germany have all greatly increased their school systems in the last two or three generations.
But in those countries also literature is rather decaying than improving. It is a common observation that it is a weariness to the
flesh to study the massive learning of German scholars, philosophers, historians, and critics, because the German brain seems
impenetrable to the charm of literary form; and all this ponderous
erudition has to be smelted down by French or English minds
before it can be assimilated by the average student. No! What we
now call education, primary or academic, is the atrophy of literature. An age which boasts as types of the historian such conscientious annalists as Freeman and Gardiner, makes it impossible to
have a Gibbon. They who love the epigrams of Browning and
Meredith so that they despise the fire of Byron and the glow of
Scott, prefer poety that has neither ease nor music. And when we
are surfeited with journalism, short stories, and the slang of the
gutter, we cannot expect to rear again another Lamb, another Jane
Austen, another Coleridge, or even a new Macaulay.

The double effect of making life a race or a scramble, working
with the ceaseless cataract of commonplace print, just good enough
to occupy the average mind having a superficial school training,
debases the general intellectual currency, and lowers the standard.
Scientific and historical research piles up its huge record of facts
with a sort of scholiast's attention to minute scholarship and inattention to impressive form. It would seem as if the higher order
of literature were produced in inverse ratio to the number of the
reading public and the volume of literary product. The immortal
literature of Athens was created when those who could enjoy and
judge literature were a few thousand and the books available were
hardly one hundred. And Virgil and Horace, Cicero and Livy had
not so very many more readers or libraries around them. Victor
Hugo, in his *Notre Dame*, has a powerful chapter on the text—*ceci
tuera cela. Le livre tuera l'édifice.* The printed book was the death
of the cathedral. To-day we may say—the school has been the

death of literature. Not the true school that is to be—but the patent high-pressure Reading Machine that we now call the School.

Art, like literature, is in the same anarchic, expectant, transitional state. There is a fierce desire to secure Art, to discover new forms of Art, to put beauty into our lives. The new feature about the Art of our generation is to have opened it to women within narrow limits and in given fields. There never was such talk about Art, such criticism, such controversy, rivalry, dogmatism, and sacrifice. And there never was such a chaos of ideals, convention, and methods—idealist, realist, impressionist, grotesque, obscene, and vulgar. Modern Art is an orchestra wherein many excellent performers and many mere pretenders each play their own instrument with perfectly separate compositions, that have neither note nor key in harmony together. A picture show is like a fancy ball in which every costume is a separate choice of the wearer; where a Crusader, or a Pierrot, and a Red Indian dance with Nell Gwyn, a nun, and a Maid of Athens. Immense pains have been bestowed on the costumes; the individual result is often pleasing; but the effect of the whole is dissonance. In painting, as in literature, drama, music, sculpture, or architecture, a feverish effort is made to get hold of something new, to shake off the old ideals, to see what can be done without ideals, by giving rein to every fresh impulse and to each untried talent.

In all the allied arts we find to-day vehement efforts to try experiments, to get rid of mental effort, and to make everything short, rapid, and easy. These conditions, eminently demanded by an age in a hurry, exclude all dominant conventions and ideals, and all the grander types of Art. No fashionable audience can endure the *Trilogy* of Aeschylus, the *Antigone*, or *Lear*. A smart audience comes to the play to laugh, to talk, and to smoke, and for choice will rather at a Music Hall sit through a dozen lively "turns," with acrobatic interludes. There is a keen and growing interest in music; but the musical world cannot decide what is the end of music, or what it should aim at—whether to charm, to astound, or to instruct its audience. What are we to paint, what are we to build, and what is the proper aim or purpose of painting or of building? Is sculpture to be classical, ideal, direct imitation of everyday things, beautiful, gross, familiar, or commonplace? It may be that a new art world is to be evolved out of this welter of "go-as-you-please," but the immediate effect is rather bewildering than soothing. And one who has trained his spirit on the immortal masterpieces of Art in ages which were generally held to be great, does somehow feel that behind all Art there have to be thought, hope, love, and reverence of a spiritual kind that compels common assent—in short, a philosophy, a moral ideal, a religion.

In things far deeper and more vital than manners, literature, and art, the signs of transition press on us everywhere. The break-up of philosophical and religious certainties inevitably brings about re-settlement in the aspects of social institutions, of family life, and of moral standards. It cannot be doubted that, with the accession of Victoria, a wide-spread improvement in moral standards began and has been maintained and raised. And not merely a higher moral standard, but an improved moral practice resulted. The steady and almost universal increase of temperance, the diminution of crime and of sexual debauchery are the most conspicuous and most blessed triumphs of seventy years of the new moral gospel of social and personal life. And it is a lay and ethical gospel far more than a clerical or theological gospel. It is common to all classes, all professions, and all churches—and eminently to the churches and the societies which have no theology at all. The great advance of moral judgment and of all forms of beneficent social agencies, the relief of suffering and the reduction of crime, are the noblest title of the nineteenth century.

Amongst the most conspicuous and the most beneficent modes of social evolution are the wholly new relations between Capital and Labour, the all-round improvement in the rank and file of the workers, and the new attitude towards their claims in the class which controls power and wealth. It has advanced to the point at which the possession of property in the abstract is a burning question, and the duties of property for the first time become a dominant problem. We are certainly not "all Socialists now"; but Socialism, especially as a vague aspiration, is in the air. The origin of wealth, the obligations of wealth, the social possibilities and the moral justification of wealth are the problems of our time. And it has no more burning task to answer, and no more worthy boast to make. The answer—the hundred answers—are as yet conflicting and contradictory. Everything relating to the social economy of civilised man is quite in flux and unformed. But the universal sense amongst rich and poor, rulers and ruled, the thoughtful and the thoughtless, that social, political, and economic problems face us and must be solved—this marks the twentieth century as one of the great epochs of transition in modern times.

The character of doubt, unsettlement, resettlement, applies to all our public life in every form, and with it comes an insatiable eagerness to refashion society, recast instituitons, and try a new departure. But a similar character marks the personal and domestic life of our age. It is more subtle and far less general or conspicuous. But it would be a paradox if the melting away of religious, moral, and social canons of public life did not react on our persons and on our homes. There has been an astonishing advance in longevity, in good health, in sobriety, in sexual purity, and in bodily culture, as statistics and a multitude of habits testify. They who, as I have done, knew men and women in various classes having lived through the times of the Georges, can verify all this from what they have heard from eye-witnesses of the times described by Thackeray and Bulwer, and the biographies of Byron, Sheridan, Fox, and Brougham. We are a far cleaner, healthier, kindlier race than the men and women of *Vanity Fair*, not to say than the contemporaries of Squire Western and Tom Jones.

The most conspicuous change of all will be found in the vastly increased development in the life of women—women's education, industry, opportunities for culture and self-maintenance. Much of all this is entirely blessed, much of it is mere waste of effort, and some of it even morally debasing. I have said so much about the horrors attending the factory labour of young girls and mothers that I do no more now than record my conviction that it is one of the prime dangers of our age. The fierce struggle of women to wrest the labour field from men, to undersell their own husbands, fathers, and brothers, is a monstrous perversion alike of industrial, domestic, and moral order. A society which continues to develop in this line is lost. The quite modern cry for political rights is already being defeated by the good sense of the immense majority of women and by the revived honesty of politicians who have played or trafficked with the question too long. The higher training, the new fields open to women, their greater freedom, are admirable conquests of the nineteenth century, and, along with the Legislation of 1882 and more recent Acts, have gone far already to satisfy the anarchic demand for political equality with men.

It is fortunate that the claim for political equality and other extravagant pretensions of the kind are of mushroom growth. In a really serious form, they are hardly more than one generation old. At the time of the women's protest against the Suffrage Bill in 1889, the claim for votes was a purely academic or rather a drawing-room movement. And as to the social emancipation of the "New Woman," my own recollection is that it took no startling form until the last quarter of the nineteenth century. Till that date, or until about thirty years ago, when the great colonial and trans-atlantic immigration set in, and impecunious noblemen went over-seas for heiresses, the manners of educated women of social position were those of their mothers and their grandmothers, but with a much higher education and even superior grace and refine-ment. The "undergraduate" and "man-about-town" ways of smart ladies are too recent to be lasting. We shall soon be rid of this folly.

The industrial independence and the political ambition of women are obviously but manifestations of a profound moral revolution. It is but one wave issuing out of that vast upheaval of Democracy which for a century has run round the civilised world. And Democracy has affected not only social and political ideals, but domestic ideals in subtle and indirect ways. It has suggested new conceptions of family life and family duty. Our old ideas about the sanctity of the family, of the sacred responsibilities of wife, mother, and daughter, of their relation to husband, father, and son, and of each to each,—all are undergoing a silent loosening and weakening process. The last word of Democracy is, "every man, woman, and child for himself, herself, and itself." But the English of this high-sounding Greek word is—"the weaker to the wall." I suppose the very last institution of civilisation which stands in need of regeneration is the family. And I am so old-fashioned as to hold that the fashionable nostrums for regenerating the family are retrogressions towards primitive savagery. Civilised society consists not of individuals, but of families.

Assaults on the family are assaults on marriage and married life. And it is plain that there are silent secret mutterings against the bonds of marriage as hitherto accepted and respected in Christen-dom. The rapid increase of divorce, mainly in Protestant countries, and the literary glorification of concubinage and free love, are the advance-guard of the attack on the foundations of marriage— which to-day is sounded in various notes by philosophers and romancers, English, American, Scandinavian, and Slavonic. The Latin races are content with the practice and the poetry of a freer life, without worrying themselves about a revised code of ethics to be brought up to date. All this as yet is fitful, unsystematic, and generally personal to the situation and history of the male or female reformer. But those who look below the surface of things must see that there is a wide and correlated yearning to have family duties and ties, marriage, the functions of the sexes and relations to each other, cast in new moulds, so as to install novel forms of social organisation.

I am neither optimist nor pessimist in this, nor any other matter. I am far from satisfied that our present ideal of family life is perfect—much less that our ideal or our practice in married life is not in want of some future regeneration in the way of discipline and fortifying. Nor, again, do I feel any sympathy for the satirists and cynics who make a trade of caricaturing the vices and grossness of their age. But I feel bound to point to the growing disbelief in the family, which must always remain the true source and centre of our social life. This is, in my judgment, the most dangerous symptom of our age. It is the last word I have to utter at the close of a long, happy, busy life—in which I cannot recall, in my personal experience of family life, any memories that are not blessed and consoling, nor any thought of those I have lost, of those I have still, or of those whom I may leave behind me, which is not such a memory as may fitly soothe a death-bed.

EPITAPH

I close this book with words that indeed resume in themselves all that I have ever written or spoken during half a century, which is this—that all our mighty achievements are being hampered and often neutralised, all our difficulties are being doubled, and all our moral and social diseases are being aggravated by this supreme and dominant fact—that we have suffered our religion to slide from us, and that in effect our age has no abiding faith in any religion at all. The urgent task of our time is to recover a religious faith as a basis of life both personal and social. I feel that I have done this, in my own poor way, for myself, and am closing my quiet life in resignation, peace, and hope. And this book is the simple story of how this faith was slowly and for ever borne in upon my life; how it secured me unbroken happiness in good fortune and in evil times; and what, under its inspiration, I have tried to do in my own opportunities, as I understood them to be possible and good.

DOCUMENTARY HISTORY OF WESTERN CIVILIZATION
Edited by Eugene C. Black and Leonard W. Levy

---

* In preparation